Casey Hawthorne
102 - 3720 Cambie Street
Vancouver, BC
V5Z 2X5

Aspect-Oriented Software Development

ROBERT E. FILMAN

TZILLA ELRAD

SIOBHÁN CLARKE

MEHMET AKŞIT

Addison-Wesley

Boston • San Francisco • New York • Toronto • Montreal
London • Munich • Paris • Madrid
Capetown • Sydney • Tokyo • Singapore • Mexico City

Library of Congress Cataloging-in-Publication Data
A CIP catalog record for this book can be obtained from the Library of Congress
LOC Number: 2004107799

Publisher: *John Wait*
Acquisitions Editor: *Paul Petralia*
Marketing Manager: *Chris Guzikowski*
International Marketing Manager: *Tim Galligan*
Managing Editor: *Gina Kanouse*
Senior Project Editor: *Sarah Kearns*
Copy Editor: *Ben Lawson*
Indexer: *Brad Herriman*
Proofreader: *Sheri Cain*
Composition: *ICC*
Cover Design: *Nina Scuderi*
Manufacturing Buyer: *Dan Uhrig*

Many of the designations used by manufacturers and sellers to distinguish their products are claimed as trademarks. Where those designations appear in this book, and Addison-Wesley was aware of a trademark claim, the designations have been printed with initial capital letters or in all capitals.

The authors and publisher have taken care in the preparation of this book, but make no expressed or implied warranty of any kind and assume no responsibility for errors or omissions. No liability is assumed for incidental or consequential damages in connection with or arising out of the use of the information or programs contained herein.

The publisher offers discounts on this book when ordered in quantity for bulk purchases and special sales. For more information, please contact:

U.S. Corporate and Government Sales
(800) 382-3419
corpsales@pearsontechgroup.com

For sales outside of the U.S., please contact:

International Sales
international@pearsoned.com

Visit Addison-Wesley on the web: www.awprofessional.com

Copyright © 2005 by Pearson Education, Inc.

All rights reserved. No part of this publication may be reproduced, stored in a retrieval system, or transmitted, in any form, or by any means, electronic, mechanical, photocopying, recording, or otherwise, without the prior consent of the publisher. Printed in the United States of America. Published simultaneously in Canada.

For information on obtaining permission for use of material from this work, please submit a written request to:

Pearson Education, Inc.
Rights and Contracts Department
75 Arlington Street, Suite 300
Boston, MA 02116
Fax: (617) 848-7047

ISBN 0-321-21976-7
Text printed on recycled paper
1 2 3 4 5 6 7 8 9 10—08 07 06 05 04
First printing, September 2004

REPRINTS AND REVISIONS

Reprints

The following papers are reprints (reprinted by permission):

N *Degrees of Separation: Multi-Dimensional Separation of Concerns*. Peri Tarr, Harold Ossher, Stanley M. Sutton, Jr., and William Harrison.
Proc. 21st Int'l Conf. Software Engineering (ICSE'1999), pp. 107–119

Inserting Ilities by Controlling Communications. Robert E. Filman, Stuart Barrett, Diana D. Lee, and Ted Linden. *Communications of the ACM*, vol. 45, no. 1, January 2002, pp. 116–122.

Structuring Operating System Aspects. Yvonne Coady, Gregor Kiczales, Mike Feeley, Norm Hutchinson, and Joon Suan Ong. *Comm. ACM*, vol. 44, no. 10, Oct 2001, pp. 79–82.

Revisions

The following papers are revisions of earlier printed articles, along with a citation of the earlier version:

Composition Patterns: An Approach to Designing Reusable Aspects. Siobhán Clarke and Robert J. Walker. *Proc. 23rd Int'l Conf. Software Engineering (ICSE-01)*, Toronto, May 2001, pp. 5–14.

Aspect-Oriented Modeling: Bridging the Gap Between Implementation and Design. Tzilla Elrad, Omar Aldawud, and Atef Bader. *ACM SIGPLAN/SIGSOFT Conference on Generative Programming and Component Engineering (GPCE'02)*, Pittsburgh, October 2002.

An Initial Assessment of Aspect-Oriented Programming. Robert J. Walker, Elisa L. A. Baniassad, and Gail C. Murphy. *Proc. 21st Int'l Conf. Software Engineering (ICSE '99)*, pp. 120–130.

In memory of my grandparents, Jack, Minnie, Sidney, and Helen—R. E. F.

In memory of my parents, Menahem and Pnina Holzer—T. E.

In memory of my parents, Peter and Maura Clarke—S.C.

For my parents, Baha and Nevruz Akşit—M.A.

Contents

16 Aspect-Oriented Software Development with Java Aspect Components 343

Renaud Pawlak, Lionel Seinturier, Laurence Duchien, Laurent Martelli,
Fabrice Legond-Aubry, and Gérard Florin

Contents

Acknowledgments

We would like to thank Craig Thompson and Tom Poppendieck for their careful readings of a draft of this manuscript, Ryan Van Roode for help with production, and the contributing authors for their efforts and patience in bringing this project to fruition.

About the Editors

Robert E. Filman is a senior scientist at the Research Institute for Advanced Computer Science at NASA Ames Research Center, working on frameworks for distributed applications. He has worked and published in the areas of software engineering, distributed computing, network security, programming languages, artificial intelligence, algorithms, and human-machine interface. He received his Ph.D. in Computer Science in 1979 from Stanford University.

Tzilla Elrad is a research professor in the Department of Computer Science at Illinois Institute of Technology, where she heads the Concurrent Software Systems research group. She received her B.S. in mathematics and physics from the Hebrew University and her M.S. and Ph.D. in Computer Science from Syracuse University, NY and the Technion, Israel, respectively. Her research interests include concurrent programming languages design, adaptive software systems development, and formal reasoning.

Siobhán Clarke is a lecturer in the Department of Computer Science at Trinity College, Dublin. Her research interests include aspect-oriented software development, context-aware computing and programming models for mobile, sentient, context-aware systems. She received her B.S. and Ph.D. degrees from Dublin City University. Prior to her career in research, she worked as a software engineer with IBM for 11 years.

Mehmet Akşit holds an M.S. from the Eindhoven University of Technology and a Ph.D. from the University of Twente. He is a professor in the Department of Computer Science, University of Twente, and he is also affiliated with the Centre for

Telematics and Information Technology. He (and his group) have developed the composition filters aspect-oriented programming technique, synthesis-based architecture/software design, and techniques to synthesize architectures from solution domains for creating stable software systems, have applied fuzzy-logic to software design, and have created design formalisms such as Design Algebra for balancing various quality factors at different stages of software development.

About the Contributors

Franz Achermann is a software engineer at Swisscom, a Swiss telecommunications operator. His research interests include languages and tools for object-orientation, software engineering, and formal methods. He holds a Ph.D. in Computer Science for his work on the composition language Piccola.

Omar Aldawud is a software architect at Lucent Technology. He received his Ph.D. in Computer Science from Illinois Institute of Technology, where he is currently a lecturer and a senior member of the Concurrent Software Systems research group. Omar's interests include OO, AO, DOT net, and advanced modeling with UML.

Gustavo Alonso is professor of Computer Science at the Swiss Federal Institute of Technology (ETH Zurich). He received his engineering degree in telecommunications from Madrid Technical University (1989) as well as his M.S. (1992) and Ph.D. (1994) degrees in Computer Science from the University of California, Santa Barbara.

João Araújo is an assistant professor at the New University of Lisbon, Portugal. He received a B.S. and an M.S. in Computer Science from UFPE, Brazil, and a Ph.D. in software engineering from the University of Lancaster, United Kingdom. His research interests include requirements engineering and object-oriented and aspect-oriented software development.

Michael Austermann has developed the JMangler framework as part of his diploma thesis at the University of Bonn (2000). Since completing his degree, he has been a consultant at SCOOP Software GmbH, Cologne. There he has continued evolving JMangler and has initiated and led work on the development of CC4J, a powerful code coverage application developed using JMangler.

Atef Bader is a member of the technical staff at Lucent Technologies and adjunct assistant professor at Illinois Institute of Technology, where he is also a member of the Concurrent Software Systems research group. His research interests include object-oriented technology, aspect-oriented software development, automated software testing, concurrent software systems, and software architecture. He received his Ph.D. in Computer Science from Illinois Institute of Technology.

Elisa L. A. Baniassad received her Ph.D. in Computer Science from the University of British Columbia in 2003 and is now an NSERC post-doctoral fellow at Trinity College, Dublin. She is interested in empirical studies of developers' practices for finding and dealing with aspects in code. Based on these observations, she works on software-design analysis for elucidation of aspects in system requirements and establishing traceability links to detailed design and implementation.

Ted Bapty is a research assistant professor in electrical engineering at Vanderbilt University and a senior research scientist at the Institute for Software Integrated Systems. His research interests are in technologies to build large-scale, real-time, distributed, embedded systems at multiple levels of granularity.

Stu Barrett is a consultant in Austin, Texas. He has worked at Texas Instruments, Raytheon, Microsoft, and CALEB Technologies on topics including embedded OS design, networking, artificial intelligence, distributed systems/applications, and middleware. He received his B.S.E.E. from Michigan Technological University in 1972. When not consulting, Stu relaxes by firing high-power rockets.

Lodewijk Bergmans is an assistant professor at the University of Twente, the Netherlands, where he obtained his Ph.D. His primary research interests are understanding how to compose stable and evolvable software from separate modules and achieving this through developing (AOP) models based on Composition Filters.

Gordon S. Blair is professor of distributed systems at Lancaster University. He is on the steering committee of the International Middleware Conference and was general chair for that event in 1998. His research interests include next generation middleware and reflection.

Lynne Blair is a senior lecturer in the Computing Department at Lancaster University. She has a background in the formal specification and verification of distributed multimedia systems and is currently working on both aspect-oriented software development and also problems of (feature) interaction that occur in such complex systems.

Noury Bouraqadi founded the Computer Science Lab of the Ecole des Mines of Douai (France) in 2001. Since 1995, his research has aimed at easing development of complex software. For this purpose, Dr. Bouraqadi has been working on reflection, aspect-oriented programming, and software components in the context of distributed systems.

Marcelo R. Campo is an associate professor in the Computer Science Department and head of the ISISTAN Research Institute at the UNICEN University, Tandil, Argentina. He received his Ph.D. degree in Computer Science from the Universidade Federal de Rio Grande do Sul, Porto Alegre, Brazil in 1997. His research interests include intelligent aided software engineering, software architecture and frameworks, agent technology, and software visualization. He is a research fellow of the National Council for Scientific and Technical Research of Argentina (CONICET).

Richard Cardone is a researcher at the IBM Watson Research Center in New York. He received his Ph.D. in Computer Science from the University of Texas at Austin in 2002. He enjoys developing useful software and discovering ways of making that development more fun and efficient. Away from the computer, his interests include hiking, bicycling, and motorcycling.

Ruzanna Chitchyan is a Ph.D. candidate in the Computing Department at Lancaster University. Her principal research interests are in multi-dimensional separation of concerns, synthesis of aspect-oriented design approaches, and development of dynamic composition mechanisms. She co-organized the First Workshop on Analysis of Aspect-Oriented Software at ECOOP 2003.

Pedro J. Clemente graduated in 1998 in Computer Science from the University of Extremadura, where he is currently a lecturer. He is a member of the Quercus Software Engineering Group, and his research is focused on component-based software engineering and aspect-oriented software development.

Yvonne Coady is a recent Ph.D. graduate from the University of British Columbia and is currently an assistant professor at the University of Victoria. Her research interests include aspect-oriented software development, systems engineering, and sustainability of systems infrastructures.

Geoff Cohen is a researcher and consultant on future software technologies. He was a founding program committee member of OOPSLA's *Onward! Seeking New Paradigms and New Thinking* track and its 2004 chair. He was a member of the research staff that produced the National Academy of Science report on the intersection of Computer Science and biology. He holds a Ph.D. in Computer Science from Duke University and a B.A. from the Woodrow Wilson School of Public and International Affairs at Princeton University.

Adrian Colyer is an IBM senior technical staff member based in the United Kingdom. Within IBM, Adrian leads a team that is both developing core aspect-oriented (AO) technologies and helping development groups around the corporation to adopt and apply them. Adrian also leads the open source AspectJ and AspectJ Development Tools projects on Eclipse.org. Prior to his involvement with AO, Adrian worked on enterprise middleware in a variety of roles including product development, strategy, and emerging technology.

Pascal Costanza is a research associate at the Institute of Computer Science III of the University of Bonn. His research interests include the design of programming languages, especially language constructs for unanticipated software evolution and aspect-oriented programming. He has been involved in the design and implementation of the programming languages Gilgul and Lava, the JMangler framework, and aspect-oriented extensions for Common Lisp.

Bart De Win is a research assistant in the Distributed Systems and Computer Networks (DistriNet) research group in the Department of Computer Science of the Katholieke Universiteit Leuven. His main research interests are in security, in particular secure software engineering, anonymity control, and security in the context of embedded systems.

J. Andrés Díaz Pace is an assistant professor in the Computer Science Department at the UNICEN University, Tandil, Argentina. He received his master's degree from the UNICEN University in 2001, where he is currently pursuing his Ph.D. His research interests include object-oriented frameworks, architecture-based design, AI techniques, and separation of concerns.

Remi Douence has been an assistant professor at Ecole des Mines de Nantes since 1998. In 1996, he defended his thesis on a formal study of functional language implementations. In 1997, he worked on software architecture languages at Carnegie-Mellon University. Remi is interested in linguistic support for software engineering in general and in AOP in particular.

Laurence Duchien is currently a professor at INRIA Lille and University of Lille, France and on the Jacquard team since 2001. She was associate professor in the Computer Science Department at CNAM, Paris, France. She received her Ph.D. degree from University Paris 6 LIP6 laboratory in 1988, and her habilitation à diriger des recherches from University Joseph Fourier, Grenoble, in 1999. Her research interests include design methodologies, proof systems for distributed object-oriented applications, and reflective and aspect-oriented programming.

Mike Feeley is an associate professor at the University of British Columbia. His active research projects are in the areas of peer-to-peer file systems, mobile ad hoc networks, and scalable system structure.

Gérard Florin is currently professor of Computer Science at CNAM, Paris, France. He was head of the CEDRIC (Centre d'Etudes et de Recherche en Informatique du CNAM) from 1990 to 1998. He graduated from ENSET Cachan ("Ecole Normale Supérieure de l'Enseignement Technique"). He received his Ph.D. degree from the University Paris 6 in 1975. His doctorat d'état degree is devoted to the formal definition of stochastic Petri nets and to a set of numerical tools that implement the theoretical results. His research interests now include distributed computing, fault tolerance, and reflective and aspect-oriented programming.

Pascal Fradet is an INRIA researcher. His research interests are in the areas of programming languages: functional programming, domain specific languages, compilation, transformation, analysis, and, since 1997, aspect-oriented programming. He is interested in the foundations and semantics issues of AOP. He views aspects as formal properties to be enforced on programs.

Daniel P. Friedman is a professor in the Computer Science Department at Indiana University. He received his bachelors from University of Houston and masters and doctorate from The University of Texas at Austin. He is interested in all facets of programming languages. He has co-authored a series of "Little" books, which emphasize a functional approach to programming, as well as some big books.

Aniruddha S. Gokhale is an assistant professor in the Electrical Engineering and Computer Science Department at Vanderbilt University and a research scientist at the Institute for Software Integrated Systems. His primary responsibilities include leading research projects involving modeling of middleware solutions.

Jeff Gray is an assistant professor in the Computer and Information Sciences Department at the University of Alabama at Birmingham, where he is co-director of the Object-Oriented Distributed Computing laboratory. His research focuses on language-independent frameworks that permit construction of aspect weavers at various levels of abstraction.

William G. Griswold is a professor of Computer Science and engineering at the University of California, San Diego. He received his Ph.D. in Computer Science from the University of Washington in 1991. In 2003, he was general chair for the 2nd International Conference on Aspect-Oriented Software Development. His research interests include ubiquitous computing, aspect-oriented software development, software evolution and design, software tools, and program analysis.

Thomas Gross is a professor of Computer Science at ETH Zurich, Switzerland. He received a Ph.D. in electrical engineering from Stanford and was on the faculty of the School of Computer Science at Carnegie Mellon. He is interested in tools, techniques, and abstractions for software construction. He has worked on many aspects of the design and implementation of software systems.

John Grundy is professor of software engineering at the University of Auckland. He has published over 100 refereed papers on software tools and methods, software architecture and component-based systems, aspect-oriented software engineering techniques, software process technology, and user interface technology.

Jan Hannemann is currently a Ph.D. candidate in the Department of Computer Science at the University of British Columbia, Canada. He received an M.S. degree in Computer Science from the Georgia Institute of Technology and a Diplom degree in applied systems science from the University of Osnabrück, Germany.

William Harrison has been a researcher at the IBM Thomas J. Watson Research Center since 1970. He has made contributions in optimizing compiler technology, software development technology, cooperative software development, and software-by-composition. He is co-originator of subject-oriented programming and one of the leaders of the Concern Manipulation Environment effort.

Juan Hernández is an associate professor in the Computer Science Department of Extremadura University (Spain), where he leads the Quercus Software Engineering Group. He received his B.S. in mathematics from the University of Extremadura and Ph.D. in Computer Science from the Technical University of Madrid. His research interests include component-based software development, aspect orientation, and distributed systems.

José Luis Herrero is currently an associate professor at the Computer Science Department of Extremadura University. He belongs to the Quercus Software Engineering Group. He received the B.S. in Computer Science from the University of Granada and the Ph.D. degree in Computer Science from the Extremadura University in 2003. His research interests include aspect orientation with UML and e-commerce.

John Hosking is a professor and head of the Computer Science Department at the University of Auckland. He has research interests and publications in software tools, software engineering, consistency management, and applications in health informatics and construction IT.

Norm Hutchinson is an associate professor at the University of British Columbia. His research interests include concurrent and distributed operating systems, soft real-time systems, and mobility in distributed systems.

Wouter Joosen is a professor in the Distributed Systems and Computer Networks (DistriNet) research group at the Department of Computer Science of the Katholieke Universiteit Leuven. His main research interests are in the areas of software architecture for distributed systems, aspect-oriented and component-based development, middleware, software security and embedded systems

Gregor Kiczales is a professor at the University of British Columbia. While at the Palo Alto Research Center, he was a principal scientist and the founder of the AOP and AspectJ projects. He is a co-author, with Danny Bobrow and Jim des Rivieres, of *The Art of the Metaobject Protocol*.

Günter Kniesel is a substitute professor of applied Computer Science at the University of Osnabrück and a lecturer at the University of Bonn. His research interests includes object-based inheritance, roles, aspect-oriented programming, dynamic software evolution, program transformations, refactoring, and analysis of interferences between transformations. Dr. Kniesel obtained an honors diploma in Computer Science from the University of Dortmund in 1989 and an honors Ph.D. in Computer Science from the University of Bonn in 2000.

Thomas Ledoux has been an assistant professor at the Ecole des Mines de Nantes (EMN) since 1998. His main Ph.D. contribution was OpenCorba, a reflective broker implemented on the top of a Smalltalk meta-object protocol. He is currently investigating context-awareness for middleware computing and self-adaptive component-based applications within the Obasco group (EMN/INRIA).

Diana Lee is a mathematical scientist with Science Applications International Corporation working in the Neural Engineering Lab at NASA Ames Research Center. Ms. Lee is also an adjunct faculty member at Santa Clara University's School of Engineering. Prior to working at NASA, Ms. Lee worked at Microelectronics and Computer Research Corporation, Lockheed-Martin, and International Business Machines. She has an M.S. in applied mathematics from Santa Clara University and a B.A. in mathematical sciences from Rice University.

Fabrice Legond-Aubry is a Ph.D. student at Conservatoire National des Arts et Metiers in Paris, France since 2001. He is currently working with the University Paris 6 LIP6 laboratory. He is involved in the development of the JAC (Java Aspect Components) core framework. He also works on component adaptability and reusability through aspects and contracts. In 2000, he graduated from the Ecole Francaise d'Electronique et d'Informatique engineering school.

Wesley Leong received his masters degree in Computer Science from the University of California, San Diego. He is currently at NVIDIA Corporation.

Karl Lieberherr Dr. Lieberherr is a professor in the College of Computer and Information Science at Northeastern University, where he has directed the Demeter project since 1985. He is a member of the steering committee of the conference series on Aspect-Oriented Software Development (AOSD), and was a keynote speaker at the International Conference on Software Engineering 2004 and program chair for AOSD 2004 in Lancaster, England.

Calvin Lin is an associate professor in the Department of Computer Sciences at the University of Texas at Austin. He received his B.S.E. from Princeton University in 1985 and his Ph.D. from the University of Washington in 1992. His research interests include languages and compilers. In his spare time, he plays and coaches ultimate frisbee.

Ted Linden managed the Object Infrastructure Project (OIP) project at the former Microelectronics and Computer Technology Corporation (MCC). His other research interests and publications include artificial intelligence, planning and scheduling, software security and reliability, robotics, and flexible software development methods. He received his Ph.D. in mathematics from Yeshiva University in 1968. He currently works as a consultant in Palo Alto, California.

Cristina Videira Lopes is an assistant professor in the School of Information and Computer Science, University of California, Irvine. She conducts research in programming languages and ubiquitous computing. She was one of the founders of the AOP project at PARC. She has a Ph.D. in Computer Science from Northeastern University.

David Lorenz is an assistant professor in the College of Computer Science, Northeastern University. He has a Ph.D. from the Technion. Prof. Lorenz's research interests include concepts of software components, with special interest in adaptive components and component-based design (particularly JavaBeans technology).

Laurent Martelli is a co-founder of AOPSYS, a company dedicated to offering competitive and easy-to-use programming tools based on the aspect-oriented programming paradigm. He graduated from Institut d'Informatique d'Entreprise, Evry, France in 1997. He is one of the developers of the JAC (Java Aspect Components) framework and is currently using it to develop applications for AOPSYS's customers.

Mira Mezini is a professor of Computer Science at Darmstadt University of Technology, Germany. She is the author of several papers and is leading several projects in the area of aspect-oriented programming involving not only the development of aspect-oriented technology but also technology transfer to software companies. She has been involved in research on improving the modularity of object-oriented systems for more than 10 years.

Ana Moreira is an assistant professor at the New University of Lisbon. Her research interests include object technology, requirements engineering, and aspect-orientation. She has been a member of the ECOOP and UML program committees for several years and has organized various workshops and conferences. She received her Ph.D. in formal methods from the University of Stirling in 1994.

Juan Manuel Murillo is an associate professor in the Computer Science Department of Extremadura University. He belongs to the Quercus Software Engineering Group. He received his B.S. in Computer Science from the Technical University of Barcelona and Ph.D. degree in Computer Science from the Extremadura University in 2001. His research interests include aspect orientation, web services orchestration, and software architectures.

Gail C. Murphy is an associate professor at the University of British Columbia. She received her graduate degrees from the University of Washington. Her research interests are in software evolution, software design, source code analysis, aspect-oriented software development, and empirical evaluation.

Sandeep Neema is a research scientist at ISIS, Vanderbilt University. His research interests include design space exploration and constraint-based synthesis of parallel/distributed, real-time, embedded systems, as well as dynamic reconfiguration of hardware and software in an embedded, real-time context.

Oscar Nierstrasz is a professor of Computer Science at the Institute of Computer Science of the University of Berne where he leads the Software Composition Group. Prof. Nierstrasz is the co-author of the book *Object-Oriented Reengineering Patterns* (Morgan Kaufmann, 2003). He is interested in all aspects of component-oriented software technology, particularly the design and implementation of high-level specification languages and tools to support reusability and evolution. He completed his B.Math at the University of Waterloo (1979) and his M.S. (1981) and Ph.D. (1984) at the University of Toronto.

Martin E. Nordberg III is a senior software architect with Blueprint Technologies, Inc. He has close to 20 years experience in software development, ranging from technically complex projects to organizationally complex projects. His interests include programming language details, object and aspect-oriented analysis and design, design patterns, and model-driven software architecture. He received his B.S. and M.B.A. degrees from Rensselaer Polytechnic Institute and his Ph.D. from the University of Massachusetts.

Joon Suan Ong is a recent Ph.D. graduate from the University of British Columbia. His research interests include network architectures, user-level networking, and distributed systems.

Harold Ossher has been a researcher at the IBM Thomas J. Watson Research Center since 1986. He is one of the originators of subject-oriented programming, multidimensional separation of concerns and Hyper/J, and the Concern Manipulation Environment. He currently leads the group conducting research and technology transfer in this area.

Klaus Ostermann is a research associate at Darmstadt University of Technology. He has an M.S. from the University of Bonn and a Ph.D. from Darmstadt University of Technology. His research focuses on the design and implementation of aspect-oriented languages as well as aspect-oriented type systems, foundations, and applications.

Renaud Pawlak holds a Ph.D. in Computer Science from the Conservatoire National des Arts et Métiers in 2002. He is currently a post-doctoral fellow at INRIA Lille, working on the Jacquard team. His research interests include software engineering in general and aspect-oriented programming in particular. He is currently researching AOP within distributed environments and promoting AOP use in industry.

Frank Piessens is a professor in the Distributed Systems and Computer Networks (DistriNet) research group in the Department of Computer Science of the Katholieke Universiteit Leuven. His main research interests are in software security, especially language-based security, security in software engineering, middleware security, and software vulnerabilities.

Andrei Popovici received a masters degree in Computer Science from the Darmstadt University of Technology (1998). After his studies, he joined the Computer Science Department at ETH Zurich as a teaching and research assistant. He completed his Ph.D. in June 2003 with a thesis on dynamic adaptation and aspect-oriented programming.

Awais Rashid is a lecturer in the Computing Department at Lancaster University. His principal research interests are in aspect-oriented requirements engineering, hybrid aspect-oriented programming, aspect-oriented databases, and object data management.

Martin P. Robillard is a recent Ph.D. graduate from the Department of Computer Science at the University of British Columbia and is currently an assistant professor at McGill University, Montréal. His research interests include program understanding, evolution, and modularization.

Isabelle Rouvellou is a research staff member and manager of the Advanced Enterprise Middleware department at the IBM's T. J. Watson Research Center, working on the design and implementation of middleware enabling the next generation of distributed applications. Isabelle holds several IBM awards for the contributions she made to IBM's WebSphere family of products. She is also a co-author of papers and patents in the field of distributed object technology, messaging, and software engineering. She received a Ph.D. from Columbia University.

Fernando Sánchez is currently an associate professor at the Computer Science Department of Extremadura University (Spain). He belongs to the Quercus Software Engineering Group. He received his B.S. in Computer Science from the University of Sevilla in 1992 and Ph.D. in Computer Science from the Extremadura University in 1999. His research interests include aspect orientation and web engineering. He is involved in several research projects and agreements with Internet companies.

Douglas C. Schmidt is a professor in the Electrical Engineering and Computer Science Department at Vanderbilt University. His research focuses on patterns, optimization techniques, and empirical analyses of object-oriented frameworks for distributed real-time and embedded middleware running over high-speed networks and embedded system interconnects.

Lionel Seinturier is an associate researcher at INRIA Lille, France in the Jacquard team, on leave from University Paris 6 LIP6 laboratory. His research interests include system services for middleware platforms and reflective and aspect-oriented programming. He received his Ph.D. degree from CNAM Paris in 1997, where he worked on design principles for distributed applications.

Mario Südholt is an assistant professor at École des Mines de Nantes and holds a doctoral degree from Technische Universität Berlin. He is a member of INRIA's OBASCO research group. His research work is focused on AOSD and component-based programming, particularly on foundations of AOP and applications of formal approaches.

Stanley M. Sutton Jr. received a Ph.D. from the University of Colorado, Boulder. He is currently a consulting software engineer at IBM's T. J. Watson Research Center, where he works on aspect-oriented and model-driven software development in the Software by Composition department. He is also employed at the Laboratory for Advanced Software Engineering Research at the University of Massachusetts, Amherst, where he works in the area of software-process and workflow.

Janos Sztipanovits is the E. Bronson Ingram Distinguished Professor of Engineering in the Electrical Engineering and Computer Science Department of Vanderbilt University. He is founding director of the Institute for Software Integrated Systems. Recently, he was program manager and acting deputy director of DARPA Information Technology Office. He is an IEEE Fellow.

Peri Tarr has been a researcher at IBM's Thomas J. Watson Research Center since 1996. She co-originated multi-dimensional separation of concerns and Hyper/J and co-invented the Concern Manipulation Environment. Her research focuses on AOSD throughout the software lifecycle and morphogenic software (software that remains malleable throughout its life).

Federico U. Trilnik is a research assistant in the Computer Science Department at the UNICEN University, Tandil, Argentina. He received his systems engineering degree from the UNICEN University in 2000, where he is currently pursuing his masters degree. His research interests include object-oriented frameworks, multi-agent systems, and aspect-oriented technologies.

Robert J. Walker is an assistant professor at the University of Calgary. He completed his Ph.D. in March 2003 on a mechanism for performing localized transformations of source modules (called implicit context) and its application to easing software evolution and reuse. His other interests include empirical validation and software visualization.

Preface

Software development is changing. The opportunities of the Internet, computerized businesses, and computer-savvy consumers, the exponential decline in the cost of computation and communication, and the increasingly dynamic environment for longer-living systems are pressing software developers to come up with better ways to create and evolve systems. There is fomenting in software development process, system structure, programming, quality assurance, and maintenance.

Software is about building computational models of some part of the elements or information flow of the world. For all but the most trivial software systems, conquering the engineering of the system requires (perhaps recursively) dividing the system into chunks that can be (by and large) separately created and managed. The last decade of the twentieth century saw the rise (and perhaps dominance) of the object-oriented perspective on system modularization. Object-orientation focuses on selecting *objects* as the primary unit of modularity and associating with these objects all the system's behavior. Objects are typically elements of the domain or of the computational process.

Object-orientation is reaching its limits. Many things one cares about in creating a software system (*concerns*) are not neatly localized to the behavior of specific "things." Building diverse systems requires simultaneously manipulating many concerns. Examples of concerns range from non-functional notions such as security, reliability, and manageability to precise implementation techniques such as concurrency control, caching, and error recovery. Since conventional programming technologies are centered on producing a direct sequence of instructions, they require the programmer to remain cognizant of all such concerns throughout the programming process. The programmer must explicitly intermix the commands to achieve these concerns with the code for the primary application functionality. This produces tangled code and erroneous and difficult-to-maintain systems.

New technologies are emerging to allow richer specifications of programs and better modularization of these specifications. Along with these new technologies, we are also seeing novel software engineering methodologies for using them. One of the most exciting of these new technologies is *aspect-oriented software development* (AOSD). AOSD programming technologies (aspect-oriented programming, or AOP) provide linguistic mechanisms for separate expression of concerns, along with implementation technologies for weaving these separate concerns into working systems. *Aspect-oriented software engineering* (AOSE) technologies are emerging for managing the process of developing systems within this new paradigm.

ABOUT THIS BOOK

This book grew out of our experience with the special issue on aspect-orientation in the October, 2001 *Communications of the ACM*. Seven times as many papers were submitted to that issue as we could print; those that appeared proved among the most popular in the ACM digital library. Simultaneously, we saw a growing number of increasingly popular workshops on aspect-oriented topics. There was clearly great interest in the computer science community for learning more about aspects. This led to two ideas—establishing an international conference on aspect-oriented software development and creating a book to illustrate to the advanced software development community the diversity of ideas in this space. The conference, organized by the Aspect-Oriented Software Association and co-sponsored by ACM, has recently had its third annual meeting; the proceedings are in the ACM digital library.

We intend this book as a volume for advanced software engineers interested in learning about this new direction in software development. To populate the book, we sent out invitations to selected researchers in the field either to submit a new paper presenting an overview of their work or to nominate an appropriate existing paper for reprinting. This book is the result of selecting from and editing those submissions.

HOW TO READ THIS BOOK

We recommend the first chapter, which is an introduction to the ideas of aspect-oriented software development, to all readers. Beyond that, system development rests on a basis of programming languages and models, though actual system development demands all the processes of an engineering activity. The ultimate test of a software technology is the systems whose construction it has supported, though aspects are not sufficiently mature to have an impressive portfolio. Correspondingly, after the introduction, the book is structured in three parts: Part 1, "Languages and Foundations," is primarily descriptions of languages for implementing aspects, with some attention to the place of aspects in the programming language universe. Part 2, "Software Engineering," describes technologies for the aspect-oriented software development process. Finally, Part 3, "Applications," details some of the first application experiences using aspect technology. Each part has an introductory section delimiting the space of aspect technology within the topic and outlining the place of each chapter in that space. Beyond that introduction, the chapters (as befits a contributed book on the state-of-the-art) are fundamentally independent. While the authors make the typical reference to other's works, almost every chapter is self-contained.

Chapter 1

Introduction

This book is about aspect-oriented software development (AOSD), a set of emerging technologies that seeks new modularizations of software systems. AOSD allows multiple concerns to be separately expressed but nevertheless be automatically unified into working systems. We intend this book to be an overview of these technologies for the computer professional interested in learning about state-of-the-art developments.

In general, programming is about realizing a set of requirements in an operational software system. One has a (perhaps evolving) set of properties desired of a system, and proceeds to develop that system to achieve those properties. Software engineering is the accumulated set of processes, methodologies, and tools to ease that evolutionary process, including techniques for figuring out what we want to build and mechanisms for yielding a higher-quality resulting system.

A recurrent theme of software engineering (and engineering in general) is that of modularization: "separation and localization of concerns." That is, we have "concerns"—things we care about—in engineering any system. These concerns range from high-level, user-visible requirements like reliability and security to low-level implementation issues like caching and synchronization. Ideally, separating concerns in engineering simplifies system development by allowing the development of specialized expertise and by producing an overall more comprehensible arrangement of elements.

Traditional software development has focused on decomposing systems into units of primary functionality, recognizing the other issues of concern, and leaving it to programmers both to code modules corresponding to the primary functionality and to make sure that all other issues of concern are addressed in the code wherever appropriate. Sometimes these other concerns can be packaged into modules of behavior themselves (e.g., subroutines, methods, or procedures). However, often the degree of shared context or the cost of contextual change (for example, the cost of a subprogram call) necessitates intermixing (crosscutting) the instructions for the primary functionality and the other concerns. In any case, conventional development requires programmers to keep in mind all the things that need to be done, how to deal with each issue, the problems associated with the possible interactions, and the execution of the right behavior at the right time.

Spreading out the responsibility for invoking the code for multiple concerns to all programmers produces a more brittle system. Each programmer who has to do something right is one more person who can make a mistake; each spot where something needs to be done is a potential maintenance mishap. The distribution of the code for realizing a concern becomes especially critical as the requirements for that concern evolve—a system maintainer must find and correctly update a variety of (likely poorly identified) situations.

We use the term aspect-oriented programming (AOP) to describe the activity of programming with multiple crosscutting concerns or aspects. The general *modus operandi* of programming AOSD systems is to let system developers express the behavior for each concern in its own module. Such a system must also include some directions for how the different concerns are to be knitted together into a working system (for example, to which program entities each separate concern applies) and a mechanism for actually producing a working system from these elements. For example, many AOSD systems provide a way to say, "High security is achieved by doing X. Reliability is achieved by doing Y. I want high security in the following places in the code and reliability on these operations." The AOSD system then produces an object that invokes the high security and reliability codes appropriately.

Concern-level illustrations of the application of AOP techniques include replication, configuration, debugging, mobility, program instrumentation, security, code movement, and synchronization. AOP is only beginning to penetrate commercial applications, but interesting prototypes have been demonstrated in areas such as application servers, operating systems kernels, real-time distributed event channels, distributed middleware, distributed quality-of-service, multi-agent system architectures, object databases, domain-specific visual modeling, collaboration, workflow, e-commerce, software visualization, engineering design, and data processing.

1.1 BOOK ORGANIZATION

Just like object-oriented programming, aspect technology started with aspect-oriented programming languages. Currently, several aspect-oriented languages are in widespread availability, and researchers are continually inventing new ones. Part 1 of this book, "Languages and Foundations," examines this area, including descriptions of not only proposed AOP languages but also programming models based on aspect ideas and chapters discussing the fundamental and historical nature of AOP.

Just as object-oriented programming led to the development of a large class of object-oriented development methodologies, AOP has encouraged a nascent set of software engineering technologies. Part 2, "Software Engineering," examines these issues, include methodologies for dealing with aspects, modeling techniques (often based on the ideas of the Unified Modeling Language, UML), and testing technology for assessing the effectiveness of aspect approaches.

Of course, the ultimate aim of programming is to develop software systems. In Part 3, "Applications," we present descriptions of the application of aspect technology to particular software problems, including examples that range from the systems to application levels.

Each part of the book includes an introduction to that area and chapters by contributors describing their own work. We invited each contributor to either create an original chapter, targeted at the advanced programmer, or to nominate reprinting an existing paper meeting those criteria. Several of our contributors chose to meld the two approaches, revising existing work in light of new experience and the intended audience.

AOSD is a rapidly evolving area. This format has enabled us to present the reader with a wider overview, a more current set of work, and a clearer sense of the diversity of opinions than a synopsis of different research or an in-depth study of one particular research direction would have provided.

1.2 COMMON TERMINOLOGY

Certain common terminology and themes pervade these papers. Different authors have variations on the meaning they assign to these ideas. This is a symptom of intellectual youth and ferment. They use certain terms freely. Thus, it is helpful to begin with a brief glossary of common AOSD concepts.

Concerns.   Any engineering process has many things about which it cares. These range from high-level requirements ("The system shall be manageable") to low-level implementation issues ("Remote values shall be cached"). Some concerns are localized to a particular place in the emerging system ("When the M key is pressed, the following menu shall pop up"), some refer to measurable properties of the system as a whole ("Response time shall be less than a second"), others are aesthetic ("Programmers shall use meaningful variable names"), and others involve systematic behavior ("All database changes shall be logged"). Generically, we call all these concerns, though AOSD technology is particularly directed at the last, systematic class.

Crosscutting concerns. Software development addresses concerns, both concerns at the user/requirements levels and at the design/implementation level. Often, the implementation of one concern must be scattered throughout the rest of an implementation. We say that such a concern is *crosscutting*. Note that what is crosscutting is a function of both the particular decomposition of a system and the underlying support environment. A particular concern might crosscut in one view of an architecture while being localized in another; a particular environment might invisibly support a concern (for example, security) that needs to be explicitly addressed in another.

Code tangling. In conventional environments, implementing crosscutting concerns usually results in code tangling—the code for concerns becomes intermixed. Ideally, software engineering principles instruct us to modularize our system software in such a way that (1) each module is cohesive in terms of the concerns it implements and (2) interfaces between modules are simple. Software that complies with these principles tends to be easier to produce, more naturally distributed among different programmers, easier to verify and test, and easier to maintain, reuse, and evolve to future requirements. Crosscutting works against modularization. Code for crosscutting concerns finds itself scattered through multiple modules; changes to that code now require changing all the places it touches, and (perhaps more importantly and less obviously) all changes to the system must conform to the requirements of the crosscutting concern. That is, if certain actions require, say, a security or accounting action, then in maintaining the code, we must consider how every change interacts with security and accounting.

Aspects. An *aspect* is a modular unit designed to implement a concern. An aspect definition may contain some code (or *advice,* which follows) and the instructions on where, when, and how to invoke it. Depending on the aspect language, aspects can be constructed hierarchically, and the language may provide separate mechanisms for defining an aspect and specifying its interaction with an underlying system.

Join points. *Join points* are well-defined places in the structure or execution flow of a program where additional behavior can be attached. A join point model (the kinds of joint points allowed) provides the common frame of reference to enable the definition of the structure of aspects. The most common elements of a join point model are method calls, though aspect languages have also defined join points for a variety of other circumstances, including field definition, access, and modification, exceptions, and execution events and states. For example, if an AOP language has method calls in its join point model, a programmer may designate additional code to be run on particular method calls.

Advice.   *Advice* is the behavior to execute at a join point. For example, this might be the security code to do authentication and access control. Many aspect languages provide mechanisms to run advice *before, after, instead of,* or *around* join points of interest. Advice is *oblivious* in that there is no explicit notation at the joint point that the advice is to be run here—the programmer of the original base code may be oblivious to the evolving requirements. This contrasts with conventional programming languages, where the most common concern modularization mechanism, the subprogram, must be explicitly called.

Pointcut designator.   A *pointcut designator* describes a set of join points. This is an important feature of AOP because it provides a *quantification mechanism*—a way to talk about doing something at many places in a program with a single statement. A programmer may designate all the join points in a program where, for example, a security code should be invoked. This eliminates the need to refer to each join point explicitly and thereby reduces the likelihood that any aspect code would be incorrectly invoked.

Composition.   Abstractly, the idea of bringing together separately created software elements is *composition*. Different languages provide a variety of composition techniques, including subprogram invocation, inheritance, and generic instantiation. An important software engineering issue in the composition of components is the guarantees and mechanisms that a language provides to make sure that elements being composed "fit together." This allows warning of incompatibilities during system development, rather than being surprised by them during system execution. Common mechanisms for such guarantees include type checking the signatures of subprogram calls and the interface mechanism of languages like Java.

Weaving.   *Weaving* is the process of composing core functionality modules with aspects, thereby yielding a working system. Various AOP languages have defined several mechanisms for weaving, including statically compiling the advice together with base code, dynamically inserting aspects when loading code, and modifying the system interpreter to execute aspects.

Wrapping, before and after.   One of the most common AOP techniques is to provide method calls as (sometimes the only) join points and to allow the advice to run either *before, after,* or *around* the method call. This notion can be generalized into the idea of *wrapping*—providing a filter or container around a component, which mediates communications to that component and enforces the desired aspects.

Statics and dynamics. The terms *static* and *dynamic* appear in some of the following discussions. In general, *static* elements are ones that can be determined before the program begins execution, typically at compile time; *dynamic* things happen at execution. A weaving process can be either static or dynamic, depending on whether it relies on a compilation or loading mechanism (static) or run-time monitoring (dynamic) for its realization. Somewhat orthogonally, an AOP language can be characterized as having static or dynamic join points, depending on whether the places that aspects are to be invoked are dependent purely on the compile-time structure of the original code or the run-time events of program execution.

The tyranny of the dominant decomposition. The previous discussion spoke of aspects as something to be imposed on a "base" program. However, one can make a perfectly coherent argument that all code elements should be treated as equals and that the best way to build AOSD systems is by providing a language for weaving together such elements. Some of the systems discussed in this book adopt that point of view. A key subtext of that discussion is whether aspect behavior can be imposed on aspects themselves. Doing so makes the contractual assertions of aspects more complete at the cost of complicating the underlying implementations.

1.3 HISTORICAL CONTEXT

The history of programming has been a slow and steady climb from the depths of direct manipulation of the underlying machines to linguistic structures for expressing higher-level abstractions. Progress in programming languages and design methods has always been driven by the invention of structures that provide additional modularity. Subroutines assembled the behavior of unstructured machine instructions, structured programming argued for semantic meaning for these subroutines, abstract data types recognized the unity of data and behavior, and object-orientation (OO) generalized this to multiplicity of related data and behaviors.

The current state-of-the-art in programming is object-oriented (OO) technology. With objects, the programmer is supposed to think of the universe as a set of instances of particular classes that provide methods, expressed as imperative programs, to describe the behavior of all the objects of a class.

Object-orientation has many virtues, particularly in comparison to its predecessors. Objects provide modularization. The notion of sending messages to objects helps concentrate the programmer's thinking and aids understanding code. Inheritance mechanisms in object systems provide a way both to ascribe related behaviors to multiple classes and to make exceptions to that prescription.

Objects are not the last word in programming organization. This book is about an emerging candidate for the next step in this progression, aspect-oriented software development. Aspects introduce new linguistic mechanisms to modularize the implementation of concerns. Each of the earlier steps (with the minor exception of multiple inheritance in OO systems) focused on centralizing on a primary concern. AO, like its predecessors, is about recognizing that software systems are built with respect to many concerns and that programming languages, environments, and methodologies must support modularization mechanisms that honor these concurrent concerns. AO is technology for extending the kinds of concerns that can be separately and efficiently modularized.

PART 1

Languages and
Foundations

The ultimate goal of software engineering is to create running software systems, usually for a von Neumann architecture of instructions, registers, and memory locations. Formally, almost all programming languages are computationally equivalent—almost any programming language can be used to create Turing-machine-equivalent systems and control von Neumann machines. Why not just program in assembler or FORTRAN? Because programming is a human activity. Alternative programming models and languages facilitate building systems with better "-ilities:" evolvability, adaptability, reusability, efficiency, ease of implementation, and so forth.

We have seen a historical progression of language structures for taming the von Neumann beast: imperative, functional, logical, object-oriented. The earliest programming languages such as Algol and FORTRAN were imperative, mapping fairly straightforwardly to a von Neumann architecture: the abstractions of an imperative program (procedures, statements, record structures) have a fairly direct correspondence to von Neumann instructions and addressable memory locations. This provided efficient execution and straightforward compiler implementation. This machine-oriented approach to programming was not immediately perceived to be a problem, since software systems of that time were mainly applied to solving well-structured and relatively simple problems. We lacked the processing power to undertake harder problems or to apply more complex programming notations.

Computers got faster and larger, encouraging us to tackle more complicated problems. Programming language designers began to search for means to express problems and their solutions without being so closely tied to the details of the underlying machine. Some languages, such as functional and logic-based programming, have used mechanisms that break away from the imperative model. While these are good for certain classes of problems, they have failed to capture much mindshare. Most programmers are comfortable with languages that are primarily sequences of stateful and imperative commands.

Progress in imperative languages was marked by inventions that moved away from a simple map of the von Neumann architecture, such as subprograms, abstract data types, and modules. Although these abstractions provided modularizations and thereby reduced the complexity of programs, the organizational influence of von Neumann architecture still dominated. A data abstraction is roughly equivalent to a memory location accessed through a (privileged) set of user-defined instructions.

Within the context of imperative languages, introducing the concept of inheritance (and later delegation) was probably the most significant deviation from the von Neumann architecture. Object-oriented systems trace their roots to Simula[4], Ole-Johan Dahl and Kristen Nygaard's language for simulating complex systems, such as the vehicles, roads, and bridges of traffic flow. Simula enhanced Algol with the concepts of classes and class inheritance. In the following years, many language designers and programmers adopted this approach and contributed to the vast expansion of the application of object-oriented languages.

TRADITIONAL ENGINEERING

Perhaps the greatest effect of the progression to object orientation has been to shift the focus of programmers and designers from a machine-oriented view to a problem-centric view. This naturally led to adopting problem solving techniques in software engineering. In traditional engineering disciplines, design is a problem solving process. It aims to map problems to realizable solutions, expressed using the artifacts in the corresponding engineering domain. Problem solving consists of analyzing and dividing the problems into sub problems, solving each (sub) problem by applying the relevant knowledge in the engineering domain, and synthesizing (composing) the solutions into an integrated working system.

Traditional engineering disciplines have introduced the concepts of *canonical component models, systemic (system-wide) models, system construction rules,* and *multiple* (simultaneous) *models.* A *canonical component model* (such as a transistor model) defines the common properties of a set of its instances (such as transistors). Good canonical component models are *succinct*: they do not include redundant or irrelevant abstractions. A canonical model defines the *essential operations* on the model. This "algebraic" approach makes component models highly predictable and usable, especially in constructing more complex systems. However, such composition can introduce unwanted redundancy. In addition, it may also be necessary to identify a new set of essential operations over the constructed system. Traditional engineering disciplines address this problem by mapping the individual component models to a well-defined common model. For example, electronic engineers define models for the individual components (for example, transistors and resistors) and map these models into a common model (for example, circuits) that represents the *systemic properties* of the composed system. For electronic engineers, the common model is generally based on Kirschoff's law, and for mechanical engineers, Newton's laws. Preferably, common models should be canonical as well (for example, well-defined circuit models such as amplifiers).

Interestingly, in traditional engineering disciplines, the main focus of engineers is models that express *systemic* properties. For example, while designing an amplifier, electronic engineers define models that enable the computation of systemic properties such as the amplification factor, frequency bandwidth, and harmonic distortion. To carry out the desired computations, systemic models *quantify* (reason about) adopted components and/or other systemic models. In traditional engineering disciplines, designers generally have the precise knowledge of how systemic models *quantify* the related models. In fact, these quantifications define the basis of the *system construction rules*.

However, although traditional engineering disciplines generally use precise models, finding the optimal composition of solution models (synthesis) for solving a given problem can be difficult (NP-complete for a general case [7]). In that respect, software engineering is just like other engineering disciplines.

Another common practice of traditional engineering disciplines is to create *multiple systemic models* that represent different characteristics of the system. For example, within the context of designing an electronic amplifier, one model may be used for computing the frequency bandwidth, another model for computing the amplification factor, and so forth. Normally, a component participates in more than one systemic model. In principle, component models are independent of their containing systemic models. This obliviousness makes component models more reusable. Systemic models, on the other hand, qualify the component models.

Fulfilling the requirements of one model may have adverse effects on other models. For example, large bandwidth may compromise the amplification factor, low harmonic distortion may require decreasing amplification efficiency, and so forth. Within a given context, much of the skill of engineers is leveraging different solutions to obtain an optimal balance among quality factors.

SOFTWARE DEVELOPMENT IS ENGINEERING

Software development is an engineering activity, and as such, it progresses along the evolutionary path of traditional engineering disciplines [8]. The emerging phenomena of aspect-oriented software development techniques can be explained and motivated within this context. The concepts of *component models*, *systemic models*, *system construction rules*, and *multiple models* as defined in traditional engineering disciplines correspond respectively to the concepts of *base-level models, aspect models, join point models,* and *multi-dimensional separation of concerns* of aspect-oriented languages. Like traditional engineering methods, aspect-oriented languages seek stability by adopting canonical models. These models can be seen as a distinguishing characteristic of aspect-oriented languages.

Aspect-oriented languages can model the natural systemic properties of problem domains. This allows them to be a better representation than conventional object-oriented languages. Because of the conceptual divergence of aspect-oriented languages from the von Neumann machines, efficient implementation of aspect-oriented languages remains a challenging problem. Aspect-oriented languages therefore have to compromise within the context of the following two constraints [1]:

Abstractness constraint.   The constructs of an aspect-oriented programming language must be abstract enough to match the natural abstractions of the problem domain. However, they also must be concrete enough to match the realization of the implementation platform. This constraint aims to minimize the implementation effort and enable efficiency.

Standardization constraint.   The realization of an implementation platform must be standardized to ease sharing among multiple languages but must be differentiated enough to match the individual needs of each target language. This constraint aims to reduce costs through sharing implementations.

These two constraints depict a design spectrum for aspect-oriented programming (AOP) implementations. The first constraint defines the concern of balancing modeling expressiveness of aspect-oriented languages with efficient implementation. The second constraint balances the breadth of application of an AOP language with its efficient implementation with respect to a particular computational environment.

THE CHAPTERS

In the first chapter in this part, Chapter 2, "Aspect-Oriented Programming Is Quantification and Obliviousness," Robert Filman and Daniel Friedman introduce the terms *quantification* and *obliviousness* as the two distinguishing characteristics of aspect-oriented languages. The term *quantification* refers to the fact that the expression of a single aspect may affect multiple program modules; the term *obliviousness* refers to the fact that the affected modules do not contain any particular notation preparing them for this action. Within that framework, the chapter presents several dimensions for the understanding of aspect-oriented languages, the most important of which is whether the quantification is to take the place of the structural (static) or behavioral (dynamic) properties of the system. The chapter then compares various (non-aspect oriented) languages and techniques with respect to the concepts of quantification and obliviousness. These ideas echo our notions of the important features of systemic models and component models in traditional engineering disciplines.

In Chapter 3, "*N* Degrees of Separation: Multi-Dimensional Separation of Concerns," Peri Tarr, Harold Ossher, Stanley M. Sutton, Jr., and William Harrison emphasize the value of defining *simultaneous models* incorporating separate concerns. In this approach, models are built by using primitive units (for example, operations and attributes) and compound units (for example, classes). Each model expresses a solution along a given dimension (for example, persistency). *Hyperslices* are used to capture such models. Multiple hyperslices may exist simultaneously; different hyperslices can conflict with each other. Models in different hyperslices are integrated into a single system through the application of *composition rules*. These rules also specify how to resolve conflicts. This approach allows defining multiple models simultaneously; the flexibility of the composition rules avoids differentiating between aspects and components.

In the software engineering literature, there have been several attempts for representing conflicting design models simultaneously [2, 3, 5]. However, most of these approaches cover only the early phases of the software development process. This contrasts with the hyperslice approach, where tools such as Hyper/J support translating hyperslices to executable programs.

From the perspective of the *abstractness constraint*, the canonical model of this approach is quite general. It can be considered more of a design model than a language model. Specific implementations of this approach choose specific definitions of the primitives, compound units, and composition rules. The *standardization constraint* is determined by the available implementation tools. For example, Java is the implementation platform for the hyperslice language Hyper/J. Currently defined models in hyperslices and the composition rules restrict this approach to static composition of aspects. Hyperslices traces its intellectual roots to work in the early 1990s on subject-oriented programming [6].

Composition filters, described by Lodewijk Bergmans and Mehmet Akşit in Chapter 4, "Principles and Design Rationale of Composition Filters," introduce a linguistic construct, the *concern,* as a mechanism for uniformly expressing crosscutting and non-crosscutting concerns. Concern specifications have three (optional) parts: *filter modules,* a *superimposition specification,* and an *implementation*. A concern specification with just an implementation corresponds to an element (such as a class) in a conventional program. Filter modules are used to express crosscutting concerns. They are specified using a declarative message-manipulation language based on a set of primitive and/or user-defined filter types. Filter modules are attached to object instances[1] through a declarative constraint-based superimposition specification. Multiple concerns may superimpose their filter modules on the same object.

The canonical model of composition filters assumes that aspects can be added to objects by manipulating the interaction patterns of objects. Message manipulation is achieved by superimposing filter modules, using the composition operators of the filter module specification language. The composition filters approach supports a variety of filter types, ranging from primitive language-independent filters to stateful user-defined types.

Composition filters aim at language independence and easy verification of aspect compositions. Due to their declarative nature (and depending on the adopted implementation technique), aspects can be composed at compile time, runtime, or both.

From the perspective of the abstractness constraint, this approach is limited to adding aspects only at the level of interacting program modules. The standardization constraint of composition filters is a common interaction interface for multiple languages.

The composition filters model goes back to the late 1980s. In the ensuing years, this model evolved from hardwired filter modules on singular objects towards flexible superimposition of separately specified filter modules on multiple objects.

The next two chapters illustrate the third major family of aspect-oriented languages. In Chapter 5, "AOP: A Historic Perspective (What's in a Name)," Cristina Lopes elucidates the derivation of the word "aspect" in the context of separating software concerns. This chapter presents a personal history of her work on the topic, starting with her graduate studies at Northeastern, progressing to specialized aspect languages for particular concerns like distribution, and culminating with her work at Xerox PARC on the team that developed AspectJ.

In Chapter 6, "AspectJ," Adrian Colyer provides a brief introduction to the goals of the AspectJ project and gives an overview of the AspectJ language and supporting tools. AspectJ is a general-purpose programming language. AspectJ and AspectJ tools are designed to be easy to integrate into existing Java-based environments. Today, AspectJ is by far the most popular aspect-oriented language in use.

The most important extension to Java in AspectJ is the concept of *join points*. Join points are identifiable events in the execution of the program. *Pointcut expressions* are used to refer to the join points in an AspectJ program. For example, a pointcut expression may specify join points for the execution of a method or constructor, a call to a method or constructor, read or write access to a field, etc. *Advice* is a set of program statements that are executed at join points referred to by a pointcut

---

1. In principle, filter modules can be superimposed on any identifiable program piece that interacts with other program pieces through operation calls.

specification. AspectJ has three kinds of advice: *before* advice, *after* advice, and *around* advice. These execute *before, after,* and *around* join points matched by the advice's pointcut expression. *Aspects* are the unit of modularity by which AspectJ implements crosscutting concerns. Aspects can contain methods and fields, point-cuts, advice, and *inter-type declarations*. Inter-type declaration mechanisms allow an aspect to provide an implementation of methods and fields on behalf of other types.

The canonical model of AspectJ is derived from the Java language. The abstract-ness constraint of the language is determined by the combination of pointcut specifications, advices, and inter-type declarations. The standardization constraint of the language is determined by the compilation mechanisms of AspectJ within Java environments.

In Chapter 7, "Coupling Aspect-Oriented and Adaptive Programming," Karl Lieberherr and David Lorenz contrast and unify their work on adaptive programming with AOP. The abstract data type/object-oriented tradition argues for reducing the mutual interdependence of code by hiding implementations within abstractions. However, in practice that is not sufficient to keep components from becoming depen-dent on each other's structural implementation—the actual parts of composite objects often become visible to code using those objects. Adaptive programming argues that a major cause of increased software coupling is due to complex interac-tions along the nested object structures. The canonical model of this approach is based on a succinct graph-based representation of object and class hierarchies with a set of graph manipulation operations. Aspects can be superimposed over the graph structures using these operations. The abstractness constraint of this approach is determined by the succinct graph models. The standardization constraint is defined by the algorithms that transform conventional (object-oriented) programs to the graph representations and vice versa.

The authors claim that both adaptive programming and AOP can benefit from each other: adaptive programming concepts can enhance the separation of concern characteristics of aspect-oriented languages, and AOP, as illustrated by AspectJ, can provide a better implementation platform for adaptive programming.

In Chapter 8, "Untangling Crosscutting Models with CAESAR," Mira Mezini and Klaus Ostermann assert that conventional AOP languages are too limited in abstract-ing and reusing aspects. The programming model CAESAR provides constructs for better aspect modularization, for flexibly binding aspects to different implementation modules, and for dynamically combining aspects into a running system. The reuse mechanism is called *aspectual polymorphism*; it generalizes subtype polymorphism to aspect-oriented models. The model uses virtual classes and family polymorphism to help enable type-safe reuse.

The canonical model of CAESAR is a novel generalization of the object-oriented model to the aspect-oriented model. Its abstractness constraint is mainly determined by the language construct called Aspect Collaboration Interface, the unit of aspect reuse. Its standardization constraint is determined by the algorithms that translate CAESAR to existing languages and run-time environments.

Chapter 9, "Trace-Based Aspects," by Remi Douence, Pascal Fradet, and Mario Südholt, argues that conventional object-oriented languages are inadequate for expressing relations between execution events of aspects. To overcome this limitation, this paper introduces an event-based crosscut specification, where events refer to the relevant states of program execution. With this model, one can invoke aspects based on the dynamic history of program execution. Crosscut specifications are controlled by event matching and propositional and sequential logic.

From the abstractness constraint point of view, the canonical model of this approach is a state-based crosscut program. The standardization constraint is determined by the algorithms and techniques that capture the state of executions.

Chapter 10, "Using Mixin Technology to Improve Modularity," by Richard Cardone and Calvin Lin, revisits the themes of the ability of multiple-inheritance-like mechanisms to add concerns to an object system from Chapters 2 and 3 and aspectual polymorphism from Chapter 8. In conventional object systems like Java (or at least Java before Java 5), the types of a system are constants. Mechanisms such as C++ templates and Ada and Java 5 generics allow constructing types by instantiating generic type descriptions. *Mixins* carry this idea of instantiated types into the inheritance mechanism. That is, one can parameterize with respect to the superclasses of a type. Cardone and Lin describe mixins and show how mixins can be used for aspects. Just as CAESAR in Chapter 8 was concerned with coordinating the instantiation of multiple types, Cardone and Lin describe a layering mechanism for collecting related mixins together. They illustrate the power of this mechanism with a graphical user interface library that can be parameterized with respect to its target device.

In Chapter 11, "Separating Concerns with First-Class Namespaces," Oscar Nierstrasz and Franz Achermann present a model of separation of concerns based on *forms*, a structure of first-class namespaces, *agents*, or processes, and *channels*, communication structures between processes. This work strives for a canonical model that is capable of expressing a large category of language abstractions. A critical element of this model is that forms can describe both required and provided operations of a component, thereby enabling statically checking the consistency of architectural structures. The standardization constraint of this approach is determined by a layered set of implementation techniques, where forms, agents, channels, and services define the most concrete layer. Nierstrasz and Achermann demonstrate how their model can be used to describe mixins and mixin layers.

The last five chapters of Part 1 turn toward issues of implementing aspect-oriented languages. Several of the systems described in the earlier chapters can be understood as compiler-based systems that take descriptions of base-level code, aspects, and some language mapping the aspects to the base-level code (though symmetric systems treat the base-level code and aspects as the same stuff, and the mapping commands in some languages are intermixed with the code). These compilers output object code that implements the desired functionality. There are four primary alternatives to this "compilation-based" approach. The first, illustrated in Chapter 12, "Supporting AOP Using Reflection," by Noury Bouraqadi and Thomas Ledoux, modifies the process of interpreting a program to intermix aspect behavior. Controlling the execution of interpreter of a language is meta-programming; Bouraqadi and Ledoux provide an introduction to meta-programming and illustrate how meta-programming can be used to support aspects.

The second implementation technology is to wrap base-level components with aspects. One way of implementing composition filters (Chapter 4) relies directly on such a wrapping. A similar but decidedly more programmatic approach is illustrated in Chapter 13, "Inserting Ilities by Controlling Communications," by Robert E. Filman, Stu Barrett, Diana Lee, and Ted Linden, which describes the Object Infrastructure Framework (OIF). OIF is based on wrapping communicating components; using the wrappers to manipulate their communications. The OIF approach is programmatic: wrappers are themselves objects; they embody aspects and can be dynamically apportioned around base-level components. The system supports mechanisms such as intra-aspect and inter-aspect and base component communication channels to aid the pragmatics of programming. The composition languages of composition filters emphasize expressing permanent semantic relationships about the base components; the composition language in OIF describes default initializations.

The next two chapters of this part are unified by the theme of modifying or manipulating the output of the ordinary compilation process to achieve aspects. In Chapter 14, "Using Bytecode Transformation to Integrate New Features," Geoff Cohen describes one of the earlier implementations of this idea. Bytecode transformation adds concerns by modifying compiled Java classfiles. Günter Kniesel, Pascal Costanza, and Michael Austermann extend this idea in Chapter 15, "JMangler—A Powerful Back-End for Aspect-Oriented Programming." JMangler provides class-loading-time bytecode transformation. Transformation at load-time ensures that no code that has avoided aspectization can run in the system, an important security and integrity guarantee. Both bytecode transformation mechanisms take advantage of the fact that some operations of interest to aspects are more explicitly visible in the object code than in the source.

The final chapter of Part 1, Chapter 16, "Aspect-Oriented Software Development with Java Aspect Components," by Renaud Pawlak, Lionel Seinturier, Laurence Duchien, Laurent Martelli, Fabrice Legond-Aubry, and Gérard Florin, builds on the natural dynamics of run-time class-loading manipulation to describe the final implementation technology, framework-based mechanisms. With a framework, the application program "fits in," in some sense, to a run-time environment. The JAC framework is powered by run-time bytecode transformation and features elements such as containers, instance-based methods, and dynamic reconfiguration. As a lead-in to Part 2, "Software Engineering," this chapter also describes a UML-based process for building JAC applications.

DIMENSIONS OF ASPECT LANGUAGE DESIGN

One of the advantages of bringing together this collection of papers is the opportunity to perform a comparative analysis of the different approaches. Dimensions to consider for each system include:

Symmetry versus asymmetry. Does the model differentiate between "base-level" and "aspect" elements, or is all programming done with a single kind of stuff? Proponents of the latter have characterized the former as supporting "the tyranny of the dominant decomposition," though many programmers may find it comforting to have a dominant decomposition to program against.

Join point models. At which points in the program can aspect behavior be introduced? Critical considerations in this element include join points that refer to the structural or dynamic properties of program execution and which structural or dynamic features are accessible.

Composition mechanism. What linguistic mechanisms does the system provide for describing where aspects should be applied? Choices include providing a separate language for describing the composition, intermixing composition commands with the actual code, and making composition an executable operation. Composition also interacts with object-oriented inheritance. A worthwhile side note is the issue of whether aspects can be applied to aspects. This is important because we don't want the semantic guarantees that aspects provide to be subverted by the aspect system itself. That is, if using the "security" aspect ensures that a system is secure, we don't want to run aspects that have not also been made secure.

Quantification. What mechanisms does the programmer have for making systematic application of aspects? What kinds of predicates can the programmer use to describe a class of situations that call for an aspect? Examples of such predicates include elements with the same syntactic structure (e.g., method calls, conditionals), elements with the same lexical structure (e.g., things with the same name or name prefix), elements with the same semantic structure (e.g., all methods that support a particular interface), and elements with the same execution history (e.g., all events of a particular type, or all events that match a particular temporal logic).

Encapsulation.   Consider what mechanisms the language provides for constraining the visibility and effect of aspects and aspect interactions.

Type safety.   To what extent does the language provide static mechanisms for checking the compatibility of composed components? The languages and models in this part range from almost no such checking to elaborate multi-level organizations for guaranteeing mutually and collectively appropriate roles.

Obliviousness.   Does code to which an aspect is to be applied need to be prepared in any particular way? Though there are no examples of this in the following papers, is there a way to protect a component from aspect application?

Domain specificity.   Does the language provide general aspect-oriented programming (in the sense that Java or C++ is a general-purpose language), or is it restricted or enhanced for a particular class of problems?

Reuse and aspect parameterization.   To what extent can one create aspects that are reusable in multiple contexts? How can such aspects be parameterized or specialized to the needs of a particular context?

Conflict resolution.   Are there mechanisms to describe and resolve possible conflicts from the use of multiple aspects? A common example of an aspect is a "logging aspect" that records that something has happened in a software system. This is particularly useful for debugging, accounting, and security auditing. Transactions (in the database sense) have also been proposed as good for aspects. Transactions, on the other hand, are supposed to either totally complete or leave no trace of their failure. Logging and transaction aspects thus conflict.

Legacy relationships.   Is the proposed system meant to augment an existing programming environment or extend that environment, or does the model require the programmer to employ entirely new constructs?

Run-time aspect dynamics.   Can the aspects in use be altered at runtime, or are they fixed before program execution, typically by a compilation process? Are the quantification targets of aspects (which aspects apply to which situations) fixed, or can they be altered at runtime?

Analyzability.   How does the aspect language affect the ability to statically analyze the source system?

Debugability.   How does the aspect language affect the ability to debug a system?

Testability.   Can aspects be tested without base code?

Software process.   What does the particular language have to say about the process of its use?

Implementation mechanism.   How can the language be implemented? As we discussed previously, the following chapters have examples of compilation-based systems, reflection, frameworks, wrapping, and bytecode transformation-based systems.

Available run-time environment.   What additional mechanisms does the system provide to support run-time applications?

Every aspect language or model makes choices in each of these dimensions. These dimensions are separate but not completely orthogonal. The complexity of aspect language design is the compound interactions of making a set of choices that give the language its unique design structure and application.

REFERENCES

1. AKŞIT, M. 2003. The 7 C's for creating living software: a research perspective for quality-oriented software engineering, University of Twente (Enschede).

2. AKŞIT, M. AND MARCELLONI, F. 2001. Deferring elimination of design alternatives in object-oriented methods. *Concurrency and Computation: Practice and Experience*, 13, 1247–1279.

3. BALZER, R. 1991. Tolerating inconsistency, In *13th Int'l Conf. of Software Engineering (ICSE)*, (Austin). IEEE.158–163.

4. BIRTWISTLE, G. M., DAHL, O. J., MYHRHAUG, B., AND NYGAARD, K. 1973. *Simula Begin*, Auerbach, Philadelphia.

5. FINKELSTEIN, A. C. W., GABBAY, D., HUNTER, A., KRAMER, J., AND NUSEIBEH, B. 1994. Inconsistency handling in multiperspective specifications. *IEEE Transactions on Software Engineering*, 20, 569–578.

6. HARRISON, W. AND OSSHER, H. 1993. Subject-oriented programming—a critique of pure objects. In *8th Conf. Object-Oriented Programming, Systems, Languages, and Applications (OOPSLA)*, (Washington, D.C.). ACM, 411–428.

7. MAIMON, O. AND BRAHA, D. 1996. On the complexity of the design synthesis problem, *IEEE Transactions on Systems, Man, And Cybernetics Part A: Systems and Humans*, 26, 1, 141–150.

8. TEKINERDOGAN, B. 2000. On the notion of software engineering: a problem solving perspective. Chapter 2. In *Synthesis-based software architecture design*, Ph.D. thesis, University of Twente (Enschede).

Chapter 2

Aspect-Oriented Programming Is Quantification and Obliviousness

ROBERT E. FILMAN AND DANIEL P. FRIEDMAN

We argue that the distinguishing characteristic of aspect-oriented programming (AOP) languages is that they allow programming by making quantified programmatic assertions over programs that lack local notation indicating the invocation of these assertions. This suggests that AOP systems can be analyzed with respect to three critical dimensions: the kinds of quantifications allowed, the nature of the interactions that can be asserted, and the mechanism for combining base-level actions with asserted actions. Consequences of this perspective are the recognition that certain systems are not AOP and that some mechanisms are meta-AOP: They are sufficiently expressive to allow straightforwardly programming an AOP system within them.

2.1 INTRODUCTION

We are concerned with aspect-oriented programming (AOP) qua programming language—determining what makes a language AOP. This work was prompted by a question from Tzilla Elrad, who asked whether event-based publish-and-subscribe (EBPS) mechanisms (for example, [21]) are AOP. After all, in a publish-and-subscribe system, separate concerns can be realized by having concerns subscribe to the events they care about. In thinking about that question, we have come to the belief that two properties, *quantification* and *obliviousness* (which we have also referred to as *implicit invocation* [15]), are necessary for AOP. Understanding these relationships clarifies the variety of possible AOP languages and suggests research directions for AOP.

Here we address the structural essence of AOP, not its application—somewhat similar to the difference between defining object-oriented programming (OOP) systems in terms of polymorphic methods and inheritance versus waxing euphoric about objects as the appropriate way to model the world. (We take inspiration here from Wegner [42], who early in the history of object-oriented programming discussion tried to clarify the dimensions of OOP language design.) Our definition clarifies why some systems that might seem to be AOP are not and why some systems are stronger than just AOP—their primitives allow straightforward construction of AOP mechanisms at the user level.

2.2 *LOCAL AND UNITARY STATEMENTS*

Programming languages are about writing a structure of *statements* that a compilation or interpretation process will elaborate as a series of primitive directions. (The directions themselves will be a finite text, though their interpretation may be unbounded.) The earliest computer machine-language programs had a strict correspondence between the program text and the execution pattern. Generally, each programming language statement was both *unitary* and *local*—unitary in that it ended up having effect in precisely *one* place in the elaborated program, and local in that it was almost always proximate to the statements executing around it.

The history (of this part) of programming languages has been about moving away from purely local and unitary languages and toward mechanisms that let the programmer separate concepts into pragmatic assemblages or modules, instead of being tied to saying things just where they happen. The first exceptions to locality were subprograms (i.e., procedures, subroutines, functions). Subprograms were a great invention, enabling abstracting out some behavior to someplace else. They have many virtues for separating concerns. For example, expertise in, say, Runge-Kutta methods could be embodied in the writer of the Runge-Kutta library. The application programmers were users of that library. They still had to know something about Runge-Kutta (when to use it, how to invoke it) and had to locally and *explicitly* call it in their code. The program was still unitary: It exhibited a direct correspondence between one statement in the programming language written and one sequence of machine instructions executed.

Inheritance (and related mechanisms like delegation) in object-oriented programming was another important introduction of non-locality. Executing inherited behavior is non-local. How explicit this execution was depended on whether the OO language used send-super or mixins.

Send-super systems like Java and Smalltalk allow the programmer to explicitly invoke the behavior of its parent class or classes without knowing exactly what behavior is being invoked. Adding behavior to classes higher in the class structure allows a limited form of *quantified* program statements—that is, statements that have effect on many places in the underlying code. For example, suppose we wish to introduce a "display" aspect to a program about simulating traffic movement. We will want to make quantified statements like "Whenever something moves (executes its move method), the screen must be updated." Imagine that all things that move are descendants of the class of moveable-object. We can accomplish this with send-super inheritance if we have a cooperative base-class programmer—one who will consistently follow directions. We make the behavior of the move method in movable-object be the display update, and we request that the programmers of derivative classes invoke send-super at the end of their code. This requires the derived class programmers to know that they have to do something, but it relieves them of having to know what exactly it is that they have to do. We're also restricted with respect to the locus of behavior—we can ask programmers to do the send-super at the start of their code or at the end, but our directions probably need to be consistent throughout the system.

Requiring cooperation is not good enough. Programmers may fail to be systematically cooperative, and the base program may itself be already written or otherwise out of our control. For true AOP, we want our system to work with programmers who don't have to be thinking about every concern as they program. The behavior of the other concerns must be invoked implicitly. An early example of something close to obliviousness is *mixin inheritance,* found in MacLisp and Symbolics Lisp [6, 36]. With mixins, the derived-class functionality is determined by assembling the code of the derived class with the advice of its super classes. The aspect programmer can make quantified statements about the code by adding mixins, while the derived class programmer remains (almost) ignorant of these actions. The scope of quantification is controlled by which classes inherit the mixin. That is, we can quantify over the descendants of some superclass for a given single method. In the screen update example, adding an "after" mixin to movable-object's move accomplishes the automatic update. Except that class inheritance relationships are part of a class's definition, we would have an AOP system (and even this caveat has an exception [16]).

In general,

> *AOP can be understood as the desire to make quantified statements about the behavior of programs and to have these quantifications hold over programs that have no explicit reference to the possibility of additional behavior.*

We want to be able to say, "This code realizes this concern. Execute it whenever these circumstances hold." This breaks completely with local and unitary demands— we can organize our program in the form most appropriate for coding and maintenance. We do not even need the local markings of cooperation. The weaving mechanism of the AOP system can, by itself, take our quantified statements and the base program and produce the primitive directions to be performed.

2.3 OBLIVIOUSNESS

Obliviousness states that one can't tell that the aspect code will execute by examining the body of the base code. Obliviousness is desirable because it allows greater separation of concerns in the system creation process—concerns can be separated not only in the structure of the system, but also in the heads of the creators. Obliviousness in AOP contrasts with the primary mechanism for separation of concerns in programming languages: subprograms. One invokes a subprogram or sends a specific message to a particular target. With AOP, the crosscutting behavior is intermixed by higher-level specifications, not low-level programming.

This is not to ignore the disadvantages of obliviousness—that systems melded from separate minds may not function the way anyone intended and that systems composed by formal rules may produce surprising behavior. Nor is it the assertion that AOP techniques must always be used obliviously—there's no great harm in knowing what's going on, either. The argument is that one of the two things that distinguish aspect-oriented programming languages from their predecessors is the ability to be oblivious.

2.4 QUANTIFICATION

AOP is thus the desire to make programming statements of the form

> *In programs* P, *whenever condition* C *arises, perform action* A.   (1)

over "conventionally" coded programs *P*. This suggests three major choice dimensions for the designer and implementer of an AOP system:

- ◆ **Quantification.** What kinds of conditions can we specify?
- ◆ **Interface.** How do the actions interact with the programs and with each other?
- ◆ **Weaving.** How will the system arrange to intermix the execution of the programs with the actions?

In an AOP system, we make quantified statements about which code is to execute in which circumstances. We note that there has periodically appeared in the AOP literature discussions of "symmetric" and "asymmetric" AOP systems. In symmetric languages, all program elements are equal, and following the directions of a composition language, the equal pieces are composed together into a whole. Hyper/J [37] is the canonical example of a symmetric language. An asymmetric language divides the world into a base program and aspects. We are agnostic to this religious divide, merely noting that if one is allowed to quantify over one's aspects, the two can be understood to be equivalent.

Over what can our AOP systems let us to quantify? Broadly, we can quantify over the static structure of the system and over its dynamic behavior.

2.4.1 Static Quantification

The static structure is the program as text. Two common views of program text are in terms of the public interfaces of the program (typically methods, but occasionally also public variables) and the complete structure of the program—typically, the parsed-program as abstract syntax tree (though occasionally the object code [8]).

Black-box AOP systems quantify over the public interface of components like functions and object methods. Examples of black-box systems include Composition-Filters [2], synchronization advice [25], aspect moderators [9], and OIF [18]. A simple implementation mechanism for black-box AOP is to wrap components with the aspect behavior.

Clear-box AOP systems allow quantification over the internal (parsed) structure of components. Examples of such systems include AspectJ, which allows (among other things) quantifying over both the calling and accepting calls in subprograms [27, 28], Hyper/J, whose composition rules allow quantifying over elements such as the interpretation of variables and methods within modules [37], meta-interpreter-based systems, where the process of program interpretation is modified to run aspects [3, 38], and transformation systems, where actual object, intermediate, or source code is transformed to include aspect behavior [8, 12, 20, 22, 29].

A given AOP system will present a quantification language that may be as simple as just allowing aspect decoration of subprogram calls or complex enough to represent pattern matching on the abstract syntax tree or compiled structure of the program. Understood this way, a clear-box AOP system could allow static quantifications such as "add a print statement to show the new value of any assignment to a variable within the body of a while loop if the variable occurs in the test of the while loop."

Clear-box and black-box techniques each have advantages and disadvantages. Clear-box techniques require source or object code. They provide access to all the (static) nuances of the program. They can straightforwardly implement "caller-side" aspects (aspects associated with the calling environment of a subprogram invocation). Black-box techniques are typically easier to implement. (In environments like Lisp, where calls are ordinarily routed through a modifiable function symbol, black-box techniques can be downright trivial.) Black-box techniques can also be used on components where the source code is lacking.

Because black-box techniques can't quantify over anything besides a program's interface, clear-box techniques are especially useful for debugging. For example, a clear-box system could implement a concern like a statement-execution counting profiler, or writing to a log file on every update of a variable whose name starts with "log." However, black-box techniques are more likely to produce reusable and maintainable aspects—an aspect tied to the code of a module can easily slip into dependence on the coding tricks of that module. Interfaces imply contracts.

Clear-box techniques are more difficult to implement, as they usually imply developing a major fraction of a compiler. A typical clear-box implementation of structural quantification needs to obtain a parsed version of the underlying program, run transformation rules realizing the quantified aspects over that abstract syntax tree, and output the resulting tree back in the source language for processing by the conventional language compiler. That can be a lot of work.

2.4.2   *Dynamic Quantification*

Dynamic quantification is tying the aspect behavior to something happening at run-time. Examples of such occasions include:

- The raising of an exception.
- The call of a subprogram X within the temporal scope of a call of Y. (The call of X within the context of Y problem is an instance of the "jumping aspect" problem [2].)
- The size of the call stack exceeding some value.
- Some pattern of more primitive events in the history of the program being matched; for example, after the "try password" routine has failed five times with no intervening successes.
- The swapping of the running thread.

The abstractions most programming languages present about the structure and execution of a program are only a subset of the possible available abstractions: Scheme allows a programmer to capture the "current context" and reinvoke the current behavior. C programmers glibly rummage around on the stack, content in the knowledge that the pattern of procedure calls is straightforwardly recognizable so long as the machine and compiler remain constant. 3-Lisp and similar reflective systems allow the programmer access to the interpreter's state [13]. Elephant allows reference to previous variable values [35]. The ability to program with respect to such properties is an ingredient of programming language design. Even if such elements are absent in the underlying language, an aspect language may still allow quantification over them. Filman and Havelund present a more detailed discussion of the possibility of dynamic AOP mechanisms [20]; a recent implementation of an AOP system based on event response is [14].

2.5 IMPLEMENTATION ISSUES

Assertion (1) suggests a design space for AOP languages. It implies choices in each of the three dimensions: quantification, interface, and weaving.

Quantification. Quantification incorporates the notions of defining the "join points" of the code along with the language and mechanisms for selecting when a particular join point deserves a particular aspect. Examples of possible join points include subprogram calls, variable references, and statements. As mentioned earlier, one can quantify over the static structure of the program or over its dynamic behavior. Examples of the predicates one can use to describe a static quantification include discriminating by package, by the inheritance structure of the program, by the structure of call arguments, by the lexical structure of program element names, and by the nested structure of program elements. (Masterscope is an early example of a quantification language for programs that has a rich language for describing points in program structures [39].) Examples of dynamic quantification scope include the dynamic nesting structure of calls and the occurrence of particular events (e.g., "after x is assigned 3, while y is greater than 7"). There have also been suggestions that the program of the base code could be provided mechanisms to prevent aspect interactions and that the system check for incompatible aspect applications.

Interface. Interface includes the structure of the "aspect code," the interactions among aspects, and the relationships and information sharing among the aspects and base code. Issues of interface include what context of the underlying program is available to an aspect, how aspects communicate among themselves and with the underlying program, ordering of aspects at the same locus, and aspect parameterizations.

Weaving. Weaving expresses how the system intertwines the execution of the base code and aspects. Key elements include the actual weaving mechanism (for example, compile-time weaving, altering the interpretation process, or meta- or reflective mechanisms) and the ability to dynamically change quantifications in a running system.

2.6 ASPECT-ORIENTED LANGUAGES

To return to Elrad's question, what qualifies as an aspect-oriented language? Let us consider some possibilities:

Rule-based systems. Roughly speaking, rule-based systems like OPS-5 [5] or, to a lesser extent, Prolog, are programming with purely dynamically quantified statements. Each rule says, "Whenever the condition is true, do the corresponding action." (We are ignoring the tendency of some rule-based systems to execute exactly one matching rule and then recompute the matching rule set.) If we all programmed with rules, we wouldn't have AOP discussions. We would just talk about how rules that expressed concerns X, Y, and Z could be added to the original system, with some mention of the tricks involved in getting those rules to run in the right order and to communicate with each other. The base idea that other things could be going on besides the main flow of control wouldn't be the least bit strange. (Laddaga et al. proposed doing AOP with AI-style inference [30].)

But by and large, people don't program with rule-based systems. This is because rule-based systems are notoriously difficult to code. They've destroyed the fundamental sequentiality of almost everything. The sequential, local, unitary style is really very good for expressing most things. The cleverness of classical AOP is augmenting conventional sequentiality with quantification, rather than supplanting it wholesale.

Event-based publish-and-subscribe. In EBPS systems, the subscription mechanism is precisely a quantification mechanism. ("Let me know whenever you see something like. . . .") The question, then, is "Is EBPS oblivious?" If the application's programming style is to use events as the interface among components or if the underlying system automatically generates interesting events, then EBPS can be used as a black-box AOP mechanism. On the other hand, if we expect the programmer to scatter event generation for our purposes throughout otherwise conventional programs, then one cannot program EBPS obliviously, and hence it is not AOP.

Frameworks. Framework systems [10] provide a high-level organization (a main flow of control) into which the application programmer plugs behavior at particular points. In some sense, a framework comes with a particularly defined set of concerns and allows plugging in (and separately specifying) just those concerns. Often frameworks will have default behaviors for these concerns. While frameworks provide a way of separating certain concerns, their restriction to a set of predefined concerns and often predefined though parameterized behaviors keeps the framework mechanism from rising to the level of a *language* for separating concerns.

Domain-specific languages.   Domain-specific languages (DSLs) offer small, often declarative syntax and semantics for programming a particular domain [43]. Examples of domain-specific languages are SQL, HTML, and yacc. DSLs succeed in intermixing crosscutting concerns into programs but, like frameworks, crosscut only the concerns anticipated by the language designer and often only with the mechanisms built into the language.

Intentional programming and meta-programming.   Intentional programming (IP) [1] and meta-programming (MP) [26] provide the ability to direct the execution order in arbitrarily defined computational patterns. They can be seen as environments for writing transformation compilers (that is, a mechanism for implementing clear-box AOP), rather than as self-contained realizations of the AOP idea.

Generative programming.   Similarly, generative programming [11] works by transforming higher-level representations of programs into lower-level ones (that is, by compiling high-level specifications). By incorporating aspects into the transformation rules, one can achieve AOP in a generative programming environment.

2.7   RELATED WORK

Earlier versions of these ideas have been expressed at the AOP workshops in Minneapolis [19] and Budapest [17]. Those publications have sparked a certain amount of discussion on the foundational question of the nature of aspect-oriented programming. Wand describes aspect-orientation as an alternative specification language for programs [40]. He argues that aspects are modular units of specification and that a join-point model is a shared ontology between programs and aspects. Masuhara and Kiczales examined four AOP languages, attempting to extract the essence of their AOPness through understanding their interpretation/weaving process [34]. There have also been numerous examples of providing denotational semantics for AOP, particularly when restricted to advice on functions. A good source for discussions of this kind is the series of "Foundations of Aspect-Oriented Languages" (FOAL) workshops at the AOSD conference [31, 32, 33].

2.8   CLOSING REMARKS

Understanding something involves both understanding how it works (*mechanism*) and what it's good for (*methodology*). In computer science, we're rarely shy about grandiose methodological claims (see, for example, the literature of AI or the

Internet). But mechanism is important—appreciating mechanisms leads to improved mechanisms, recognition of commonalities and isomorphisms, and plain old clarity about what's actually happening. The understanding gained through the examination of mechanism leads to generalization and richer systems. The quantification and obliviousness argument is about looking for the common mechanism in AOP systems, seeing how to understand particular AOP systems with respect to those mechanisms, and looking for the places where those mechanisms can be generalized. We're trying to answer the question, "Is *X* an AOP system?" where the answer is not based on whether the creator of the system called it AOP, but rather on whether its mechanisms can be used to do AOP.

Imagine, if you will, Anne, a computer scientist working in isolation, who has invented a language exactly like AspectJ, except that she believes the purpose of the language is to insert debugging statements into conventional Java code. She's called the language "DebugJ," and everywhere AspectJ uses the word "aspect," she uses "debug." Her methodological explanations are all about temporarily inserting only debugging statements into code under development. Is DebugJ an AOP language?

Consider Betty, who believes she has invented a new aspect-oriented language called "AspectTran." AspectTran looks just like Fortran, except that "subroutine" has been replaced by the word "aspect." Betty explains that users should encode concerns separately in these aspect routines, and if a concern crosscuts another, they should invoke the aspect code with a CALL statement. Shared state between the aspect and the base routine is passed in parameters to the aspect call. Since Fortran is call-by-reference, one can even have an aspect change the value of a local variable! Betty is proud of how little she had to modify the Fortran compiler to create AspectTran. Is AspectTran an AOP language?

If this seems far-fetched, keep in mind how long it took to convince Ada aficionados that Ada83 was not an object-oriented language. Dahl, Myhrhaug, and Nygaard never mentioned that Simula 67 was an object-oriented language. Nevertheless, it's universally acclaimed as the first. Decide for yourself if Ada95 is an object-oriented language: One can do all the object-oriented things by using particular features in specific and non-obvious ways, but the term "object" is not part of the language's lexicon.

We have identified AOP with the ability to assert quantified statements over programs without explicit reference to these statements. This implies

AOP is not about OOP.   OOP is a popular programming language technology. Most implementations of new language ideas are done in the context of OOP. The class hierarchy of OO systems is a convenient structure over which to quantify. However, "quantification" and "obliviousness" are independent of OO. Therefore, it is perfectly reasonable to develop AOP for functional or imperative languages. Work illustrating this point includes Coady et. al's AspectC for C [7] and Wand's ADJ/PROC for a first-order mini-language [41].

AOP is not useful for singletons.   If one has an orthogonal concern that is about exactly one place in the original code, and that orthogonal concern will not propagate to other loci as the system evolves, it is probably a bad idea to use AOP for that concern. Just write a call to the aspect procedure into that place, or permute the source code in whatever way necessary to achieve the aspect. The cost to the software maintenance and evolution process by the existence of an additional aspect probably exceeds the benefit of using a singleton aspect.

AOP language designs ought to be more implicit.   Our goal should be to minimize the degree to which programmers (particularly the programmers of the primary functionality) have to change their behavior to realize the benefits of AOP. It's a really nice bumper sticker to be able to say, "Just program like always, and we'll be able to add the aspects later." (And change policies later, and we'll painlessly transform the code for that, too.) Realizing that bumper sticker is a challenge to the developers of AOP.

ACKNOWLEDGMENTS

Our thanks to Siobhán Clarke, Tzilla Elrad, Gregor Kiczales, Diana Lee, and Tarang Patel for comments on the drafts of this chapter and its predecessors.

REFERENCES

1. AITKEN, W., DICKENS, B., KWIATKOWSKI, P., DE MOOR, O., RICHTER, D., AND SIMONYI, C. 1998. Transformation in intentional programming. In *5th Int'l Conf. Software Reuse*, (Victoria, British Columbia). IEEE, 114–123.

2. BERGMANS, L. AND AKŞIT, M. 2001. Composing crosscutting concerns using composition filters. *Comm. ACM 44*, 10 (Oct.), 51–57.

3. BOURAQADI-SAÂDANII, N. M. N. AND LEDOUX, T. 2001. How to weave? In *Workshop on Advanced Separation of Concerns (ECOOP)*, (Budapest). http://trese.cs.utwente.nl/Workshops/ecoop01asoc/papers/Bouraqadi.pdf.

4. BRICHAU, J., MEUTER, W. D., AND DEVOLDER, K. 2000. Jumping aspects. In *Workshop on Aspects and Dimensions of Concerns (ECOOP)*, (Cannes, France). http://trese.cs.utwente.nl/Workshops/adc2000/papers/Brichau.pdf.

5. BROWNSTON, L., FARRELL, R., KANT, E., AND MARTIN, N. 1985. *Programming Expert Systems in OPS5: An Introduction to Rule-Based Programming*. Addison-Wesley, Reading, Massachusetts.

6. CANNON, H. 1982. Flavors: A non-hierarchical approach to object-oriented programming. Tech. rep., Symbolics Inc.

7. COADY, Y., KICZALES, G., FEELEY, M., AND SMOLYN, G. 2001. Using AspectC to improve the modularity of path-specific customization in operating system code. In *8th European Software Engineering Conference*, (Vienna). ACM, 88–98.

8. COHEN, G. A. 1999. Recombining concerns: Experience with transformation. In *Workshop on Multi-Dimensional Separation of Concerns (OOPSLA)*, (Denver). http://www.cs.ubc.ca/~murphy/multid-workshop-oopsla99/position-papers/ws23-cohen.pdf.

9. CONSTANTINIDES, C. A. AND ELRAD, T. 2001. Composing concerns with a framework approach. In *Int'l Workshop on Distributed Dynamic Multiservice Architectures (ICDCS), Vol. 2*, (Phoenix), Z. Choukair, Ed. IEEE, 133–140.

10. COTTER, S. AND POTEL, M. 1995. *Inside Taligent Technology*. Addison-Wesley, Reading, Massachusetts.

11. CZARNECKI, K. AND EISENECKER, U. W. 2000. *Generative Programming: Methods, Tools, and Applications*. Addison-Wesley, Reading, Massachusetts.

12. DEVOLDER, K. AND D'HONDT, T. 1999. Aspect-oriented logic meta programming. In *Meta-Level Architectures and Reflection, 2nd Int'l Conf. Reflection*, P. Cointe, Ed. LNCS, vol. 1616. (Springer Verlag, Berlin), 250–272.

13. DES RIVIERES, J. AND SMITH, B. C. 1984. The implementation of procedurally reflective languages. In *Symp. LISP and Functional Programming* (Austin). ACM, 331–347.

14. DOUENCE, R. AND SÜDHOLT, M. 2002. A model and a tool for event-based aspect-oriented programming (EAOP). Tech. Rep. 02/11/INFO, Ecole des Mines de Nantes.

15. ELRAD, T., FILMAN, R. E., AND BADER, A. 2001. Aspect-oriented programming. *Comm. ACM 44*, 10 (Oct.), 29–32.

16. FIKES, R. E. AND KEHLER, T. 1985. The role of frame-based representation in reasoning. *Comm. ACM 28*, 904–920.

17. FILMAN, R. E. 2001. What is aspect-oriented programming, revisited. In *Workshop on Advanced Separation of Concerns (ECOOP)*, (Budapest). http://trese.cs.utwente.nl/Workshops/ecoop01asoc/papers/Filman.pdf.

18. FILMAN, R. E., BARRETT, S., LEE, D. D., AND LINDEN, T. 2002. Inserting ilities by controlling communications. *Comm. ACM 45*, 1 (Jan.), 116–122.

19. FILMAN, R. E. AND FRIEDMAN, D. P. 2000. Aspect-oriented programming is quantification and obliviousness. In *Workshop on Advanced Separation of Concerns (OOPSLA)*, (Minneapolis). http://trese.cs.utwente.nl/Workshops/OOPSLA2000/papers/filman.pdf.

20. FILMAN, R. E. AND HAVELUND, K. 2002. Source-code instrumentation and quantification of events. In *Foundations of Aspect-Oriented Languages (FOAL, AOSD)*, (Enschede, The Netherlands) G. T. Leavens and R. Cytron, Eds. Department of Computer Science, Iowa State Univ., 45–49. ftp://ftp.cs.iastate.edu/pub/technreports/TR02-06/TR.pdf.

21. FILMAN, R. E. AND LEE, D. D. 2000. Managing distributed systems with smart subscriptions. In *Int'l Conf. Parallel and Distributed Processing Techniques and Applications (PDPTA)*, (Las Vegas). CSREA Press, Bogart, Georgia, 853–860.

22. FRADET, P. AND SÜDHOLT, M. 1998. AOP: Towards a generic framework using program transformation and analysis. In *Workshop on Aspect-Oriented Programming (ECOOP)*, (Brussels). ftp://ftp.emn.fr/pub/objet/publications/ecoop98/aop.ps.gz.

23. FRIEDMAN, D. P., HAYNES, C. T., AND WAND, M. 2001. *Essentials of Programming Languages (2nd Ed.)*. MIT Press, Cambridge, Massachusetts.

24. GARLAN, D. AND NOTKIN, D. 1991. Formalizing design spaces: Implicit invocation mechanisms. In *4th Int'l Symp. of VDM Europe on Formal Software Development-Volume I*. LNCS, vol. 552. Springer-Verlag, Berlin, 31–44.

25. HOLMES, D., NOBLE, J., AND POTTER, J. 1998. Towards reusable synchronisation for object-oriented. In *Workshop on Aspect-Oriented Programming (ECOOP)*, (Brussels). http://trese.cs.utwente.nl/aop-ecoop98/papers/Holmes.pdf.

26. KICZALES, G., DES RIVIERES, J., AND BOBROW, D. G. 1991. *The Art of the Metaobject Protocol*. MIT Press, Cambridge, Massachusetts.

27. KICZALES, G., HILSDALE, E., HUGUNIN, J., KERSTEN, M., PALM, J., AND GRISWOLD, W. G. 2001. An overview of AspectJ. In *ECOOP 2001—Object-Oriented Programming, 15th European Conference*, (BUDAPEST), J. L. KNUDSEN, Ed. Lncs, vol. 2072. (Springer-Verlag, Berlin), 327–353.

28. KICZALES, G., HILSDALE, E., HUGUNIN, J., KERSTEN, M., PALM, J., AND GRISWOLD, W. G. 2001. Getting started with AspectJ. *Comm. ACM 44*, 10 (Oct.), 59–65.

29. KNIESEL, G., COSTANZA, P., AND AUSTERMANN, M. 2001. JMangler—a framework for load-time transformation of Java class files. In *1st Int'l Workshop on Source Code Analysis and Manipulation (SCAM 2001)*, (Florence, Italy). http://www. informatik.uni-bonn.de/~costanza/SCAM_jmangler.pdf.

30. LADDAGA, R., ROBERTSON, P., AND SHROBE, H. 2001. Aspects of the real-world. In *Workshop on Advanced Separation of Concerns in Object-Oriented Systems (OOPSLA)*, (Tampa, Florida). http://www.cs.ubc.ca/~kdvolder/Workshops/ OOPSLA2001/submissions/23-robertson.pdf.

31. LEAVENS, G. T. AND CYTRON, R. Eds. 2002. *Proc. FOAL: Foundations of Aspect-Oriented Languages* (Enschede, Netherlands). http://www.cs.iastate.edu/ ~leavens/FOAL/papers-2002/TR.pdf.

32. LEAVENS, G. T. AND CLIFTON, C., Eds. 2003. *Proc. FOAL: Foundations of Aspect-Oriented Languages* (Boston). http://www.cs.iastate.edu/~leavens/FOAL/index-2003.shtml.

33. LEAVENS, G. T., CLIFTON, C., AND LÄMMEL, R. Eds. 2004. *Proc. FOAL: Foundations of Aspect-Oriented Languages* (Lancaster, England). http://www.cs.iastate.edu/ ~leavens/FOAL/papers-2004/proceedings.pdf.

34. MASUHARA, H. AND KICZALES, G. 2003. Modeling crosscutting in aspect-oriented mechanisms. In *Proc. ECOOP 2003—Object-Oriented Programming, 17th European Conference*, (Darmstadt, Germany), L. CARDELLI, Ed., LNCS vol. 2743. Springer-Verlag, Berlin, 2–28.

35. MCCARTHY, J. 1996. Elephant. Tech. rep., Stanford University. http://www-formal. stanford.edu/jmc/elephant.html.

36. MOON, D. A. 1986. Object-oriented programming with flavors. In *1st Conf. Object-Oriented Programming, Systems, Languages, and Applications (OOPSLA)*, (New York). ACM, 1–8.

37. OSSHER, H. AND TARR, P. 2001. The shape of things to come: Using multi-dimensional separation of concerns with Hyper/J to (re)shape evolving software. *Comm. ACM 44*, 10 (Oct.), 43–50.

38. SULLIVAN, G. T. 2001. Aspect-oriented programming using reflection and meta-object protocols. *Comm. ACM 44*, 10 (Oct.), 95–97.

39. TEITELMAN, W. AND MASINTER, L. 1981. The Interlisp programming environment. *IEEE Computer 14*, 4 (Apr.), 25–34.

40. WAND, M. 2003. Understanding aspects: extended abstract. IN *Proc. 8th SIGPLAN International Conference on Functional Programming (ICFP)*, (Uppsala, Sweden). ACM, 299–300.

41. WAND, M., KICZALES, G., AND DUTCHYN, C. in press. A semantics for advice and dynamic join points in aspect-oriented programming. *ACM Transactions on Programming Languages and Systems*.

42. WEGNER, P. 1987. Dimensions of object-based language design. In *2nd Conf. Object-Oriented Programming, Systems, Languages, and Applications (OOPSLA)*, (Orlando, Florida). ACM, 168–182.

43. WILE, D. S. AND RAMMING, J. C. 1999. Guest editorial: Introduction to the special section: Domain-specific languages (DSLs). *IEEE Transactions on Software Engineering 25*, 3, 289–290.

Chapter 3

N *Degrees of Separation: Multi-Dimensional Separation of Concerns*

**PERI TARR, HAROLD OSSHER, STANLEY M. SUTTON, JR.,
AND WILLIAM HARRISON**

Done well, *separation of concerns* can provide many software engineering benefits, including reduced complexity, improved reusability, and simpler evolution. The choice of boundaries for separate concerns depends on both requirements on the system and on the kind(s) of *decomposition* and *composition* a given formalism supports. The predominant methodologies and formalisms available, however, support only *orthogonal* separations of concerns, along *single* dimensions of composition and decomposition. These characteristics lead to a number of well-known and difficult problems.

This paper describes a new paradigm for modeling and implementing software artifacts, one that permits separation of *overlapping* concerns along *multiple* dimensions of composition and decomposition. This approach addresses numerous problems throughout the software lifecycle in achieving well-engineered, evolvable, flexible software artifacts and traceability across artifacts.

3.1 INTRODUCTION

The primary goals of software engineering are to improve software quality, to reduce the costs of software production, and to facilitate maintenance and evolution. In pursuit of these goals, software engineers constantly seek development technologies and methodologies that reduce software complexity, improve comprehensibility, promote reuse, and facilitate evolution. These properties, in turn, induce several specific requirements on the formalisms used to develop software artifacts. Reduced complexity and improved comprehensibility require *decomposition* mechanisms to carve software into meaningful and manageable pieces. They also require *composition* mechanisms to put pieces together usefully. Reuse requires the development of large-scale reusable components, low coupling, and powerful, *non-invasive* adaptation and customization capabilities. Ease of evolution depends on low coupling and also requires *traceability* across the software lifecycle, mechanisms for minimizing the impact of changes, and substitutability.

Despite much good research in the software engineering domain, many of the problems that complicate software engineering still remain. Software comprehensibility tends to degrade over time (if, indeed, it is present at all). Many common maintenance and evolution activities result in high-impact, invasive modifications. Artifacts are of limited reusability, or are reusable only with difficulty. Traceability across the various software artifacts is limited, which further complicates evolution.

These somewhat diverse problems are due, in large part, to limitations and unfulfilled requirements related to *separation of concerns* [19]. Our ability to achieve the goals of software engineering depends fundamentally on our ability to keep separate *all* concerns of importance in software systems. All modern software formalisms support separation of concerns to some extent, through mechanisms for decomposition and composition. However, existing formalisms at all lifecycle phases provide only small, restricted sets of decomposition and composition mechanisms, and these typically support only a single, "dominant" dimension of separation at a time. We call this the "tyranny of the dominant decomposition."

We believe that achieving the primary goals of software engineering requires support for *simultaneous* separation of *overlapping* concerns in multiple dimensions. We will illustrate how limitations on current mechanisms prevent this and thereby lead directly to the failure to achieve these goals. We propose a model of software artifacts, decomposition, and composition to overcome these limitations. This model allows for simultaneous, multi-dimensional decomposition and composition. It is *not* a "universal" artifact modeling formalism; rather, it complements existing formalisms, giving developers additional modularization flexibility while continuing to use the formalisms of their choice. Moreover, this model is not particular to any phase of the software lifecycle. The extra flexibility to represent alternative decompositions of artifacts within a development phase also enables us to relate artifacts in multiple ways across phases, and even to *co-structure* artifacts—permit different artifacts, developed during different phases of the software lifecycle, to be structured in such a way that corresponding elements align clearly. We show how this increased flexibility can help to address the problems of software complexity and comprehensibility and difficulties with reuse, facilitate software evolution, and enhance traceability between artifacts, both within and across development phases.

The rest of this paper is organized as follows. Section 3.2 motivates the need for multiple dimensions of decomposition and rich mechanisms for composition.

Section 3.3 describes our abstract model of software artifacts. It also shows how this model can address many of the issues raised in Section 3.2. Section 3.4 describes the issues involved in instantiating the model for particular artifact development formalisms, such as UML [21] or Java [6]. Section 3.5 describes related work and shows how our approach has been partially realized in some existing work. Finally, Section 3.6 presents some conclusions and future work.

3.2 MOTIVATION

To illustrate some pervasive and serious problems in software engineering that help motivate our work, we present a running example involving the construction and evolution of a simple software engineering environment (SEE) for programs consisting of expressions. We assume a simplified software development process, consisting of informal requirements specification in natural language, design in UML, and implementation in Java.

3.2.1 The First Go-Round

The initial set of requirements for the SEE are simple:

> *The SEE supports the specification of expression programs. It contains a set of tools that share a common representation of expressions. The initial toolset should include: an evaluation capability, which determines the result of evaluating an expression; a display capability, which depicts an expression textually; and a check capability, which checks an expression for syntactic and semantic correctness.*

Based on these requirements, we design the system using UML. Figure 3-1 shows a subset of the design, which represents expressions as abstract syntax trees (ASTs) and defines a class for each kind of AST node. Each class contains accessor and modifier methods, plus methods `eval()`, `display()`, and `check()`, which realize the required tools in a standard, object-oriented manner.

The code that implements this design has a similar structure, except that it separates *interfaces* to AST nodes from *implementation classes*, resulting in two hierarchies instead of one.

This simple example raises some noteworthy issues that occur commonly in software. Despite being representations of the same system, each of the three kinds of artifacts decomposes the system differently. The requirements decompose by tool, or *feature* (e.g., [23]), while the design and code decompose by *object*. The code further separates interface from implementation parts. The difference in decomposition models leads directly to *scattering*—a single requirement affects multiple design and code modules—and *tangling*—material pertaining to multiple requirements is interleaved within a single module. These problems compromise comprehension and evolution, as we will see shortly.

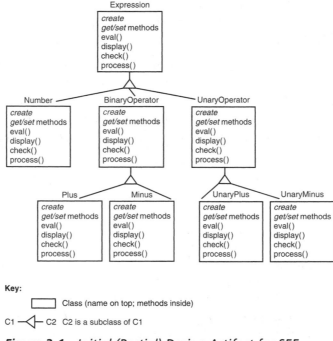

Figure 3-1   *Initial (Partial) Design Artifact for SEE.*

3.2.2 Evolving the SEE: An Environmental Hazard

After using the SEE for some time, clients request some changes in the system:

- ◆ Expressions should be optionally persistent.
- ◆ Style checking should be supported as well as syntax and semantic checking. It should be possible to check expressions against multiple styles. Any meaningful combination of checks (e.g., syntax only; syntax plus style(s)) should be permitted.

Unfortunately, these seemingly straightforward enhancements have a significant impact on the design and code. Figure 3-2 shows the impact on the Java implementation class hierarchy. A simple implementation of persistence requires adding "save" and "retrieve" methods to all AST classes, and inserting additional code into all accessor and modifier methods to retrieve persistent objects upon first access and to flush modifications back to the database. This represents a non-trivial, invasive change to all AST design classes and to all of the interfaces and implementation classes in the code, a serious case of scattering.[1] Code to support retrieval and update of persistent objects becomes tangled with other code in the accessor and modifier methods, impeding comprehensibility and future evolution. Further, the persistence code also has an impact on the new style checkers. If the persistence option is present, the style checkers must include their state information in the persistent representation of expressions. This kind of context-dependent feature is extremely difficult to represent in modern formalisms.

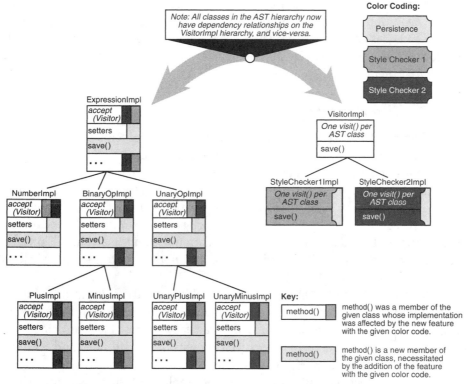

Figure 3-2 *The Java Implementation Classes, Post-Evolution.*

---

1. Subclassing is a non-invasive mechanism for change, but it is not a reasonable option here. It produces combinatorial explosions of classes and still requires invasive changes to any client that creates instances of the original classes.

The ability to permit arbitrary combinations of checks is also problematic. It requires special infrastructure support, in both the design and implementation. This infrastructure is not present—it comes at high cost in terms of conceptual complexity and run-time overhead, so it was not included originally, as it was not necessary. We choose to address this problem by retrofitting the Visitor design pattern [5], which permits optional combinations of features, into the design and code. Visitor requires us to replace all AST `check()` methods with `accept(Visitor)` methods, and to define a separate Visitor class for each type of check. The modifications to the check feature needed to support this capability are invasive, affecting every module in the design and code, and complicating all the artifacts and their interrelationships. The presence of arbitrary checks further complicates the persistence capability, since the information to be made persistent depends on the particular combination of syntax and/or style checkers. Finally, these modifications significantly impede the future evolution of the artifacts. They introduce a higher degree of coupling between the AST classes and the visitor classes, as evident in Figure 3-2, and the presence of visitors in the design will necessitate extensive changes to accommodate modifications to the AST hierarchy [5].

3.2.3 *The Postmortem*

This example demonstrates, in a microcosm, many problems that plague software engineers and suggests why we still fall short of our goals.

Impact of change: The goal of low impact of change requires *additive*, rather than *invasive*, change. Yet conceptually simple changes, like those in the expression SEE, often have widespread and invasive effects, both within the modified artifact and on related pieces of other artifacts. This is primarily because units of change often do not match the units of abstraction and encapsulation within the artifacts. Thus, additive changes in one artifact, like requirements, may not translate to additive changes in other artifacts, like design and code.

Modern extensibility features, such as subclassing and design patterns, help but are not sufficient [16] because they require significant pre-planning. It is not feasible to pre-enable artifacts for all possible extensions, even if it were possible to anticipate them.

Reuse: Despite wide recognition of its benefits, reuse is limited and occurs mostly on code, not requirements or designs. Part of the impediment to large-scale reuse is that larger artifacts entail more design and implementation decisions, which can result in tangling of concerns and coupling of features, reducing reusability. Given large and complex artifacts, plus the weak set of adaptation and customization capabilities available in most formalisms, developers face a significant amount of invasive work to adapt a component for a given context.

Traceability: Different artifacts are written for different purposes and include different levels of abstraction. Thus, they are specified in different formalisms and are often decomposed and structured differently. A case in point is the requirements scattering and tangling problem illustrated earlier. No clear correspondence of abstraction or structure across artifacts exists, in general, to aid traceability. Instead, developers must create connections among related artifacts explicitly (e.g., [9]). These connections are complex, can be invalidated readily, and, most importantly, they do not reduce scattering or tangling. They can help developers assess the impact of a given change, but they cannot localize it or reduce its impact. Developers must therefore make invasive, time-consuming changes to multiple artifacts to propagate the effects of a given change. When time constraints are tight, they often choose to make changes only to code, letting other artifacts become obsolete.

We believe that a major cause of these impact of change, reusability, and traceability problems is the "tyranny of the dominant decomposition." Existing modularization mechanisms typically support only a small set of decompositions, and usually only a single "dominant" one at a time. This dominant decomposition satisfies some important needs, but usually at the expense of others. For example, a decomposition may be chosen to limit the impact of some changes, but traceability may thereby be sacrificed (or, indeed, the ability to limit the impact of other changes); or, in a data decomposition designed to match application-domain concepts, code for a feature may be scattered across multiple application modules and tangled with code for other features. To make matters worse, different formalisms typically support different dominant decompositions, reducing traceability across artifacts. Many different kinds of concern are important in a software system, and designating one of them as dominant in each context, at the expense of the others, contributes significantly to the problems identified above.

3.2.4 *Breaking the Tyranny*

To achieve the full potential of separation of concerns, we need to break the tyranny of the dominant decomposition. In the example and related discussion, several kinds of concerns were identified:

- *Feature:* These include display, basic check, evaluate, persistence, and style check. Features may also be required or optional.
- *Unit of change:* Additions made due to user requests
- *Customization:* The additions or changes needed to customize a component for a particular purpose
- *Data or object:* The classes involved in the system

If the system could be modularized according to concerns of all these kinds, *simultaneously,* the problems described above would be greatly ameliorated.

Traceability would be improved by encapsulating features separately, with clear correspondence between the representation of a particular feature in different artifacts (i.e., co-structuring). Impact of change would be reduced by the ability to encapsulate each unit of change separately. Reuse would be enhanced by the improved traceability, and by separating customization details from the base component, provided composition is rich enough to apply them effectively.

These are just a few of the dimensions of concern along which separation may be desirable. Others include: to match conceptual abstractions; to conform to a given modeling paradigm (object-oriented, functional, etc.) or to take advantage of special-purpose formalisms; to separate "optional" from "required" pieces; to separate variants for different host systems, classes of users, etc.; to permit distribution or parallel processing; to facilitate concurrent or cooperative development; etc. The possibilities are limitless, and vary with context. What is more, different dimensions of concern are seldom orthogonal: they overlap, and can affect one another. A truly flexible approach to modularization must allow any and all that are needed to apply simultaneously, and must be able to handle overlap and interactions among them.

3.3 MULTI-DIMENSIONAL SEPARATION OF CONCERNS

This section introduces a model of decomposition and composition that we believe satisfies these needs. The model is used in conjunction with developers' artifact formalism(s) of choice, giving developers additional power without requiring changes to the formalisms.

We begin with a model of conventional software, to set the context and introduce some terminology, then describe our model and show how it addresses many of the issues raised earlier.

3.3.1 A Model of Conventional Software

A particular software system is written to address some problem or provide some service within a problem *domain*. To do this, it must model or implement a variety of *concepts* of importance in that domain. These concepts include objects (e.g., "expression" in the example), functionality (e.g., "evaluation"), and properties (e.g., "persistence"). Concepts derived directly from the domain as well as internal software concepts (e.g., data structures) are both important.

The software system itself consists of a set of *artifacts,* such as requirements specifications, designs, and code. Each artifact consists of descriptive material in some formalism, whose purpose is to model needed concepts in a manner appropriate for that artifact. The formalisms differ for different projects, different phases, and different artifacts, and perhaps even within an artifact. Different artifacts often share the same concepts, with each concept potentially being described in a different way, and with different details, in the different artifacts. For example, the word `expression` in the requirements and the class `Expression` in the design and code all describe the concept "expression" in their rather different ways and at different levels of detail.

It is convenient to think of the descriptive material in each artifact as being made up of *units*. What constitutes a unit depends on the formalism, and perhaps on the context. For example, in object-oriented design formalisms or programming languages, classes are one kind of unit. If one looks below the class level, individual methods may also be considered units. This illustrates the important point that formalisms typically consist of at least some basic elements, which we call *primitive units*, and some grouping construct(s), which we call *compound units* or *modules*.

We treat primitive units as indivisible; our model works with them, but never looks inside them. A single concept is typically modeled by a collection of many units (primitive or compound). Perhaps surprisingly, a single unit often participates in modeling more than one concept. For example, the `eval()` method within the `Plus` class participates in modeling both the "plus expression" concept and the "evaluation" concept.

The purpose of modules is to accomplish *separation of concerns* [19]. Even software systems of moderate size contain so many primitive units that they cannot all be held in one's mind at once. When performing some development task, a developer must be able to focus on those units that are pertinent to that task and ignore all others. To accomplish this, software engineers identify *concerns* of importance, and seek to localize units representing concepts that pertain to each concern into a module. Ideally, one only need look inside a module if one is interested in a given concern. For example, a class is a module containing units (describing methods and instance variables) that model a particular kind of object; all internal details of such objects, such as their representation, are described within the class.

Many kinds of concerns are important during the software lifecycle. These *dimensions of concern* help to organize the space of concepts and units. Common dimensions of concern are data or object (leading to data abstraction) and function (leading to functional decomposition). Others include feature (both functional, such as "evaluation," and cross-cutting, such as "persistence"), role, and configuration. As illustrated by these examples, some dimensions of concern derive from the domain, often aligning with important domain concepts, while others come from system requirements, from the development process, and from internal details of the system itself. In short, there are any number of dimensions of concern that might be of importance for different purposes (e.g., comprehension, traceability, reusability, evolvability, etc.), for different systems, and at different phases of the lifecycle.

Modern artifact formalisms typically allow decomposition (i.e., grouping of units) into modules according to only a single dimension of concern, which we term the *dominant dimension*. The formalism often dictates specifically what the dominant dimension must be. For example, object-oriented formalisms support decomposition based on the object (or data) dimension, while procedural and functional programming languages permit decomposition based on function. Even formalisms that do not impose a specific dominant dimension typically do not support simultaneous decomposition according to multiple dimensions, so the developer ultimately chooses a dominant dimension. In either case, the modular structure of the artifact achieves separation of concerns only along this dominant dimension.

Thus, in our model, a conventional software system is a set of artifacts that model domain concepts in appropriate formalisms. Artifacts contain modules, which contain units. The modular structure reflects decomposition based on one dominant dimension of concern.

3.3.2 *Multi-Dimensional Decomposition: Hyperslices*

As discussed in Section 3.2, decomposition according to concerns along a single, dominant dimension is valuable, but usually inadequate. Units pertaining to concerns in other dimensions end up "scattered" across many modules and "tangled" with one another. Separation according to these concerns is, therefore, not achieved. To alleviate this problem, we introduce *hyperslices* as an additional, flexible means of decomposition.

A *hyperslice* is a set of conventional modules, written in any formalism. Hyperslices are intended to encapsulate concerns in dimensions other than the dominant one. The modules within it contain all, and only, those units that pertain to, or address, a given concern. Hyperslices can overlap, in that a given unit may occur, possibly in different forms, in multiple hyperslices. This supports simultaneous decomposition according to multiple dimensions of concern. A system is written as a collection of hyperslices, thereby separating all the concerns of importance in that system, along as many dimensions as are needed. The hyperslices are composed to form the complete system (discussed below).

The choice of the term "hyperslice" is intended to reflect relationships to both "program slicing" [25] and "hyperplane." Hyperslices are similar to program slices in that both involve cuts through a system that do not align with the standard modules. They differ, however, in that program slices are at the code level only, generally consist specifically of statements that affect particular variables, and are extracted from existing programs by analysis, rather than being used to build systems by composition. Hyperslices are hyperplanes in that they encapsulate concerns that cut across multiple dimensions in a space defined by the dimensions of concern.

To demonstrate the utility of hyperslices, we consider the initial version of the expression SEE described in Section 3.2. We identified two separate dimensions of concern applicable to the initial design: object (different kinds of expressions) and feature (display, evaluation, and basic checking). Since we used object-oriented formalisms for the design and code, the object dimension was the dominant one, and separation of concerns along that dimension was effective. Separation by feature could not be accomplished, however, leading to scattering and tangling of feature-specific units. We therefore introduce five hyperslices, one to encapsulate each of these concerns (features), as shown in Figure 3-3. One hyperslice encapsulates the basic ("kernel") expression AST capabilities (node creation, accessor, and modifier methods), modularized using UML classes in the design and Java classes and interfaces in the code. The other hyperslices encapsulate, respectively, the display, evaluation, and syntax and semantic checking features. Note that these hyperslices also contain many of the same class modules as found in the kernel hyperslice (i.e., their concerns *overlap*), but the modules in these hyperslices contain only those units that pertain to the particular concern they encapsulate. Thus, e.g., the display hyperslice defines `display()` methods and instance variables (units) in AST node classes (modules), while the evaluation hyperslice defines `eval()` methods and instance variables.

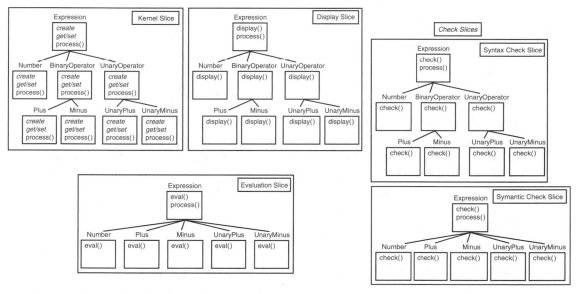

Figure 3-3 *Defining the SEE with Hyperslices.*

Note that hyperslices have been introduced without requiring the definition of new artifact formalisms. We deliberately do not modify the artifact formalisms themselves, preferring instead to allow developers to use their familiar formalisms throughout the lifecycle. The modules within a hyperslice are standard modules in the desired formalism, except that they contain only those units pertinent to the hyperslice's concern. That means that these modules might not satisfy all of the completeness constraints that the formalism normally requires. For example, the implementation code in the display hyperslice might refer to accessor methods that it does not define, on the expectation that the kernel hyperslice will provide them. This is not legal in Java, which requires modules to define any methods they use. It is fine in our model, however, because hyperslices are eventually composed together to form a "complete" hyperslice that must satisfy all of the formalism's constraints.

The definition of hyperslice above is sufficiently broad that it is possible, for any concern, to form a hyperslice consisting of exactly those units pertaining to that concern. For example, hyperslices can correspond to features, to units of change, or to specific customizations or components. If this approach is followed for all concerns of interest in a system, there is likely to be a good deal of overlap: the same unit, or different units describing the same concept, might be involved in multiple concerns. We saw this in the expression example—each of the hyperslices includes expression concepts in the form of class modules, but it defines those concepts in a way that is appropriate to its task. Overlap is acceptable; indeed, it is responsible for much of the power of this approach. Composition must be able to resolve the overlap, as discussed later.

This great flexibility raises the question of how developers should choose hyperslices for decomposing a given system, and whether the freedom is likely to lead to error and abuse. Simple uses, such as for major features or units of change, provide great benefit with little difficulty. Formulation of guidelines for more complex use of hyperslices is an issue for future research. Even with outstanding guidelines, however, use of hyperslices, like any other modularization mechanism, requires good judgement. If key structural decisions turn out to be incorrect because of design error or dramatic changes to requirements, system restructuring may be necessary, as with conventional technology. The support for simultaneous separation of concerns along multiple dimensions, however, opens the possibility of introducing new dimensions and ignoring obsolete ones, without dismantling the system. This, too, needs further research.

3.3.3 Composing Hyperslices Using Hypermodules

Hyperslices provide a flexible means of decomposing artifacts. To be useful, however, it must be possible to compose them to produce complete and consistent artifacts in unchanged artifact formalisms of choice.

A *hypermodule* is a set of hyperslices, together with a *composition rule* that specifies how the hyperslices must be composed to form a single, new hyperslice that synthesizes and integrates their units. Because of this composition property, a hypermodule is appropriate wherever a hyperslice may be used. Hypermodules can thus be nested. An entire artifact can be modeled as a hypermodule; the artifact consists of all the modules in the composed hyperslice and must satisfy whatever consistency and completeness constraints are required by the artifact formalism. The system as a whole—all of its artifacts—can also be modeled as a hypermodule, whose composition rule describes the relationships between the artifacts. The simplification of these relationships, made possible by hyperslices, and their reification in the composition rule, is a key advantage of this model.

Figure 3-4 shows a hypermodule consisting of the hyperslices from Figure 3-3. The composition rule must indicate which units in the hyperslices describe the same concepts, and how those units must be integrated. In this case, it asserts that classes in different hyperslices with the same name model the same concept and should be "merged" into a new, composed class with the same name and combined details. When the composition rule is applied, the resulting hyperslice contains exactly the modules shown in Figure 3-1. Notice that the syntax and semantic checking hyperslices can be grouped optionally into a "check" hypermodule that is nested within the SEE hypermodule. The result of (optionally) composing the syntax and semantic checking hyperslices within the "check" hypermodule is a check hyperslice, which can then be composed with the other SEE hyperslices. The ability to nest hypermodules in this manner promotes abstraction and encapsulation.

Details of composition vary greatly depending on the formalism in which units are written, and on which of the formalism's constructs are treated as units and modules. These are details that are specified as part of an *instantiation* of this model (described in detail in Section 3.4, which represents a mapping between a particular formalism and the concepts embodied within the model. They are also dependent on the details of the particular units involved, and can vary from straightforward to highly complex. Nonetheless, some general properties are worth discussing.

Composition is based on commonality of concepts across units: different units describing the same concept (usually, though not necessarily, differently) are composed into a single unit describing that concept more fully. This process involves three steps: *matching* units in different hyperslices that describe the same concept, *reconciliation* of differences in these descriptions, and *integration* of the units to produce a unified whole. Clearly, composition cannot be a fully automatic process. It is the task of the composition rule in the hypermodule to specify the details of composition.

One approach to composition rules, suggested by our work on subject-oriented programming [7, 17], is for the rule to be a combination of a concise, general rule, and detailed, specific rules that specify exceptions to the general rule or handle cases

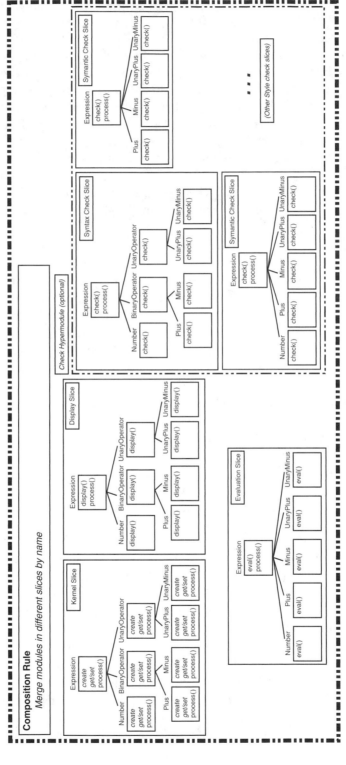

Figure 3-4 *Composing Hyperslices using Hypermodules.*

50

that it cannot handle. The general rule essentially names an automatic approach to apply as a starting point or default, such as matching by unit name (i.e., the name denotes the concept). General rules can be applied to an entire composition, or selectively to portions of it; different automatic approaches can thus be applied to different areas of a composition. Only in cases where no automatic rule suffices are detailed rules needed, in which the developer says explicitly exactly what to do. Detailed rules can handle such issues as matching units with different names that do describe the same concept, not matching units with the same names that do not describe the same concept, and reconciling different module structures, such as matching units nested at different depths in different hyperslices that nonetheless describe the same concept. The degree of mismatch in module structure and abstraction level that can be handled effectively is an issue for future research, as is determining how much mismatch occurs in practice in composed hyperslices.

An alternative is to split the composition rule across the hyperslices, allowing each hyperslice itself to specify how it is to be composed. If the rule in a hyperslice can refer to other hyperslices, this increases coupling and reduces reusability of hyperslices; if it cannot, this limits the flexibility with which overlap can be handled. Putting the composition rule a level higher, in the hypermodule, allows both flexible overlap and enhanced reuse.

In this model, therefore, developers write each artifact as a hypermodule. For each concern of importance that cannot be encapsulated effectively using the artifact formalism, they write a hyperslice that consists of modules in the artifact formalism. They also write a composition rule that specifies how these hyperslices are to be composed into a set of legal modules that make up the artifact. They also write an enclosing hypermodule that contains all the artifacts and whose composition rule specifies the relationships between them.

3.3.4   Using the Model

We have already begun to see how this artifact model can help to address some of the software lifecycle problems identified in Section 3.2.3. We now explore its impact on these problems in more detail, by revisiting the expression SEE example. We apply the same software development and evolution process, but this time, we use the proposed artifact model. We then evaluate how well the resulting artifacts address the problems presented earlier.

3.3.4.1   Revised First Go-Round

As described in Section 3.3.2, Figure 3-3 shows a somewhat different decomposition of the design and code artifacts than that produced during the initial design and coding process (depicted in Figure 3-1). The model has allowed us to separate the major non-object concerns identified during requirements-gathering: the "kernel," which encapsulates basic functionality pertaining to expressions, and display, evaluation, and checking features. Each of these concerns is encapsulated in a hyperslice. Since we chose to decompose the check feature further, we represent it as a nested hypermodule, which includes two subhyperslices, one each for the syntax and semantic checkers.

This decomposition has some significant benefits. First, hyperslices permit decomposition along multiple dimensions—in this case, object and feature—even within object-oriented formalisms that generally support only the object dimension. Second, the improved separation of concerns eliminates the scattering and tangling problems we saw earlier, by keeping units pertaining to separate requirements and features separate. A key benefit is that we have achieved encapsulation of coherent concerns *across the lifecycle*. This improves traceability and can significantly simplify the interrelationships among different artifacts that are traditionally so difficult to maintain. This approach also improves reusability considerably. For example, the entire expression AST concept, from requirements all the way to code, has been defined in a context-independent manner and can be reused readily, since the context-specific pieces are encapsulated in other hyperslices.

The use of composition to assemble hyperslices into the final SEE provides some substantial benefits as well. Observe that because composition of hyperslices is always optional, we have managed, just by separating the concerns, to ensure that we will later be able to "mix-and-match" syntax and style checking. We can also create versions of the SEE that contain different combinations of checking, evaluation, and display features—an ability we did not have in the original SEE. Notice also that we have a choice over how we define our hypermodules. We could, for example, define three hypermodules: one each that includes all hyperslices pertaining to a particular *artifact*. This allows us to compose the full requirements specification, design, and code artifacts. But we could also choose to define one hypermodule per *concern*— e.g., an "expression" hypermodule, which contains the requirements, design, and code hyperslices that encapsulate the "kernel," a "display" hypermodule that encapsulates all artifact hyperslices pertaining to display, etc. Both kinds of composition are valid and are useful for different purposes; the former permits the creation of the final artifacts, while the latter facilitates reuse of concerns and permits certain forms of inter-artifact completeness and consistency checking. As noted earlier, developers may need to decompose *or* compose differently for different reasons. This model permits them to do just that.

3.3.4.2   SEE Evolution: Saving the Environment

Clients eventually requested support for optional persistence of expressions and for multiple forms of style checking and the ability to "mix-and-match" types of checks.

Persistence is a new concern; it represents both a new feature and a unit of change. As such, its addition is not supported well by object-oriented separation of concerns, as we saw in Section 3.2.2. This time, we choose to model persistence as an independent concern (hyperslice), which both encapsulates it and provides us the opportunity to use ASTs with or without persistence. Adding style checkers is trivial—the checking hyperslice already separates syntax and semantic checking, so we need only define the style checkers as hyperslices and compose any set of them together with the syntax and/or semantic check hyperslices. Notice that these new capabilities do not require any modifications to existing hyperslices or artifacts—they can be encapsulated as separate concerns and composed with the existing artifacts.

3.3.4.3 Postmortem Revisited

We now revisit the set of software engineering problems discussed in Section 3.2.3.

Impact of change: Much of the reason for high impact of change is the mismatch between the units of change and the units of abstraction and encapsulation within artifacts. With our model, however, units of change can be separated and encapsulated like any other concern. This can, in many common cases, significantly reduce or eliminate the impact of change.

Reuse: As noted above, this model may significantly improve reuse of *all* artifacts. It permits the separation of generally useful capabilities from special-purpose ones, and it provides composition as a very powerful, non-invasive customization and adaptation mechanism. Thus, it is simpler to create reusable components and to pick up and tailor a component to a particular need.

Traceability: The ability to identify, encapsulate, and co-structure similar concerns across different artifacts greatly facilitates traceability and propagation of change across the lifecycle.

While the appropriate use of the model can directly result in the benefits we have described (and many we have not), it is not a panacea for bad design, bad code, or poor modularization. Further, overseparation of concerns is as bad as underseparation—it leads to large numbers of hyperslices with complex interrelationships, and may actually reduce comprehension and increase complexity. Nonetheless, we believe the model is a valuable tool with potentially high benefit, if used properly.

3.4 INSTANTIATION

To use this artifact model, one must instantiate it for particular artifact development formalisms. Instantiation entails determining which notational constructs map to units and modules, deciding how to represent hyperslices, and providing support for composition of hyperslices. The mapping to units is especially important, as it significantly affects how well the hypermodules will achieve various software engineering goals and properties. This section briefly describes some of the issues involved. A fuller discussion appears in [18].

3.4.1 *Mapping to Units and Modules*

Units: Choosing "units" from the set of artifact formalism constructs requires an instantiator to decide the level of *granularity* at which it is appropriate, in the given formalism, to separate and integrate concepts. We illustrate this by example, using the Java language. Java defines both *declarator* constructs (e.g., packages, interfaces, classes, methods) and *statements*. Some subset of these constructs must be treated as units. A decision in favor of fine granularity might include all declarators and statements as units. This potentially provides the flexibility to compose any pieces of Java source, but it has all of the concomitant problems of determining how to match and reconcile different statements and of trying to analyze the properties of the result. Using a coarser level of granularity might result in treating only a subset of declarators (e.g., classes and their members) as units, which simplifies composition and understanding of the composed result, at the cost of generality.

The selection of units has significant ramifications for some important software engineering properties of artifacts [18], including effects on evolution and modular development. If the set of units includes entities that are typically "hidden," such as method implementation code, composition rules and their results become sensitive to "hidden" changes. Modular development relies on important properties of individual modules being preserved by composition. If composition can occur at too fine-grained a level, such properties might not be preserved, and must be re-examined afresh in the context of each composition.

Data and *functionality* are fundamental and ubiquitous concepts in software. They are frequently the concepts that are described by artifacts, and the concepts that span hyperslices and artifacts. Formalisms generally have constructs for declaring or defining them. For example, UML has boxes representing classes, and entries within class boxes representing instance variable and method declarations. Java has classes, interfaces, instance variable declarations and methods. We believe that constructs related to data and functionality are excellent candidates for units, and hypothesize that they might, in general, be the best choices.

Modules: The selection of formalism constructs to map to modules is somewhat simpler than the choice of units. Essentially, it requires examining the particular modularization constructs the formalism provides in light of the set of units chosen. For example, suppose we choose Java methods, instance variable declarations, classes, and interfaces as units. Instance variable declarations and methods are grouped together into classes and interfaces, which in turn are grouped together into packages. We would therefore choose to map Java classes, interfaces, and packages to modules in our model. An obvious choice for UML is to map classes and package diagrams to modules.

3.4.2 Representation of Hyperslices

Hyperslices are sets of modules. They need not occur explicitly in any given artifact formalisms, though some formalisms may provide a construct to which it is convenient to map hyperslices. For example, C++'s *namespace* construct, which represents arbitrary collections of program units, Java's *package* construct, which represents collections of classes and interfaces, and UML's package diagram, which represents collections of packages and classes, may be used to model hyperslices. For formalisms that do not have such constructs, it is necessary either to enhance them or to provide a separate hyperslice-specification mechanism, such as named lists of modules.

3.4.3 Support for Composition

To provide support for composing hyperslices, it is necessary to define a means for specifying composition rules—a language, an interactive tool, or both—and to build a *compositor* that is able to apply the rules to hyperslices. Composition by hand is conceptually possible, but totally unrealistic for actual development.

Providing this support is a large job. That is a powerful reason to make mapping decisions based on formalism, not on content, to avoid the need for project-specific compositors. Compositors specialized to understand particular semantic dimensions may be useful in some circumstances, however, as demonstrated by recent work on aspect-oriented programming [10].

3.5 RELATED WORK

We discuss two categories of related work: approaches that can (loosely, perhaps) be considered instantiations of our model for particular types of artifacts, and different approaches to similar problems.

Subject-oriented programming [7, 17] partially realizes our model for object-oriented code artifacts. The units are classes, methods and instance variables. Systems are built as compositions of *subjects*—hyperslices—each of which is a class hierarchy modeling its domain from a particular point of view. We have built composition support for C++ and CORBA IDL, prototype support for Smalltalk, and are currently building support for Java. Composition rules, specified textually for C++ and through an interactive user interface for the other systems, provide considerable matching and reconciliation flexibility, and the support is a framework allowing addition of new matchers and reconcilers. We have several small, running examples that demonstrate the value of decomposition into subjects. We are also currently exploring the manifestation of subjects and composition rules in UML, to allow co-structuring of subject-oriented designs and code.

Aspect-oriented programming (AOP) [10] expands on the concepts of subject-oriented programming by identifying and illustrating several useful, *non-functional* concerns to be separated, such as concurrency properties, distribution properties, persistence and other "emergent entities" [11]. Initial work used different aspect languages (e.g., [12]) to represent different aspects. This is appealing, since a programming language is not necessarily the best formalism for expressing non-functional requirements, but it results in a need for special-purpose compositors (called *weavers*. More recent work is aimed at providing a general-purpose weaver for hyperslices written in Java [10].

AOP distinguishes the notion of "core classes," which encapsulate a system's functional requirements, from "aspects," which encapsulate non-functional, cross-cutting requirements. Aspects are written with respect to core classes and are essentially orthogonal to one another. Relative to our model, each aspect is a hyperslice, and a set of aspects together with the core classes approximate a hypermodule. The core classes are distinguished; all aspects refer to them, and therefore share the same view of the overall class structure. The hypermodule does not have a central composition rule. Instead, each aspect contains its part of the rule, specifying how that aspect is to be *woven* into the base classes. This makes the approach subject to the disadvantages discussed in Section 3.3.3, particularly that handling of overlapping concerns (i.e., interaction among aspects) is perforce done in a standard, default manner by the weaver.

Holland discusses the building of systems using compositions of *contracts* [8]. Each contract specifies a set of participant objects and their interactions, expressed as *obligations*. Its primary intent is to encapsulate these particular interactions and obligations so that they are clearly separated from other interactions involving the same objects. A single object can participate in multiple contracts, in which case it must satisfy all their obligations. Holland describes a variety of combination rules for contracts. A contract corresponds to a hyperslice in our model, cutting across classes that describe objects. The combination rules provide some alternative means of combining specifications in different contracts that apply to the same participant.

Similarly, role models (e.g., in OORAM/OORAS [1]) are essentially hyperslices. Each model describes particular roles played by objects, and how those roles interact. Role models must be composed, usually manually, to produce object definitions that satisfy all needed roles. VanHilst and Notkin propose an approach to implementing roles with templates [24]. Each template defines a role, and instantiation expressions create classes that satisfy all required roles. Collections of related templates, such as those defining similar or interacting roles for objects, constitute hyperslices in our model, and instantiation expressions are composition rules.

Adaptive programming is another approach to providing modules other than classes within object-oriented systems. A *class graph* describes some classes and their relationships, from a particular point of view. Class graphs do not contain code; instead, code is written in separate *propagation patterns*. Propagation patterns can be used with any collection of concrete classes that conform to the class graph against which they were defined. Adaptive programs are transformed into standard object-oriented programs by the Demeter tools [3]. With respect to this generated program, each propagation pattern is a hyperslice, since it contains method code that cuts across classes. The composition is performed by the Demeter tool, with matching being based on specification of class graph conformance. Propagation patterns do not overlap, however—each defines its own method—so reconciliation is not an issue. In a recent paper [13], collaboration-based decomposition is discussed, of which contracts are an example. Collaborations are hyperslices, cutting across classes.

Catalysis [4] facilitates building reusable design frameworks in UML. It incorporates a simple notion of composition based on the union of design models. It therefore represents an instantiation of our model for UML. Catalysis' matching and reconciliation rules are fairly simple, which limits the dimensions along which design models can be decomposed and composed, but makes reasoning about properties of the composed design in terms of its component design models more tractable.

The *Viewpoints* project [15] is an approach to requirements engineering. Modules, called viewpoints, encapsulate developers' views of both the requirements-building process and the pieces of the requirements artifact being developed. Different viewpoints may describe the same requirements artifacts in different notations, and they may create conflicting definitions for given requirements. The Viewpoints system defines mechanisms (based on theorem proving) for identifying and helping developers cope with inconsistency.

The Viewpoints approach shares a number of points in common with ours but also has corresponding differences. Both approaches are predicated on the belief that not all concerns can be modularized orthogonally, and that it must be possible to view systems as potentially overlapping pieces. Another similarity is a concern with resolving semantic differences between different aspects or elements of a system (views or hyperslices). Viewpoints emphasizes the detection and characterization of inconsistencies while deferring their resolution (reconciliation) to the encompassing requirements process. We have focused on the activity of composing concerns after they have been separated, including identifying and, especially, reconciling inconsistencies according to a composition rule. Finally, we are primarily concerned with how artifacts are constructed, while the Viewpoints approach is primarily concerned with how they are viewed.

Some of the problems addressed by our approach can be tackled differently. Attempts have been made to address the problem of traceability with environment support for capturing and maintaining the relationships among artifacts (e.g., [9]). The disparate structures of the artifacts make this a particularly tough problem.

The problem of limiting the impact of change has been addressed by various architectures and mechanisms, like implicit invocation [14], mediators [22], event-based integration [20], and design patterns [5]. These are all valuable, but they suffer from the drawback that the kinds of changes they permit—the open points—must be anticipated. Retrofitting any of these mechanisms where not originally planned requires invasive change.

A great deal of work has been done to promote reuse, and other researchers and developers have recognized the importance of large-component reuse (e.g., [2]). Effective reuse requires powerful adaptation and customization mechanisms, but current customization technology is usually restricted to interface adaptation using some sort of adapter or transformation layer, or to substituting alternative modules at predetermined points, such as in object-oriented frameworks. Interesting recent work builds on adaptive programming to support "adaptive plug-and-play components" [13].

3.6   CONCLUSIONS AND FUTURE WORK

A number of important problems in software engineering have resisted general solution, including problems related to software understanding, maintenance, evolution, and reuse. We believe that these problems share a common cause: failure of modern artifact formalisms to satisfy the *separation of concerns* requirement adequately. Numerous reasons exist to separate and integrate software artifacts, and these reasons may result in different artifact structures. Moreover, many concerns may be relevant simultaneously, and the entire set of concerns may evolve over time. Despite this observation, artifact formalisms include weak decomposition and composition mechanisms that permit only a small, "dominant" set of concerns to be separated. This leads directly to our inability to achieve many of the goals of software engineering as a discipline.

Our model of multi-dimensional software decomposition helps to overcome these limitations. It permits encapsulation of particular concerns in a software system, both *within* and *across* artifacts, and it allows kinds of separation of concerns that may not be separable in artifact formalisms, such as units of change, features, and overlapping concerns. This improves traceability across the lifecycle. The model also provides a powerful composition mechanism that facilitates integration, adaptation, and "plug-and-play." In so doing, it promotes reuse, improves comprehension, and eases maintenance and evolution. Thus, the approach addresses some fundamental limitations in software engineering. For these reasons, we believe that support for multi-dimensional decomposition and composition represents a key to advances along a broad front of software engineering challenges.

This work is clearly at an early stage, largely unproven yet. Still, a considerable body of experience and related research now exists to support the claim that multi-dimensional separation of concerns is one of the key software engineering issues today. The model presented is just a starting point. It must be refined, stretched, and modified, and it must be instantiated for a variety of formalisms to explore issues that arise for different methodologies and at different phases of the software lifecycle. These instantiations must be used for real development, to evaluate them and create new development methods that exploit their strengths; to explore issues in intra- and inter-artifact matching and reconciliations; and to explore the impact of multi-dimensional separation of concerns on areas like development methodology, software process, analysis, testing, reverse engineering, reengineering, and software architecture.

ACKNOWLEDGMENTS

Joyce Vann, Mark Wegman, and the reviewers provided valuable feedback on earlier versions of this paper. Siobhán Clarke produced the SEE design in UML.

REFERENCES

1. ANDERSEN, E. A. AND REENSKAUG, T. 1992. System design by composing structures of interacting objects. In *ECOOP '92 European Conf. Object-Oriented Programming* (Kaiserslautern), O. L. Madsen, Ed. LNCS, vol. 615. Springer-Verlag, Berlin, 133–152.

2. BOEHM, B. W. AND SCHERLIS, W. L. 1992. Megaprogramming. In *DARPA Software Technology Conference*. Meridien Corp., Arlington, Virginia, 63–82.

3. DEMETER RESEARCH GROUP. Online material on adaptive programming Demeter/ Java, and APPCs. http://www.ccs.neu.edu/research/demeter/.

4. D'SOUZA, D. F. AND WILLS, A. C. 1999. *Objects, Components, and Frameworks with UML: The Catalysis Approach*. Addison-Wesley, Reading, Massachusetts.

5. GAMMA, E., HELM, R., JOHNSON, R., AND VLISSIDES, J. 1995. *Design Patterns: Elements of Reusable Object-Oriented Software*. Addison-Wesley, Reading, Massachusetts.

6. GOSLING, J., JOY, B., AND STEELE, G. L. 1996. *The Java Language Specification*. Addison-Wesley, Reading, Massachusetts.

7. HARRISON, W. AND OSSHER, H. 1993. Subject-oriented programming—a critique of pure objects. In *8th Conf. Object-Oriented Programming, Systems, Languages, and Applications (OOPSLA)*, (Washington, D.C.). ACM, 411–428.

8. HOLLAND, I. M. 1992. Specifying reusable components using contracts. In *ECOOP '92 European Conf. Object-Oriented Programming* (Utrecht, Netherlands), O. L. Madsen, Ed. LNCS, vol. 615. Springer-Verlag, Berlin, 287–308.

9. KADIA, R. 1992. Issues encountered in building a flexible software development environment: Lessons from the Arcadia project. In *5th Symp. Software Development Environments (SESPSDE)*, (Tyson's Corner, Virginia). ACM, 169–180.

10. KICZALES, G., LAMPING, J., MENDHEKAR, A., MAEDA, C., LOPES, C., LOINGTIER, J. M., AND IRWIN, J. 1997. Aspect-oriented programming. In *ECOOP'97 Object-Oriented Programming, 11th European Conference*, M. Akşit and S. Matsuoka, Eds. LNCS, vol. 1241. Springer-Verlag, Berlin 220–242.

11. KICZALES, G. AND LOPES, C. V. 1998. ECOOP '98 aspect-oriented programming tutorial notes. Tech. rep., AITO. July.

12. LOPES, C. V. AND KICZALES, G. 1997. D: A language framework for distributed programming. Tech. Rep. SPL-97-010, Palo Alto Research Center.

13. MEZINI, M. AND LIEBERHERR, K. 1998. Adaptive plug-and-play components for evolutionary software development. In *13th Conf. Object-Oriented Programming, Systems, Languages, and Applications (OOPSLA)*, (Vancouver). ACM, 97–116.

14. NOTKIN, D., GARLAN, D., GRISWOLD, W. G., AND SULLIVAN, K. 1993. Adding implicit invocation to languages: Three approaches. In *Object Technologies for Advanced Software: 1st JSSST Int'l Symposium* (Janazawa, Japan), S. Nishio and A. Yonesawa, Eds. LNCS, vol. 742. Springer-Verlag, Berlin, 489–510.

15. NUSEIBEH, B., KRAMER, J., AND FINKELSTEIN, A. 1994. A framework for expressing the relationships between multiple views in requirements specifications. *IEEE Transactions on Software Engineering 20*, 10, 760–773.

16. OSSHER, H., HARRISON, W., BUDINSKY, F., AND SIMMONDS, I. 1994. Subject-oriented programming: Supporting decentralized development of objects. In *7th IBM Conf. Object-Oriented Technology*, (Santa Clara, California).

17. Ossher, H., Kaplan, M., Katz, A., Harrison, W., and Kruskal, V. 1996. Specifying subject-oriented composition. *Theory and Practice of Object Systems 2*, 3, 179–202.

18. Ossher, H. and Tarr, P. 1998. Operation-level composition: A case in (join) point. In *Workshop on Aspect-Oriented Programming (ECOOP),* (Brussels). http://trese.cs.utwente.nl/aop-ecoop98/papers/Tarr.pdf.

19. Parnas, D. L. 1972. On the criteria to be used in decomposing systems into modules. *Comm. ACM 15*, 12 (Dec.), 1053–1058.

20. Reiss, S. P. 1990. Connecting tools using message passing in the Field environment. *IEEE Software 7*, 4 (July), 57–66.

21. Rumbaugh, J., Jacobson, I., and Booch, G. 1998. *Unified Modeling Language Reference Manual*. Addison-Wesley, Reading, Massachusetts.

22. Sullivan, K. J. 1994. Mediators: Easing the design and evolution of integrated systems. Ph.D. thesis, University of Washington.

23. Turner, C. I., Fuggetta, A., Lavazza, L., and Wolf, A. L. 1998. Feature engineering. In *9th Int'l Workshop on Software Specification and Design* (Ise-Shima, Japan), IEEE, 162–164.

24. VanHilst, M. and Notkin, D. 1996. Using roles components to implement collaboration-based designs. In *11th Conf. Object-Oriented Programming, Systems, Languages, and Applications (OOPSLA),* (San Jose). ACM, 359–369.

25. Weiser, M. 1984. Program slicing. *IEEE Transactions on Software Engineering 10*, 4 (July), 352–357.

Chapter 4

Principles and Design Rationale of Composition Filters

LODEWIJK BERGMANS AND MEHMET AKŞIT

A wide range of aspect-oriented programming languages has appeared in the past years [7]. Current research on future generation AOP languages is addressing issues like flexibility, expressive power, and safety. We think that it is important to understand the motivations and design decisions of the first generation AOP languages. The Composition Filters model [4, 8, 12] is one example of such a first-generation AOP language. The goal of this chapter is two-fold: First, it aims to explain the principles of composition filters, in particular their aspect-oriented composition capabilities. Second, it aims to provide insight into the motivations and design rationale behind the composition filters model.

4.1 INTRODUCTION

During the last several years, many aspect-oriented languages have been proposed, including such representative examples [19] as adaptive programming [29], hyperspaces [32], AspectJ [25], and Composition Filters (CFs) [12]. The idea of CFs dates back to as early as 1986. As such, it is among the earliest, if not the first, aspect-oriented language. Like other approaches, the CF model has evolved. This chapter presents the contemporary CF model, illustrating how it can address certain modeling problems and providing insight into its motivations and design rationale.

The structure of this chapter is as follows: in Section 4.1, we introduce the background and objectives of the CF model. Section 4.2 introduces an example, which is used to illustrate the issue of composing and reusing multiple concerns in object-oriented programs when requirements evolve. In Section 4.3, the CF model is presented as an approach to address the identified problems. This section introduces the CF model, focusing on its application to concerns that crosscut within an object. Section 4.4

extends this discussion by explaining how the CF model can address crosscutting over multiple objects. Section 4.5 evaluates the CF model, Section 4.6 discusses common misconceptions about the CF model, and Section 4.7 presents our conclusions.

4.1.1 Background and Aims of the Composition Filters Model: Finding the Right Abstractions

The CF model has originated from the *Sina* language, which was first published in 1988 [6]. The concepts and ideas of Sina have since evolved, with the main objective being to improve the composability characteristics of object-oriented and, ultimately, aspect-oriented programming languages.

We use the term *composability* to refer to the ability to define a new program entity—with a behavior as required—as the construction of two or more program entities. We distinguish two key elements of composability. The first element refers to the mechanisms (or *composition operators*) used to compose software units (objects, aspects, etc.). Typical composition operators are inheritance, aggregation, and weaving mechanisms. The second key element refers to the properties or restrictions imposed on software units to make them safe for composition. For example, well-defined interfaces and declarative join point models may contribute to safe composition; these can be used for early detection of problems such as references to non-existent program elements and naming conflicts. The challenge is to find the right balance between the expressiveness of composition mechanisms and the restrictions imposed on software units. Addressing this challenge has been the main focus of the work on composition filters.

A fundamental design decision of the CF model is to distinguish two kinds of abstractions: (class-like) *concerns* and *filters*. Briefly, a concern is the unit for defining the primary behavior, while a filter is used to extend or enhance concerns so that (crosscutting) properties can be represented more effectively.

The main objectives of the composition filters model are summarized here. Later in this chapter, we discuss how these objectives are addressed.

Composability. Support composition (of the behavior) of modules into new modules with the desired behavior.

Evolvability. Extend existing (object-oriented) programming models in a modular way, instead of replacing or adapting them.

Robustness. Support the creation of correct programs through appropriate language abstractions that avoid common programming mistakes and enable verification of certain quality properties.

Implementation-independence. Allow multiple implementations of the same behavior, including both static and dynamic implementations, tradeoffs between time and space efficiencies, and execution on different platforms.

Dynamics.   Support dynamic adaptation of structure and behavior to meet changes in requirements or context, without compromising the above objectives.

4.2 EXAMPLE: SOCIAL SECURITY SERVICES

We first present a simple example to illustrate the issue of composing and reusing multiple concerns in object-oriented programs when the requirements evolve. The example is a simplified version of the pilot study conducted in [17]. Due to the evolving business context, the initial software has undergone a series of modifications. We use a change scenario to explain the concepts and the application of the CF approach.

4.2.1 An Overview of the Application

The context of the example is a (Dutch) government-funded agency that is responsible for the implementation of disability insurance laws. As illustrated in Figure 4-1, the agency implements five tasks. Task `RequestHandler` creates a case for clients. Cases are represented as documents. `RequestDispatcher` implements the initial evaluation and distribution of the requests to the necessary tasks. A request can be dispatched to `MedicalCheck`, `Payment`, and/or `Approval`. `MedicalCheck` is responsible for evaluating a client's degree of disability. `Payment` is responsible for issuing bank orders. `Approval` is the (management) task of approving the proposed decisions, such as rewarding or rejecting a claim. Once a request is forwarded by `RequestDispatcher`, the further processing and routing of documents between tasks is a responsibility of the participating tasks. We would like to emphasize that Figure 4-1 only shows a small part of the actual system [17].

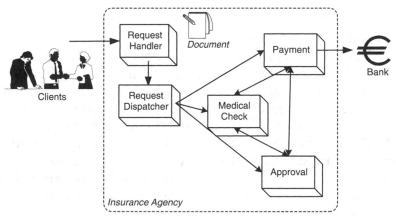

Figure 4-1   *Tasks in the example system.*

4.2.2   The Software System

The implementation of the system is based on a set of *tasks* and a number of *documents*. For now, assume that tasks and documents are implemented using classes. Each client request results in the creation of a document instance. Depending on the document type and input from the client, the document is edited and sent to the appropriate tasks (objects). Each involved task processes the document according to its specific needs.

As shown in Figure 4-2, class `Document` is the *abstract* root class of all document types. Every document inherits its attributes and methods (a number of getters and setters and several additional methods, e.g., for accessing the status of the document, or for printing and mailing it). Class `Document` has several subclasses. For example, `ClaimDocument` is used to represent the clients' claims. Its attributes are typically written—through the appropriate methods—by various tasks as the document is processed.

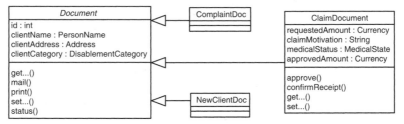

Figure 4-2   *Part of the class hierarchy of documents that represent client requests.*

As shown in Figure 4-3, the interface `TaskProcessor` declares the basic methods for all tasks. The method `process()` accepts a document as an argument and starts the task processing for the document; this might be a partially or fully automated process. In the cases where human interaction is required, an "editor" UI tool is opened that presents the document and offers a task-specific interface to perform the manual part of processing. This is handled by the method `startEditor()`. Typically the last action of a task consists of forwarding the document to the next task(s); this is handled by the method `forward()`. The actual selection of all permitted tasks in the given state of the system has been factored out into the method `selectTask()`; the method `forward()` has the responsibility of choosing one of the permitted tasks.

These methods must be defined by classes that implement this interface. Figure 4-3 shows some classes for different tasks. Each of these may inherit (task-specific) methods from different superclasses; this is not shown in the figure.

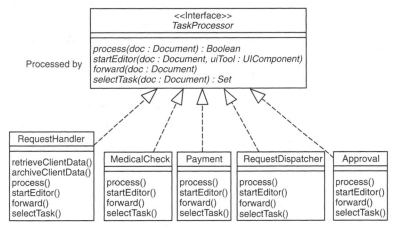

Figure 4-3 *Class definitions for tasks.*

RequestHandler implements the front-end of the office. For example, if a client wants to issue a claim, this task creates an object of ClaimDocument, retrieves the necessary client data, and opens an editor for the document object. The responsible clerk can then perform actions specific for RequestHandler. When the task is completed, the clerk selects a subsequent task—from the permitted ones—and forwards the document. This causes the invocation of method process() on the next task, with the document passed as an argument.

In this system, new activities are introduced by creating a new structural document class. (In the actual system from which this example has been derived, there were approximately 30 different document types.)

4.3 INTRA-OBJECT CROSSCUTTING WITH COMPOSITION FILTERS

In this section, we begin by briefly explaining the CF object model, focusing on concerns that crosscut *within* an object. We discuss the basic mechanisms of the CF model using the example that was introduced in Section 4.2. This chapter presents a conceptual model of composition filters, explained in an operational way. Actual implementations may vary substantially, as we discuss in Section 4.5.1.

4.3.1   Concern Instance = Object + Filters

The CF model is a modular extension to the conventional *object-based* model [38] used by programming languages such as Java, C++, and Smalltalk, as well as component models such as .NET, CORBA, and Enterprise JavaBeans. The core concept of this extension is the enhancement of conventional objects by manipulating all sent and received messages. This allows expressing many different behavioral enhancements since in an object-based system all the externally visible behavior of an object is manifest in the messages it sends and receives. Figure 4-4 illustrates this extension by "abstracting" the *implementation object* with a layer[1] that contains filters for manipulating sent and received messages. These filters are grouped into subcomponents called *filter modules*. Filter modules are the units of reuse and instantiation of filter behavior. In addition to the specification of filters, the filter modules may provide some execution context for the filters.

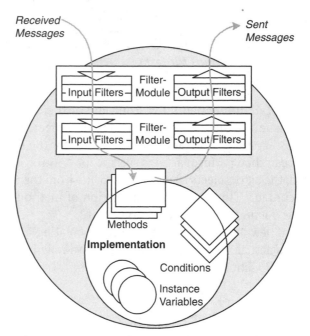

Figure 4-4   *Simplified representation of concern instances with filters.*

---

1.   This is different from straightforward object wrapping—e.g., problems such as object schizophrenia [33] are avoided because in the CF case, there is only one object with a single identity.

The *filters* define enhancements to the behavior of objects. Each filter specifies a particular inspection and manipulation of messages. *Input filters* and *output filters* can manipulate messages that are respectively received and sent by an object. After the composition of filter modules and filters, received messages must pass through the input filters and be sent through the output filters.[2]

The enhanced object, which we refer to as the *implementation object,* may be defined in any object-based language, given the availability of proper tool support for that language. The main requirement is that the object offers an interface of available methods. Two types of methods are distinguished: *regular methods* and *condition methods* (*conditions* for short). Regular methods implement the functional behavior of the object. They may be invoked through messages if the filters of the object allow this. Conditions must implement side-effect free Boolean expressions that typically provide information about the state of the object.

Conditions serve three purposes:

1. They offer an abstraction of the state of the implementation object, allowing filters to consider only relevant states.
2. They allow filters to remain independent of the implementation details of the implementation object. This has the additional benefit of making the filters more reusable.
3. Conditions can be reused by multiple filter (modules) and concerns.

In summary, conditions enforce the separation of the state abstraction and the message filtering concerns.

4.3.2 Evolution Step 1: Protecting Documents

In the initial system, each task could access all the attributes of a document. A request dispatcher clerk, for instance, could accidentally edit the medical data properties. To overcome this problem, the second release placed restrictions on the execution of messages. Within a given document-processing phase, only the appropriate tasks should have access to the interface methods of the corresponding document. A possible implementation for this is to test the role of the sender of the

---

2. More precisely, both filter modules and filters are composed together using dedicated composition operators. In this chapter, we assume that both filter modules and filters within those modules are composed with a fixed order that depends on the declaration order of various elements.

received message[3] before executing the corresponding method, throwing an exception if the method was invoked by an inappropriate object.

In the evolution steps that follow, we reuse all the functionality that has been implemented so far, incrementally introducing the new requirements through modular extensions.

With conventional objects, there are two primary extension alternatives: subclassing an existing document class or aggregating an instance of an existing document class and reusing its behavior internally by sending ("forwarding") messages to it. Both of these patterns require overriding many methods of the reused class. These methods must implement the verification of the identity of the sender object, in addition to invoking the behavior of the original method. We refer to [12] for an extensive discussion on advantages and disadvantages of inheritance-based and aggregation-based composition.

In the actual pilot project, the number of required method redefinitions was substantially high, due to the quantity of document types and the number of methods for each document type that had to be protected.

4.3.3   A Composition Filters Solution

We describe filter specifications in more detail using the `ProtectedClaim Document` example described in the previous section. The code for `Protected ClaimDocument` is shown in Listing 4-1. Using inheritance, `Protected ClaimDocument` extends the existing class `ClaimDocument` with a protection mechanism to prevent inappropriate objects from invoking certain methods. We refer to this mechanism as *multiple views*. We first introduce the overall structure of a composition filters specification, show how messages are processed by filters, illustrate how filters can express inheritance, and finally explain how filters can express views in a modular way.

Class `ProtectedClaimDocument` consists of a filter module, `Document WithViews` (lines 2–19), and an implementation part, which is defined as a Java class named `ProtectedClaimDocumentImpl` (lines 20–31). In principle, any object-based language can be used to realize the implementation part. In this example, the implementation defines the conditions and methods that are newly introduced by class `ProtectedClaimDocument`.

---

3. Depending on the implementation language, it may be non-trivial to identify the sender of a message and its role.

Listing 4-1 *Implementation of* ProtectedClaimDocument *with composition filters*

```
(1)    concern ProtectedClaimDocument begin
(2)    filtermodule DocumentWithViews begin
(3)      internals
(4)        document: ClaimDocument;
(5)      conditions
(6)        Payment; MedChck; ReqHndlr; ReqDisp; Approval;
(7)      methods
(8)        activeTask():String;
(9)        document.*;   //all methods on interface of ClaimDocument
(10)     inputfilters
(11)       protection: Error = {
(12)         Payment=>{setApprovedAmount, getApprovedAmount},
(13)         MedChck=>{setMedStatus, getMedStatus, getClaimMotivation},
(14)         ...//etc. for the other views
(15)         True=>{mail, print, status, getClientName, getCategory} };
(16)       inh : Dispatch = { inner.* , document.* };
(17)   end filtermodule DocumentWithViews;

(18)   implementation in Java   //for example
(19)     class ProtectedClaimDocumentImpl {
(20)       boolean Payment() { return this.activeTask()!="Payment" };
(21)       boolean MedChk()    { ... };
(22)       boolean ReqHndlr()  { ... };
(23)       boolean ReqDisp()   { ... };
(24)       boolean Approval()  { ... };
(25)       String  activeTask() { ... };
(26)       }
(27)   end implementation
(28)   end concern ProtectedClaimDocument;
```

The filter module `DocumentWithViews` contains four parts: The first is the declaration of `internals` (lines 3–4); these are internal objects, encapsulated by the filter module. A new instance of an internal is created for each instantiation of the filter module that declares it. In this example, an instance of `ClaimDocument` named `document` is created for each instantiation of the filter module. A filter module can also declare `externals`; these are references to instances created outside the filter module and concern and are used for representing shared state. Typically, the reference consists of a name that is bound according to lexical scoping rules.

The second part refers to the `conditions` (lines 5–6). Conditions serve to abstract the state of the implementation object. In this case, five conditions are declared. It is possible to reuse conditions declared elsewhere by using the syntax `<instance name>.<condition name>`, where `<instance name>` must be a valid internal or external object. The form `<instance name>.*` can be used to 'import'[4] all conditions from an instance. Possible name conflicts are resolved by selecting the first occurrence of a condition name based on the order of declaration.

The third part of the filter module refers to the lines 7–9, where the `methods` that are used within the filter expressions are declared, including the types of arguments and return values. Line 8 shows the declaration of method `activeTask()`, which takes no arguments and returns an instance of type `String`. For the purpose of language independence, the adopted notation follows the UML conventions [31] where appropriate. Line 9 shows the use of a wildcard `*` as a shorthand notation to declare all the methods in the signature of class *ClaimDocument*.[5] Again, possible name conflicts are resolved by selecting the first method according to the order of declaration.

The fourth and the last part of this example filter module is the specification of the *input filters* in lines 10–17. Two filters are declared in this part; *protection* and *inh*. The first filter handles the multiple views, and the second specifies the inheritance relation from the "previous version"; i.e. from *ClaimDocument*. We will go into more detail about the way filters work in the next subsection.

All the named instances, conditions, and methods within filter specifications must always be declared within the filter module. The resulting *declarative completeness* (as in Hyper/J [32]) improves the ability to do modular and incremental reasoning about the correctness of the program. In addition, when instantiating a filter module, it is straightforward to verify that all the declared entities within the filter module can actually be bound to concrete implementations.

4.3.4 *Message Processing*

We explain the process of *message filtering* with the aid of Figure 4-5. The description focuses on input filters, but output filters work in exactly the same manner. In

---

4. This is semantically close to the notion of inheritance of conditions.

5. This shorthand notation can be seen as a compromise between explicitly declaring all the methods on one hand and convenience and open-endedness on the other hand. A particular property of the wildcard is that extensions to the interface of the reused class (in the current example, `ClaimDocument`) will be automatically available to the reusing concern (`ProtectedClaimDocument`).

Figure 4-5, three filters, *A*, *B*, and *C*, are shown. We assume sequential composition of these three filters. Each filter has a *filter type* and a *filter pattern*. The filter type determines how to handle the messages after they have been matched against the filter pattern. The filter pattern is a simple, declarative expression to match and modify messages. Typically, messages travel sequentially along the filters until they are dispatched. Dispatching here means either to start the execution of a local method or to delegate the message to another object.

Figure 4-5 illustrates how a message[6] is rejected by the first filter (*A*) and continues to the subsequent filter (*B*). At filter (*B*) it matches immediately, and is modified . Then the message continues to the last filter (*C*). In the example, at the last filter, the message matches and is then subject to a dispatch.

Each filter can either accept or reject a message. The semantics associated with acceptance or rejection depend on the type of the filter. Typically, these are the

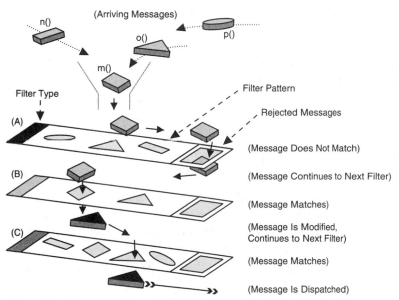

Figure 4-5   *An intuitive schema of message filtering.*

---

6.   Messages are first reified; i.e., a first-class representation is created. Composition filters thus *conceptually* apply a form of message reflection [20], but note that actual implementations may "optimize away" the reification.

manipulation (modification) of the message or the execution of certain actions. Examples of predefined filter types are:

Dispatch.   If the message is accepted, it is dispatched to the current target of the message; otherwise, the message continues to the subsequent filter (if there is none, an exception is raised) [2].

Substitute.   Is used to modify (substitute) certain properties of messages explicitly.

Error.   If the filter rejects the message, it raises an exception; otherwise, the message continues to the next filter in the set [2].

Wait.   If the message is accepted, it continues to the next filter in the set. The message is queued as long as the evaluation of the filter expression results in a rejection [8, 10].

Meta.   If the message is accepted, the message is reified and sent as a parameter of a new message to a named object; otherwise the message just continues to the next filter. The object that receives the message can observe and manipulate the reified message and reactivate its execution [4].

We will see examples of the application of various filter types throughout the remainder of this chapter. Although filters can also be defined by the programmer, we do not discuss that in this chapter.

A composition filter specification corresponds to the creation of an instance of a filter type; for example, in Listing 4-1, *ProtectedClaimDocument* declares the following filter in line 18:

```
(18)      inh : Dispatch = { inner.* , document.* };
```

This expression declares a filter instance with name *inh* of filter type *Dispatch*, which is initialized with the filter pattern between the curly brackets. The filter pattern consists of a number of *filter elements*, connected with composition operators. In this particular case, the two filter elements are `inner.*` and `document.*`. A filter element is mainly used for matching messages. In addition, a filter element may modify certain parts of messages. Evaluation of a filter element always yields at least a Boolean result indicating whether the message actually matched the filter element.

We discuss only one filter element composition operator: the sequence operator ','. The semantics of this operator are similar to a conditional OR—when the filter element on the left side matches, the whole expression is satisfied, and no further filter elements should be considered. However, if the filter element on the left side does not match, the filter element on the right side will be evaluated, and so on, until either a filter element matches or all filter elements have been evaluated. The total expression always yields a Boolean result, i.e., *true* if the message did *match* one of the filter elements and *false* if it could not match any of them—a so-called *reject*.[7]

In the example shown previously, the message matches the first filter element if the selector of the received message is within the signature of `inner`. This is the case when a corresponding method has been declared by the implementation object itself. If so, the `target` property of the message is replaced by a reference to the `inner` object. If the selector of the message is not in the signature of *inner*, the message is matched with the second filter element, `document.*`. This is successful if the selector of the message is in the signature of class `ClaimDocument`. If the message does match, it has reached the end of the filter elements, yielding a *reject*.

After this matching process, an action is performed based on the filter type, the result of the matching process (i.e., *accept* or *reject*), and the potentially modified message. In the previous example, either this means the dispatch of the message to the new target, or the original, unchanged message simply continues to the subsequent filter. Dispatching by a `Dispatch` filter means one of three things:

1. If the target of the message is `inner`, this implies the execution of a method of the inner (implementation) object with the name that equals the selector of the message.

2. If the target of the message has been declared as an *external object,* dispatching is equivalent to (true) *delegation* [28] of the message to the target object. This means that the message is forwarded to the target, where the essential difference with message invocation is that the *server* pseudovariable (usually referred to as 'this' in C++ and Java, and 'self' in Smalltalk) still refers to the original receiver of the message invocation, not to the new target. In the literature, this property is also described as "allowing the ancestor to be part of the extended identity of the delegating object" [28]. A key feature of delegation is that it allows multiple instances to share (reuse) both the behavior (i.e., methods) *and* state (value) of an instance.

3. If the target of the message has been declared as an *internal object,* dispatching is again equivalent to true delegation, but the intuitive meaning is different—because each instance has its own copy of a declared internal object, delegating to

---

7. For an impression of the possible alternative composition operators, consider for example operators based on pure *OR*s or *AND*s, where multiple matches might lead to multiple dispatch of the same received messages, either sequential or in parallel.

an internal object is equivalent to inheriting from the class of the internal object. This is because both the behavior and the data structure (but not the actual values) of the superclass are reused.

This is exemplified by the dispatch filter in the previous example. This filter accepts and executes all received messages that are declared and implemented by the inner (implementation) object (in lines 21–30 of Listing 4-1). All other messages that are in the signature of internal object document (i.e., available on its interface), as defined by concern ClaimDocument, match at the second part of the filter and are thus dispatched (delegated) to the document object. Remaining messages that are in neither of the two signatures continue to the next filter; if there is none, this yields a run-time error ("message not understood").[8]

We now consider the first filter in this example implementation, the filter named protection with filter type Error. The semantics of filter type Error are that it does nothing when a message is accepted and raises an exception[9] when the message is rejected. The filter contains several elements, separated by the ',' sequence composition operator:

```
protection : Error = {
   Payment => {setApprovedAmount, getApprovedAmount},
   MedChck => {setMedStatus, getMedStatus,
               getClaimMotivation},
   ...  //etc. for the other views
   True => {mail, print, status, getClientName, getCategory}
};
```

Each of these elements has the form <condition> => {<list of messages>}. Its semantics are that the expression on the right side of the characters '=>' is only evaluated if the condition on the left side evaluates to true.

The aim of this example is to ensure that only the relevant messages are allowed to pass, and all others should result in an exception. To achieve this, the above Error filter uses conditions (Payment, MedChck, etc.) that evaluate to *true* if the invocation was sent by respectively the tasks Payment, MedicalCheck, etc. In combination with the enable operator '=>', the protection filter only allows messages setApprovedAmount() and getApprovedAmount() if the condition Payment

---

8. Run-time errors can be avoided through static type checking, with some reduction of flexibility.

9. It is possible to add the type of exception as a parameter to the filter type; for example, "protection: Error(AuthorizationException)=...".

is true. This means the sender of the message was a payment task. The filter expresses such constraints for all the different tasks, ending with a list of messages that are always acceptable; hence these are associated with the condition `true`.

4.3.5   *Intra-Object Crosscutting*

The previous example of adding views exemplifies so-called *intra-object crosscutting:* each view constraint applies to a set of messages. For example, the `MedChk` condition is used to ensure authorized access for the messages `setMedStatus()`, `getMedStatus()`, and `getClaimMotivation()`. Instead of reimplementing the restriction in each of the corresponding methods, a filter defines this crosscutting constraint in a modular way.

However, the range of the crosscut specification is limited: Although a filter expression may refer to messages that are inherited from or delegated to other concerns, only messages on the interface of a single concern are considered. In the next section, we show how to extend the application of composition filters in a broader (crosscutting) scope.

4.4   *INTER-OBJECT CROSSCUTTING*

From a software engineering perspective, the distinction between intra-object and inter-object crosscutting is more fundamental than just the expressiveness of the pointcut mechanism. Typically, software engineers consider classes or concerns as the unit of development and change. In addition, all specifications that are part of a single concern specification are assumed to be potentially interdependent and are likely to be developed and evolve mutually, typically by one or a few closely cooperating software engineers. In accordance with this view, software engineers should design filters as an integral part of the concerns.[10] This is a sharp contrast with inter-object crosscutting concerns, which are assumed to be developed independently, typically at a different time and potentially by different software engineers. As a result, the interfaces between the crosscutting concerns and the concerns that are affected by them are substantially more critical. The CF model reflects this distinction by introducing a different ("higher-level") mechanism for inter-object

---

10. This may seem in contradiction with the idea that filters are a modular extension to the object-oriented model, but as we explain in the sidebar "Common Misconceptions about Composition Filters," the fact that the language model is an extension does not mean that applications should be designed by first designing objects and adding the interface part afterward.

crosscutting. Its basic concept is to use groups of filters and related definitions, called *filter modules*, which are composed with concerns through the so-called *superimposition*[11] mechanism. The *superimposition* specifications describe the locations within the program where concern behavior is to be added in the form of filter modules.

4.4.1 Evolution Step 2: Adding Workflow Management

To explain the mechanism of superimposition, we introduce a second extension to our running example. In the design of the example so far, each clerk (i.e., human user) has to choose which task is to be executed next for a given document. Accordingly, the document is forwarded to the appropriate task object. To enforce a better-managed business process, we introduce a new concern, called `WorkFlowngine`.

Based on a workflow specification, the concern `WorkFlowEngine` is responsible for implementing the task selection process. In the current version, task selection is implemented within the method `forward()`. This method further calls on the method `selectTask()`, which returns a task selected among a set of alternatives. The method `selectTask` is implemented specifically for each `TaskProcessor` concern.

The concern `WorkFlowEngine` declares the attribute `workFlowSpec`, which represents the process to be enforced. This concern also implements the method `choose()`, which returns the task to be forwarded based on the workflow specification and the set of alternatives available.

The method `forward()` first calls `selectTask()` of `WorkFlowEngine`, followed by an invocation on `choose()`. Adding workflow management to the system in an object-oriented implementation would require redefinition of method `forward()` for all task classes. The method `forward()` cannot be implemented by a superclass since every task implements this method in a specific manner. An aspect-oriented implementation is a preferable solution.

We use this example to illustrate how crosscutting can be expressed using the CF model. As shown in Listing 4-2, this concern consists of four parts: (1) a (crosscutting) filter module named `UseWorkFlowEngine` that ensures that all relevant concerns in the application actually use the engine for determining the next tasks (lines 2–10); (2) a (shared) filter module named `Engine` that implements the behavior of the workflow engine itself (lines 11–19); (3) a `superimposition`

---

11. Our notion of superimposition bears resemblance to, but is truly distinct from, the technique of superimposition as proposed by Bougé and Francez [14] and Katz [24]. Conceptually, superimposition as proposed by Bosch [13] is very close, but it refers to instantiation-time composition and does not include any support for crosscutting.

specification (lines 20–28); and (4) the implementation of the necessary functionality
(lines 29–42).

Listing 4-2 *Specification of* `WorkFlowEngine`, *illustrating a crosscutting CF concern*

```
(1)    concern WorkFlowEngine begin     //introduces global workflow control
(2)      filtermodule UseWorkFlowEngine begin    //declares crosscutting code
(3)        externals
(4)          wfEngine : WorkFlowEngine;        //*declare* a shared instance
(5)        methods                    //declare the -intercepted- messages
(6)          Set selectTask(Document);
(7)          workflow(Message);
(8)        inputfilters
(9)          redirect: Meta = {[selectTask]wfEngine.workflow};
(10)     end filtermodule useWorkFlowEngine;

(11)     filtermodule Engine begin       //defines interface of workflow engine
(12)       methods
(13)         workflow(Message);
(14)         choose(Document, TaskProcessor, Set) :
(15)         TaskProcessor;
(16)         setWorkFlow(WorkFlow);
(17)       inputfilters
(18)         disp : Dispatch = { inner.* };      //accept all my methods
(19)     end filtermodule engine;

(20)     superimposition begin      //defines actual crosscutting composition
(21)       selectors        //queries set of all instances in the system
(22)         allTasks = {*=RequestHandler,
(23)                     *=MedicalCheck, *=Payment,
(24)                     *=RequestDispatcher, *=Approval };
(25)       filtermodules
(26)         self <- Engine;
(27)         allTasks <- UseWorkFlowEngine;
(28)     end superimposition;

(29)     implementation in Java;
(30)       class WorkFlowEngine {
(31)         WorkFlow workFlowRepr;
(32)         void workflow(Message mess {
(33)           Document doc = mess.getArg(1);
(34)           TaskProcessor curTask = mess.target();
(35)           Set alternatives = mess.send();
(36)           mess.return( choose(doc, curTask, alternatives) );
```

```
(37)          };
(38)       TaskProcessor choose(Document, TaskProcessor, Set){ ... };
(39)       void setWorkFlow(WorkFlow wf) { ... };
(40)        }
(41)     end implementation;
(42)  end concern WorkFlowEngine;
```

The filter module `UseWorkFlowEngine` defines a filter of type `Meta`, which intercepts the calls on the method `selectTask()` and sends them in reified[12] form to the external object `wfEngine` as the argument of a message `workflow()`. This filter module represents the crosscutting behavior that must be superimposed upon all the `TaskProcessor` concern instances. In this case, the crosscutting behavior consists mostly of connecting the various task instances to the central workflow engine.

The filter module `Engine` and the implementation part together implement the workflow engine. In addition to some methods for accessing and manipulating the workflow representation (here only `setWorkFlow()` is shown), this filter module defines the method `workflow()`. This method `selectTask()` first determines the next task that should handle the document, then modifies the corresponding argument of the message object, and finally *fires* the message so that the message continues its original execution with an updated argument.

The `superimposition` clause specifies how the concerns crosscut each other. The `superimposition` clause starts with a `selectors` part that specifies a number of *join point selectors,* abstractions of all the locations that designate a specific crosscut. Selectors are defined as queries over the instance space, expressed using OCL (Object Constraint Language), which is part of the UML specification [31]. The concern `WorkFlowEngine` defines a single selector named `allTasks`. This selector repeatedly uses the expression `*=<ConcernName>` to specify all objects that are instances of the various classes that represent tasks. The `selectors` part can be followed by a number of sections that can specify respectively which objects, conditions, methods, and filter modules are superimposed on locations designated by selectors. In this example, the filter module `Engine` is superimposed upon `self`. This means that instances of `WorkFlowEngine` include an instance of the filter module `Engine`. In addition, the filter module `useWorkFlowEngine`[13] is superimposed on all the instances defined by the selector `allTasks`.

---

12. A *reified form* is a representation of the message as an object (an instance of the *Message* concern) from which information about the message, such as target, selector, arguments, and sender, can be retrieved and modified.

13. Names on the right side can be prefixed with the concern name followed by a double semicolon. Otherwise, the prefix "`self::`" is assumed.

The sidebar, "Unification of Classes, Filter Modules, and Superimposition into Concerns," discusses the effects of combining filter modules, the superimposition clause, and the implementation clause within a single concern and the ramifications of omitting some of these parts.

Unification of Classes, Filter Modules, and Superimposition into Concerns

The composition filters model adopts a single abstraction as the major module concept, the *concern* abstraction. In this sidebar, we discuss some of the ramifications of this design decision.

A concern abstraction consists of three optional parts: (1) the filter module specifications; (2) the superimposition specification; and (3) the implementation of the behavior. This is illustrated in the Figure 4-6, especially by the concern on the left side of the picture.

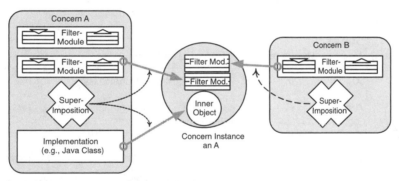

Figure 4-6   *The elements of concerns and their mapping to concern instances.*

The figure shows on the left side a *concern specification* for concern *A*, consisting of two filter modules, a superimposition specification, and an implementation. On the right side of the figure, another concern specification, *B*, is depicted that consists only of a filter module and a superimposition specification. In the middle, an example *concern instance*, an *A*, is shown, which is an instance of concern *A*, including the implementation defined by *A* and one filter module superimposed by *A*, as well as an additional filter module that has been superimposed by *B*.

As a result of the unification into concerns, the model does not distinguish between "aspect" and "base" module abstractions, which has a couple of advantages: (1) It makes the model 'cleaner': no different syntax and/or semantic rules need to be defined for the various possible configurations. (2) This structure allows for modeling base-level functionality and state together with crosscutting behavior into a single module abstraction (rather than two separate modules for respectively the "aspect" and the "base" level abstractions).

This offers a degree of symmetry [22] between concerns that avoids design compromises and allows for more stable designs where the decisions about what to model as base and what to model as aspect abstractions can be avoided. However, depending on the particular implementation, the structure of the run-time model may be different; for example, when the superimposition specifications are resolved statically, there are no equivalent abstractions at runtime.

Not all three parts of the concern specification are obligatory. Table 4-1 outlines the various possible combinations of leaving out one or more parts and summarizes their intuitive meaning.

Table 4-1   *The Parts of a Concern and Their Mapping to Concern Instances*

Filter Module(s)	Super- Imposition	Implementation	Explanation
✗	✗	✓	c.f. conventional class
✓	only to self	✓	c.f. conventional composition filters class
✓	✓	✓	Crosscutting concern with implementation
✓	✓	✗	'Pure' crosscutting concern, no implementation
✓	✗	✗	c.f. abstract advice without crosscutting definition
✗	✓	✗	Superimposition only (of reused filter specs)
✗	✓	✓	CF class or aspect with only reused filter specs

4.4.2   Evolution Step 3: Adding Logging

One important concern of the workflow system is monitoring the process, detecting the bottlenecks, and rescheduling and/or reallocating resources when necessary. Determining which methods need to be monitored is difficult a priori (i.e., at compile time) since it depends on the purpose of monitoring. Therefore, all interactions among objects may potentially need logging. More precisely, logging the reception of messages by an instance is sufficient. For each instance, actual logging of the message receptions can be turned on or off at runtime.

The definition of concern Logging in Listing 4-3 starts with the filter module NotifyLogger, which defines the crosscutting behavior needed to collect the information to be logged from all over the application. Logging is implemented by sending all received messages as objects to the global object logger using a Meta filter. The Logging concern creates an internal Boolean object logOn for every instance, which is used to enable or disable the logging of messages. More details of the implementation are shown in Listing 4-3. Note that logging is also supported for the methods of the WorkFlowEngine concern, but we exclude the instances of Logging, especially to avoid recursive logging of the log() messages.

Listing 4-3 *Specification of the* Logging *concern*

```
(1)   concern Logging begin              //introduces centralized logger
(2)     filtermodule NotifyLogger begin    //declares the crosscutting code
(3)       externals
(4)         logger : Logging;    //declare a shared instance of this concern
(5)       internals
(6)         logOn : boolean;      //created when the filtermodule is imposed
(7)       methods
(8)         loggingOn();               //turn logging for this object on
(9)         logginOff();               //turn logging for this object off
(10)        log(Message);       //declared here for typing purposes only
(11)      conditions
(12)        LoggingEnabled;
(13)      inputfilters
(14)        logMessages : Meta =
(15)        { LoggingEnabled=>[*]logger.log };
(16)        dispLogMethods : Dispatch =
(17)        { loggingOn, loggingOff };
(18)    end filtermodule NotifyLogger;
(19)    filtermodule Logger begin       //defines interface of logger object
(20)      methods
(21)        log(Message);    //and methods for information retrieval from log
(22)      inputfilters
(23)        disp : Dispatch =
(24)        { inner.* };                //accept all my own methods
(25)    end filtermodule Logger;
(26)    superimposition begin
```

```
(27)        selectors
(28)          allConcerns = { *->reject(oclIsTypeOf(Logging)) };
(29)              //selects all concern instances except instances of Logging
(30)        methods
(31)          allConcerns <- { loggingOn(),
(32)          loggingOff() };                              //bind methods
(33)        conditions
(34)          allConcerns <- LoggingEnabled;               //bind condition
(35)        filtermodules
(36)          allConcerns <- NotifyLogger; //superimpose NotifyLogger on all
(37)          self <- Logger;         //superimpose Logger filtermodule on self
(38)      end superimposition;
(39)      implementation in Java;
(40)        class LoggerClass {
(41)          boolean LoggingEnabled() { return logOn };
(42)          void loggingOn()  { logOn:=true; };
(43)          void loggingOff()  { logOn:=false; };
(44)          void log(Message mess) { ... }; // collect information & store
(45)        }
(46)      end implementation;
(47)   end concern Logging;
```

The shared part of the logging functionality is defined by filter module `Logger`. This declares the method `log()`, which takes an instance of `Message` as an argument and logs the information about the message. Typically, a range of methods for retrieving and/or displaying the logged information should be declared by `Logger` as well; we omit these for brevity. The filter module also contains a filter definition `disp` that ensures that these method(s) are made available on the interface of the `Logging` concern.

The superimposition part of this example is interesting since it involves a slightly more complicated binding process. This is illustrated by Figure 4-7. The set of join points where logging must be added is defined by `allConcerns`. This selector uses an OCL expression to select all instances in the system, except for the instances of concern `Logging`. The last part of the superimposition clause defines the superimposition of the `Logger` filter module to the `Logging` concern itself and the superimposition of the `NotifyLogger` to the join points defined by the `allConcerns` selector. The latter filter module declares an external global instance of `Logging` named `logger`, an internal `logOn`, which is created for each superimposed filter module, and several methods. The `loggingOn()` and `loggingOff()` methods must be available for execution in the context of the superimposed instance (because of the dispatch filter `dispLogMethods`), but they are declared by concern `Logging`. Therefore, the superimposition specification must explicitly bind the declared methods to the implementation within concern `Logging`, which is done in lines 31-32. Similarly, the condition `LoggingEnabled` is declared in the filter module `NotifyLogger` (line 12). When this condition is evaluated in the `logMessages` filter in lines 14–15, normally the condition would be searched in the local context. Therefore, in line 34, the implementation of the `LoggingEnabled` condition from concern `Logging` is bound to all other concerns.

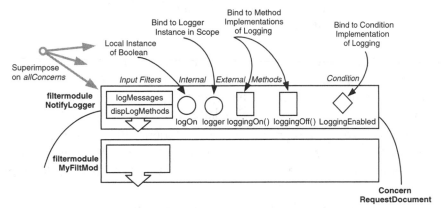

Figure 4-7   *Illustration of superimposition and binding of filter module* `NotifyLogger`.

4.5   EVALUATION

We begin this section with a discussion of a variety of prototype implementations. In Section 4.5.2, we address the technique of inlining since this is an important implementation technique that also demonstrates the ability to generate efficient code for (at least for a subset of) composition filters. Finally, in Section 4.5, we evaluate the CF model based on the objectives that were presented in Section 4.1 and the example case of this paper, and we relate these issues to some other work in this area. In the sidebar, "Common Misconceptions about Composition Filters," we have listed a number of examples of what composition filters are *not* and what they *do not do*.

4.5.1   Implementations of the CF Model

Throughout the years, a wide range of implementations of the composition filters model has been realized. These differ from each other in several respects:

The adopted base language.   That is, the language that expresses the implementation part.

The level of integration with the base language. For example, whether the syntax of the interface part is adapted to the syntax of the base language.

Translation time. Ranging from a pure interpreter to a byte code interpreter to a compiler.

These implementations have been proof-of-concept research prototypes. We now present various implementations, focusing on their distinguishing characteristics. The aim of this presentation is to give an impression of the wide range of possible implementation strategies.

Sina. The *Sina* language [36] was the first implementation of composition filters, which were at that time referred to as interface predicates [6]. The Sina compiler translated the Sina language into a byte code representation that was interpreted by a dedicated virtual machine. The latter was built on top of Smalltalk.

Sina/st. *Sina/st* [27] was another implementation of the Sina language on top of Smalltalk, but this version supported the full composition filters mechanism. The implementation was based on an interpreted, reflective, runtime, first-class model of filters and messages.

CFIST. *CFIST* [37] aimed at the integration of Smalltalk programming and composition filters, both at the language level and at the tool level. A key concept of this prototype was that it kept the Smalltalk class definitions completely separate and independent of the composition filters part.

C++/CF. The *C++/CF* language [21] investigated the integration of composition filters with C++. It was based on the explicit reification of message invocations (implemented through macros).

ComposeJ. *ComposeJ* [39] is an inlining compiler for an integrated Java/CF language.

ConcernJ. *ConcernJ* [34] is the implementation of composition filters including the superimposition mechanism as a front-end to ComposeJ. It resolves the crosscutting and generates corresponding filter specifications for ComposeJ.

JCFF. An alternative, more pragmatic, approach has been taken in JCFF (*Java Composition Filters Framework*) [35], where composition filters are implemented in Java as a library. This has the advantage of allowing software engineers to remain completely in a familiar programming language.

Compose*.NET. Recently, we have initiated the design and development of Compose*.NET [18, 23, 30], which adds the capability of adding composition filters to .NET assemblies. The latter are a universal, object-oriented representation of programs in any (one of many) programming language. This gives us the ability to add composition filters to any programming language that has been implemented by .NET.

Further, we would like to point out that composition filters seem to be well suited to extend (other) component models such as CORBA. This has been investigated, for example, in [16].

4.5.2 Inlining Composition Filters

As another example of the benefits of the implementation-independent model and to address the issue of performance, we present an example of *inlining* of filters as a compilation technique to achieve efficient execution of composition filters. The principle of filter inlining is to generate a custom version of the filter code for a specific message selector, thereby typically eliding the bulk of the filter code. This custom version is then inserted at the start of the method with the corresponding selector.

To demonstrate the effect of inlining, we show how the example filter code in Listing 4-4 is translated by the ComposeJ tool.

Listing 4-4 *Example filter code from an email application*

```
inputfilters
  verifyUserView : Error = {
    userView()=>{putOriginator, putReceiver,
                 putContent, getContent,
                 send, reply },
    true~>{putOriginator, putReceiver,
           putContent, getContent, send,
           reply }   };
  verifySystemView : Error = {
    systemView()=>{approve, putRoute, deliver},
    true~>{approve, putRoute, deliver}   };
dis: Dispatch = { inner.*, mail.* };
```

This example consists of three filters that every message should pass. It uses two conditions that must be evaluated at runtime. Further, the last line involves signature matching. Obviously, literally processing the full filter specifications for every message is, even when generating efficient code, quite expensive.

However, a look at the generated code that is inlined in `USVMail::reply()` after a clean-up reveals that the amount of code to be executed for this message is quite limited:

```
if (!userView())
   throw new FilterException("Error filter exception");
return mail.reply();
```

For message `reply()`, this is the full code that is needed to execute the filters in Listing 4-4.

The ability to inline filters is simplified by the fact that the filter specifications are declarative and easy to analyze statically.

There are a few considerations, however:

◆ Not all the messages that an object receives may correspond to the execution of an inlined filter implementation. In those cases, a potentially more elaborate execution of the whole set of filters is required.

◆ The code above does not show some overhead in our implementation; e.g., for the purpose of bookkeeping pseudovariables.

◆ Code inlining generally results in increased code size.

An important lesson to be learned from this example, as well as from the range of examples in the previous subsection, is that general conclusions about the efficiency of the implementation of filters must be drawn with great care.

Common Misconceptions About Composition Filters

Composition filters have been around for a substantial amount of time. Among the feedback we have received, we have discovered some common misconceptions. By explicitly addressing these issues, we hope that the readers of this chapter will gain an improved understanding of these specific issues.

Composition filters can only "filter out" messages. The term *filtering* may suggest that the only purpose of filters is to selectively allow certain messages. In general, filters can observe and *manipulate* messages, as well as trigger certain actions.

Composition filters objects are equivalent to "wrappers." Traditional object wrapping is similar to the composition filters approach, but it differs in at least two important ways. First, the behavior of object wrappers is implemented by regular methods, whereas composition filters are tailor-made abstractions for composing the behavior of objects. Second, object wrapping suffers from some modeling problems such as object schizophrenia [33]. Composition filters, among others by the merit of the dispatching mechanism, do not suffer from these problems.

Composition filters are a tool for adapting existing classes. The fact that the implementation object is separate and can be an already implemented class does not mean that this is the actual purpose. Although there certainly are useful applications in this area, it is important to realize that the filters depend only on the offered interface of methods and conditions. This interface must in general be designed before constructing the implementation and the filters. Hence, the approach of choice is to identify the filters along with other properties of classes during the design phase.

The filtering mechanism must be very inefficient. The declarative style of composition filters allows for various optimizations, in particular avoiding overhead that is irrelevant for specific messages. We refer to Section 4.5.2 for more details about this topic. It should be noted that some mechanisms that are offered by filters, such as synchronization and message reflection, have inherent performance penalties that cannot be avoided.

There are only a few composition filter types. Most publications about composition filters, including this chapter, discuss only a limited set of filter types. The presented filter types are the result of our attempts to define filter types that are canonical models for some common aspects of software systems. However, there are no inherent restrictions on the number or behavior of filter types.

Composition filters cannot express application-specific "advice." Clearly, the aim of the composition filters model is to offer predefined and programmer-defined abstractions to address common problems. To attach application-specific advice to messages, a Meta filter can be defined, which designates a specific method for the implementation of the advice. This was exemplified by the logging example in this paper (Listing 4-3).

Composition filters implementations must be multi-language. We have stressed that the CF model is language-independent; the filtering mechanism can be made to work with implementation parts expressed a variety languages. However, we make no claims about the support of multi-language systems or for heterogeneous platforms: This depends strictly on a particular implementation. Typically, existing implementations work with a single language/platform [21, 27, 37, 39]. Clearly, a multi-language implementation is possible, in particular by relying on a multi-language platform such as CORBA [16] or .NET [23, 30].

Composition filters are strictly reactive.   This would mean that filters can only be active when triggered by incoming messages. Although this is an important category (e.g., *Error*, *Substitute*, and *Dispatch* filters), some other filters can be active without being triggered by incoming messages. For example, the *Wait* filter must repeatedly reconsider whether some of the blocked messages in the queue can be activated again. Similarly, the *RealTime* filter is responsible for continuously rescheduling threads such that deadlines are met.

4.6   CONCLUSION

In Section 4.1.1, we presented the objectives for the CF model: composability, evolvability, robustness, implementation-independence, and dynamics. In this section, we briefly discuss each of these objectives—to what extent they are met with the present model and how they relate to the presented example whenever applicable, and in some cases, we refer to related or future work.

Composability.   The CF model supports composability at two levels: composition of filters and composition of concerns. Composition of filters is supported because all filters are based on the same underlying model of message manipulation. Only specific semantic dependencies between filters can cause interference problems. Second, filter expressions support the composition of behavior of concerns, most notably the signatures of concerns. The example evolution scenario that we used in this paper illustrates the stepwise composition of the final application from several concerns. For example, an instance of `ProtectedClaimDocument` after the final evolution is a composition of the `ClaimDocument` and `ProtectedClaimDocument` concerns, with the (superimposed) filter modules `DocWithViews` and `NotifyLogger`. As a result, such an instance composes the redirect `Meta` filter (line 9 of Listing 4-2), the `protection` filter of type `Error` (lines 11-17 of Listing 4-1), and the `inh` filter of type `Dispatch` (in line 18 of Listing 4-1).

Crosscutting concerns require the composition of filter modules; this is essentially similar to the composition of (multiple) filters. Further, declarative completeness of filter modules makes it easier to check composability at compile time or instantiation time. Superimposition among crosscutting concerns is also possible, as demonstrated by the workflow and logging concern in our example.

Evolvability. The CF model extends traditional object models with possibly cross-cutting behavior. This is achieved by extending objects with filters (filter modules). This is possible for virtually any object or component model. The only possible issue is that inheritance of the implementation language and inheritance of the CF model are orthogonal: developers must take care to avoid implementation language inheritance relations between CF objects.

Robustness. A number of properties of the CF model contribute to robustness, including the overall language design and the chosen abstractions and their syntax and semantics. Verifying or even discussing robustness in general is quite hard; hence, we focus on the following properties:

1. **Encapsulation.** The implementation of a CF concern is strongly encapsulated; superimposition of filter-interfaces, objects, methods, and conditions is restricted to the interface level. Therefore, superimposed concerns do not rely on the details of the implementation (even the implementation language is encapsulated). Several other approaches, such as AspectJ [25], allow the crosscutting concerns (aspects) to refer to, and depend on, implementation details of the base-level abstractions. This makes the aspects less reusable and more vulnerable to implementation changes. Although researchers do not all agree whether the benefits of respecting encapsulation outweigh the limitations, it seems fair to state that encapsulation is beneficial for robustness.

2. **High-level semantics.** Filter specifications use a common pattern matching language and adopt filter types to add concern semantics. The semantics of filter types are well defined and highly expressive in their specific concern domains [8, 10]. As shown in the example, `Error`, `Dispatch`, and `Meta` filters could effectively express multiple views, delegation and message reflection, respectively. Given the availability of suitable filter types, this enables the programmer to express his intents clearly and concisely.

3. **Analyzable aspect description language.** Most aspect-oriented approaches adopt general-purpose programming languages for specifying concern. In general, reasoning about the semantics of such concerns is hard to do (e.g., consider the undecidability problems of Turing-complete languages). The restricted (pattern matching) language used to define filters provides better opportunities for automated analysis of correctness. We have started to explore this area in [9, 18].

Implementation-independence. The CF model is largely independent of specific implementation techniques, programming language, and platforms. This was demonstrated in Section 4.5.1 through the discussion of eight implementations of the composition filters model that are all substantially different in one or more respects. In particular, this is made possible by the declarativeness of filter specifications.

Dynamics. To a large extent, the implementation independence supports the dynamic adaptation of structure and behavior. Again, declarative specifications of filters and superimposition are helpful, but in particular, it must be possible to explain and implement the language through an operational model.

The CF model addresses the quality objectives as depicted in Section 4.3; for each objective, one or more specific properties of the CF model contributes to meeting the objective. Our future work will mainly focus on new verification techniques, new filter types, and robust CF development tools. In addition, we continue to explore ways to improve composability.

REFERENCES

1. AKŞIT, M. AND BERGMANS, L. 2001. Guidelines for identifying obstacles when composing distributed systems from components. In *Software Architectures and Component Technology*, M. Akşit, Ed. Kluwer Academic Publishers, Boston, 29–56.

2. AKŞIT, M., BERGMANS, L., AND VURAL, S. 1992. An object-oriented language-database integration model: The composition-filters approach. In *ECOOP '92 European Conf. Object-Oriented Programming* (Kaiserslautern), O. L. Madsen, Ed. LNCS, vol. 615. Springer-Verlag, Berlin, 372–395.

3. AKŞIT, M., BOSCH, J., V. D. STERREN, W., AND BERGMANS, L. 1994. Real-time specification inheritance anomalies and real-time filters. In *8th European Conf. Object-Oriented Programming* (Bologna), M. Tokoro and R. Pareschi, Eds. Springer-Verlag, Berlin, 386–407.

4. AKŞIT, M., WAKITA, K., BOSCH, J., BERGMANS, L., AND YONEZAWA, A. 1993. Abstracting object-interactions using composition-filters. In *Object-Based Distributed Processing*, R. Guerraoui, O. Nierstrasz, and M. Riveill, Eds. LNCS, vol. 791. Springer-Verlag, Berlin, 152–184.

5. AKŞIT, M., DIJKSTRA, J. W., AND TRIPATHI, A. 1991. Atomic delegation: Object-oriented transactions. *IEEE Software 8*, 2, 84–92.

6. AKŞIT, M. AND TRIPATHI, A. 1988. Data abstraction mechanisms in SINA/ST. In *3rd Conf. Object-Oriented Programming, Systems, Languages, and Applications (OOPSLA)*, (San Diego, California). ACM, 267–275.

7. ASPECT-ORIENTED SOFTWARE ASSOCIATION. Aspect-oriented software development-tools and languages. http://aosd.net/tools.htm.

8. BERGMANS, L. 1994. Composing concurrent objects. Ph.D. thesis, University of Twente.

9. BERGMANS, L. 2003. Towards Detection of Semantic Conflicts between Crosscutting Concerns. In *Analysis of Aspect-Oriented Software (AAOS, ECOOP) (Darmstadt, Germany)*. http://www.comp.lancs.ac.uk/computing/users/chitchya/AAOS2003/Assets/bergmansl.pdf.

10. BERGMANS, L. AND AKŞIT, M. 1996. Composing synchronisation and real-time constraints. *Journal of Parallel and Distributed Computing 36*, 32–52.

11. BERGMANS, L. AND Akşit, M. 2001. Composing crosscutting concerns using composition filters. *Comm. ACM 44*, 10 (Oct.), 51–57.

12. BERGMANS, L. AND AKŞIT, M. 2001. Constructing reusable components with multiple concerns using composition filters. In *Software Architectures and Component Technology*, M. Akşit, Ed. Kluwer Academic Publishers, Boston.

13. BERGMANS, L. AND COINTE, P. 1997. Workshop report of the ECOOP'96 workshop on composability issues in object-orientation. In *Special Issues in Object-Oriented Programming*, M. Mühlhaüser, Ed. dpunkt verlag, Heidelberg, 53–124.

14. BOSCH, J. 1997. Composition through superimposition. In *Workshop Report of the ECOOP'96 Workshop on Composability Issues in Object-Orientation, Special Issues in Object-Oriented Programming*, M. Mühlhaüser, Ed. dpunkt, Heidelberg, 94–101.

15. BOUGÉ, L. AND FRANCEZ, N. 1988. A compositional approach to superimposition. In *15th Symp. Principles of Programming Languages (POPL)*, (San Diego, California). ACM, 240–249.

16. BURGGRAAF, A. 1997. Solving modelling problems of CORBA using Composition Filters. M.S. thesis, Department of Computer Science, University of Twente.

17. DE GREEF, N. 1991. Object-oriented system development. M.S. thesis, University of Twente.

18. DÜRR, P. 2004. Detecting Semantic Conflicts Between Aspects. M.S. thesis, University of Twente.

19. ELRAD, T., FILMAN, R. E., AND BADER, A. 2001. Aspect-oriented programming. *Comm. ACM 44*, 10 (Oct.), 29–32.

20. FERBER, J. 1989. Computational reflection in class based object-oriented languages. In *4th Conf. Object-oriented Programming, Systems, Languages, and Applications (OOPSLA)*, (New Orleans). ACM, 317–326.

21. GLANDRUP, M. 1995. Extending C++ using the concepts of composition filters. M.S. thesis, University of Twente.

22. HARRISON, W., OSSHER, H., AND TARR, P. 2003. Asymmetrically vs. symmetrically organized paradigms for software composition. In *Software engineering Properties of Languages for Aspect Technologies (SPLAT, AOSD)*, (Boston). http://www.daimi.au.dk/~eernst/splat03/papers/William_Harrison.doc.

23. HOLLJEN, F. 2004. Compilation and Type-Safety in the Compose*.NET environment. M.S. thesis, University of Twente.

24. KATZ, S. 1993. A superimposition control construct for distributed systems. *ACM Transactions on Programming Languages and Systems 15*, 2 (Apr.), 337–356.

25. KICZALES, G., HILSDALE, E., HUGUNIN, J., KERSTEN, M., PALM, J., AND GRISWOLD, W. G. 2001. An overview of AspectJ. In *ECOOP 2001—Object-Oriented Programming, 15th European Conference*, (Budapest), J. L. Knudsen, Ed. LNCS, vol. 2072, Springer-Verlag, Berlin, 327–353.

26. KICZALES, G., LAMPING, J., MENDHEKAR, A., MAEDA, C., LOPES, C., LOINGTIER, J.-M., AND IRWIN, J. 1997. Aspect-oriented programming. In *ECOOP'97 Object-Oriented Programming, 11th European Conference*, M. Akşit and S. Matsuoka, Eds. LNCS, vol. 1241, Springer-Verlag, Berlin, 220–242.

27. KOOPMANS, P. 1995. Sina user's guide and reference manual. Tech. rep., Dept. of Computer Science, University of Twente.

28. LIEBERMAN, H. 1986. Using prototypical objects to implement shared behavior in object-oriented systems. In *1st Conf. Object-Oriented Programming, Systems, Languages, and Applications (OOPSLA)*, (New York). ACM, 214–223.

29. MEZINI, M. AND LIEBERHERR, K. 1998. Adaptive plug-and-play components for evolutionary software development. In *13th Conf. Object-Oriented Programming, Systems, Languages, and Applications (OOPSLA)*, (Vancouver). ACM, 97–116.

30. NOGUERA, C. 2003. Compose*; a run-time for the .NET platform. M.S. thesis, Vrije Universiteit, Brussel.

31. OBJECT MANAGEMENT GROUP. 1999. The unified modeling language specification, version 1.3.

32. OSSHER, H. AND TARR, P. 2001. Multi-dimensional separation of concerns and the hyperspace approach. In *Software Architectures and Component Technology*, M. Akşit, Ed. Kluwer Academic Publishers, Boston, 293–323.

33. SAKKINEN, M. 1989. Disciplined inheritance. In *ECOOP 89—3rd European Conf. Object-Oriented Programming*, S. Cook, Ed. Cambridge University Press Cambridge, UK, 39–56.

34. SALINAS, P. 2001. Adding systemic crosscutting and super-imposition to Composition Filters. M.S. thesis, Vrije Universiteit, Brussel.

35. SAVARESE, L. 2003. Aspect oriented software development applied to track modeling for command and control. M.S. thesis, University of Twente.

36. TRIPATHI, A., BERGE, E., AND AKŞIT, M. 1989. An implementation of the object-oriented concurrent programming language Sina. *Software Practice and Experience 19*, 3 (Mar.), 235–256.

37. VAN DIJK, W. AND MORDHORST, J. 1995. CFIST-composition filters in SmallTalk. Graduation thesis, HIO, Enschede, The Netherlands.

38. WEGNER, P. 1987. Dimensions of object-based language design. In *2nd Conf. Object-Oriented Programming, Systems, Languages, and Applications (OOPSLA)*, (Orlando, Florida). ACM, 168–182.

39. WICHMAN, J. C. 1999. The development of a preprocessor to facilitate composition filters in the Java language. M.S. thesis, University of Twente.

Chapter 5

AOP: A Historical Perspective (What's in a Name?)

CRISTINA VIDEIRA LOPES

The term "aspect-oriented programming" (AOP) came into existence sometime between November of 1995 and May of 1996 at the Xerox Palo Alto Research Center (PARC). AOP was based on an extensive body of prior work, but somehow the existing terminology wasn't appropriate for describing what we were doing. The new programming technology we were beginning to devise was going to change the world!

In this chapter, I will give my own account of how AOP—the ideas, the technologies, and the name—came to be. But, history is just marginally interesting if one doesn't make the effort to learn from it and apply that knowledge to things that are still to come. AOP didn't quite "change the world," but no doubt it had an impact in research communities and in programming at large. There are valuable lessons to be learned from the emergence of AOP, and an analysis of those is the ultimate goal of this chapter.

5.1 A MATTER OF STYLE

Giving an historical perspective of a technology involves stating facts as much as it involves describing the technical context in which the technology emerged and understanding the dynamics of the group of people who created it. Having been part of that group, I am in a privileged position to tell the AOP story, or at least a rendition of that story. I have not been active in the AOP project since the summer of 2000, so I can't report the project's history since then. Many people have joined the team after I left and have made significant contributions to the current version of the language.

Like most historical perspectives, this one is based on facts, but the interpretations and comments are entirely my own. Also like most historical perspectives, this one is incomplete: It focuses on the period 1995–1998, the time when AOP and, later, AspectJ emerged. A lot had happened before, and a lot has happened since then.

AOP, as such, started emerging in 1995 when I was already at PARC as a visiting student. In the years that followed, one of the types of questions I was often asked was, "What is AOP?" Is it a programming language? Macros in disguise? A design methodology? A clever pre-processor? Meta-programming? How is this different from X (replace X with your favorite programming trick or language feature)? The other frequent question was, "What are aspects?" Synchronization and tracing *feel* like aspects, but what else? And what makes an aspect an aspect, anyway?

As I'm writing this chapter, eight years later, I have good answers for all of these questions, but that wasn't the case back in 1995–1998. In fact, many brilliant minds have blamed the AOP group for propagating subversive ideas without having clear definitions for what we were trying to do. They were right: Our definitions were fuzzy and got clearer over time. Back then, we had two options: We could lock ourselves in the office for a few years, brainstorm and beat the thing to death until we figured it all out; or we could bring a semi-baked idea to the public and iterate it with a larger community until the clear definitions would emerge. We chose the latter. The reasons for this choice are as much pragmatic as they are a matter personal style. The pragmatic reasons included the following. First, we all believed that the validation of the AOP thesis (i.e., that it led to better programs) could only be done outside the controlled environment of our offices. So there was no point in locking ourselves up to come up with a beautiful formal semantics, because that would miss the core of the thesis. Second, we also believed that what we were doing crosscut the boundaries of the traditional communities in software engineering and programming languages. We needed to get early input from different kinds of people, especially from "real programmers," our ultimate evaluators.

Many researchers will probably identify with this need to reach out in order to validate their work; others won't. Again, a matter of style. But among those that do, not many can do it successfully, even when their work is impressive. It takes financial support, a good team and a good team leader—these are all management issues that many researchers tend to overlook. The popularity of AOP and AspectJ is due, firstly, to Gregor Kiczales, not only for his technical leadership but also for his natural ability to secure resources and attract people.

5.2 RESEARCH TRENDS IN THE EARLY '90S

In writing this section, I have consulted a technical report written by my colleague Walter Hürsch and myself at the end of 1994 [12]. That report was titled "Separation of Concerns," and it was written when I was still at Northeastern

University. In retrospect, it is evident that we missed a few important pieces of work and that we had a somewhat narrow vision of what was being separated. But overall, that report did a good job of capturing a trend that was in the air, and that is the reason why I am reproducing it here. People were talking about "separation of concerns;" our report captured the building blocks and the conceptual glue of what later became AOP and the AOP community. For reasons that fall out of the scope of this chapter, Walter and I stopped working on that report. I continued working on my thesis, which focused on concurrency and distribution Aspects.

What follows is a summary of that report. Parts in italics are verbatim text. In reading it, the reader should place him/herself in 1994. The reader should also be aware that the projects mentioned here have evolved considerably since 1994.

5.2.1   *Formulation of the Problem*

The increasing complexity of today's software applications and the advent of novel and innovative technology make it necessary for programs to incorporate and deal with an ever greater variety of special computing concerns such as concurrency, distribution, real-time constraints, location control, persistence, and failure recovery. Underlying all of these special purpose concerns is the basic concern responsible for the fundamental computational algorithm and the basic functionality. Special purpose concerns exist to either fulfill special requirements of the application (real-time, persistence, distribution) or manage and optimize the basic computational algorithm (location control, concurrency).

Typical approaches to integrate an additional concern have been to extend a given programming language by providing a few new programming language constructs that address the concern. An example of such an extension is the Distributed Real-time Object Language DROL (Takashio and Tokoro 1992), an extension of C++ with the capability of describing distributed real-time systems.

Even though the concerns may be separated conceptually and incorporated correctly, commingling them in the code brings about a number of problems:

- *Programming intertwined code is hard and complex since all concerns have to be dealt with at the same time and at the same level. The extended programming language provides no adequate abstraction of concerns at the implementation level.*

- *Intertwined code is hard to understand because of the above lack of abstraction.*

- *Commingled code is hard to maintain and modify because the concerns are strongly coupled.*

♦ *Specific to object-oriented systems, the intertwined code gives rise to inheritance anomalies (Akşit et al. 1994, Matsuoka and Yonezawa 1993) due to the strong coupling of the different concerns. It becomes impossible to redefine a method implementation or the commingled special concern in a subclass without redefining both.*

Many researchers have recognized the above problems for single concerns in their specific area of expertise and have started to address them. Many devised techniques for separating individual concerns (Akşit et al. 1992, Akşit et al. 1994, Honda and Tokoro 1992, Okamura and Ishikawa 1994, Akşit, Wakita et al. 1994, Lopes and Lieberherr 1994, Lieberherr et al. 1994).

5.2.2 Analysis of the Problem and Specialized Solutions

For software concerns, we distinguished two different levels of separation:

Conceptual level. *At the conceptual level, the separation of concerns needs to address two issues. 1) Provide a sufficient abstraction for each concern as an individual concept. 2) Ensure that the individual concepts are primitive, in the sense that they address the natural concerns in the mind of the programmer.*

Implementation level. *At the implementation level, the separation of concerns needs to provide an adequate organization that isolates the concerns from each other. The goal at this level is to separate the blocks of code, which address the different concerns, and provide for a loose coupling of them.*

The concerns identified at the conceptual level are mapped into the implementation level through programming language constructs. [. . .] Separation of concerns at the conceptual level is generally considered important and a primary means to manage complexity in all engineering disciplines. [. . .] However, few programming languages allow these abstractions to actually be separately programmed. The resulting code organization is monolithic, intertwining statements for different purposes [. . .].

We then turned to some approaches that had been suggested in the literature, including the work of our own group, Demeter [22, 24, 41]. We identified a set of papers that focused on the separation of some concern from the basic algorithmic concern. Table 5-1 gives an overview of this survey; I have now added more references than what we originally had.

Casey Hawthorne
102 - 8720 Cambie Street
Vancouver, BC
V5Z 2X5

Table 5-1   *Approaches for Separation of Certain Concerns*

Technique → Concern ↓	Meta-Level Programming	Adaptive Programming	Composition Filters	Others
Class organization		Lieberherr [24]		
Process synchronization	Watanabe [48]	Lopes [29]	Akşit [3]	Frølund [7] Reghizzi [39]
Location control	Okamura [36]			Zeidler [50] Takashio [46]
Real-time constraints			Akşit [2]	Barbacci [5]
Others				Liskov [25] Jacobson [14] Magee [32]

5.2.3   *Identifying Concerns That Can Be Separated*

In the "Separation of Concerns" report, Walter and I went on to analyze the major software concerns that had been referenced in the literature. We focused on class organization, synchronization, location control (configuration issues), real-time constraints, and failure recovery. We stressed the point that such a list was, by no means, exhaustive; we believed it was open-ended. For the purposes of that report, we were simply compiling a set of software engineering concerns that had been frequently referred to in different papers as problematic. We mentioned other examples such as debugging, persistence, and transaction management.

In the years that followed, these concerns would again be the central focus of AOP-related work. Later on, AspectJ introduced general-purpose aspect programming constructs that made the concept of "aspect" more general and helped open up the list.

5.2.4   *Separation Techniques*

In the report, we made a distinction between separation of concerns at the conceptual level and at the implementation level. The former may exist without the latter, and that was pretty much the state-of-the-art in 1994. There were, however, some programming techniques that looked promising for achieving the separation at the implementation level. Refer to Table 5-1 to see the techniques we identified at the time. What follows are the highlights of our analysis.

5.2.4.1 Meta-Level Programming

Meta-level programming is a well-know paradigm that has been documented in several publications (Smith 1984, Maes 1987, Watanabe and Yonezawa 1990, Kiczales et al. 1991, Okamura and Ishikawa 1994, among others). [. . .] A reflective system incorporates structures for representing itself. The basic constructs of the programming language, such as classes or object invocation, are described at the meta-level and can be extended or redefined by meta-programming. Each object is associated with a meta-object through a meta-link. The meta-object is responsible for the semantics of operations on the base object.

How does meta-level programming support the separation of concerns at the implementation level? *By trapping message sends and message receives to objects, meta-objects have the opportunity to perform work on behalf of the special purpose concerns. For example, they can check for synchronization constraints, assure real-time specifications, migrate parameters between machines, write logs, and so forth. This allows the base-level algorithms to be written without the special purpose concerns, which in turn can be programmed in the meta-objects. Also, by having structural reflection (meta-knowledge about the relations between classes), meta-level programming can achieve separation between algorithms and data organization.*

5.2.4.2 Adaptive Programming

The work described in Lieberherr et al. 1994 and Lopes and Lieberherr 1994 presents adaptive software, a programming model based on code patterns. Code patterns are classified in different categories, each one capturing abstractions in programming:

Propagation patterns *define operations (algorithms) on the data. Propagation patterns identify subgraphs of classes that interact for a specific operation. References to the data are made in a structure-shy manner through succinct subgraph specifications, and the actual code is defined in code wrappers along traversal paths.*

Transportation patterns *abstract the concept of parameterization. They are used within propagation patterns in order to carry parameters in and out along the subgraphs.*

Synchronization patterns *define synchronization schemes between the objects in concurrent applications. Their purpose is to control the processes' access to the execution of the operations.*

How does adaptive programming support the separation of concerns at the implementation level? *Each pattern category addresses a different concern and can be viewed as a high-level software component that interacts with other components in a very loose manner through name resolution. Each pattern is quasi-independent of both the other patterns and the data organization. This has the effect, for example, that changes in the class organization don't necessarily imply updates in the patterns, and modifications of the algorithm (propagation patterns) don't necessarily imply changes in the synchronization scheme.*

5.2.4.3   Composition Filters

The composition filter model is an extension of the conventional object-oriented model through the addition of object composition filters. We will focus here on the filterpart and how it can achieve separation. For a detailed description of the model and its various applications we refer to Akşit et al. 1992, Bergmans 1994, Akşit et al. 1994.

   Filters are first class objects and thus are instances of filter classes. The purpose of filters is to manage and affect message sends and receives. In particular, a filter specifies conditions for message acceptance or rejection and determines the appropriate resulting action. Filters are programmable on a per class basis. The system makes sure that a message is processed by the filters before the corresponding method is executed: once a message is received, it has to pass through a set of input filters, and before a message is sent, it has to pass through a set of output filters.

How do composition filters support the separation of concerns at the implementation level? *Separation of concerns is achieved by defining a filter class for each concern. For example, in Akşit et al. 1994, a real-time filter RealTime was proposed to affect the real-time aspects of incoming messages. RealTime filters have access to a time object that is carried with every message and which specifies the earliest starting time and a deadline for the message.*

   Each filter class is responsible for handling all aspects of its associated concern. The filter mechanism gives programmers a chance to trap both message receives and sends, and to perform certain actions before the code of the method is actually executed. The resulting code is thus nicely separated into the special purpose concern (in the filter) and basic concern (in the method).

5.2.4.4   Discussion

Common to the above techniques is the fact that they provide some mechanism to intercept message sends and receives. Meta-object protocols perform the interception at the meta-level through computational reflection and reification of messages. Composition filters trap messages through the built-in filter mechanism. In both cases, interception was done at run-time. Pattern-oriented programming achieves message interception at compile time; the pattern compiler detects when a method needs to be extended with code for special purpose concerns and inserts that code directly, similar to a preprocessor—no interception is done at run-time. [. . .]

An important aspect of meta-level programming is that the separation of concerns is not imposed by the model. [. . .] Rather, meta-level programming facilitates the separation of concerns by providing the reflective information about the constructs of the language itself. Programming the special purpose concerns at the meta-level is a strategy that may or may not be followed by the programmers. This is contrary to filters and code patterns, which provide specific language constructs to achieve the separation of concerns. As a consequence, both the filters approach and the code patterns approach require new language construct for each new concern, while in the meta-level programming that is not the case.

In retrospect, we missed at least one important piece of related work: Subject-Oriented Programming [10]. We also missed the opportunity to compare all these approaches with an emerging wave, design patterns [8]. But the important thing about our paper was that it pointed out how the search for better expression mechanisms that focused on certain software development concerns were, in fact, driving a large number of research efforts at the time. This research was being driven by some common goal, and it was important for me to understand what that was. I wanted to formulate the kernel of the problem that was prompting so many solutions. Why weren't C++ and Lisp good enough?

5.3   THE BIRTH OF AOP AT PARC

In the summer of 1995, as I was starting to devise a thesis proposal based on some of these ideas, I took an internship in Gregor Kiczales's group at Xerox PARC. The group at the time was working on Open Implementations [15, 17, 19]. During that summer, I implemented Demeter's traversals in a dialect of Scheme that supported OO reflection [30], reinforcing the idea that reflection was a powerful programming technique that could support Demeter's useful concepts for software evolution. Following that internship, I got an invitation to stay at PARC and continue my thesis work there. And so I did. The three years that followed were crucial both to the foundations of AOP and to me, personally: I defended my thesis at the end of the summer of 1997. Between 1995 and 1997, I continued to work under Karl Lieberherr's supervision, but I had Gregor Kiczales as a co-advisor.

I can't remember the exact date when we decided to call our work "aspect-oriented programming," but I remember the term was suggested by Chris Maeda, the most business-oriented person of the group. Another name being tossed around was

Aspectual Decomposition and Weaving (ADW), which was dropped. In my notebook, the first reference to "AOP" occurs at the end of November 1995. In January 1996, my notebook indicates that we were using Open Implementation and AOP at the same time, although for different pieces of the group's work. By June of 1996, Gregor Kiczales gave a couple of public talks about AOP, one in the ACM Workshop on Strategic Directions in Computing Research, and another one in one workshop at ECOOP organized by Mehmet Akşit. That month we submitted a proposal to DARPA entitled "Aspect-Oriented Programming." By the end of 1996, the references to Open Implementation in my notebook disappeared, although by that time we produced a paper about it [17].

One other word that defined AOP was the word "weaver." Again, I can't remember the exact date when that word emerged and who suggested it, but it must have happened in late 1995 or early 1996. Weaver was the name we gave to the pre-processors that would merge the components and aspect modules into base language source code. Later, this word was disfavored because it had a strong connotation with text pre-processing. But "weaver" is still a good word for the AOP language processors, even though they are more than simple text pre-processing. The latest version of the AspectJ compiler is a good example of bytecode weaving that supports the join point model.

In October of 1996, we held a workshop at PARC to which we invited certain people who were pursuing work related to separation of concerns. That was the kick-off meeting for discussing AOP beyond our group; I'll say more about that in the next section. In this section, I'll focus on work done by the group at PARC.

5.3.1 RG

One of the projects going on at PARC when I got there was RG [33, 35]. The concern that was targeted in that project was optimizing memory usage when composing functions containing loops over matrices. Although optimizing memory usage has never since then been analyzed as an aspect, the RG example was actually very interesting, and it was chosen as the leading example in the first AOP paper [18]. The reason RG is interesting is that the problem in it illustrates quite well, even better than the AspectJ examples, what I think is the essence of AOP: the need for more powerful referencing mechanisms in a programming language. The aspects in RG expressed issues like the following (citing from [35]):

> For every message send invoking a primitive filter, before computing its arguments, examine each argument and determine whether the loop structure needed to calculate the filter is compatible with the loop structure needed to calculate the argument. In that case, generate a single loop structure that computes

both the argument value and the filter value, and replace the original message send with a send to the fused loop.

While I might have chosen a slightly different wording, what this quote shows is that there is the need to refer to lots of different things: "every message send" of a certain kind, "before computing its arguments," and certain "loop structures" in the target object and the arguments. These are all referencing needs that are not supported by most programming languages and that the group at PARC was trying to support.

5.3.2 AML

A second project under way was Annotated MatLab, or AML [13]. The problem addressed here was the optimization of certain MatLab programs, again focusing on memory usage and operation fusion. The AML solution was to annotate the MatLab code with special directives, mostly declarative, that augmented the code with information so that a language processor could produce optimized code.

There were many discussions within the group at PARC regarding whether AML was AOP or not. The final language annotations didn't look like our other systems in that they weren't separated from the base code but rather were still embedded in it. But, more importantly, it was hard to express in plain English the abstractions that those directives captured. For this reason, AML didn't make it to the ECOOP paper. It served, however, as a data point to formulate what aspect-oriented programming should or shouldn't be like.

5.3.3 ETCML

Between the summer of 1995 and the summer of 1997, John Lamping was working, among other things, on a little system called Evaluation Time Control Meta Language (ETCML). The idea was to provide a set of directives that programmers could use in order to instruct the language processor about when to evaluate certain pieces of code. This work was in the sequence of the work in Reflection more precisely, to identify whether certain parts of the code should be evaluated at compile-time or at runtime. This came from the need to optimize meta-object protocols, making them be compiled away. The thesis there was that the language processor could not always determine the best evaluation time and that input from the programmer would simplify immensely the task of the language processor. In ETCML, evaluation time was being analyzed as a software development concern that had important consequences on run-time performance.

This work served as another interesting data point to think about software development concerns that were relatively independent from the functional code.

5.3.4   *DJ*

Prior to the doctorate program, my background was in distributed operating systems [43]. That led me to the search for better expression mechanisms for distributed programming. When I went to PARC, I had outlined my thesis in two publications: an ECOOP paper [29] and an ISOTAS paper [26]. Those were the pillars of my dissertation: a couple of small languages for distributed programming, which I called D (as in *D*istributed Programming) and their specification as an extension to Java, DJ [27]. The two little languages were called COOL and RIDL.[1]

DJ was different from RG, AML, and ETCML and used a technical approach more similar to that of Demeter [22, 24] than that used at the time by the group at PARC, i.e., Reflection [16] and Open Implementation [15, 19]. For starters, DJ didn't target run-time optimizations; it targeted program-time expressiveness for some distributed programming concerns. RG, AML, and ETCML had a top-down flavor: There was the notion of what a well-designed program should look like, and they were adding more instructions for tuning the performance without modifying the original well-designed programs. DJ had a bottom-up flavor: Based on what distributed programs looked like, usually messy, I was trying to reorganize the code so that certain concerns that were tangled in Java could be untangled. In the process, I was defining language constructs that would allow me to do that. In the end, the combination of the top-down and bottom-up approaches proved to be fruitful.

I didn't particularly like the meta-level programming model. Certainly that model and the resulting techniques could be used to separate the concerns I was studying, but it felt awkward, though it was the only decent model at the time. Meta-objects have a beautiful run-time interpretive semantics; I wanted a compile-time process. Compile-time reflection loses the beautiful simplicity of the run-time reflection model: Meta-objects start to feel and act like macros. Therefore, one is led to question whether that is the right model for compile-time processes at all. I didn't think so. I thought compile-time reflection introduced unnecessary complexity to the expression mechanisms I was looking for. Here is what I was looking for.

For synchronization, I wanted to be able to say things like, "Before executing the operation, take in `BoundedBuffer` objects, make sure no other thread is executing it in the same object, and make sure the buffer is not empty; otherwise wait," or "After executing the operation, take in `BoundedBuffer` objects, check if the buffer is empty, and if so, mark it as empty; also, check if the buffer was previously full, and if

---

1. A few years later, in 2000 or so, my advisor Karl Lieberherr decided to rename "Demeter/Java" to "DJ" [22, 36]. Are you confused yet? Throughout this article, DJ refers to my DJ back in 1995–1997; my advisor's system will be called Demeter/Java, as it was at the time.

so, mark it as not full." I also wanted to allow the expression of multi-object coordination schemes for concurrent agents like "Before executing the operation activate in the `Engine` object, make sure the `Door` object is closed." It seemed awkward to me that in order to say this, I would have to define metaclasses, instantiate and associate a meta-object for every base object, trap every message sent to the base objects, and execute their meta-objects code at those points. For multi-object coordination schemes, the one-to-one association between base and meta-objects wasn't even appropriate: we would want one single coordinator associated with the objects involved in the coordination scheme.

For remote parameter passing, I wanted to be able to say things like, "When the operation `getBook` of `Library` objects is invoked remotely, the returned `Book` object should be copied back to the client, but the field `shelfCopies` shouldn't be included," or "When the operation `borrowedBooks(User)` of `Library` objects is invoked remotely, the only information that's needed from the `User` parameter is the `User`'s name, so copy only that." Again, it seemed awkward that in order to express this, I would have to use the reflection model.

Things would get even more confusing when these directives were to have a static code generation effect, which was what I was looking for. Although the reflection model might be a reasonable *implementation* model for the process, it certainly wasn't true to the intentions of synchronization and remote parameter passing directives, as expressed in plain English. The problem, then, was the expression of referencing.

So I came up with a simpler referencing mechanism, which was inspired by a body of previous work done by other people, but especially by my advisor Karl Lieberherr's Demeter system [22]. The directives, expressed separately from the classes, would refer to the object's operations and internals by name:

```
coordinator BoundedBuffer {
  selfex put, take;
  mutex {put, take};
  condition empty = true, full = false;
  put: requires !full;
      on_exit {
        if (empty) empty = false;
        if (usedSlots == capacity) full = true;
      }
  take: requires !empty;
      on_exit {
        if (full) full = false;
        if (usedSlots == 0) empty = true;
      }
}
```

and

```
portal LibrarySystem {
  boolean registerUser(User user) {
    //Only strings. Everything else of User is excluded.
    user: copy {User only all.String;}
  };
  Book getBook(int isbn){
    //for return object, exclude the field shelfCopies
    return: copy {Book bypass shelfCopies;}
  };
  BookList borrowedBooks(User user) {
    //for return object, exclude the field shelfCopies
    return: copy {Book bypass shelfCopies;}
    // for User, bring only the name
    user: copy {User only name;}
  };
}
```

The binding, by direct naming, was unidirectional from these modules to the classes they referred to, and not the other way around. In other words, contrary to the dominating paradigm that said that each module must specify itself and its dependencies completely, this scheme allowed the definition of modules that would "impose" themselves on other modules without an explicit request or permission from the latter. With this scheme, it was trivial to plug in and unplug concern-specific modules with a compilation switch.

This scheme also scaled nicely for multi-object schemes: just add more class names to the list of classes the coordinators and the portals were associated with, and we could refer to the operations and internals of those classes. For example:

```
coordinator Engine, Door {...}
```

5.3.5 DJava

Up until 1997, DJ was my own little piece of work, a system that I had carried with me from Northeastern, and one among others that we, as a group, were working on. In 1997, things changed.

I spent most of that year locked in my apartment writing my dissertation, so I didn't participate much in the group's activities. In the spring, Gregor decided to invest the group's resources into the implementation of a DJ weaver, a pre-processor written in Lisp. That first language implementation, called DJava, supported COOL and some of RIDL. Over that summer, they planned a usability study. The users were four summer interns. They wrote a distributed space war game with it. (This came in handy, as I was writing the Validation chapter.) A report of those activities can be found in my dissertation ([27], Chapter 5). We used that application as an example for a long time.

At the end of the summer, Gregor decided to use DJava as the flagship system, the seed of what later became AspectJ.

In the meantime, back at Northeastern, Karl Lieberherr also decided to incorporate DJ into Demeter/Java. That happened from the end of 1997 throughout 1998.

5.3.6 AspectJ

The first version of AspectJ, made public in March of 1998, was a reimplementation of DJava. It supported only COOL. Another release followed soon; I believe it was AspectJ 0.1. It included RIDL. A group at the University of British Columbia did some preliminary usability tests with this version. The results can be found in [47].

As release 0.1 was coming out, at the end of April of 1998, AspectJ suffered a transfiguration. Gregor wanted to develop a general-purpose aspect language. DJ was a couple of concern-specific languages; it wasn't very useful for general-purpose programming. The decision to make AspectJ general-purpose wasn't simple, at least for me. We had already released two versions, and changing the language's philosophy would probably confuse those who had been using it as a reference for AOP. But more importantly, it wasn't at all obvious to me how a general-purpose aspect language would, indeed, be useful at the time, given the limited number of crosscutting concerns we had previously identified. What examples would we use to justify and explain it?

In retrospect, it is clear my fears were inconsequential. AspectJ is a lot more useful for a larger number of software development needs than it would have been if we had continued the path we initially set, which was, by design, limited. DJ served AOP well, but it was time to grow it. What follows is a brief analysis of what it took to make the shift from concern-specific to general-purpose.

In a paper we published in the summer of 1998 [28], we used the image shown in Figure 5-1 to describe the range of languages we had been designing.

How did we move from concern-specific to general purpose? What was preserved, what was added, and what was thrown away? This is my view about the transition process.

Significant differences:

♦ The concept of having coordinators and portals as first-order elements of the language went away. AspectJ has "aspects." Aspects could, then, be coordinators and eventually portals too. In fact, the subsequent releases of AspectJ had examples of aspects acting as coordinators and even reusable coordinator library aspects, which, because of the elimination of syntax, had a lot more lines of code than their DJ counterparts. But the good thing was that aspects could play lots of other roles without having to add more syntax. This was the design change that made AspectJ general purpose.

- Central to DJ and Demeter was the concept of programming crosscutting concerns separately from the "primary" concerns, using special kinds of modules that could not be referenced back by the objects. The existence of aspect instances, and the possibility of their being handled in programs, was a point of much discussion, and during the first 2+ years of development, we went back and forth on this issue (I call it "the meta-object syndrome"). The compromise was to use a singleton aspect instance by default. This is still the policy in the latest version of AspectJ, although it now provides a richer set of aspect instance associations. Unlike DJ, AspectJ provides handlers to aspect instances through the `aspectOf()` operation.

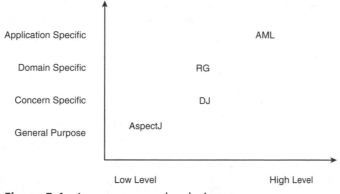

Figure 5-1   *Languages under design.*

Significant clarifications:

- The concept of join point, which had been identified in DJ, RG, and other systems, was cleaned up. DJ had only two kinds of join points: the reception of messages by objects (in COOL and RIDL) and the sending of messages to objects (in RIDL). Gregor envisioned a much richer set of join points that are now part of the AspectJ join point model. This extension, by itself, didn't make AspectJ general purpose, but it certainly expanded the kinds of crosscuts it could express.

In particular, this clarification allowed for the definition of control flow pointcuts in later versions of AspectJ.

Significant preservations:

+ Two basic principles were preserved: the presentation of AspectJ as an extension to Java and the implementation of the weaver as a compile-time process. Up until recently, the weaver was a pre-processor, transforming AspectJ programs into Java programs. Now it operates on bytecodes.

+ Central to DJ and Demeter was the concept of referring to the join points using a very simple direct naming scheme based on the names of the classes and the fields. Since in DJ the "aspect" modules could refer to several classes, it used qualified names such as `ClassName.FieldName`, which could include wild cards. One design point was very important: *There was no notion of this naming process being a reflective operation.* To understand this, we have to look at the alternatives. In other languages, such as CLOS [45], once we have an object, we can get the names of classes and members through a reflective API, and we can build meta-programs with that. DJ did not have the base-meta distinction and the API that goes with it; it had a simple declarative form for naming join points. That was preserved in AspectJ. The denotation of join points suffered several syntactic changes over the years, especially as we started to extend the kinds of join points supported by AspectJ. But unlike meta-programming, the naming is not programmatic but declarative: Therefore, it feels very "natural," as declarative programming usually does.

+ The temporal referencing before/after associated with join points existed in DJ and was preserved in AspectJ. (Note that before/after existed in other systems prior to DJ, namely in CLOS and in Demeter.)

+ The static introduction of structure and behavior had been defined early on for COOL [29]. CLOS [45] also supported a similar feature but for runtime. Introduction generated much discussion, as it didn't fit the run-time semantics of join points too well, but it was preserved in AspectJ. Over the years, it suffered several changes and clarifications.

Past the transition from concern-specific to general-purpose aspect language, which happened in 1998, AspectJ evolved considerably. Part of that evolution was due to the commitment to a solid advanced development plan. The support from DARPA, starting in 1998, allowed Gregor to get the resources he needed. In early 1999, the weaver was rewritten in Java, which made the system much more portable than the previous Lisp version. At the end of that year, there were extensions to existing Integrated Development Environments. The design of AspectJ stabilized when it got to release 0.7 in the first half of 2000. That was also the time I started pursuing other interests.

In concluding this section, I should note that many people were directly involved in the AOP project at PARC at various times besides Gregor Kiczales and myself. In the early days of AOP, the group included John Lamping, Anurag Mendhekar, Chris Maeda, Jean-Marc Loingtier, and John Irwin. Venkatesh Choppella was there during the transition from DJ to the general-purpose AspectJ. Jim Hugunin and Mik Kersten joined in the transition to advanced development. Others, including Erik Hilsdale, joined after I left the project and helped solidify the technology even further. Over the years, more than a dozen summer students contributed to the project; I can't remember all of their names, so I will leave them anonymous.

5.4 BUILDING COMMUNITIES

Communities rarely happen spontaneously. It takes time and planning to create and expand them. The AOP group at PARC has put a significant effort in building communities around the technology. Lots of people outside our group were instrumental in helping clarify the concepts by providing alternative technologies and all sorts of feedback. There were/are two kinds of communities: researchers and practitioners. The bridge was built by very special people: early adopters, those people who work in industry but have the curiosity and the will to try out beta systems.

5.4.1 Researchers

As mentioned earlier in the paper, in October of 1996, we held a workshop at PARC to which we invited researchers we knew were working in similar things. There were about 15 people in that meeting. The goal of that workshop was to discuss the major characteristics of and compare the work we all were doing. That included AOP (i.e., the PARC people), subject-oriented programming (Ossher and Tarr), Composition Filters (Akşit and Bergmans), Reflection (Matsuoka et al.), and adaptive programming (Lieberherr). It was a fruitful workshop. One of the outcomes was the plan for a larger workshop associated with ECOOP'97, with the title "Aspect-Oriented Programming." That workshop attracted over 40 people and was a big success. AOP felt like the new kid on the OOP block. After that, there was an AOP workshop at ECOOP every year and one AOP workshop at ICSE'98. At every workshop, I always met new people whose work would fit and enrich the separation of concerns/AOP umbrella.

5.4.2 Practitioners

Building communities of users, especially the "real" ones, is much harder than building communities of researchers. By "real" users, I mean software engineers developing products in companies. Researchers thrive on ideas; practitioners thrive on solid systems that solve their problems without introducing new problems. Nobody in the industry will use a system just because it embodies an interesting idea that will potentially help him or her.

Our first users were graduate students linked to the research community. They were the only ones who were motivated enough to skip through all the bugs! They weren't really using the language to build anything; they were using it as a reference point. Our first "real" users started to show up in the beginning of 2000. At this point, the compiler was solid enough to handle a few hundred classes. The first users who contacted us had read about AOP, had played a bit with the examples in AspectJ, and wanted to try it in parts of their projects with our support for debugging aspects.

Early adopters are essential, but they are also hard to deal with. They try something and they either like it—pushing it to the limit and asking for more—or silently drop it. A handful of early users were patient enough to point out defects and weaknesses and persisted in using AspectJ until it got a lot more solid. The vast majority was put off by the beta-ness of the language. Given that I left the AOP project later that year, I can't say much about what happened next. Based on the traffic in the mailing list, the articles in industry magazines, and the third-party IDE support, it looks like AspectJ has been embraced by a large community. Some of the AOP ideas are here to stay!

5.5 LOOKING BACK

It is quite interesting to look back to the period 1994–1997 and to compare my vision of AOP at the time with what AOP is now. My notion of Aspects[2] was based on systems I had worked on or studied. So, back then, according to my "Separation of Concerns" report, Aspects, independent of the techniques used to program them, were things like synchronization, remote parameter passing, configuration issues, real-time constraints, object structure, failure handling, persistence, security, debugging, etc. When I went to PARC, I found out about run-time performance Aspects such as memory optimization, loop fusion, and evaluation time. Recently, I did a quick survey of

---

2.   I am using Aspect with a capital A to denote crosscutting concerns at the conceptual (design) level, not at the implementation (AspectJ) level.

what users are using AspectJ for by looking at articles in industry magazines [9, 20, 21, 44] and posting a question in the users list. The following categorization is an attempt at organizing my findings:

1. Debugging and instrumentation Aspects such as tracing, logging, testing, profiling, monitoring, and asserting. Most of the usages fall into this category, but some usages are very sophisticated. For example, one user reported having built a "virtual internal information bus" inside his company's application.

2. Program construction Aspects such as mixins, multiple-inheritance (e.g., for bean construction), and views.

3. Configuration Aspects such as managing the specifics of using different platforms and choosing appropriate name spaces for property management.

4. Enforcement and verification Aspects such as making sure the types of a framework are used appropriately, performing components' contract validation, and ensuring best programming practices.

5. Operating Aspects such as synchronization, caching, persistence, transaction management, security, and load balancing.

6. Failure handling Aspects such as redirecting a failed call to a different service.

The ability to use aspects as add-ons over classes, as well as to plug in and unplug different aspects with a compilation switch, is being perceived as the major advantage of AspectJ/AOP.

In retrospect, although we missed a few kinds of Aspects and mentioned a couple that didn't yet emerge in practice, the analysis that Walter and I made back in 1994, which was voicing a trend that was in the air, was a self-fulfilling prophecy! It is actually quite amazing that later we at PARC were able to design a language that supports this diversity of crosscutting concerns . . . *with just a few key concepts*. In other words, the path I had started on—the design of concern-specific languages—wouldn't scale!

Another interesting observation is that AspectJ does not support any of the runtime performance Aspects that the group at PARC was focusing on before I joined. This doesn't mean that those Aspects are irrelevant; it simply means that AspectJ doesn't provide the kinds of referencing mechanisms that are necessary to support them.

One last comment on whether the broad AOP thesis—that it leads to *better* programs—has been validated or not: I don't have enough data to be able to draw any scientific conclusion. My recent poking at the AspectJ users gave me anecdotal evidence, as some users described their systems and commented on their positive experiences. From where I stand now, which is relatively far from where I used to be, I can see that AOP is extremely popular. Maybe the academic thesis doesn't matter, as it never mattered for all other languages (Lisp, C++, Java, etc.). The academic thesis may not matter as long as AOP helps solving some practical software problems.

5.6 THE ESSENCE OF AOP

What is it about Aspects that makes them both attractive to researchers and useful to practitioners? And where can we go from here? I haven't worked in AOP for a couple of years, but being as fascinated by languages as I was then, it's very interesting to try to answer these questions.

First of all, programming languages are incredibly restrictive programming systems. They all have one fundamental weakness. They emphasize the fact that they are a means to define computational processes, and they ignore the fact that they are a means for *humans* to write and read computational processes. Humans don't think using any of the existing programming languages. Even if we do, we certainly haven't been writing down structured ideas for thousands of years using those languages. We have been using natural languages. That has worked out quite well. Natural languages are as general purpose as languages can get. They contain an extremely rich and diverse set of constructs that allow us to write down an enormous amount of ideas concisely in modular ways that can be easily understood by others.

Computer systems, of course, are different. I am not suggesting that programming languages should have a natural language interface. That was suggested a long time ago (Sammet [40], Ballard, and Biemann [4]) and it has been done before (Hypertalk [49] and NaturalJava [38]); the result is always limited or dubious. However, I am suggesting that programming language designers should pay more attention to the way natural languages work and the way we structure ideas with them. This is related to what I think is the major contribution of AOP to the next generation of programming systems.

Take tracing, for example. When we think of tracing, we formulate something like this: "For all methods, call `Trace.in` before they start executing and `Trace.out` after they finish executing." However, all programming languages will force us to transform this sentence into something like this: "In method A, call `Trace.in`; . . . call `Trace.out`; return. In method B, *etc.*" So what is it about the first representation of the intention that's better than the second, and how does the natural language help? In this case, it's the references to "all methods," "before . . . executing," and "after . . . executing." *That's the power of AspectJ: it supports a richer set of structural and temporal referencing that follows what we have in natural languages.* AspectJ does it in a way that seems to be very useful for practitioners: It allows the encapsulation of these forms in modules that can be added to or removed from the applications with a compilation switch. In other words, writing a tracing aspect is like writing a different chapter, or section, in a book.

So, what makes an Aspect be an Aspect, before we even think of programming it with AspectJ? Given the name we chose for it, which clearly influences our perception, Aspects are software concerns that affect what happens in the Objects but that are more concise, intelligible, and manageable when written as separate chapters of the imaginary book that describes the application. This pseudo-definition of Aspect aligns well with what users have been using AspectJ for. The structural and temporal referencing in AspectJ are essential mechanisms for achieving the separation between the Objects and those other concerns. Those mechanisms are also *natural:* We would use those kinds of referential relations if we were to write it in English or Portuguese. But the need for better referencing mechanisms doesn't end with what the word "Aspect" conveys.

5.7 FUTURE CHALLENGES

On the way to future challenges, I'll do a brief incursion into Linguistics. Linguistics has been studying a large super-set of the constructs that AspectJ supports: referentiality between utterances—the subject matter of binding theory draws its roots from Chomsky's pioneering work. In natural languages, pronouns (e.g., this, that, it, her, which, etc.) are examples of such referential relations, but they are not the only ones. In general linguistics, referential dependence is studied regardless of morphological form, regardless of whether it is context-dependent or context-free, and regardless of whether it is about objects or about time. For example, references can be lists of nouns such as "president, the cat, the resident, and the hat," constraints on nouns such as "colorless liquids," temporal references such as "after reading the input stream," and combinations of the above. Note that we use these forms intuitively, that they make texts concise, and that they allow us to organize our ideas as optimally as we can. This rich set of references is what allows us, for example, to divide specification manuals into chapters and sections that are related but loosely coupled; it is also what allows us to make a statement and add more to it at a later point. If we didn't have these referential forms, we would have a hard time communicating indeed.

Programming languages support a very small set of referential relations. In particular, reflective references, groups, and temporal references are practically nonexistent. They can be simulated by combinations of computation and new nouns. And that's exactly one of the things that make programs much more complex than they should be: Programmers have to express a rich set of referencing forms using a very small set of referencing forms. In the process, intentions get diluted and tangled.

The future of AOP will probably benefit from removing the word "Aspect" from its name! What's important for the next generation of programming languages is the exploration of the rich set of referential relations we find in natural languages. That will allows us to appropriately implement pieces of program specification not only as separate chapters, but also as sections, paragraphs, and even sentences in a way that's much more *natural*. This will help avoid redundancy, temporary variables, and all sorts of programming oddities. This is, of course, a challenge for language designers. I have only some fuzzy ideas about how those languages should look. It seems to me that the conceptual framework that's available from Linguistics is an excellent framework for programming languages, too.

ACKNOWLEDGMENTS

Thanks to John Lamping for reading an earlier draft of this chapter and pointing out some memory lapses and inconsistencies. Thanks also to Mik Kersten for proofreading.

REFERENCES

1. AKŞIT, M., BERGMANS, L., AND VURAL, S. 1992. An object-oriented language-database integration model: The composition-filters approach. In *ECOOP '92 European Conf. Object-Oriented Programming*, (Kaiserslautern), O. L. Madsen, Ed. LNCS, vol. 615. Springer-Verlag, Berlin, 372–395.

2. AKŞIT, M., BOSCH, J., V. D. STERREN, W., AND BERGMANS, L. 1994. Real-time specification inheritance anomalies and real-time filters. In *8th European Conf. Object-Oriented Programming* (Bologna), M. Tokoro and R. Pareschi, Eds. LNCS, vol. 821. Springer-Verlag, Berlin, 386–407.

3. AKŞIT, M., WAKITA, K., BOSCH, J., BERGMANS, L., AND YONEZAWA, A. 1993. Abstracting object-interactions using composition-filters. In *Workshop on Object-Based Distributed Processing (ECOOP)*, R. Guerraoui, O. Nierstrasz, and M. Riveill, Eds. LNCS, vol. 791. Springer-Verlag, Berlin, 152–184.

4. BALLARD, B. AND BIERMANN, A. 1979. Programming in natural language: NLC as a prototype. In *CSC-ER Annual Conference*. ACM, 228–237.

5. BARBACCI, M. AND WING, J. 1986. Specifying functional and timing behavior for real-time applications. Tech. Rep. CMU/SEI-86-TR-4 ADA178769, Software Engineering Institute, Carnegie Mellon University, Pittsburgh.

6. BERGMANS, L. 1994. Composing concurrent objects. Ph.D. thesis, University of Twente.

7. FRØLUND, S. AND AGHA, G. 1993. A language framework for multi-object coordination. In *ECOOP '93—Object-Oriented Programming, 7th European Conference*, (Kaiserslautern), O. M. Nierstrasz, Ed. LNCS, vol. 707. Springer-Verlag, Berlin, 346–360.

8. GAMMA, E., HELM, R., JOHNSON, R., AND VLISSIDES, J. 1995. *Design Patterns: Elements of Reusable Object-Oriented Software*. Addison-Wesley, Reading, Massachusetts.

9. GROSSO, W. 2002. Aspect-oriented programming and AspectJ. *Dr. Dobbs Journal*. http://www.ddj.com/articles/2002/0208/.

10. HARRISON, W. AND OSSHER, H. 1993. Subject-oriented programming—a critique of pure objects. In *8th Conf. Object-Oriented Programming, Systems, Languages, and Applications (OOPSLA)*. ACM, 411–428.

11. HONDA, Y. AND TOKORO, M. 1992. Soft real-time programming through reflection. In *Int'l Workshop on Reflection and Meta-Level Architecture*, (Tokyo). JSSST. 12–23.

12. HÜRSCH, W. L. AND LOPES, C. V. 1995. Separation of concerns. Tech. Rep. NU-CCS-95-03, College of Computer Science, Northeastern University. February.

13. IRWIN, J., LOINGTIER, J. M., GILBERT, J. R., KICZALES, G., LAMPING, J., MENDHEKAR, A., AND SHPEISMAN, T. 1997. Aspect-oriented programming of sparse matrix code. In *Int'l Scientific Computing in Object-Oriented Parallel Environments (ISCOPE)*. LNCS, vol. 1343. Springer-Verlag, Berlin.

14. JACOBSON, I. 1986. Language support for changeable large real time systems. In *1st Conf. Object-Oriented Programming, Systems, Languages, and Applications (OOPSLA)*, (Portland, Oregon). ACM, 377–384.

15. KICZALES, G. 1996. Beyond the black box: Open implementation. *IEEE Software 13*, 1 (Jan.), 8–11.

16. KICZALES, G., DES RIVIERES, J., AND BOBROW, D. G. 1991. *The Art of the Metaobject Protocol*. MIT Press, Cambridge, Massachusetts.

17. KICZALES, G., LAMPING, J., LOPES, C., MAEDA, C., MENDHEKAR, A., AND MURPHY, G. 1997. Open implementation design guidelines. In *19th Int'l Conf. Software Engineering (ICSE)*, (Boston). ACM, 481–490.

18. KICZALES, G., LAMPING, J., MENDHEKAR, A., MAEDA, C., LOPES, C., LOINGTIER, J. M., AND IRWIN, J. 1997. Aspect-oriented programming. In *ECOOP'97 Object-Oriented Programming, 11th European Conference*, M. Akşit and S. Matsuoka, Eds. LNCS, vol. 1241. Springer-Verlag, Berlin, 220–242.

19. KICZALES, G. AND PAEPCKE, A. 1995. Open implementations and metaobject protocols: Tutorial slides and notes. Tech. rep., Xerox Palo Alto Research Center. http://www2.parc.com/csl/groups/sda/publications/papers/Kiczales-TUT95/for-web.pdf.

20. LADDAD, R. 2002. I want my AOP! *JavaWorld magazine*. http://www.javaworld.com/javaworld/jw-01-2002/jw-0118-aspect.html.

21. LESIECKI, N. 2002. Test flexibility with AspectJ and mock objects. Tech. rep., Java Technology Zone for IBM's Developer Works. http://www-106.ibm.com/developerworks/java/library/j-aspectj2/?open&l = 007,t = gr.

22. LIEBERHERR, K., ORLEANS, D., AND OVLINGER, J. 2001. Aspect-oriented programming with adaptive methods. *Comm. ACM 44*, 10 (Oct.), 39–41.

23. LIEBERHERR, K. J. 1996. *Adaptive Object-Oriented Software: The Demeter Method with Propagation Patterns*. PWS Publishing Company, Boston.

24. LIEBERHERR, K. J., SILVA-LEPE, I., AND XIAO, C. 1994. Adaptive object-oriented programming using graph-based customization. *Comm. ACM 37*, 5 (May), 94–101.

25. LISKOV, B. AND SCHEIFLER, R. 1983. Guardians and actions: Linguistic support for robust, distributed programs. *ACM Transactions on Programming Languages and Systems 5*, 3 (July), 381–404.

26. LOPES, C. V. 1996. Adaptive parameter passing. In *2nd Int'l Symp. Object Technologies for Advanced Software (ISOTAS)*, (Kanazawa, Japan). LNCS, vol. 1049. Springer-Verlag, Berlin, 118–136.

27. LOPES, C. V. 1997. D: A language framework for distributed programming. Ph.D. thesis, College of Computer Science, Northeastern University.

28. LOPES, C. V. AND KICZALES, G. 1998. Recent developments in AspectJ. In *Workshop on Aspect-Oriented Programming (ECOOP)*, (Brussels). http://trese.cs.utwente.nl/aop-ecoop98/papers/Lopes.pdf.

29. LOPES, C. V. AND LIEBERHERR, K. J. 1994. Abstracting process-to-function relations in concurrent object-oriented applications. In *8th European Conf. Object-Oriented Programming* (Bologna), M. Tokoro and R. Pareschi, Eds. LNCS, vol. 821. Springer-Verlag, Berlin, 81–99.

30. LOPES, C. V. AND LIEBERHERR, K. J. 1996. AP/S++: Case-study of a MOP for purposes of software evolution. In *Reflection '96* (San Francisco), G. Kiczales, Ed.

31. MAES, P. 1987. Concepts and experiments in computational reflection. In *2nd Conf. Object-Oriented Programming, Systems, Languages, and Applications (OOPSLA)*, (Orlando). ACM, 147–155.

32. MAGEE, J., KRAMER, J., AND SLOMAN, M. 1989. Constructing distributed systems in CONIC. *IEEE Transactions on Software Engineering 15*, 6 (June), 663–675.

33. MAHONEY, J. V. 1995. Functional visual routines. Tech. Rep. SPL95-069, Xerox Palo Alto Research Center.

34. MATSUOKA, S. AND YONEZAWA, A. 1993. Analysis of inheritance anomaly in object-oriented concurrent programming languages. In *Research Directions in Concurrent Object-Oriented Programming*, G. Agha, P. Wegner, and A. Yonezawa, Eds. The MIT Press, Cambridge, Massachusetts, 107–150.

35. MENDHEKAR, A., KICZALES, G., AND LAMPING, J. 1997. RG: A case-study for aspect-oriented programming. Tech. Rep. SPL-97-009, Palo Alto Research Center.

36. OKAMURA, H. AND ISHIKAWA, Y. 1994. Object location control using meta-level programming. In *8th European Conf. Object-Oriented Programming* (Bologna), M. Tokoro and R. Pareschi, Eds. LNCS, vol. 821. Springer-Verlag, Berlin, 299–319.

37. ORLEANS, D. AND LIEBERHERR, K. 2001. DJ: Dynamic adaptive programming in Java. In *Metalevel Architectures and Separation of Crosscutting Concerns 3rd Int'l Conf. (Reflection 2001)*, (Kyoto), A. Yonezawa and S. Matsuoka, Eds. LNCS, vol. 2192. Springer-Verlag, Berlin, 73–80.

38. PRICE, D., RILOFF, E., ZACHARY, J., AND HARVEY, B. 2000. NaturalJava: A natural language interface for programming in Java. In *5th Int'l Conf. On Intelligent User Interfaces*, (New Orleans). ACM, 207–211.

39. REGHIZZI, C. S. AND DE PARATESI, G. G. 1991. Definition of reusable concurrent software components. In *ECOOP '91 European Conf. Object-Oriented Programming*, (Geneva), P. America, Ed. LNCS, vol. 512. Springer-Verlag, Berlin, 148–166.

40. SAMMET, J. 1966. The use of English as a programming language. *Comm. ACM 9*, 3, 228–230.

41. SILVA-LEPE, I., HURSCH, W., AND SULLIVAN, G. 1994. A report on Demeter/C++. *C++ Report 6*, 2 (Feb.), 24–30.

42. SMITH, B. C. 1984. Reflection and semantics in Lisp. In *Symp. Principles of Programming Languages (POPL)*, (Salt Lake City). ACM, 23–35.

43. Sousa, P., Sequeira, M., Zúquete, A., Ferreira, P., Lopes, C., Pereira, J., Guedes, P., and Alves Marques, J. 1993. Distribution and persistence in the IK platform: Overview and evaluation. *Computing Systems Journal 6*, 4 (Fall), 391–424.

44. Spurlin, V. 2002. Aspect-oriented programming with Sun ONE studio. Tech. rep., Sun Microsystems. http://forte.sun.com/ffj/articles/aspectJ.html.

45. Steele Jr., G. 1990. *Common Lisp: The Language, 2nd Edition*. Digital Press, Bedford, Massachusetts.

46. Takashio, K. and Tokoro, M. 1992. DROL: An object-oriented programming language for distributed real-time systems. In *7th Conf. Object-Oriented Programming, Systems, Languages, and Applications (OOPSLA)*, (Vancouver). ACM, 276–294.

47. Walker, R. J., Baniassad, E. L. A., and Murphy, G. C. 1999. An initial assessment of aspect-oriented programming. In *21st Int'l Conf. Software Engineering (ICSE)*, (Los Angeles). ACM, 120–130.

48. Watanabe, T. and Yonezawa, A. 1990. Reflection in an object-oriented concurrent language. In *ABCL: An Object-Oriented Concurrent System*, A. Yonezawa, Ed. MIT Press, Cambridge, Massachusetts, 45–70.

49. Winkler, D., Kamins, S., and DeVoto, J. 1994. *Hypertalk 2.2: The Book*. Random House, New York.

50. Zeidler, C. and Gerteis, W. 1992. Distribution: Another milestone of application management issues. In *Technology of Object-Oriented Languages and Systems (TOOLS Europe)*, (Dortmund, Germany), G. Heeg, B. Magnusson, and B. Meyer, Eds. Prentice Hall, Englewood Cliff, New Jersey, 87–99.

Chapter 6

AspectJ

ADRIAN COLYER

AspectJ is a seamless aspect-oriented extension to the Java programming language that is designed to be easy to learn and use and fully Java platform-compatible. This chapter provides a brief introduction to the goals of the AspectJ project and gives an overview of the AspectJ language and supporting tools. We conclude by looking at future directions for AspectJ.

6.1 ASPECTJ GOALS

The AspectJ project seeks to provide an aspect-oriented programming environment that is:

- General purpose
- Supported directly in the programming language
- Easy to learn
- Incrementally adoptable
- Easy to integrate with existing processes and tools
- Suitable for commercial use

6.1.1 General Purpose

AspectJ is designed as a general purpose programming language. It neither has specialized language constructs for particular aspects nor is targeted at a particular application domain (such as enterprise application development). AspectJ is general purpose in the same way that an object-oriented language such as Java is general purpose.

Over and above the forms exposed in the Java programming language, AspectJ lets the programmer express crosscutting concerns using *aspects*. The kinds of aspects that people write (or reuse) can be broadly divided into three categories: general-purpose aspects, domain-specific aspects, and application-specific aspects. *General-purpose aspects* are applicable to almost any program. Examples include aspects such as tracing, logging, caching, and pooling. *Domain-specific aspects* have broad applicability within a given domain. For example, aspects for transaction management, persistence, and security are specific to the domain of enterprise application development. *Application-specific aspects* are unique to the particular program under construction. In object-oriented systems, there are classes that fall into each of these three categories too, and just as there are many more application-specific classes than general-purpose ones, so there are many more application-specific aspects than there are general-purpose ones.

6.1.2 *Direct Support in the Programming Language*

A key decision in the design of AspectJ was that aspects should be first class entities in the programming language. In AspectJ, `aspect` is a keyword. One can create aspect types just as easily as class types. At runtime, Aspects have instances with their own state and behavior. The designers of AspectJ took the view that the best long-term strategy for aspect-orientation is to have the concepts directly represented in the programming language. This is in contrast to approaches such as Hyper/J [8], which work within the confines of an existing object-oriented programming language and have the programmer specify additional aspect-related directives in side-files.

Language shapes thought. The real power of aspect-orientation comes when a programmer starts to think in terms of aspects and to reason about a program using an aspect-oriented metamodel ("aspect-oriented thinking"). Aspect-oriented thinking is harder to achieve when you have an object-oriented language (and hence an object-oriented metamodel that structures your thinking), and you have to layer aspect notions on top of it. AspectJ lets you take a statement in the design document that "all SQL exceptions thrown by the data layer need to be logged for subsequent analysis" and encode it directly as:

```
after() throwing(SQLException ex) : inDataLayer() {
  logException(ex);
}
```

6.1.3   Easy to Learn

AspectJ is designed to be easy to learn. This goal led to the early decision to base the language on top of Java, a popular object-oriented language: Every legal Java program is a legal AspectJ program. When programming with AspectJ, a developer can use any Java class libraries, continuing to benefit from any prior investment made in learning them. The strategy is analogous to the history of C++, where expressing C++ as an extension to C built a bridge into the world of object-orientation for procedural programmers.

The AspectJ model adds aspect-oriented features to Java through a few additional constructs and retains a distinction between aspects and classes (aspects have powers that classes do not). A "more pure" or "stronger" form of aspect-orientation, in which *everything* is an aspect, was considered early in the design of the AspectJ language, but this proved to be too big a conceptual gulf for object-oriented programmers to easily cross in one step.

6.1.4   Incremental Adoption

AspectJ is designed to allow incremental adoption. It is important that users coming to AspectJ can take a few early steps without needing to make a big investment in the technology and concepts. Adoption of AspectJ typically proceeds in three phases. First, AspectJ is used to write simple aspects that police design and implementation constraints (for example, that only types in the persistence component should make calls to the database). These aspects introduce users to the notions of *join points* and *pointcuts* (see Section 6.2) but do not affect the compiled program or its runtime execution in any way. In the second phase of adoption, AspectJ is additionally used to write "auxiliary" or "infrastructure" aspects—aspects that handle things such as tracing, error handling, monitoring, and other concerns that are an important part of an application but that are not its reason for being. In the final phase of adoption, aspects are also used to help modularize the core application functionality—for example, encoding business rules as aspects.

6.1.5   Easy to Integrate

AspectJ and the AspectJ tools are designed to be easy to integrate into existing environments—there is no requirement to throw everything away and start anew. The first important part of this is that the AspectJ compiler produces 100% legal Java bytecodes that can be run on any standard JVM.

The AspectJ distribution contains Ant [1] tasks that make it easy to switch an application build process from using the Java compiler to using the AspectJ compiler.

It also contains the `ajdoc` tool that extends `javadoc`-generated documentation to include cross-references to aspects and documentation of the aspects themselves. As of the 1.2 release, AspectJ includes a simple API for integrating AspectJ's aspect linking (*weaving*) capability into an existing classloader hierarchy so that aspects from aspect libraries can be linked with application classes as they are loaded. AspectJ support is available in a wide range of Java programming environments, including Eclipse, JBuilder, NetBeans, and Emacs.

6.1.6   Suitable for Real Applications

AspectJ is intended to be used on real applications, not just for research examples. This requires a robust compiler that produces high-quality error messages, runs quickly with a small enough footprint, and produces quality generated code. This is also the reason that AspectJ provides features such as incremental compilation support—essential when developing anything other than toy examples.

6.2   THE ASPECTJ LANGUAGE

The AspectJ language is designed as an extension to the Java language. It adds one fundamental concept—*join points.* On top of that are layered AspectJ's *pointcut* and *advice* mechanisms. In addition, AspectJ supports a form of open-class composition through a mechanism known as *inter-type declarations*. Pointcuts, advice, and inter-type declarations can be combined as needed and encapsulated inside a unit of modularity (a type) known as an *aspect*.

6.2.1   Join Points

Join points are identifiable points (events) in the execution of a program. Not all such points are interesting: For example, AspectJ exposes join points for the execution of a method and for a call made to a method, but not for the execution of the ninth line of source code in a source file. AspectJ's *join point model* determines the types of join points that can be referred to in an AspectJ program (via pointcut expressions). The join point model defines join points for:

- The execution of a method or constructor
- Execution of advice
- A call to a method or constructor
- Read or write access to a field

- The execution of an exception handler (catch block)
- The static initialization of a class
- Initialization of an object or aspect

While some of these may seem to be static, syntactic elements of a program's text, it is important to understand that join points are dynamic: they arise during program execution. Thus, the best way to illustrate join points is not a static model of the structure of a system, but through an object collaboration or sequence diagram. Figure 6-1 illustrates execution and call join points in a simple sequence diagram.

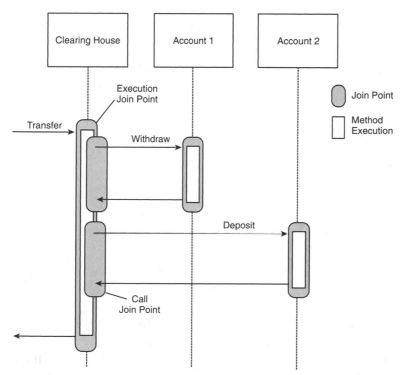

Figure 6-1   *Execution and call join points shown in a sequence diagram.*

6.2.2   Pointcuts

Pointcuts are predicates that match join points. Pointcut expressions are built up using AspectJ's primitive pointcut designators, of which there are three basic types. The first set of pointcut designators matches based on the kind of join point (is it a method call or a field access?). The second set of designators matches join points based on context at the join point (is the executing object an instance of Foo?), and the third set of designators matches based on scope (is the join point resulting from code within the org.xyz package?).

AspectJ provides pointcut designators that match based on kind for each kind of join point in AspectJ's join point model. The designators are: call, execution, get, set, handler, adviceexecution, staticinitialization, preinitialization, and initialization. Wildcarding within pointcut expressions is allowed. Table 6-1 shows some example pointcut expressions and their meanings in AspectJ.

Table 6-1 *Example Pointcut Expressions Matching on Kind of Join Point*

Pointcut Expression	Meaning
execution(public * get*(..))	The execution of any public method returning any type and taking any arguments, where the method name begins with "*get.*"
set(int Point.x)	An update to the value of the field x in the Point class.
handler(IOException+)	The excecution of an exception handler for IOException or any of its subclasses.
call(* org.xyz..*(..))	A call to any method declared in a type in a package whose name begins with "org.xyz."
staticinitialization (Serializable+)	The static initialization of any serializable class.

AspectJ's context matching pointcut designators are this, target, and args. The expression this(String) matches any join point where the currently executing object is an instance of String. The expression target(Foo) matches any join point where the target object (of a call for example) is an instance of Foo. Referring to the sequence diagram of Figure 6-1, for the withdraw call made by the "clearing house" object to the "account 1" object, the "clearing house" object is bound to this, and the "account 1" object is bound to target.

AspectJ's scoping pointcut designators are within, withincode, cflow, and cflowbelow. The within pointcut matches any join point where the associated source code is defined within a given scope (such as a type or package). The withincode pointcut matches join points where the associated source code is defined within a given set of methods or constructors. The cflow and cflowbelow pointcuts match join points based on the control flow in which they occur. For example, the pointcut expression `cflow(execution(* IBankAccount.*(..))` matches any join point arising as a result of the execution of a method defined by the `IBankAccount` interface, including all join points in the method's call graph. Referring again to Figure 6-1, both the calls to and the execution of the `withdraw` and `deposit` methods are in the control flow of the execution of the `transfer` method. Both `cflow` and `cflowbelow` below take as their argument another pointcut expression. They differ in that `cflow` also matches the join points matched by its pointcut expression, whereas `cflowbelow` excludes those join points.

AspectJ provides one final primitive pointcut, `if`, that takes a Boolean expression as its argument. The `if` pointcut can be used to extend AspectJ's join point matching. A common use is to test a Boolean flag, as, for example, in the expression `if(enabled)`.

An important part of the AspectJ language is that pointcuts support abstraction and composition. Abstraction is supported through the `pointcut` keyword that allows the programmer to define a named pointcut. Composition is achieved by combining both named and primitive pointcuts using the `&&`, `||`, and `!` operators. Listing 6-1 shows a simple example of the power this gives: expressions can be easily built up, and the `illegalJDBCCall` pointcut reads naturally.

Listing 6-1   *Pointcut abstraction and composition*

```
pointcut jdbcCall() :
  call(* java.sql..*(..)) || call(* javax.sql..*(..));

pointcut inDataLayer() :
  within(org.xyz.persistence..*);

pointcut illegalJDBCCall() :
  jdbcCall() && !inDataLayer();
```

As well as simply matching join points, pointcuts can provide contextual information about those join points to their consumers. A pointcut can declare a formal parameter list of context it provides, and the contextual values are extracted based on name binding, as in the following example:

```
pointcut ejbCall(EJBObject anEJB) :
  call(* EJBObject+.*(..)) && target(anEJB);
```

AspectJ also provides a declare warning/error mechanism that allows the programmer to enforce certain rules and constraints in their design or implementation by producing a compilation warning or error if a pointcut expression matches any join points. Using the example from Listing 6-1, a programmer could write:

```
declare warning : illegalJDBCCall() :
  "Don't make database calls outside of data layer";
```

This would cause the compiler to issue a warning if any database calls were coded outside of the data layer.

6.2.3 Advice

Advice is simply a set of program statements that are executed at join points matched by a pointcut. Each piece of advice in AspectJ has an associated pointcut. That pointcut determines the join points at which the advice executes. AspectJ has three basic kinds of advice: *before* advice, *after* advice, and *around* advice. These execute before, after, and around join points matched by the advice's pointcut expression. After advice is further subdivided into *after returning* advice, *after throwing* advice, and *after (finally)* advice. After returning advice executes only on successful return from the join point, and after throwing advice executes only if the join point was exited as a result of throwing an exception. After finally advice always executes however the join point is exited, and thus the programmer must be careful to deal with both normal and exceptional return conditions when using it. The source fragment in Listing 6-2 shows how pointcuts and advice could be combined to implement dirty tracking in a data access object.

Listing 6-2 *Dirty tracking example*

```
/**
 * setting a non-transient field in a DataAccessObject
 * is considered a dirtying action.
 */
pointcut dirtyingAction(DataAccessObj dao) :
  set(!transient * *) && target(dao);

/**
 * after returning from a dirtying action, set
 * the dirty flag.
 */
after(DataAccessObj dao) returning :
  dirtyingAction(dao) {
  dao.setDirty();
}
```

```
pointcut saveOrRestore() :
  execution(* DataAccessObj+.save(..)) ||
  execution(* DataAccessObj+.restore(..));

/**
 * Successful completion of a save or restore
 * operation clears the dirty flag.
 */
after(DataAccessObj dao) returning :
  saveOrRestore() && this(dao) {
  dao.clearDirty();
}
```

The example also shows how advice can be associated with both named and anonymous pointcut expressions and how context provided by pointcuts can be bound to variables used within the body of the advice. The invocation of advice at join points matched by the pointcut expression associated with it is implicit—no program source statements explicitly call the advice. Figure 6-2 shows an example of the implicit

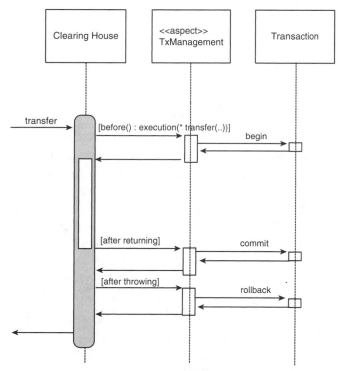

Figure 6-2 *Advice invocations shown in a sequence diagram.*

invocation of before and after advice to wrap the execution of an account transfer operation in a transaction.

Around advice is the most powerful form of advice in AspectJ, since it has the power to decide whether or not a matched join point should actually execute (for example, whether or not a call should proceed). Within the body of around advice, the special form `proceed()` is called at the point at which the computation at the join point should proceed (if at all). The arguments to the `proceed` are the same as those in the advice declaration. They can be altered by the body of the advice, affecting, for example, the arguments that a call proceeds with, or even the target object of a call. The example in Listing 6-3 shows the use of around advice to ensure that the value of a field stays within range.

Listing 6-3   *Using proceed inside around advice*

```
/**
 * For some markets the engine speed is limited by
 * software...
 */
void around(int speed) :
  set(int Car.currentSpeed) && args(speed) {
  int newSpeed = (speed < MAX_SPEED) ? speed : MAX_SPEED;
  proceed(newSpeed);
}
```

6.2.4   Inter-Type Declarations

Sometimes, a crosscutting concern involves not just dynamic considerations (advice) but also static ones. Returning to the theme of dirty tracking in data access objects, the solution presented in Listing 6-2 requires that each data access object support the `setDirty()` and `clearDirty()` operations. We would like everything concerned with dirty tracking to be encapsulated in one place, including the definition of these methods. AspectJ's inter-type declaration mechanisms allow an aspect to provide an implementation of methods and fields on behalf of other types. Listing 6-4 shows one way of addressing the static crosscutting elements of dirty tracking using AspectJ.

Listing 6-4   *Inter-type declarations for the dirty tracking concern*

```
(1) interface IDirtyStateTracking {};
(2)
(3) declare parents : org.xyz.persistence..*
```

```
(4)    implements IDirtyStateTracking;
(5)
(6) private boolean IDirtyStateTracking.isDirty = false;
(7)
(8) private void IDirtyStateTracking.setDirty() {
(9)   isDirty = true;
(10) }
(11)
(12) private void IDirtyStateTracking.clearDirty() {
(13)   isDirty = false;
(14) }
```

Line 1 simply declares an empty interface, `IDirtyStateTracking`. Lines 3 and 4 use AspectJ's `declare parents` statement to indicate that all the types in the `org.xyz.persistence` package should implement the `IDirtyStateTracking` interface. Line 6 declares that all implementers of the `IDirtyStateTracking` interface have a field `isDirty`. This field is declared private to the aspect making the inter-type declaration. Lines 8 through 14 provide a default implementation of the `setDirty()` and `clearDirty()` operations for implementers of `IDirtyStateTracking`. Again, these operations are visible only to the aspect making the inter-type declarations. (If they were declared public, then any type in the application could see them.)

In addition to the forms illustrated by this example, AspectJ also supports `declare parents ... extends`, which changes a type's parent class in a type-safe manner, and a `declare soft` statement, which can soften exceptions occurring at a given set of join points (used for modularizing certain kinds of exception handling policies).

6.2.5 *Aspects*

Aspects are the unit of modularity by which AspectJ implements crosscutting concerns. Aspects are declared using the `aspect` keyword and can contain methods and fields (just like a class), pointcuts, advice, and inter-type declarations. Listing 6-5 shows a complete aspect declaration for a dirty tracking aspect.

Just like classes, aspects can have their own state and behavior defined in methods and fields. Aspect instances are implicitly created by AspectJ at runtime. By default, there is a single instance of each aspect type, but other aspect lifecycles are possible by declaring that an aspect should be created `pertarget`, `perthis`, `percflow`, or `percflowbelow` of a pointcut expression. For example, using `percflow` causes a new aspect instance to be created every time a new control flow starts at a join point matched by the pointcut expression.

Listing 6-5   *The complete dirty tracking aspect*

```
public aspect DirtyTracking {

  /*
   * Marker interface for objects with tracking
   */
  interface IDirtyStateTracking {};

  declare parents : org.xyz.persistence..*
    implements IDirtyStateTracking;

  // implementation of interface

  private boolean IDirtyStateTracking.isDirty = false;

  private void IDirtyStateTracking.setDirty() {
   isDirty = true;
  }

  private void IDirtyStateTracking.clearDirty() {
   isDirty = false;
  }

  // setting and clearing dirty flag

  pointcut dirtyingAction(IDirtyStateTracking dao) :
    set(!transient * *) && target(dao) &&
    !within(DirtyTracking);

  after(IDirtyStateTracking dao) returning :
    dirtyingAction(dao) {
    dao.setDirty();
  }

  pointcut saveOrRestore() :
    execution(* IDirtyStateTracking+.save(..)) ||
    execution(* IDirtyStateTracking+.restore(..));

  after(IDirtyStateTracking dao) returning :
    saveOrRestore() && this(dao) {
    dao.clearDirty();
  }
}
```

So the aspect declaration:

```
public aspect AccountOperation :
percflow(execution(* *.*(..)) && target(Account)) {
  ...
```

creates a new instance of the `AccountOperation` aspect every time a method is executed on an `Account` object. The aspect instance lives until the execution of the method has completed.

When several aspects have advice executing at the same join point, the order in which the advice executes is undefined. For many programs, this is perfectly acceptable, but if the order of execution matters, AspectJ provides a `declare precedence` construct for specifying a (partial) ordering among aspects. *Before* advice defined in an aspect of higher precedence executes ahead of *before* advice defined in an aspect of lower precedence; *after* advice in an aspect of higher precedence executes following *after* advice of lower precedence.

6.2.6   *Further Reading*

This has, of necessity, been a brief and incomplete overview of the AspectJ language. Of course, the AspectJ Programming Guide [3] provides a more complete definition of the language. The reader's attention is particularly called to the appendix defining the language's semantics.

6.3   *ASPECTJ TOOLS*

This section presents a brief history and overview of the AspectJ compiler and the accompanying IDE support, `ajdoc` tool, and Ant tasks.

6.3.1   *History*

A good overview of the early history of aspect-oriented programming and AspectJ can be found in Chapter 5 of this book [7]. Table 6-2 summarizes the history of AspectJ since that time.

6.3.2   *The Compiler*

The AspectJ compiler translates AspectJ source code into Java bytecodes. It supports a variety of options for achieving that end, and these are discussed in Section 6.3.2.1.

Section 6.3.2.2 provides a high-level overview of the internal architecture of the compiler.

Table 6-2   *The Recent History of AspectJ*

AspectJ Version	Released	Significant Features
0.1	4/98	Domain specific languages: COOL (for synchronization) and RIDL (for remote invocation).
0.2	6/98	General purpose language.
0.3	5/99	Rewrite of AspectJ compiler from Lisp to Java.
0.5	1/00	ajdoc and first IDE support.
	8/00	Compiler and core tools released as open-source.
1.0.0	11/01	First version to compile directly to bytecodes. Ant tasks and AspectJ Browser added.
	2/02	AspectJ Development Tools project started on Eclipse.org.
1.1beta	12/02	AspectJ no longer a PARC project but an Eclipse technology project. Compiler extends Eclipse compiler and includes back-end weaving.
1.1.0	6/03	Aspect libraries, weaving into jar files, and incremental compilation.
1.2	4/04	Improved compiler (faster compilation, better error messages, and better generated code). Load-time weaving support.

6.3.2.1   Features

The simplest way to use the AspectJ compiler (`ajc`) is to present it with a list of source files (`.java` or `.aj`). The compiler produces the corresponding Java bytecode class files.

The compiler can also take as input Java class files (`.class`), either in directories or in jar files, and link (weave) these with aspects to produce new versions of those classes. The aspects can be passed to the compiler in either source or binary form. Binary form aspects are packaged in jar files as aspect libraries: `ajc` supports the `-aspectpath` option to pass aspect libraries to the compiler and the `-outjar` option to assist in creating them in the first place.

As of AspectJ 1.2, class files produced by the `ajc` compiler can be re-linked with new versions of aspects and with additional aspects without needing to go back to the source files. This is supported by the `-Xreweavable` option. The binary linking capabilities of the AspectJ compiler mean that the linker portion can be used to link classes with aspects as late as class definition time during class loading. AspectJ ships with a sample class loader that exploits this and an API for integrating the linker into an existing class loader hierarchy.

The AspectJ compiler also supports incremental compilation. If the source files for one or more classes are updated (or added, or deleted), then the AspectJ compiler recompiles and re-links just the classes defined in those files. The compiler can also detect updates to and incrementally re-link classes passed to it in binary form (.class files). If a change is detected in an aspect, then only the aspect is recompiled, but all the class files defined to the compiler are re-linked.

6.3.2.2   Implementation

The front-end of the compiler is responsible for translating AspectJ source files into class files. It is built as an extension to the Eclipse Java Development Tools (JDT) compiler. Aspects are compiled into class files that contain methods (with mangled names) for advice and inter-type declarations and have pointcut, advice, and other AspectJ-specific information encoded in attributes in the constant pool. The back-end of the compiler (the *weaver*) implements the bytecode transformations indicated by the encoded attributes to produce the final linked versions of the class files. Figure 6-3 provides an overview of the compilation process.

The front-end part of the compilation process is complicated by inter-type declarations and privileged aspects—these constructs all require changes to the Java compiler's default name-binding and static checking behavior.

The back-end of the compiler instruments classes by (for example) inserting calls to the precompiled advice methods. Crudely, each class file is processed in turn, and for each place in the bytecode that represents a join point in AspectJ's join point model, the pointcut expressions associated with all the advice in the system are checked to see if they could match at the join point. If a match is possible, then a call to the advice is inserted. Sometimes a definite match cannot be determined until run-time, in which case a run-time test is also inserted to guard the call to the advice. A good overview of AspectJ's weaving is found in [5]. An AspectJ developer's guide to the compiler and weaver is also available [6].

6.3.3   *IDE Support for AspectJ*

The goal of the IDE support provided for AspectJ is to make it as easy as possible for programmers to develop, understand, and work with AspectJ programs. A lot of emphasis is placed on showing crosscutting structure—for example, the advises and advised-by relationships that are shown for advice.

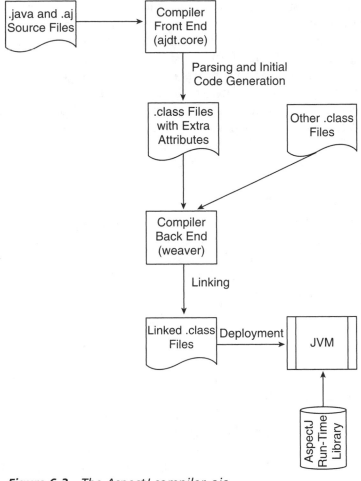

Figure 6-3 *The AspectJ compiler, ajc.*

Figure 6-4 shows the `DirtyTracking` aspect from Listing 6-5 in AJDT under Eclipse. Syntax highlighting and code-completion are available in the editor buffer, and the outline view shows the places affected by advice, allowing the programmer to navigate among them.

For working with larger software systems, AJDT also provides an aspect visualization perspective that uses a SeeSoft style presentation [4] to display the places in the source code that are affected by an aspect. The display can also be used for navigation—clicking on a bar takes you to the source line. Figure 6-5 shows an example of the visualizer in action.

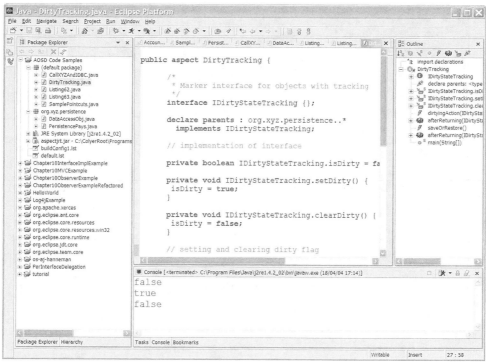

Figure 6-4 *DirtyTracking aspect in AJDT.*

Debugging AspectJ programs is also supported, as shown in Figure 6-6. More details about the features and functions of AJDT can be found on the AJDT project home page [2].

For users not working in the Eclipse environment, AspectJ support is also available in Emacs, JBuilder, and NetBeans. The AspectJ distribution includes a simple browser, `ajbrowser`, which also shows the crosscutting structure of AspectJ programs.

6.3.4 Generating Documentation with ajdoc

The `ajdoc` tool produces `javadoc`-like documentation for AspectJ programs. Figures 6-7 and 6-8 show the output of `ajdoc` for an aspect and for a class with methods advised by an aspect. The goal of the tool is once more to make the crosscutting nature of the aspects in the program explicit, this time in the documentation.

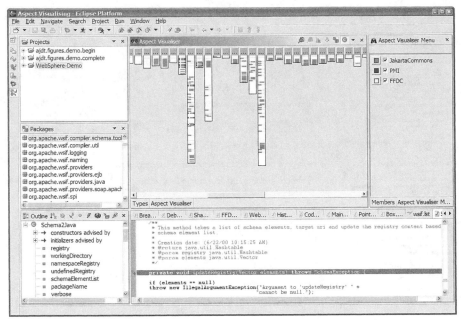

Figure 6-5 *Aspect visualization.*

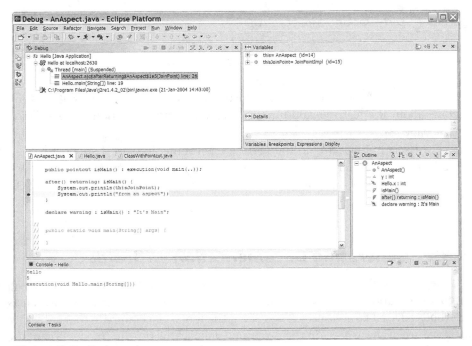

Figure 6-6 *Debugging support.*

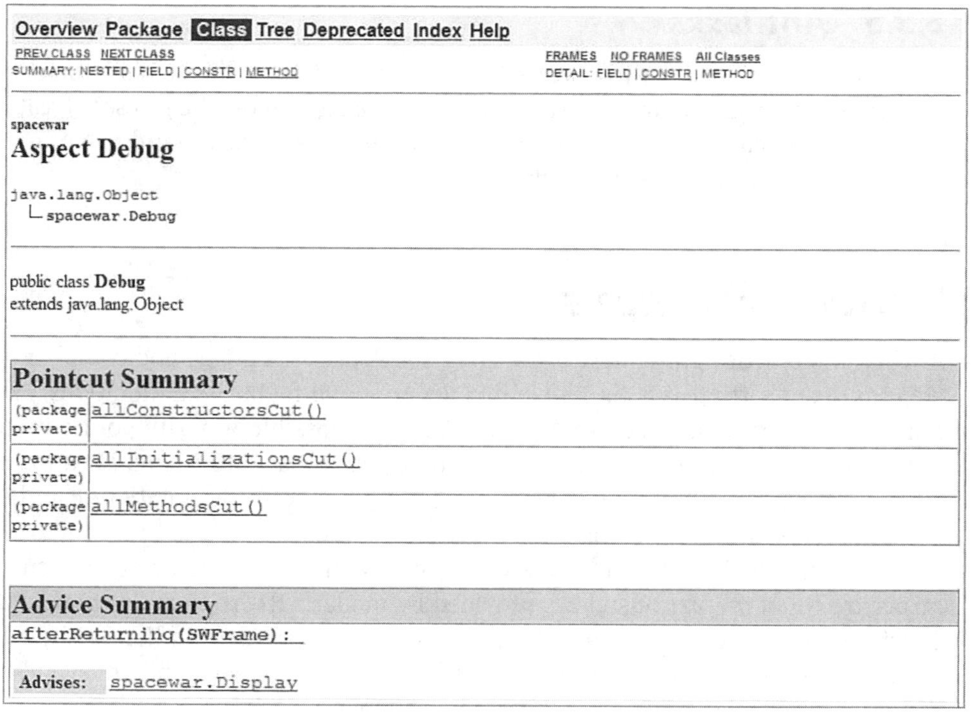

Overview Package **Class** Tree Deprecated Index Help
PREV CLASS NEXT CLASS   FRAMES NO FRAMES All Classes
SUMMARY: NESTED | FIELD | CONSTR | METHOD   DETAIL: FIELD | CONSTR | METHOD

spacewar
Aspect Debug

```
java.lang.Object
  └ spacewar.Debug
```

public class **Debug**
extends java.lang.Object

Pointcut Summary

(package private)	allConstructorsCut()
(package private)	allInitializationsCut()
(package private)	allMethodsCut()

Advice Summary

afterReturning(SWFrame) :

Advises:	spacewar.Display

Figure 6-7   *ajdoc of an aspect.*

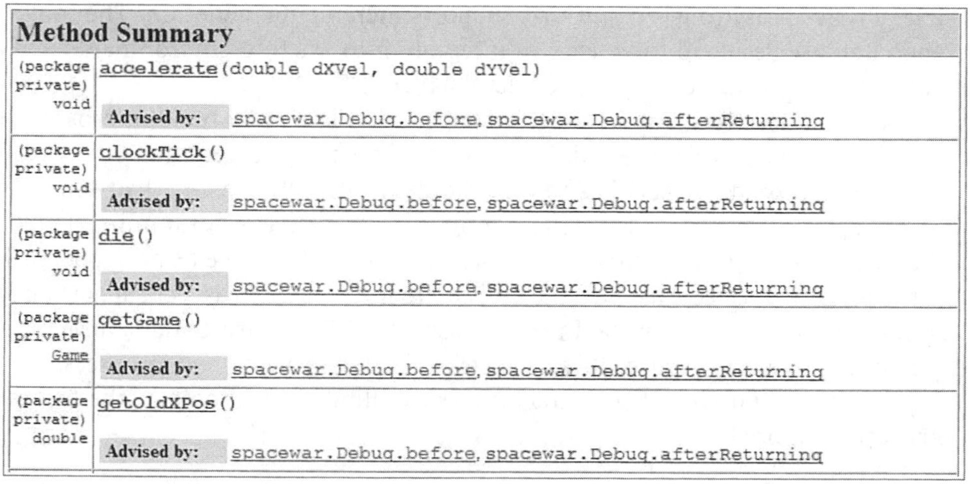

Method Summary

(package private) void	accelerate(double dXVel, double dYVel)
	Advised by: spacewar.Debug.before, spacewar.Debug.afterReturning
(package private) void	clockTick()
	Advised by: spacewar.Debug.before, spacewar.Debug.afterReturning
(package private) void	die()
	Advised by: spacewar.Debug.before, spacewar.Debug.afterReturning
(package private) Game	getGame()
	Advised by: spacewar.Debug.before, spacewar.Debug.afterReturning
(package private) double	getOldXPos()
	Advised by: spacewar.Debug.before, spacewar.Debug.afterReturning

Figure 6-8   *Crosscutting structure shown in advised methods.*

6.3.5 Ant Tasks

The Ant tasks included in the AspectJ distribution are designed to be plug-compatible with their Java counterparts wherever possible. The tasks allow the full set of features of the AspectJ compiler to be exploited, including the creation and use of aspect libraries and linking into existing class files.

6.4 FUTURE DIRECTIONS

At the time of writing, the next big step for the AspectJ language and compiler is to step up to supporting Java 5.0, including generics and metadata annotations. When annotation support is added to AspectJ, it will be possible to write pointcuts that match join points based on metadata annotations and also to introduce a form of `declare annotation` (analogous to `declare parents`)—annotations can themselves be crosscutting concerns.

In the IDE tools, the next steps are to complete the work of showing crosscutting structure in all the various views provided by modern IDEs (such as showing the effect of `declare parents` in a type hierarchy browser), ensuring that existing Java refactorings behave correctly in the presence of aspects, and to begin to add new aspect-oriented refactorings into the refactoring menu.

6.5 CONCLUDING REMARKS

The AspectJ project provides a general-purpose aspect-oriented programming language that is easy to learn and that supports incremental adoption. The tools and approach are designed to be easy to integrate into existing environments and are aimed at supporting real application development.

AspectJ goes to great lengths to support developers by making crosscutting structure explicit in IDEs and documentation. This much is required of any aspect-oriented approach. AspectJ has to work harder at its IDE support than some other approaches that work within the confines of the Java programming language (because it needs a dedicated compiler, a structure model, and editing support). This is the price that AspectJ pays for the decision to implement its aspect support directly in the programming language. In return, AspectJ makes it direct and natural for programmers to express crosscutting concerns. With a growing body of users and the availability of numerous books and articles extolling the technology, the future for AspectJ looks bright.

ACKNOWLEDGMENTS

The phrase "standing on the shoulders of giants" may be a cliché, but in this case, it is undeniably true. I consider myself fortunate to have stewardship of the AspectJ and AspectJ Development Tools projects for a time, but the credit for the success of AspectJ belongs to many people including, but not limited to, Gregor Kiczales, John Lamping, Cristina Lopes, Bill Griswold, Jeff Palm, Erik Hilsdale, Jim Hugunin, Mik Kersten, Wes Isberg, Ron Bodkin, and Andy Clement.

REFERENCES

1. APACHE ANT PROJECT. http://www.apache.org.

2. ASPECTJ DEVELOPMENT TOOLS. http://www.eclipse.org/ajdt.

3. ASPECTJ TEAM. 2004. AspectJ Programming Guide. http://www.eclipse.org/aspectj.

4. EICK, S., STEFFEN, J., AND SUMNER, E. 1992. Seesoft—A Tool for Visualizing Line Oriented Software. *IEEE Transactions on Software Engineering SE-2*, 18 (11), 957–968.

5. HILSDALE, E., AND HUGUNIN, J., 2004. Advice Weaving in AspectJ. In *3rd Int'l Conf. Aspect-Oriented Software Development (AOSD)*, (Lancaster, England), K. Lieberherr, Ed. ACM, 26–35.

6. HUGUNIN, J. 2004. Guide for developers of the AspectJ compiler and weaver. http://dev.eclipse.org/viewcvs/index.cgi/~checkout~/org.aspectj/modules/docs/developer/compiler-weaver/indext.html?rev=HEAD&content-type=text/html&cvsroot=Technology_Project.

7. LOPES, C., 2004. Aspect-Oriented Programming: A Historical Perspective. In *Aspect-Oriented Software Development*. R. Filman, T. Elrad, S. Clarke, M. Aksit Eds. Addison-Wesley, Chapter 5.

8. OSSHER, H. AND TARR, P., Using Multidimensional Separation of Concerns to (re)shape Evolving Software. *Comm. ACM 44*, 10, 43–49.

Chapter 7

Coupling Aspect-Oriented and Adaptive Programming

KARL LIEBERHERR AND DAVID H. LORENZ

Adaptive programming (AP) is a programming technique for developing *concern-shy* programs. AP can be viewed as a special case of aspect-oriented programming (AOP), and vice-versa. In this chapter, we examine the close relationship between AP and AOP and discuss their integration. The integration of AP and AOP produces better support for ubiquitous traversal-related concerns and for *concern-shy aspect-oriented programming*. We illustrate the coupling of AOP and AP by describing DJ [29, 31], a hybrid tool of Demeter and Java, and by describing DAJ [33], a hybrid tool of Demeter [32] and AspectJ.

7.1   INTRODUCTION

Aspect-oriented programming (AOP [12]) and adaptive programming (AP [16]) are closely related. Conceptually, AP techniques are a subset of general AOP techniques, but chronologically, AP appeared first. Both AP and AOP deal with separation of concerns, and both aspire to better modularize otherwise crosscutting concerns, but their perspectives are different. AOP enables the programmer to modularize crosscutting concerns. AP enables the programmer to practice concern-shy programming.

7.1.1   Concern-Shy Programming

A program is *concern-shy* if it abstracts away from some concerns it cuts across. Shy programming builds on the observation that traditional black-box composition is not abstract (disciplined) enough. Conventional black-box composition isolates the implementation from the interface, allowing the implementation to evolve independently of its interface. However, interfaces also evolve [27]. Interfaces become strongly coupled to their clients unless programmers use considerable self-discipline in coding. This discipline of programming abstracted away from certain parts of the interface is referred to as *shy programming;* shy programming lets the program recover from (or adapt to) interface changes. This principle is similar to the shyness metaphor in the Law of Demeter (LoD [18]; see Section 7.2.3) that argues that since structure evolves over time, it is best to restrict communication to just a subset of the visible objects. The AP principle, contrasted with the principle of black-box abstraction, is summarized as follows:

- **Black-box principle.** The representation of an object can be changed without affecting clients.
- **AP principle.** The interface of an object can be changed within certain parameters without affecting clients.

7.1.2   Structure-Shy Programming

Current implementations of AP apply concern-shy programming primarily to structure. Structure-shy programming provides a special-purpose embedded language that controls the traversal of objects in complex object-graph structures. Because knowledge of the graph structure is confined to small, specific statements in this special-purpose language, programs that use only these statements are immune to most effects of changing the underlying object relationships (i.e., changes to the class graph). For this reason, we sometimes use structure-shy programming as a synonym for AP. We have created several implementations of this technology. The most recent ones, DJ and DAJ, respectively, use the reflective mechanisms in Java and the aspect-oriented mechanisms in AspectJ to search the graph.

The next section presents shyness in human behavior as a motivating metaphor for adaptive behavior in structure-shy programming. Section 7.3 presents DJ, and Section 7.4 presents DAJ. Related works are described in Section 7.5.

7.2   SHYNESS AS A METAPHOR FOR ADAPTIVE BEHAVIOR

Knowledge relationships among software components can be understood by analogy to human organizations. Humans create hierarchies—such as managers, group leaders, and individual workers—so that changes in knowledge state follow restricted paths and so that not everyone has to know about all changes (see Figure 7-1). We relate those restrictions to shyness in human behavior.

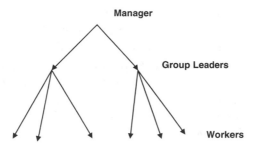

Figure 7-1   *Manager, group leaders, and workers.*

This *shyness* has three elements:

(a) Minimizing information sharing

(b) Minimizing the number of communication channels

(c) Reducing the scattering of communications

The structural alternative is organizational bedlam: having arbitrary people dependent on the work structure of arbitrary other people, requiring considerable routing and analysis with each change in process or organization.

Better software design mimics the shyness of good organizations rather than the disorderliness of bad ones. In object-oriented software systems, an important locus of shared knowledge is the class graph. It is better to have components that rely only on local information in the class graph than global knowledge of its structure. It is better to have *shy* workers and components that minimize the external knowledge of their internal behavior than ones that become trapped into the *doing* of something a particular way because others rely not just on the output but also on the process.

Better organizations also minimize communications channels so that not everyone is bothered by the chatter of routine activities. Similarly, better software systems follow a parallel in the Law of Demeter, which states that an object should "talk" only to closely related objects. The closely related object for a worker is the group leader, not the manager.

Finally, better organizations restructure information so that higher managers deal with summarized and coalesced versions of the raw facts. This allows high-level managers to better understand the many projects they are responsible for and to optimize with respect to the overall system behavior. The orders of high-level managers affect many worker projects. Each order cuts across one or more projects, and it is important that those orders are not too tied to the details in the projects. Otherwise, orders are brittle, and the managers would have to spend too much time writing and revising them. The same point applies to programming: Instead of sending an object a lot of individual requests, it is better to send one complex request that can be understood as a whole and that is not tied to many details in the object. Consider an SQL query as another example of a complex request. The SQL query abstracts away from the physical database organization, but the query optimizer will use it. Therefore, it is more efficient to send one complex SQL query to a database rather than 50 very simple SQL queries. The query optimizer of the database system can coordinate the responses to the simple queries, and the overall response time will be better.

7.2.1 How Shyness Relates to AP

The arguments for AP parallel those for structured organizations. Pure information hiding does not hide enough. Information hiding makes all public interfaces available, but minimizing sharing (shyness trait (a)) asserts that only an abstraction of those interfaces should be visible at higher levels. In AP, only high-level information about the class graph is visible at the (adaptive) programming level. This shields the program from many changes to the class graph in the same way that the manager is shielded from many of the changes in the workers' projects. The role of the group leader is played by the glue code that maps high-level information to low-level information and vice-versa (see Table 7-1).

Table 7-1   *The Correspondence Between Management and Programs*

Worker	Group Leader	Manager
Class graph	Glue code	Adaptive program

AP is related to complex requests (shyness trait (c)) by offering a declarative way of navigating through objects and executing operations along the way. This is better than sending many small data accessing requests and allows for optimal generation of correct traversal code that contains accidental details from the class graph.

7.2.2 How Shyness Relates to AOP

Aspect-oriented programming is about abstractions that cut across multiple modules [19, 34]. It can best achieve its potential if it follows the same principles as AP. Good AOP minimizes information sharing (shyness trait (a)) when aspects are only loosely coupled to base programs. Often, good aspect systems provide glue code that maps the aspect to the detailed usage context. AOP is related to complex requests (shyness trait (c)) by observing that an aspect is a complex request to modify the execution of a program. These relationships are illustrated in Table 7-2.

Table 7-2 *The Relationship Between Management and AOP*

Worker	Group Leader	Management
Program	Glue code	Aspect

7.2.3 Law of Demeter

An example of the overlap between AP and AOP is apparent in the Law of Demeter. The Law of Demeter [18, 20] is a style rule for object-oriented programming whose goal is to reduce the behavioral dependencies between classes. Its primary form asserts that a method M should only call methods (and access fields) on objects that are *preferred suppliers:* immediate parts on `this`, objects passed as arguments to M, objects that are created directly in M, and objects in global variables (in Java, `public static` fields). Limiting which methods call which other methods keeps programmers from encoding too much information about the object model into a method, thus loosening the coupling between the structure concern and the behavior concern.

To obey the Law of Demeter, methods whose ad-hoc implementation is scattered across several classes need to be cleanly localized. The result is a clean separation of various behavioral concerns from concerns about the structural information (class graph).

AP allows one to minimize the number of communication channels (shyness trait **(b)**) while nevertheless following the Law of Demeter. A study of three medium-sized object-oriented systems found that following the Law of Demeter can result in a large number of small methods that scatter and duplicate class graph information: In all three systems, 50% of the methods were fewer than two C++ statements or four Smalltalk lines long [38]. This can make it hard to understand the high-level picture of what a program does. Adaptive programming with traversal strategies and adaptive visitors in DAJ avoids this problem while providing even better support for loose coupling of concerns.

7.2.4 Law of Demeter for Concerns

The Law of Demeter for Concerns (LoDC [17]) is a style rule for programming, which states that an object should "talk" only to closely related objects that share its current concerns. A concern is any issue the designer is concerned with, such as a use case or the synchronization or logging policy for the system. Following the Law of Demeter induces adaptive programming, while following the Law of Demeter for Concerns induces aspect-oriented programming.

7.3 REFLECTIVE ADAPTIVE PROGRAMMING WITH DJ

Consider the processing of XML schema definitions [6]. Listing 7-1 is an example of an XML schema taken from an aspect-oriented web development system [14]. The schema consists of a sequence of items. Some are type definitions, and some are declarations. Verifying that all types used in the schema are either standard or locally defined is a typical consistency check.

Listing 7-1 *An example of an XML schema*

```
<xsd:schema xmlns:xsd="http://www.w3.org/2001/XMLSchema"
            xmlns:ddd="http://webjinn.org">
 <xsd:element name="structure">
  <xsd:complexType>
   <xsd:sequence>
    <xsd:element name="fields" type="Fields"/>
    <xsd:element name="comment" type="xsd:string"/>
   </xsd:sequence>
  </xsd:complexType>
 </xsd:element>
 <xsd:complexType name="Fields">
  <xsd:sequence>
   <xsd:element name="field" type="Field"/>
  </xsd:sequence>
 </xsd:complexType>
 <xsd:complexType name="Field">
  <xsd:sequence>
   <xsd:element name="attribute" type="Attribute"/>
  </xsd:sequence>
  <xsd:attribute name="name" type="xsd:NMTOKEN"/>
 </xsd:complexType>
 <xsd:complexType name="Attribute">
  <xsd:attribute name="name" type="xsd:NMTOKEN"/>
  <xsd:attribute name="value" type="xsd:string"/>
 </xsd:complexType>
</xsd:schema>
```

Figure 7-2 shows a UML class diagram that represents a small subset of the XML schema definition language. A simple algorithm for checking a schema for undefined types involves two traversals of the object structure representing the schema definition: one to collect all the types defined in the schema, and another to check each type reference to see if it is in the set of defined types.

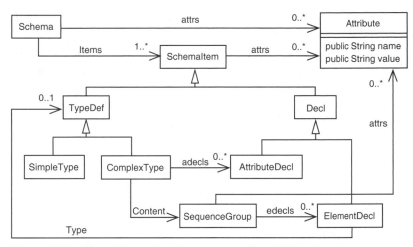

Figure 7-2   *Class hierarchy for representing XML schema.*

The actual traversal behavior, however, is quite complex. The functional behavior must be split between the `Schema`, the `Attribute`, and the other classes in order to comply with the Law of Demeter. Moreover, deciding whether to traverse a field requires knowledge of the overall class structure: for example, in `SequenceGroup`, the finding type definitions traversal method only needs to traverse the `edecls` field because an `ElementDecl` element declaration may include a `TypeDef` type definition; if the object model were extended so that an `AttributeDecl` attribute declaration could also include a type definition, the traversal method in `ComplexType` would have to be changed to traverse the `adecls` field, even though nothing about `ComplexType` itself changed.

DJ is a library of classes that make traversals like collecting all defined types and verifying all type references much easier to define, understand, and maintain. Listing 7-2 shows an implementation of the `Schema` class that defines the two traversals succinctly using the `ClassGraph` and `Visitor` classes from the `dj` package.

A `ClassGraph` instance is a simplified representation of a UML [2] class diagram; its nodes are types (classes and primitive types), and its edges are (unidirectional) associations and (bi-directional) generalizations. The default `ClassGraph` constructor builds a graph object using reflection from all the classes in the default package; a string containing a package name can be provided as a constructor argument to build a class graph from another package.

Calling the traverse method on a `ClassGraph` object does a traversal. It takes three arguments: the root of the object structure to be traversed; a string specifying the traversal strategy to be used; and an adaptive visitor object describing what to do at points in the traversal. A traversal strategy specifies the end points of the traversal, using the from keyword for the source and the to keyword for the target objects. In between, any number of constraints can be specified with via or bypassing.

Listing 7-2   *Using traverse from the DJ library*

```
import edu.neu.ccs.demeter.dj.ClassGraph;
import edu.neu.ccs.demeter.dj.Visitor;

class Schema {
  Attribute attrs[];
  SchemaItem items[];
  static final ClassGraph cg = new ClassGraph();
  public Set getDefinedTypeNames() {
    final Set def = new HashSet();
    cg.traverse(
      this,
      "from Schema via ->TypeDef,attrs,* to Attribute",
      new Visitor() {
        void before(Attribute host) {
          if (host.name.equals("name"))
            def.add(host.value);
        }
      });
    return def;
  }
  public Set getUndefinedTypeNames() {
    final Set def = getDefinedTypeNames();
    final Set undef = new HashSet();
    cg.traverse(
      this,
      "from Schema via ->Decl,attrs,* to Attribute",
      new Visitor() {
        void before(Attribute host) {
          if (host.name.equals("type")
              && !def.contains(host.value))
            undef.add(host.value);
        }
      });
    return undef;
  }
}
```

The two traversals in Listing 7-2 traverse from `Schema` to `Attribute`; in other words, they visit attributes in a schema because type names appear in attribute values for both definitions and references. They differ in their constraints: to find the names of types defined by the schema, the first traversal looks only at attributes of type definitions (`TypeDef` objects); to find the names of types referenced by the schema, the second traversal looks only at attributes of declarations (`Decl` objects). The `->TypeDef,attrs,*` syntax is a pattern specifying the set of association edges whose source is class `TypeDef` and whose label (field name) is `attrs`; the asterisk means that an edge in the set can have any target type.

Traversals of object structures are done efficiently [22]: For each object in the traversal, associations that can possibly lead to a target object are traversed sequentially (including inherited associations, subject to any constraints specified in the traversal strategy). If an object that has no possible path leading to a target object is encountered, the traversal omits searching it. For example, in the XML schema example, the items field of schema contains an array of `SchemaItem` objects; this array may contain `TypeDef` objects; since `TypeDef` is a subclass of `SchemaItem`, the elements of the array are traversed as part of the `getDefinedTypeNames` traversal. However, some of the elements may be `AttributeDecl` objects. There is no possible path to a `TypeDef` object. If one of these elements is encountered in the array, it is skipped. The `adecls` field of `ComplexType` is never traversed since it can only contain an array of `AttributeDecl` objects. Note that if the `adecls` field were a vector instead of an array, it could contain objects of any type, and so DJ would have to traverse it in case one of its elements were a `TypeDef` object or some other object that could lead to a `TypeDef`. Using the parametric polymorphism of Java 1.5 [3], this problem can be avoided: the type of `adecls` could be `List<AttributeDecl>`, and DJ would know it could avoid it.

The anonymous inner visitor class is a subtype of the `Visitor` class in the `dj` package. During a traversal with a visitor of type *V*, when an object *o* of type *T* is reached in the traversal, if there is a method on *V* named `before` whose parameter is type *T*, that method is called with *o* as the argument. Then, each field on the object is traversed if needed. Finally, before returning to the previous object, if there is a method on *V* named `after` whose parameter is type *T*, that method is called with *o* as the argument. The `Visitor` subclasses defined inline in Listing 7-3 only define one `before` method each, which is executed at `Attribute` objects, the end point of the traversal.

DJ also provides support for generic programming [28]: The `asList` method on `ClassGraph` adapts an object structure and a traversal strategy into a `List`, part of Java's Collections framework [10]. The object structure is viewed as a collection of objects whose type is the target of the traversal strategy; the collection's `iterator` performs the traversal incrementally with each call to `next`. Listing 7-3 shows how to rewrite the previous example using `asList`.

Listing 7-3 *Using the collection adaptor asList*

```
import edu.neu.ccs.demeter.dj.*;
class Schema {
  Attribute attrs[];
  SchemaItem items[];
  static final ClassGraph cg = new ClassGraph();
  public Set getDefinedTypeNames() {
    final Set def = new HashSet();
    List typeDefAttributes =
      cg.asList(
        this,
        "from Schema via ->TypeDef,attrs,* to Attribute");
    Iterator it =
    typeDefAttributes.iterator();
    while (it.hasNext()) {
      Attribute attr = (Attribute) it.next();
      if (attr.name.equals("name"))
      def.add(attr.value);
    }
    return def;
  }

  public Set getUndefinedTypeNames() {
    final Set def = getDefinedTypeNames();
    final Set undef = new HashSet();
    List declAttributes =
      cg.asList(
        this,
        "from Schema via ->Decl,attrs,* to Attribute");
    Iterator it = declAttributes.iterator();
    while (it.hasNext()) {
      Attribute attr = (Attribute) it.next();
      if (attr.name.equals("type")
          && !def.contains(attr.value))
        undef.add(attr.value);
    }
    return undef;
  }
}
```

DJ also has edge visitor methods that get executed whenever certain edges in the object graph are traversed. (So far, in our examples, visitor method execution depended only on the class of the object being traversed.)

An edge has the form `n_1(source, target)` or `n(source, 1, target)`. In the first case, the name of the part-of edge is fixed (`1`); in the second case, it is variable. `n` is either `before` or `after`. `around` is only available in an alpha version of DJ.

For a part-of edge, the signatures are matched in the order shown in Listing 7-4, where n starts with `before` or `after`. `S` is the source type of the edge, `1` is the label of the edge, and `T` is the target type of the edge. For example, if an edge `->Employee, salary, Currency` is traversed, then first the visitor method `before_salary (Employee, Currency)` is invoked if it exists, followed by `before_salary (Employee,Object)`, etc.

Listing 7-4 *The order of signature matching*

```
1.  n_1(S, T)
2.  n_1(S, Object)
3.  n_1(Object, T)
4.  n_1(Object, Object)
5.  n(S, String, T)
6.  n(S, String, Object)
7.  n(Object, String, T)
8.  n(Object, String, Object)
```

From an AOP perspective, expressions 1 through 8 in Listing 7-4 are pointcut designators for execution join points of traversals. For example, `n_1(S, Object)` selects all join points during a traversal where we traverse a part-of edge called `1` starting from an object of type `S` (bound in the first argument) and going to any kind of object (bound to the second argument).

DJ pointcut designators can only select join points in traversals, while AspectJ has a much richer set of join points [1]. The DJ pointcut designators can be simulated in AspectJ using pointcuts such as `this`, `target`, `args`, and `call`.

7.3.1 *Implementation Highlights*

In this section, we present some highlights of the implementation of DJ and some examples of interesting uses. When the `ClassGraph` constructor is called, it creates a graph object containing reflective information about all the classes in a package. However, in Java, there is no way to get a list of all classes in a package; packages are just namespaces, not containers. Moreover, the JVM only knows about classes that have already been loaded, and it only loads classes when they are referenced. Since a class graph might be constructed before many of the classes in the package have been referenced, the constructor has to discover classes some other way: it searches the class path (provided by the JVM as `System.getProperty("java.class.path")`) for all .class files in subdirectories corresponding to the package name. For each class file that is found, it calls `Class.forName()` with the class name, which causes the JVM to load the class if it hasn't already been loaded. If there are classes that need to be added to a class graph that do not exist as .class files in the class path (for example if they are loaded from the network or constructed dynamically), they must be added explicitly by calling `addClass()`.

A class graph may also be created from another class graph and a traversal strategy, forming the subgraph of classes and edges that would be traversed according to that pair. This can be used to remove unwanted paths from a class graph, such as backlinks, rather than having to add bypassing constraints to every traversal strategy.

The traverse method on `ClassGraph` is implemented in a two-stage process. First, a traversal graph is computed from the class graph and the traversal strategy (which itself is converted into a strategy graph, whose nodes are the classes mentioned in the traversal strategy and whose edges each have constraints attached to that leg of the traversal); then the object structure is traversed, using information from the traversal graph to decide where to go next at each step, and visitor methods are invoked as needed. The traversal graph computation takes time proportional to the product of the number of edges in the class graph and the number of edges in the strategy graph; since the same traversal strategy is often reused multiple times with the same class graph, the traversal graph can be saved and reused without needing to be recomputed every time. The class `TraversalGraph` has a constructor that takes a traversal strategy and a `ClassGraph` object, as well as methods `traverse` and `asList`. The traversal computation algorithm is also available as a separate package, the AP Library [21].

At each step in a traversal, the fields and methods of the current object, as well as methods on the visitor object, are inspected and invoked by reflection. Some of this reflective overhead could be avoided by generating a new class (at runtime) that invokes the appropriate fields and methods directly; this is planned for a future addition to DJ. Applications of pluggable reflection [27] combined with partial evaluation to speed up the traversal may be possible as well. The implementation of `asList` is somewhat trickier than regular traversal: the list iterator must return in the middle of the traversal whenever a target object is reached and then resume where it left off when called again. An earlier version created an ad-hoc continuation-like object that was saved and restored at each iteration, but this was error-prone and not very efficient; the current version uses a separate Java thread as a `coroutine`, suspending and resuming at each iteration. An additional method, `gather`, can be used to copy all the target objects into an `ArrayList`. This is faster still, but the list returned by `asList` has the advantage that calls to `set` on the iterator can replace target objects in the original object structure.

Java's reflection system, unlike many other meta-object protocols [11], has no mechanism for intercession: there is no way to make a new subclass of `Class` that behaves differently for certain meta-operations such as method invocation [27]. However, DJ's `Visitor` class does allow a limited form of intercession. It has the method `before(Object obj, Class cl)` (and corresponding `after`), which is invoked by the `ClassGraph.traverse` method at each traversal step. It looks for a method named `before` with a single parameter whose type is the class represented by `cl` and invokes it with `obj` as argument. This method can be overridden by a sub-class to perform more dynamic behavior based on the reified class object of the object being traversed.

7.4   ASPECTUAL ADAPTIVE PROGRAMMING WITH DAJ

DJ exemplifies how AP is conceptually integrated with Java. DJ makes the concepts of AP available as Java classes: `ClassGraph`, `Strategy`, and `Visitor`. It is interest-ing to see how AP is integrated with AspectJ. This has been the objective of the DAJ project [33, 37].

DAJ achieves a couple of goals. First, it is easy for AspectJ programmers to use AP. Only two new declarations need to be learned to use DAJ, namely strategy and traver-sal declarations. Second, it improves the performance of AP. The implementation is an order of magnitude faster than DJ and class dictionaries have been added as an optional feature.

7.4.1   Strategy Graph Intersection

While DJ works with any number of class graph views using a strategy to define each view, DAJ works with only one main class graph. Making the strategy language more expressive, particularly by adding a strategy intersection capability, compensates for this restriction. For example, we can define a strategy `eachFile` as

```
declare strategy: eachFile:
    "intersect(from CompoundFile to File, down)";
declare strategy: down:
    "from * bypassing -> *,parent,* to *";
```

where strategy `down` selects only the down links in a recursive data structure by bypassing all parent links. Strategy `eachFile` reaches all `File`-objects reachable from a `CompoundFile`-object, but only following down links.

To get the equivalent of `cg.traverse(o, whereToGo, whatAndWhenToDo)` in DAJ, a second kind of declaration, called a traversal declaration, is introduced. It defines a new method using the strategy `whereToGo` and the class of `WhatAndWhenToDo`:

```
WhatAndWhenToDo.
  declare traversal:
  void someName(): whereToGo (WhatAndWhenToDo);
```

7.4.2 Visitor Classes

`WhatAndWhenToDo` is a Java identifier naming a class (declared elsewhere) containing visitor methods that are invoked during the traversal. Arguments to the traversal will be passed to the constructor of the visitor. There are five kinds of visitor methods:

- **void** `start()` is invoked at the beginning of the traversal.
- **void** `before(ClassName)` is invoked when an object of the given class is encountered during the traversal before its fields are traversed.
- **void** `after(ClassName)` is invoked when an object of the given class is encountered during the traversal after its fields have been traversed.
- **void** finish() is invoked at the end of the traversal, that is, after all the fields of the root object have been traversed.
- `Object getReturnValue()` is invoked at the end of the traversal, and its value is returned as the result of the traversal (suitably cast to the traversal's return type).

In the future, all the capabilities in DemeterJ [32] will be added to DAJ.

Having added strategy and traversal declarations to AspectJ, it also makes sense to add a new pointcut designator to AspectJ: `traversal(s)` for a traversal strategy s. It selects all join points in the traversal defined by s and can be freely combined with other pointcut designators.

The implementation of DAJ translates the class dictionary files to class definitions with parsing methods using the ANTLR tools [36], and it translates the strategy and traversal declaration files to AspectJ introductions defining the appropriate traversal methods using the AP Library [21, 22]. It then weaves all the AspectJ files together.

In the current implementation of DAJ, we have the restriction that traversal and strategy declarations must be put into separate files. This is a small inconvenience but has the advantage that the AspectJ compiler does not need modification.

7.5   RELATED WORK

The notion of shyness is linked to the notion of quantification [7]. AOP is quantification because an aspect works with an entire family of base programs [24]. DJ [29, 31] is closely related to DemeterJ [32], a preprocessing tool that takes a *class dictionary file* (containing a textual representation of a UML class diagram, with syntax directives for parsing and printing object structures) and some *behavior files* (containing regular Java methods to be attached to the classes in the class dictionary, plus traversal method specifications, visitor methods, and *adaptive methods* that connect a traversal with a visitor class) and generates plain Java code for those classes with traversal methods attached along with a parser and some custom visitors such as for printing, copying, or comparing object structures. Demeter/C++ [15, 23] is a predecessor of DemeterJ with similar capabilities. DJ shares the same traversal strategy language and traversal graph algorithms as DemeterJ but does no code generation and is a pure-Java library.

Besides being easier to use with existing Java code, DJ has a few other advantages over DemeterJ. One is the ability to traverse classes for which the programmer does not have source code or when he or she is not able or willing to modify the source code. For example, one might traverse parts of Java's Swing library of GUI widgets. DJ can traverse public accessor methods or may even use private methods and fields if the JVM's security manager allows reflective access to private parts. Another new feature of DJ is the ability to work with subgraphs of a class graph; in DemeterJ, all traversals are computed in the context of the whole class graph defined in the class dictionary, but in DJ, you can create new class graphs by selecting a subgraph with a traversal strategy. In addition, DJ, allows components to be more generic by taking class graphs, traversal strategies, or classes to be visited as run-time parameters. These latter two advantages are due to the reification of concepts that only exist at compile-time in DemeterJ as first class objects in DJ.

An adaptive object-model [39] is an object model that is interpreted at runtime. If an object model is changed, the system changes its behavior. Java's object model can't be changed at runtime (other than dynamic class loading), but DJ interprets the object model when doing traversals.

DJ's `Visitor` class is similar to reflective visitor-beans [25] and `Walkabout` classes [35]. However, neither of those provides a language for customizing traversals. Java Object Query Language (OQL), a binding of OQL from ODMG 2.0 [4] to Java, treats query specifications much like DJ treats traversal strategy specifications [9]. An OQLQuery object can be constructed from a string describing a query; the query can then be executed by calling the execute() method on the OQLQuery object. Queries are either compiled dynamically at runtime or interpreted. An example of a query is:

```
OQLQuery query = new OQLQuery
     ("select p.getSpouse from p in persons");
Set spouses = (Set) query.execute();
```

7.6 CONCLUSION

AOP and AP have the same benefit list, namely understandability, maintainability, and reusability. The key idea behind AOP is "better modularization of concerns;" the key idea behind AP is "concern-shyness." Before the introduction of AOP, AP tried to fill both roles.

Traversal specifications can be applied to graphs other than the object graph. In particular, traversals can be applied to the dynamic call graph in AspectJ. In fact, AspectJ already uses structure-shy regular expressions to specify traversals. In AspectJ, we can write a traversal strategy: "from jp to *" in the form cflow(jp), and this qualifies as an application of structure-shy programming.

Generally, AP can benefit from AOP in that AP capabilities can be more easily implemented with an AOP language than with an object-oriented language. AOP can also benefit from AP in that those AP abilities can help in decoupling aspects from graph structures. For example, type patterns are complex pointcut descriptors that can be made structure-shy by using a traversal specification. Similarly, aspectual polymorphism [5] and parameterizing introductions with traversal specifications can help express complex introductions in AspectJ via a single structure-shy expression. Hence, the premise is that AP is a variety of AOP and AOP is a variety of AP.

In this chapter, we discussed how AOP and AP could be coupled. "Shyness" is an important concept not only for AP but also for AOP. When a module M_1 keeps only limited information about another module M_2, we say that M_1 is M_2-shy. If aspects are not "shy," their usefulness greatly decreases. There are three facets to shyness: (a) sharing only limited information, (b) communicating only to a few other modules, and (c) avoiding scattered communications. We have presented DJ, a pure-Java library supporting dynamic adaptive programming. DJ makes it easier to follow the Law of Demeter, loosening the coupling between the structure and behavior concerns and adapting to changes in the object model. It is more flexible and dynamic than the preprocessing approach taken by DemeterJ, using interpreting traversal strategies at runtime and reflection to traverse object structures with adaptive visitors. Expression of pointcuts at a higher level of abstraction is an important issue in AOP. Traversal-strategy-based pointcuts show one interesting way that this can be accomplished; contract-based pointcuts is another way [26]. AOP, specifically AspectJ, has developed a good model for expressing sets of join points in a call graph in a structure-shy way. Indeed, AspectJ is excellent for writing an object-form Law of Demeter checker that is so structure-shy that it works with any legal Java program [20, 30].

REFERENCES

1. ATTIE, P. C., KOJARSKI, S., AND LORENZ, D. H. 2003. Formalizing the Temporal Order of Join-Points. Tech. Rep. NU-CCS-03-17, College of Computer and Information Science, Northeastern University, Boston. Dec. http://www.ccs.neu.edu/ home/ lorenz/papers/reports/NU-CCIS-03-17.html.

2. BOOCH, G., RUMBAUGH, J., AND JACOBSON, I. 1999. *The Unified Modeling Language User Guide*. Addison Wesley, Reading, Massachusetts.

3. BRACHA, G., ODERSKY, M., STOUTAMIRE, D., AND WADLER, P. 1998. Making the future safe for the past: Adding genericity to the Java programming language. In *13th Conf. Object-Oriented Programming, Systems, Languages, and Applications (OOPSLA)*, (Vancouver). ACM, 183–200.

4. CATTELL, R. G. G., BARRY, D. K., BARTELS, D., BERLER, M., EASTMAN, J., GAMERMAN, S., JORDAN, D., SPRINGER, A., STRICKLAND, H., AND WADE, D. 1997. *The Object Database Standard: ODMG 2.0*. Morgan Kaufmann, San Mateo, California.

5. ERNST, E. AND LORENZ, D. H. 2003. Aspects and Polymorphism in AspectJ. In *2nd Int'l Conf. Aspect-Oriented Software Development (AOSD)*, (Boston), M. Akşit, Ed. ACM, 150–157.

6. FALLSIDE, D. C. 2000. XML Schema part 0: Primer. Tech. rep., W3C. Oct. http://www.w3.org/TR/xmlschema-0/.

7. FILMAN, R. E. AND FRIEDMAN, D. P. 2000. Aspect-oriented programming is quantification and obliviousness. In *Workshop on Advanced Separation of Concerns (OOPSLA)*, (Minneapolis). http://trese.cs.utwente.nl/Workshops/OOPSLA2000/papers/filman.pdf.

8. GAMMA, E., HELM, R., JOHNSON, R., AND VLISSIDES, J. 1995. *Design Patterns: Elements of Reusable Object-Oriented Software*. Addison-Wesley, Reading, Massachusetts.

9. HARRISON, C. 1994. AQL: An adaptive query language. M.S. thesis, Northeastern University, Boston. ftp://ftp.ccs.neu.edu/pub/people/lieber/theses/harrison/thesis.ps.

10. JAVASOFT. Collections framework overview. http://java.sun.com/products/jdk/1.2/docs/guide/collections/overview.html.

11. KICZALES, G., DES RIVIERES, J., AND BOBROW, D. G. 1991. *The Art of the Metaobject Protocol*. MIT Press, Cambridge, Massachusetts.

12. KICZALES, G., LAMPING, J., MENDHEKAR, A., MAEDA, C., LOPES, C., LOINGTIER, J.-M., AND IRWIN, J. 1997. Aspect-oriented programming. In *ECOOP'97 Object-Oriented Programming, 11th European Conference,* M. Akşit and S. Matsuoka, Eds. LNCS, vol. 1241. Springer-Verlag, Berlin, 220–242.

13. KOJARSKI, S., LIEBERHERR, K., LORENZ, D. H., AND HIRSCHFELD, R. 2003. Aspectual reflection. In *Software engineering Properties of Languages for Aspect Technologies (SPLAT, AOSD),* (Boston). http://www.daimi.au.dk/~eernst/splat03/papers/Sergei_Kojarski.ps.

14. KOJARSKI, S. AND LORENZ, D. H. 2003. Domain Driven Web Development with WebJinn. In *OOPSLA 2003 Special Track on Domain Driven Development,* Int' Conf. Object-Oriented Programming, Systems and Applications (OOPSLA), (Anaheim, California), ACM, 53–65. http://www.webjinn.org.

15. LIEBERHERR, K. J. 1992. Component enhancement: An adaptive reusability mechanism for groups of collaborating classes. In *Information Processing '92, 12th World Computer Congress* (Madrid), J. van Leeuwen, Ed. Elsevier, 179–185.

16. LIEBERHERR, K. J. 1996. *Adaptive Object-Oriented Software: The Demeter Method with Propagation Patterns*. PWS Publishing Company, Boston.

17. LIEBERHERR, K. J. 2004. Controlling the Complexity of Software Designs. Keynote invited talk at *26th Int'l Conf. Software Engineering (ICSE),* (Edinburgh, Scotland).

18. LIEBERHERR, K. J. AND HOLLAND, I. 1989. Assuring good style for object-oriented programs. *IEEE Software 6,* 5 (Sept.), 38–48.

19. LIEBERHERR, K. J., LORENZ, D. H., AND OVLINGER, J. 2003. Aspectual Collaborations: Combining Modules and Aspects. *The Computer Journal 46,* 5 (Sept.), 542–565. Special issue on AOP. http://www.ccs.neu.edu/home/lorenz/papers/ac/.

20. LIEBERHERR, K. J., LORENZ, D. H., AND WU, P. 2003. A case for statically executable advice: Checking the Law of Demeter with AspectJ. In *2nd Int'l Conf. Aspect-Oriented Software Development (AOSD),* (Boston), M. Akşit, Ed. ACM, 40–49.

21. LIEBERHERR, K. J. AND PATT-SHAMIR, B. 1997. Traversals of object structures: Specification and efficient implementation. Tech. Rep. NU-CCS-97-15, College of Computer Science, Northeastern University, Boston. Sept. http://www.ccs.neu.edu/research/demeter/AP-Library/.

22. LIEBERHERR, K. J., PATT-SHAMIR, B., AND ORLEANS, D. 2004. Traversals of object structures: Specification and efficient implementation. *ACM Transactions on Programming Languages and Systems 26*, 2, 370–412.

23. LIEBERHERR, K. J., SILVA-LEPE, I., AND XIAO, C. 1994. Adaptive object-oriented programming using graph-based customization. *Comm. ACM 37*, 5 (May), 94–101.

24. LOPES, C. V., DOURISH, P., LORENZ, D. H., AND LIEBERHERR, K. 2003. Beyond AOP: Toward Naturalistic Programming. In *OOPSLA 2003 Special Track on Onward! Seeking New Paradigms & New Thinking. ACM SIGPLAN Notices 38*, 12 (Dec), 34–43.

25. LORENZ, D. H. 1998. Visitor beans: An aspect-oriented pattern. In *Workshop on Aspect Oriented Programming (ECOOP)*, (Brussels). http://trese.cs.utwente.nl/aop-ecoop98/papers/Lorenz.pdf.

26. LORENZ, D. H. AND SKOTINIOTIS, T. 2003. Contracts and Aspects. Tech. Rep. NU-CCS-03–13, College of Computer and Information Science, Northeastern University, Boston. Dec. http://www.ccs.neu.edu/home/lorenz/papers/reports/NU-CCIS-03-13.html.

27. LORENZ, D. H. AND VLISSIDES, J. 2003. Pluggable reflection: Decoupling meta-interface and implementation. In *Int'l Conf. Software Engineering (ICSE)*, (Portland, Oregon). ACM, 3–13.

28. MUSSER, D. R. AND STEPANOV, A. A. 1994. Algorithm-oriented generic libraries. *Software Practice and Experience 24*, 7 (July), 623–642.

29. NEERAJ SANGAL, N., FARRELL, E., LIEBERHERR, K., AND LORENZ, D. H. 1999. Interaction Schemata: Compiling Interactions to Code. In *Technology of Object-Oriented Languages and Systems (TOOLS 30)*. (Santa Barbara, California), IEEE, 268–277.

30. NG, D., KAELI, D. R., KOJARSKI, S., AND LORENZ, D. H. 2004. Program Comprehension Using Aspects. In *ICSE 2004 Workshop on Directions in Software Engineering Environments (WoDiSEE'2004)*, (Edinburgh, Scotland). http://www.ccs. neu.edu/home/lorenz/papers/wodisee04/.

31. ORLEANS, D. AND LIEBERHERR, K. 2001. DJ: Dynamic Adaptive Programming in Java. In *Reflection'01, 3rd Int'l Conf.*, A. Yonezawa and S. Matsuoka, Eds. LNCS, vol. 2192. Springer-Verlag, Berlin, 73–80.

32. ORLEANS, D. AND LIEBERHERR, K. 2001. DemeterJ. Tech. rep., Northeastern University, Boston. http://www.ccs.neu.edu/research/demeter/DemeterJava/.

33. ORLEANS, D. AND LIEBERHERR, K. 2003. DAJ: Demeter in AspectJ. Tech. rep., Northeastern University, Boston. Jan. http://www.ccs.neu.edu/research/demeter/DAJ/.

34. OVLINGER, J. 2004. Combining Aspects and Modules. Ph.D. thesis, Northeastern University, Boston. http://www.ccs.neu.edu/ research/demeter/ theses/ovlinger/ thesis.pdf.

35. PALSBERG, J. AND JAY, C. B. 1998. The essence of the visitor pattern. In *22nd Int'l Computer Software and Applications Conference (COMPSAC)*, (Vienna). IEEE, 9–15.

36. PARR, T. AND QUONG, R. 1995. ANTLR: A predicated-LL(k) parser generation. *Software Practice and Experience 25*, 7, 789–810.

37. SUNG, J. 2002. Aspectual concepts. M.S. thesis, Northeastern University, Boston. http://www.ccs.neu.edu/research/demeter/DAJ/index-john.html.

38. WILDE, N. AND HUITT, R. 1992. Maintenance support for object-oriented programs. *IEEE Transactions on Software Engineering 18*, 12 (Dec.), 1038–1044.

39. YODER, J. W. AND RAZAVI, R. 2000. Metadata and adaptive object-models. In *ECOOP 2000 Workshop Reader*. LNCS, vol. 1964, Springer-Verlag, Berlin, 104–112.

Chapter 8

Untangling Crosscutting Models with CAESAR

MIRA MEZINI AND KLAUS OSTERMANN

Since the structured programming movement in the 1970s, programming language research has concentrated on mechanisms for encoding *hierarchical* models, that is, mechanisms for viewing a system at more or less detail. This works well if we assume that real-world systems can be organized in mind-independent concept hierarchies. However, different perspectives on a system may yield models that are not hierarchically related to each other. Since it is not possible to represent such *crosscutting models* in traditional languages, we are forced to structure software systems into hierarchical models by arbitrarily choosing one of the crosscutting models as the primary decomposition criteria. This arbitrary choice of the primary model results in code tangling and scattering.

We argue that aspect-oriented (AO) languages need better support for crosscutting models. We emphasize that join point interception, while an important cornerstone to modularizing crosscutting models, does not alone solve these problems.

To alleviate these problems, we propose CAESAR. With CAESAR, it is possible to implement different pieces of software with respect to different crosscutting models (encoded as so-called *collaboration interfaces*) and later combine them on-demand by means of a special translator called *binding*. CAESAR's strengths are in the reuse and componentization of aspects, allowing us to use aspects polymorphically. We introduce the notion of aspectual polymorphism as a generalization of subtype polymorphism to crosscutting models and propose a novel concept for dynamic aspect deployment in order to realize aspectual polymorphism. Static type safety is preserved due to the introduction of virtual classes and family polymorphism.

8.1 INTRODUCTION

As early as 1972, Parnas [22] noted that the criteria that we choose for decomposing software systems into modules have an important impact on the software engineering properties of the resulting system. For example, a data-centric decomposition eases changes in the representation of data structures [22], whereas function-centric decomposition makes it easy to modify functions of the system or add new features [10]. With the aspect-oriented software development paradigm, the decomposition problem is considered under a new light: The question is now not as much about which criteria to choose as it is about how to support the decomposition of systems simultaneously according to several independent criteria. Such simultaneous decompositions are needed because our perception of the world and especially our perception of software systems depend heavily on this idea: Observing a software system from different perspectives may imply completely different decompositions of the concerns, yielding *crosscutting models*.

For a technical definition of the term "crosscutting," the reader is referred to Masuhara and Kiczales [16]. Here we give an informal (graphical) characterization. Consider Figure 8-1. Each shape stands for a particular object (in the most general sense) of a software system. We have three options for organizing this space: by size (see Figure 8-2), by shape (see Figure 8-3), or by color (see Figure 8-4). The resulting classifications are all equally reasonable models of the space, but they are not hierarchically related. That is, they do not represent more or less detailed views of the space.

Figure 8-1 *Abstract concern space.*

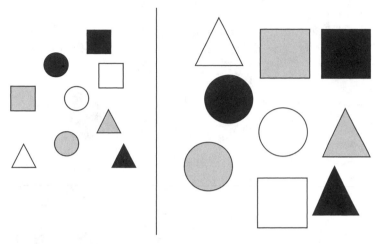

Figure 8-2 *Divide by size.*

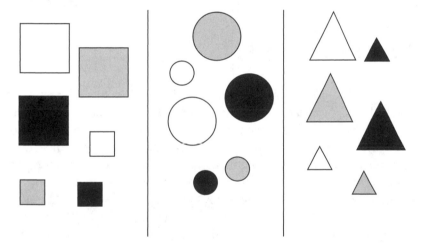

Figure 8-3 *Divide by shape.*

Informally speaking, a model M_1 would be a specialization of another model M_2 if, for each class[1] $C_1 \in M_1$, there is a class $C_2 \in M_2$ such that C_1 is contained in C_2. Indeed, if we consider, for example, the *size* and *shape* of the models, some of the objects in the class *rectangle* in the *shape* model are classified as *big* in the *size*

---

1. The term "class" is used here to denote an element of the partition of the space implied by a model.

model, while others are contained in the class *small*. Being independent, not specializations of each other, is (roughly speaking) what characterizes "crosscutting models"—their units of decomposition intersect but do not subsume each other.

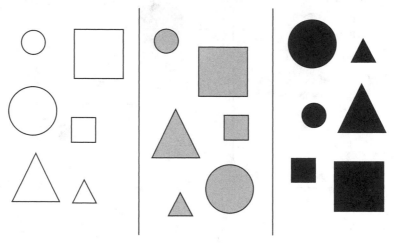

Figure 8-4 *Divide by color.*

The motivation for the AO paradigm is that traditional software decomposition techniques lack appropriate support for crosscutting models. They assume that real-world systems have mind-independent concept hierarchies. As a result, most parts of a software system are defined in terms of the same global program structure. While multiple models of the system might actually be supported, these models are hierarchical, rather than crosscutting, views of a system. With decomposition techniques so far, we organize the system as a hierarchy of packages/classes/procedures, and we can have a more or less detailed view of the system. This is also reflected in the idea of organizing software in *layers,* another invention of structured programming [7]. The key point here is that crosscutting is not appropriately supported.

With a mind-independent hierarchical decomposition, we have to choose one fixed classification sequence, such as the one shown in Figure 8-5. In this example, the classification sequence was *color, shape, size*. The problem with such a fixed classification sequence is that all relevant independent decomposition criteria have to be forced into it. The result is code scattering and tangling. Figure 8-5 illustrates the scattering problem by means of the concern *circle*, whose definition is scattered around the hierarchical decomposition (cuts across the modular units of the color-driven decomposition of the system). Only the color concern (the first element in the classification sequence) is cleanly separated into *white, grey*, and *black*, but even this decomposition is not satisfactory because the color concern is still blended (tangled) with other concerns. We call this problem the *arbitrariness of the primary model.*

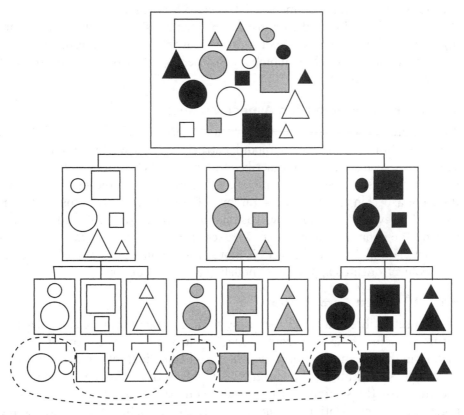

Figure 8-5 *Arbitrariness of the decomposition hierarchy.*

The 'arbitrariness of the primary model' problem is related to the 'tyranny of the dominant decomposition' [25], meaning that "existing languages and formalisms generally provide only one, dominant dimension along which to separate—e.g., by object or by function" [25]. We prefer the term 'arbitrariness of the primary model' and its formulation given here, because it emphasizes that the problem arises not because only one dominant decomposition *mechanism*, such as classes versus functions, is supported. One can actually simulate functional decomposition in an object-oriented language [28]. The problem is the primary mental model: Hierarchical decomposition requires a primary model and other models that are subordinate, as illustrated in Figure 8-5.

8.1.1   *Requirements on Language Support*

Having characterized the term "crosscutting model" and the problems resulting from the lack of support for such models, let us consider the requirements they impose on the module definition and composition mechanisms. In this discussion, the term *aspect* is used to denote a piece of software that is expressed in terms of a particular model and that needs to be combined with other aspects, which are encoded in different crosscutting models.

8.1.1.1   Multi-Abstraction Aspect Modules

Appropriate module constructs are needed to express an aspect as a set of collaborating abstractions comprising the modular structure of the world as seen by the aspect. This allows each aspect to be described in terms of its *own* model, thereby escaping the arbitrariness of the primary model. For example, it should be possible to define the color aspect in terms of the hierarchy in Figure 8-4, i.e., in terms of the concepts "white," "grey," and "black," as well as relations between them. The advantage of supporting the definition of an aspect as a set of mutually recursive abstractions that interact via well-defined interfaces is more or less a direct derivate of the advantages of the object-oriented approach to modeling a world of discourse.

8.1.1.2   Aspect Composition

Given a set of independent crosscutting multi-abstraction models, we need mechanisms to define how they come together during the execution of the system, including the specification of *when/where* and *how* different models join the execution. The specification of *when/where* involves the definition of points in the execution of the system and eventually conditions under which models come together. The specification of *how* involves mappings between abstractions in different models. This is because values comprising the state of the system at a certain execution point are, in general, simultaneously instances of different abstractions (are classified under different classes) in different crosscutting models.

8.1.1.3   Reuse of Aspect Implementation and Bindings

Modules for expressing individual aspects should follow the open-closed principle [17]. On the one hand, they should be self-contained, capturing the "inherent" structure and behavior of one particular aspect independent of other aspects. On the other hand, due to being partial, perspective-specific views of a system, individual aspects cannot alone capture the complete system definition. They must somehow rely on compositions to fill in the other parts of the definition. Given this distinction between the "closed" and "open" parts of an aspect, the question is how to capture the interaction between them so that their definitions, the *aspect implementation* and *aspect binding*, can be reused independently. In the following, we briefly explain why such reuse makes sense.

An aspect implementation that is tightly coupled with a particular aspect binding, by the virtue of being defined within the same module, cannot be reused with other possible bindings. Hence, this particular aspect implementation must be rewritten for every meaningful binding, thereby rendering the application tangled, as the aspect implementation itself becomes crosscutting. Especially for non-trivial aspects with complex implementations, this rewriting of the aspect implementation is tedious and error-prone.

An aspect binding that is tightly coupled to a specific aspect implementation is also undesirable. A binding translates the concepts, terms, and abstractions of the application's world into the world of the particular aspect domain. Its usage is better not limited to a specific aspect implementation. For example, consider the calculation of shortest paths graphs modeled as an aspect in terms of edge and node abstractions. Consider now the calculation of shortest paths in a computer network for efficient routing. Binding a shortest path calculation aspect would involve mapping concepts of edges and nodes to respective abstractions in the aspect defining the structure of a computer network. Now, it makes sense to reuse this binding with different possible shortest path algorithms, taking advantage of their different performance properties.

8.1.1.4 Aspectual Polymorphism

Given that the intelligence of the system, i.e., of the entities making up the running system, is distributed among several equally important crosscutting models, it is important to support a new kind of polymorphism, *aspectual polymorphism*. Aspectual polymorphism is the counterpart of the subtype polymorphism in object-oriented languages. *Subtype polymorphism* allows us to write some polymorphic functionality *pf* to a high-level model of the system *HM* (a set of types, *TS*) and polymorphically reuse it with any detailed model conforming to *HM* (consisting of subtypes of the types in *TS* used within the definition of *pf*). We could also say that usual subtype polymorphism is *hierarchical:* It fits the hierarchical decomposition mechanisms available in object-oriented languages.

The idea behind aspectual polymorphism is that we want to be polymorphic not only within a hierarchy of models but also across independent crosscutting models. Aspectual polymorphism allows us to write polymorphic functionality to one of the crosscutting models of the system and combine it polymorphically with code that is written to any other crosscutting model.

To make things more concrete, consider a hierarchy that divides figures into different shapes, as in Figure 8-3.[2] This means that it is possible to write a method with a `Figure` parameter that is polymorphic with respect to the shape of the figure. Aspectual polymorphism means that polymorphism is available with respect to any hierarchical decomposition. In terms of the example, this means that the code can simultaneously be used polymorphically with respect to color and size of figures as well!

Aspectual polymorphism is strongly related to the idea of *fluid aspect-oriented programming,* the "ability to temporarily shift a program (or other software model) to a different structure to do some piece of work with it, and then shift it back" [13]. Let us see how usual object-oriented polymorphism via late binding fits into this picture: Calling a method `m(X x)` with a parameter x that can be assigned polymorphically (i.e., x might refer to an instance of a subclass of X) at runtime can be seen as temporarily (during the execution of the method) shifting or transforming this method so that calls to methods of the parameter object are dispatched to the method implementations of the respective class of x. In this way, usual late binding can be seen as a primitive form of fluidity. It is limited, because one can only "transform" with respect to our single decomposition hierarchy.

8.1.2   Contribution and Structure of the Chapter

In this chapter, we argue that existing aspect-oriented approaches do not properly satisfy the requirements stated previously. Section 8.2 argues that the concepts that have been in the focus of aspect-oriented research, join points (points in the execution of a base program to intercept) and advice (how to react at these points), are only a *part* of the solution concerning the arbitrariness of the primary model. More powerful means for structuring aspect code are needed on top of join point interception (JPI). To keep the discussion focused and to clarify our terminology, in Section 8.2, we concentrate on join point/advice approaches only. In Section 8.6, we consider the deficiencies of other approaches.

To resolve the problems discussed in Section 8.2, we propose the CAESAR model in Section 8.3. CAESAR is based on the notion of collaboration interfaces (CIs) [19] as a means to better support a-posteriori integration of independent components into existing applications. We show that CIs and the related notions of separated CI implementations and CI bindings, once properly adapted to the needs of aspect-orientation, can also be applied to support a more modular structuring of aspect code and better

---

2. In Figure 8-3, the figures represent abstract concepts and not graphical figures, but for the purpose of this example, let's just consider them as graphical figures.

aspect reuse. In Section 8.4, we evaluate CAESAR with respect to the problems identified in Section 8.2. The current state of an implementation of the model is discussed in Section 8.5, related work in Section 8.6, and future directions in Section 8.7.

8.2 JOIN POINT INTERCEPTION

In this section, we discuss the deficiencies of a JPI-based approach to aspect structuring. The discussion in this section is in no way a critique of the notions of JPIs and advices. On the contrary, these are pivotal concepts of aspect-oriented languages. This work emphasizes the need for higher-level module concepts *on top* of them.

To illustrate the problems with JPI, we examine the implementation of the observer pattern in AspectJ proposed by Hannemann and Kiczales [12], shown in Listings 8-1 and 8-2. Listing 8-1 shows a reusable implementation of the observer protocol in AspectJ, while Listing 8-2 binds it to particular classes.

Listing 8-1 *Reusable observer protocol in AspectJ*

```
public abstract aspect ObserverProtocol {
 protected interface Subject { }
 protected interface Observer { }
 private WeakHashMap perSubjectObservers;
 protected List getObservers(Subject s) {
   if (perSubjectObservers == null)
      perSubjectObservers = new WeakHashMap();
   List observers =
    (List) perSubjectObservers.get(s);
   if ( observers == null ) {
     observers = new LinkedList();
     perSubjectObservers.put(s, observers);
   }
   return observers;
 }
 public void addObserver(Subject s,Observer o){
   getObservers(s).add(o);
 }
 public void removeObserver(Subject s,Observer o){
   getObservers(s).remove(o);
 }
 abstract protected void
   updateObserver(Subject s, Observer o);

 abstract protected pointcut subjectChange(Subject s);
```

```
after(Subject s): subjectChange(s) {
  Iterator iter = getObservers(s).iterator();
  while ( iter.hasNext() )
     updateObserver(s, ((Observer)iter.next()));
}
}
```

Listing 8-2 *Binding of observer protocol in AspectJ*

```
public aspect ColorObserver extends ObserverProtocol
  declare parents: Point implements Subject;
  declare parents: Line implements Subject;
  declare parents: Screen implements Observer;

  protected pointcut subjectChange(Subject s):
    (call(void Point.setColor(Color)) ||
    call(void Line.setColor(Color)) ) && target(s);

  protected void updateObserver(Subject s, Observer o) {
     ((Screen)o).display("Color change.");
  }
}
```

The basic idea in Listing 8-1 is that the aspect `ObserverProtocol` declares an *abstract pointcut* that represents change events in the `Subject` classes. The empty interfaces `Subject` and `Observer` are marker interfaces that are used in the binding to map the application classes to their roles. The observers for each subject are stored in a global `WeakHashMap` (the weak references are required in order to prevent a memory leak) that maps a subject to a list of observers. In case of a subject change, all observers are notified by means of the abstract method `updateObserver()`. This method is overridden in the binding aspect in order to fill in the appropriate update logic.

This organization has two primary advantages. First, the code in Listing 8-1 is indeed a reusable implementation of the observer protocol: Nothing in the implementation is specific to a particular binding of this functionality. This is because the authors recognize the need to separate aspect implementation and aspect binding. Second, the same role, e.g., `Subject`, can be mapped to multiple different classes, e.g., `Point` and `Line`, as in Listing 8-2. It would also be no problem to assign two roles, e.g., `Subject` and `Observer`, to the same class or to assign the same role twice to the same class in two different bindings. For example, a `Point` can be simultaneously a subject concerning coordinate changes as well as color changes. In terms of [24], the observer "component" in Listing 8-1 is independently extensible.

These features are probably the rationale for the author's decision against an alternative (simpler) implementation: declaring `addObserver()` and `removeObserver()` in the interface `Subject` and then (in the binding) injecting these methods into the corresponding classes by means of a so-called *introduction*, AspectJ's open class mechanism. Similarly, a `LinkedList` could be introduced into every `Subject` class, thereby rendering the `perSubjectObservers` map unnecessary. However, with this solution, a class could not have two different instantiations of the `Subject` role, because then the class would have multiple implementations of the same method (e.g., `addObserver()`), producing a compilation error. We would lose independent extensibility.

Now, let us take a critical look at this solution and identify the problems.

8.2.1 *Lack of Support for Multi-Abstraction Aspects*

Note that all methods in Listings 8-1 and 8-2 are top-level methods of the enclosing aspect class. For example, `addObserver()`, which is conceptually a method of the subject role, is a top-level method whose first parameter is the respective `Subject` object. This design leads to a poor separation of concerns inside the aspect: The enclosing class contains all methods of all abstractions that are defined in the particular aspect, and therefore easily becomes bloated. In a way, this is a rather procedural style of programming, contradicting one of the fundamentals of object-oriented programming: A type definition contains all methods that belong to its interface. It also contradicts the aspect-oriented vision of defining crosscutting modules in terms of their own modular structure. The structure of the aspect in Listing 8-1 is one of empty abstractions and unstructured method definitions. As such, it is not particularly modular.

The implications of this design decision are not only conceptual but also practical. First, we cannot pass objects that play a role to other classes that expect an instance of that role. Envisage, for illustration, a role `Comparable` with a method `compareTo()`. If we want to pass an object as a `Comparable` to another class, e.g., a sorting class, then the approach in Listings 8-1 and 8-2 based on introducing an empty interface and encoding all methods as top-level methods of the enclosing class does not work. The alternative would be to use AspectJ's introduction mechanism to introduce the interface and its methods directly into the respective classes. However, doing that loses independent extensibility, as discussed previously. For example, a `Point` could be compared to another `Point` by means of their geometrical distance $\sqrt{x^2 + y^2}$ as well as their Manhattan distance $|x| + |y|$ to the origin, which would require two independent implementations of the `Comparable` abstraction.

A similar problem shows up when there are interactions between the abstractions that build up the aspect's model of the world—`Subject` and `Observer` in our example—is needed. The interaction in Listing 8-1 is very simple: A subject passes itself on, calling the `notify` method on each observer, but the parameter never gets used in the binding of the aspect in Listing 8-2. It is more realistic that observers would want more detailed information of the state change that actually happened on the subject's site. This would require some query methods in the interface of the subject. Using the AspectJ design "pattern" exemplified in Listings 8-1 and 8-2, where abstractions are type-less, we would have to declare such query methods also at the top level, e.g., `getState(Subject s)`. The query methods would have to be declared abstract in Listing 8-1 since their implementation is binding-specific and should be implemented by the concrete binding subaspect in Listing 8-2. However, it is not possible to implement different query methods for `Point` and `Line`. That is, it is not possible to dynamically dispatch with regard to the type of the base objects being decorated with the subject functionality.

With the solution in Listings 8-1 and 8-2, it is also awkward to associate state with the individual abstractions in the definition of the aspect. For example, the observers of all subjects are stored in a global hash map `perSubjectObservers`. Besides the dangers of such a global bottleneck, the access and management of state becomes clumsy. The example in Listing 8-1 is relatively simple, because state is associated with only one of the abstractions (`Subject`), and this state consists of only one "field." However, the general case is that multiple abstractions in the module structure of the aspect may declare multiple fields. A simple example would be an implementation where observers maintain a history of the observed state change, e.g., when they need to react on sequences of events rather than on individual changes. If we consider the case that all roles need many different fields, then the code might very easily become a mess if all these fields are hosted by the outer aspect.

The problem with modeling state becomes worse when we consider the case of role inheritance, e.g., `SpecialSubject` inheriting from `Subject`. In this case, we would end up simulating shared data fields manually. This problem with modeling state applies to the aspect binding as well. There, we might want to associate state with the objects that are mapped to the aspect roles, for example, in order to cache computed values.

Summarizing the problems so far, what we would like to have is a nested class structure of aspect implementation and aspect binding within which we can assign methods and state to every aspect role in isolation.

8.2.2 Lack of Support for Sophisticated Mapping

The second kind of problem with the solution in Listings 8-1 and 8-2 is that the mapping from aspect abstractions to base classes by means of the `declare parents` construct works only when each aspect abstraction has a corresponding base class to which it is mapped directly. However, this is not always the case. For example, consider a scenario in which there is no class `Line` and every `Point` object has a collection of adjacent points. If we want to map this data structure to a graph aspect defined in terms of `Node` and `Edge` abstractions, then an edge would be represented by two adjacent points, but there is no abstraction in the base application to which we can map the `Edge` abstraction. The latter is only implicitly and indirectly represented by the collections of adjacent points.

8.2.3 *Lack of Support for Reusable Aspect Bindings*

Third, every aspect binding is coupled to one particular implementation. For example, the `ColorObserver` binding in Listing 8-2 is hardwired to the observer pattern implementation in Listing 8-1, although the binding itself is not dependent on the implementation details of the observer pattern. The observer pattern is not a very good example to illustrate the usefulness of a binding that can be used with many different implementations. A better example is that of an aspect binding that maps an arbitrary data structure, such as the classes of an abstract syntax tree, to a general tree representation. Many different implementations of a tree make sense in conjunction with such a binding, for example, one that displays trees on the screen or one that performs algorithms on trees. That is, one might want to be able to write some functionality that is parameterized with a particular binding type but that is polymorphic with respect to the implementation. However, this is not possible when the binding is coupled to the implementation.

8.2.4 *Lack of Support for Aspectual Polymorphism*

The fourth deficiency concerns aspect deployment. We say that the `ColorObserver` aspect in Listing 8-2 is statically deployed. By this, we mean that once compiled together with the package containing the figure classes, the changes in the particular points in the execution of point and line objects implied by the `ColorObserver` aspect are effective. It is not possible to determine at runtime whether to apply the aspect at all or which implementation of the aspect to apply, e.g., a LinkedList version or one with asynchronous notifications. We say that *aspectual polymorphism* is missing in the sense that the code is not polymorphic with respect to the types and implementations of the aspects affecting it after compilation.

8.3 *THE CAESAR MODEL*

A core feature of CAESAR is the notion of an *aspect collaboration interface (ACI for short)*—an interface definition for aspects with multiple mutually recursive nested types. The purpose of an ACI is the decoupling of aspect implementations and aspect bindings, which are defined in independent but indirectly connected modules. The idea is that while being independent of each other, these modules implement disjoint parts of a common ACI, which indirectly relates them as parts of a whole. We illustrate our ideas also by means of the observer example. Listings 8-3, 8-4, and 8-5 show an ACI for the observer protocol, an aspect implementation, and an aspect binding, respectively. We discuss each in turn.

Listing 8-3 *ACI for observer protocol*

```
interface ObserverProtocol {
   interface Subject {
     provided void addObserver(Observer o);
     provided void removeObserver(Observer o);
     provided void changed();
     expected String getState();
   }
   interface Observer { expected void notify(Subject s); }
}
```

Listing 8-4 *Sample impl. of observer protocol*

```
class ObserverProtocolImpl implements ObserverProtocol {
   class Subject {
     List observers = new LinkedList();
     void addObserver(Observer o) { observers.add(o);}
     void removeObserver(Observer o) {
        observers.remove(o);
     }
     void changed() {
        Iterator it = observers.iterator();
        while ( iter.hasNext() )
          ((Observer)iter.next()).notify(this);
     }
   }
}
```

Listing 8-5 *Sample binding of observer protocol*

```
class ColorObserver binds ObserverProtocol {
   class PointSubject binds Subject wraps Point {
     String getState() {
```

```
      return "Point colored "+wrappee.getColor();
  }
}
class LineSubject binds Subject wraps Line {
  String getState() {
    return "Line colored "+wrappee.getColor();
  }
}
class ScreenObserver binds Observer wraps Screen {
  void notify(Subject s) {
    wrappee.display("Color changed: "+s.getState());
  }
}
after(Point p): (call(void p.setColor(Color)))
    { PointSubject(p).changed(); }
after(Line l): (call(void l.setColor(Color)))
    { LineSubject(l).changed(); }
}
```

8.3.1 *Aspect Collaboration Interfaces*

An ACI consists, in general, of several mutually recursive nested ACIs, one for each abstraction in the modular structure of the aspect. The ACI `ObserverProtocol` in Listing 8-3, for example, has two nested ACIs, `Subject` and `Observer`, that are mutually recursive in that the name of each type is used in the definition of the other. A simple ACI which does not contain other nested ACIs (e.g., `Subject`) is a special kind of interface. It lays down a bidirectional communication protocol between any possible implementation and binding of the corresponding abstraction. It does so by distinguishing between two part-interfaces: the *provided* and the *expected facets* of the abstraction, consisting of methods declared with the modifiers `provided` and `expected`, respectively. Hence, we can redefine an ACI as consisting of expected and provided declarations for the aspect as a whole as well as a set of mutually recursive nested ACIs, one for each abstraction in the modular structure of the aspect. The provided facet of an aspect lays down what the aspect provides to any context in which it is applied. The observer ACI in Listing 8-3 specifies that any implementation of `ObserverProtocol` must provide an implementation of the three provided methods of `Subject`.[3] On the other hand, the expected facet of an aspect makes explicit

---

3. In this example, the `Observer` abstraction does not have any provided methods. However, one can easily think of other examples where more than one abstraction declares a non-empty provided facet.

what the aspect requires of the context in which it is applied in order to be able to supply what the provided facet promises. Hence, the expected facet declares methods whose implementation is binding-specific.

Consider for instance the part of the observer protocol concerned with communicating relevant state from the subject to observers on change notification. The relevant part of the subject's state and how this state should be extracted are highly dependent on what classes play the subject and observer roles in a particular composition. Furthermore, the operation to be called on the observer as part of the notification is also binding-specific. This is why `notify()` and `getState()` are declared with the modifier `expected` in Listing 8-3.

An ACI's provided and expected facets are implemented in different modules, called *aspect implementations* and *aspect bindings* respectively. However, all implementations and bindings of the same ACI are indirectly connected to each other since they implement two facets of the same whole. The common ACI serves as a medium for bidirectional communication between them: Any module that implements one of the facets can freely use declarations in the other facet. This loose coupling is the key to independent reuse of implementations and bindings.

8.3.2 Aspect Implementations

An aspect implementation must implement all methods in the provided facet of the corresponding ACI, i.e., all aspect-level `provided` methods, as well as provided facets of all nested ACIs. Listing 8-4 shows a simple implementation of the `ObserverProtocol` ACI. Similarly, we could write another implementation of `ObserverProtocol`, say, a class `AsyncObserverImpl` that implements `ObserverProtocol` and that realizes a notification strategy with asynchronous updates.

As illustrated in Listing 8-4, an aspect implementation is a class that declares itself with an `implements` clause. Provided facets of the nested ACIs are implemented in nested classes that have the same names as their respective nested ACIs (see `ObserverProtocolImpl.Subject` in Listing 8-4). The implementation of provided methods can call `expected` methods of the same or of other abstractions of the same aspect. For example, `Subject.changed()` calls `notify()`, which is declared in the expected facet of `ObserverProtocol.Observer`. Nested implementation classes are free to define additional state and behavior (for example, as the `observers` field in `Subject`). Since `ObserverProtocol.Observer` has no provided methods, there is no `Observer` class in Listing 8-4, but we could have added additional state and behavior with `Observer`, if necessary.

8.3.3 Aspect Bindings

An aspect binding implements all expected methods in the aspect's CI and in its nested interfaces. Listing 8-5 shows a binding of `ObserverProtocol`, which maps the subject role to `Point` and `Line` and the observer role to `Screen`. The class `ColorObserver` declares itself as a binding of `ObserverProtocol` by means of a `binds` clause.

For each nested ACI of `ObserverProtocol`, i.e., `Subject` and `Observer`, there might be zero, one, or more nested bindings inside `ColorObserver`. The latter are also declared with a `binds` clause and must implement all `expected` methods in the corresponding interface. The relation between nested types in an ACI and their binding classes is not established by name identity since there might be more than one binding for the same abstraction within the same binding class, as in Listing 8-5.

Aspect binding is almost pure OO: A binding class refers to one or more base objects and uses their interface for implementing the expected facet of the aspect abstraction. The aspect binding in Listing 8-5 uses only three non-OO features: (a) the `wrap` clause and the `wrappee` keyword, (b) wrapper recycling and (c) pointcuts and advices. Features (b) and (c) are explained in Sections 8.3.4 and 8.3.6. The `wrap` clause and the keyword `wrappee` are syntactic sugar for the common case, when each aspect abstraction is mapped to exactly one base class. For example, `class PointSubject binds Subject wraps Point ...` is syntactic sugar for:

```
class PointSubject binds Subject {
  Point wrappee;
  PointSubject(Point wrappee) { this.wrappee = wrappee; }
  ...
}
```

In general, a wrapper class may have an arbitrary number of "wrappees" that can be initialized or computed in the constructor.

Due to bindings being almost pure OO in CAESAR, the programmer can encode more complicated cases, where the relation to application objects has to be computed or is represented by multiple application objects. Consider, for example, an observer that is to be notified when the coordinates of points `p1` and `p2` are changed, reducing their distance to less than some δ. In this case, there is no direct mapping from the subject role to any application class—the subject role is represented by a *pair* of point objects.

8.3.4 Wrapper Recycling

A subtle issue when using wrappers is avoiding creating multiple wrappers for the same base object (what we have called *wrapper identity hell* [19]). Our solution is a mechanism called *wrapper recycling*. Syntactically, wrapper recycling refers to not simply creating an instance of a wrapper `W` with a standard `new W(construc-torargs)` constructor call but instead retrieving a wrapper with the construct `outerClassInstance.W(constructorargs)`. For illustration, consider the expressions `PointSubject(p)` and `LineSubject(l)`[4] in the after-advice in Listing 8-5. We use the usual Java scoping rules. For example, `PointSubject(p)` is just an abbreviation for `this.PointSubject(p)`.

The semantics of wrapper recycling is that it guarantees a unique wrapper for every (set of) wrappees in the context of an `outerClassInstance`. This is due to the semantics of a wrapper recycling call, which caches nested wrappers. The outer class instance maintains a map `mapW` for each nested wrapper class `W`. An expression `outerClassInstance.W(wrapperargs)` corresponds to the following sequence of actions:

1. Create a compound key for the constructor arguments and look up this key in `mapW`.

2. If the lookup for the key fails, create an instance of `outerClassInstance.W` with the annotated constructor arguments, store it in the hash table `mapW`, and return the new instance. Otherwise, return the object already stored in `mapW` for the key.

Hence, the call to the wrapper recycling operation `PointSubject(p)` is equivalent to the corresponding constructor call only if a wrapper for `p` does not already exist. That is, two subsequent wrapper retrievals for a point yield the same `PointSubject` instance. The identity and state of the wrapper are preserved.

A naïve implementation of wrapper recycling in a language with garbage collection would imply a memory leak because wrapped objects would never be collected by the garbage collector. However, this can easily be reconciled by more advanced memory management techniques such as weak references and reference queues. Java, for example, has a standard API class `WeakHashMap` that could be used instead of a usual map. The discussion about what technique to use concerns the implementation of a compiler (runtime system) for CAESAR. It remains transparent to the programmer, who works with the concept of wrapper recycling rather than with low-level realization details of this concept. This is different from the use of the `WeakHashMap` data structure in the AspectJ implementation of the observer protocol discussed in Section 8.2.

---

4. Recall that the clauses `wraps Point` and `wraps Line` imply corresponding constructors.

8.3.5 Most Specific Wrappers

Another interesting feature of CAESAR is its notion of *most specific wrappers*: A mechanism that determines the most specific wrapper for an object based on the object's run-time type when multiple nested binding classes with the same name are available. Consider, for example, MovableFigures in Listing 8-6, which contains three nested classes named MovableFigure. These classes have different constructors, though. (Recall that the wraps clause is just syntactic sugar for a corresponding constructor.) On a constructor or wrapper recycling call, the dynamic type of the argument determines the actual nested binding to instantiate/recycle. For example, if Test.move(Figure) in Listing 8-6 is called with a Point as the actual parameter f, the wrapper recycling call mv.MovableFigure(f) returns an instance of the MovableFigure implementation that wraps Point.

Listing 8-6   *Using most specific wrappers*

```
class MovableFigures {
  class MovableFigure implements Movable wraps Figure {
    void moveBy(int x, int y) {};
  }
  class MovableFigure implements Movable wraps Point {
    void moveBy(int x, int y) {
      wrappee.setX(wrappee.getX()+x);
      wrappee.setY(wrappee.getY()+y);
    }
  }
  class MovableFigure implements Movable wraps Line {
    void moveBy(int x, int y) {
      MovableFigure(wrappee.getP1()).moveBy(x,y);
      MovableFigure(wrappee.getP2()).moveBy(x,y);
    }
  }
}
class Test {
  MovableFigures mv = new MovableFigures();
  void move(Figure f) {
    mv.MovableFigure(f).moveBy(5,7);
  }
}
```

The mechanism of most specific wrapper is very similar to multiple dispatch in languages such as CLOS, Cecil [5], or MultiJava [6]. More precisely, if one thinks of the constructors of nested classes as factory methods of the enclosing instance, then our mechanism is an application of multiple dispatch at these factory methods.

8.3.6 Pointcuts and Advices

As illustrated in Listing 8-5, CAESAR also has advices and pointcuts, which while being similar to AspectJ differ from it in two ways. The first concerns the decoration of executing (target) objects at a join point with aspect types. This decoration is implicit in AspectJ. For example, consider the pointcut `subjectChange` in Listing 8-2: The base object, s, brought into the scope of `ColorObserver` by the join point `target`, whose type is either `Line` or `Point`, is automatically seen as being of type `Subject` within `ColorObserver` (as per the parameter type of the pointcut).

In CAESAR, the conversion is explicit via wrapper recycling calls. In Listing 8-5, we avoided type conversions in a pointcut in order to avoid mingling the discussion on wrapper recycling with that of pointcuts and advices. For this reason, we defined different pointcuts for `Point` and `Line`. A shorter variant of the same binding, where we use conversions in the pointcuts, is given in Listing 8-7. Note that the explicit calls to wrapper recycling operators within the `with` clauses in Listing 8-7 allow us to decorate basis objects with different aspect facets in each "case" of the pointcut. We prefer the explicit variant, because it increases the programmer's expressiveness: The programmer can choose among several constructors of the binding classes, if more than one is available. For instance, we could create an observer binding that reacts on both color changes and coordinate changes. In the case of coordinate changes, the `getState()` method should give us information about the new coordinates and not about the color as in Listing 8-5. In this case, we could add another `Point` binding `PointSubject2` to the code in Listing 8-5 that has a different implementation of `getState()` and select the `PointSubject2` binding in the respective case (coordinate changes) of the pointcut definition.

Listing 8-7 Alternative binding of observer

```
public class ColorObserver binds ObserverProtocol {
    ... as before ...
  after(Subject s):
    ( call(void Point.setColor(Color))
        with s = PointSubject(target)) ||
    ( call(void Line.setColor(Color))
        with s = LineSubject(target) ) {
    s.changed();
  }
}
```

The second and more important difference between CAESAR and AspectJ pointcuts and advices is at the semantic level. Compiling a binding class that contains advice definitions does not have any effect on the base application's semantics. This is because an aspect (its implementation and binding) must be explicitly deployed in CAESAR. Only the advice definitions of explicitly deployed aspects are executed, as we discuss in the next section.

8.3.7 Weavelets and Deployment

In order to gain a complete realization of an aspect type, an implementation-binding pair needs to be composed into a new unit called a *weavelet*. An example of a weavelet is the class CO in Listing 8-8, which represents a complete realization of the ObserverProtocol interface that combines the implementation ObserverProtocolImpl with the binding ColorObserver, denoted by the declaration after the extends clause.

Listing 8-8 *Weavelet composition*

```
class CO extends
    ObserverProtocol<ColorObserver,ObserverProtocolImpl> {};
```

A weavelet is a new class within which the respective implementations of the expected and provided methods from the binding and implementation parts are composed. The composition takes place recursively for the nested classes; all nested classes with a binds declaration are combined with the corresponding implementation from the implementation class.

A weavelet has to be *deployed* in order to activate its pointcuts and advices. A weavelet deployment is syntactically denoted by the modifier deploy and comprises basically two steps: (a) create an instance of the weavelet at hand and (b) call the deploy operation on it. One can choose between *static* (load time) and *dynamic* deployment.

8.3.7.1 Static Deployment

Static deployment is expressed by using the deploy keyword as a modifier of a final static field declaration. Semantically, it means that the advices and pointcuts in the instance that has been assigned to the field become active. For example, co is deployed when Test is loaded in the following code extract:

```
class Test ... {
    deploy public static final CO co = new CO();
    ...
}
```

The object assigned to `co` could also be computed in a `static` method; hence, the weavelet that is actually deployed might also be a subtype of `CO`, thereby enabling static aspectual polymorphism. The `deploy` keyword can also be used as a class modifier. This variant should be regarded syntactic sugar in the sense that `deploy class CO ... { ... }` is equivalent to declaring a deployed field named `THIS` as in:

```
class CO ... {
   deploy public static final CO THIS = new CO();
   ...
}
```

Listing 8-9 shows the declaration of a statically deployed color observer protocol together with sample code that shows how the deployed weavelet instance can be accessed (`register()`). Since `CO.THIS` is deployed, the pointcuts of the observer protocol are active, i.e., color changes in points and lines are propagated to `CO.THIS`.

Listing 8-9 *Static aspect deployment*

```
deploy class CO extends
  ObserverProtocol<ColorObserver,ObserverProtocolImpl>{};
...
void register(Point p, Screen s) {
  CO.THIS.PointSubject(p).addObserver(
  CO.THIS.ScreenObserver(s));
}
```

Using `deploy` as a class modifier is appropriate if we need only one instance of the aspect and if aspectual polymorphism is not required. By means of `deploy` as a field modifier, we can create and deploy multiple instances of the same weavelet and select from different weavelets using aspectual polymorphism. Having two instances of, say, the `CO` weavelet in the observer example would mean that every `Point` and `Line` would have two independent facets as subject with independent lists of observers. An example that makes more sense is the association of color to elements of a data structure, which can be seen as nodes of a graph. Multiple independent instances of the corresponding weavelet would represent multiple independent colorings of the graph. Other examples can be derived from role modeling, where frequently one object has to play the same role twice. An example of this situation is when a person is an employee in two independent companies. Static aspectual polymorphism is useful if we want to select a particular weavelet based on conditions that are known at load-time. For example, based on the number of processors or the multi-threading support, one might either choose a usual observer pattern implementation or one with asynchronous updates.

8.3.7.2 Dynamic Deployment

Dynamic deployment is denoted by the keyword `deploy` used as a block statement. The rationale behind dynamic deployment is that frequently we cannot determine which variant of an aspect should be applied (or whether we need the aspect at all) until runtime. Consider, for example, a program with different logging options, i.e., without logging, with standard logging, and with "verbose" logging. In CAESAR, this can be implemented as in Listing 8-10.[5] We have two different logging aspects related by inheritance, `Logging` and `VerBoseLogging`, and we choose one of them at runtime, depending on the command line arguments with which the program has been started.

Listing 8-10 Polymorphic aspect deployment

```
class Logging {
  after(): (call(void Point.setX(int)) ||
    call(void Point.setY(int)) ) {
    System.out.println("Coordinates changed");
  }
}
class VerboseLogging extends Logging {
  after(): (call(void Point.setColor(Color)) {
    System.out.println("Color changed");
  }
}
class Main {
  public static void main(String args[]) {
    Logging l = null;
    Point p[] = createSamplePoints();
    if (args[0].equals("-log"))
      l = new Logging();
    else if (args[0].equals("-verbose"))
      l = new VerboseLogging();
    deploy (l) { modify(p); }
  }
```

---

5. In order to keep the example simple, we do not use separate binding and implementation here. If separation of implementation and binding would be overkill, we can collapse both parts into a single unit.

```
public static void modify(Point p[]) {
  p[3].setX(5);
  p[2].setColor(Color.RED);
  }
}
```

The `deploy` block statement in `Main.main` specifies that the advices defined in the annotated aspect instance 1 become active in the control flow of the `deploy` block; in this case, during the execution of `modify(f)`. In particular, other independent threads that execute the same code are not affected by the `deploy` clause. The advice and pointcuts that will be activated in the deploy block are not statically known; 1 is only known by its upper bound `Logging` (1 could have also been passed as a parameter). In other words, the advices are late-bound, similarly to late method binding; hence our term *aspectual polymorphism*. If 1 is `null`, the `deploy` clause has no effect at all.

The usefulness of dynamic deployment becomes clear when we consider a "simulation" of this functionality by means of static deployment. With static deployment, we would have to encode the different variants by conditional logic in the aspect code.[6] The structure of the aspect would be awkward, because all variants of the aspect are tangled inside a single aspect module. In a way, this is similar to simulating late binding in a non-OO language. Dynamic aspectual polymorphism can be seen as an imperative consequence of integrating aspects into the OO concept world. Without aspectual polymorphism, programs would also be fragile with respect to concurrent programs; additional synchronization measures would be required.

An interesting question is whether the aspect deployment code should also be separated from the rest of the code. This can easily be done with another aspect whose responsibility is the deployment of the logging aspect, as illustrated in Listing 8-11. In this code, the aspect `LoggingDeployment` (which is itself deployed statically) computes and deploys an appropriate logging aspect by means of an `around` advice; i.e., the `proceed()` call is executed in the context of the logging aspect.

Listing 8-11   *Aspect deployment aspects*

```
deploy class LoggingDeployment {
  around(final String s[]): cflow(Main.main(String[])
```

---

6. Our example also uses conditional logic in `Main.main`. However, we select the logging variant once and never have to do any checks again (a factory object could have been used, as well), whereas without dynamic deployment, the check would be redone at every joinpoint.

```
        && args(s)  && (call(void Main.modify(Point[])) {
      Logging l = null;
      if (...) l = new Logging(); else ... ;
      deploy (l) in { proceed(s); }
   }
}
class Main {
  public static void main(String args[]) {
    Point p[] = createSamplePoints();
    modify(p);
  }
  public static void modify(Point p[]) {...}
}
```

8.3.8   *Virtual Classes and Static Typing*

In CAESAR, all nested interfaces of a CI and all classes that implement or bind such interfaces are *virtual types/classes*, as in the family polymorphism approach [9]. Similar to fields and methods, virtual types also become properties of objects of the class in which they are defined. Hence, their denotation can only be dynamically determined in the context of an instance of the enclosing class. The rationale behind using family polymorphism lies in its power with respect to reuse and polymorphism at the level of multiple related abstractions.

If we want to have a variant of a binding, weavelet, or CI, we can refine the respective entity by creating an extension within which the nested virtual types/classes can be overridden. LazyColorObserver in Listing 8-12 refines the behavior of ColorObserver in Listing 8-5 by using virtual class overriding (declared with the keyword override)—a lazy ScreenObserver reacts only after being notified ten times about a change. The important observation to make here is that even if the definition of PointSubject and LineSubject are inherited unchanged, references to Observer within their respective implementations are automatically bound to LazyColorObserver.ScreenObserver during the execution of any method on an instance of LazyColorObserver.

Listing 8-12   *Lazy color observer*

```
public class LazyColorObserver extends ColorObserver {
  override class ScreenObserver {
    int count = 0;
    void notify(Subject s) {
      count++;
```

```
      if (count >= 10) { super.notify(s); count = 0; }
    }
  }
}
```

However, this flexibility is not paid for with loss of static typing: An improvement of the type system proposed in [9] preserves the ability to detect type errors at compile time. The integration of virtual classes [15] and family polymorphism [9] with collaboration interfaces and their implementation and binding units has already been described in [19].

8.4 EVALUATION

This section discusses how CAESAR copes with the problems outlined in Section 8.2. In addition, we elaborate on how CAESAR'S explicit aspect instantiation and deployment relate to AspectJ-like languages, where aspects are only implicitly created and which do not have a notion of aspect deployment.

8.4.1 Problems Revisited

Recall that we identified the following problems for 'conventional' AOP in Section 8.2:

1. Lack of support for multi-abstraction aspects.
2. Lack of support for sophisticated mapping of aspect abstractions to base classes.
3. Lack of support for reuse of aspect bindings.
4. Lack of support for aspectual polymorphism.

In the following, we explain how each of these problems is solved in CAESAR.

8.4.1.1 Multi-Abstraction Aspects

As was shown in the code in Listings 8-3, 8-4, and 8-5, each abstraction in the vocabulary of the world as it is decomposed from the point of view of an aspect is defined in its own full-fledged module with a well-defined interface. Methods in the interface of one abstraction can be called by methods of other abstractions within the same aspect or from the outside. For example, consider the call of `Subject.notify(...)` in the implementation of `ObserverProtocolImpl` in Listing 8-4, or the invocation of `CO.THIS.addObserver(...)` in Listing 8-9.

This finer-grained modularization of the aspect itself allows the run-time system to dispatch methods based not only on the instance of the aspect but also on the particular abstraction in execution. Consider, for example, the `getState()` method in the definition of `Subject`, which was implemented differently for point-subjects and for line-subjects, while being used uniformly in the update logic (cf. Listing 8-5). As was pointed out in Section 8.2, the same polymorphism would not be possible if there were only aspect-level methods. Furthermore, due to the incorporation of virtual classes, it is easy to encode different variants of a multi-abstraction aspect, as illustrated in Listing 8-12.

Let us now consider the issue of defining state for the individual abstractions pertaining to an aspect. The examples in the previous section show that each abstraction in the modular structure can declare its own state, e.g., `observers` in `Subject`. Hence, there is no need for defining data structures that "globally" maintain aspect-related state of all base objects in a single place, such as `perSubjectObservers` in Listing 8-1. Similarly, state can be added to the abstractions at the binding side, such as the `count` field in Listing 8-12.

8.4.1.2 Sophisticated Aspect to Base Class Mapping

In our model, bindings are Java classes with some additional features. As such, the definition of mappings from aspect abstractions to the classes of a base application can make use of the full expressiveness of a general purpose OO language. There is nothing to prevent a CAESAR programmer from coding any mapping, no matter how sophisticated (cf. the example at the end of Section 8.3.3, see also [19] for more examples).

8.4.1.3 Reusing Aspect Bindings

Different weavelets can combine an aspect binding with different aspect implementations. On the other hand, different weavelets can combine (and reuse) a particular aspect implementation with multiple different bindings. For example, we can combine the observer protocol binding to `JButton` and `MyActionListener` with the `LinkedList` or the `AsynchronousUpdate` observer implementation. On the other hand, we can combine the same observer implementation, say `AsynchronousUpdate`, with multiple different bindings, e.g., to `JButton`/ `MyActionListener` and `ListModel`/`JList`. Consequently, one can define functionality that is polymorphic with respect to (a) aspect implementations by being written to a certain aspect binding type, (b) aspect bindings by being written to a certain aspect implementation type, or (c) both of them by being written to an ACI.

8.4.1.4 Aspectual Polymorphism

As discussed in Section 8.3.7, our approach does support aspectual polymorphism. For example, the `modify(Point p[])` method in Listing 8-10 is polymorphic with respect to aspects that might be defined in the future. It is even possible to run the same method concurrently within two different threads with and without the logging aspect.

8.4.2 *Explicit Versus Implicit Aspect Instantiation/Deployment*

The question we pose here is: How does our notion of explicit aspect instantiation and deployment relate to AspectJ-like languages, within which aspects are only implicitly created and which do not have a notion of aspect deployment? In AspectJ, aspect instantiation can be controlled by means of the aspect modifiers isSingleton (this is the default), perThis/perTarget, and percflow/percflowbelow. In CAESAR, these aspect instantiation strategies turn out to be special cases or "patterns" of the more general model in CAESAR.

Table 8-1 describes how the AspectJ instantiation strategies can be simulated in CAESAR. The isSingleton case is obvious. The perThis modifier can be simulated by creating a wrapper class and using wrapper recycling to refer to the state that is associated with each point. Simulating perTarget is identical to perThis, except that we would have to exchange this(p) by target(p). More interesting is AspectJ's percflow modifier, which means that an instance of the aspect is created for each flow of control of the join points picked out by the annotated pointcut. The semantics of percflow can be simulated by using a deployment aspect ADepl that uses dynamic deployment at the respective starts of control flow.

Table 8-1 *Aspect Instantiation in AspectJ and* CAESAR

AspectJ	CAESAR
```aspect A isSingleton { State s; }```	```deploy class A {State s;}```
```aspect A perThis(pointChanges) {```	```deploy class A {```
``` pointcut pointChanges() :```	``` class PointWrapper```
``` call (Point.setX(int));```	``` wraps Point { State s}```
``` State s;```	``` after(Point p):```
``` after(Point p): pointChanges() &&```	``` call(Point.setX(int)) &&```
``` this(p) { ...s...}```	``` this(p) {```
```}```	``` ...PointWrapper(p).s; ...```
	``` }```
```aspect A percflow(pointChanges) {```	```class A {```
``` pointcut pointChanges():```	``` State s;```
``` call (Point.setX(int));```	``` after(): somePointcut() { ...```
``` State s;```	``` }```
``` after(): somePointCut() { ... }```	```}```
```}```	```deploy class ADepl {```
	``` around():```
	``` call (Point.setX(int)) {```
	``` deploy(newA()){proceed();}```
	``` }```

What do we gain if all the cases in Table 8-1 can already be handled very well by AspectJ? Recall that AspectJ instantiation strategies are just special cases of a more general model in CAESAR. This has two implications. First, we do not need special new keywords to express the semantics of AspectJ instantiation. Second, and more importantly, our model allows us to express instantiation and deployment semantics that cannot easily be expressed in AspectJ.

When using AspectJ's `perThis` of `perTarget` modifiers, state can be only associated with objects that are caller or callee, respectively, in a pointcut. In CAESAR, state can be associated with arbitrary objects and arbitrary relations between objects. For example, we could associate state with every *pair* of `this` and `target`, or with any argument of a method call. In the `percflow` case, we can not only simulate the AspectJ semantics but also express more sophisticated behaviors, such as deploying an instance of an optimization aspect only if the number of calls to the method to be optimized is executed more than a certain number of times.

8.5 IMPLEMENTATION

Most parts of a Java-based implementation of the CAESAR model, called CAESARJ, have already been implemented. With the FamilyJ compiler [27], we have integrated the notion of dependent virtual types into the Java programming language. We have also extended AspectJ with the notion of dynamic deployment described in this chapter. In current work, these two building blocks are being integrated together and extended with mechanisms for collaboration interfaces. We are also working on a CAESARJ plug-in and debugger for the Eclipse [8] environment. The project web site includes up-to-date news on the implementation [4].

8.6 RELATED WORK

8.6.1 Open Classes

An open class is a class to which new fields or methods can be added without editing the class directly. For example, in MultiJava [6] additional methods can be attached to a class. In AspectJ, methods as well as fields can be added to a class by means of *introductions*. As already discussed in Section 8.2, open classes are in contrast to the concept of independent extensibility [24], an essential prerequisite for reusable and extensible software. CAESAR offers an alternative to open classes that is even more powerful and that does not violate independent extensibility.

CAESAR is also related to Hyper/J and its notion of multi-dimensional separation of concerns (MDSOC) [25]. Tarr et al.'s observation about the "tyranny of the dominant decomposition" is in the vein of our term "arbitrariness of the decomposition hierarchy." Our aspect bindings serve as a translator from one hierarchy to another and allow viewing and using a system from different perspectives. This is similar to the MDSOC idea of having multiple concern dimensions such that the program can be projected on each concern hyper plane. However, on the technical level, CAESAR is very different from Hyper/J. In Hyper/J, one can define an independent component in a hyperslice. Hyperslices are independent of their context of use because they are declaratively complete. That is, they declare as abstract method everything that they need but cannot implement themselves. A hyperslice is integrated into an existing application by means of composition rules specified in a hypermodule. As the result, new code is generated by mixing the hyperslice code into the existing code. Similar to PCAs, Hyper/J [25] also lacks the notion of collaboration interfaces and the reuse of bindings related to it. Either the modules to be composed are not independent due to the usage of the "merge-by-name" composition strategy, or the modules are independent, but then the non-reusable composition specification gets very complex. Similar to Adaptive Plug and Play Components (APPCs) and aspectual component models (Section 8.6.2), Hyper/J's approach is class-based. It is not possible to add the functionality defined in a hyperslice to individual objects. Furthermore, Hyper/J's sublanguage for mapping specifications from different hyperslices is fairly complex and not well integrated into the common OO framework.

Lasagne [26] is a run-time architecture that features aspect-oriented concepts. An aspect is implemented as a layer of wrappers. Aspects can be composed at runtime, enabling dynamic customization of systems. Lasagne also allows context-sensitive selection of aspects, enabling client-specific customization of systems. Although Lasagne is an architectural approach focusing on middleware (instead of a general purpose language extension as CAESAR), it has some similarity to CAESAR. In particular, Lasagne also features extensions that are created and deployed at runtime, and it also provides means to restrict the visibility of an extension to a particular scope (as our `deploy` block statement).

Bergmans and Akşit have presented an extension of the composition filter model [1, 2] geared toward aspect-oriented programming. With composition filters, it is possible to define various filters for incoming and outgoing messages of an object. By means of *superimposition* [2], these filters can be applied to objects that are specified via a join point declaration similar to AspectJ pointcuts. Composition filters have no dedicated means to separate aspect implementation and binding, and there is no notion of deployment or aspectual polymorphism. In comparison with CAESAR, where almost everything is specified as usual OO code, composition filters are more declarative. On one hand, this makes it easier to express kinds of concerns that are easily expressible with the declarative sublanguage, but on the other hand it restricts its applicability to arbitrary kinds of concerns.

8.6.2   *Adaptive Plug and Play Components*

Adaptive Plug and Play Components (APPCs) [18] and their aspect-oriented variant of *aspectual components* (AC) [14] are related to our work in that both approaches support the definition of multi-abstraction components/aspects and have a vague definition of required and provided interfaces. However, the latter feature was not well integrated with the type system. Recognizing this deficiency, the successor model of *Pluggable Composite Adapters* (PCAs) [20] even dropped this notion and reduced the declaration of the expected interface to a set of standard abstract methods. With the notion of collaboration interfaces, CAESAR represents a qualitative improvement over all three models in support for multi-abstraction aspects. Due to the lack of a CI notion, connectors and adapters in APPC, AC, and PCA models are bound to a fixed implementation of an aspect and cannot be reused. In addition, APPCs and AC rely on a dedicated mapping sublanguage that is less powerful than our object-oriented wrappers with wrapper recycling. Finally, these approaches lack the notion of virtual types.

8.6.3   *Collaboration-Based Decomposition*

Finally, the question rises of how to position the work presented here with respect to previously published work on generic programming and *collaboration-based decomposition* (CBD). Generic programming and CBD approaches aim at providing modules that encapsulate a whole collaboration of classes; classes are decomposed into the roles they play in the different collaborations. The idea is nicely visualized by a two-dimensional matrix, with the classes as the column indexes and collaborations in which these classes are involved as the row indexes.

Mixin layers [23] and delegation layers [21] are two representatives of approaches to CBD. The former makes heavy use of generic programming as provided by C++ templates, whereas the latter uses a combination of virtual classes and delegation. Both approaches provide concepts for composing and decomposing a collaboration into *layers* such that a particular collaboration variant can be obtained by composing the required layers. Neither of these approaches support on-demand re-modularization. The definition of a collaboration layer in these approaches also encodes how the collaboration is integrated. The vocabulary of abstractions that are involved in an application is defined a-priori to the definition of any collaboration layer and is consequently shared by all layer definitions.

Collaboration layers are especially useful when we have many different variants of a particular collaboration (for example, `Graph`, `ColoredGraph`, and `WeightedGraph`) and want to mix-and-match these variants at runtime (for example, create a `ColoredWeightedGraph` by composing the color and the weight layer). Collaboration layers nicely complement the concepts proposed in this chapter, as they allow us to decompose both components and connectors into layers that can be combined on-demand. In the future, we plan to combine the dynamic composition features of the delegation layers approach with the concepts of the work presented here.

8.6.4   Implementation of Dynamic Deployment

Dynamic deployment brings about new challenges for the implementation of aspects. Implementing dynamic deployment via static preparation of the code is only possible if many dynamic checks (checking for deployed aspects in the current thread) are inserted into the code. A more elegant solution to implement dynamic deployment is to use run-time weaving. The Steamloom virtual machine [3] supports run-time weaving and has dedicated support for dynamic deployment of aspects. Hanenberg et al describe an approach to continous weaving [11] within which the instrumentation of code locations can be deferred until other dependent join points are triggered.

8.7   SUMMARY AND FUTURE WORK

We have identified the arbitrariness of the primary model as the most important cause of code tangling. We argued that join point interception is an important foundation for dealing with code tangling but does not alone suffice to cope with the identified problems. We proposed CAESAR, a model for aspect-oriented programming with dedicated support for crosscutting models. CAESAR's strengths are in the reuse and componentization of aspects, allowing us to use aspects polymorphically. We introduced the notion of aspectual polymorphism as a generalization of subtype polymorphism to crosscutting models and proposed a novel concept for dynamic aspect deployment in order to realize aspectual polymorphism. Static type safety is preserved due to the introduction of virtual classes and family polymorphism.

There are a few limitations and further extensions of the model. First, our virtual class mechanism is currently not powerful enough to associate virtual types with other types that are defined outside the enclosing type. This might eventually prove to be too restrictive. We are investigating ways of "importing" external types within a collaboration interface. Second, we believe that the modularity of pointcut specifications can be improved to enhance reuse and incremental definition of pointcuts. Third, similar to other AO approaches, CAESAR builds on top of run-time environments designed with a procedural or object-oriented execution model in mind. We believe that aspect-aware execution models result in more expressive aspect-oriented languages. Last but not least, the concepts in CAESAR are the result of lab research, and their usefulness has to be evaluated in real-life case studies. We are currently involved in a project with software companies aiming at evaluating aspect-oriented concepts, in general, and CAESAR, in particular, in real industrial projects.

REFERENCES

1. AKŞIT, M., BERGMANS, L. AND VURAL, S. 1992. An object-oriented language-database integration model: The composition-filters approach. In *ECOOP '92 European Conf. Object-Oriented Programming*, (Kaiserslautern), O. L. Madsen, Ed. LNCS vol. 615. Springer-Verlag, Berlin, 372–395.

2. BERGMANS, L. AND AKŞIT, M. 2001. Composing multiple concerns using composition filters. Tech. rep., University of Twente, The Netherlands. http://trese.cs.utwente.nl/composition_filters/.

3. BOCKISCH, C., HAUPT, M., MEZINI, M., AND OSTERMANN, K., 2004. Virtual Machine Support for Dynamic Join Points. In *4th Int'l Conf. Aspect-Oriented Software Development (AOSD)*, (Lancaster, UK), K. Lieberherr, Ed. ACM, 83–92.

4. CAESARJ. Caesarj homepage. http://caesarj.org.

5. CHAMBERS, C. 1992. Object-oriented multi-methods in Cecil. In *ECOOP '92 European Conf. Object-Oriented Programming*, (Kaiserslautern), O. L. Madsen, Ed. LNCS, vol. 615. Springer-Verlag, Berlin, 33–56.

6. CLIFTON, C., LEAVENS, G. T., CHAMBERS, C., AND MILLSTEIN, T. 2000. MultiJava: Modular open classes and symmetric multiple dispatch for Java. In *15th Conf. Object-Oriented Programming, Systems, Languages, and Applications (OOPSLA)*, (Minneapolis). ACM, 130–145.

7. DIJKSTRA, E. W. 1967. The structure of the "THE'" multiprogramming system. In *Symp. Operating System Principles (SOSP)*. ACM, 10.1–10.6.

8. ECLIPSE HOMEPAGE. http: //www.eclipse.org.

9. ERNST, E. 2001. Family polymorphism. In *ECOOP 2001—Object-Oriented Programming, 15th European Conference*, (Budapest), J. L. Knudsen, Ed. LNCS, vol. 2072. Springer-Verlag, Berlin, 303–326.

10. GARLAN, D., KAISER, G. E., AND NOTKIN, D. 1992. Using tool abstraction to compose systems. *IEEE Computer 25*, 6, 30–38.

11. HANENBERG, S., HIRSCHFELD, R., AND UNLARND, RAINER. 2004. Morphing aspects: incompletely woven aspects and continous weaving. In *4th Int'l Conf. Aspect-Oriented Software Development (AOSD)*, (Lancaster, UK), K. Lieberherr, Ed. ACM, 46–55.

12. HANNEMANN, J. AND KICZALES, G. 2002. Design pattern implementation in Java and AspectJ. In *17th Conf. Object-Oriented Programming, Systems, Languages, and Applications (OOPSLA)*, (Seattle). ACM, 161–173.

13. KICZALES, G. 2001. Aspect-oriented programming—the fun has just begun. In *Workshop on New Visions for Software Design and Productivity: Research and Applications* (Nashville, Tennessee). http://www.hpcc.gov/iwg/sdp/vanderbilt/position_papers/gregor_kiczales_aspect_oriented_programming.pdf.

14. LIEBERHERR, K., LORENZ, D., AND MEZINI, M. 1999. Programming with Aspectual Components. Tech. Rep. NU-CCS-99-01, College of Computer Science, Northeastern University.

15. MADSEN, O. L. AND MØLLER-PEDERSEN, B. 1989. Virtual classes: A powerful mechanism in object-oriented programming. In *4th Conf. Object-Oriented Programming, Systems, Languages, and Applications (OOPSLA)*, (New Orleans). ACM, 397–406.

16. MASUHARA, H. AND KICZALES, G. 2003. Modular crosscutting in aspect-oriented mechanisms. In *ECOOP 2003—Object-Oriented Programming, 17th European Conference*, (Darmstadt), L. Cardelli, Ed. LNCS, vol. 2743. Springer-Verlag, Berlin, 2–28.

17. MEYER, B. 1997. *Object-Oriented Software Construction, 2nd Ed.* Prentice Hall, Englewood Cliffs, New Jersey.

18. MEZINI, M. AND LIEBERHERR, K. 1998. Adaptive plug-and-play components for evolutionary software development. In *13th Conf. Object-Oriented Programming, Systems, Languages, and Applications (OOPSLA)*, (Vancouver). ACM, 97–116.

19. MEZINI, M. AND OSTERMANN, K. 2002. Integrating independent components with on-demand remodularization. In *17th Conf. Object-Oriented Programming, Systems, Languages, and Applications (OOPSLA)*, (Seattle). ACM, 52–67.

20. MEZINI, M., SEITER, L., AND LIEBERHERR, K. 2001. Component integration with pluggable composite adapters. In *Software Architectures and Component Technology*, M. Akşit, Ed. Kluwer Academic Publishers, Boston, 325–356.

21. OSTERMANN, K. 2002. Dynamically composable collaborations with delegation layers. In *ECOOP 2002—Object-Oriented Programming: 16th European Conference*, (Málaga, Spain), B. Magnusson, Ed. LNCS, vol. 2374. Springer-Verlag, Berlin, 89–110.

22. PARNAS, D. L. 1972. On the criteria to be used in decomposing systems into modules. *Comm. ACM 15*, 12 (Dec.), 1053–1058.

23. SMARAGDAKIS, Y. AND BATORY, D. 1998. Implementing layered design with mixin layers. In *ECOOP'98 Object-Oriented Programming, 12th European Conference*, (Brussels), E. Jul, Ed. LNCS, vol. 1445. Springer-Verlag, Berlin, 550–570.

24. Szyperski, C. 1996. Independently extensible systems—software engineering potential and challenges. In *19th Australian Computer Science Conference* (Melbourne). 203–212.

25. Tarr, P., Ossher, H., Harrison, W., and Sutton Jr., S. M. 1999. *N* degrees of separation: Multi-dimensional separation of concerns. In *21st Int'l Conf. Software Engineering (ICSE)*, (Los Angeles). IEEE, 107–119.

26. Truyen, E., Vanhaute, B., Joosen, W., Verbaeten, P., and Jørgensen, B. N. 2001. Dynamic and selective combination of extensions in component-based applications. In *23rd Int'l Conf. Software Engineering (ICSE)*, (Toronto). ACM, 233–242.

27. Wittmann, A. 2003. Towards Caesar: Family polymorphism for Java. M.S. thesis, Darmstadt University of Technology. www.st.informatik.tu-darmstadt.de/ pages/projects/familyj/.

28. Wolber, D. 1997. Reviving functional decomposition in object-oriented design. *Journal of Object-Oriented Programming 10*, 6, 31–38.

Chapter 9

Trace-Based Aspects

REMI DOUENCE, PASCAL FRADET, AND MARIO SÜDHOLT

This chapter presents *trace-based aspects,* a model that takes into account the history of program execution in deciding what aspect behavior to invoke. That is, aspect behavior is invoked depending on relations among events of the execution history. With trace-based aspects, weaving is accomplished through an execution monitor that modifies the program execution to include the behavior specified by the aspects. We motivate trace-based aspects and explore the trade-off between expressiveness and property enforcement/analysis.

More concretely, we first present an expressive model of trace-based aspects enabling proofs of aspect properties by equational reasoning. Using a restriction of the aspect language to regular expressions, we address the difficult problem of interactions between conflicting aspects. Finally, by restricting the actions performed by aspects, we illustrate how to keep the semantic impact of aspects under control and how to implement weaving statically.

9.1 INTRODUCTION

Aspect-oriented programming (AOP) is concerned with providing programmatic means to modularize crosscutting functionalities of complex applications. By encapsulating such functionalities into aspects, AOP facilitates development, understanding, and maintenance of programs. An important characteristic of aspects is that they are built from *crosscuts* (pointcuts), which define where an aspect modifies an application, and *inserts* (advice), which define the modifications to be applied. Typically, crosscuts denote sets of program points or execution points of the base application, and inserts are expressed in a traditional programming language. For instance, an aspect for access control could be defined in terms of crosscuts denoting sets of access methods and inserts performing the access control tests. However, because aspect languages are rather limited, it is often necessary to use inserts to pass information from one crosscut to another. Consider, for example, an aspect performing some access control for logged-in users. An aspect language that cannot refer to the historical login event must use an extra insert to set a flag in the login code and must write the access control aspect to recognize this flag.

Conventional aspect languages allow unrestricted inserts; the role of inserts overlaps with that of crosscuts. This makes reasoning on aspects and woven programs difficult. In this chapter, we present an approach that uses expressive aspect languages and restrictions on inserts to enable reasoning about different aspect properties.

Trace-based aspects are defined on traces of events occurring during program execution. Trace-based aspects are more expressive than those based on atomic points because they can express relations between execution events, including those involving information from the corresponding execution states. For example, an aspect for access control could express that a user has to log in first in order to pass an access check later. Such aspects are called *stateful:* Their implementation must use some kind of state to represent their evolution according to the event encountered. Conceptually, weaving is modeled by an execution monitor, whose state evolves according the history of program execution and that, in case of a match, triggers the execution of the corresponding action. By strictly separating crosscuts and inserts by means of two different, well-defined languages, we address the formalization of aspects and weaving. Restrictions on these languages allow us to design static analysis of aspect properties as well as an optimized implementation of aspect weaving.

In Section 9.2, we informally introduce the main features of trace-based AOP: observable execution traces, stateful aspects (composed of crosscuts and inserts), and weaving (based on execution monitoring). In Sections 9.3 through 9.5, we explore three different options within the trade-off between expressiveness and property enforcement/analysis. The first provides an expressive crosscut language with no restrictions on the inserts. However, the expressive power of this option precludes automatic proofs of most aspect properties. The second option is characterized by more restricted, but still stateful, aspects corresponding to regular expressions over execution traces. Because of this restriction, it is possible to statically detect whether several aspects interact (e.g., testing whether an encryption aspect interacts with a system logging aspect). We also suggest operators for the resolution of such interactions. The last option is characterized by a very restricted insert language where aspects can be seen as formal safety properties. We present how these aspects/properties can be statically and efficiently woven. An application of this technique is the securing of mobile code upon receipt. Finally, we discuss related work and conclude in Section 9.6.

This chapter is a unified presentation of three distinct studies: [3], [7] (which has recently been extended in [8]), and [9]. These studies share a trace-based approach to AOP. To make the presentation more intuitive, we have deliberately omitted many extensions and technical details.

9.2 CHARACTERISTICS OF TRACE-BASED ASPECTS

Trace-based aspects have two main characteristics. First, aspects are defined over sequences of observable execution states. Second, weaving is more naturally performed on executions rather than program code. The weaver can be seen as a monitor interleaving the execution of the base program and execution of inserts.[1]

9.2.1 Observable Execution Trace

The base program execution is modeled by a sequence of observable execution states (a.k.a. join points). This trace can be formally defined on the basis of small-step semantics [16] of the programming language. Each join point is an abstraction of the execution state. Join points may denote not only syntactic information (e.g., instructions) but also semantic information (e.g., dynamic values). For example, when the user Bob logs in, the function `login()` is called in the base program with `"Bob"` as a parameter. This join point of the execution can be represented by the term `login("Bob")`.

9.2.2 Aspect Language

The basic form of an aspect is a rule of the form $C \blacktriangleright I$ where C is a crosscut and I is an insert. The insert I is executed whenever the crosscut C matches the current join point. Basic aspects can be combined using operators (sequence, repetition, choice, etc.) to form stateful aspects.

Crosscuts. A crosscut defines execution points where an aspect should perform an action. In general, a crosscut C is a function that takes a join point as a parameter. This function returns either `fail` when the join point does not satisfy the crosscut definition or a substitution that captures values of the join point. For example, we can define a crosscut *isLogin* that matches session logins and captures the corresponding user name. It would return `fail` when it is applied to the join point `logout()` and the substitution *uid* = `"Bob"` when it is applied to `login("Bob")`.

---

1. This model does not preclude implementing weaving as a compile-time process (see Section 9.5).

Inserts. An insert is an executable program fragment with free variables. For instance, the insert `addLog(`*uid* `+ "logged in")` prints the name of a logged user when it is executed. In this insert, the name of the user is represented by the variable *uid* to be bound by a crosscut. In the remainder of the paper, the special insert `skip` represents an instruction doing nothing.

Stateful aspects. The intuition behind a basic aspect $C \blacktriangleright I$ is that when C matches the current join point and yields a substitution ϕ, the program ϕI is executed. For example, we can define a basic security aspect that logs sessions as follows:

isLogin $\blacktriangleright$ `addLog(`*uid* `+ "logged in")`

In order to build stateful aspects, basic aspects can be combined using control operators. Using a C-like syntax, we can define an aspect that logs all sessions as follows:

`while(true){` *isLogin* $\blacktriangleright$ `addLog(`*uid* `+ "logged in") }`

This definition applies the basic security aspect again and again. Control operators allow us to define sophisticated aspects on execution traces. For instance, the following aspect tracks sequences of sessions (`login` followed by `logout`).

`while(true){` *isLogin* $\blacktriangleright$ `addLog (`*uid* `+ "logged in") ;`
 isLogout $\blacktriangleright$ `addLog(`*uid* `+ "logged out") }`

9.2.3 Weaving

In general, several aspects addressing different issues (e.g., debugging and profiling) can be composed (using a parallel operator ||) and woven together. The weaver takes a parallel composition of n aspects $A_1 \| \ldots \| A_n$ and tries to apply each of them (in no specific order) at each join point of the execution trace.

Conceptually, the weaver is an execution monitor that selects the current basic aspects of $A_1, \ldots, A_n$ and tries to apply them at each join point. When a crosscut matches the current join point, the corresponding insert is executed. After all basic aspects have been considered, the base program execution is resumed and proceeds until the next join point.

When a basic aspect of a stateful aspect A_i has been applied and its insert executed, the state of A_i evolves. The control structure of A_i (e.g., repetition or sequence) specifies which basic aspect must be considered next. For instance, the previous security aspect remains in its initial state until a login occurs. After the aspect has matched a `login` event, it waits to match a `logout` event before returning to its initial state.

In the remainder of this chapter, we instantiate this framework to form a variety of different definitions of crosscuts, inserts, and stateful aspects. We thereby obtain different aspect languages and enable reasoning about aspect-oriented programs, both manually and, using static analysis techniques, automatically.

9.3   *EXPRESSIVE ASPECTS AND EQUATIONAL REASONING*

We present a first instantiation of the general framework for AOP introduced in the previous section. This instantiation, inspired by the work presented in [9], is intended to illustrate two main points:

- The usefulness of expressive aspect definitions
- The application of general proof techniques for the analysis and transformation of AO programs

Crosscuts.   In this section, we instantiate the general framework by allowing crosscuts C to be arbitrary predicates. For instance, a predicate *isWeakPassword* could recognize the event of changing a password to a word a dictionary. Note that we do not define the language of crosscuts; they are to be defined using some general-purpose language.

Stateful Aspects.   Aspects are defined as a collection of mutually recursive definitions of the form *var = A*. Since one of our main interests lies in the definition of *stateful* crosscuts, we base an aspect definition on the following grammar:

$$
\begin{aligned}
A ::= \ & C \blacktriangleright I && \text{; basic aspect} \\
| \ & A_1 ; A_2 && \text{; sequence} \\
| \ & A_1 \ \blacksquare \ A_2 && \text{; choice} \\
| \ & var && \text{; invocation}
\end{aligned}
$$

The grammar allows us to compose aspects by sequentialization, deterministic choice, and aspect invocation. In a deterministic choice $A_1 \blacksquare A_2, A_1$ is always chosen if it is applicable; A_2 is chosen only if it is applicable, and A_1 is not. Using composed aspects, we can define, for example, an aspect *tryOnce* trying to apply $C \blacktriangleright I$ only on the current join point and doing nothing afterward as:

$$
\begin{aligned}
tryOnce &= (C \blacktriangleright I \, ; void) \ \blacksquare \ void \\
void &= isAny \blacktriangleright \texttt{skip} \ ; void
\end{aligned}
$$

If C matches the current join point, the weaver chooses the first branch and executes the insert I, and the aspect becomes *void* that keeps doing nothing. Otherwise, the weaver chooses the second branch (*void*), which keeps doing nothing right from the start.

In order to illustrate how such expressive aspects may be used, consider the following definition:

$$\log = (isLogin \blacktriangleright \texttt{addLog}\,(uid)\,;\log\,;isLogout \blacktriangleright \texttt{skip})$$
$$\blacksquare isLogout \blacktriangleright \texttt{skip}$$
$$logNestedLogin = isLogin \blacktriangleright \texttt{skip}\ ;\log\ ;logNestedLogin$$

The aspect *logNestedLogin* considers sessions starting with a call to the `login` function with the user identifier as a parameter (whose occurrence is matched by the crosscut *isLogin*) and ending with a call to the function `logout` (matched by the crosscut *isLogout*). This aspect logs nested (i.e., non top-level) calls to the login function, which may be useful because such a call may log into a non-local network and be therefore dangerous. The recursive definition of the aspect is responsible for pairing logins and logouts, thus detecting non top-level calls to `login`.

Now, let us consider the following aspect:

$$initAtFirstLogin = isLogin \blacktriangleright \texttt{initNetworkInfo()}\ ;void$$

This aspect *initAtFirstLogin* detects the first call to login in order to initialize network information. Then the following calls to login are ignored.

It is easy to prove that the two aspects *logNestedLogin* and *initAtFirstLogin* are equivalent to a single sequential aspect. Basically, this can be proven by unfolding recursive definitions and induction principles [9]. The proof starts with a parallel composition *logNestedLogin* || *initAtFirstLogin* and eliminates the parallel operator by producing all the possible pairs of crosscuts from the two aspect definitions and by folding. The resulting sequential aspect can be simplified if a pair of crosscuts has no solution. In our example we get the following sequential aspect:

$$initAndLog = isLogin \blacktriangleright \texttt{initNetworkInfo()}\,;log\,;logNestedLogin$$

9.4 DETECTION AND RESOLUTION OF ASPECT INTERACTIONS

By restricting the expressiveness of our aspect language (while still adhering to stateful aspects), it is possible to automatically prove (certain) aspect properties. In this section, we consider a second instantiation of the general framework that supports a more restrictive yet expressive crosscut language in which static checking of interactions is feasible.

Crosscuts. A crosscut is defined by conjunctions, disjunctions, and negations of terms

$$C ::= T \mid C_1 \textbf{ and } C_2 \mid C_1 \textbf{ or } C_2 \mid \textbf{not } C$$

where T denotes terms with variables. The formulas used to express these crosscuts belong to the so-called quantifier-free equational formulas [5]. Whether such a formula has a solution is decidable. This is one of the key properties making the analysis in this section feasible.

We can define, for example, a crosscut matching logins performed by the user `root` on any machine, or by any non-root user on any machine but the `server` as follows:

$$login(\texttt{root}, m) \textbf{ or } (login(u,m) \textbf{ and } (\textbf{not } login(u, \texttt{server})))$$

In this context, checking whether the current join point (which, remember, is represented by a term) matches the crosscut definition is computed by a generalized version of the unification algorithm that is well-known, e.g., from logic programming.

Note that, for the sake of decidability (i.e., static analyses), the crosscuts C defined by the equation above are less expressive than those considered in the previous section. They can only denote join points as term patterns (as opposed to arbitrary term predicates).

Stateful aspects. The main idea of the aspect language presented in this section is to restrict stateful aspects to regular expressions using the following grammar:

$$
\begin{aligned}
A ::= &\ C \blacktriangleright I \,; A && \text{; sequence} \\
\mid &\ C \blacktriangleright I \,; var && \text{; end of sequence} \\
\mid &\ A_1 \blacksquare A_2 && \text{; choice}
\end{aligned}
$$

Using this aspect language a security aspect *logAccess* that logs file accesses (calls to `read`) from a call to `login` until a call to `logout` (assuming non-nested sessions) can be expressed as

$$
\begin{aligned}
logAccess &= login(u, m) \blacktriangleright \texttt{skip} \,; logRead \\
logRead &= (\texttt{logout}() \blacktriangleright \texttt{skip} \,; logAccess) \\
&\quad \blacksquare (read(x) \blacktriangleright \texttt{addLog}(x) \,; logRead)
\end{aligned}
$$

where x matches the name of the accessed file.

9.4.1 Aspect Interactions

Remember that a parallel composition of n aspects $A_1 \| \ldots \| A_n$ does not define any specific order of aspect application; the result of weaving may be non-deterministic. This situation arises when aspects interact, that is to say when at least two inserts must be executed at the same join point. For instance, consider the following aspect:

$$cryptRead = \texttt{read}(x) \blacktriangleright \texttt{crypt}(x); \; cryptRead$$

This aspect states that the reads should be encrypted. It interacts with the aspect *logAccess* defined previously, which describes logging for all users. When a user logs in and accesses a file, this access must be logged, *and* the file name must be encrypted.

The algorithm to check aspects interaction is similar to the algorithm for finite-state product automata. It terminates due to the finite-state nature of our aspects. Starting with a composition $A \| A'$, the algorithm eliminates the parallel operator by producing all the possible pairs (conjunction) of crosscuts from A and A'. A conjunction of crosscuts C_1 and C_2 is a solvable formula, and we can check if it has a solution using the algorithm of [5]. A crosscut with no solution cannot match any join point and can be removed from the aspect [7]. In the case of the example *logAccess* $\|$ *cryptRead*, we get:

$$
\begin{aligned}
logAccess \; \| \; cryptRead & \\
= \texttt{login}(u, m) &\blacktriangleright \texttt{skip} \quad ; logCrypt \\
\blacksquare \; \texttt{read}(x) &\blacktriangleright \texttt{crypt}(x) \; ; \; logAccess \; \| \; cryptRead \\
logCrypt = \texttt{logout}() &\blacktriangleright \texttt{skip} \; ; \; logAccess \; \| \; cryptRead \\
\blacksquare \; \texttt{read}(x) &\blacktriangleright (\texttt{addLog}(x) \blacklozenge \texttt{crypt}(x)) \; ; \; logCrypt
\end{aligned}
$$

Conflicts are represented using the non-deterministic function $(I_1 \blacklozenge I_2)$, which returns either $I_1 ; I_2$ or $I_2 ; I_1$. Here, we have $(\texttt{addLog}(x) \blacklozenge \texttt{crypt}(x))$, so the two aspects are not independent. Note that spurious conflicts have already been eliminated with the help of the rule

$$(I \blacklozenge \texttt{skip}) = (\texttt{skip} \blacklozenge I) = I.$$

This analysis does not depend on the base program to be woven. When there is no ($\blacklozenge$) in the resulting sequential aspect, the two aspects are independent for all programs. This property does not have to be checked again after any program modification. However, this property is a sufficient but not a necessary condition for aspect interaction. A more precise analysis is possible by taking into account the possible sequences of join points generated by the base program to be woven [7].

9.4.2   Support for Conflict Resolution

When no conflicts have been detected, the parallel composition of aspects can be woven without modification. Otherwise, the programmer must get rid of the nondeterminism by making the composition more precise. In the following, we present some linguistic support aimed at resolving interactions.

The occurrences of rules of the form $C \blacktriangleright (I_1 \blacklozenge I_2)$ indicate all potential interactions. They can be resolved one by one. For each $C \blacktriangleright (I_1 \blacklozenge I_2)$, the programmer may replace each rule $C \blacktriangleright (I_1 \blacklozenge I_2)$ by $C \blacktriangleright I_3$ where I_3 is a new insert that combines I_1 and I_2 in some way. For instance, in the previous example, $(\texttt{addLog}(x) \blacklozenge \texttt{crypt}(x))$ can be replaced by $\texttt{crypt}(x)$; $\texttt{addLog}(x)$ in order to generate encrypted logs.

This option is flexible but can be tedious. Instead of writing a new insert for each conflict, the programmer may indicate how to compose inserts at the aspect level. We propose a parallel operator $\|_{seq}$ to indicate that whenever a conflict occurs, $(I_1 \blacklozenge I_2)$ must be replaced by I_1 ; I_2 (where ";" denotes the sequencing operator of the programming language). Other parallel operators are useful, such as $\|_{fst}$, which replaces $(I_1 \blacklozenge I_2)$ by I_1 only.

Let us reconsider the two aspects *logAccess* and *cryptRead*:

- *logAccess* $\|_{seq}$ *cryptRead* generates plaintext logs for super users.
- *cryptRead* $\|_{seq}$ *logAccess* generates logs for users by logging (possibly encrypted) accesses.

9.5   STATIC WEAVING OF SAFETY PROPERTIES

The previous restrictions allow detecting interactions during weaving. However, they are not sufficient to detect semantic interactions. The code inserted by an aspect may still influence the application of another independent aspect. Our notion of independence only ensures that aspects can be woven in any order. In order to prevent semantic interactions and, more generally, to control the semantic impact of weaving, one has to restrict the language of inserts. Here, we consider the same aspect language as the previous section, except for the language of inserts, which becomes:

$$I ::= \texttt{skip} \mid \texttt{abort}$$

Even if this restriction is quite drastic (aspects can only abort the execution), interesting aspects can still be expressed. The expressive crosscut language allows us to specify safety properties (properties stating that no "bad thing" happens during the execution). Aspects can be used to rule out unwanted execution traces and to express security policies [3].

This restriction has several benefits:

- Aspects are semantic properties, and the impact of weaving is clear.
- Inserts always commute. There are no interactions between aspects, which can be composed freely in parallel.

The woven program satisfies the property/aspect: For executions in accordance with the property, it has the same behavior as the base program. Otherwise, it produces an exception and terminates just before violating the property.

The main drawback of execution monitors is their run-time cost. They are not specialized to the program, and each program instruction may involve a run-time check. In the remainder of this section, we present how to weave such trace-based aspects statically and efficiently.

9.5.1 Example

Consider the following aspect:

safe = `accountant()` ▶ `skip` ;
  (`manager()` ▶ `skip` ;`critical()` ▶ `skip` ; *safe*
  ■ `critical()` ▶ `abort` ; *safe*)
■ `manager()` ▶ `skip` ;
  (`accountant()` ▶ `skip` ;`critical()` ▶ `skip` ; *safe*
  ■ `critical()` ▶ `abort` ; *safe*)
■ `critical()` ▶ `abort` ; *safe*

The property defined by the aspect states that a critical action cannot take place before the clearance of the manager and the accountant (i.e., at least a call to `manager` and to `accountant` must occur before each call to `critical`).

Figure 9-1 illustrates weaving of this property on a very simple imperative base program.

Since the property is specified by a finite state aspect, it can be encoded as an automaton with alphabet {m, a, c} corresponding to the calls to `manager`, `accountant`, and `critical`, respectively. Notice that the base program may violate this property whenever the condition of the first `if` statement is false. The woven program, where two assignments and a conditional have been inserted, satisfies the property (i.e., aborts whenever the property is about to be violated).

An important challenge is to make this dynamic enforcement as inexpensive as possible. In particular, if we are able to detect statically that the base program satisfies the property, then no transformation should be performed.

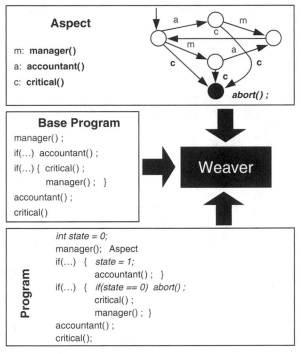

Figure 9-1   *Weaving safe on a simple imperative base program.*

9.5.2   Weaving Phases

Our aspects define a regular set of allowed finite executions. An aspect is encoded as a finite state automaton over events. The language recognized by the automaton is the set of all authorized sequences of events.

The weaver is a completely automatic tool that takes the automaton and the base program and produces an instrumented program [3]. We now outline its different phases (depicted in Figure 9-2).

Base Program Annotation.   The first phase is to locate and annotate the instructions of the base program corresponding to events (crosscuts). Depending on the property we want to enforce, the events can be calls to specific methods, assignments to specific variables, opening of files, etc. A key constraint is that an instruction of the base program must be associated with at most one event. This is easy to ensure when events are specified solely based on the syntax. In order to take semantic crosscuts into account, the base program must be transformed beforehand. Consider the event *"x is assigned the value 0."* It cannot be statically decided whether an assignment $x:=e$ will generate this event or not. A solution is to transform each assignment $x:=e$ into the statement `if e=0 then x:=e else` $x:=e$ where each instruction is now associated with a single event. Such pre-transformations rely on static program analyses to avoid insertion of useless tests.

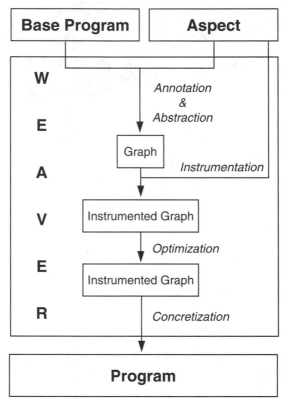

Figure 9-2 Phases of weaving.

Base Program Abstraction. The base program is abstracted into a graph whose nodes denote program points and whose edges represent instructions (events). The abstraction makes the next two phases independent of a specific programming language. Since the aspect is a trace property, the abstraction is the control-flow graph of the base program. In order to produce a precise abstraction, this phase relies on a control-flow analysis.

Instrumentation. The next phase is to transform the graph in order to rule out the forbidden sequences of events. We integrate the automaton by instrumenting the graph with additional structures (states and transition functions) that mimic the evolution of the automaton. Intuitively, this instrumentation corresponds to the insertion of an assignment (to implement the state transition of the underlying automaton) and a test (to check whether the property is about to be violated) before each event. This naïve weaving is optimized by the next phase.

Optimizations. The instrumented graph is refined in three steps. The automaton specifies a general property independent of any particular program. The first step is to *specialize* the automaton with respect to the base program. Second, a transformation similar to the classical automaton *minimization* yields a normalized instrumented graph. Finally, static analyses are used to optimize the automaton by removing useless state transitions.

The graph after optimization represents a program where at most one test and/or assignment (state transition) have been inserted at each `if` and `while` statement.

Concretization. The optimized graph must be translated back into a program. The graph has remained close to the base program since its nodes and edges still represent the same program points and instructions. We just need a way to store, fetch, and test a value (the automaton state) without affecting the normal execution. This is easily done using a fresh global variable.

9.5.3 Just-In-Time Weaving

The most interesting application of this technique is securing mobile code on receipt. The local security policy is declared as a property (aspect) to be enforced on incoming applets. The just-in-time weaver secures (i.e., abstracts, instruments, optimizes, and concretizes) an applet before loading it. Since some steps are potentially costly, our implementation uses simple heuristics that make the time complexity of weaving linear in the size of the program.

There are several benefits to this separation of security concerns. First, it is easier to express the policy declaratively as a property. Second, the approach is flexible and can accommodate customized properties. This feature is especially important in a security context where it is impossible to foresee all possible attacks and where policies may have to be modified quickly to respond to new threats.

9.6 CONCLUSION

In this chapter, we have presented a model (and three instantiations) for AOP based on execution traces. We have focused on the following points:

- Expressive and stateful aspect definitions
- A model conceptually based on weaving of executions

- Reasoning about and analysis of aspect properties, in particular aspect interaction
- Enforcement of properties by program transformation (i.e., static weaving)

We now briefly consider these contributions in turn and compare our approach with related work.

We have advocated and presented expressive (i.e., stateful) aspect languages. The crosscut language of AspectJ [14] consists mostly of *single instruction patterns* matching events such as a method calls or field accesses. AspectJ's patterns are very similar to our basic aspects $C \blacktriangleright I$. Expressing stateful aspects in AspectJ requires bookkeeping code in advice to pass information between crosscuts (e.g., increment a counter in an advice to check for the counter value later). The AspectJ construction `cflow` is the only exception allowing the definition of a form of stateful aspect. For example, `cflow(call(critical)) && call(read)` matches join points where `read` is called whenever there is a pending call to `critical` in the execution stack.

Our model is conceptually based on a monitor observing execution events and weaving execution traces, similar to the approach proposed by Filman and Havelund [11]. Other techniques can be related to execution monitors. Computational reflection is a general technique used to modify the execution mechanisms of a programming language. Restricted approaches to reflection have been proposed in order to support AOP. For instance, the composition filter model [2] proposes method wrappers in order to filter method calls and returns. De Volder *et al.* [6] propose a meta-programming framework based on Prolog. Unfortunately, these approaches do not allow stateful aspects.

By appropriate restrictions of the aspect language, we have proposed some solutions to the difficult problem of aspect interactions. Few other program analyses for AO programs have been proposed, most notably by Sereni and de Moor for the optimization of AspectJ's `cflow` construction [18] and by Shiman and Katz to verify applicability of aspects using model checking techniques [19]. At the tool-level, AspectJ provides limited support for aspect interaction analysis using IDE integration: the base program is annotated with crosscutting aspects. This graphical information can be used to detect conflicting aspects. However, the simple (i.e. stateless) crosscut model of AspectJ would entail an analysis detecting numerous spurious conflicts because the bookkeeping code cannot be taken into account. In case of real conflicts, AspectJ programmers must resolve conflicts by reordering aspects using the keyword `dominate`. When two aspects are unrelated with respect to the domination or hierarchy relations, the ordering of inserts is undefined.

In order to define static interaction analysis, we had to formally define aspects and weaving (see [7] for a formal treatment of Section 9.4). There are several approaches to the formalization of AOP. Wand *et al.* [22] propose a denotational semantics for a subset of AspectJ. Lämmel [15] formalizes method call interception with big-step semantics. Andrews' model [1] relies on algebraic processes. He focuses on equivalence of processes and correctness (termination) of the weaving algorithm. Other operational approaches to the formalization of AO systems have been proposed by Walker et al. [21] and Tucker and Krishnamurti [20] using different forms of abstract machines, as well as Jagadeesan *et al.* [13] based on process calculi.

Finally, we have shown in Section 9.5 that by restricting the insert language, aspects can be seen as formal properties, which can be enforced by program transformation. Dynamic monitors (such as VeriSoft [12] and AMOS [4]) or "security kernels" (such as Schneider's security automata [17]) have been used to enforce security properties. By contrast, our programming language approach permits many optimizations and avoids extending the run-time system or the language semantics.

The different aspect languages presented suggest several extensions. For example, allowing crosscuts of the same aspect to share variables makes the aspect language more expressive (cf. [8]). The possibility of associating an instance of an aspect with a run-time entity (e.g., each instance of a class in a Java program) would facilitate the application of our model to object-oriented languages. It would have been interesting to characterize a larger class of inserts (beyond `abort`) allowing us to keep the semantic impact of weaving under strict control. More generally, we believe that an important avenue for further AOP research is to provide more safeguards in terms of static analyses and specially tailored aspect languages. In order to make these analyses applicable in the context of large-scale application, their integration with standard model checking techniques [10] seems promising.

REFERENCES

1. ANDREWS, J. H. 2001. Process-algebraic foundations of aspect-oriented programming. In *Metalevel Architectures and Separation of Crosscutting Concerns 3rd Int'l Conf. (Reflection 2001)*, (Kyoto), A. Yonezawa and S. Matsuoka, Eds. LNCS, vol. 2192. Springer-Verlag, Berlin, 187–209.

2. BERGMANS, L. AND AKŞIT, M. 2001. Composing crosscutting concerns using composition filters. *Comm. ACM 44*, 10 (Oct.), 51–57.

3. COHEN, D., FEATHER, M. S., NARAYANASWAMY, K., AND FICKAS, S. S. 1997. Automatic monitoring of software requirements. In *19th Int'l Conf. Software Engineering (ICSE)*, (Boston). ACM, 602–603.

4. COLCOMBET, T. AND FRADET, P. 2000. Enforcing trace properties by program transformation. In *27th Symp. Principles of Programming Languages (POPL)*, (Boston). ACM, 54–66.

5. COMON, H. 1991. Disunification: A survey. In *Computational Logic: Essays in Honor of Alan Robinson*, J. L. Lassez and G. Plotkin, Eds. MIT Press, Cambridge, Massachusetts, 322–359.

6. DE VOLDER, K. AND D'HONDT, T. 1999. Aspect-oriented logic meta programming. In *Meta-Level Architectures and Reflection, 2nd Int'l Conf. Reflection*, P. Cointe, Ed. LNCS, vol. 1616. Springer, Verlag, Berlin, 250–272.

7. DOUENCE, R., FRADET, P., AND SÜDHOLT, M. 2002. A framework for the detection and resolution of aspect interactions. In *1st ACM Conf. Generative Programming and Component Engineering* (Pittsburgh). LNCS, vol. 2487. Springer-Verlag, Berlin, 173–188.

8. DOUENCE, R., FRADET, P., AND SÜDHOLT, M. 2004. Composition, reuse, and interaction analysis of stateful aspects. In *3rd Int'l Conf. Aspect-Oriented Software Development (AOSD)*, (Lancaster, UK). ACM, 141–150.

9. DOUENCE, R., MOTELET, O., AND SÜDHOLT, M. 2001. A formal definition of crosscuts. In *Metalevel Architectures and Separation of Crosscutting Concerns 3rd Int'l Conf. (Reflection 2001)*, (Kyoto), A. Yonezawa and S. Matsuoka, Eds. LNCS, vol. 2192. Springer-Verlag, Berlin, 170–186.

10. FELTY, A. P. AND NAMJOSHI, K. S. 2003. Feature specification and automated conflict detection. *ACM Transactions on Software Engineering and Methodology 12*, 1, 3–27.

11. FILMAN, R. E. AND HAVELUND, K. 2002. Realizing aspects by transforming for events. In *Automated Software Engineering (ASE), Workshop on Declarative Meta Programming to Support Software Development* (Edinburgh). http://www.cs.ubc.ca/~kdevolder/Workshops/ASE2002/DMP/papers/DMPWorkshop-Proceedings.pdf.

12. GODEFROID, P. 1997. Model checking for programming languages using Verisoft. In *24th Symp. Principles of Programming Languages (POPL)*, (Paris). ACM, 174–186.

13. JAGADEESAN, R., JEFFREY, A., AND RIELY, J. 2003. A calculus of untyped aspect-oriented programs. In *ECOOP 2003—European Conference on Object-Oriented Programming*, (Darmstadt), L. Cardelli, Ed. LNCS, vol. 2743. Springer-Verlag, Berlin, 54–73.

14. KICZALES, G., HILSDALE, E., HUGUNIN, J., KERSTEN, M., PALM, J., AND GRISWOLD, W. G. 2001. An overview of AspectJ. In *ECOOP 2001—Object-Oriented Programming, 15th European Conference*, (Budapest), J. L. Knudsen, Ed. LNCS, vol. 2072. Springer-Verlag, Berlin, 327–353.

15. LÄMMEL, R. 2002. A semantical approach to method-call interception. In *1st Int'l Conf. Aspect-Oriented Software Development (AOSD)*, (Enschede, The Netherlands), G. Kiczales, Ed. ACM, 41–55.

16. NIELSON, F. AND NIELSON, H. R. 1992. *Semantics with Applications—A Formal Introduction*. Wiley, New York.

17. SCHNEIDER, F. B. 2000. Enforceable security policies. *ACM Transactions on Information and System Security 3*, 1 (Feb.), 30–50.

18. SERENI, D. AND DE MOOR, O. 2003. Static analysis of aspects. In *2nd Int'l Conf. Aspect-Oriented Software Development (AOSD)*, (Boston). ACM, 30–39.

19. SHIMAN, M. AND KATZ, S. 2003. Superimpositions and Aspect-Oriented Programming. *The Computer Journal, 46*, 5, 529–541.

20. TUCKER, D. B. AND KRISHNAMURTI. 2003. Pointcuts and advice in higher-order languages. In *2nd Int'l Conf. Aspect-Oriented Software Development (AOSD)*, (Boston). ACM, 158–167.

21. WALKER, D., ZDANCEWIC, S., AND LIGATTI, J. 2003. A theory of aspects. In *Functional Programming*, (Upsala). ACM.

22. WAND, M., KICZALES, G., AND DUTCHYN, C. in press. A semantics for advice and dynamic join points in aspect-oriented programming. *ACM Transactions on Programming Languages and Systems*.

Chapter 10

Using Mixin Technology to Improve Modularity

RICHARD CARDONE AND CALVIN LIN

In object-oriented languages, aspects can be defined by generalizing the idea of a class to that of a *mixin,* a form of generic type. Mixins become aspects when they contain code for multiple classes. In this chapter, we describe mixins and explain how they can be used to define aspects. We demonstrate the flexibility of mixin programming by prototyping a graphical user interface library that can be configured to run on dissimilar devices. We also describe additional language and compiler support that increases the effectiveness of mixin programming. We conclude by proposing some new ideas about how mixins and generic types in general can be better supported in object-oriented languages.

10.1   INTRODUCTION

One approach to reducing the cost of software is to make software easier to reuse. Doing so reduces the risk and expense of developing new applications. The ability to reuse code depends on two properties: *modularity* and *easy composition*. Modularity allows us to separate concerns [26], making code easier to understand, maintain, and treat as a unit. Easy composition allows us to combine the capabilities of different code modules in different applications.

Unfortunately, today's object-oriented languages, such as Java, are limited in their ability to modularize and compose code. Modularity is limited because the basic unit of encapsulation and reuse is the class. Once the organization of a class hierarchy is fixed, it is always possible to define new features whose implementations *crosscut* the existing set of classes. For example, it is common for features that add global properties, such as security, thread safety, fault tolerance, or performance constraints, to affect code in multiple classes. It is difficult to encapsulate such features in a single class. Instead, object-oriented programs generally consist of sets of collaborating classes [16], and changes to one class often require coordinated changes to others.

Current object-oriented languages are also limited in their ability to compose features. Java's support for composition depends primarily on single inheritance and subtype polymorphism. These mechanisms do not scale well when there are a large number of features. For example, there are three possible ways to organize two features, A and B, into classes (see Figure 10-1): (1) put them in the same class, (2) make A a subclass of B, or (3) make B a subclass of A.

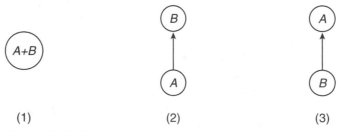

(1)   (2)   (3)

Figure 10-1 *Organizing features in classes.*

Each choice has different implications regarding the composition of A and B. For example, the first two choices force B to be included whenever A is included. Thus, by forcing the programmer to choose a single fixed class hierarchy, Java makes it difficult to compose a collection of features in an orthogonal manner. As the number of features grows, this problem becomes more severe, because the number of possible feature combinations grows rapidly, but the number of feature combinations that can be practically supported does not.

This chapter describes how *mixins* [9], a kind of generic type, can improve the flexibility of Java class hierarchies, thereby improving the ability to modularize code and compose features. The purpose of this chapter is threefold. First, we provide an introduction to mixin programming. We describe our mixin extension to Java and the additional language support that we implemented to increase the effectiveness of programming with mixins. Second, to give a concrete example, we summarize our previously published evaluation [13] of how mixins allow us to build customizable GUI libraries. In particular, we explain how a nested form of mixins, called *mixin layers* [27, 28], can be used to implement a configurable GUI that runs on platforms with widely dissimilar capabilities, such as cell phones, PDAs, and PCs. We also show how mixin layers support the implementation of crosscutting features, so mixin layers can be thought of as aspects [23]. Third, we propose a new approach of integrating mixins into object-oriented type systems and a new way of reconciling the implementation tradeoffs inherent in parametric polymorphism.

10.2 *MIXIN TECHNOLOGY*

Our approach to increasing reuse is to build into programming languages better support for modularization and composition. To test this approach, we have developed the *Java Layers* (JL) language [12, 20], which extends the compositional capability of Java.

Java Layers extensions include support for constrained *parametric polymorphism* [11] and mixins. Parametric polymorphism allows types to be declared as parameters to code. Parametric polymorphism enhances reuse by allowing the same generic algorithm to be applied to different types; the collection classes in C++'s Standard Template Library [29] are an example of this kind of reuse. JL's implementation is similar to C++'s templates, but in keeping with most proposals [1, 2, 10, 19] for adding generic types to Java, JL allows type parameters to be constrained.

Mixins are types whose supertypes are specified parametrically. Mixins further enhance reuse over non-mixin parametric polymorphism by allowing the same subtype specialization to be applied to different supertypes. We give an example of mixin reuse in Section 10.2.1.

Mixin layers [27, 28] are a special form of mixins that can be used to coordinate changes in multiple collaborating classes. Mixin layers are mixins that contain nested types, which can themselves be mixins. Fidget, our GUI framework described in Section 10.3, is built using mixin layers.

10.2.1 *Mixins*

The term *mixin* was first used to describe a style of LISP programming that combines classes using multiple inheritance [21, 24]. Since then, the mixin concept has evolved to be that of a type whose supertypes are declared parametrically [9, 33]. We use the term in this sense and limit ourselves to languages such as Java that support single inheritance of classes. JL supports mixins and other generic types by implementing parametric classes and interfaces.

Mixins are useful, because they allow multiple classes to be specialized in the same manner, with the specializing code residing in a single reusable class. For example, suppose we wanted to extend three unrelated classes—`Car`, `Box`, and `House`—to have a "locked" state by adding two methods, `lock()` and `unlock()`. Without mixins, we would define subclasses of `Car`, `Box`, and `House` that each extended their respective superclasses with the `lock()` and `unlock()` methods. This approach results in replicating the lock code in three places.

Using mixins, however, we would instead write a single class called `Lockable` that could extend any superclass, and we would instantiate the `Lockable` class with `Car`, `Box`, and `House`. This approach results in only one definition of the lock code. In JL, the `Lockable` mixin would be defined as shown in Listing 10-1.

Listing 10-1 *Lockable mixin in JL*

```
class Lockable<T> extends T {
  private boolean _locked;
  public lock(){_locked = true;}
  public unlock(){_locked = false;} }
```

This class is *parametric,* because it declares *type parameter* T. JL's parametric types are similar in syntax and semantics to C++ template classes. When `Lockable<T>` is compiled, T is not bound. To use `Lockable<T>`, T must be bound to a type to create an *instantiation* of the parametric class. Each distinct binding of T defines a new *instantiated type,* which can then be used like a conventional Java type.

What makes `Lockable<T>` a mixin, however, is that its instantiated types inherit from the types bound to T. Mixins are distinguished from other parametric types, because the supertypes of mixins are specified using type parameters. Thus, a mixin's supertypes are not precisely known at *compile-time* but instead are specified at *instantiation-time.*

Mixin instantiations generate new class hierarchies. For example, `Lockable<Box>` generates the hierarchy shown in Figure 10-2.

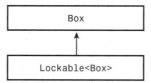

Figure 10-2 `Lockable<Box>` *Hierarchy.*

In its current form, `Lockable`'s capabilities are limited, because nothing can be presumed about the type that gets bound to the type parameter T. In JL, however, constraints can be specified to restrict the types used in instantiations. For example, the redefinition of `Lockable` in Listing 10-2 guarantees that T's binding type implements the physical object interface (not shown). This constraint on T means members of `PhysicalObject` can be used within `Lockable` in a type-safe manner.

Listing 10-2 *Redefining* `Lockable`

```
class Lockable<T implements PhysicalObject>
  extends T {...}
```

10.2.2 Stepwise Refinement

The GenVoca software component model [6] provides a conceptual framework for programming with mixins. The model supports a programming methodology of *step-wise refinement* in which types are built incrementally in layers. The key to stepwise refinement is the use of components, called *layers,* that encapsulate the complete implementation of individual application features. Application features are any characteristic or requirement implemented by an application. Stepwise refinement allows custom applications to be built by mixing and matching features.

Mixins implement GenVoca layers. To show how mixins can be used to build applications incrementally, we define the `Colorable` and `Ownable` mixins in the same way that we defined the `Lockable` mixin above. `Colorable` manages a physical object's color, and `Ownable` manages ownership properties. We can now create a variety of physical objects that support various combinations of features in Listing 10-3.

Listing 10-3 *Incrementally building applications*

```
Colorable<Ownable<Car>>
Colorable<Lockable<Box>>
Lockable<Ownable<Colorable<House>>>
```

We can think of each of these instantiations as starting with the capabilities of some base class, `Car`, `Box`, or `House`, and refining those capabilities with the addition of each new feature. In the end, a customized type supporting all the required features is produced. Mixins can be used in this way to provide some of the flexibility of multiple inheritance while avoiding pitfalls such as name collisions and repeated inheritance [33].

10.2.3 Mixin Layers

The compositional power of mixins can be increased with mixin layers. *Mixin layers* are mixins that contain nested types. A single mixin layer can implement a feature that crosscuts multiple classes. To see how this works, consider an example from our evaluation of customizable GUI libraries, which we call *Fidget* (*F*lexible w*idget*s).

Listing 10-4 shows simplified versions of the basic *Fidget* class and the mixin layer that adds color support.

Listing 10-4 *BaseFidget*

```
class BaseFidget<> {
  public class Button {...}
  public class CheckBox {...} ...}

class ColorFidget<T> extends T {
  public class Button extends T.Button {...}
  public class CheckBox
     extends T.CheckBox {...} ...}
```

`BaseFidget` takes no explicit type parameters; we show two of its nested widget classes above. In the instantiation `ColorFidget<BaseFidget<>>`, the behavior of each of the nested classes in `BaseFidget` is extended by its corresponding class in `ColorFidget`. In this way, feature code scattered across multiple classes is encapsulated in a single mixin layer. In Section 10.3.4, we explain why some parameterized classes don't have explicit type parameters.

10.3 FIDGET DESIGN

For many years, software portability meant running similar software on different general-purpose computers, each with its own operating system and architecture. Software developers minimized the cost of supporting multiple platforms by reusing the same code, design, and programming tools wherever possible. Today, miniaturization has led to a wide diversity of computing devices, including embedded systems, cell phones, PDAs, set-top boxes, consumer appliances, and PCs. Though these devices are dissimilar in hardware configuration, purpose, and capability, the same economic forces that drove software reuse among general-purpose computers now encourage reuse across different device classes.

To make it easier to reuse code across devices, several standardization efforts are defining new Java run-time environments [31]. These environments are customized for various classes of devices while still remaining as compatible as possible with the Java language, JVM, and existing libraries. For example, Sun's KVM [32] virtual machine, which is designed to run on devices with as little as 128K of memory, has removed a number of Java language features, such as floating point numbers and class finalization, and a number of JVM features, such as native methods and reflection. In addition, the capabilities of run-time libraries have also been reduced to accommodate limited memory devices. This redesign of the Java libraries leads to two questions that directly concern code reuse and the ability to support crosscutting concerns:

- How does one scale an API to accommodate different devices capabilities?
- How does one reuse the same library code across different devices?

Fidget explores the above questions by implementing a prototype GUI that works on cell phones, Palm OS devices [25], and PCs. The challenge is to provide a single GUI code-base that runs on all these devices, yet accommodates the input, output, and processing capabilities of each device. For example, a device may or may not support a color display, so in building our libraries, we would like to be able to easily include or exclude color support. Thus, we need a way to encapsulate features that crosscut multiple classes to a degree that is not possible with standard programming technologies. The goal of Fidget is to test the hypothesis that mixins and mixin layers provide a convenient mechanism for encapsulating crosscutting concerns.

10.3.1   Architecture

Fidget is structured as a stack of the three architectural layers highlighted in Figure 10-3: the Hardware Abstraction layer (HAL), the Kernel layer, and the User layer. On the bottom, the HAL interacts with the underlying device's graphics system and is the only Fidget code that is device-dependent. On top, the User layer is a thin veneer that provides a familiar, non-nested, class interface to application programmers. Our discussion focuses on the Kernel layer.

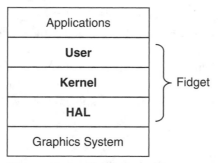

***Figure 10-3**   Fidget's architecture.*

The Kernel layer defines all widgets and all optional widget features. The kernel sits on top of the HAL and uses the HAL's drawing and event handling capabilities to create displayable widgets. Fidget widgets are modeled after those of Java's AWT [17, 30], so widget classes such as `Window`, `Button`, and `TextField` serve the same purpose in Fidget as their analogs do in AWT. The kernel implements nine such widgets, which is sufficient for our prototyping purposes. Even though some optional features cannot be used with all devices, there is only a single kernel code-base.

The Fidget kernel uses a *lightweight* implementation [17] to accommodate devices with constrained memory resources. Lightweight widgets do not have associated peer widgets in the underlying graphics system, which for Fidget is a small subset of either the Java SDK [30] or the J2ME [31] graphic subsystems.[1] Thus, a Fidget window that displays two buttons and a text field creates only one widget, a window, in the underlying Java system. Fidget then draws its own buttons and text field on this underlying window.

10.3.2   Components

The design of the Fidget kernel classes is based on the `BaseFidget` class introduced in Listing 10-4 in Section 10.2.3. `BaseFidget` provides the minimal implementation for each widget in a nested class. We implemented nine widgets in our prototype; Listing 10-4 shows two of these. These nested widget classes are `Button`, `CheckBox`, `CheckBoxGroup`, `Label`, `Panel`, `TextArea`, `TextComponent`, `TextField`, and `Window`.

Optional features are implemented in mixin layers that extend `BaseFidget`. These mixin layers can contain code for one widget class, or they can implement crosscutting features and contain code for more than one widget class. For example, the `TextFieldSetLabel` layer affects only one class by adding the `setLabel()` method to `TextField`. Conversely, the `LightWeightFidget` layer implements lightweight widget support and contains code for most widgets. Fidget's features are listed in Table 10-1.

`BaseFidget` also contains two nested classes that serve as superclasses for the nested widget classes. `Component` implements common widget function and is a superclass of all widgets. `Container`, a subclass of `Component`, allows widgets to

---

1. For experimental ease, we scaffold Fidget on top of Java instead of writing low-level graphics code for each device.

contain other widgets. `Window` is an example of a container widget. In the next section, we explore the design consequences of defining these superclasses in `BaseFidget`.

Table 10-1 *Fidget Kernel Mixins*

Kernel Mixin	Multi-Class?	Description
ButtonSetLabel	No	Re-settable Button label
BorderFidget	No	Draws Container borders
CheckBoxSetLabel	No	Re-settable Checkbox label
TextComponentSetFont	No	Changeable fonts
TextFieldSetLabel	No	Re-settable TextField label
AltLook	Yes	Alternative look and feel
ColorFidget	Yes	Color display support
EventBase	Yes	Basic event listeners/handlers
EventFidget	Yes	All event listeners/handlers
EventFocus	Yes	Focus event handling
EventKey	Yes	Keyboard event handling
EventMouse	Yes	Mouse event handling
LightWeightFidget	Yes	Lightweight support

10.3.3 The Sibling Pattern

The *Sibling design pattern* uses inheritance relationships between classes nested in the same class to enhance code modularity. The pattern itself can be implemented in Java, but mixin layers make it more practical.

We begin our discussion of this pattern by looking at a problem that occurs when certain crosscutting features are implemented with mixin layers. We then show how the Sibling pattern solves this problem and how additional JL language support simplifies the solution.

The advantage of nesting `Component`, `Container`, and all widget classes inside of `BaseFidget` is that a single mixin layer can affect all of these classes. We reintroduce `BaseFidget` in Listing 10-5, this time showing the widget `Button` and its superclass `Component` (type parameter constraints and most nested classes are not shown). As Listing 10-5 illustrates, in Fidget, features like color support modify the behavior of `Component` as well as its widget subclasses.

Listing 10-5 *Incorrect BaseFidget*

```
class BaseFidget<> {
  public abstract class Component {...}
  public class Button extends Component {...} ...}

class ColorFidget<T> extends T {
  public class Component
    extends T.Component {...}
  public class Button
    extends T.Button {...} ...}

ColorFidget<LightWeightFidget<BaseFidget<>>>
```

There is, however, a potential pitfall when parent and child classes are nested in the same class. To see the problem, Listing 10-5 also shows an instantiation of a Fidget GUI with color support. The instantiation includes the `LightWeightFidget` mixin (code not shown), which is structured like `ColorFidget`.

The class hierarchies generated by the instantiation are shown in Figure 10-4. The enclosing classes form a class hierarchy, as do like-named nested classes.

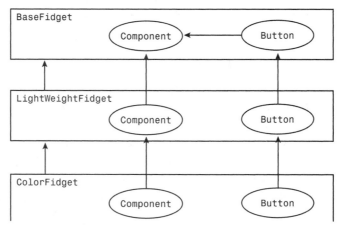

Figure 10-4 *Incorrect hierarchy.*

In addition, `Button` inherits from `Component` in `BaseFidget`. Note that `ColorFidget.Button` does not inherit from `ColorFidget.Component`, which means that the color support in the latter class is never used. As a matter of fact, it would be useless for any mixin layer to extend `Component`, because no widget will ever inherit from it.

The inheritance relationship we really want is shown in Figure 10-5, where `ColorFidget.Button` inherits from all `Button` classes and `Component` classes in the mixin-generated hierarchy. We call this the *Sibling pattern,* which we define as the inheritance pattern in which a nested class inherits from the *most specialized subclass* of one of its siblings. In Figure 10-5, `BaseFidget.Button` inherits from the most specialized subclass (`ColorFidget.Component`) of its sibling (`BaseFidget.Component`).

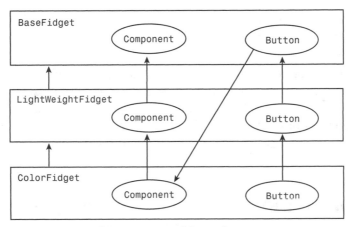

Figure 10-5   *Sibling pattern hierarchy.*

The Sibling pattern can be implemented in Java by using a distinguished name for the leaf class of all mixin-generated hierarchies. Once this well-known, predetermined name is established by programming convention, it can be used in any class or mixin in the application. This solution, however, limits flexibility and can lead to name conflicts when different instantiations are specified in the same package. By contrast, JL provides a more flexible naming solution that avoids the need for ad-hoc naming conventions. We describe that solution now.

10.3.4   *JL's Implicit* **This** *Type Parameter*

JL provides a better way to express the Sibling pattern using its implicit **This** type parameter [12]. Parameterized types in JL have one implicit type parameter and zero or more explicitly declared type parameters. **This** is automatically bound to the leaf class type in a mixin-generated hierarchy, which provides JL with a limited, static, virtual typing [35] capability.

Listing 10-4 shows how `BaseFidget`, which declares no type parameters explicitly, uses its implicit **This** parameter to implement the Sibling pattern. JL binds **This** to the leaf class in the generated hierarchy, which is `ColorFidget` in our example from Listing 10-5. The redefined `Button` class in Listing 10-6 now inherits from `ColorFidget.Component`, as shown in Figure 10-5.

Listing 10-6 *Correct BaseFidget*

```
class BaseFidget<> {
  public abstract class Component {...}
  public class Button
     extends This.Component {...} ...}
```

The Sibling pattern allows a Fidget layer to extend individual widget classes and their common superclass simultaneously. In this way, established object-oriented methods of class decomposition, in which common function is placed in superclasses, are extended to work with mixins layers. In Fidget's mixin layers, refinements to `Component` are inherited by all widget classes in all layers.

10.4 USING FIDGET

To build a Fidget library, we first select the SDK or J2ME Hardware Abstraction Layer (HAL) based on the target device's underlying Java support. PCs use the SDK; Palm devices and cell phones use J2ME. As described in Section 10.3.1, the HAL provides a small set of line and curve drawing primitives that is consistent across all platforms.

Next, we specify and compile the features we need in our library. The code implementing the different features resides in mixin layers in the `kernel` package, which corresponds to the Kernel layer in Figure 10-3. The actual Fidget libraries are assembled in the User layer, which we implement in the `widget` package. The code in Listing 10-7 shows the feature selection for two different libraries.

Both of the preceding libraries are lightweight implementations (Section 10.3.1), the only kind currently available in Fidget. The first library supports all events and, by overriding the drawing methods in `LightWeightFidget`, provides an alternative look and feel. The second library supports color displays, resettable labels, and key and mouse event handling. If a library feature is not supported by the device on which it runs, then executing the feature code either has no effect or throws an exception.

Listing 10-7 *Feature selection for different libraries*

```
package widget;

class Fidget extends AltLook<EventFidget<
  LightWeightFidget<BaseFidget<>>>> {}

class Fidget extends ColorFidget<
  ButtonSetLabel<EventKey<EventMouse<
  EventBase<LightWeightFidget<
  BaseFidget<>>>>>>> {}
```

In addition to the `Fidget` class, the User layer contains wrapper classes for each widget. These classes allow Fidget widgets to replace AWT widgets in application code. For example, the definitions for the `Button` and `Window` wrapper classes are shown in Listing 10-8.

Listing 10-8 *Wrapper class definitions*

```
public class Button extends Fidget.Button{}
public class Window extends Fidget.Window{}
```

To use a Fidget library, application code simply imports `widget.*` and uses the Fidget widgets in the same way that AWT widgets are used. The sample code in Listing 10-9 functions in a similar way using either Fidget or AWT. The code creates a window with a single button. The button's label is set to "ButtonLabel," and then the window is displayed on the screen.

Listing 10-9 *Replacing AWT widgets*

```
// import widget.* or java.awt.*
public class Sample {
  public static void main(String[] args) {
    Window win = new Window(...);
    Button b = new Button("ButtonLabel");
    win.add(b);
    win.setVisible(true)
  } }
```

10.5 MIXIN PROGRAMMING SUPPORT

In addition to the implicit **This** type parameter described in Section 10.3.4, JL introduces three other language features and one compiler feature that make mixin programming more effective [12]. In this section, we briefly characterize two language features that have been implemented in JL.

10.5.1 Constructor Propagation

Superclass initialization is not straightforward in mixin classes, because the superclass of a mixin is not known when the mixin is defined [37]. To make constructors convenient to use with mixins, JL introduces the **propagate** modifier for constructors. Constructors are propagated from parent to child class, with constructors marked **propagate** in the parent only able to affect constructors marked **propagate** in the child. (The default constructor in a child class is also considered propagatable.) Constructor propagation is more than the simple inheritance of constructors, because constructor signatures and bodies can change when constructors are propagated to child classes.

In Fidget, one measure of the effectiveness of automatic constructor propagation is that many constructors do not need to be hand-coded. In `BaseFidget`, 20 constructors are declared with **propagate.** On average, the 13 kernel layers that extend `BaseFidget` declare just over one constructor each, which indicates that automatic constructor generation is sufficient in most cases.

10.5.2 Deep Conformance

Mixins provide a powerful way to compose software, but to avoid composing incompatible features, mechanisms are needed to restrict how mixins are used. Type parameter constraints are one mechanism for restricting the use of mixins to avoid incompatibilities. In addition, JL extends the semantics of constrained type parameters to work with the nested structure of mixin layers.

JL's notion of *deep interface conformance* [27] extends Java's idea of interface constraints to include nested interfaces. Normally, a Java class that implements an interface is not required to implement the interface's nested interfaces. JL introduces the **deeply** modifier on `implements` clauses to require classes to implement the nested interfaces of the classes' super-interfaces. In addition, by using the **deeply** modifier on `extends` clauses, JL also defines *deep subtyping* [27]. Deep subtyping requires that a subtype have the same nested structure as the supertype it extends.

In JL, mixin layers that deeply conform to the same interface or mixin layers that deeply subtype the same supertype can be composed with each other, because they are compatible at all nesting levels. This compatibility is guaranteed by the compiler.

10.6 FUTURE WORK

In this section, we describe two prospective extensions to JL: semantic checking and class hierarchy optimization. We also propose two topics for future research: a treatment of mixins as types and a reconciliation of two approaches to implementing parametric polymorphism in object-oriented languages.

10.6.1 Semantic Checking

Even with deep conformance, undesirable mixin compositions can still be easily created. The ability to restrict how mixins are ordered or how many times a mixin can appear in an instantiation requires a higher level of checking than is convenient using OO-type systems. We call this extended capability *semantic checking* because mixin compositions should be not only type-safe but also meaningful.

JL's semantic checking uses semantic *attributes,* which are identifiers or tags chosen by programmers to represent meaningful characteristics in an application. At compile-time, an *ordered attribute list* is associated with each class hierarchy. Attributes are added to lists using **provides** clauses in class definitions. Attribute lists are tested using **requires** clauses in class definitions. These tests use regular expression pattern matching and a count operator to validate the presence, absence, cardinality, and ordering of mixins in a composition. Semantic checking occurs only at compile-time; there is no run-time overhead. Chapter 4 of Cardone's dissertation provides greater detail about the design of the JL's semantic checking facility [12].

10.6.2 Class Hierarchy Optimization

JL's programming methodology of stepwise refinement can create deep hierarchies of small classes. The use of many small classes can increase load time and the memory footprint of an application. In addition, stepwise refinement can also increase method call overhead, because multiple mixin methods are often called to perform the work of a single method in a conventionally written application.

At design time, we want the modularity of stepwise refinement; At runtime, we want fast code unimpeded by multiple layers of indirection. By extending existing technology [36] that compresses class hierarchies, we believe the run-time effects of design time layering can be largely eliminated. Chapter 5 of Cardone's dissertation provides greater detail about the design of the Class Hierarchy Optimization [12].

10.6.3 Mixins as Types

Most mixin research falls into one of two categories. The first uses parametric polymorphism to implement mixins by generalizing the idea of a parameterized type. The second defines *mixins as types* and generalizes the idea of a class. In this section, we propose a way to bring these two approaches together.

Using parametric polymorphism, mixins and other parameterized types are typically treated as *type functions* or *type schemas,* which generate types but are not themselves types. In languages that already support parametric types, adding mixins can be an almost trivial extension. Mixin research in this category often uses C++ template classes, which already support mixins. Such research [14, 27, 37] emphasizes software engineering concerns and often includes experiments that test the effectiveness of different mixin programming techniques. Java Layers builds directly on this line of research.

On the other hand, mixins can be defined as types that extend their supertypes without relying on parametric polymorphism. The research [4, 8, 15] in this area focuses on the formal semantics of mixins and on the integration of mixins into existing type systems. This integration typically uses the keyword *mixin* to declare new types, which either replace or work in conjunction with existing types (e.g., classes).

JAM [3] is a recently implemented language that treats mixins as types. JAM integrates mixin types into Java by adding two new keywords and by extending Java's type system. The JAM code in Listing 10-10 illustrates how mixin type M is declared and how it is used to define two subclasses (Child1 and Child2) of two parent classes (Parent1 and Parent2).

Listing 10-10 *Mixins as types in Java*

```
mixin M { ... }
class Child1 = M extends Parent1;
class Child2 = M extends Parent2;
```

Since mixins are types in JAM, Child1 is a subtype of both M and Parent1 in the Listing 10-10. Child2 is also a subtype of M, which allows objects of types Child1 and Child2 to be treated as type M objects.

To avoid some of the restrictions of JAM, such as the inability to compose mixins with other mixins, and to support parametric polymorphism, we propose an implementation of parametric types that supports *full* and *partial instantiation*. A parametric type is fully instantiated when all type parameters are bound; a parametric type is partially instantiated when at least one type parameter is unbound. The asterisk (*) is used to indicate unbound type parameters in instantiations.

A key component of this proposal is that all instantiations are types, but only full instantiations can be constructed. The code in Listing 10-11 depicts mixin M and two lines of code that appear outside of M. The variable `partial` has type M<*>, which is a partial instantiation of mixin M. Any full instantiation of M can be constructed and assigned to `partial`, as objects of types M<Parent1> and M<Parent2> here have been.

Listing 10-11 *Constructing full instantiations*

```
class M<T> extends T { ... }
M<*> partial = new M<Parent1>();
partial = new M<Parent2>();
```

In this proposal, parametric polymorphism (with mixin support) is fundamentally integrated into the type system. In addition, partial instantiation implies partial evaluation: In partial instantiations, members of parametric types that are not dependent on unbound type parameters are accessible.

10.6.4 *Implementing Parametric Polymorphism*

There are two basic ways to implement parametric polymorphism in object-oriented languages. *Homogeneous* implementations execute the same compiled code for all instantiations of a parametric type. *Heterogeneous* implementations, on the other hand, generate a specialized version of compiled code for each distinct instantiation of a parametric type. In this section, we propose a way to realize the benefits of both approaches in the same implementation.

The homogeneous approach is implemented by Generic Java (GJ) [10] and will be used in future versions of Java [19]. These implementations work by *erasing* type parameters at compile time and replacing them with general types that are appropriate for all instantiations.

Figure 10-6 shows parametric class C and its erasure, which gets compiled. In GJ, no type parameter information is available at runtime. Instead, the GJ compiler inserts dynamic type casts into code to guarantee type safety. It also inserts bridge methods to guarantee that method overriding works properly.

```
class C<T> {                        class C {
  T f;                                Object f;
  T m(T t) {…} }                      Object m(Object t) {…} }
```
Erasure

Figure 10-6 *Homogeneous type parameter erasure.*

In general, homogeneous implementations are memory-efficient, because a single class implements all instantiations of a parametric type. Homogeneous implementations, however, also have a number of disadvantages. Type erasure loses information because actual type parameter bindings known at compile time are not available at runtime. This means, for example, that a type parameter cannot specify the (non-array) type in a **new** expression, since the actual type is not known at runtime and cannot be allocated. For the same reason, type parameters cannot be used as the types in cast, **catch**, or **instanceof** expressions. Most significant, however, is that *pure homogeneous implementations in Java cannot support mixins* because different mixin instantiations require different supertypes.

Alternatively, the heterogeneous approach is implemented by C++ and Java Layers. JL uses a heterogeneous implementation, because mixins can be supported and because of its increased expressiveness; i.e., the ability to use type parameters wherever a type is legal.

Figure 10-7 shows parametric class C and the instantiation of C<String>, which gets compiled. Since each instantiation generates specialized code, heterogeneous implementations, like JL and C++, can experience code bloat if a large number of instantiations is used. In addition, the substitution of actual type parameters in instantiated types can lead to access control restrictions when the actual type and the parametric type are in different packages [10].

```
class C<T> {                        class C_String {
  T f;                                String f;
  T m(T t) {…} }                      String m(String t) {…} }
```
C<String>

Figure 10-7 *Heterogeneous instantiation.*

Unfortunately, the choice between homogeneous and heterogeneous implementation affects the programming language and its usage. Homogeneous implementations place numerous restrictions on the use of type parameters; heterogeneous implementations require programmers to consider code size and package placement issues. Rather than lock a language into one approach or the other, we propose to combine the two approaches and to give the programmer control over their use.

Specifically, we propose that parametric types declared with the new **special-ize** modifier be instantiated using the heterogeneous approach; otherwise, the homogenous approach is used.[2] Heterogeneously instantiated parametric types can support mixins and the less restrictive use of type parameters. Thus, **specialize** determines how type parameters are used in parametric types. Our proposal gives programmers explicit control over instantiation, whereas programmers currently are implicitly controlled by the implementation choice made by the language.

10.7 RELATED WORK

AspectJ [22, 23] is an extension to the Java programming language in which concerns are encapsulated in a new construct called an *aspect*. Aspects implement features that crosscut class boundaries, just as mixin layers do in JL. Both aspects and mixin layers can add new methods to existing classes. Aspects can weave code before or after the execution of a method, an effect JL achieves using method overriding and explicit calls to **super**. Aspects can refine the behavior of any group of existing classes, while mixin layers can only refine the classes nested in their superclasses. Thus, aspects are more expressive and can address more kinds of concerns than JL mixins. On the other hand, aspects must express explicit ordering constraints, while the order of mixin application is implicit in their instantiations. Also, as generic classes, mixins are probably easier to integrate into existing type systems than aspects.

Hyper/J [18] provides Java support for *multi-dimensional separation of concerns* [34]. This approach to software development is more general than that of JL, because it addresses the evolution of all software artifacts, including documentation, test cases, and design, as well as code. Hyper/J focuses on the adaptation, integration, and on-demand remodularization of Java code. Like JL, encapsulated feature implementations, called *hyperslices* in Hyper/J, can be mixed and matched to create customized applications. Unlike JL, Hyper/J can extract and possibly reuse feature code not originally separated into hyperslices. That is, Hyper/J supports the unplanned re-factorization of code to untangle feature implementations. While JL generalizes current OO technology, Hyper/J represents a more radical shift in thinking that also requires the development of new composition techniques.

---

2. Alternately, a **generalize** modifier could be defined, but **specialize** fits in better with the current plan for Java generics.

10.8 CONCLUSION

In this chapter, we discussed mixins and mixin layers, and we described how mixin layers implement reusable software components. We summarized an evaluation in which custom GUI libraries are generated using mixin layers. We also described supplemental language support that makes mixin programming easier and more effective.

Additionally, we made two proposals concerning parametric types and mixins. Our first proposal brings together two lines of mixin research by defining partially instantiated parametric types as types. Our second proposal bridges the gap between homogeneous and heterogeneous implementations of parametric polymorphism by giving programmers the choice of implementation when they define parametric types.

ACKNOWLEDGMENTS

This work has been supported by NSF CAREER grant ACI-9984660 and a grant from Tivoli.

REFERENCES

1. AGESEN, O., FREUND, S. N., AND MITCHELL, J. C. 1997. Adding type parameterization to the Java language. In *12th Conf. Object-Oriented Programming, Systems, Languages, and Applications (OOPSLA)*, (Atlanta). ACM, 49–65.

2. ALLEN, E., BANNET, J., AND CARTWRIGHT, R. 2003. A First-Class Approach Genericity. In *18th Conf. Object-Oriented Programming, Systems, Languages, and Applications (OOPSLA)*, (Anaheim). ACM, 96–114.

3. ANCONA, D., LAGORIO, G., AND ZUCCA, E. 2000. Jam—a smooth extension of Java with mixins. In *ECOOP 2000—Object-Oriented Programming: 14th European Conference*, (Cannes, France), E. Bertino, Ed. LNCS, vol. 1850. Springer-Verlag, Berlin, 154–178.

4. ANCONA, D. AND ZUCCA, E. 2002. A theory of mixin modules: Algebraic laws and reduction semantics. *Mathematical Structures in Computer Science 12*, 6, 701–737.

5. ARNOLD, K., SCHEIFLER, R., WALDO, J., O'SULLIVAN, B., WOLLRATH, A., O'SULLIVAN, B., AND WOLLRATH, A. 1999. *JINI Specification*. Addison-Wesley, Reading, Massachusetts.

6. BATORY, D. AND O'MALLEY, S. 1992. The design and implementation of hierarchical software systems with reusable components. *ACM Transactions on Software Engineering and Methodology (TOSEM) 1*, 4 (Oct.), 355–398.

7. BATORY, D., SINGHAL, V., SIRKIN, M., AND THOMAS, J. 1993. Scalable Software Libraries. *Proceedings of the 1st Symposium on the Foundations of Software Engineering (FSE)*, (Los Angeles). ACM, 191–199.

8. BONO, V., PATEL, A., AND SHMATIKOV, V. 1999. A core calculus of classes and mixins. In *ECOOP '99—Object-Oriented Programming: 13th European Conf.*, R. Guerraoui, Ed. LNCS, vol. 1628. Springer-Verlag, Berlin, 43–66.

9. BRACHA, G. AND COOK, W. 1990. Mixin-based inheritance. In *Conf. Object-Oriented Programming: Systems, Languages, and Applications; European Conf. Object-Oriented Programming* (Ottawa, Canada). ACM, 303–311.

10. BRACHA, G., ODERSKY, M., STOUTAMIRE, D., AND WADLER, P. 1998. Making the future safe for the past: Adding genericity to the Java programming language. In *13th Conf. Object-Oriented Programming, Systems, Languages, and Applications (OOPSLA)*, (Vancouver). ACM, 183–200.

11. CARDELLI, L. AND WEGNER, P. 1985. On understanding types, data abstraction, and polymorphism. *ACM Computing Surveys 17*, 4 (Dec.), 471–523.

12. CARDONE, R. 2002. Language and compiler support for mixin programming. Ph.D. thesis, University of Texas at Austin.

13. CARDONE, R., BROWN, A., MCDIRMID, S., AND LIN, C. 2002. Using mixins to build flexible widgets. In *1st Int'l Conf. Aspect-Oriented Software Development (AOSD)*, (Enschede, The Netherlands), G. Kiczales, Ed. ACM, 76–85.

14. EISENECKER, U. W., BLINN, F., AND CZARNECKI, K. 2000. A solution to the constructor-problem of mixin-based programming in C++. In *1st Workshop on C++ Template Programming* (Erfurt, Germany). Also published in Dr. Dobbs Journal, No. 320, January 2001.

15. FLATT, M., KRISHNAMURTHI, S., AND FELLEISEN, M. 1998. Classes and mixins. In *Symp. Principles of Programming Languages (POPL)*. ACM, 171–183.

16. GAMMA, E., HELM, R., JOHNSON, R., AND VLISSIDES, J. 1995. *Design Patterns: Elements of Reusable Object-Oriented Software*. Addison-Wesley, Reading, Massachusetts.

17. GEARY, D. M. 1999. *Graphic Java, Mastering the JFC, 3rd ed.* Prentice-Hall, Englewood Cliffs, New Jersey.

18. IBM RESEARCH. Hyperspaces. http://www.research.ibm.com/hyperspace/.

19. JAVA COMMUNITY PROCESS. JSR-14: Add generic types to the Java programming language. http://www.jcp.org.

20. JAVA LAYERS HOME PAGE. http://www.cs.utexas.edu/users/richcar/JavaLayers.html.

21. KEENE, S. 1989. *Object-Oriented Programming in Common Lisp: A Programming Guide in CLOS*. Addison-Wesley, Reading, Massachusetts.

22. KICZALES, G., HILSDALE, E., HUGUNIN, J., KERSTEN, M., PALM, J., AND GRISWOLD, W. G. 2001. An overview of AspectJ. In *ECOOP 2001—Object-Oriented Programming, 15th European Conference*, (Budapest), J. L. Knudsen, Ed. LNCS, vol. 2072. Springer-Verlag, Berlin, 327–353.

23. KICZALES, G., LAMPING, J., MENDHEKAR, A., MAEDA, C., LOPES, C., LOINGTIER, J. M., AND IRWIN, J. 1997. Aspect-oriented programming. In *ECOOP'97 Object-Oriented Programming, 11th European Conference*, M. Akşit and S. Matsuoka, Eds. LNCS, vol. 1241. Springer-Verlag, Berlin, 220–242.

24. MOON, D. A. 1986. Object-oriented programming with flavors. In *1st Conf. Object-Oriented Programming, Systems, Languages, and Applications (OOPSLA)*, (New York). ACM, 1–8.

25. PALM INC. http://www.palm.com.

26. PARNAS, D. L. 1972. On the criteria to be used in decomposing systems into modules. *Comm. ACM 15*, 12 (Dec.), 1053–1058.

27. SMARAGDAKIS, Y. 1999. Implementing large-scale object-oriented components. Ph.D. thesis, University of Texas at Austin.

28. SMARAGDAKIS, Y. AND BATORY, D. 1998. Implementing layered design with mixin layers. In *ECOOP'98 Object-Oriented Programming, 12th European Conference*, (Brussels), E. Jul, Ed. LNCS, vol. 1445. Springer-Verlag, Berlin, 550–570.

29. STROUSTRUP, B. 1997. *The C++ Programming Language, 3rd. Ed.* Addison Wesley.

30. SUN MICROSYSTEMS, INC. Java. http://java.sun.com/.

31. SUN MICROSYSTEMS, INC. Java 2 platform, micro edition, (j2me). http://java.sun.com/j2me.

32. SUN MICROSYSTEMS, INC. 2000. Connected, limited device configuration, specification 1.0a.

33. TAIVALSAARI, A. 1996. On the notion of inheritance. *ACM Computing Surveys 28*, 3 (Sept.), 438–479.

34. TARR, P., OSSHER, H., HARRISON, W., AND SUTTON JR., S. M. 1999. *N* degrees of separation: Multi-dimensional separation of concerns. In *21st Int'l Conf. Software Engineering (ICSE)*, (Los Angeles). IEEE, 107–119.

35. THORUP, K. K. 1997. Genericity in Java with virtual types. In *ECOOP'97 Object-Oriented Programming, 11th European Conference*, M. Akşit and S. Matsuoka, Eds. LNCS, vol. 1241. Springer, Berlin, 444–471.

36. TIP, F., LAFFRA, C., SWEENEY, P. F., AND STREETER, D. 1999. Practical experience with an application extractor for Java. In *14th Conf. Object-Oriented Programming, Systems, Languages, and Applications (OOPSLA)*, (Denver). ACM, 292–305.

37. VANHILST, M. AND NOTKIN, D. 1996. Using C++ templates to implement role-based designs. In *JSSST Int'l Symp. Object Technologies for Advanced Software*, (Kanazawa, Japan). LNCS, vol. 1049. Springer-Verlag, Berlin, 22–37.

Chapter 11

Separating Concerns with First-Class Namespaces

OSCAR NIERSTRASZ AND FRANZ ACHERMANN

As applications evolve, it becomes harder and harder to separate independent concerns. Small changes to a software system increasingly affect different parts of the source code. AOP and related approaches offer various ways to separate concerns into concrete software artifacts, but what is the *essence* of this process? We claim that first-class namespaces—which we refer to as *forms*—offer a suitable foundation for separating concerns by offering simple yet expressive mechanisms for defining composable abstractions. We demonstrate how forms help a programmer to separate concerns by means of practical examples in Piccola, an experimental composition language.

11.1 INTRODUCTION

It is well accepted that complex software systems should be developed as sets of manageable pieces, where each piece ideally addresses a single concern. These pieces are then composed together to achieve the desired behavior of the application. However, carving a complex system up into suitable pieces may be far from trivial since concerns typically overlap and interfere. Tarr and coworkers [32] argue that we cannot achieve this separation in a single-paradigm language due to the single dominant dimension of separation supported by the language. For instance, while object-oriented programming separates everything into objects, concerns like persistence and synchronization are not naturally represented as objects, so they get tangled into several objects in the application. The fact that each concern cannot be factored out into a single abstraction leads to components incorporating several varying aspects. This hinders their reusability in other contexts.

AOP and related approaches offer various techniques and mechanisms that make it easier to factor out concerns into composable software artifacts [13]. Many of these approaches attempt to augment a host language with features or tools that compensate for the shortcomings of the dominant paradigm.

We propose, instead, to ask a different question, namely: *Is there a simple programming model that can serve as a good basis for defining arbitrary kinds of composable abstractions?*

Such a model should be capable of expressing not only conventional programming abstractions, such as procedures, objects, classes, and modules, but also higher-order abstractions, such as (for example) mixins, metaclasses, wrappers, and coordination abstractions.

As a typical example, consider a generic readers/writers synchronization policy. Although it is reasonably straightforward in most programming languages to implement such a policy for a given data abstraction, it can be difficult to impossible to implement a *generic* policy as a composable software artifact that can be applied in a straightforward way to any existing data abstraction.

Furthermore, we seek to raise the level of abstraction so that instead of "wiring" software components together at a low level, we are able to *plug* them together using high-level connectors. A *compositional style* (also referred to in the literature as an "architectural style" [28]) specifies a set of component *interfaces*, *connectors* to plug together components, and *rules* governing valid compositions of components. In short, we seek to make the way in which software systems are composed explicit and manipulable so they can be easily understood and adapted.

We propose *forms* as a suitable foundation for developing composable software abstractions. Forms unify extensible records, services, and first-class namespaces. On one hand, they offer a familiar mechanism for modeling various kinds of data abstractions as records. On the other hand, they offer a fine degree of control in manipulating, extending, and composing the namespaces available to running applications. A *service* is just an abstraction over a form, that is, a function that takes a form as an argument and returns a form. Since a service is also a form, forms offer a suitable basis for modeling high-order software abstractions. Forms can thus be conveniently used to model composable namespaces that both provide and require sets of services.

Piccola [4, 23] is an experimental composition language based on forms. In addition to forms and services, Piccola provides *agents* (concurrent processes) and *channels* (unbounded buffers providing non-blocking *send* and blocking *receive* services) as core mechanisms. With these basic mechanisms, Piccola can be used to easily express the kind of composable abstractions we are targeting.

In Section 11.2, we provide a brief overview of Piccola and its design rationale. In particular, we show how forms, agents, and channels support a layered approach to defining compositional styles. In Section 11.3, we present a non-trivial example of composing mixin layers with forms. In Section 11.4, we briefly survey some of the ways in which forms support software composition. We conclude in Section 11.5 with some remarks concerning the current status of Piccola and ongoing work.

11.2 PICCOLA

In this section, we give an overview of the layered architecture of Piccola itself, a brief example of generic wrappers in Piccola, and an overview of the kinds of composition abstractions that can be conveniently expressed in Piccola.

Piccola is designed to be a *composition language,* rather than a general purpose programming language. As such, it reduces software composition to a bare minimum of core mechanisms, that is, forms, agents, and channels, which can then be used to define higher-level abstractions.

Forms.   A *form* is an extensible record. For example, `a=(x=1, y=2)` defines a form a that binds labels `x` and `y`. We can *project* a label in a form, such as `w=a.x`, or we can *extend* a form with new bindings; for example, `b=(a, z=3)` extends a with a binding for label `z`. A form is also a *namespace*; *for example*, `('a, x+y)` evaluates `x+y` in the namespace `a`.

Services.   A *service* is a function over forms. `println` is a standard Piccola service that prints its argument form. `newPoint p:(x=p.x, y=p.y)` takes a form `p` as its argument and returns a form that extracts just the `x` and `y` bindings from `p`. Note that a service is also a form, so we can bind labels to services, extend services with bindings, or extend forms with services. (A service can be thought of as a form with single "call" label, just as a function object in C++ is an object with an `operator()` member function.)

Agents.   The standard Piccola service `run` invokes the `do` service of its argument as a new, concurrent agent. (The code `run(do:println "hello")` creates a new agent that asynchronously prints "hello".)

Channels.   A channel is an unbounded buffer that can be used to synchronize agents. `newChannel()` returns a form with `send` and `receive` services. `send` is non-blocking, while `receive` blocks if there is no data on the channel. As a simple example, `stop:newChannel().receive()` is a service that causes an agent to stop dead (i.e., it tries to read from a channel that no other agent ever writes to).

The formal semantics of Piccola is compactly expressed with the help of the Piccola-calculus [2, 22], a process calculus that extends Milner's π-calculus [19] with forms and services.

With these mechanisms, Piccola can express three complementary kinds of composition:

Namespace composition. A form can be *extended* with another form, yielding a new form.

Functional composition. Services can be *invoked* with a form as an argument, yielding a form as a result.

Agent composition. Concurrent agents can be composed and *coordinated* by means of shared channels.

11.2.1 Piccola Layers

Piccola is intended to be used in a layered fashion (see Table 11-1) to ultimately support a paradigm of "scripting" applications together from a set of software components [6]. In the ideal case, components constitute a kind of "component algebra" in which operators connect components and again yield components. Scripts, then, compose components, yielding up bigger components.

At the lowest level, the Piccola run-time system provides nothing but the core mechanisms of the Piccola-calculus. Programming at this level would be like programming in a concurrent assembly language.

The next level defines the Piccola language. In Piccola, *everything is a form*, so Piccola hides the operators of the Piccola-calculus and models everything in terms of *forms* and *services*. There is no special syntax to express agents and channels, just standard services `run` and `newChannel`. Mechanisms for defining infix and prefix operators are also provided, which is convenient for specifying component connectors as compositional operators. More importantly, reflective mechanisms are provided for exploring forms, wrapping them, and wrapping existing components from a host programming language (i.e., Java or Squeak [11], in the current Piccola implementations).

Table 11-1 *Piccola Layers*

Applications	Components + Scripts
Compositional styles	Streams, events, GUI composition, . . .
Standard libraries	Basic coordination abstractions, built-in types
Piccola	Operator syntax, introspection, component wrappers
Piccola-calculus	Forms, agents, channels, services

When Piccola starts up, a number of standard libraries are loaded. At this level, Piccola provides access to a number of built-in types (i.e., Booleans, numbers, strings, collections, file streams, and so on). In most cases, these standard types wrap existing Java components to provide them with more convenient compositional interfaces. The standard libraries also provide a number of standard services that implement various common control structures in terms of forms, agents, and channels. Exception handling, for example, is implemented using two agents to run the *try* and *catch* blocks and a channel to coordinate them in case an exception is raised [6].

On top of the standard libraries, one may define various compositional styles that abstract away from the low-level wiring of the Piccola-calculus and provide instead higher-level plugs, or connectors corresponding to a problem domain. A simple GUI style, for example, that wraps Java AWT and Swing components can easily be defined in Piccola. Furthermore, the style gives us a simple component algebra in which a composition of GUI components is again a GUI component.

Finally, at the top level, one may use these styles to script together components. For example, the GUI style is used to build an interactive console for developing and testing JPiccola scripts (see Figure 11-1).

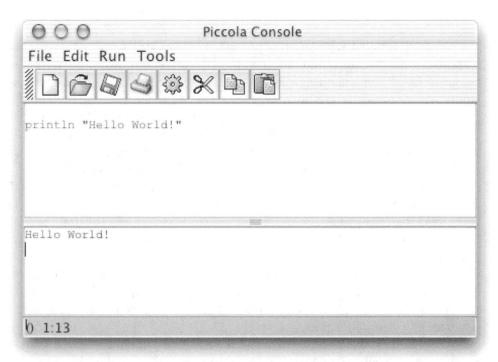

Figure 11-1   *The JPiccola console—scripted from wrapped Java GUI components.*

11.2.2 Generic Wrappers

Let us first consider the problem of defining a generic wrapper. wrapPrePost wraps each service of its argument form by invoking pre- and post-services before and after the original body. The implementation uses the built-in service forEachLabel to iterate over the labels of the argument.

```
wrapPrePost Arg:
  'wrappedForm = newVar()      # local variable
  forEachLabel
    form = Arg.form
    do Label:                    # wrap each service in Arg.form
      wrappedForm.set            # update the result
        'wrappedService Args:
          Arg.pre()                        # invoke the pre-service
          Label.project(form)(Args)  # invoke original service
          Arg.post()                       # invoke the post-service
        wrappedForm.get()        # get the result so far
        Label.bind(wrappedService)  # add the new binding
  wrappedForm.get()                        # return the wrapped form
```

Although detailed explanation of the code is beyond the scope of this discussion (please see the JPiccola Guide for details [23]), a few observations may help the reader to follow this example. wrapPrePost is a service being defined that takes a single Arg form as its argument. Arg is expected to provide bindings for pre, post, and form. wrappedForm is a local binding (made local by the Piccola ' operator). newVar is a standard service that returns a persistent variable with get and set services. forEachLabel is another standard service, whose argument is the *indented* form on the following lines. This argument provides bindings for form (a value) and do (a service). forEachLabel generates a first-class representation of each label bound in the form. A first-class label is a form that represents a label and provides services such as bind, project, and restrict. The first-class labels are use to reflect over the structure of the argument form and build a new, wrapped representation.

A key point to notice is that all services in Piccola are monadic; that is, they always take a single form as an argument, rather than a tuple of forms. This makes the task of wrapping services much simpler than it would be in most programming languages.

We could now use this generic wrapper to wrap a component with an arbitrary synchronization policy. Suppose, for example, we define semaphores like this:

```
newSemaphore:
  'sem = newChannel()
  p: sem.receive()
  v: sem.send()
  'v()
```

and a mutual exclusion synchronization policy like this:

```
newMutexPolicy:
  'sync = newSemaphore()
  pre:  sync.p()
  post: sync.v()
```

Now if F is some form, we can wrap each of its services with a mutual exclusion policy as follows:

```
MutexF = wrapPrePost
  form = F
  newMutexPolicy()
```

A readers/writers synchronization policy could be similarly defined. In this case, however, we must distinguish between reader and writer services and use the wrapPrePost service to wrap them separately with their own policies:

```
bindRWPolicy Arg:
  wrapPrePost
    form = Arg.reader
    pre  = Arg.policy.preR
    post = Arg.policy.postR
  wrapPrePost
    form = Arg.writer
    pre  = Arg.policy.preW
    post = Arg.policy.postW
```

We must now explicitly list the services to be wrapped:

```
RWsynchedF = bindRWPolicy
  policy = newRWPolicy()           # create rw policy
  reader = (r1 = F.r1, r2 = F.r2)  # the reader methods
  writer = (w = F.w)               # the writer method
```

Generic wrappers play an important part in compositional styles, since they constitute a form of reusable "glue code" that can adapt components to different styles. Automatically invoked wrappers are used in Piccola, for example, to adapt Java components to compositional styles. Java AWT and Swing components, for example, are automatically wrapped when they are accessed by a Piccola script, allowing them to be connected using the GUI style defined in Piccola.

11.3   EXAMPLE: MIXIN LAYER COMPOSITION

In this section, we give a concrete example of mixin layer composition [30] implemented as a compositional style in SPiccola (the Squeak implementation of Piccola [25]). Mixin layers are (in our view) a less well-known and non-trivial composition style. Implementing mixin layers requires an object-oriented language that supports nested classes and mixins. The language P++, for example, extends C++ to support static and type-safe mixin layer composition [29]. Implementing mixin layer composition in Piccola thus serves to validate that Piccola is expressive enough to tackle high-level composition abstractions. Finally, mixin layers are a good candidate to illustrate component algebras, because composed mixin layers are again mixin layers.

We present the graph traversal application proposed by Holland [10]. This application defines different operations on an undirected graph. *VertexNumbering* numbers the nodes in a depth-first order, *CycleChecking* determines whether the graph contains a cycle, and *ConnectedRegions* partitions the nodes of the graph into connected regions. Holland implemented the application based on a framework. Later, Van Hilst and coworkers [33] reimplemented it using roles and mixins. Smaragdakis and Batory finally used mixin layers to implement the same application [30, 31].

The three main implementation classes are `Graph`, `Vertex`, and `Workspace`. The `Graph` class defines a container of vertices with the usual graph properties. The nodes are stored as instances of the class `Vertex`. The `Workspace` class includes the specific part of a traversal. For instance, the `workspace` object plays the role *WorkspaceNumber* in the *VertexNumbering* application to associate numbers to the nodes. This role specifies a slot in which to store a current number and to assign and increment this number each time a new node is visited during depth-first traversal. We can implement such a role using a mixin. The mixin adds the specific members and operations to its superclass when composed. Similarly, a mixin adds the number slot to a vertex class.

Smaragdakis and Batory use the GenVoca model [9] to keep the different mixins applied to classes in synch. A GenVoca component is a mixin layer. In essence, a mixin layer encapsulates all the mixins necessary for a single collaboration. For instance, the mixin layer *Number* to implement the *VertexNumbering* collaboration contains two mixins: one to add the vertex numbering during traversal and one to add the number to a vertex. The advantages of using mixin layers instead of isolated mixins are clear: Design or change elements in the application are encapsulated and implemented in a single component.

11.3.1   Mixin Layers in Piccola

We now seek a simple way to model and compose mixins and mixin layers. We would like to achieve the kind of simplicity illustrated by the following example. `graph` provides constructors for graphs and vertices. We then compose it, using the `**` mixin layer composition operator, with mixin layers `dft`, `numberNodes`, and `cycle`, which, respectively, provide services for depth-first traversal, automatic numbering of nodes, and cycle detection:

```
layers = graph ** dft ** numberNodes ** cycle
newGraph: layers.asGraph()
asVertex: layers.asVertex()
g = newGraph()
...
```

We claim that the model of explicit namespaces offered by forms provides us with a good way of modeling compositional abstractions like mixin layers.

First of all, although Piccola provides only forms, not objects or classes, it is relatively simple to model objects and classes as forms. An object is just a form providing services that access some private state, such as the semaphores we saw earlier. A class is a form offering services shared by all instances, such as constructors, and services to create subclasses [6].

In our example, `graph` represents a base-level mixin layer, that is, one that provides services `asGraph` and `asVertex` to create new graphs and vertices. A graph itself provides services like `insert` and `each` to insert a new vertex or visit each vertex. The other mixin layers wrap the `asGraph` and `asVertex` of the layer below to create graphs and vertices with new or adapted services. In each case, it is important that the mixin layer *simultaneously* wrap both constructors since the new and adapted services typically depend on each other.

How do the mixin layers work? Let's consider the `numberNodes` layer:

```
numberNodes =
  asVertex V:
    V
    number = newVar(0)
```

```
asGraph G:
  G
  visit:
    n = newCounter()
    G.each(do V: V.number.set(n.inc()))
```

`asVertex` wraps a vertex to provide it with a number. `asGraph` wraps a graph to provide it with a `visit` service that increments the `number` of each of its vertices. These two services simultaneously wrap vertices and graphs from the layer below, so we are sure that when a vertex is visited, it actually provides a `number` binding.

Next, we need to implement a composition operator `**` such that "*A ** B*" is a composite mixin layer, provided that *A* and *B* are mixin layers. We could implement a generic mixin layer composition operator in the style of our `wrapPrePost` service, but for simplicity we just consider the specific problem of composing graph mixin layers:

```
'Defaults = (asVertex X:X, asGraph X: X)
_**_ A B:
  'A = (Defaults, A) # set defaults
  'B = (Defaults, B)
  asVertex X: B.asVertex(A.asVertex(X))
  asGraph X: B.asGraph(A.asGraph(X))
```

The form `Defaults` contains default values for the `asVertex` and `asGraph` wrappers, namely the identity function. We rebind A and B so that the actual arguments may override these defaults. Finally, we compose new `asVertex` and `asGraph` wrappers from those provided by the arguments.

Note that the order in which the mixin layers are composed affects the end result. `numberNodes`, for example, depends on the `each` service provided by graphs of the layer below. The `graph` layer provides such a service, but the `dft` layer happens to replace this service by a depth-first traversal `each` service. As a consequence, `graph**dft**numberNodes` and `graph**numberNodes**dft` exhibit different behaviors.

11.3.2 Software Evolution with Mixin Layers

The resulting separation of concerns enables us now to combine or replace mixin layers in a straightforward way. Suppose, for example, that graphs may be exposed to concurrent clients. In this case, we might want to apply a synchronization policy to the graph. The mixin layer `exclusive` applies a mutual exclusion synchronization policy to all the methods of graph. Since the order of mixin layer composition is significant, we apply this layer last of all:

```
layers = graph ** dft ** numberNodes ** cycle ** exclusive
```

We can also change the depth-first traversal to a breadth-first traversal by replacing a component:

```
layers = graph ** bft ** numberNodes ** cycle
```

We can adapt a layer that (by chance) does not follow the naming conventions by introducing some *glue code*:

```
myLayer =
  asGraph = legacyLayer.addFancyFeatureToGraph
  asVertex = legacyLayer.addFancyFeatureToNode
```

In case there are many components that need to be adapted in the same way, we can abstract from the glue code to obtain a general-purpose *glue abstraction*:

```
LegacyAdaptor legacyLayer:
  asGraph = legacyLayer.addFancyFeatureToGraph
  asVertex = legacyLayer.addFancyFeatureToNode
myLayer = legacyAdaptor(myLegacyLayer)
```

As a final validation of mixin layers, we found it straightforward to extend the graph traversal mixin layer framework with a new mixin layer for visualizing graphs.

The `visual` layer in Piccola packages the glue code needed to display graphs in Squeak:

```
visual =
  asGraph G:
    G
    'defaultColor = Smalltalk("Color").yellow()
    morph = newVar(0)
      ...
    # replace G.each by an animated version
    each Block:
      ...
```

This new mixin layer can now be added to any graph traversal mixin layer composition at the appropriate point.

In Figure 11-2, we see visualizations of thread-unsafe and thread-safe graphs that have been subjected to two concurrent traversals that mark and unmark the nodes (i.e., by changing their color).

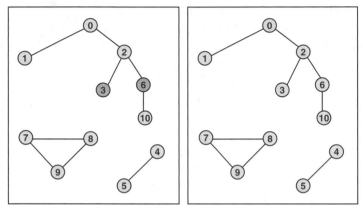

Figure 11-2 `graph()**dft**visual` vs. `graph()**sdft**visual`.

The visualization clearly shows that only the thread-safe graph is uniformly colored at the end.

11.4 SPECIFYING COMPOSITIONAL STYLES WITH FORMS

We now briefly survey some of the typical compositional styles and techniques that are used to make software more flexible and adaptable. We demonstrate how Piccola forms support them. Note that these styles are not orthogonal.

Component algebras. A *component algebra* is a compositional style in which the composition of two or more components is again a component. The best-known example of a component algebra is pipes and filters. The components are sources, filters, and sinks, and the principle operator is the pipe. A source composed with a filter yields a source, and a filter composed with a filter is again a filter.

We believe that any compositional style can be conveniently expressed as a component algebra. In addition to pipes and filters, we have developed and experimented with component algebras for GUI components [6], input/output streams [4], coordination of concurrent agents [3], and mixin layers [21].

Higher-order wrappers. Many kinds of extensions can be factored out as simple wrappers, adding "before and after" behavior. Since all values (including abstractions) are forms in Piccola, abstractions are higher-order, making it easy to specify higher-order wrappers. As we have seen in Section 11.2.2, services in Piccola are *monadic*, always taking a single form as an argument. This makes it possible to define *generic wrappers* that do not depend on the number of arguments. Piccola uses wrappers heavily to adapt components to conform to a particular style.

Glue abstractions. Many glue abstractions can be expressed as simple wrappers. Glue abstractions can wrap known services or add new ones while leaving others undisturbed [16, 26]. A simple glue abstraction, for example, can wrap a `java.math.BigInteger` to provide it with the usual arithmetic operators. (Java does not provide operator overloading, so a `Biginteger` provides methods like `add` and `multiply` instead of + and * .)

Mixins and metaobjects. Higher-order wrappers make it possible to define mixins and other composition mechanisms for building objects. Piccola provides only forms as "primitive objects," but one can define a variety of other object models on top of forms [26]. One of Piccola's few keywords is `def`, used to define a fixpoint, but it is also possible to delay binding of self, which makes object models with explicit metaobjects attractive. Metaobjects enable run-time reflection [12].

Coordination abstractions. Piccola provides primitives to instantiate concurrent agents or to explicitly create new channels within scripts. The formal semantics of Piccola is in terms of a process calculus, so concurrency is built-in, not added on [16, 26]. This makes it easy to define coordination abstractions as abstractions over scripts. Furthermore, coordination can be seen as a special case of scripting, and many coordination styles can be naturally expressed as component algebras [3].

Implicit policies. Forms are also used in Piccola to represent *namespaces* [5]. Whenever a script is evaluated, it has access to two special namespaces, representing respectively the *root* context and the *dynamic* context. The root context defines the global environment, but can be specialized to define a "sandbox" for an untrusted agent or to override or extend global services (like `println`). The dynamic context is the environment provided by a client of an agent and can be used to define implicit policies. This mechanism can be used, for example, to define an exception handling mechanism for Piccola [5, 6] (the handler is always passed in the dynamic context). The same mechanisms are used more generally to optionally override any kind of default policy.

Default arguments. Since abstractions are monadic, taking a single form as an argument, and since forms can be extended, it is straightforward to define default arguments for services, as we did in defining the ** mixin layer composition operator.

11.5   CONCLUSION

As we have argued elsewhere [4], Piccola lies somewhere between a *scripting language*, like Python or TCL, an *architectural description language* (ADL), like Wright [7] or Rapide [15], a *coordination language*, like Darwin [18] or Manifold [8], and a *glue language*, like Smalltalk or C.

A type system has been developed for Piccola [16], but it too is at the level of the process calculus. We would like to reason about higher-level types in terms of components and their composition. Ideally, we might like a type system that can express not only required and provided services, but even some more detailed dependencies [14, 20, 24].

In previous papers, we have presented the conceptual framework of *components*, *scripts*, and *glue* [27], the formal underpinnings of Piccola in terms of the Piccola-calculus [4, 17, 22], and a tour of the Piccola language features [6]. We have demonstrated how Piccola forms can model different notions of *explicit namespaces* [5], we have shown how different forms of *coordination* can be expressed as compositional styles [3], and we have argued that aspect-oriented programming [13] can be expressed as *feature mixins* in Piccola [1]. We have also argued that software systems can evolve gracefully only if they are designed in such a way as to cleanly separate stable and flexible aspects into *components* and *scripts* [21].

Here, we have argued that the mechanism of explicit namespaces provided by forms is crucial to achieving a clean separation of concerns.

Piccola is designed to be a *composition language*, good at expressing different kinds of *compositional styles*, each of which may be suitable for composing components for different application domains. We are still experimenting with applications of Piccola. Although we believe that Piccola provides the right abstractions needed to express applications as flexible compositions of software components, we still have to prove that these techniques can succeed in separating concerns for complex domains where other approaches have failed.

Our long-term goal is to develop a framework that supports the definition of higher-level composition operators and in which we can reason about properties of composite components. Piccola should serve as a platform to develop a composition environment hosting components and supporting the flexible scripting of components within user-defined architectural styles.

ACKNOWLEDGMENTS

This work has been supported by the Swiss National Science Foundation under Projects #20-53711.98, "A Framework Approach to Composing Heterogeneous Applications," #20-61655.00, "Meta-models and Tools for Evolution Towards

Component Systems," and the Swiss Federal Office for Education and Science under Project BBW #96.00335-1, within the Esprit Working Group 24512: "COORDINA: Coordination Models and Languages."

Thanks to Robert Filman and Markus Gaelli for numerous suggestions and corrections.

REFERENCES

1. ACHERMANN, F. 2000. Language support for feature mixing. In *Workshop on Multi-Dimensional Separation of Concerns in Software Engineering (ICSE)*, (Limerick, Ireland). http://www.research.ibm.com/hyperspace/workshops/icse2000/Papers/achermann.pdf.

2. ACHERMANN, F. 2002. Forms, agents, and channels—defining composition abstraction with style. Ph.D. thesis, University of Berne, Switzerland.

3. ACHERMANN, F., KNEUBÜHL , S., AND NIERSTRASZ, O. 2000. Scripting coordination styles. In *4th Int'l Conf. Coordination Languages and Models*, (Limassol, Cyprus), G. Catalin-Roman and A. Porto, Eds. LNCS, vol. 1906. Springer-Verlag, Berlin, 19–35.

4. ACHERMANN, F., LUMPE, M., SCHNEIDER, J. G., AND NIERSTRASZ, O. 2001. PICCOLA—a small composition language. In *Formal Methods for Distributed Processing: A Survey of Object-Oriented Approaches*, H. Bowman and J. Derrick, Eds. Cambridge University Press, Cambridge, UK, 403–426.

5. ACHERMANN, F. AND NIERSTRASZ, O. 2000. Explicit Namespaces. In *Modular Programming Languages*, J. Gutknecht and W. Weck, Eds. LNCS, vol. 1897. Springer-Verlag, Berlin, 77–89.

6. ACHERMANN, F. AND NIERSTRASZ, O. 2001. Applications = Components + Scripts—A Tour of Piccola. In *Software Architectures and Component Technology*, M.Aksit, Ed. Kluwer, Boston, 261–292.

7. ALLEN, R. AND GARLAN, D. 1996. The Wright architectural specification language. Tech. Rep. CMU-CS-96-TB, School of Computer Science, Carnegie Mellon University, Pittsburgh.

8. ARBAB, F. 1996. The IWIM model for coordination of concurrent activities. In *1st Int'l Conf. Coordination Languages and Models*, (Cesena, Italy), P. Ciancarini and C. Hankin, Eds. LNCS, vol. 1061. Springer-Verlag, Berlin, 34–56.

9. BATORY, D., SINGHAL, V., THOMAS, J., DASARI, S., GERACI, B., AND SIRKIN, M. 1994. The GenVoca model of software-system generators. *IEEE Software 11*, 5, 89–94.

10. HOLLAND, I. M. 1992. Specifying reusable components using contracts. In *ECOOP '92 European Conf. Object-Oriented Programming*, (Utrecht, Netherlands), O. L. Madsen, Ed. LNCS, vol. 615. Springer-Verlag, Berlin, 287–308.

11. INGALLS, D., KAEHLER, T., MALONEY, J., WALLACE, S., AND KAY, A. 1997. Back to the future: The story of Squeak, a practical Smalltalk written in itself. In *12th Conf. Object-Oriented Programming, Systems, Languages, and Applications (OOPSLA)*, (Atlanta). ACM, 318–326.

12. KICZALES, G., DES RIVIERES, J., AND BOBROW, D. G. 1991. *The Art of the Metaobject Protocol*. MIT Press, Cambridge, Massachusetts.

13. KICZALES, G., LAMPING, J., MENDHEKAR, A., MAEDA, C., LOPES, C., LOINGTIER, J. M., AND IRWIN, J. 1997. Aspect-oriented programming. In *ECOOP'97 Object-Oriented Programming, 11th European Conference*, M. Akşit and S. Matsuoka, Eds. LNCS, vol. 1241. Springer-Verlag, Berlin, 220–242.

14. KNEUBÜHL, S. 2003. Typeful compositional styles. M.S. thesis, University of Berne, Switzerland.

15. LUCKHAM, D. C. AND VERA, J. 1995. An event-based architecture definition language. *IEEE Transactions on Software Engineering 21*, 9 (Sept.), 717–734.

16. LUMPE, M. 1999. A Pi-calculus based approach to software composition. Ph.D. thesis, University of Berne, Switzerland.

17. LUMPE, M., ACHERMANN, F., AND NIERSTRASZ, O. 2000. A formal language for composition. In *Foundations of Component-Based Systems*, G. T. Leavens and M. Sitaraman, Eds. Cambridge University Press, Cambridge, UK, 69–90.

18. MAGEE, J., DULAY, N., EISENBACH, S., AND KRAMER, J. 1995. Specifying distributed software architectures. In *European Software Engineering Conference (ESEC)*, (Sitges, Spain). LNCS vol. 989. Springer-Verlag, Berlin, 137–153.

19. MILNER, R., PARROW, J., AND WALKER, D. 1992. A calculus of mobile processes, part I/II. *Information and Computation 100*, 1, 1–77.

20. NIERSTRASZ, O. 2003. Contractual types. Tech. Rep. IAM-03-004, Institut für Informatik, Universität Bern, Switzerland.

21. NIERSTRASZ, O. AND ACHERMANN, F. 2000. Supporting compositional styles for software evolution. In *Int'l Symp. Principles of Software Evolution (ISPSE)*, (Kanazawa, Japan). IEEE, 11–19.

22. NIERSTRASZ, O. AND ACHERMANN, F. 2003. A calculus for modeling software components. In *1st Int'l Symp. Formal Methods for Components and Objects 2002*, (Leiden, The Netherlands), F. S. De Boer, M. M. Bonsangue, S. Graf and W-P. de Roever, Eds. LNCS, vol. 2852. Springer-Verlag, Berlin, 339–360.

23. NIERSTRASZ, O., ACHERMANN, F., AND KNEUBÜHL, S. 2003. A guide to JPiccola. Tech. Rep. IAM-03-003, Institut für Informatik, Universität Bern, Switzerland.

24. NIERSTRASZ, O., SCHNEIDER, J. G., AND ACHERMANN, F. 2000. Agents everywhere, all the time. In *Workshop on Component-Oriented Programming (ECOOP)*, (Cannes, France). www.cs.rug.nl/~bosch/WCOP2000/.

25. SCHÄRLI, N. 2001. Supporting pure composition by inter-language bridging on the meta-level. M.S. thesis, University of Berne, Switzerland.

26. SCHNEIDER, J. G. 1999. Components, scripts and glue: A conceptual framework for software composition. Ph.D. thesis, University of Berne, Switzerland.

27. SCHNEIDER, J. G. AND NIERSTRASZ, O. 1999. Components, scripts, and glue. In *Software Architectures—Advances and Applications*, L. Barroca, J. Hall, and P. Hall, Eds. Springer-Verlag, Berlin, 13–25.

28. SHAW, M. AND GARLAN, D. 1996. *Software Architecture: Perspectives on an Emerging Discipline*. Prentice-Hall, Englewood Cliffs, New Jersey.

29. SINGHAL, V. P. 1996. A programming language for writing domain-specific software system generators. Ph.D. thesis, University of Texas at Austin.

30. SMARAGDAKIS, Y. AND BATORY, D. 1998. Implementing layered design with mixin layers. In *ECOOP'98 Object-Oriented Programming, 12th European Conference*, (Brussels), E. Jul, Ed. LNCS, vol. 1445. Springer-Verlag, Berlin, 550–570.

31. SMARAGDAKIS, Y. AND BATORY, D. 1998. Implementing reusable object-oriented components. In *5th Int'l Conf. Software Reuse* (Victoria, Canada). IEEE, 36–45.

32. TARR, P., OSSHER, H., HARRISON, W., AND SUTTON JR., S. M. 1999. *N* degrees of separation: Multi-dimensional separation of concerns. In *21st Int'l Conf. Software Engineering (ICSE)*, (Los Angeles). IEEE, 107–119.

33. VANHILST, M. AND NOTKIN, D. 1996. Using C++ templates to implement role-based designs. In *Int'l Symp. Object Technologies for Advanced Software*. JSSST, 22–37.

Chapter 12

Supporting AOP Using Reflection

NOURY BOURAQADI AND THOMAS LEDOUX

Aspect-oriented programming (AOP) allows applications to be developed by implementing crosscutting concerns (i.e., *aspects)* in a loosely coupled fashion [27]. The application results from a weaving process that knits aspects with core functionalities (i.e., *base code).* This weaving is done at *join points,* which are points within the base code execution flow [16]. Isolating aspects and weaving them with base code are two critical issues of the AOP paradigm. One possible approach for implementing these mechanisms is *reflection.*

Reflection is the ability of a system to observe and change its own execution [29, 36]. In an object-oriented reflective programming language, this is made possible by representing program entities (e.g., classes, methods) and execution mechanisms (e.g., interpreter, garbage collector) as full-fledged *meta-objects.* Since meta-objects control the execution of *base objects* (i.e., plain objects), a change in a meta-object alters program behavior. This control is done through an explicit link between base and meta-objects, the *meta-link.*

This chapter explores the relationship between reflection and AOP. The duality between base and meta-objects and their connection through the meta-link makes reflection a natural solution for supporting AOP. Separation is achieved by making base objects represent base code and meta-objects represent aspect code. Weaving relies on the meta-link that connects base objects (and then base code) to meta-objects (and then aspect code). In this context, *Meta-Objects Protocols (MOP)* support join points.

The chapter is organized as follows. In Section 12.1, we present reflection, emphasizing that reflective systems are structured into layers (*meta-levels*). This presentation also covers the concepts of meta-objects, MOP, and meta-link. To illustrate these concepts, we provide a reflective programming language, MetaclassTalk,[1] and present examples of its use. In Section 12.2, we show the capability of reflection to support AOP. More precisely, we demonstrate that aspects can be represented using meta-objects. We also show that aspect weaving in this context relies on the meta-link and meta-object composition. In Section 12.3, we discuss the advantages and drawbacks of using reflection for AOP. Section 12.4 ends the chapter with a discussion of open issues.

12.1 WHAT IS REFLECTION?

Reflection is the ability of a system to observe and change its own execution [29, 36]. A programming language is said to be reflective if it provides an explicit representation (i.e., *reification*) of entities that either represent program building blocks (e.g., classes, methods) or are involved in program execution (e.g., stack, garbage collector). Thus, using a reflective language, developers can not only define system (i.e., software) functionalities, but can also define new program building blocks or execution mechanisms (i.e., define how functionalities will be performed). Put another way, developers can not only write the program, but can also extend the interpreter.

12.1.1 Base-Level Versus Meta-Level

Separation between functionalities and execution mechanisms leads to a system with different levels (i.e., layers[2]). On one hand, system functionalities are defined on the *base-level* (e.g., deposits and withdrawals in a banking system). On the other hand, reified entities such as system's building blocks (e.g., fields, methods) and execution mechanisms (e.g., message handling, process scheduling) are located on the *meta-level*. The meta-level can be viewed as an interpreter that evaluates the base-level. This layering allows some separation of concerns and hence provides a first support for AOP, as we will discuss in Section 12.2.

As shown in Figure 12-1, a reflective system can have more than two levels. After all, the meta-level itself is part of the system. Since a reflective system can reason and act on itself, then the system can reason and act on the meta-level. Thus, the meta-level can be viewed as a program that is interpreted by some meta-meta-level. The meta-meta-level is also part of the system, so we need an extra level, and so on.

Although the tower of levels can be arbitrarily high, the number of levels should always be finite—we require that the system be able to perform its tasks within a

---

1. A reflective extension of Smalltalk is available at http://csl.ensm-douai.fr/MetaclassTalk.

2. In the context of reflective systems, people prefer the term "level" instead of "layer."

finite amount of time and memory. Thus, reflective systems rely on the existence of some default interpreter that acts as the topmost level. The evaluation of this topmost level is hardwired so as to keep the tower of meta-levels finite.

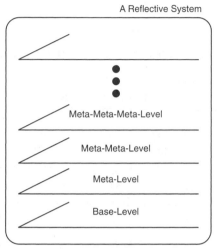

Figure 12-1   *Levels of a reflective system.*

Note that the relationship between the base-level and the meta-level can be translated along the reflective tower. For any pair of contiguous levels, the higher will be the "meta-level" of the lower. Thus, we can simplify the remainder of this section by focusing only on the two first levels (base-level and meta-level).

12.1.2   *Meta-Objects and Their Protocols*

In the context of object-oriented reflective systems, both the base-level and the meta-level consist of collections of objects. Objects that define program functionalities are called *base-level objects* (base objects for short). Objects defining program building blocks or execution mechanisms are called *meta-level objects* (meta-objects for short).

APIs (Application Programming Interfaces) that manipulate meta-objects are called *Meta-Object Protocols (MOPs)* [24]. MOPs allow you to access program structures such as class, inheritance relationships, methods, and fields defined within classes. They also provide access to execution mechanisms. Object creation, message sending and receptions, method lookup and evaluation, and field reading and writing are all examples of execution mechanisms. Section 12.2 shows that by providing access to execution mechanisms, MOPs give access to join points.

Since meta-objects are objects, they are instances of some classes that define fields and methods to properly handle these execution mechanisms. Using inheritance, you can build new meta-object classes that extend the execution mechanisms. You can even define meta-objects with completely different semantics (e.g., single *vs.* multiple inheritance).

12.1.3 Meta-Link and Meta-Object Cooperation

Abstraction levels of a reflective system introduce a new kind of relationship between objects: base objects and meta-objects are connected through a *meta-link*. Functionalities provided by each base object are then executed using the execution mechanisms defined in that base object's meta-object. Thus, a meta-object *controls* its linked base object. For example, consider a meta-object that extends the default message reception action with a logging mechanism. Linking any object to the "log meta-object" then causes its messages to be logged.

In the previous example, we linked a single base object to one meta-object. However, other alternatives exist [19, 29, 30, 34, 41, 43]. A single base object can be controlled by several meta-objects, and a single meta-object can be shared among several base objects. When many meta-objects control the same base object, they have to *cooperate* somehow in order to handle the execution. Often, the cooperation policy is not hardwired, so it can be extended and adapted like most of a system's other features.

Figure 12-2 shows four objects (o1 to o4) that are linked to different meta-objects (mo1 to mo5). The mo1 meta-object controls the o1 object. Three meta-objects (mo2, mo4, and mo5) cooperate in order to control the o2 object.

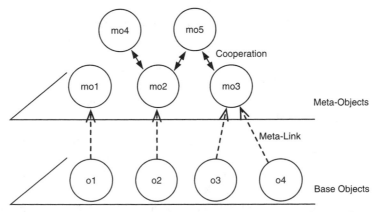

Figure 12-2 *Base versus meta-objects and their relationships.*

Meta-objects mo3 and mo5 cooperate in order to control objects o3 and o4. Thus, o3 and o4 share meta-objects mo3 and mo5. Meta-object mo5 is also shared with object o2.

12.1.4 Example of a Reflective Programming Language and its MOP

Our example is a running reflective programming language named MetaclassTalk [2, 3]. MetaclassTalk is a reflective extension of Smalltalk [18, 21, 23] for simplifying experiments with new programming paradigms. Smalltalk has been chosen to implement MetaclassTalk, because it provides many reflective facilities [35]. For example, classes, methods, and the execution stack are reified and can be handled like plain objects.

Although Smalltalk has many reflective facilities, they provide little help for changing the execution mechanisms. MetaclassTalk addresses this weakness by opening up the execution process. For example, MetaclassTalk allows changing the message dispatch schema, memory allocation, and the inheritance policy.

12.1.4.1 The MetaclassTalk MOP

MetaclassTalk provides control of most execution mechanisms of a reflective OO language. The methods defined by the root class for meta-objects include

send: methodName **from:** sender **to:** receiver **arguments:** argArray **superSend:** superFlag **originClass:** originClass

controls message sends (i.e., outgoing messages). Its arguments are:

- **methodName.** The name of the method to invoke. Because we use Smalltalk, this name is also the signature of the method.[3]
- **sender.** The object that emits the message.
- **receiver.** The object that should receive the message.
- **argArray.** An array with message parameters.
- **superFlag.** Is true if the message is sent to super.
- **originClass.** The class where the message is emitted. This is useful for super sends since it makes it possible to find out the starting class for method lookup.

---

3. Smalltalk is dynamically typed, and the name of a method reflects the number of its arguments. A Smalltalk method name is a compound of many words separated by colons. The number of colons is equal to the number of method arguments.

receive: methodName **from:** sender **to:** receiver **arguments:** argArray **superSend:** superFlag **originClass:** originClass

controls message receptions (i.e. incoming messages). It takes the same arguments as the previous method. The only difference is that it is performed by the meta-object of the receiver of the message.

atIV: fieldIndex of: anObject

controls field (instance variable in Smalltalk jargon) read access. This method takes two arguments:

- **fieldIndex**. The index (within the array representing the object structure) of the field to access.
- **anObject**. The object that holds the field.

atIV: fieldIndex of: anObject **put:** value

controls fields write accesses. The last parameter denotes the value to store.

This list is only part of the actual MetaclassTalk MOP. Other reflective facilities are also available, including mechanisms for memory allocation for created objects, method lookup, and evaluation.

12.1.4.2   Meta-Link and Meta-Object Cooperation in MetaclassTalk

MetaclassTalk makes it possible to implement a variety of relationships between base objects and meta-objects. At this time, three policies have been implemented:

- A single meta-object shared between instances of a same class
- A single specific meta-object private to each base object
- Many meta-objects shared among many base objects

In the following section, when many meta-objects cooperate to control one or many base objects, we use a simple cooperation rule that relies on the "chain of responsibility" design pattern [17]. All meta-objects that control the same base object are arranged into a single chain [31]. The head of the chain is the meta-object that is actually linked to the base object. Whenever this meta-object takes control of some base object activity (e.g., handling messages received by the base object), it first performs its meta-processing and then forwards information about the activity to control to the next meta-object on the chain. Once the last meta-object of the chain performs its meta-processing, the flow of control goes back through the chain. This cooperation scheme requires the explicit cooperation of the meta-objects [31].

12.1.4.3 Example: Logging

Suppose we have a banking application, and we want to log the activity of a specific account (e.g., deposits, withdrawals). First, we need to build a class of meta-objects that perform logging, as shown in Figure 12-3.

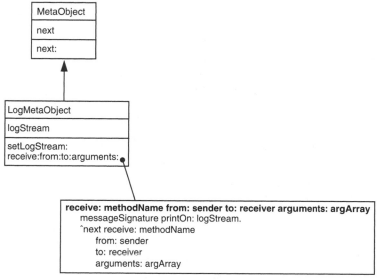

Figure 12-3 *Logging meta-object class.*

The `LogMetaObject` class defines a field named `logStream`, which references the stream where logs are written (e.g., a stream on some log file). `LogMetaObject` also defines a method for setting the stream and redefines the method for handling received messages. This method simply prints the message signature into the log stream. Then the default behavior for reception handling is performed.

In order to log the behavior of a given account, we need to use a "log" meta-object. Listing 12-1 shows code that:

♦ Declares two temporary variables `myAccount` and `myMeta` (line 1).

♦ Creates a new account and references it using `myAccount` (line 2).

♦ Creates a new log meta-object and stores it in `myMeta` (line 3).

- Sets up the stream where logs should be stored (line 4).
- Links myAccount to myMeta (line 5). As suggested by the protocol used for this linking (addMetaObject:), a base object can be linked to many meta-objects. Those meta-objects cooperate in order to control the behavior of the base object. Of course, some (or all) of these meta-objects can be shared with another base object.

Listing 12-1   *Setting up a specific meta-behavior for a base object*

```
1. | myAccount myMeta |
2. myAccount := BankAccount new.
3. myMeta := LogMetaObject new.
4. myMeta logStream: (WriteStream...)
5. myAccount addMetaObject: myMeta.
```

Once myAccount is linked to the MyMeta log meta-object, its activity gets logged. So, whenever the myAccount receives the deposit: 100 message, its meta-object (myMeta) takes control. Concretely, an implicit message is sent to myMeta as shown in Figure 12-4. As a result, first myMeta performs the logging, and then it evaluates the deposit: 100 message.

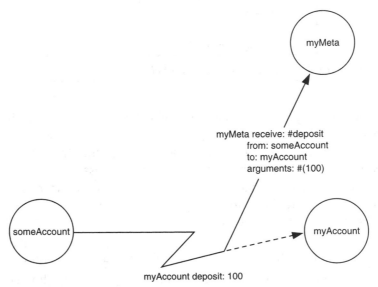

Figure 12-4   *Handling the reception of the* deposit: *message.*

In this example, among all instances of the `BankAccount`, only the one referenced by `myAccount` is logged. Now, imagine that we want to log every instance of `BankAccount`, including ones that are not created yet. This can be done by sending the `addMetaObjectClass:` message to the `BankAccount` class as `BankAccount addMetaObjectClass: LogMetaObject`.

This message makes the `BankAccount` class link every new instance with a new meta-object instance of `LogMetaObject` at initialization. Thus, logs of every new account go into a specific stream.

12.2 AOP USING REFLECTION

In this section, we show how to support AOP using reflection. We provide an example of this support based on a real-world application with multiple aspects. Aspects definitions and weaving are illustrated using MetaclassTalk and its MOP.

12.2.1 From Reflection to AOP

To show the relationships between reflection and AOP, we present a mapping from the concepts of AOP to those of reflection. This mapping illustrates how reflection can be used to separate aspect code and base code and to weave them together.

Aspect code is separated from base code thanks to the natural separation between the base-level and the meta-level. Base code is defined at the base-level, while aspects are defined at the meta-level. Base objects represent base code, and meta-objects represent aspects. Separating aspect definitions one from another is done by making use of a specific set of meta-objects for each aspect. Thus, each meta-object participates in a single aspect.

Weaving is performed using the meta-link and meta-object cooperation. Aspects are woven with base code using the meta-link. Indeed, the meta-link connects meta-objects, representing aspects, to base objects, representing base code. Usually, when weaving multiple aspects with base code, a given base object requires linking to multiple meta-objects. Conflicts arise when two meta-objects compete to control the same execution mechanism (e.g., the same message reception) of the same base object. Such conflicts can be solved by making meta-objects cooperate (whenever possible), as presented in Section 12.1.3.

One important notion related to weaving is the concept of join points. Join points correspond to particular points in the base code execution flow. The MOP provided by a reflective language defines and gives access to these points. For example, the MOP can state that meta-objects are active on message receptions. However, this definition is *generic* because it is not bound to base-code: It does not refer to a particular set of message receptions. The exact set of message receptions controlled by a given meta-object *mo* remains undefined until *mo* is linked to some base object *o*. Once this linkage is performed, the *mo* meta-object controls all messages received by *o*. So, reflection looses the coupling between aspect definitions and base-code, paving the way for aspect reuse.

To conclude, we draw an analogy between a reflective programming language and AspectJ [25, 26, 28]. Methods of meta-object classes play the role of sets of *advice*. The MOP can be viewed as a set of *abstract pointcuts*. Concreteness is obtained by linking a given base object to some meta-object since the meta-object acts on some concrete execution flow (i.e., some concrete join points such as a particular message send or field access).

12.2.2 Example of an Application with Multiple Aspects

Consider the example of a digital bookstore that sells books on the web (Figure 12-5). Among objects comprising the digital bookstore, we have customers, managers, books, and orders. The digital bookstore supports various functionalities such as searching for books, ordering books, adding and removing books, and updating price lists.

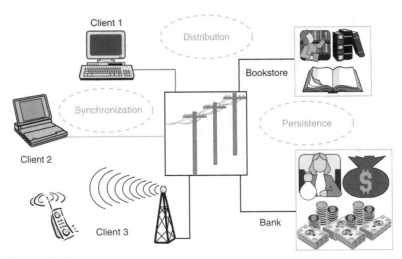

Figure 12-5 *A digital bookstore.*

The digital bookstore system also has several aspects with which developers should be concerned. Obviously, distribution is one of them. The digital library system should interact with remote entities (e.g., customers, bank). Another aspect is concurrency. Multiple customers can search for books or make orders while library managers handle orders or update the price list. Yet another aspect is persistence. It is crucial to make objects such as orders or books persist, even if the application stops running.

12.2.3   Separating Aspects

Thanks to the base-meta separation provided by reflection, we can decompose our digital bookstore application, as shown on Figure 12-6. On one hand, aspects are defined at the meta-level using meta-objects. On the other hand, application core functionalities are defined at the base-level using base objects.

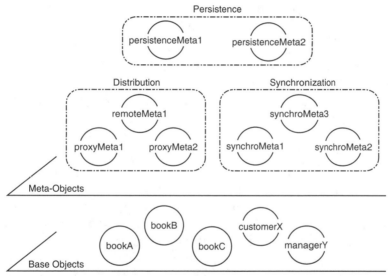

Figure 12-6   *Separating aspects in the bookstore application.*

Separating aspects from each other is done by decomposing the meta-level into sets of meta-objects. Each set includes meta-objects specific to a single aspect.

The set of meta-objects specific to the distribution aspect includes meta-objects that make some base objects be remotely accessible or behave as proxies (possibly with cache). Meta-objects for a proxy forward all received messages to some remote-objects and take care of marshaling. Meta-objects for remote-objects register these in some name server and take care of marshaling.

The synchronization aspect is represented by a set of meta-objects that allow defining critical sections of code (e.g., mutually exclusive methods). For example, such a meta-object handles accesses to the price field of a book so that:

◆ When the price is changed by some thread, other threads attempting either a read or a write access of the same field are locked.

◆ When the price is read by some thread, other threads attempting a write access to the price field are locked.

The persistence aspect is represented by a set of meta-objects that define how base objects should be stored and when the storage should be updated. For example, a meta-object could handle accesses to book fields in order to update a database on changes.

Besides a set of meta-objects, an aspect definition in MetaclassTalk includes a *configuration script*. This latter is a code that

◆ Creates meta-objects.

◆ Performs any required initialization for meta-objects (e.g., linking persistence meta-objects to some database).

◆ Sets up the meta-link, that is, links the aspect's specific meta-objects to application base objects.

For example, Figure 12-7 provides the code defining the synchronization aspect. This definition is quite simple. There is only one meta-object class named `SynchronizationMetaObject`, and the configuration script only ensures the creation of a synchronization meta-object for every instance of classes `Book` and `Order`. So, an instance of the `SynchronizationMetaObject` is created and linked to every new instance of one of these two classes.

The `SynchronizationMetaObject` class defines a new field named `lock`. This field holds a lock object that prevents critical sections of code from being executed by more than one thread simultaneously. We ensure this synchronization by making the `SynchronizationMetaObject` class redefine methods for controlling fields reads and writes. In each of those two methods (`atIV:of:` and `atIV:of:put:`), the critical section of code is between square brackets.

As stated previously, an aspect definition distinguishes between:

◆ Aspect-specific processing provided by meta-object classes

◆ When and where to perform this processing (i.e., join points) provided by the configuration script

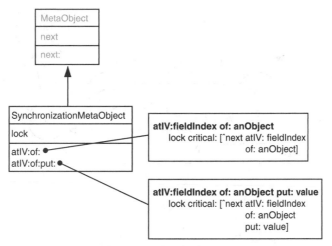

Figure 12-7 *Definition of a synchronization aspect.*

Since the specification of join points is provided by the configuration script, meta-object classes are generic. Thus, they can be reused in different applications, paving the way for aspect reuse.

12.2.4 *Weaving Aspects*

In the context sketched in Section 12.2.3, weaving consists of performing configuration scripts of all aspects. As a result, each new base object involved in multiple aspects is linked to multiple meta-objects. These meta-objects cooperate in order to control the activity of the newly created base object. This cooperation can rely on the chain of responsibility design pattern described in Section 12.1.3.

For example, consider a book base object in our digital bookstore. It should be both synchronized and persistent. Each of these two concerns is represented by a specific meta-object. The synchronization meta-object ensures that only one thread can access (read or write) some field of a book. The persistence meta-object ensures that whenever a field value is changed (i.e., write access), the new value is stored on some database. We organize these two meta-objects in a chain, as shown in Figure 12-8. The synchronization meta-object is the head of the cooperation chain, and thus it is linked to the book object.

In order to show the meta-object cooperation in action, let's examine what happens when the bookstore manager tries to update the price of some book. The price update means assigning a new value to the `price` field of the given book. Figure 12-9 shows the main steps for the processing of this assignment.

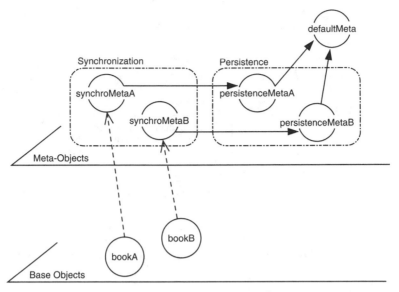

Figure 12-8 *Weaving aspects using meta-objects cooperation.*

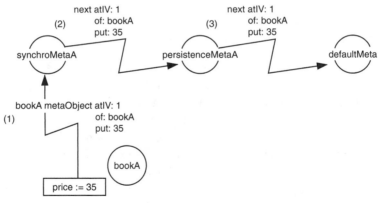

Figure 12-9 *Interaction between cooperating meta-objects.*

The evaluation of the assignment of the new price to the `price` field is performed by sending a message `atIV:of:put:` to the meta-object linked to the `bookA` book. The first parameter of this message is the index of the accessed field (we suppose that `price` is the first field of the class `Book`), the second parameter is the object holding the field, and the last parameter is the new value. Note that the message `metaObject` allows the retrieval of the meta-object linked to some base object.

In the case of the `bookA` object, its direct meta-object is `synchroMetaA`, which is in charge of synchronization.

When `synchroMetaA` receives the `atIV:of:put:` message (step 1 in Figure 12-9), it first locks field access to other threads. Then it requests the next meta-object in the cooperation chain to perform the field access (step 2 in Figure 12-9). The next meta-object in the chain is `persistenceMetaA`, which enforces persistence. When this latter meta-object receives the `atIV:of:put:`, it updates the database with the new price. Then it requests the next meta-object in the cooperation chain to perform the field access (step 3 in Figure 12-9). The next meta-object is `defaultMeta`, which provides the default semantics for the MetaclassTalk MOP. It is `defaultMeta` that actually writes the new value into the price field. Once the `price` value is updated, the control flow goes back through the inverse path (`defaultMeta`, `persistenceMeta`, and then `synchroMeta`). So, `synchroMeta` is given the opportunity to release the lock on accesses to the `price` field.

As stated above, the meta-object cooperation policy presented here is not the only possible one. Many other strategies to perform meta-object cooperation (and hence deal with conflicting aspects) are possible. One can even imagine a completely different approach for weaving. Instead of doing it at the instance (meta-object) level, it is possible to do it at the level of meta-object classes. In this context, each base object is controlled by a single meta-object. The latter is an instance of a class that "merges" definitions provided by classes related to aspects relevant to the base object. The "merge," for example, can rely on multiple inheritance or mixin-based inheritance [4].

To conclude this section, we should recall that aspect weaving (and particularly weaving non-orthogonal aspects) is still an open issue in AOP [6, 13, 14]. Although reflection does not solve or even avoid possible conflicts, it has two advantages: (1) it expresses the aspect weaving issue in a more familiar way, which is object or class composition, and (2) it makes possible the exploration of various strategies for weaving and conflict handling.

12.3 DISCUSSION

In this section, we discuss advantages and drawbacks of the use of reflection to support AOP.

12.3.1 Flexibility

Many reflective systems make meta-objects exist during runtime. This is the case in MetaclassTalk and other MOPs [32, 33, 39, 42]. One of the main benefits of this approach is *flexibility*: the set of meta-objects controlling a base object can be changed dynamically at runtime. Since aspects are represented using meta-objects, it becomes possible *to weave or unweave aspects dynamically* [1, 9, 11, 22, 33].

Weaving and unweaving aspects dynamically is an interesting feature for applications dealing with problems such as pervasive or automatic computing and unplanned or context-aware evolution. For example, in the context of critical systems that should not be stopped for maintenance or unplanned evolution, new aspects can be added, and existing ones can be removed or upgraded dynamically.

Quality of Service (QoS) is another benefit of flexibility provided by dynamic weaving [15]. QoS is mandatory in application domains where resources are constrained and variable in time (e.g., in embedded systems). Aspects can be (un)weaved at runtime according to the execution conditions [9]. For example, the bandwidth of a wireless connection on a PDA can undergo variations, which must be taken into account to provide a correct QoS [10]. A typical PDA has limited CPU power and memory size, except when it is docked at a desktop. When the network bandwidth is high, the remote communication aspect should save CPU and memory. But when the bandwidth decreases under some threshold, QoS requires replacing the previous aspect. The new remote communication aspect should sacrifice some CPU and memory for caching.

Concretely, remote communication requires having some base objects on the PDA that act as proxies for some remote objects. This behavior is introduced by means of some meta-objects that should be replaced according to the network load. When the bandwidth decreases, a meta-object that makes some base object behave as a plain proxy should be replaced by another one that makes our base object behave as a proxy with cache.

12.3.2 *Performance*

Flexibility is an advantage of reflection, but its cost is a non-negligible overhead. Indeed, meta-objects act like interpreters. This difficulty is compounded, because in a reflective system, meta-objects can be controlled by some meta-meta-objects.

Various approaches exist to deal with this overhead. One possible solution is to "merge" base and meta-levels at compile time or load time. This is done in OpenC++ 2.0 [7] and OpenJava [8]. This approach, from which AspectJ technology was derived [40], suppresses any "indirection" by flattening the reflective tower. The program is transformed so as to have only one level of objects. However, while this considerably speeds computing, it detracts from flexibility.

Another approach, adopted by Iguana [20, 34] and Reflex [38, 39], consists of restricting the activity of meta-objects to just those places where it is required. This *partial reflection* makes it possible to limit the overhead to only cases where some special meta-processing is required. However, flexibility is restricted to planned scenarios, and unplanned evolution is not possible. Indeed, meta-objects' capabilities are defined statically and cannot be changed at runtime.

An alternative solution consists of using *partial evaluation* [5, 37]. This approach promises to keep the flexibility of reflection while drastically reducing performance overhead. Roughly, the idea behind this approach is to assume that meta-objects will not change, and to generate an optimized version of application code under this assumption. This optimized code is run instead of the original code. When the meta-objects change, the optimized code is regenerated.

12.3.3   Complexity

Reflection is one powerful tool for reaching the goal of AOP [27]. Indeed, reflection opens up the programming language and makes it extensible and adaptable. However, reflection has been criticized for its complexity. The underlying concepts tend to be hard to learn and may make programs difficult to understand [12].

Nevertheless, we believe that this complexity can be at least partially hidden Aspect developers can be provided some aspect-specific (i.e., domain-specific) language that compiles into a reflective language. The aspect-specific language eases expressing aspects while restricting the access to available reflective facilities.

12.3.4   Tooling

One of the issues in building programs using AOP is the lack of appropriate development tools. This is particularly true for debugging. The difficulty of building such tools is among the reasons behind this scarcity. Aspects usually cannot be tested in isolation, and it is difficult to retrieve aspect-specific code by analyzing weaved code.

Reflection provides the benefit of using existing development tools. Aspects can be expressed in terms of classes of meta-objects, whose code can be viewed and edited using class browsers. Testing and debugging can also be done using existing tools. Debugging is made easier since meta-objects aspects remain decoupled one from another. Indeed, each aspect is represented by a set of meta-objects that can be distinguished from other (meta-) objects even after weaving. One can argue that these tools are rather "low-level" and do not suit aspects. However, (1) they are a first answer to the tooling issue, and (2) they can be extended (especially by means of reflection) to better support aspect development.

12.3.5   Reuse

Software reuse is one of the holy grails of software engineering. In order to reuse aspects in different applications, aspects should be generic. That is, the definition of an aspect should not explicitly reference application components. However, weaving requires linking aspects to application components. This is somewhat contradictory with aspect genericity.

By expressing aspects using meta-objects, reflection brings to AOP reuse solutions provided by object-oriented programming (e.g., inheritance). One can easily build new aspects using new meta-object classes that inherit from existing meta-object classes. Furthermore, meta-objects classes can easily be made generic (that is, independent of any application). Indeed, only configuration scripts that link meta-objects to base objects need to be application-specific.

12.4 CONCLUSION

In this chapter, we presented reflection and how it can be used to support AOP. We described the MetaclassTalk MOP and showed one possible approach to use it in order to implement isolated aspects and then weave them together.

An aspect can be implemented in isolation since its definition is a compound of a set of generic meta-object classes and a configuration script. Meta-object classes define aspect specific processing (e.g., synchronization), while the configuration script expresses when and where to perform this processing (i.e., it specifies join points). In fact, the configuration script allows you to create meta-objects, initialize them, and link them to base objects. Since the specification of the join point is provided by the configuration script, meta-object classes are generic. Thus, they can be reused in other applications, paving the way for aspect reuse.

In the previously described context, weaving is performed by evaluating aspect configuration scripts. As a result, each base object can be linked to many cooperating meta-objects. This relationship can be updated at runtime by adding or removing meta-objects. Thus, the use of reflection provides flexibility. Applications can be adapted or evolved by dynamically weaving and unweaving aspects.

It's worth recalling that the approach presented previously is only one possible way to support AOP. Many other approaches to represent and weave aspects can be developed using reflection. Particularly, different strategies for dealing with non-orthogonal aspect weaving can be studied. Reflection is not only a way to support AOP, but it is also an ideal test bed to evaluate solutions for AOP open issues.

REFERENCES

1. BOURAQADI, N. 2000. Concern-oriented programming using reflection. In *Workshop on Advanced Separation of Concerns (OOPSLA)*, (Minneapolis). http://trese.cs.utwente.nl/Workshops/OOPSLA2000/papers/bouraqadi.pdf.

2. BOURAQADI, N. 2004. Safe metaclass composition using mixin-based inheritance. In *Journal of Computer Languages Systems & Structures, Volume 30, Special issue: Smalltalk Language, Issues 1-2,* Ducasse, S., and Wuyts, R. Eds., 49–61.

3. BOURAQADI, N. 1999. Un mop smalltalk pour l'étude de la composition et de la compatibilité des métaclasses. application à la programmation par aspects. Ph.D. thesis, Faculté des Sciences et des Techniques, Université de Nantes.

4. BRACHA, G. AND COOK, W. 1990. Mixin-based inheritance. In *Conf. Object-Oriented Programming: Systems, Languages, and Applications; European Conf. Object-Oriented Programming,* (Ottawa). ACM, 303–311.

5. BRAUX, M. AND NOYÉ, J. 1999. Towards partially evaluating reflection in Java. In *2000 Workshop on Partial Evaluation and Semantics-Based Program Manipulation,* (Boston). ACM, 2–11.

6. BRICHAU, J., MENS, K., AND DE VOLDER, K. 2002. Building composable aspect-specific languages with logic metaprogramming. In *1st ACM Conf. Generative Programming and Component Engineering,* (Pittsburgh). LNCS, vol. 2487. Springer-Verlag, Berlin, 110–127.

7. CHIBA, S. 1995. A metaobject protocol for C++. In *10th Conf. Object-Oriented Programming, Systems, Languages, and Applications (OOPSLA),* (Austin). ACM, 285–299.

8. CHIBA, S. AND TATSUBORI, M. 1998. Yet another java.lang.Class. In *Workshop on Object-Oriented Technology: Ecoop'98 Workshop Reader.* Springer-Verlag, Berlin, 372–373.

9. DAVID, P. C. AND LEDOUX, T. 2002. Dynamic adaptation of non-functional concerns. In *1st Int'l Workshop on Unanticipated Software Evolution (USE-ECOOP),* (Malaga, Spain). http://joint.org/use2002/sub/david-ledoux.pdf.

10. DAVID, P. C. AND LEDOUX, T. 2002. An infrastructure for adaptable middleware. In *On the Move to Meaningful Internet Systems, 2002—DOA/CoopIS/ODBASE 2002 Confederated Int'l Conferences.* LNCS, vol. 2519. Springer-Verlag, Berlin, 773–790.

11. DAVID, P. C., LEDOUX, T., AND BOURAQADI, N. 2001. Two-step weaving with reflection using AspectJ. In *Workshop on Advanced Separation of Concerns in Object-Oriented Systems (OOPSLA),* (Tampa, Florida). http://www.cs.ubc.ca/~kdvolder/Workshops/OOPSLA2001/submissions/02-david.pdf.

12. DE VOLDER, K. AND D'HONDT, T. 1999. Aspect-oriented logic meta programming. In *Meta-Level Architectures and Reflection, 2nd Int'l Conf. Reflection,* P. Cointe, Ed. LNCS, vol. 1616. Springer Verlag, Berlin, 250–272.

13. DOUENCE, R., FRADET, P., AND SÜDHOLT, M. 2002. A framework for the detection and resolution of aspect interactions. In *1st ACM Conf. Generative Programming and Component Engineering* (Pittsburgh). LNCS, vol. 2487. Springer-Verlag, Berlin, 173–188.

14. DOUENCE, R., FRADET, P., AND SÜDHOLT, M. 2004. Composition, Reuse and Interaction Analysis of Dynamic Aspects. In *3rd Int'l Conf. on Aspect-Oriented Software Development (AOSD 2004)*, (Lancaster), Murphy, G., and Lieberherr, K. Eds. ACM, 141–150.

15. DUZAN, G., LOYALL, G., SCHANTZ, R., SHAPIRO, R., AND ZINKY, J. 2004. Building Adaptive Distributed Applications with Middleware and Aspects. In *3rd Int'l Conf. on Aspect-Oriented Software Development (AOSD 2004)*, (Lancaster), Murphy, G., and Lieberherr, K. Eds. ACM, 66–73.

16. ELRAD, T., FILMAN, R. E., AND BADER, A. 2001. Aspect-oriented programming. *Comm. ACM 44*, 10 (Oct.), 29–32.

17. GAMMA, E., HELM, R., JOHNSON, R., AND VLISSIDES, J. 1995. *Design Patterns: Elements of Reusable Object-Oriented Software*. Addison-Wesley, Reading, Massachusetts.

18. GOLDBERG, A. AND ROBSON, D. 1983. *Smalltalk-80: The Language and Its Implementation*. Addison-Wesley, Reading, Massachusetts.

19. GOLM, M. AND KLEINÖDER, J. 1999. Jumping to the meta level: Behavioral reflection can be fast and flexible. In *2nd Int'l Conf. Meta-Level Architectures and Reflection*. LNCS, vol. 1616. Springer-Verlag, Berlin, 22–39.

20. GOWING, B. AND CAHILL, V. 1996. Meta-object protocols for C++: The Iguana approach. In *Reflection '96*, (San Francisco), G. Kiczales, Ed. 137–152.

21. GUZDIAL, M. AND ROSE, K. EDS. 2002. *Squeak—Open Personal Computing and Multimedia*. Prentice Hall, Upper Saddle River, New Jersey.

22. HIRSCHFELD, R. 2003. AspectS—Aspect-Oriented Programming with Squeak. In *Objects, Components, Architectures, Services, and Applications for a Networked World, Int. Conference NetObjectDays (NODe 2002)*, (Erfurt), October 2002, Akşit, M., Mezini, M., and Unland, R. Eds., Revised Papers, LNCS 2591, Springer, 216–232.

23. INGALLS, D., KAEHLER, T., MALONEY, J., WALLACE, S., AND ALLAN KAY 1997. Back to the Future. The Story of Squeak, A Practical Smalltalk Written in Itself. In *12th Conf. on Object-Oriented Programming, Systems, Languages, and Applications (OOPSLA'97)*, (Atlanta), Berman, A. M., Loomis, M., and Bloom, T. Eds. ACM, 318–326.

24. KICZALES, G., DES RIVIERES, J., AND BOBROW, D. G. 1991. *The Art of the Metaobject Protocol*. MIT Press, Cambridge, Massachusetts.

25. KICZALES, G., HILSDALE, E., HUGUNIN, J., KERSTEN, M., PALM, J., AND GRISWOLD, W. G. 2001. An overview of AspectJ. In *ECOOP 2001—Object-Oriented Programming, 15th European Conference*, (Budapest), J. L. Knudsen, Ed. LNCS, vol. 2072. Springer-Verlag, Berlin, 327–353.

26. KICZALES, G., HILSDALE, E., HUGUNIN, J., KERSTEN, M., PALM, J., AND GRISWOLD, W. G. 2001. Getting started with AspectJ. *Comm. ACM 44*, 10 (Oct.), 59–65.

27. KICZALES, G., LAMPING, J., MENDHEKAR, A., MAEDA, C., LOPES, C., LOINGTIER, J. M., AND IRWIN, J. 1997. Aspect-oriented programming. In *ECOOP'97 Object-Oriented Programming, 11th European Conference*, M. Akşit and S. Matsuoka, Eds. LNCS, vol. 1241. Springer-Verlag, Berlin, 220–242.

28. LADDAD, R. 2003. *AspectJ in Action*. Manning Publications, Greenwich, Connecticut.

29. MAES, P. 1987. Concepts and experiments in computational reflection. In *2nd Conf. Object-Oriented Programming, Systems, Languages, and Applications (OOPSLA)*, (Orlando). ACM. 147–155.

30. MCAFFER, J. 1995. Meta-level programming with CodA. In *ECOOP'95 Object-Oriented Programming, 9th European Conference*, W. Olthoff, Ed. LNCS, vol. 952. Springer-Verlag, Berlin, 190–214.

31. MULET, P., MALENFANT, J., AND COINTE, P. 1995. Towards a methodology for explicit composition of metaobjects. In *10th Conf. Object-Oriented Programming, Systems, Languages, and Applications (OOPSLA)*, (Austin). ACM, 316–330.

32. OLIVA, A. AND BUZATO, L. E. 1999. The design and implementation of Guaraná. In *5th Conf. Object-Oriented Technologies & Systems (COOTS)*, (San Diego). USENIX, 203–216.

33. PAWLAK, R., SEINTURIER, L., DUCHIEN, L., AND FLORIN, G. 2001. JAC: A flexible solution for aspect-oriented programming in Java. In *Metalevel Architectures and Separation of Crosscutting Concerns 3rd Int'l Conf. (Reflection 2001)*, (Kyoto), A. Yonezawa and S. Matsuoka, Eds. LNCS vol. 2192. Springer-Verlag, Berlin, 1–24.

34. REDMOND, B. AND CAHILL, V. 2002. Supporting Unanticipated Dynamic Adaptation of Application Behaviour. In *Proceedings of 16th European Conf. on Object-Oriented Programming (ECOOP 2002)*, (Malaga), Boris Magnusson, Ed. LNCS vol. 2374. Springer-Verlag, Berlin, 205–230.

35. RIVARD, F. 1996. Smalltalk: A reflective language. In *Reflection '96* (San Francisco), G. Kiczales, Ed. 21–38. http://www2.parc.com/csl/groups/sda/projects/reflection96/docs/rivard/rivard.pdf.

36. SMITH, B. C. 1984. Reflection and semantics in lisp. In *Symp. Principles of Programming Languages (POPL)*, (Salt Lake City). ACM, 23–35.

37. SULLIVAN, G. T. 2001. Aspect-oriented programming using reflection and meta-object protocols. *Comm. ACM 44*, 10 (Oct.), 95–97.

38. TANTER, E., BOURAQADI, N., AND NOYÉ, J. 2001. Reflex towards an open reflective extension of Java. In *Metalevel Architectures and Separation of Crosscutting Concerns 3rd Int'l Conf. (Reflection 2001)*, (Kyoto), A. Yonezawa and S. Matsuoka, Eds. LNCS vol. 2192. Springer-Verlag, Berlin, 25–43.

39. TANTER, E., NOYÉ, J., CAROMEL, D., AND COINTE, P. 2003. Partial behavioral reflection: Spatial and temporal selection of reification. In *18th Conf. Object-Oriented Programming, Systems, Languages, and Applications (OOPSLA)*, (Anaheim). ACM, 27–46.

40. THOMAS, D. 2002. Reflective software engineering—from MOPs to AOSD. *Journal of Object Technology 1*, 4 (Sept.), 17–26.

41. WATANABE, T. AND YONEZAWA, A. 1988. Reflection in an object-oriented concurrent language. In *3rd Conf. Object-Oriented Programming, Systems, Languages, and Applications (OOPSLA)*, (San Diego). ACM, 306–315.

42. WELCH, I. AND STROUD, R. 1999. From Dalang to Kava—the evolution of a reflective Java extension. In *Reflection '99,* (Saint-Malo, France), P. Cointe, Ed. LNCS, vol. 1616. Springer-Verlag, Berlin, 2–21.

43. YOKOTE, Y. 1992. The Apertos reflective operating system: The concept and its implementation. In *7th Conf. Object-Oriented Programming, Systems, Languages, and Applications (OOPSLA)*, (Vancouver). ACM, 414–434.

Chapter 13

Inserting Ilities by Controlling Communications

ROBERT E. FILMAN, STUART BARRETT, DIANA D. LEE, AND TED LINDEN

For many applications, most code is not devoted to implementing the desired input-output behavior but to providing system-wide properties like reliability, availability, responsiveness, performance, security, and manageability. We call such qualities *ilities*. This article describes a system that enables a more complete separation of ility implementations from functional components, allowing ilities to be developed, maintained, and modified with minimal impact on functional implementations.

Ilities can seldom be entirely implemented simply as discrete services. For example, many replication algorithms require logging and distributed update on every object modification. Similarly, performance, security, and manageability enhancements demand systematic and widespread code changes, complicating a clean design. While object-oriented design and programming has provided effective ways to modularize functional requirements into separately maintainable components, it has been less successful in enabling programmers to modularize code devoted to ilities. Object orientation does not provide programming structures that allow ilities and functionality to evolve independently over the software lifecycle.

Separating ility support from functional components becomes significantly more important and complex in distributed applications. Distributed applications typically have more stringent ility requirements and need more complex ility algorithms. This article defines an approach that supplements standard object-oriented methods with a general mechanism for injecting ility implementations into the communications between functional components. Algorithms that support ilities are separated from functional components but may be invoked whenever functional components communicate. This allows ilities and functionality to be modified and maintained with minimal impact on each other.

13.1   *ACHIEVING ILITIES BY CONTROLLING COMMUNICATION*

Our research integrates the following key ideas:

Intercepting communications.   Our primary claim is that ilities can be achieved by intercepting and manipulating communications among functional components and by invoking appropriate "services" on all inter-component communications.

Discrete injectors.   Our communication interceptors are first class objects, discrete components that have (object) identity and can be sequenced, combined, and treated uniformly by utilities. We call them *injectors*. In a distributed system, an ility may require injecting behavior on both the client and the server. For instance, security requires authenticating on the server credentials generated on the client. Figure 13-1 illustrates injectors on communication paths between components.

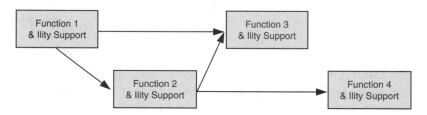

Traditional designs mix ility support within functional components.

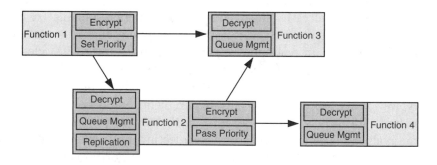

The Object Infrastructure Framework inserts services into the communication paths between functional components.

Figure 13-1   *Injectors on communication paths.*

Injection by object/method.   Each instance and each method on that object can have a distinct sequence of injectors.

Dynamic injection.   Dynamic configuration allows us to place debugging and monitoring probes in running applications and to create software that detects its own obsolescence and updates itself. There is a tradeoff, however, since security and manageability require rigorous configuration control over injector changes.

Annotations.   Injectors need to communicate among themselves. For example, the authentication injector needs to know the identity and credentials of a service requestor. Our solution is to provide a general mechanism for annotating communications with meta-information. Injectors are capable of reading and modifying the annotations of requests (and reading and modifying the request arguments and target function name).

Thread contexts.   Our goal is to keep the injection mechanism invisible to the functional components. However, sometimes clients and servers need to communicate with injectors. For example, a quality-of-service injector may want to process requests in order of their priority, but the only reasonable source of request priority is the client application. While some annotations must originate from the functional applications, separation of concerns would be destroyed if functional components have to be aware of all annotations. We make annotations largely transparent to functional components by providing an "alternative communication channel." Each client and server thread has its own set of annotations, the *thread context*. The system arranges to copy annotations among the client's thread context, the request, and the server's thread context.

High-level specification compiler.   There is a large conceptual distance between abstract ilities and discrete sequences of injectors. To span this gap, we have created Pragma, a compiler that takes a high-level specification of desired properties and ways to achieve these properties, and maps that specification to an appropriate set of injector initializations.

13.2   OBJECT INFRASTRUCTURE FRAMEWORK

We have illustrated these ideas by defining an architecture (the Object Infrastructure Framework or OIF), instantiating that architecture for a particular environment (CORBA®/Java™), and creating several validating applications within that framework [2, 8].

Current technology for building distributed, component-based applications uses sockets, messages, remote procedure calls such as DCE™, or Object Request Brokers (ORBs, such as CORBA, JavaRMI™, and DCOM). Without too much loss of generality, we focus on ORB frameworks and use CORBA as our exemplar. CORBA implements distribution by building *proxy* objects on both the client (caller environment) and server (called environment) to represent a particular server object. The client-side proxy (or *stub*) is responsible for *marshaling* a client request into a form that can be transmitted over the network; the server-side proxy (or *skeleton*) *demarshals* the request into native data structures for the server to process. ORB technology provides object location transparency and hides the details of marshaling and communication protocols. What it doesn't do is handle ility concerns like partial failures, security, and quality of service. ORBs such as CORBA and Enterprise JavaBeans™ provide different discrete mechanisms for particular ility issues, but such mechanisms typically provide only a finite number of choices for the application architect, and require a good understanding and diligent application of the mechanism by the application programmer.

13.2.1   Injectors

OIF's key implementation idea is to modify ORB proxies so that: (1) each stores a map from proxy methods to a sequence of injectors, and (2) in the proxy processing for a given method, that sequence is invoked between the application and marshaling. The action method of the injector gets an object representing the request. It can interrogate and modify that object for the request's target, method name, arguments, and annotations. Being code, it can perform arbitrary other operations, such as invoking methods on other (remote) objects and changing its local static state. Figure 13-2 illustrates CORBA proxies extended with injectors.

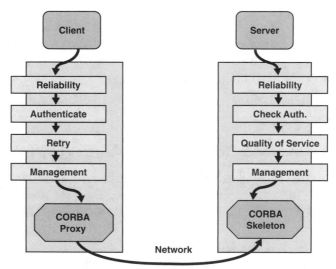

Figure 13-2   *OIF inserts injectors between the application and the network.*

Injector processing is in "continuation style," meaning injectors invoke the rest of the injector sequence between their "before" and "after" behaviors. (With the continuation pattern, one of the parameters of a routine is a representation of "the rest of the work to be done" after this routine has finished. In OIF, the continuation is represented as a list of injectors, and invoking the continuation is simply calling the first injector in this list, providing it the rest of the list as its continuation.) This has the advantages of allowing the injector stack to naturally catch exceptions, and permitting an injector to forgo or transform the continuation sequence. Our authentication injector illustrates the former advantage. A server-side authentication injector dissatisfied with a request's credentials raises an exception that a client-side injector catches. The client side injector interrogates the user and reinvokes the request with the additional annotation.

Similarly, when methods return static values and do not have side effects, an injector can cache values returned from previous calls. When a request is already in the cache, the caching injector can omit the remote call and return the local value. This has the effect of doing "objects by value" for selected parts of a remote object.

13.2.2   Annotations

Annotations provide a language for applications and injectors to communicate regarding requests. That is, they are a meta-language for statements about requests and the processing state. Annotations can express notions like "This request is to be done at high priority," "Here are the user's credentials," and "Here is the cyberwallet to pay for this request." Annotations can be associated with both requests (*request annotations*) and processing threads (*thread contexts*).

OIF annotations are name-value pairs. The names are strings and the values are CORBA ANY types, allowing object references as annotation values. This requires annotation readers and writers to have an implicit agreement about annotation types. Object references in annotations are used for patterns such as continuations ("Send the results of this computation to X") and agencies ("Y can verify my identity"), but not strings; encoding object references as strings would burden the recipient with demarshaling. The framework defines certain common annotations, including session identification, request priority, sending and due dates, version and configuration, cyber wallet, public key, sender identity, and conversational thread. Programs can rely on the common meanings of these annotations. Applications and injectors can create other annotations. Annotations can be implemented as hash tables or property lists. OIF proxies marshal and demarshal request annotations like ordinary procedure arguments.

Requiring injectors to declare the annotations they read and write, and enforcing those declarations, can improve security. We may feel safer using an injector that is restricted to only read the due dates of messages rather than one that can alter user identification or method arguments.

Thread contexts, (annotations associated with processing threads), allow applications to communicate with injectors. On each call, the framework copies the client thread's annotations to the annotations of the nascent request. On the server side, the framework builds the context of the service thread from the request's annotations. On return, the framework copies the server's context to the annotations of the response and then back to update the context of the original client. This scheme has the feature of propagating context through a chain of calls: Client A's call of B at priority x becomes B's context's priority of x. B's request of C (in furtherance of A's call) goes out with priority x. Figure 13-3 illustrates this pattern.

Thread contexts have the advantage of permitting client/injector communication without modifying the application interfaces. They have two disadvantages: newly spawned threads need to copy or share the context of their parents, and there is no primitive linguistic mechanism for neatly "block structuring" a change to a thread's context—allowing, for example, a thread to simply timeshare among tasks.

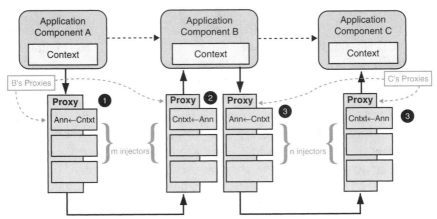

Figure 13-3 *Propagating annotations. ❶ When object A makes a call on method m in Object B, its thread context is copied over into the annotation of the request. ❷ After creating the thread to serve A's request, the annotations of the request are copied to that thread's context. ❸ B calls method n on C. This process is repeated for B's calls when handling that request. Thus, an annotation (e.g., priority) set in A is carried over through B to C.*

Declarations can control annotation copying. For example, the number of times the (client) retry-on-failure injector retries is not sent downstream. Similarly, we do not want a server to be able to update a client's user identification. The default behavior is to copy, enabling creating new annotations without modifying existing application code.

13.2.3   Pragma

Our high-level goal is to take functional code, ility specifications, and reusable ility service implementations and weave them together into the actual system code. Ideally, we would like to be able to press the "application: be secure," key, and, lo and behold, the application code is pervasively modified as necessary. That said, we have the sad task of reminding the reader of the dearth of magic in the world. Ilities must be implemented by invoking actual services. Saying you want security does not create security. Rather, you have to define security, as, for example encrypting all communications using { 64 | 128 | 7 } bit { DES | RSA | ROT-13 }, checking the user's { password | fingerprints | DNA } for { every | occasional } access to { all | sensitive } methods, recognizing intrusions { from strange sites | trying a series of passwords | asking too many questions }, keeping track of privileges by { proximity | job function | dynamic agreements }, and so forth. We need the ility architect both to have implementations of the appropriate algorithms (injectors that actually do that work), and to specify where each set of injectors is applied.

Pragma posits a two-level structure to achieve these goals. The architect defines:

1. A number of ilities (symbolic names like "reliability").
2. Methods (*actions*), to achieve each ility. For example, the ility "security" might have an action "high security" that authenticates through fingerprints and includes extensive monitoring and intrusion detection, while the action "low security" might require only passwords and limited monitoring.
3. A map from the actions to locations in the program. A location can be on a particular method in the implementations of a particular interface, on all the methods of a particular interface, on all the methods of a given name, or everywhere. These definitions can also include assertions about injector ordering.

Pragma also includes constructs for declaring annotations (including their type, default values, and copying context) and for constraining the use of injectors. We support the latter in two ways: an assertion mechanism allows an injector to preclude or demand another, and a cascade mechanism allows the successive refinement of policies within an organization. More specifically, a *policy* (collection of Pragma statements) may import other policies. A policy may also specify a set of alternatives for an ility. Policies that import such restrictions can choose among (or further restrict) this set, but may not offer new choices. Thus, an enterprise architect may define three acceptable security alternatives, an application suite architect may restrict these to two, and the ility architect for a particular program may choose to use only one.

The Pragma compiler takes as input both a policy and the application IDL™, and generates injector initializations and annotation declarations. Pragma, for each method, interface, and ility, finds the "most specific" way of doing that ility on that method of that interface. (Subinterfaces are more specific than superinterfaces; method-mentions more specific than not, and, arbitrarily, method-mentions more specific than interfaces.) It then orders the actions on that ⟨interface, method⟩ pair and outputs the results as data to the initialization mechanism. Pragma flags as errors combinations that violate constraints. Figure 13-4 shows the Pragma for Vendoom [8], a demonstration system developed using OIF.

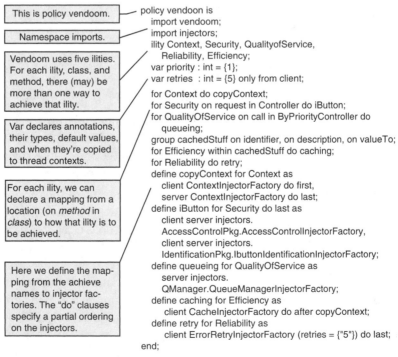

Figure 13-4 *Pragma for Vendoom.*

13.3 APPLIED ILITIES

Our work has been driven by demonstrating these ideas in a pair of prototypical applications. DisDev [2] implements a distributed repository and illustrates the use of injectors to achieve reliability through replication. Vendoom implements a simulation of a distributed, competitive network management application. It uses injectors to achieve quality of service (such as real-time performance), manageability, and security [8]. We review the lessons learned in pursuing these ilities in our framework.

13.3.1 Reliability

Our primary experiments in supporting reliability have centered on injecting replication algorithms into DisDev, a document management application. Replication algorithms typically send copies of messages to replicants. That is, if operation f is invoked on x and y, (and f mutates the application state), all replicants need to be aware of this action. Our work suggests this is more easily supported if x and y are symbolic, rather than pointers into a replicant's memory space.

Other reliability injectors we have demonstrated include the retry injector, which repeats attempts that time out or otherwise fail, and the rebind injector, which seeks alternative servers under the recognized failure of one.

Transactions are a reliability mechanism that illustrates the limits of this approach. Transactions require application objects that can start and end transactions and rollback on failure. If the application objects have these interfaces, injectors can be used to coordinate their invocation. For example, transaction identity is a straightforward application of request annotations. Sadly, however, transactions cannot be transparently achieved by injection to objects that lack them.

13.3.2 Quality of Service

By quality of service, we include a variety of requirements for getting things done within time constraints. The real-time community recognizes two varieties of real-time systems, *hard real-time* and *soft real-time*. A correct hard real-time system must complete all tasks by their deadlines. Soft real-time systems seek to allocate resources to more important tasks. Hard real-time requires cooperation throughout the processing chain (for example, in the underlying network), since the promise of particular service can be abrogated in too many places. (Doug Schmidt's work on real-time CORBA ORBs [11] illustrates this point: commercial CORBA ORBs, built without constant real-time mindfulness, conceal FIFO queues and exhibit anti-real-time behavior.)

Soft real-time is amenable to several communication control tactics. These include using queue control to identify the most worthwhile thing to do next [8], calling the underlying system's quality of service primitives, using side-door mechanisms to efficiently transport large quantities of data, and choosing among multiple problem solving approaches. We have demonstrated the first of these tactics in Vendoom. All except the last are easily done with injectors. If the application supplies the alternative problem solving methods (either by replicating the problem solving sites, allowing load balancing, or providing genuinely different algorithms), the communication control mechanism can apply the most effective problem solvers. Injectors, as stateful objects, can determine the best message target using tactics such as learning from historical experience and consulting traffic-reporting agencies.

13.3.3 Manageability

We take a network control perspective on manageability, dividing manageability into five elements: performance measurement, accounting, failure analysis, intrusion detection, and configuration management. The first four are amenable to generating events in relevant circumstances and directing those events to the appropriate recipients. For example, in Vendoom we have used injectors to publish events to update graphic displays, report payment data, and debug the application. In general, to the extent that the semantics of interesting events are tied to communication acts, such as when a micro-payment is processed each time a service is called, or the trace of inter-component messages is sent to a system's debugger, the events can be realized through external communication controls. This technique is inadequate when the interesting actions happen completely within the application components. Examples of such internal activity include when payment is directly proportional to the number of records accessed by a database service, or debugging occurs wholly within a component.

We have also designed a configuration management injector that dynamically tests for incompatible versions and automatically updates stale configurations. Such management can be done only for clients and servers that provide the appropriate interfaces.

13.3.4 Security

Security, at least in a software sense, is primarily a combination of access control, intrusion detection, authentication, and encryption. Controlling the communication process allows us to encrypt communications, reliably send user authentication from client to server (and pass it along to dependent requests), and check the access rights of requests. All this is independent of the actual application code. (However, we may only be able to encrypt the message data, not its headers. Similarly, encrypting object references may confuse the marshaling code. In general, encryption is better done after marshaling.) Watching communications provides a locus for detecting intrusion events [5], although not, of course, specifying the actual algorithms for recognizing an intrusion. We have illustrated security in Vendoom with injectors that perform access control and, (by checking the user's Java ring), authentication.

Can such mechanisms yield security? Somewhat. Such mechanisms reflect common notions of security, but cannot prevent hazards such as subverting a system's personnel, tapping communication lines, brute-force cracking of encryption codes, or components that cheat. Magic has its limits.

13.4   RELATED WORK

We have described a mechanism for separately specifying system-wide concerns in a component-based programming system and then weaving the code handling those concerns into a working application. This is the theme of Aspect-Oriented Programming (AOP). OIF is an instance of AOP, and brings to AOP a particularly elegant division of responsibilities. Key work on AOP includes Harrison and Ossher's Subject-Oriented Programming [6] which extends OOP to handle different subjective perspectives; Akşit and Tekinerdogan's message filters [1], which, like OIF, reify communication interceptors; Lieberherr's Adaptive programming [9], which proposed writing traversal strategies against partial specifications; and Kiczales and Lopes' [7] language for separate specifications of aspects, which effectively performs mixins at the source-code language level. Czarnecki and Eisenecker's book [3] includes a good survey of AOP technology.

The idea of intercepting communications has occurred several times in the history of computer science. Perhaps the earliest examples were in Lisp: the Interlisp advice mechanism and mixins of MacLisp.

It is common to tackle ility concerns by providing a framework with specific choices about those concerns. Examples include transaction monitors like Encina™ and Tuxedo® and distributed frameworks like Enterprise Java Beans and CORBA. It is worth noting that the CORBA security specification and many commercial CORBA implementations are emerging with some form of user-defined filter mechanism on communications. While these mechanisms are not as general as OIF, our work can be understood as a methodology for using CORBA filters.

The use of a separate specification language for creating filters parallels the work at BBN on quality of service [10], where the IDL-like Quality Description Language is woven with IDL to affect system performance.

13.5 CONCLUSION

Elsewhere, we argued that requirements come in four varieties: *functional* requirements that exhibit the primary semantic behavior of a system and are typically locally realized, *systematic* requirements that can be achieved by "doing the right thing" consistently throughout the program, *combinatoric* requirements that are computationally intractable expressions of overall system behavior, and *aesthetic* requirements that express non-computable qualities of the system [4]. Conventional development does a good job of supporting the first of these, and the last two are difficult to automate in any case.

We believe the mechanisms described in this article—injectors on communication, annotations, and high-level specification languages—are a comprehensive approach to satisfying systematic requirements. While not all systematic algorithms can be implemented without application cooperation, we have demonstrated a technology for taking a high-level expression of desired systematic requirements and automatically propagating this behavior to the components of a distributed system. We believe our results generalize to other contexts.

We thank Lockheed Martin Corporation; Motorola Incorporated; National Aeronautics and Space Administration, Ames Research Center; Raytheon Company; Office of the Assistant Secretary of Defense for Health Affairs (OASD(HA)), Composite Health Systems (CHCS); and Southwestern Bell Information Services for their financial support.

Encina is a trademark of Transarc Corporation. DCE is a trademark of The Open Software Foundation. Java, Enterprise Java Beans, and Java RMI are trademarks of Sun Microsystems, Inc. CORBA is a registered trademark and IDL is a trademark of Object Management Group, Inc. TUXEDO is a registered trademark of Novell, Inc.

REFERENCES

1. AKŞIT, M. AND TEKINERDOĞAN, B. 1998. Solving the modeling problems of object-oriented languages by composing multiple aspects using composition filters. In *Workshop on Aspect-Oriented Programming (ECOOP)*, (Brussels). http://trese.cs.utwente.nl/aop-ecoop98/papers/Aksit.pdf.

2. BARRETT, S. AND FOSTER, P. 1998. Turning Java components into CORBA components with replication. In *OMG-DARPA-MCC Workshop on Compositional Software Architectures*, (Monterey, California). http://www.objs.com/workshops/ws9801/papers/paper067.doc.

3. CZARNECKI, K. AND EISENECKER, U. W. 2000. *Generative Programming: Methods, Tools, and Applications*. Addison-Wesley, Reading, Massachusetts.

4. FILMAN, R. E. 2001. Achieving ilities. In *OMG-DARPA-MCC Workshop on Compositional Software Architectures*, (Monterey, California). http://www.objs.com/workshops/ws9801/papers/paper046.doc.

5. FILMAN, R. AND LINDEN, T. 1996. Communicating security agents. In *5th Workshops on Enabling Technologies: Infrastructure for Collaborative Enterprises—Int'l Workshop on Enterprise Security*, (Stanford, California). IEEE, 86–91.

6. HARRISON, W. AND OSSHER, H. 1993. Subject-oriented programming—a critique of pure objects. In *8th Conf. Object-Oriented Programming, Systems, Languages, and Applications (OOPSLA)*, (Washington, D. C.). ACM, 411–428.

7. KICZALES, G., LAMPING, J., MENDHEKAR, A., MAEDA, C., LOPES, C., LOINGTIER, J. M., AND IRWIN, J. 1997. Aspect-oriented programming. Tech. Rep. SPL97-008 P9710042, Xerox PARC. Feb. http://www.parc.xerox.com/spl/projects/aop/tr-aop.htm.

8. LEE, D. AND FILMAN, R. 2001. Verification of compositional software architectures. In *OMG-DARPA-MCC Workshop on Compositional Software Architectures*, (Monterey, California). http://www.objs.com/workshops/ws9801/papers/paper096.doc.

9. LIEBERHERR, K. J. 1996. *Adaptive Object-Oriented Software: The Demeter Method with Propagation Patterns*. PWS Publishing Company, Boston.

10. SCHANTZ, R., BAKKEN, D., KARR, D., LOYALL, J., AND ZINKY, J. 1998. Distributed objects with quality of service: An organizing architecture for integrated system properties. In *OMG-DARPA-MCC Workshop on Compositional Software Architectures*, (Monterey, California). http://www.objs.com/workshops/ws9801/papers/paper099.doc.

11. SCHMIDT, D. C., BECTOR, R., LEVINE, D. L., MUNGEE, S., AND PARULKAR, G. 1997. An ORB endsystem architecture for statically scheduled real-time applications. In *Workshop on Middleware for Distributed Real-Time Systems and Services*, (San Francisco). IEEE, 52–60.

Chapter 14

Using Bytecode Transformation to Integrate New Features

GEOFF COHEN

An aspect-oriented software development system typically contains some mechanism that integrates multiple concern-handling constructs at a single point in code. This functionality is necessary because many different dimensions or aspects of the overall design could influence behavior at that single point. This chapter describes the technique of *bytecode transformation* to accomplish such integration. Bytecode transformation adds concerns to existing code by modifying compiled Java classfiles, transforming the original code through a set of changes specified by a user-supplied program. While bytecode transformation is a common implementation technique for aspect-oriented programming in Java [11], its full functionality is rarely exposed to the end-programmer. The use of user-defined transformation and the targeting of compiled classes (rather than source code) provide improved expressiveness and flexibility for the aspect-oriented software design process.

As part of our research into bytecode transformation, we built a prototype transformation environment called JOIE [4]. Although in principle bytecode transformation could apply to other bytecode formats, such as P-Code [15], the Microsoft Common Language Runtime [9], or some implementations of Smalltalk [8], our implementation is in Java, and this discussion considers only Java classfiles as a target.

This chapter describes the ways in which bytecode transformation can be an effective mechanism for implementing aspect-oriented software development systems. It begins with a short description of how the concept of transformation relates to aspect-oriented programming and then presents an overview of the technique of bytecode transformation. It describes programming with bytecode transformation, discusses its use in the broader context of aspect-oriented software development, and relates some lessons learned from experience.

14.1   ASPECTS AND TRANSFORMATION

The impetus for aspect-oriented programming is that in other coding paradigms, the code that implements some features can be scattered across the body of the program, tangled in with code that implements other features. This occurs in features such as logging, caching, and security, where often code of a similar form is invoked many times throughout the program. This code has many disadvantages: It is tedious to write, it is error-prone, it complicates the program, and the calls can add overhead that may be needless for many users.

By inserting these calls automatically, transformation lifts the burden from the programmer and reduces the number of potential errors. This technique gains even more weight when the inserted code is a more complex series of operations that may change at some later point; centralizing the point of programming allows quicker development and enables a higher degree of reuse. However, the task of inserting code can in turn become tedious and error prone. For example, how do you specify where all the insertions must happen? What if the insertions must be customized somehow for each insertion point? Providing a higher-level conceptual interface to describe such changes is a promising technique [2].

The integration of new feature-handling code into a target application has three components: traversal, selection, and generation. A *traversal* defines an order in which the transformer will visit the code. (Generally, we consider traversal of code statements within a method, but the principle is similar for ordering the visits of methods or classes.) A *filter* operates on the output of a traversal, selecting individual join points as necessary or not for a given transformation. Finally, a *generator* creates a new code sequence to insert at the selected point (technically, it may also edit or remove code); it may alter its behavior based on the context passed to it by the traversal or filter. The simplest and most common type of generator uses a statically defined sequence, but the idea is generalizable to the dynamic creation of custom code. Each of these components can be independently specified and can be replaced by alternate implementations to achieve different goals.

For example, consider a transformation to add the Observable design pattern to a target. Its goal is to insert code that marks the object as dirty wherever a change of state occurs. One possible implementation uses a traversal that iterates through the code by basic block. The filter would identify instructions that modify the state of the object, and the generator would insert code marking the object as dirty. Once the filter had identified a valid target, the traversal could then skip the remainder of the basic block, bundling the notification of observers until the end of the method.

14.2 AN OVERVIEW OF BYTECODE TRANSFORMATION

Bytecode transformation is an example of a late code modification technique [21], targeting an executable program after compilation. Traditional late code modification systems suffer for lack of certain useful information available only in source code. However, Java classfiles retain symbolic information that enables a wide range of transformations. Additionally, bytecode transformation can be used on code for which source is not available.

Bytecode transformation can make a wide array of changes to a target class, including adding or removing fields, methods, or constructors; changing the superclass, changing the types or signatures of fields or methods, redirecting method invocations to new targets, and inserting new code into methods at arbitrary points.

Bytecode transformation can take place at any point, from initial class creation by the compiler to class loading. This section discusses transformation at two important stages in the lifecycle: *static* transformation, performed immediately after compilation when the entire program is complete, present, and visible, and *dynamic* transformation, performed at load time, one class at a time at the client. Static transformation allows transformations based on knowledge of the entire program, while dynamic transformation enables transformations that are aware of the run-time environment.

14.2.1 Static Transformation

Static transformation occurs after compilation and operates on class files on disk, writing the changes back and thus making them durable until the classes are recompiled. The entire program might be present when the system applies the transformation (the "closed-world" assumption). This means that no unseen classes subclass application classes and that the application does not dynamically load new classes. If so, a range of more sophisticated inter-method and inter-class optimizations and analyses is possible. This is similar to link-time optimizers [19], which use whole-program analysis to enable the optimizations they perform. Even without the closed-world assumption, the transformer can use information present in the classfile to determine and manipulate the class hierarchy. Interprocedural analysis can reveal valid targets for inlining or parameter elimination; dead code removal can remove unused code, methods, or even classes.

Transforming statically, rather than during the loading process, shifts transformation out of the critical path. Running the transformation at this point makes it unnecessary to run at load time; if the developer is certain that the transformation is necessary, then performing the transformation after compiling is advantageous.

14.2.2   Dynamic Transformation

Dynamic transformation operates at some time between the JVM request for a class and the loading of that class. Dynamic transformation may occur at the server as specific clients request the class, at an intermediate proxy that transforms classes as they pass through the network [17], or at load time as the classes enter the JVM.

The classloader architecture provided in Java provides a convenient mechanism to alter the semantics of loading a class. A classloader is a user-defined object in Java responsible for locating and obtaining classfiles and handing them to the JVM. While classloaders are intended to enable programmers to control the source location or time of class, they also provide an opportunity for transformation.

Performing the transformation at load time is the only way to guarantee transformation of foreign code, such as applets or servlets loaded from the network. It can apply whole-program transformations to such applications.

In addition to ensuring that every application class supports a given feature, a transformation can also be *restrictive*, guaranteeing that no application class uses a forbidden feature. For example, a restrictive transformer can limit access to a secure resource by simply disallowing any code that references that resource. The transformer can then safely add its own calls to that resource. Given Java's type-safety, all calls to that resource are guaranteed to be legitimate. (However, see the discussion later on reflection).

Load-time transformation is *incremental*: The transformer processes individual classes one at a time as they are loaded. The transformer does not control the load order of the classes, and most current JVMs do not allow modification or reloading of already-loaded classes. Transformers thus have only one chance to transform classes and often must do so with incomplete information about the entire application.

This constraint limits the applications for load-time transformation. For example, a dynamic transformer cannot, in general, apply optimizations requiring interprocedural analysis (such as leaf method removal) because the transformation may operate on a call site before the matching method is loaded. Transformer control over the class load order would improve the generality of dynamic transformation but would not solve the problem. For method invocations for which the transformer cannot determine the run-time type of the object, the classloader would require all possible descendents of that object to determine the safety of that method invocation. The current specification of the classfile does not provide that information, and in general, new subclasses may dynamically appear.

14.3   PROGRAMMING TRANSFORMATION

In the transformation architecture employed by JOIE, there are four main roles: the target program, the transformer, auxiliary code, and run-time support classes. The *target* is the original, untransformed program. The *transformer* is a class—or collection of classes—that contains the logic to edit and manipulate the target. As part of that manipulation, transformers may insert new, already compiled, units of functionality directly into the target; these units are found in *auxiliary classes*, which may be bundled together with the transformer.

Auxiliary classes do not appear by name in the final running program; the transformer copies portions of their definitions into the target classes. Finally, a set of classes provides *run-time support* for the transformed classes. Typically, a transformer author bundles together the transformer, auxiliary classes, and run-time classes.

The distinction between auxiliary classes and transformer classes is important. Auxiliary classes are not classes that assist the transformer. They do not execute during the transformation process. Rather, they contain fragments of code that the transformer inserts into the target. Auxiliary classes lose their identity during transformation. The transformed application contains their code but no references to their names. This is analogous to the "base/meta" distinction in metaprogramming [12]. Here, both the target and the auxiliary classes are base code, while the transformer is the metaprogram that operates on both. Additionally, the transformer can obtain base code from other sources, such as by internally containing or referencing program fragments or by dynamic generation during transformation. However, the use of auxiliary classes represents good transformer-programming style.

Run-time classes are akin to auxiliary classes in that they do not execute during the transformation and are part of the resulting application. In contrast, however, the run-time classes are not copied into the target but retain their identity. Typically, the code found in auxiliary classes refers to run-time classes by name.

Making the transformer an executable (rather than declarative) program has implications for both selecting sites for transformation and inserting code. Since the transformer is a fully fledged program with private state, it can be extremely selective and customized about where and how it chooses to operate. For example, it could choose transformation sites based on the other content of the target method, apply only a set number of transformations, or act only when a method met some criteria (such as being a leaf method).

14.3.1 Selection

Key to the design of JOIE is its ability to carefully specify the selection of targets of transformation, including the points at which to insert code and the selection of target classes. Contrast this to systems that provide a set of permissible join points, including call sites, field accesses, and method boundaries; these systems are more intuitive and simpler. JOIE, by allowing arbitrary access to instructions, provides a more powerful and more dangerous interface, especially when coupled with the programmable nature of transformers described previously. For example, a transformer in JOIE can limit a transformation to once per basic block or, more powerfully, can insert code only if that location is not dominated by code inserted earlier.

Bytecode transformation can also target the entire program. *Whole-program* transformation can add a feature to every class of an application or, conversely, verify that certain properties are true of every loaded class. For example, one could extend every object in a system to be Observable. Whole-program transformation is best done at load time, as classes cannot execute in the JVM until they have been through the classloading process.

In contrast, a *selective* transformation targets a specific subset of application classes. The targets for a selective transformer might be listed in a configuration file, or the transformer can infer the targets from inspection of classes that reference them.

Sometimes, the programmer of the original, unmodified program will want to pass information about that program to a transformer to aid in selection. For example, while it can be difficult for a transformer to determine which methods leave a data structure in a consistent state, the programmer usually knows. In these cases, the programmer can define a *labeling interface* whose name is known to the transformer. A labeling interface is simply a standard Java interface (that is, a named set of method names with no implementations) that is used to pass information to the transformer. For example, if a method of a class were part of an interface called `Consistent`, the transformer would know to treat that method as one that left the data structure intact.

14.3.2 Use in AOSD

Separating the transformation logic from the inserted content is another important design choice. In *binary* architectures, aspects define their own placement. In *composer* architectures such as JOIE, a third entity applies aspects to designated locations in the code. These designs are not mutually exclusive, and most systems allow some mixture of the two, for example, by letting aspects refer to others. In general, however, composer architectures, especially when coupled with late or dynamic application of aspects (through transformation or otherwise), are an important building block for a more distributed and dynamic model of software development.

Binary architectures are best suited toward the use of aspect-oriented programming as an augmentation to traditional programming, improving the ability of a single programmer or coordinated team of programmers to separate concerns. However, composer architectures additionally support a model in which applications can be assembled, transformed, and adapted by third parties, including the end user. This has particular application toward adding aspects to legacy code [10]; in an important sense, however, all code is legacy code.

This broader model offers two advantages over tightly-bound aspect development: programs can be smaller, incurring the size cost of additional features only when clients request them, and transportable code can adapt to new services or interfaces made available by some hosts.

Lightweight.   Placing certain aspects of functionality in transformers allows applications to be shipped with only their core functionality; no extras, such as logging or instrumentation, are included. This makes the resulting application cleaner and more lightweight and thus easier to transport over the Internet. The cost to transform the code and support the additional features is borne only by those sites that specifically request that functionality.

This has advantages for software management as well. Imagine an application that has five optional features implemented as bytecode transformations. That means there are thirty-two potential executable images of that program, one for every combination of included features. In a system that applies transformations only when requested, only the original (untransformed) program is stored. While postponing the decision of applying features does incur a (small) performance cost, it may be a preferable option when the potential executable images number in the hundreds or even thousands and when different users may require different subsets of available features.

Adaptable.   Transportable programs assume a standard set of APIs that they use to invoke system services. Some hosts may offer extended services, such as a replication service or persistent store of objects. Standard transportable code will not know about these APIs and thus will be unable to use them. If appropriate, load-time transformation can modify the applications to use a new service's API (for example, by redirecting constructors to the persistent store). This allows the original version of the application to be platform-independent and still take advantage of new features on enhanced platforms.

However, most broadly, the advantage of this model of code development is that the potential number of programs increases significantly. If aspects, in whatever implementation form, remain locked inside development groups, they will only be used for a single application. If aspects are designed to be as orthogonal as possible, applicable to a broad range of target programs, then the number of potential programs increases as the product of available programs and aspects.

14.4   LESSONS LEARNED

The introduction of transformation as a new program development tool raises important issues, including interface design, safety and correctness, the existence of multiple namespaces, interactions between base code and inserted code, and difficulties with debugging. Many of these issues arise from the lack of maturity of tools and programming techniques associated with transformation.

JOIE has been available for free to academic researchers since 1997; since then, many research projects have employed it as a transformation environment. These projects include security architectures [22] [6], a framework for automated testing of object-oriented programs [20], a meta-object protocol for Java [23], groupware [14], program termination [16], and a voice-enabling toolkit [7]. The feedback from these researchers, as well as our own experience developing applications, has led to continued refinements in the implementation and interface of JOIE. This section discusses some of the lessons learned from experience.

14.4.1   Interface Design

First, it is important to provide transformer developers with a platform that includes common sequences of operations on bytecode, especially for difficult or dangerous operations. For example, early versions of JOIE did not provide an interface that abstracted individual bytecode details. Not only were the resulting transformers prone to errors, but also each of them repeated similar sequences of code for safety checks and updates. Providing an interface that hid the majority of details of type and local addressing mode simplified the task of assembling transformations and improved their safety and correctness (also see [3] and [18] for alternate interface approaches).

Second, it is easier to construct and reuse transformers that maintain a strong separation between the transformation logic and the content of the inserted code. For example, early implementations of transformers constructed code sequences by manually creating each instruction. This was difficult and tedious and was equivalent to programming in assembly. The resulting transformer was also difficult to reuse, as it hardwired the instructions. Transformers written for later versions of JOIE could simply refer to a separate class containing the splice written in Java. The current interface extends this principle by providing a mechanism to separate different aspects of the transformation logic—traversal, target selection, and new code generation—into separate modules.

Third, the concerns best suited to implementation through transformation are those that are orthogonal to the functionality of the original application. These sorts of concerns tend to supply system functionality such as security, monitoring, or language features. The common element of these features is that each assists the base application in providing the same service, but with some additional independent functionality.

14.4.2 *Safety, Security, and Correctness*

We want transformers to be correct, secure, and safe. A transformer must produce a transformed class that does not violate the security or safety guarantees of Java; it must not interfere with the correct functioning of the target class, except where explicitly intended by the author; and it must correctly perform whatever change on the class the author intended. However, the use of third-party transformers, especially if executed at load time and potentially loaded over the network, raises concerns over whether the resulting transformed code will still be safe, that is, whether it can gain unauthorized access to resources or memory.

Java security is supported by two pillars: the verifier and the `Security-Manager`. The Java verifier guarantees, among other things, that code is type-safe and particularly that pointers cannot be created or manipulated. This prevents a malicious or buggy program from walking through memory and reading or writing in a way that violates type safety. The `SecurityManager` is a user-extensible class that is queried by library code at execution time about whether specific classes have permission to access specific resources. For example, a program loaded over the Internet might not be permitted to read from the file system, but it could spawn a new thread. Since load-time transformations occur before the verifier runs, transformed code must still comply with the same type-safety restrictions as non-transformed code.

With respect to security, transformers are no more powerful than any imported code. Put another way, transformed code is no less secure than any code produced by an untrusted compiler. The `SecurityManager` has the same ability to restrict transformed code's access to system resources as before.

There are also important security policy issues. For example, is it safe for classes to instantiate and register new transformations during the execution of the program? Is it safe to load transformers over the network and apply them? How does a system determine the access permissions of a transformed class? Can classes ever gain or lose permissions as a result of the transformation?

While the verifier prevents outright abuses of the type system (such as pointer arithmetic), a transformer could translate one type-safe program to a subtly different type-safe program but have violated certain aspects of the language model. For example, a class with private data members could be translated into a similar class but with the members redefined to be public. Accesses to those newly public members are perfectly valid and legal, but they violate the original intent of the programmer and thus the source-code language specification. The addition of transformation to program development suggests that the verifier could be extended to include formal analysis of transformations as well [1].

Here, we describe three different security paradigms in which transformers can exist. The first and most secure is to consider the transformers to be a trusted subsystem and only allow transformations supplied by the system provider or installer. For example, a transformer might transform incoming code to comply with a different local security system. User code would have no access to the transformation process.

The second is to allow class providers to supply their own transformers designed to accompany their code. This still allows them to decompose the program into a base functionality and attributes obtainable through transformation, similar, for example, to the programming model for AspectJ [13]. However, this would prevent transformations from one source being applied to another.

The final and most general policy is to allow transformations full access to other classes. While this seems fundamentally unsafe, recall that transformed code is still verified and runs subject to the `SecurityManager`. And while it is true that the loader might unknowingly attempt to load malicious code, this risk is no higher for transformers than it is for base code.

If the transformer comes from a trusted source, then it should be as trusted as original code. A refinement of this policy is to provide a set of permissions in the `SecurityManager` that restrict the kinds of transformations the platform currently allows. For example, a particular policy might allow changing the type of classes but not changing private members to public.

14.4.3   Multiple Namespaces

The use of multiple classloaders can complicate an application. Each instance of a classloader in a JVM defines a new namespace for types. That is, an instance of a class loaded by one classloader is not the same type as an instance of that class loaded by a different classloader. This means, for example, that an attempt to assign one to the other results in a type mismatch error. This feature is intended for security, as it provides a measure of isolation between different applications that might share the same run-time context, as is the case with applets or servlets. However, it can make programming with classloaders tricky, as classes that compile correctly can throw run-time type mismatch errors when components are loaded by different classloaders.

This collision points out that two fairly different program mechanisms—namespaces and class loading—are tied together in the JVM specification. Implementing load-time transformation would be cleaner and more convenient if combined with a mechanism that redefined loading semantics but did not create a new namespace. The Load-Time Adaptation project [5] simulated this by interposing class editing between the JVM and the file system, avoiding the classloader altogether.

14.4.4 *Reflection*

Java offers a capability at runtime to discover the fields and methods of classes, to invoke methods and get and set fields, and to instantiate objects. While this is a useful and powerful technique, it can interfere with some of the functionality of transformation, especially in security-oriented transformation.

Since many security-oriented transformations seek to prevent an application from invoking sensitive methods without going through accounting calls, this ability presents a threat. More seriously, applications could use reflection to access or change the security runtime's state, call its methods, or instantiate objects associated with protected resources. There are a number of possible solutions, including disabling reflection, disabling only reflective method invocation and allocation, or wrapping reflection with checks that prevent access to unwrapped methods. Disabling reflection or some portion of it is the easiest solution but may also prevent legitimate usage.

Similar concerns and responses are associated with the ability to explicitly and dynamically load new classes by name.

14.4.5 *Addressing Transformed Functionality*

When the original program is written, the transformation is still in the future. Thus, references to classes or methods that will be introduced during transformation are invalid and will not compile. This can have advantages for security-oriented transformations; if methods dealing with the security state are inserted, the runtime can be assured that they are legitimate (since they would not have compiled in the original).

However, this inability to address transformed code can create difficulties when source code needs to access the transformed functionality, such as subscribing to an Observable object. In this case, the fact that the target class has not yet been transformed prevents code from invoking `subscribe`; that method is at that point not a part of the class. This can be solved with a simple but inelegant pass to a method that receives types `Object`, typecasts arguments to the appropriate type, and invokes a particular method. (A substantially less strict compiler would solve the problem as well.)

14.4.6 *Debugging Transformed Code*

When a bug in a transformed application arises, it is often unclear if it is a bug in the original code, a bug in the transformation code, or a bug that arose from the interaction of the two. Currently, debugging transformers demands an understanding of both the original code and the transformer. The problem is particularly severe if multiple transformations are active.

Some specific debugging support is essential to facilitate load-time transformation as a useful programming tool. At the very least, the environment must be able to determine if the failed code was transformed, if transformed code appears in the call chain, and which transformers were responsible for any transformed code.

14.5 *CONCLUSION*

Bytecode transformation is a powerful technique for modifying or adding new functionality to compiled Java classes, especially when performed at load time. The design and features of the Java classfile and the JVM, including the stack-oriented nature of the instructions, the use of symbolic references, and the class loading architecture, render bytecode a convenient and amenable target for late transformation.

As implementations of extra features are concentrated at a single point, there are increased opportunities for code reuse. A single transformation may serve as the implementation of a feature for many different programs; improvements to that code result in improvements in all applications that use that transformation. This is a natural extension of the promise of object-oriented code.

The programmatic nature of transformations and the ability of transformers to target individual instructions make bytecode transformation a powerful, albeit dangerous, tool. However, given a robust implementation with a layered interface that allows programmers to trade off protection and expressiveness, bytecode transformation is a useful and promising mechanism by which to apply new features and concerns into already compiled code.

REFERENCES

1. BENTON, N. 2004. Simple relational correctness proofs for static analyses and program transformations. In *Proceedings of the Annual Symposium on Principles of Programming Languages*, (Venice, Italy), 14–25.

2. BOSHERNITSAN, M. 2003. Program manipulation via interactive transformations. In *Companion of the 18th Annual ACM SIGPLAN Conference on Object-Oriented Programming, Systems, Languages, and Applications*, (Anaheim, California), 120–121.

3. CHIBA, S. AND NISHIZAWA, M. 2003. An Easy-to-use Toolkit for Efficient Java Bytecode Translators. In *Proceedings of the second international conference on Generative programming and component engineering*, (Erfurt, Germany), 364–376.

4. COHEN, G., CHASE, J., AND KAMINSKY, D. 1998. Automatic program transformation with JOIE. In *Annual Technical Conference*, (New Orleans). USENIX, 167–178.

5. DUNCAN, A. AND HÖLZLE, U. 1999. Load-time adaptation: Efficient and non-intrusive language extension for virtual machines. Tech. Rep. TRCS99-09, Department of Computer Science, University of California, Santa Barbara.

6. EVANS, D. AND TWYMAN, A. 1999. Flexible policy-directed code safety. In *Symp. Security and Privacy*, (Oakland, California). IEEE, 32–45.

7. FULKERSON, M. S. AND BIERMANN, A. W. 2000. Javox: A toolkit for building speech-enabled applications. In *6th Applied Natural Language Processing Conference*, (Seattle). Association for Computational Linguistics, 105–111.

8. GOLDBERG, A. AND ROBSON, D. 1983. *Smalltalk-80: The Language and its Implementation*. Addison-Wesley, Reading, Massachusetts.

9. GORDON, A. D. AND SYME, D. 2001. Typing a multi-language intermediate code. In *28th Symp. Principles of Programming Languages (POPL)*, (London). ACM, 248–260.

10. GRAY, J. AND ROYCHOUDHURY, S. 2004. A technique for constructing aspect weavers using a program transformation engine. In *Proceedings of the 3rd International Conference on Aspect-Oriented Software Development*, (Lancaster, UK), 36–45.

11. HILSDALE, E. AND HUGUNIN, J. 2004. Advice Weaving in AspectJ. In *Proceedings of the 3rd International Conference on Aspect-Oriented Software Development*, (Lancaster, UK), 26–35.

12. KICZALES, G. 1992. Towards a new model of abstraction in software engineering. In *Int'l Workshop on New Models in Software Architecture, Reflection and Meta-Level Architecture*, (Tokyo). http://www.parc.xerox.com/spl/groups/eca/pubs/papers/ Kiczales-IMSA92/for-web.pdf.

13. KICZALES, G., HILSDALE, E., HUGUNIN, J., KERSTEN, M., PALM, J., AND GRISWOLD, W. G. 2001. An overview of AspectJ. In *ECOOP 2001—Object-Oriented Programming, 15th European Conference*, (Budapest), J. L. Knudsen, Ed. LNCS, vol. 2072. Springer-Verlag, Berlin, 327–353.

14. LI, W., WANG, W., AND MARSIC, I. 1999. Collaboration transparency in the DISCIPLE framework. In *Int'l Conf. Supporting Group Work (GROUP)*, (Phoenix, Arizona). ACM, 326–335.

15. NORI, K., AMMANN, U., JENSEN, K., NAGELI, H., AND JACOBI, C. 1981. P-code compiler: Implementation notes. In *Pascal: The Language and its Implementation*, D. W. Barron, Ed. Wiley, (New York), 125–170.

16. RUDYS, A. AND WALLACH, D. S. 2002. Termination in language-based systems. *Information and System Security 5*, 2, 138–168.

17. SIRER, E. G., GRIMM, R., GREGORY, A. J., AND BERSHAD, B. N. 1999. Design and implementation of a distributed virtual machine for networked computers. In *17th Symp. Operating Systems Principles (SOSP)*, (Charleston, South Carolina). ACM, 202–216.

18. SITTAMPALAM, G., DE MOOR, O., AND LARSEN, K. F. 2004. Incremental execution of transformation specifications. In *Proceedings of the Annual Symposium on Principles of Programming Languages*, (Venice, Italy), 26–38.

19. SRIVASTAVA, A. AND WALL, D. W. 1993. A practical system for intermodule code optimization at link-time. *Journal of Programming Languages 1*, 1 (Mar.), 1–18.

20. VOGELHEIM, D. 1999. Ein rahmenwerk zur untersuchung zustandsbasierter testverfahren für objektorientierte software. Tech. rep., Lehr- und Forschungsgebiet Informatik III, RWTH Aachen.

21. WALL, D. W. 1992. Systems for late code modification. Tech. Rep. TR 92/3, Western Research Laboratory, Digital Equipment Corporation.

22. WALLACH, D. S. AND FELTEN, E. W. 1998. Understanding Java stack inspection. In *Symp. Security and Privacy*, (Oakland, California). IEEE, 52–63.

23. WELCH, I. AND STROUD, R. 1999. Dalang—a reflective extension for Java. Tech. Rep. CS-TR-672, Department of Computer Science, University of Newcastle-upon-Tyne, United Kingdom.

Chapter 15

JMangler—A Powerful Back-End for Aspect-Oriented Programming

GÜNTER KNIESEL, PASCAL COSTANZA, AND MICHAEL AUSTERMANN

Aspect-oriented software development (AOSD) improves separation of concerns in software development by enabling the modular expression of crosscutting aspects. However, modular implementation of an aspect requires techniques for "weaving" the aspect into the code of all classes that require it. Often, weaving is complicated by the unavailability or dynamic creation of source code.

In this chapter, we present JMangler, a freely available framework for load-time transformation of compiled Java programs. We introduce the notions of *generic class file interception* and *order-independent composition* and explain JMangler's contribution in these areas. Then we show how JMangler can be used for load-time weaving and for injecting hooks that enable run-time weaving. JMangler enables behaviors beyond the ability of current high-level AOSD languages and systems.

15.1 INTRODUCTION

AOSD improves separation of concerns by enabling the modular expression of crosscutting concerns. Modular implementation of a concern as one aspect[1] requires techniques to "weave" this implementation back into the code of all classes that require the concern. For instance, logging behavior expressed in one aspect must be "woven" into all the classes of a system whose activities should be recorded.

---

1. We use *aspect* as a generic term for a module that encapsulates the implementation of one concern, abstracting from the particular language concepts of AspectJ [30], ComposeJ [6, 45], DJ [38], Hyper/J [39, 40], and other AOSD systems.

311

15.1.1 Challenges for Aspect Weaving

A general solution for aspect weaving must deal with different times and development contexts.

Weaving can be performed before a program starts (compile-time or *static weaving*), at load-time (*load-time weaving*), or after a class is loaded (*dynamic weaving*). Static weaving has the advantage of adding no unnecessary run-time penalty to a program's execution. However, in a dynamic class-loading context, static weaving has the weakness that it cannot enforce aspect application to dynamically loaded classes. With static weaving, we have to trust the programmer to identify the classes that belong to a program. In Java,[2] the only way to be sure of which classes are actually used by a program is by checking during dynamic class loading.

Weaving might be applied in *fully controlled contexts* or in *partly controlled contexts,* depending on how the woven entities are created and stored and in which format they are available. A program can be available as source code or in compiled form. Source code and compiled code can be entirely available beforehand, or parts of it can be generated at runtime. Code can be stored locally or on a remote host. Full control means that every part of the program is available as source code, *and* the code is stored locally *and* is entirely available beforehand. Otherwise, we have only partial control. These relationships are illustrated in Table 15-1.

Table 15-1 *Contexts of Weaving*

	Controlled	**Uncontrolled**
Format	source code	compiled code
Creation	beforehand	during runtime
Storage	local	remote

Another challenge for weaving is managing variants. Not every incarnation of a system requires every aspect. In general, the number of possible variants grows exponentially with the number of possible adaptations. Depending on its context of use, an application might need to integrate a logging aspect, might apply an observer aspect for monitoring different subsets of the program state [24], might need to apply various security or synchronization exception handling policies [7], and so forth. In their

---

2. Since JMangler targets Java class files, all our discussions are in the context of the Java language (and conservative extensions thereof).

discussion of "jumping aspects," for instance, Brichau, Meuter, and de Volder [7] show that different exception handling policies are required if an application is deployed standalone or as a component of another application.

It could be prohibitive to generate all these variants statically and in advance. For these reasons, we need means for instrumenting the code base "on-the-fly," depending on the actual needs of an application in a concrete deployment scenario.

15.1.2 Promises of Load-Time Analysis and Transformation (LAT)

Processing binaries at load time makes it possible to address many of the challenges mentioned above. Load-time analysis and transformation of class files (subsequently called LAT) can be used to implement *load-time weaving* or to insert code that performs *run-time weaving*. With a tool that can store transformed classes, LAT can also be used for *static weaving* of binary code.

LAT is inherently applicable to black-box components delivered by third parties in binary format and is oblivious of the local or remote origin of binaries and of their static or dynamic creation.

LAT processes only classes relevant in a given application context. It can further prevent *static version proliferation* by taking advantage of dynamic information for selection of relevant transformations and for their specialization to current run-time conditions.

15.1.3 Aspect-Oriented LAT with JMangler

The advantages of load-time transformation have motivated the development of various LAT tools and frameworks for Java class files. JMangler differs from other approaches in four main regards:

- It provides "*generic interception*" of application class files, allowing transformation of any application classes independent of a custom JVM and of whether the transformed application uses its own class loaders [33]. Therefore, it enables load-time adaptation in environments like application servers, which make heavy use of custom class loaders [31].

- As of version 3, JMangler has an open architecture that facilitates the integration of "weavers," which perform the real transformation of Java class files. Weavers inherit JMangler's generic interception ability, so they can be implemented on top of all existing class file transformation frameworks [4, 8, 9, 11, 12, 34, 35], including those that were not designed for load-time use.

- JMangler extends the Java class-loading model by providing nested class loading: while loading and transforming a class, it is possible to load, analyze, and transform further classes. This enables non-local load-time transformations, which depend on the contents of multiple class files.

- JMangler includes a weaver that provides a partial solution to the problem of aspect interference. For a certain class of transformations, it can guarantee that their joint use will not lead to undesired effects (interferences) even if the transformations have been developed independently [33].

JMangler and its relation to other LAT tools are described in [10, 33]. Details of its use and various features that go beyond the scope of this paper are described in the tutorial that is available online and as part of the JMangler distribution [26]. A commercial development tool built with JMangler is presented in [31].

In Section 15.2, we introduce the notion of generic interception and explain how JMangler achieves generic interception. Then we present its open architecture, which enables other frameworks to be used as plug-ins for JMangler (Section 15.3), and we describe the treatment of non-local dependencies (Section 15.4).

In Section 15.5, we introduce the concepts behind the weaver included in JMangler as far as necessary to understand its use in different AOSD scenarios. In Section 15.6, we discuss a few typical application scenarios: development of higher-level aspect tools, load-time weaving, run-time weaving, and applications beyond the expressive power of existing high-level AOSD languages. Section 15.7 examines related work. In Section 15.8, we summarize ongoing and future work before concluding. Appendix 15.A illustrates the implementation of a code transformer.

15.2   GENERIC INTERCEPTION

One of the main challenges in the design of JMangler was to hook into the class loading system in a way that ensures interception of all application class files without compromising portability. In this section, we first review related approaches in order to explain why this is an issue. Then we present the solution used by JMangler. The class loading architecture and the resulting interception options are illustrated in Figure 15-1.

15.2.1   Java's Class Loader Architecture

Java's class loading mechanism [20, 21, 36] is implemented partly in the JVM, which contains the native implementation of the *bootstrap class loader,* and partly in the Java APIs, which contain the pure Java class `java.lang.ClassLoader` and subclasses thereof (see Figure 15-1). The bootstrap class loader is responsible for loading system classes (that is, all classes that are part of the Java Development Kit and of standard extensions). The class `ClassLoader` is the common superclass of all classloaders for application-specific classes.

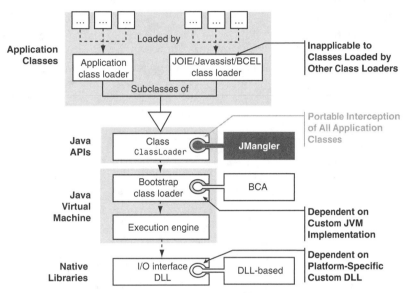

Figure 15-1 *Four ways of intercepting classes at load time: Use of a custom classloader, extension of the class* `java.lang.ClassLoader`, *use of a custom JVM implementation, and use of a custom I/O DLL. Only the second option provides portable generic interception.*

Programmers can customize the class loading system by writing their own subclasses of `ClassLoader`. Custom class loaders are used for two reasons:

Customization. Custom class loaders can customize the class loading process to fit the special needs of an application (e.g., remote or mobile code). Preprocessing of loaded class files also falls into this category.

Namespaces. Every class loader *instance* provides a separate namespace. Even if *different copies of the same class* are loaded by different classloaders, they live in different namespaces and are treated as *different classes* by the JVM. So more than one "subapplication" can run in the same host application on the same JVM without interfering with each other. This is a typical scenario in application servers.

15.2.2   Class-Loader Dependent Interception

The common way of intercepting class files at load time is by writing a custom sub-class of `ClassLoader`. For instance, BCEL, Javassist, and JOIE include custom classloaders.

The applicability of this approach is limited by the namespace mechanism. Loading a class with one class loader automatically excludes processing the same copy of that class with another classloader. Therefore, classloader-dependent interception is not possible in applications that have their *own* custom class loader(s). Common uses of custom classloaders include application servers, distributed applications, and mobile code.

15.2.3   JVM-Dependent Interception

Classloader-independent interception is achieved by Keller and Hölzle's Binary Component Adaptation (BCA) [27, 28, 29]. This was the first approach that enabled modifying compiled Java classes at load time. However, BCA is implemented as a customized version of the Java Virtual Machine of JDK 1.1 for Solaris. It is therefore JVM-dependent.

15.2.4   Platform-Dependent Interception

Duncan and Hölzle [18] propose a non-intrusive alternative to BCA, *library-based load time adaptation*. They avoid having to customize the JVM by supplying a modified version of the dynamically linked standard C library. To make their approach work with all JVMs on a given platform, they modify each file routine to check for class files. Unfortunately, library-based adaptation requires a custom DLL to be provided for every operating system. Therefore, it is platform-specific.

15.2.5   Portable Generic Interception

In contrast to the previous approaches, JMangler provides a portable and generic interception facility. JMangler achieves this by providing a modified version of the `final` method `defineClass()` in the class `java.lang.ClassLoader`. Because the modified behavior is enforced for every subclass of `ClassLoader`, JMangler is activated whenever an application-specific class is loaded. This way, interception of all loaded application classes is possible, independently of a custom JVM or a platform-specific DLL. The limitation of this approach compared to BCA and DLL-based load-time adaptation is that JMangler cannot transform system classes.

Every version of JMangler (1 through 3) is an alternative implementation scheme for this same basic idea. Version 1 provides the modification statically and enforces its utilization by prepending it to Java's `BootstrapClassPath` when starting the JVM. Version 2 does not modify `java.lang.ClassLoader`. However, it achieves the same effect by intercepting all instantiations of concrete subclasses of `java.lang.ClassLoader` and by replacing them with instantiations of adapted versions these classes. Analysis and replacement of calls as well as creation of adapted version of classloaders is done at load time. Versions 3 and higher use the "HotSwap" API for Java[3] [15, 16] to replace `java.lang.ClassLoader` with a version created at runtime. Discussion of further implementation issues, including the tradeoff between the different schemes, is outside the scope of this paper.

15.3 OPEN ARCHITECTURE

JMangler (version 3 and higher) is more than just a load-time transformation framework. It has an open architecture, which lets existing class file transformation frameworks transparently take advantage of its generic interception mechanism. Thus it is a generic enabler for the load-time use of existing frameworks. Figure 15-2 illustrates the essential parts of the architecture.

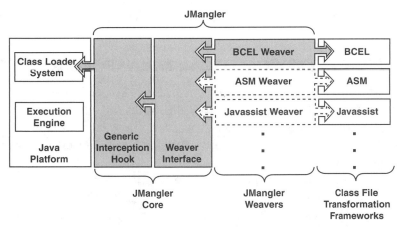

Figure 15-2 *JMangler's open architecture makes its generic interception mechanism available to every class file transformation framework.*

---

3. HotSwap provides dynamic class exchange as an extension of the Java Platform Debugger Architecture (JPDA). See http://java.sun.com/j2se/1.4/docs/guide/jpda/enhancements.html.

Key items include the following:

Hook.   The "hook" implements the generic interception mechanism and extends Java's linear class loading scheme by nested class loading (see Section 15.4). It manages intercepted class files as byte streams.

Weavers.   Weavers provide the real weaving functionality. Because generic interception is already performed by the hook, weavers can be implemented on top of all existing class file transformation frameworks [4, 8, 9, 11, 12, 34, 35], including those that were not designed for load-time use. Weavers are not constrained in any way. In the simplest case, a weaver consists of a few classes that implement the *weaver interface* on the basis of a particular transformation framework. However, weavers can provide arbitrary additional functionality beyond the one supported by the underlying framework. For instance, the JMangler distribution includes a weaver based on BCEL [4, 11, 12]. In addition to the functionality of BCEL, it provides specific support for controlling the weaving process to enable composition of independently developed transformer components (see Section 15.5). Other researchers have already expressed their interest in implementing weavers for ASM [8] and Javassist [9].

Weaver interface.   The weaver interface is a collection of Java interfaces that establish the connection between the hook and the weavers. They mediate the passing of class file representations from the hook to the weavers and back again.

15.4   SUPPORT FOR NON-LOCAL TRANSFORMATIONS

The class-loading mechanism of Java is *linear:* Every class is loaded completely before another class starts loading. Figure 15-3 illustrates the corresponding flow of raw class files from the hook to the active weaver. The weaver creates a higher-level representation and transforms this representation before converting it back to a byte stream for the JVM.

This scheme is sufficient for the implementation of *local* analyses and transformations, which need information about just one class at a time. Examples include the introduction of accessor methods or access counters in a class and simple before, after, and around advice.

However, many analyses and transformations are *non-local* because they depend on the contents of multiple class files. For instance, the addition of forwarding methods requires information about the interface of the class being forwarded to.

Non-local dependencies impose problems for load-time weaving. On one hand, the instrumentation of one class must be completed before handing the class over to the JVM (as the HotSwap API of JDK 1.4 does not support addition of methods and fields at runtime). On the other hand, instrumentation of a class cannot be completed before further classes on which it depends are loaded and analyzed. This is not possible with the linear class-loading model of Java.

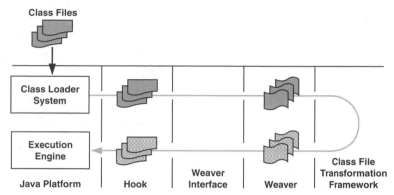

Figure 15-3   *Linear loading of class files: Every class gets loaded and transformed completely before another class can be loaded.*

To resolve this problem, JMangler extends the Java class-loading model by providing *nested class loading:* While loading and transforming a class, it is possible to load, analyze, and transform other classes. As illustrated in Figure 15-4, classes loaded and transformed during the processing of another class are stored and only passed to the JVM after completion of the suspended class loading process. Storage of transformed classes also enables their use for later non-local analyses (without having to repeat the same transformations again).

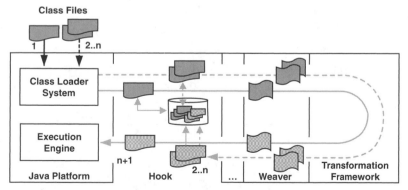

Figure 15-4   *JMangler provides* nested class loading: *While loading and transforming a class, it is possible to load, analyze, and transform further classes. All transformed classes are stored for later non-local analyses. The numbers in the figure indicate the sequence of steps performed.*

Nested loading is implemented in the `MemoryClassLoaderHook` of JMangler. It is thus available to every plug-in. Linear class loading is supported by the `SieveClassLoaderHook` to avoid the overhead of nested loading when it is not required. Applications can choose the preferred loading model simply by setting an option in a configuration file.

15.5 THE BCEL WEAVER

In addition to the generic interception and nested loading functionality available to every weaver, JMangler also includes a fully functional weaver. The *BCEL weaver* provided with JMangler offers an API for the implementation of *transformers components* (or simply, *transformers*) and the ability to load sets of transformers and apply their transformations to all classes of a program. Added benefits over the direct use of BCEL [4, 11, 12] are the notion of transformer components, the simple composition of such components based on a textual configuration file, support for enforcing binary compatibility of transformations, and support for conflict-free automatic composition of independently developed transformer components.

15.5.1 Transformations and Aspects

Weaving can be seen as transformation of classes. Accordingly, an aspect can be interpreted as the specification of such a transformation that determines *what* is to be transformed and *how* it should be transformed. This can be generalized as the specification of conditions, interface transformations, and code transformations.

Conditions.   Conditions are arbitrary Java Boolean expressions. Conditions enable implementation of the filter conditions of ComposeJ [6, 45] and the pointcut definitions of AspectJ [30].

Interface transformations.   By default, JMangler supports all transformations of class files that do not violate binary compatibility [22]:

- Addition of classes, interfaces, fields, and methods
- Changes to a method's `throws` clause
- Changes to a class's `extends` clause that do not reduce the set of direct and indirect superclasses
- Changes to a class's `implements` clause that do not reduce the set of direct and indirect superinterfaces
- Addition and changes of annotations that respect binary compatibility.

These transformations allow implementing the interface modifications express-ible in current aspect languages, such as the *introductions* of AspectJ [30] or the *hypermodule definitions* of Hyper/J [39, 40]. If desired, the system can also per-form transformations that break binary compatibility, such as the removal of methods.

Code transformations.   Code transformations are changes of method code. They allow expressing the *advices* of AspectJ, *traversals* of DJ [38], *filter actions* of Composition Filters [6, 45], and *method combination rules* of Hyper/J [39, 40].

15.5.2   Transformers

Conditions and transformations that conceptually belong together can be imple-mented in one *transformer* component.

Transformers are Java classes that implement specific interfaces (`Interface-Transformer` and `CodeTransformer`). A transformer component that implements the operations of the `InterfaceTransformer` interface can perform one or many related interface transformations. The same is true for code transforma-tions. A transformer can play both roles by implementing both interfaces. Thus, it is possible for one component to provide a consistent set of related interface and code transformations. For instance, an accessor transformer needs interface transforma-tions to create the accessor methods *and* code transformations to enforce their invocation in place of direct variable accesses.

15.5.3   Use of Transformers

Transformers are the basic unit of deployment and composition in the BCEL weaver. The transformers that should be applied to the classes of a program are specified in a configuration file that is passed as a parameter to the invocation of JMangler along with the main class of the program and the program arguments (see Appendix 15.A).

This scheme eases transformer component deployment in two ways: there is no need to write any code in order to apply and compose transformers, and the applica-tion of transformers is independent of the base programs to which they should be applied.

15.5.4   Unanticipated Composition of Transformers

Multiple transformers can be applied jointly to the same program by listing them together in one configuration file and by specifying the desired order of execution. This provides a simple way of composing existing transformers. However, it also raises one of the main challenges in the design of JMangler and of aspect systems in general: *unanticipated composition of independently developed transformers.*

The main issue here is that an execution order cannot be specified for transformers that have been developed independently without being specifically designed for joint use. Whenever independently developed transformers are provided as black boxes (which is the core idea of component-oriented development), the composer most likely does not have enough knowledge of their design and implementation in order to decide on the proper composition order. The same is true for independently developed aspects.

In this context, the problem is to determine automatically *in which order transformers should be combined* to achieve the intended semantics while avoiding unwanted side effects.

In the current version, JMangler does not have any way of determining order automatically.[4] However, we have reduced the scope of the problem by identifying a class of transformations for which *order is irrelevant*. It is possible to apply them iteratively until a fixed point is reached. In particular, *iterative application of a set of positively triggered, monotonic interface transformations*[5] *is guaranteed to produce a unique fixed point, independent of the order in which the transformations are applied.* Section 15.5.6 presents a short example that illustrates the effect of fixed point iteration. A detailed one is contained in [33].

This insight has influenced the design of JMangler in three ways:

1. There is a conceptual and API-level separation of interface transformations and code transformations.

2. JMangler supports by default only interface transformations that preserve binary compatibility, which is a different way of saying that it supports only monotonic interface transformations.

3. JMangler provides the ability to iterate interface transformations until a fixed point is reached.

15.5.5 *The Transformation Process*

Figure 15-5 illustrates the previously described transformation process. The transformers specified in the configuration file passed as parameters to JMangler are applied to every loaded class. The transformation proceeds in two phases.

---

4. We have developed an automatic conflict detection and ordering mechanism [3, 32]. However, its integration into JMangler is a topic for future work.

5. A transformation is *positively triggered* if it is initiated by the existence of a particular property of a program but must not be caused by the absence of a property. A transformation is *monotonic* if it adds properties to a program but does not remove properties.

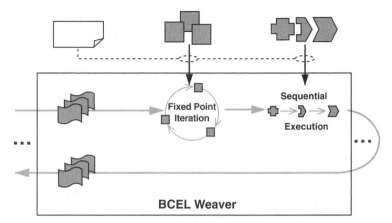

Figure 15-5   *Transformation process implemented in JMangler's BCEL weaver: First, the interface transformations are applied iteratively until a fixed point is reached, then the code transformers are applied sequentially in the order specified in the configuration file.*

In the first phase, *interface transformers* are activated:

- Each interface transformer analyzes the classes under consideration, decides which transformations are to be carried out, and requests these transformations from the BCEL weaver.
- The weaver collects the transformation requests of all interface transformers, checks the validity of the requested transformations (with respect to binary compatibility / monotonicity), and performs the transformations (in an arbitrary order).
- This process is repeated until no further interface modification requests are issued. If an illegal transformation is detected, the process is aborted.

In the second phase, the *code transformers* are activated. They are executed exactly in the order indicated in the configuration file. Each code transformer analyzes the classes under consideration, decides which transformations are to be carried out, and performs these transformations *directly,* using the BCEL API [4, 11, 12].

15.5.6   *Example*

Consider a logging transformer, whose purpose is to log execution of *all* methods that call certain security sensitive methods. It can be implemented as a combined interface and code transformer.

Assume method m in class `class` should be logged. Then the interface transformer part creates a method `m_log` in *class*, which calls m after performing logging actions. The code transformer replaces calls to the original method m by calls to `m_log` at every join point where logging should be performed.

Now assume another independently developed interface transformer that adds a method to the program, say `more2Log`, which also fulfils the criterion for being logged.

Iterative execution of the two interface transformers guarantees that there exists a `more2Log_log` method when the logging code transformer is activated. Thus, the invariant assumed by the code transformer is fulfilled.

If transformers were executed just once, their user would need to know enough of their internal working in order to determine that the second transformer needs to be activated before the first one. Even worse, if the transformers were mutually dependent, there would be no way of using them together *without* iterative application [33].

This example illustrates that fixed point iteration provides the *guarantee* that each interface transformation is applied to the *entire* program, including parts added by other interface transformers. Code transformers can therefore rely on the fact that the invariants they assume are indeed met throughout the program.

Now that we know how to compose and apply existing transformers with JMangler and understand the transformation process, the only missing part of the picture is how to write transformers. This is explained separately for interface and code transformers.

15.5.7 Creation of Interface Transformers

From a technical point of view, an interface transformer is a Java class that implements the interface `InterfaceTransformerComponent`. The main method in this interface, `ExtensionSet transformInterface(Unextendable ClassSet`[6]`)`, analyzes a set of classes and determines a set of extensions that should be performed on these classes.

For instance, the transformer shown in Listing 15-1 requests the addition of the interface `java.lang.Serializable` to each class in the class set passed as parameter.

---

6. An *UnextendableClassSet* is unextendable just in the sense that transformers cannot add or remove classes from it. However, they can modify its classes, and the framework can add new classes that get loaded during the transformation process.

Listing 15-1 *An interface transformer that adds the interface* `java.lang.Serializable` *to each class that does not implement it already*

```
public class MyTransformer implements InterfaceTransformerComponent {
  // The interface to be added.
  private String interfaceName = "java.lang.Serializable";

  // This method will be invoked by JMangler to compute the
  // interface transformations requested by this transformer
  // component.
  public ExtensionSet transformInterface (UnextendableClassSet cs) {
    ExtensionSet es = new ExtensionSet();

    // Analyze and transform all classes in the class set.
    Iterator iter = cs.getIteratorForTransformableClasses();
    while (iter.hasNext()) {
      // The BCEL representation of a class file.
      ClassGen clas = (ClassGen)iter.next();
      // The conditional transformation.
      if (!Condition.implementsInterface (clas, interfaceName)) {
        es.addInterfaceToClass(this,
                               clas.getClassName(),
                               interfaceName);
      }
    }
    return es; // Give JMangler the collected transformation
               // requests.
  }
}
```

A complete version of this and many other transformers can be found on the JMangler web site and in the samples package of the JMangler distribution. The samples can be taken as templates for writing interface transformers. This is easily done after a short study of the classes `ClassGen` and `ExtensionSet`. The class `ClassGen` is part of the BCEL library [4, 11, 12] and provides the basic operations to analyze and transform a class file. All monotonic interface modifications listed in Section 15.5.1 have their counterparts as methods of the `ExtensionSet` set class, whose purpose is to collect transformation requests and execute them under the control of JMangler, as described in Section 15.5.5.

15.5.8   Creation of Code Transformers

A code transformer is a Java class that implements the interface `CodeTrans-formerComponent`. The main method in this interface, `transformCode (UnextendableClassSet)` analyzes the set of classes passed as parameter and modifies them directly using the BCEL API.

Creating code transformations requires an above-average understanding of the internal workings of the Java Virtual Machine, its instruction set, its class file format, and the BCEL library. However, since many tasks follow quite fixed idioms, learning to program at this level is not as difficult as it may appear. A tool that is very helpful in this context is the BCELifier [4]. From a plain Java method, it creates the BCEL code that will create exactly the input method when executed. BCELifier is provided on the BCEL web site and is also included in the JMangler 3 release.

An example of an advanced application, code coverage, that can be conveniently expressed in about one page of code is presented in Appendix 15.A. A short introduction to code coverage is given in Section 15.6.3.2.

15.6   USAGE SCENARIOS

In this section, we discuss typical application scenarios for JMangler: load-time weaving (Section 15.6.1), run-time weaving (Section 15.6.2), and applications beyond the expressive power of existing high-level AOSD languages (Section 15.6.3).

15.6.1   Load-Time Weaving with JMangler

The straightforward use of JMangler for AOSD development is the implementation of load-time weaving. We talk about *load-time weaving* if functionality is introduced at load time into an application and activated permanently for the current run of the application.

In the simplest case, the introduced functionality is the intended functionality of an aspect such as tracing behavior. The examples given in the previous section all fall into this category, so we do not go into further details here. Instead, we pick the ObjectTeams project as an interesting large application that uses JMangler for load-time weaving. ObjectTeams [25, 37, 44] is a programming model that builds on research and experience concerning several recent approaches, mostly from the field of aspect-oriented software development.

ObjectTeams/Java adapts classes of the system core at load time using JMangler (with the BCEL weaver). This enables running several ObjectTeams applications with different adaptations to shared modules, although shared modules exist only as a single jar file. No source code is needed, nor are different adapted variants stored in the file system, thus significantly relieving configuration management and deployment.

Thus, on the one hand, ObjectTeams fully exploits the benefits of load-time weaving with JMangler. On the other hand, programmers using ObjectTeams/Java need not know about JMangler since input for transformations is generated by the compiler and invocation of JMangler is encapsulated in the command for starting the Java Virtual Machine.

15.6.2 Run-Time Weaving with JMangler

An advanced use of load-time weaving is to create a system that performs run-time weaving. In such a scenario, it is not the logging code that is weaved at load time but the code that enables dynamic inclusion of logging and other "aspects." This is the way AspectWerkz [2] uses load-time weaving to provide a dynamic, aspect-oriented system with a high, user-friendly abstraction level. In order to be generally applicable, AspectWerkz adopted (and adapted) the generic interception approach of JMangler.

Yet another variant of this idea is described in [42]. Starting from the formal semantics of a core language, which includes *method call interception* (MCI), different implementation models are examined regarding expressiveness, simplicity, and efficiency. One suggested alternative is to perform static weaving of code that enables dynamic method call interception and to eliminate at load time the hooks that are *not* relevant for that particular invocation of a program. In this scenario, the load-time transformation is used to unweave code that only slows down the application without providing any functional benefit. Thus, the load-time transformer behaves as an optimizer for the statically weaved code that performs dynamic weaving.

15.6.3 Advanced Features

For the sake of simplicity, ease of use, or avoidance of conceptual problems, AOSD languages abstract away some of the expressive power available at the bytecode level. We discuss here two cases: (1) *parametric* and (2) *fine-grained* analysis and transformation.

15.6.3.1 Parametric Introductions and Advices

The logging example in Section 15.5.6 illustrates that one transformer can compactly express interface and code transformations that are parametric with respect to the exact name of the manipulated entities. The italic style of the method name m (see Section 15.5.6) indicates that this is a variable ranging over the names of all methods that fulfill the conditions for being logged. Correspondingly, the name m_log is a template for names of logging methods to be created. For instance, if the transformer determines at runtime that the methods $meth_1, \ldots, meth_n$ should be logged, the template expands to $meth_1\_log, \ldots, meth_n\_log$.

In AspectJ terminology, our logging example expresses a possibly infinite number of consistent "introductions" and "advices" in one single transformer. This is impossible in AspectJ, which supports only a limited form of parametric names in pointcuts but does not support parametric names in introductions and advices. Put differently, AspectJ can perform wildcard matching of *existing* names, but it offers no mechanism to create *new* names that depend on the matched ones. Instead, one has to know statically all names of methods to be logged and write the same introduction code (up to names) for each and every method.

The step from AspectJ's wildcard substitution to "parametric aspects" is a significant change in expressiveness [23]. Moving from statically known names to *name variables* means making the step from a closed to an open world. This results in extended applicability and expressiveness but also raises additional interference problems, as illustrated by the logging example in Section 15.5.6. The lack of mechanisms for dealing with aspect interference in open worlds is one important reason that prevents many aspect systems from offering parametric transformations.

Disregarding aspect interference, ComposeJ [45] could support a similar functionality by means of meta filters [6]. However, meta filters are not yet implemented. For Hyper/J [39, 40], parametricity seems to be difficult to achieve, due to its declarative completeness requirement (every name referred to must be declared in the referring module).

It seems that the only aspect systems that already provide parametric introductions and advices are systems based on logic metaprogramming, such as TyRuBa [13, 14] and SOUL [41]. An interesting new contribution in this context is the concept of "parametric introductions" in *Sally* [23]. It is interesting to note that these systems are similar to JMangler in that the backtracking mechanism of logic programming is another way of implementing fixed point iteration.

15.6.3.2 Code Coverage

The common abstraction supported by AOSD languages is interception of variable accesses and method calls. In [19], Filman and Havelund consider the ability to "intercept" finer-grained structures as a desirable improvement to aspect languages. In this section, we give an example application where "interception" at the level of individual statements or individual lines of code is essential: code coverage.

Code coverage is a measure for the percentage of a program exercised ("covered") by the tests run on that program. Coverage is reported on the basis of metrics. For instance, *statement coverage* reports the percentage of statements in a program that have been executed during testing. A good coverage tool will also indicate the places in a program that have not been covered.

In showing how JMangler can be used to implement a coverage tool, we concentrate on *line coverage,* the percentage of lines of code covered by tests.

A code transformer for collecting line coverage information is listed and explained in detail in Appendix 15.A. CC4J, a full-fledged, commercial code coverage tool deployed in large scale industrial software projects is described in [31]. Its core is a similar transformer for the BCEL weaver of JMangler (see Figure 15-6). Unlike the vanilla version presented in the appendix, it supports collecting coverage information from multiple test runs and their user-friendly presentation that immediately directs programmers to the untested spots of the application. Also, it is considerably more efficient.

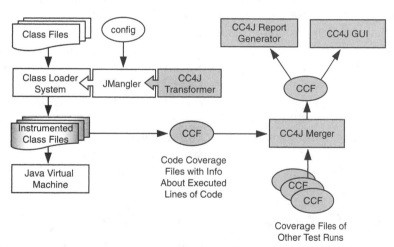

Figure 15-6 *Architecture of CC4J, a commercial code coverage tool implemented with JMangler.*

Summarizing, JMangler offers considerable expressive power but is clearly a tool for "experts." It is typically used as a back-end for the implementation of easier to use, high-level aspect tools and systems. This is reflected in all the case studies presented in this section.

15.7   RELATED WORK

JMangler has often been described as a class file transformation framework and has consequently been compared to similar tools [33]. However, JMangler version 3, described in this paper, clearly separates the concerns of generic class file interception, nested class loading, control of the weaving process, and class file manipulation. Its contributions to the state-of-the-art address the first three concerns. Its open architecture makes the system independent of a particular transformation framework. This is a step forward compared to the work we reported in [10, 33].

Related to the generic interception mechanism, we know of only one recently started similar project. As of May 2003, the BeeSee system (http://besee.sourceforge.net/) is being redesigned to provide a generic interception mechanism "largely inspired by JMangler 3.x" (see the javadoc of class "Starter"). The aim of the development is to provide a lightweight version of JMangler's basic mechanisms at the price of eliminating support for more advanced features like nested class loading and iterative application of transformers.

Related to nested class loading, we know of no similar work yet.

Related to weaving control, effects similar to the iterative application of transformers can be achieved in systems based on logic metaprogramming (e.g., SOUL) [14, 41], due to their inherent backtracking mechanism.

JMangler's iteration mechanism is a means of resolving potential conflicts between different transformations. Douence et al. present a more advanced approach to detection and resolution of aspect-aspect conflicts [17]. Their work is based on an event model of aspect-oriented programming and additional annotations of aspect programs. Bardey and Kniesel's work provides a similar effect based on detection of dependencies among conditional program transformations [3, 32]. Störzer and Krinke present an approach to aspect-base interference based on traditional program analysis techniques in [43].

15.8   CONCLUSIONS AND FUTURE WORK

In this chapter, we have discussed why load-time analysis and transformation is a promising approach to various challenges of aspect weaving: missing source code of base entities, their dynamic creation, and version proliferation.

We have introduced JMangler, a framework that enables interception and transformation of all loaded application classes. The generic interception mechanism is portable across operating systems, independent of a custom JVM implementation, and effective also in applications that use custom classloaders (application servers, for instance). JMangler provides nested class loading as an extension of the linear Java class loading model, thus enabling load-time transformations that are dependent on the contents of multiple classes. It supports the integration of weavers implemented on top of different class file transformation frameworks and provides a complete weaver implemented using BCEL.

The BCEL weaver enables composition and joint use of transformer components that have been developed independently. *Automatic* order-independent composition is possible for positively triggered, monotonic interface transformations. Only the order of code transformations has to be specified explicitly, since it is essential for the behavior of the resulting code.

An AOSD system can translate its aspects to JMangler transformer components and let them be applied at load time. Load-time transformation can be used to weave application-level functionality or to inject code that performs run-time weaving.

Load-time weaving with JMangler is also able to process classes that are created and loaded dynamically from an arbitrary local or remote origin. Since weaving is done at load time, only the aspects get weaved that are useful for that particular invocation of a program. Thus static creation of potentially unnecessary variants is avoided.

If desired, variants created at load time can be stored for later use. JMangler transformers allow the implementation of "parametric aspects" that express compactly a potentially infinite number of "introductions" and "advices." It is possible to define "pointcuts" at the level of individual statements or line numbers. This enables very fine-grained control over a program's behavior, as exemplified by the CC4J code coverage system.

Recent follow-up work has focused on improving automatic handling of aspect interference. We have developed a tool that allows automatic detection and resolution of interferences between transformations [3, 32]. The integration of the interference-checking tool with JMangler is a topic of ongoing work.

Information on the most recent state of JMangler can be found at http://javalab. cs.uni-bonn.de/research/jmangler/.

ACKNOWLEDGMENTS

We want to thank Robert Filman, Shigeru Chiba, and Tzilla Elrad, who have provided many critical remarks on an earlier draft of this paper. Their knowledgeable comments have significantly contributed to the quality of its presentation. All remaining errors are, of course, ours.

Discussions with the participants of the JMangler tutorial and demonstration at AOSD 2003 have provided much encouragement and sharpened our understanding of current needs and relevant future work. In this context, thanks go in particular to Andrew Clement, Bruno Harbulot, Eric Hilsdale, Mik Kersten, Renaud Pawlak, Andrei Popovici, Christa Schwanninger, Lionel Seinturier, and Matthew Webster.

We also want to thank Lodewijk Bergmanns and Stephan Herrmann for providing information about the JMunger and ObjectTeams projects early during their development. Stephan Herrmann, and Christine Hundt also provided a lot of helpful feedback on bugs and possible improvements in various versions of JMangler.

Most of this work has been performed within the TAILOR project, directed by Professor A. B. Cremers and partly supported by Deutsche Forschungsgemeinschaft (DFG) under grant CR 65/13.

APPENDIX 15.A SIMPLE CODE COVERAGE

In Section 15.6.3.2, we presented code coverage as an example of an application that requires "interception" at the line or statement level. Here, we show how a tool that collects line coverage information can be implemented easily as a code transformer.

In the following text, line numbers in parentheses refer to the source code shown in Listing 15-2. The example is fully functional. It can be downloaded from the JMangler web site along with other sample transformers (see http://javalab.cs.unibonn.de/research/jmangler/).

Listing 15-2 Source code for the code coverage tool

```
(1)    import de.fub.bytecode.*;
(2)    import de.fub.bytecode.generic.*;
(3)    import de.fub.bytecode.classfile.*;
(4)    import org.cs3.jmangler.*;
(5)    import org.cs3.jmangler.tau.*;
(6)    import org.cs3.jmangler.supplier.*;
(7)    import java.util.*;

(8)    public class CodeCoverTransformer
(9)       implements CodeTransformerComponent {

(10)      public static void recordCoveredLine
(11)                           (String className, int line)
(12)         {System.out.println
(13)           ("covered line "+line+" in class "+className);}
```

```
(14)     private static String recorderMethName =
(15)                            "recordCoveredLine";
(16)     private static Type recorderReturnType = Type.VOID;
(17)     private static Type[] recorderArgTypes = new Type[2];
(18)      {recorderArgTypes[0] = Type.STRING;
(19)       recorderArgTypes[1] = Type.INT;}


(20)     public void addRecordCaller
(21)       (ClassGen classGen, ConstantPoolGen poolGen,
(22)        InstructionFactory factory, int lineNo,
(23)        InstructionList intoList,
(24)        InstructionHandle beforeHandle)
(25)     {
(26)       InstructionList recordCaller =
(27)                          new InstructionList();


(28)       InstructionHandle callHandle = recordCaller.append(
(29)         new LDC_W(poolGen.addString
(30)           (classGen.getClassName()))));


(31)       recordCaller.append
(32)         (new LDC_W(poolGen.addInteger(lineNo)));


(33)       recordCaller.append(
(34)         factory.createInvoke("CodeCoverTransformer",
(35)                              recorderMethName,
(36)                              recorderReturnType,
(37)                              recorderArgTypes,
(38)                              Constants.INVOKESTATIC));


(39)       intoList.insert(beforeHandle, recordCaller);
(40)       intoList.redirectBranches(beforeHandle,
(41)                                  callHandle);
(42)     } // addRecordCaller


(43)     public void transformCode
(44)                     (UnextendableClassSet classSet)
(45)     {
(46)       Iterator classIterator =
(47)         classSet.getIteratorForTransformableClasses();
(48)       while (classIterator.hasNext()) {
(49)         ClassGen classGen =
(50)           (ClassGen)classIterator.next();
(51)         String className = classGen.getClassName();
```

```
(52)            if (className.equals(this.getClass().getName()))
(53)              continue;

(54)            ConstantPoolGen poolGen =
(55)              classGen.getConstantPool();
(56)            InstructionFactory factory =
(57)              new InstructionFactory(classGen);
(58)            Method[] methods = classGen.getMethods();

(59)            for (int methInd = 0;
(60)                 methInd < methods.length;
(61)                 methInd++) {
(62)              Method meth = methods[methInd];
(63)              if (meth.isNative() || meth.isAbstract())
(64)                continue;

(65)              MethodGen methGen =
(66)                new MethodGen(meth, className, poolGen);
(67)              InstructionList instList =
(68)                methGen.getInstructionList();
(69)              LineNumberGen[] lines =
(70)                methGen.getLineNumbers();

(71)              for (int lineInd = 0;
(72)                   lineInd < lines.length;
(73)                   lineInd++) {
(74)                LineNumberGen line = lines[lineInd];
(75)                addRecordCaller(classGen, poolGen, factory,
(76)                                line.getSourceLine(),instList,
(77)                                line.getInstruction());
(78)              }

(79)              methGen.setMaxStack();
(80)              methods[methInd] = methGen.getMethod();}

(81)            classGen.setMethods(methods);
(82)        } // while
(83)      } // transformCode

(84)    public void sessionStart() {}
(85)    public void sessionEnd() {}
(86)    public String verboseMessage() {return toString();}

(87)  } // CodeCoverTransformer
```

15.A.1 *Implementation of the* CodeCoverTransformer

First of all, we need to implement a class `CodeCoverTransformer` that implements the interface `CodeTransformerComponent` (8-9). Inside the `CodeCoverTransformer` class, we provide all the necessary ingredients for our tool, including the actual `recordCoveredLine` method (10-13). It is called at runtime, while all the other elements of `CodeCoverTransformer` are executed at load time. In our simple code coverage tool, `recordCoveredLine` just prints a message to the standard output stream.

The most interesting method required by the `CodeTransformerComponent` interface is `transformCode` (43–83) that is called by the JMangler framework at load time (according to the Hollywood principle: "Don't call us, we'll call you!"). JMangler passes an `UnextendableClassSet` to `transformCode` that contains all the classes loaded by a classloader within a session. The `getIteratorForTransformableClasses` method allows us to iterate over all classes in that set that still need to be transformed, which is what we want to do (46-48). At each step, the iterator returns an instance of `ClassGen`[7] (49).

From each `ClassGen` instance, we request the following information that we need later on:

◆ Its name (51)

◆ Its constant pool (54), a standard ingredient of java class files that contains all the constant data used within a class[8]

◆ An instruction factory (56), a BCEL utility class that allows the creation of complex bytecode instructions in a convenient way

◆ Its methods as declared in the corresponding Java source file (58)

Before we proceed, we perform a sanity check in order to prevent the `CodeCoverTransformer` from transforming itself (52–53). We then iterate over all non-native and non-abstract methods of the current transformable class (59–64)—that is, all the methods that are actually implemented in Java bytecode. We create an

---

7. This class is part of the BCEL library and represents a Java class as a modifiable data structure. BCEL distinguishes between modifiable entities that end in . . . Gen (like `ClassGen`, `MethodGen`, `FieldGen`, and so on) and their non-modifiable counterparts.

8. This includes constant numbers and string literals, but also class, method, and field names, for example.

instance of `MethodGen` for each of those methods in order to be able to modify it (65–66). Next, we request an `InstructionList` instance (67-68) and the line number table (69–70) from the current method. The instruction list is a modifiable data structure that represents the actual method code.

The line number table [36] allows us to determine the positions in the instruction list for each line of the original Java source code. For instance, in Table 15-2, the statements implementing line 3 start at program counter value 0.

Table 15-2   *A Sample Line Number Table*

Source File	Byte Code

1 public class Sample {
2   void sayHello() {
3   System.out.println
            ("Hello");
4   return;
5   }
6 }
	Method void sayHello()
	  0 getstatic #8
	  3 ldc #1
	  5 invokevirtual #9
	  8 return

Line Number	Program Counter
3	0
4	8

So we iterate over the line number table (71-78) and call the auxiliary method `addRecordCaller` (75-77) to perform the modification at each step (see the following).

Since calls to `recordCoveredLine` make use of the Java operand stack, we need to call `setMaxStack` for each `MethodGen` instance afterwards (79) in order to let BCEL determine its correct (static) size. Then we convert the `MethodGen` instance back to its non-modifiable form (as required by BCEL) (80) and finally write all the modified methods back to the `ClassGen` instance (81).

The remaining actions required by BCEL and the Java classloader framework are all performed by JMangler, so we have completed all the necessary steps by now.

The `addRecordCaller` method (20-42) works as follows. First, it creates the call sequence by generating a new instruction List (26-38). This instruction list consists of first pushing the name of the current class onto the operand stack (LDC_W[9])

---

9. Load Constant with wide index—*wide index* is an index into the constant pool possibly greater than 255.

(28–30), then pushing the line number onto the operand stack (also `LDC_W`) (31–32), and finally calling `recordCoveredLine` (33–38), which pops the two arguments from the operand stack. The latter call is generated by `createInvoke` in `InstructionFactory` that takes some meta information about `recordCoveredLine` (the name of its defining class, its own name, and its return and parameter types) and the `INVOKESTATIC` instruction for class method invocations; `createInvoke` also takes care of the correct handling of the constant pool.

This new call sequence is inserted into the instruction list (39). We insert the new call sequence *before* the given position so that a source line is recorded even when it throws an exception (which may be the correct specified behavior of your program at that line). Because the current line possibly is the branch target of other instructions (for example, of an `if/then/else` statement), we finally need to redirect all the branches from the old position to the start of the new call sequence in order to have the line number recorded in all cases (40–41).

15.A.2   Activation

In order to activate the `CodeCoverTransformer` described in the previous section, we need to define a configuration file for JMangler as partly explained in Section 15.5.3. For our purposes, the following three lines are sufficient.

```
transformer CodeCoverTransformer {
  name =
  org.cs3.jmangler.samples.codecoverage.CodeCoverTransformer;
}
```

The first line of the configuration file assigns a short name to the fully qualified class name given in the third line.[10] This declaration also activates the named transformer.

The scheme of using configuration files for transformer activation eases deployment in two ways: there is no need to write any code in order to apply a certain transformer, and the application of a transformer is independent of the base program to which it should be applied. The configuration file containing these lines, say `codecover.config`, can be used on arbitrary Java programs.

```
jmangler --cf codecover.config AnArbitraryJavaProgram
```

---

10. Such short names are convenient in more sophisticated configuration files that, for example, express relationships between different transformers.

This invocation starts the JVM, loads JMangler and the transformers specified in the configuration file, and then initiates execution of the program passed as a command line parameter.

Now suppose we are given the slightly more interesting variant of the standard "Hello, World" application:

```
(1)  public class HelloWorld {
(2)     public static void main(String[] args) {
(3)        if (args.length > 0)
(4)           {System.out.println(args[0]);}
(5)        else
(6)           {System.out.println("Hello, World!");}
(7)     }
(8)  }
```

We start the *CodeCoverTransformer* on an invocation of "HelloWorld" that has no arguments and observe the output.

```
>> jmangler --cf codecover.config HelloWorld

        covered line 3 in class HelloWorld
        covered line 6 in class HelloWorld
        Hello, World!
        covered line 7 in class HelloWorld[11]
```

Obviously, line 4 has not been covered. So we conclude that in order to guarantee complete coverage of all possible branches, we need to extend our test suite by a call of the "Hello, World" application that has a non-empty argument.

We hope that this example conveys the following facts. On the one hand, a JMangler user needs an above-average understanding of the internal workings of the Java Virtual Machine, its instruction set, its class file format, and a class file transformation framework like the BCEL library. So JMangler is clearly a tool for experts. On the other hand, JMangler allows one to implement powerful transformers in a relatively convenient way, as illustrated by the compact and straightforward code given in Listing 15-2.

---

11. Line 7 is covered because the Java compiler places the implicit return statement for method `main` at that line.

REFERENCES

1. AKŞIT, M., Ed. 2003. *2nd Int'l Conf. Aspect-Oriented Software Development (AOSD)*, (Boston), ACM.

2. ASPECTWERKZ HOME PAGE. http://aspectwerkz.codehaus.org/.

3. BARDEY, U. 2003. Abhängigkeitsanalyse für Programm-Transformationen (in German). Diploma thesis, University of Bonn.

4. BCEL HOME PAGE. http://jakarta.apache.org/bcel/.

5. BERGMANS, L. AND AKŞIT, M. 2001. Composing crosscutting concerns using composition filters. *Comm. ACM 44*, 10 (Oct.), 51–57.

6. BERGMANS, L., AKŞIT, M., AND TEKINERDOĞAN, B. 2001. Aspect composition using composition filters. In *Software Architectures and Component Technology*, M. Akşit, Ed. Kluwer Academic Publishers, Boston, 357–382.

7. BRICHAU, J., MEUTER, W. D., AND DEVOLDER, K. 2000. Jumping aspects. In *Workshop on Aspects and Dimensions of Concerns (ECOOP)*, (Cannes, France). http://trese.cs.utwente.nl/Workshops/adc2000/papers/Brichau.pdf.

8. BRUNETON, E., LENGLET, R., AND COUPAYE, T. 2002. ASM: A code manipulation tool to implement adaptable systems. In *Adaptable and extensible component systems*, (Grenoble, France). http://asm.objectweb.org/current/asm-eng.pdf.

9. CHIBA, S. 2000. Load-time structural reflection in Java. In *ECOOP 2000—Object-Oriented Programming: 14th European Conference*, (Cannes, France), E. Bertino, Ed. LNCS, vol. 1850. Springer-Verlag, Berlin, 313–336.

10. COSTANZA, P., KNIESEL, G., AND AUSTERMANN, M. 2001. Independent extensibility for aspect-oriented systems. In *Workshop on Advanced Separation of Concerns (ECOOP)*, (Budapest). http://trese.cs.utwente.nl/Workshops/ecoop01asoc/papers/Constanza.pdf.

11. DAHM, M. 1999. Byte code engineering. In *Java-Informations-Tage*. Springer-Verlag, Berlin, 267–277.

12. DAHM, M. 1999. Byte code engineering with the JavaClass API. Tech. Rep. B-17-98, Freie Universitt Berlin, Institut für Informatik.

13. DEVOLDER, K. 1998. Aspect-oriented logic meta programming. In *Workshop on Aspect-Oriented Programming (ECOOP)*, (Brussels). http://trese.cs.utwente.nl/aop-ecoop98/papers/DeVolder.pdf.

14. DeVolder, K. and D'Hondt, T. 1999. Aspect-oriented logic meta programming. In *Meta-Level Architectures and Reflection, 2nd Int'l Conf. Reflection*, P. Cointe, Ed. LNCS, vol. 1616. Springer Verlag, Berlin, 250–272.

15. Dmitriev, M. 2001. Towards flexible and safe technology for runtime evolution of Java language applications. In *Workshop on Engineering Complex Object-Oriented Systems for Evolution (ECOOSE, OOPSLA)*, (Tampa, Florida). http://www.dsg.cs.tcd.ie/ecoose/oopsla2001/ecoose_papers.zip.

16. Dmitriev, M. 2002. Hotswap technology application for advanced profiling. In *1st Int'l Workshop on Unanticipated Software Evolution (USE, ECOOP)*, (Malaga, Spain). http://joint.org/use/2002/sub/.

17. Douence, R., Fradet, P., and Südholt, M. 2002. A framework for the detection and resolution of aspect interactions. In *1st ACM Conf. Generative Programming and Component Engineering GPCE)*, (Pittsburgh). LNCS, vol. 2487. Springer-Verlag, Berlin, 173–188.

18. Duncan, A. and Hölzle, U. 1999. Load-time adaptation: Efficient and non-intrusive language extension for virtual machines. Tech. Rep. TRCS99-09, Department of Computer Science, University of California.

19. Filman, R. E. and Havelund, K. 2002. Source-code instrumentation and quantification of events. In *Foundations of Aspect-Oriented Languages (FOAL, AOSD)*, (Enschede, The Netherlands), G. T. Leavens and R. Cytron, Eds. 45–49. Department of Computer Science, Iowa State Univ., ftp://ftp.cs.iastate.edu/pub/technreports/TR02-06/TR.pdf.

20. Gong, L. 1999. *Inside Java 2 Platform Security Architecture, API Design, and Implementation*. Addison-Wesley, Reading, Massachusetts.

21. Gong, L. 1999. Securely loading classes. In *Inside Java 2 Platform Security Architecture, API Design, and Implementation*. Addison-Wesley, Reading, Massachusetts, 71–83.

22. Gosling, J., Joy, B., Steele, G., and Bracha, G. 2000. *Java Language Specification, 2nd Ed*. Addison-Wesley, Reading, Massachusetts.

23. Hanenberg, S. and Unland, R. 2003. Parametric introductions. In *2nd Int'l Conf. Aspect-Oriented Software Development (AOSD)*, (Boston), M. Akşit, Ed. ACM, 80–89.

24. Hannemann, J. and Kiczales, G. 2002. Design pattern implementation in Java and AspectJ. In *17th Conf. Object-Oriented Programming, Systems, Languages, and Applications (OOPSLA)*, (Seattle). ACM, 161–173.

25. HERRMANN, S. 2002. Object teams: Improving modularity for crosscutting collaborations. In *Net.Object Days 2002* (Erfurt, Germany), M. Akşit and M. Mezini, Eds. LNCS, vol. 2591. Springer-Verlag, Berlin, 248–264.

26. JMangler HOME PAGE. http://javalab.cs.uni-bonn.de/research/jmangler/.

27. KELLER, R. AND HÖLZLE, U. 1997. Supporting the integration and evolution of components through binary component adaptation. Tech. Rep. TRCS97-15, University of California, Santa Barbara.

28. KELLER, R. AND HÖLZLE, U. 1998. Binary code adaptation. In *ECOOP'98 Object-Oriented Programming, 12th European Conference*, E. Jul, Ed. LNCS, vol. 1445. Springer-Verlag, Berlin, 307–329.

29. KELLER, R. AND HÖLZLE, U. 1998. Implementing binary component adaptation for Java. Tech. Rep. TRCS98-21, University of California, Santa Barbara.

30. KICZALES, G., HILSDALE, E., HUGUNIN, J., KERSTEN, M., PALM, J., AND GRISWOLD, W. G. 2001. An overview of AspectJ. In *ECOOP 2001—Object-Oriented Programming, 15th European Conference*, (Budapest), J. L. Knudsen, Ed. LNCS, 2072. Springer-Verlag, Berlin, 327–353.

31. KNIESEL, G. AND AUSTERMANN, M. 2002. CC4J—code coverage for Java—a load-time adaptation success story. In *Component Deployment—IFIP/ACM Working Conference, (Berlin)*. LNCS, vol. 2370. Springer-Verlag, Berlin, 155–169.

32. KNIESEL, G. AND BARDEY, U. 2003. Static dependency analysis for conditional program transformations. Tech. Rep. IAI-TR-03-03, ISSN 0944-8535, CS Dept. III, University of Bonn.

33. KNIESEL, G., COSTANZA, P., AND AUSTERMANN, M. 2001. JMangler—a framework for load-time transformation of Java class files. In *1st IEEE Int'l Workshop on Source Code Analysis and Manipulation (SCAM 2001)*, (Florence). http://www.informatik.uni-bonn.de/~costanza/SCAM_jmangler.pdf.

34. LAFFRA, C. 2000. Jikes bytecode toolkit. http://www.alphaworks.ibm.com/tech/jikesbt.

35. LEE, H. B. AND ZORN, B. G. 1997. BIT: A tool for instrumenting Java bytecodes. In *Symp. Internet Technologies and Systems* (Monterey, California). USENIX, 73–82.

36. LINDHOLM, T. AND YELLIN, F. 1999. *The Java Virtual Machine Specification (2nd Ed)*. Addison-Wesley, Reading, Massachusetts.

37. OBJECT TEAMS HOME PAGE. http://www.ObjectTeams.org.

38. ORLEANS, D. AND LIEBERHERR, K. 2001. DJ: Dynamic adaptive programming in Java. In *Metalevel Architectures and Separation of Crosscutting Concerns 3rd Int'l Conf. (Reflection 2001)*, (Kyoto), A. Yonezawa and S. Matsuoka, Eds. LNCS, vol. 2192. Springer-Verlag, Berlin, 73–80.

39. OSSHER, H. AND TARR, P. 1999. Multi-dimensional separation of concerns using hyperspaces. Tech. Rep. 21452, IBM Research Report.

40. OSSHER, H. AND TARR, P. 2001. The shape of things to come: Using multi-dimensional separation of concerns with Hyper/J to (re)shape evolving software. *Comm. ACM 44*, 10 (Oct.), 43–50.

41. SOUL HOME PAGE. http://prog.vub.ac.be/research/DMP/soul/soul2.html.

42. STENZEL, C. 2002. Implementation models for method call interception based on formal semantics (in German: Implementationsmodelle für Methodenaufrufabfang basierend auf formaler Semantik). Diploma thesis, University of Rostock. http://www.informatik.uni-rostock.de/~stenzel/.

43. STÖRZER, M. AND KRINKE, J. 2003. Interference analysis for AspectJ. In *Foundations of Aspect-Oriented Languages (FOAL, AOSD)*, (Boston). http://www.cs.iastate.edu/~leavens/FOAL/papers-2003/stoerzer-krinke.pdf.

44. VEIT, M. AND HERRMANN, S. 2003. Model-view-controller and Object Teams: A perfect match of paradigms. In *2nd Int'l Conf. Aspect-Oriented Software Development (AOSD)* (Boston), M. Akşit, Ed. ACM, 140–149.

45. WICHMAN, J. C. 1999. The development of a preprocessor to facilitate composition filters in the Java language. M.S. thesis, University of Twente.

Chapter 16

Aspect-Oriented Software Development with Java Aspect Components

RENAUD PAWLAK, LIONEL SEINTURIER, LAURENCE DUCHIEN, LAURENT MARTELLI, FABRICE LEGOND-AUBRY, AND GÉRARD FLORIN

This chapter presents the Java Aspect Components (JAC) programming environment [10]. While the two primary goals of this framework are supporting dynamicity and distribution, JAC is nevertheless a general-purpose AOP environment, complete with a programming model, a design notation, and an API. Prior papers described the programming model [24] of JAC, its aspect composition mechanism [22], the first elements of our UML notation [21], and the architecture for distribution [23]. This article sums up the main features of JAC and describes in detail our UML notation. In Section 16.1, we introduce the JAC programming model, in Section 16.2, our UML notation, and in Section 16.3, the architecture of JAC for distribution support. Implementation details and performance measurements are provided in Section 16.4. Section 16.5 provides a comparison with other tools and closely related technologies. Finally, we conclude in Section 16.6.

16.1 JAC FRAMEWORK AND PROGRAMMING MODEL

The JAC framework is based on the notion of containers. Much like in other component frameworks (e.g., EJB [29]), a container is a host for software entities. JAC containers host both a "business" component and non-functional "aspect" component. As we discuss in Section 16.4, when working with a centralized environment, the container is simply a customized Java classloader that performs bytecode adaptations to glue the business and aspect components together. Whenever a distribution concern appears in the application, these containers become remotely accessible (either with RMI or CORBA).

16.1.1 Programming Model

JAC identifies three different roles in the development of an aspect-oriented application:

Application programmer. This role is concerned with the core business of the application. The application programmer implements the software entities coming from the functional decomposition of the problem.

Aspect programmer. This role is concerned with the implementation of non-functional services. Up to this stage, these services are independent from the ones defined by application programmers.

Software integrator. This role puts application and aspect code together. Two important tasks under the responsibility of this role are pointcut definitions and aspect composition.

For these three roles, the programming model of JAC provides the following software artifacts:

Base program. This is the set of Java objects that implements the core functionalities of applications. These are regular Java objects. This set of objects is self-sufficient and can be run on a JVM without any aspects.

Aspect components. These components implement non-functional concerns to be woven on a base program. An aspect component defines a crosscut policy (i.e., the methods of the base program whose semantics are modified by the non-functional concern) and some aspect methods (advices in AspectJ) that define the semantic modifications. Aspect methods may wrap (execute before and/or after code), replace, or extend the semantics of a base method.

16.2 DESIGN NOTATION

This section describes our UML profile to support the design of aspects with JAC. Stereotypes are proposed to qualify classes implementing a non-functional concern (Section 16.2.1) and to qualify pointcut relations (Section 16.2.2). An example using these two concepts is given in Section 16.2.3. Section 16.2.4 discusses the similarities between AOP and the use-provide relationship.

16.2.1 *Aspect Component Classes*

Aspect components (ACs) are the central point of our AO framework. They are the implementation units that define extra characteristics that crosscut a set of base objects. They are defined in classes called AC classes. The key characteristic of JAC is that the base objects that are involved in a crosscut are not necessarily located in a single container.

An AC class is tagged with the <<aspect>> stereotype. It contains attributes and methods whose semantics differ from regular methods. AC methods are meant to extend the semantics of regular classes. The extension is performed on well-defined implementation points so that these points actually use aspect services to integrate new concerns. For example, a base class can be made to use a cache interface if the aspect implements some caching concern.

Each AC method defines some code and extends the semantics of some base methods according to a modality defined by a stereotype. The stereotypes for an AC method m are:

<<before>> m(...) Method m is executed before a given point (to be specified later, see Section 16.2.2) of the base program.

<<after>> m(...) Method m is executed after a given point of the refined program.

<<around>> m(...) A part of m is executed before and another part is executed after a given point of the refined program (these two parts are defined within the implementation of m).

<<replace>> m(...) Method m modifies a given point of the extended program implementation by replacing it by the implementation of m.

<<role>> m(...) Method m can be invoked on the objects that are extended by the AC class; moreover, m can access the extended class attributes and the attributes of the AC class. This is similar to the introduction concept of AspectJ.

For example, Figure 16-1 shows the caching AC class *Caching* (with the <<aspect>> stereotype). As its name suggests, this AC class provides a caching extension mechanism. The job of storing and retrieving values from the cache is delegated to the *Cache* (regular) class. The whenWrite method of the AC class *Caching* is tagged with the <<after>> stereotype. It is executed after any base method associated with whenWrite in the pointcut definition (see Section 16.2.2). The whenRead method is tagged with <<around>>. It is executed before and after some base methods.

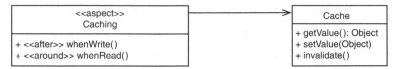

Figure 16-1   *Definition of a caching concern with an AC class.*

16.2.2   Pointcut Definition

A pointcut relation links an AC method belonging to an AC class to a set of elements of a base program. Pointcuts in JAC are limited to method calls; we do not introspect at the instruction level. Several arguments justify this decision. First, experiments with the fully reflective compiler OpenJava [32] taught us that reifying the whole code structure produces an unacceptable performance for real applications. Second, before extending the semantics of an application, it is necessary to understand its original semantics (we cannot extend something that is not clearly stated). Most of the time the original semantics are defined through an API, that is, primarily through method signatures. So base methods are definitively the best place to perform semantic extensions.

JAC supports pointcuts on both classes as on individual instances.

16.2.2.1   Class-Level Pointcut

This level is similar to the one found in AspectJ. All instances of the classes involved in the pointcut are extended by the aspect component. In this case, a pointcut relation is an oriented association from an AC class towards one or several classes. The association is stereotyped with <<pointcut>>. The roles have special semantics; they mention which methods of the client class are extended by which AC methods. The semantics of the elements mentioned in Figure 16-2 appear in the following list.

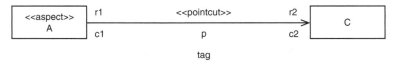

Figure 16-2   *The pointcut association: relating aspects to classes.*

- ◆ A pointcut relation p must go from an AC class A to a class C (if several classes are involved in the pointcut, several links are drawn between the AC class and the classes).

- Cardinality $c1$ is the number of aspect instances of A that can be related to one member of C (default is 0-1).

- Cardinality $c2$ is the number of members of C that can be related to one instance of A (default is * for all).

- Role $r1$ is the name of an AC method defined in A that is applied at each base program point denoted by role $r2$.

- Role $r2$ defines a base program crosscut; i.e., a set of join points. $R2$ is a logical expression (with AND, OR, and NOT operators) where each term is of the form *<qualifier> <methodExpression>*.

  - Two mains qualifiers are used: ? denotes a method execution point, and ! denotes a method invocation point.

  - *<methodExpression>* is either a fully defined method prototype (e.g., get():int) or a partially-defined one with regular expressions (e.g., get*(*):int matches all methods whose name starts with "get," that return an integer, and that take any parameters), or an expression based on the keyword defined in Table 16-1. For instance, GETTERS(a, b) matches the getter methods for fields a and b. Like in component frameworks such as JavaBeans, naming conventions are assumed on method names: getters/setters should be named get/set followed by the field name (starting in uppercase). Adders/removers should be named add/remove and take an object as a unique parameter. Introspection and bytecode analysis are performed each time a new class is loaded in the JAC framework. A meta model of the class is constructed on-the-fly with annotations that support the semantics defined in Table 16-1. For instance, each method bytecode is parsed to determine whether some fields are modified or not. If so, the method is tagged as a modifier in the RTTI aspect.

- As any UML model element, the pointcut relation can be "tag" to express extra semantics that can be used when implementing the model toward a concrete platform; some semantics examples are shown in further sections.

Figure 16-3 shows two pointcut relations that implement a caching aspect by using the AC class defined in Figure 16-1. This aspect diagram must be read as follows:

- After the execution of any setter (a method that changes the object state) of a Server object, the program must execute the whenWrite AC method.

- Around (i.e., before and after) the execution of any getter (a method that reads the object state) of a server object, the program must execute the whenRead AC method.

Table 16-1 *Keywords Allowed in Pointcut Expressions*

Keywords	Semantics
ALL	All the methods
STATICS	All the static methods
CONSTRUCTORS	All the constructors
MODIFIERS	All the methods that modify the object state, i.e., all that modify at least one of the fields
ACCESSORS	All the methods that read the object state
GETTERS[(...)]	The getters
SETTERS[(...)]	The setters
ADDERS[(...)]	The methods that add an object to a collection
REMOVERS[(...)]	The methods that remove an object from a collection
FIELDGETTERS	All the getters for primitive fields
FIELDSETTERS	All the setters for primitive fields
REFGETTERS	All the reference getters
REFSETTERS	All the reference setters
COLGETTERS	All the collection getters
COLSETTERS	All the collection setters

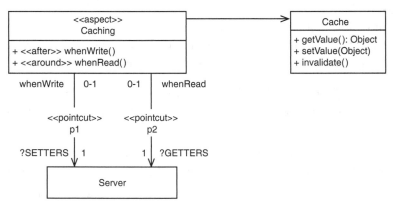

Figure 16-3 *The full caching aspect.*

16.2.2.2 **Instance-Level Pointcut**

Besides the previously described mechanism, JAC also allows developers to define pointcuts on a per-instance basis. This can be useful in several cases. For instance, a persistence framework may need to define objects as persistent roots from which other referenced objects persist. A multi-user application may want to exchange data between several users by using specific objects. In a distributed environment, server objects may need to be customized, because they must cope with heterogeneous running contexts (in terms of network properties, provided and expected quality of service, and so forth.). In all these cases, instances belonging to the same class need to be extended differently.

In Java, classes are straightforwardly named. Objects, on the other hand, present a problem: There is no direct naming scheme for identifying individual objects in Java. The solution taken in JAC is to let the framework attach a unique name to each created instance: The name is the concatenation of the class name in lowercase and of an auto-incremented integer (e.g., `server0` designates the first created instance of class `Server`). The framework provides an API a way to retrieve objects based on their name and to customize names assigned to objects. For instance, a field known to be a primary key may be used to name objects. To let designers express a per-instance pointcut, aspect component side roles in the UML diagram (i.e., `r1` in Figure 16-2) can be extended with an instance name or a regular expression on instance names. For instance, `?SETTERS|server0` designates the execution points of the setter methods of instance server0, and `?GETTERS|server[1-3]` designates the execution points of the getter methods of instances `server1`, `server2`, and `server3`.

When distribution comes into play, pointcut definitions can also be filtered based on container names (a container name being an RMI or CORBA URL depending on the chosen communication protocol between JAC remote containers). The idea is to let designers express behaviors that are dependent on the context in which components are deployed. For instance, one may want to install an authentication aspect only on specific critical hosts, whereas the rest of the application deployed on other hosts stays unmodified, or one may need to install a logging aspect only on a given container. To allow this, pointcut expressions can be extended with container names or regular expressions on container names. Merged with the previous extension for instance names, this leads to a complete scheme where pointcut expressions are of the form: `qualifier methodExpression | instanceExpression | containerExpression` with `instanceExpression` and `container Expression` being optional. For instance, `?ACCESSORS||rmi://myHost/s1` designates the accessors execution points of instances located on JAC container `rmi://myHost/s1`.

16.2.3 A First Simple Example

This section illustrates the programming model of JAC based on the Caching aspect of Figure 16-3. The details of the API and some tutorials can be found on the JAC web site [10].

Listing 16-1 gives the code of the Caching aspect component. An aspect component extends the jac.core.AspectComponent class. Among other things, this class provides a method for expressing a pointcut. The parameters of this method are the base class this pointcut designates, the qualifier methodExpression as a string, the class containing the AC method, and the AC method involved in the pointcut. Listing 16-1 defines two such pointcuts. Additional pointcut methods are available when instanceExpression and containerExpression are to be associated with the pointcut.

Listing 16-1 *A simple aspect component implementing a caching concern*

```
import jac.core.AspectComponent;
import jac.core.Wrapper;
import jac.core.Interaction;

public class Caching extends AspectComponent {
  public Caching() {
    pointcut(
      "Server","?SETTERS",CachingWrapper.class,"whenWrite");
    pointcut(
      "Server","?GETTERS",CachingWrapper.class,"whenRead");
  }

public class CachingWrapper extends Wrapper {
  private Cache cache = new Cache();
  public void whenWrite( Interaction i ) {
    proceed();
    Object value = i.arg[0];
    cache.setValue(value);
  }
  public Object whenRead( Interaction i ) {
    Object value = cache.getValue();
    if ( value == null )
      value = proceed();
    cache.setValue(value);
    return value;
} } }
```

AC methods are defined in wrapper classes (that extend the `jac.core.Wrapper` class). AC methods accept only a single parameter, a `jac.core.Interaction` instance. They may return any parameters. The rationale behind this constraint is that AC methods are upcalled by the JAC framework whenever a call to their base method is issued or executed (i.e., whenever the call matches the pointcut expression). An inter-action object `i` provides data about the current call: arguments of the call (in the `i.arg` array), a reference to the base object (`i.wrappee`), and some methods to store and retrieve context parameters; for instance, parameters that can be added by an AC method on the caller side and that can later on be retrieved on the receiver side by another AC method.

16.2.4   Extended Design Notation for Distribution

16.2.4.1   The Group Paradigm

In the caching example, the semantic modification introduced by the caching con-cern into the application is quite symmetric. Concretely, all objects modified to implement caches (the `Server` objects) can be seen as modified by the same abstract transformation rule. However, one may want to weave the caching aspect to different classes. Thus, another designation mechanism is needed to express the fact that a set of well-defined objects implements the same concern.

This need for a new kind of structured elements brings us to focus on the group paradigm. A *group* is an abstract representation of a set of instances that do not nec-essary have homogeneous functional types, but are logically grouped together, because they implement the same service (server groups) or use the same one (client groups). Elements of a group "share the same common secret."

Figure 16-4 represents the application of the caching aspect on a group of servers that implements the server part of a simple client/server application. We use an instance diagram so that it becomes obvious that the group on the top of the figure is a non-uniform set of instances (the three instances a, b, and c belong to three differ-ent classes A, B, and C). As shown in this figure, the application of the caching aspect creates a new group that contains instances of a `Cache` class that provides the caching functionality. In other words, we can say that these `Cache` instances belong to a server group that provides a caching functionality for the client group formed by the a, b, and c servers.

16.2.4.2   A Group-Based Definition of Aspects

Abstractly, the introduction of the caching concern within the original client/server application is done by the use of the services the Cache group interface provides to the servers group. This is represented in UML by using the <<use>> relation, as shown in Figure 16-5. In the general case, implementing a new concern may require using several interfaces. In these cases, several clients can be related to several servers through some <<use>> relations. Finally, a simple but sufficient definition of an aspect within this context is:

Definition 1 An *aspect* is the implementation of one or many use-provide relationship(s) between one or many client group(s) and one or many server groups.

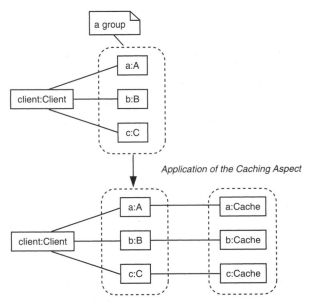

Figure 16-4 *Relating aspects to groups.*

The model of Figure 16-5 clearly brings up a use-provide relationship between a client group (the servers), and a server group (the caches) that defines the group-level services getValue(), setValue(Object), and invalidate(). The implementation of this relationship requires modifying the client group member object's implementation to introduce the caching concern.

At the analysis level, the application designer can add a tagged value aspect: aspectName to all the <<use>> relationships implemented by the aspect called aspectName to express that a use-provide relationship is implemented in an aspect-oriented fashion (see Figure 16-5). Thus group-oriented modeling allows the designer to specify in a comprehensive way which parts of the application are aspects and which parts are not. In fact, for each modeled group-level use-provide relationship, aspect-oriented techniques can be used to separate concerns within the final implementation. Note that this modeling, which is a high-level view of the application, defers the specification of pointcuts to some later stage refinements using the notation presented in Sections 16.2.1 and 16.2.2. Finally, each time the designer encounters the pattern of one or several use-provide relationships between groups, he can ask himself if an aspect would be well suited in this case.

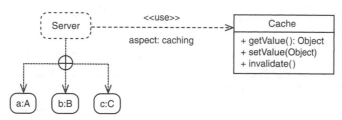

Figure 16-5   *The use relationship between a client group (the base program) and a server group (the aspect program).*

Whether to apply an aspect is mainly related to designer experience and choices. However, we can give some clues on when an aspect is better suited than a classical design. Aspects are often better when

The client group is heterogeneous.   This means that the use of the server services is spread over all the client-group member classes. This is in essence a crosscutting concern, and some extra design is necessary to cleanly modularize all the dependencies involved. In this case, the use of an aspect can greatly simplify the programmer's task and help ensure good maintainability and evolvability of the final implementation, even if some concerns are added afterwards.

Several homogeneous client groups use the same server group.   This is exactly the same situation as the previous one since several homogeneous groups can be modeled via one heterogeneous group.

Several client groups use several server groups but seem to be of the same concern.   This is a more contextual choice that depends on the knowledge of the modeled domain.

Figure 16-6 sums up the notions introduced in this section and proposes a UML metamodel where additions introduced by JAC are drawn with bold lines.

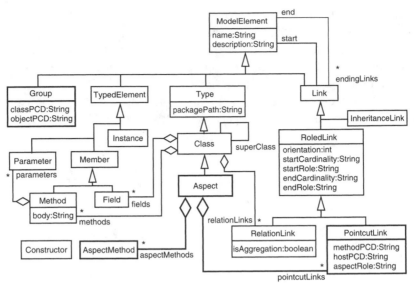

Figure 16-6   *The UML extension metamodel.*

16.3   JAC ARCHITECTURE FOR DISTRIBUTION

16.3.1   Aspects Deployment and Distribution

This section presents the features of the architecture set up in JAC to handle distribution. This architecture is called AODA (aspect-oriented distributed architecture).

The AODA provides functionalities to deploy base programs and aspect components. The idea is to allow the natural and consistent cohabitation between distribution and aspects. To do this, the AODA provides core features to support distributed aspects. Figure 16-7 shows how the AODA manages distributed aspects. The top of the figure is a simple application composed of a set of components. The curly line and the crosses symbolize the pointcut relation. The middle of the figure shows the same application, but extended by a sample aspect. Finally, the bottom part depicts the application deployed. Each container holds a local instance of the original aspect; hence, the aspect is applied on each container in the same way. The set of containers where the aspect is present is called an *aspect-space;* it can be regarded as a single but distributed aspect.

Our motivation for distributed aspect support is to allow the aspect programmer to express global and decentralized program properties. Indeed, it often happens that a non-functional property crosscuts a set of objects that are not located on the same container. For instance, when adding an authentication concern, the capacities may be checked on several server containers so that it is useful to modularize all the authentication definition in one unique aspect definition.

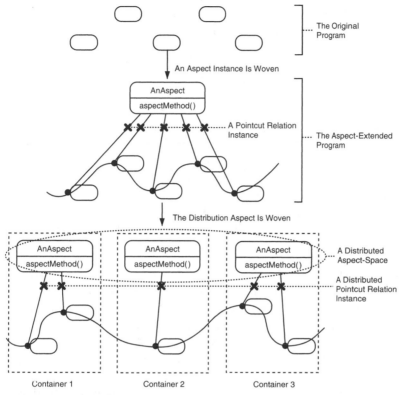

Figure 16-7   *AODA: Distributed support for aspects.*

16.3.2   *Distributed Application Example*

This section presents a simple example of a distributed application with JAC. Readers interested in more detailed examples of distributed programming with JAC can refer to [20] where, among other things, a replicated load-balanced server is described.

Consider a three-node ring that passes a token around the members of a ring. The functional base program is composed of three objects that are the nodes of the ring. The first step is to develop some base-level classes (this code sample can also be found in the JAC version that can be downloaded from [10]).

```
public class Ring {
  public static void main( String[] args ) {
    RingElement element0 = new RingElement();
    RingElement element1 = new RingElement();
```

```
      RingElement element2 = new RingElement();
      element0.setPrevious( element2 );
      element1.setPrevious( element0 );
      element2.setPrevious( element1 );
      element2.roundTrip( 9 );
} }
public class RingElement {
  public RingElement previousElement;
  public RingElement() {}
  public RingElement( RingElement previousElement ) {
    this.previousElement = previousElement;
  }
  public void setPrevious( RingElement previousElement ) {
    this.previousElement = previousElement;
  }
  public void roundTrip( int step ) {
    if( step > 0 ) previousElement.roundTrip( step-1 );
} }
```

One can develop an aspect component that deploys the three created objects in JAC containers or use the existing `DeploymentAC` aspect component provided with JAC. Each aspect component woven to an application can be associated with a configuration file that gives, with a script-like syntax, the steps needed to configure it. Each step corresponds to calling a method of the aspect component. For instance, the following script instructs the instance of `DeploymentAC` woven to the previous base program, to

1. Remotely install (AC method deploy) instances *ringelement0, ringelement1,* and *ringelement2* on containers bound to, respectively, the RMI names `rmi://host0/s0`, `rmi://host1/s1`, and `rmi://host2/s2`.

2. Create a client stub (AC method `createAsynchronousStubsFor`) for `ringelement0` on *s2*, a client stub for `ringele- ment1` on *s1*, and a client stub for `ringelement2` on *s2*. The stub delegates method calls to remote instances. This way, remote communication details are hidden from ring element objects.

```
deploy "ringelement0" "rmi://host0/s0"
createAsynchronousStubsFor "ringelement0" "rmi://host0/s0"
"rmi://host2/s2"
deploy "ringelement1" "rmi://host1/s1"
createAsynchronousStubsFor "ringelement1" "rmi://host1/s1"
"rmi://host0/s0"
deploy "ringelement2" "rmi://host2/s2"
createAsynchronousStubsFor "ringelement2" "rmi://host2/s2"
"rmi://host1/s1"
```

Figure 16-8 illustrates the topology generated by this configuration script for the deployment aspect.

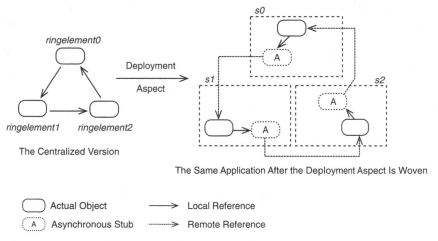

Figure 16-8 *Deployment of the ring application.*

16.3.2.1 Adding a Tracing Aspect to the Ring

Assume we want to see the round-trip progression on the different containers (in other words, where the token is). Of course, we could modify the `RingElement.roundTrip` method implementation to add a `println`. However, this technique has several drawbacks.

It is not dynamic. Once installed, removing tracing requires rebuilding the application.

It is not clean. The `RingElement.roundTrip` code is more difficult to understand, as it implements a concern that is not purely related to the ring core functionalities.

It is less reusable. What happens if you reuse a ring program that has been provided by another programmer for which you do not have the source code? What happens if you want your ring to be reused? Do you furnish the trace-free version or the traced one?

It is not safe. The trace example is simple, but imagine that you introduce a bug or a regression just because you want to add a new technical concern. For instance, you log the traces into a file, and somewhere in all the lines you add into the initial program, you forget to catch the disk full or permission denied exceptions so that the program stops because of the traces you added. Using an aspect allows you to modularize the tracing mechanism so that it is much easier to control and to ensure that your modifications do not cause any regression.

It is not simple in a distributed environment. If you want your traces centralized in a unique storage, you may need to install a tracing server. Concerns as simple as debugging or logging become more complex when the program is distributed.

For all these reasons, you may want to implement this tracing feature within an aspect. Figure 16-9 shows the tracing aspect design. The code following the figure is the straightforward JAC implementation of this model.

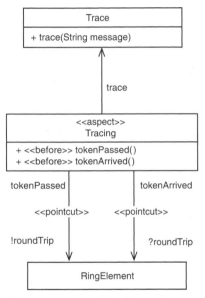

Figure 16-9 *A simple tracing aspect for the ring example.*

```
public class TracingAC extends AspectComponent {
  Trace trace = new Trace();
  TracingAC() {
    pointcut(
      "RingElement", "!roundTrip(int):void",
      TracingAC.TracingWrapper, "tokenPassed" );
    pointcut(
      "RingElement", "?roundTrip(int):void",
      TracingAC.TracingWrapper, "tokenArrived");
  }
```

```
class TracingWrapper extends Wrapper {
  public Object tokenPassed( Interaction i ) {
  trace.trace("The token has been passed by "+i.wrappee);
  return proceed();
 }

 public Object tokenArrived( Interaction i ) {
   trace.trace("The token has arrived in "+i.wrappee);
   return proceed();
}}}
```

Neither the figure nor the JAC code mention distribution. This means that the aspect works whether the application is centralized or distributed. By using the AODA, we have not only completely separated the distribution concern from the tracing one, but we have also made the aspects and their pointcut semantics inherently distributed. This distributed semantics greatly reinforces the AOP expressiveness by allowing the modularized definition of extensions that crosscut distributed applications.

The way the trace object is actually distributed can be implemented within a deployment aspect (an aspect for the tracing aspect). For instance, if you want all the traces to be centralized on the *s0* container, then just configure a distribution aspect as follows so that all the calls to the trace features are forwarded on *s0*.

```
deploy "trace0" "s0"
createStubsFor "trace0" "s0" "*"
```

The final ring application architecture is given in Figure 16-10.

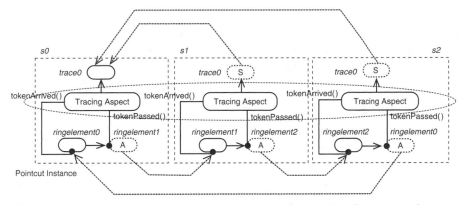

Figure 16-10   *The ring example completed with the distribution and tracing aspects.*

16.4   IMPLEMENTATION AND PERFORMANCE ISSUES FOR JAC

16.4.1   Implementation of JAC

JAC is entirely written in Java. The aspect weaving is performed at class load time using the bytecode engineering library BCEL [8]. This gives us the ability to weave applications whose source code is not available. In such a case, software integrators need only know the methods to relate to the pointcut definitions. The current distribution of JAC provides a set of predefined aspects for distribution (either with RMI or CORBA), persistence (JDBC or file system), GUI (Swing), authentication, transaction, consistency, load balancing, and broadcasting. A GUI console is provided for on-the-fly weaving or unweaving aspects in running applications. A CASE tool implementing the UML design notation defined in Section 16.1 is also available (see Figure 16-11).

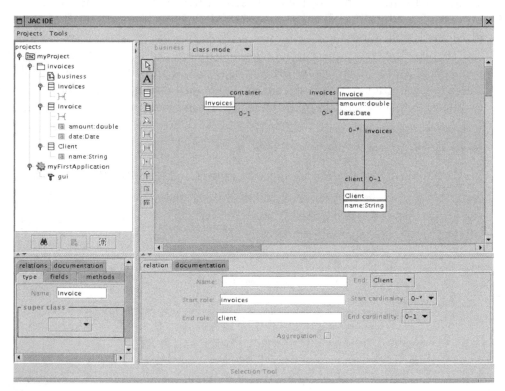

Figure 16-11   *JAC CASE tool screenshot.*

The join points considered in JAC are method invocations and executions. Hooks are introduced into woven aspects whenever these events are generated. This idea is not new and has been proposed by many authors (e.g., [2]) to implement MOPs. The approach introduces a stub method for each method of a base class. These stub method introductions are done by translating the original classes so that their instances can support aspect weaving.

We investigated several techniques to perform this translation. One of these is to use compile-time reflection by using an open compiler such as OpenJava [32]. OpenJava is very powerful, allowing all kinds of code manipulation at compile time (it takes Java code and produces a translated Java code). However, since it reifies the whole syntax tree of the program, it is slow and not well suited to our simple problem. Another solution is to perform the translation at the bytecode level. Several bytecode translators are available, and most of them can work at class load time. The idea is to use a customized classloader that reads the class file and modifies the stream contents before actually defining and registering the new class within the JVM. This solution is well suited for us. First, our translation is simple and can be performed with little overhead. Second, we can translate the classes coming from a third-party program or from external libraries with no need for the Java source code.

We implemented the translation with two different bytecode translators. Javassist 1.0 [3, 4] is a reflective high-level translator that hides the complexity of the bytecode format by instantiating a load-time meta model. It is fast and easy to use. However, because of its high-level API, Javassist introduces some restrictions on the bytecode manipulations that can be done (for instance, constructors, statics, and method invocations cannot be correctly translated). As a work-around, Javassist 2.0 proposes a low-level API in addition to the high-level one.

BCEL [8] is the most popular bytecode translator. It proposes a very low-level bytecode manipulation interface that makes it very powerful (all kinds of translations can be performed). The translation we implemented with BCEL is more complex and slower than with Javassist, but the bytecode produced is of better quality.

16.4.2 *Performance Measurements*

The critical performance point of the JAC framework is the dynamic wrappers invocation mechanism. Since this invocation relies on reflection to achieve dynamic adding or removing of aspects, the performance overhead of JAC mainly comes from the overhead of the reflective calls. Table 16-2 shows the performance of empty method calls on regular objects and on JAC wrappable objects. These tests are performed with a benchmark program that calls several methods with different prototypes and that is available in the JAC distribution [10]. The benchmark program was run under Linux with a Pentium III 600 MHz with 256KB of cache and with the SUN Java HotSpot Client VM version 1.4.

Table 16-2 *Comparative Performance Measurements for Java and JAC*

Types of Calls	Number of Calls	Total Time (ms)	Time per Call	Overhead
(A) regular object calls	6,000,000	55	~9.16 ns	—
(B) reflective calls	60,000	47	~0.78 µs	(A) × 85
(C) JAC objects calls	60,000	61	~1.00 µs	(A) × 111
(0 wrapper)				(B) × 1.29
JAC (1 wrapper)	60,000	85	~1.41 µs	(C) + 41%
JAC (2 wrappers)	60,000	110	~1.83 µs	(C) + 83%
JAC (3 wrappers)	60,000	130	~2.16 µs	(C) + 116%

One can see that a call on a JAC wrappable object is comparable to a reflective call on a regular Java object (with an overhead of 29%). Each time a wrapper is added, an overhead of about 40% of the initial time is added.

Finally, the price of adaptability is high (as for reflection) compared to compiled approaches such as AspectJ. However, with real-world aspects and especially when the application is distributed, this cost is negligible compared to the added cost of remote calls. For the moment, the JAC approach is thus more suited for middle-grained wrappable objects (only business objects are made wrappable in real-word applications; technical components that need performances are not aspectized) and for distributed and adaptable programming.

16.5   RELATED TECHNOLOGIES AND TOOLS

16.5.1   Aspect-Oriented Languages and Tools

AspectJ [11, 14] is a powerful language that provides support for the implementation of crosscutting concerns through pointcuts (collections of principle points in the execution of a program) and advice (method-like structures attached to pointcuts). Precedence rules are defined when more than one advice applies at a join point. In many features (e.g., pointcuts definition) AspectJ has rich and vast semantics. Nevertheless, we argue that in many cases that we have studied, simple schemes such as the wrapping technique proposed by JAC are sufficient to implement a broad range of solutions dealing with separation of concerns. AspectJ is a compile-time approach, whereas JAC is oriented toward run-time AOP: Aspects can be woven or unwoven on-the-fly. This feature is particularly useful for distributed applications, where application servers that cannot be stopped may still require some level of reconfiguration. For example, dynamic aspects allow introducing monitors for faults. In our opinion, the AspectJ rich syntax and compile-time approach makes it suitable for general-purpose aspect-oriented applications, whereas JAC features dedicate it for dynamic applications running in open environments. Under such circumstances, JAC also shares objectives with EJB [29] application servers such as J2EE. The main difference between the two approaches is that JAC containers are open and can be extended with any required technical services (implemented as an AC), whereas technical services are hard-coded in EJB containers and can simply be configured with XML descriptors, not changed or extended.

The composition filter object model (CFOM) [1] is an extension to the conventional object model where input and output filters can be defined to handle sending and receiving messages. This model is implemented for several languages, including Smalltalk, C++, and Java. The latter implementation is an extension to the regular Java syntax where keywords are added to declare, for instance, filters attached to classes. The goals of this model and ours are rather similar: handling separation of concerns at a meta level. Many similarities exist between composition filters and JAC wrappers. They both control the way method invocations are delivered or not to the final business objects. Nevertheless, JAC wrappers follow a programming model that does not require any extension to the Java language.

Aspectual components [15] and their direct predecessors, adaptive plug and play components [16, 17], define patterns of interaction called participant graphs (PGs) that implement aspects for applications. PGs contain participant roles (e.g., publishers and subscribers in a publish/subscribe interaction model) that (1) expect features about the classes on which they are mapped, (2) may reimplement features, and (3) provide some local features. PGs are then mapped onto class graphs with entities called connectors that define the way aspects and classes are composed. Aspectual components can be composed by connecting part of the expected interface of one component to part of the provided interface of another. Nevertheless, it seems that by doing so, the definition of the composition crosscuts the definition of the aspects, thereby losing the expected benefits of AOP.

Subject-oriented programming [9, 18] (SOP) and its direct successors, the Hyper/J tool [31] and the Concern Manipulation Environment (CME) [7], provide the ability to handle different subjective perspectives, called subjects, on the problem to model. Subjects can be composed using correspondence rules (specifying the correspondences between classes, methods, fields of different subjects), combination rules (giving the way two subjects can be glued together), and correspondence-and-combination rules that mix both approaches. Prototype implementations of SOP for C++ and Smalltalk exist, and a more recent version for Java called Hyper/J is available. This latter tool implements the notion of hyperspace [19] that permits the explicit identification of any concerns of importance.

An approach relatively close to the spirit of JAC is the Mozart project [34]. Mozart is an open distributed programming system on the Oz language that provides object/component-orientation, declarative, logic, and constraint programming. It provides a good degree of separation of concerns with support for multiple paradigms. Despite its complete nature, the core Mozart does not take full advantage of new AO programming concepts such as aspect-classes or pointcuts. In our opinion, it is therefore more difficult to comprehend and less flexible, as the provided concerns are built-in (but configurable) within the system.

Superimpositions [27] are also an approach for separation of concerns in distributed environments. This approach is a theoretical work that furnishes a language that can be applied to AOP. We are currently working on using some of the fundamental concepts of superimpositions in our aspects.

Finally, several projects such as Lasagne [33], JMangler [13], and PROSE [25, 26] provide dynamic weaving/unweaving of aspects that are similar to JAC. However, none of them fully handles the automatic distribution of aspects as JAC does.

16.5.2 Comparison with Design Notations for Aspects

Suzuki and Yamamoto's study [30] is one of the first on aspects and UML. They extend the standard UML notation and designate aspect classes with a stereotype called <<aspect>>. These classes are then related to base classes using a realization relationship. Nevertheless, nothing is said about how to express pointcuts or how to define whether advices are applied before, after, or around a join point. The stereotypes introduced in Section 16.2 answer these needs.

Theme/UML [5, 6] is an AOSD design-level language defined by Clarke and Walker and is the direct successor of work done by these authors on subject-oriented design. Theme/UML allows designing crosscutting concerns as separate models in so-called composition patterns (CP). Unless their name contains the term composition, these are units of specification for a concern. They can be seen as AspectJ abstract aspects. Strategies for merging elements from the composed models and resolving conflicts are defined. The models are packages labeled with the <<subject>> stereotype. They define a class diagram for a particular concern (e.g., the observer design pattern, with a subject and observers notified whenever state changes occur in the subject). They allow some degree of variability in the sense that they are templates. The template parameters represent exported elements from the package to be bound to elements of other base packages: they define a crosscut. The binding is specified with a `bind` clause attached to the base package. Crosscuts with JAC are relationships from the aspect class to the base class, and not between the packages containing these elements. Hence, the resulting diagrams are of lower level with JAC but are in our sense more precise. Also, the semantics of crosscuts with Theme/UML are related to a merge operation, whereas JAC aspect class diagrams reflect the before, after, and around options for an advice. Finally, the ambition of Theme/UML is to be a general-purpose aspect-oriented design notation independent of any programming approach, whereas the JAC design notation is directly linked to its programming model, allowing our CASE tool to generate code.

Stein, Hanenberg, and Unland present in [28] a design notation for the AspectJ programming model. They precisely define representations for all AspectJ language constructs. They take advantage of many UML facilities and extend four categories of diagrams to express aspect-oriented notions: interaction diagrams, class diagrams, collaboration diagrams, and use cases. First, join points are highlighted in interaction diagrams whenever they appear. UML interaction diagrams represent method invocations but leave apart instance creations and reads and writes of instance variables. Thus, they are extended with these pseudo-operations that may be concerned by join points. Second, in class diagrams, stereotypes exist to label aspects, pointcuts, and advice. When writing pointcuts and advice, an additional property named `base` is defined to hold the implementation of the pointcut. A new relationship named `<<crosscut>>` signifies the crosscutting effect of aspects on base classes. Third, parameterized collaborations are used to represent introductions of members (constructors, methods, fields) and relationships (inheritance, implementation) to the base class structure. Finally, use cases define the weaving order at each join point, e.g., whether an advice is to be executed before, after, or around the join point. This work is, as far as we know, the most advanced on defining a design notation for AspectJ constructs. As the JAC programming model is simpler than AspectJ, our design notation can be simpler than theirs. However, we think that the use cases of this work may be less intuitive than the stereotypes used in JAC. Also, introductions defined in terms of collaboration diagrams may be hard and long to write. This is the price of having a notation fully compliant with UML. The way we perform introductions with the JAC notation is more pragmatic and is completely left as an implementation issue for the CASE tool (the current version of our CASE tools let AC designers enter the introductions as lines of code). This limitation should be solved in future versions of the notation.

16.6   CONCLUSION

JAC is a framework for aspect-oriented programming (AOP) in Java. It provides a general programming model and a number of artifacts to let programmers develop aspect-oriented applications in a regular Java syntax (i.e., without any syntactical language extensions). The main elements managed by the framework are aspect components (ACs for short). They are the pieces of code that capture a crosscutting concern. Like others AOP approaches, we modularize concerns to ease maintenance and evolution. JAC provides containers to host AC and business (also called base) components. In the current version of JAC (downloadable under LGPL from our web site [10]), these containers are remotely accessible either with RMI or with CORBA. Further developments are underway for the SOAP communication protocol.

ACs define two main elements: pointcut relations and AC methods. Pointcut relations are the methods of the base program whose semantics are meant to be extended by the AC. AC methods are the blocks of code that perform the extension. The originality of pointcut relations with JAC is that they can be defined on a per-class basis (all instances of some given classes are equally extended) or on a per-instance basis (only given instances of some classes are extended). To achieve this feature, a naming scheme is provided for each base instance managed by the framework. A language for pointcuts definition is provided that lets developers filter instances based on their name or on the name of the container hosting them. The AC methods provide code that can be run before and/or after or replace the methods designated by the pointcut.

A UML notation is described in Section 16.2. The stereotypes provided enable designers to express all the previously mentioned elements concerning AC, pointcut relations, and AC method. Section 16.2.4 investigated some more advanced concepts, where AOP is compared to the use-provide relationship and to some notions of groups of heterogeneous classes. The notation is supported by a CASE tool. It generates code that can be executed by the JAC runtime. Hence, JAC covers a broad range of steps of aspect-oriented software, from the design step with UML to its implementation with aspect components and finally to execution with a run-time environment supporting dynamic weaving and unweaving of aspects.

REFERENCES

1. BERGMANS, L., AKŞIT, M., AND TEKINERDOĞAN, B. 2001. Aspect composition using composition filters. In *Software Architectures and Component Technology*, M. AKŞIT, Ed. Kluwer Academic Publishers, (Boston), 357–382.

2. CHIBA, S. 1995. A metaobject protocol for C++. In *10th Conf. Object-Oriented Programming, Systems, Languages, and Applications (OOPSLA)*, (Austin). ACM, 285–299.

3. CHIBA, S. 2000. Load-time structural reflection in Java. In *ECOOP 2000— Object-Oriented Programming: 14th European Conference*, (Cannes, France), E. Bertino, Ed. LNCS, vol. 1850. Springer-Verlag, Berlin, 313–336.

4. CHIBA, S. 2004. Javassist: Java byte code engineering made simple. In *Java Developer's Journal,* volume 9, issue 1. http://sys-con.com/story/?storyid= 38672&DE=1#RES.

5. CLARKE, S. AND WALKER, R. J. 2001. Composition patterns: An approach to designing reusable aspects. In *23rd Int'l Conf. Software Engineering (ICSE)*, (Toronto). IEEE, 5–14.

6. CLARKE, S. AND WALKER, R. 2002. Towards a standard design language for AOSD. In *1st Int'l Conf. Aspect-Oriented Software Development (AOSD)*, (Enschede, The Netherlands), G. Kiczales, Ed. ACM, 113–119.

7. COLYER, A. AND CLEMENT, A. 2004. Large-scale AOSD for middleware. In *3rd Int'l Conf. Aspect-Oriented Software Development (AOSD)*, (Lancaster, UK), K. Lieberherr, Ed. ACM, 56–65.

8. DAHM, M. 1999. Byte code engineering. In *Java-Informations-Tage*. Springer-Verlag, Berlin, 267–277.

9. HARRISON, W. AND OSSHER, H. 1993. Subject-oriented programming—a critique of pure objects. In *8th Conf. Object-Oriented Programming, Systems, Languages, and Applications (OOPSLA)*, (Washington, D.C.). ACM, 411–428.

10. JAC PROJECT HOME PAGE. http://jac.objectweb.org.

11. KICZALES, G., HILSDALE, E., HUGUNIN, J., KERSTEN, M., PALM, J., AND GRISWOLD, W. G. 2001. An overview of AspectJ. In *ECOOP 2001—Object-Oriented Programming, 15th European Conference*, (Budapest), J. L. Knudsen, Ed. LNCS, vol. 2072. Springer-Verlag, Berlin, 327–353.

12. KICZALES, G., LAMPING, J., MENDHEKAR, A., MAEDA, C., LOPES, C., LOINGTIER, J. M., AND IRWIN, J. 1997. Aspect-oriented programming. In *ECOOP'97 Object-Oriented Programming, 11th European Conference*, M. AKŞIT and S. Matsuoka, Eds. LNCS, vol. 1241. Springer-Verlag, Berlin, 220–242.

13. KNIESEL, G., COSTANZA, P., AND AUSTERMANN, M. 2001. JMangler—a framework for load-time transformation of Java class files. In *1st Int'l Workshop on Source Code Analysis and Manipulation (SCAM, ICSM)*, (Florence). IEEE, 100–110.

14. Laddad, R. 2003. *AspectJ in Action: Practical Aspect-Oriented Programming*. Manning Publications Company.

15. Lieberherr, K., Lorenz, D., and Mezini, M. 1999. *Programming with Aspectual Components*. Tech. Rep. NU-CCS-99-01, College of Computer Science, Northeastern University.

16. Mezini, M. and Lieberherr, K. 1998. Adaptive plug-and-play components for evolutionary software development. In *13th Conf. Object-Oriented Programming, Systems, Languages, and Applications (OOPSLA)*, (Vancouver). ACM, 97–116.

17. Mezini, M., Seiter, L., and Lieberherr, K. 2001. Component integration with pluggable composite adapters. In *Software Architectures and Component Technology*, M. Akşit, Ed. Kluwer Academic Publishers, (Boston), 325–356.

18. Ossher, H., Kaplan, M., Harrison, W., Katz, A., and Kruskal, V. 1995. Subject-oriented composition rules. In *10th Conf. Object-Oriented Programming, Systems, Languages, and Applications (OOPSLA)*, (Austin). ACM, 235–250.

19. Ossher, H. and Tarr, P. 2001. Multi-dimensional separation of concerns and the hyperspace approach. In *Software Architectures and Component Technology*, M. Akşit, Ed. Kluwer Academic Publishers, Boston, 293–323.

20. Pawlak, R. 2002. AOSD with JAC. Ph.D. thesis, CNAM Paris. Chapter 8.

21. Pawlak, R., Duchien, L., Florin, G., Legond-Aubry, F., Seinturier, L., and Martelli, L. 2002. A UML notation for aspect-oriented software design. In *Workshop on Aspect-Oriented Modeling with UML (AOSD)*, (Enschede, The Netherlands). http://lglwww.epfl.ch/workshops/aosd-uml/Allsubs/pawlak.pdf.

22. Pawlak, R., Duchien, L., Florin, G., and Seinturier, L. 2001. Dynamic wrappers: Handling the composition issue with JAC. In *39th Int'l Conf. and Exhibition on Technology of Object-Oriented Languages and Systems (TOOLS39)*. IEEE, 56–65.

23. Pawlak, R., Seinturier, L., and Duchien, L. 2003. JAC milestone 2003. Tech. Rep. 2003–04, Computer Science Laboratory of Lille. http://www.lifl.fr/~duchien/duchien.ps.

24. Pawlak, R., Seinturier, L., Duchien, L., and Florin, G. 2001. JAC: A flexible solution for aspect-oriented programming in Java. In *Metalevel Architectures and Separation of Crosscutting Concerns 3rd Int'l Conf. (Reflection 2001)*, (Kyoto), A. Yonezawa and S. Matsuoka, Eds. LNCS, vol. 2192. Springer-Verlag, Berlin, 1–24.

25. POPOVICI, A., GROSS, T., AND ALONSO, G. 2002. Dynamic weaving for aspect-oriented programming. In *1st Int'l Conf. Aspect-Oriented Software Development (AOSD)*, (Enschede, The Netherlands), G. Kiczales, Ed. ACM, 141–147.

26. POPOVICI, A., ALONSO, G., AND GROSS, T. 2003. Just-in-time aspects: Efficient dynamic weaving for Java. In *2nd Int'l Conf. Aspect-Oriented Software Development (AOSD)*, (Boston, Massachusetts), W. Griswold, M. AKŞIT, Ed. ACM, 100–109.

27. SIHMAN, M. AND KATZ, S. 2002. A calculus of superimpositions for distributed systems. In *1st Int'l Conf. Aspect-Oriented Software Development (AOSD)*, (Enschede, The Netherlands), G. Kiczales, Ed. ACM, 28–40.

28. STEIN, D., HANENBERG, S., AND UNLAND, R. 2002. An UML-based aspect-oriented design notation. In *1st Int'l Conf. Aspect-Oriented Software Development (AOSD)*, (Enschede, The Netherlands), G. Kiczales, Ed. ACM, 106–112.

29. SUN MICROSYSTEMS. Enterprise Java Beans technology. http://www.javasoft.com/products/ejb.

30. SUZUKI, J. AND YAMAMOTO, Y. 1999. Extending UML with aspects: Aspect support in the design phase. In *Int'l Workshop on Aspect-Oriented Programming (ECOOP)*, (Lisbon). http://trese.cs.utwente.nl/aop-ecoop99/papers/suzuki.pdf.

31. TARR, P., OSSHER, H., HARRISON, W., AND SUTTON JR., S. M. 1999. *N* degrees of separation: Multi-dimensional separation of concerns. In *21st Int'l Conf. Software Engineering (ICSE)*, (Los Angeles). IEEE, 107–119.

32. TATSUBORI, M. 1999. An extension mechanism for the Java language. M.S. thesis, University of Tsukuba. http://www.csg.is.titech.ac.jp/openjava/.

33. TRUYEN, E., VANHAUTE, B., JOOSEN, W., VERBAETEN, P., and JØRGENSEN, B. N. 2001. Dynamic and selective combination of extensions in component-based applications. In *23rd Int'l Conf. Software Engineering (ICSE)*, (Toronto). IEEE, 233–242.

34. VAN ROY, P. 1999. On the separation of concerns in distributed programming: Application to distribution structure and fault tolerance in Mozart. In *4th Int'l Workshop on Parallel and Distributed Computing for Symbolic and Irregular Applications (PDSIA)*, (Sendai, Japan). World Scientific, http://www.wspc.com.sg/books/compsci/4278.html.

PART *2*

Software Engineering

The first part of this book focused on programming language issues in software development. However, most developers know that programming is only a small fraction of the work required to produce and maintain a high-quality software system. Indeed, some experts have suggested that actual programming can be as little as 5% of total system effort. Engineering high-quality software is a difficult and uncertain undertaking, as is evidenced by the current variety of processes, methods, and tools. Processes are required (and exist to varying degrees of usefulness) to handle a myriad of complex tasks, including gathering requirements from the clients of the software, analyzing the requirements and designing and producing the software, testing the system and feeding test results back to the development team, ensuring that the new system integrates with existing business processes, deploying the system to the end users, ensuring the system stays up and running for as long as it is needed, and evolving the system as the needs of the users change. To complicate matters, these activities are not necessarily sequential. Adding to the complexity, the requirements may change at any time during the development cycle. Software engineering needs flexible development methods, technologies, and tools if there is to be any hope of a development team producing, in a timely manner, a high-quality and useful software system. Some of the key notions of software engineering are described in the sidebar.

Key Software Engineering Terminology

Software engineering.   The processes, methods, and tools that support a software development team in building a high-quality and useful software system.

371

Software process.   A series of actions that should be taken in developing a software system, such as gathering the requirements, analyzing the requirements, specifying the system, designing the system, and so forth. Most software processes break down these high-level actions to successively smaller action granularities.

Software method.   The way to achieve each action in a software process. A software method describes how to produce the required output for each step in the process, with advice on appropriate notation for representing the elements of the output. For example, in the software design step of the software process, a UML class diagram is generally part of the required output. Object-oriented methods that describe how to produce a class diagram include descriptions on identifying objects of interest, grouping them based on type, identifying relationships between objects, and so on.

Software model.   A representation of the software at varying levels of abstraction, depending on the step in the development process. For example, a UML class diagram is a model of the structure of the system.

We tend to measure system quality in terms of various properties. Often, generically termed "ilities," these properties include correctness, efficiency, maintainability, portability, reliability, predictability, interoperability, fault tolerance, recoverability, learnability, analyzability, adaptability, reusability, robustness, testability, verifiability, comprehensibility, consistency, traceability, evolvability, measurability, and modularity. High quality is clearly a tall order.

None of this is news. Currently, for each point in the development cycle, many methods purport to help control complexity, often accompanied by tools to help realize the method. Where does aspect-oriented software development fit in? The early focus on software engineering as programming has broadened, as the field has matured, to an understanding of the importance of the entire software lifecycle. Much of the work described in this section is characterized by the recognition that the benefits of an aspect-oriented approach to modularization can be realized at earlier stages in the development cycle than programming. Further work attempts to achieve another ility:—*traceability* of aspects from the requirements to the implementation. Classic software engineering lauds modularization and traceability as important properties for easing comprehensibility and maintainability of systems. Adding aspects to the development mix does not change the need for these fundamental properties—indeed, aspects emerged as a technology motivated to improve them. It is a further measure of the maturing of the field that we are also seeing a number of evaluations and experience reports of usage of AOSD in software development in this section.

Broadly speaking, all these tasks and qualities are within the realm of software engineering. Aspects extend conventional programming technology; they likewise need to extend software engineering technology. Some of the papers in this part provide insight into processes and methods for aspects at stages of the lifecycle other than programming. Some describe interesting experiences with using aspects in real projects, while still others explore the integration of aspects with existing software engineering methods, such as component-based development. Our selection is not comprehensive; a single book is too small to include all the interesting work on this topic. We hope that the set of papers here informs the reader as to the kind of work that is ongoing in aspect-oriented software engineering and provides a guide towards further investigation of the field.

THE CHAPTERS

Our first chapter, Chapter 17, "Engineering Aspect-Oriented Systems," by Gordon S. Blair, Lynne Blair, Awais Rashid, Ana Moreira, João Araújo, and Ruzanna Chitchyan, presents a study of existing approaches to aspect-oriented software engineering. The chapter begins by examining methods for including aspects in requirements engineering. Later sections examine approaches such as consideration for aspects at the specification, design, and implementation phases and discuss how approaches support evolution and aspect interaction. Each section has its own criteria for comparing approaches. For example, requirements engineering is examined with respect to issues such as support for aspectual concepts and the ability to map to artifacts later in the lifecycle; specification approaches are considered with respect to their capability for specification verification, their degree of tool support, and their extent of language independence. Many of the design comparison criteria are based on quality properties such as assessing the traceability, reusability, and comprehensibility of the designs that result from using the approaches. A theme running throughout the chapter is that of providing guidelines for the selection of a particular approach (or set of approaches) for actual use. This chapter provides an excellent starting point for those readers investigating how they can go about realizing the benefits of aspects earlier in software development than coding.

Chapter 18, "Aspect-Orientation in the Software Lifecycle: Fact and Fiction," by Pedro Clemente, Juan Hernández, José Luis Herrero, Juan Manuel Murillo, and Fernando Sánchez, illustrates the effect of introducing aspects late in the development process. The difficulties encountered by applying aspects only to the implementation and not to the design ranged from errors injected by programmers making localized changes without consideration of the design as a whole to maintenance problems that arise because the design documents no longer reflect the code.

The authors describe attempting to ameliorate these difficulties by capturing aspects earlier in the lifecycle, using two different approaches. This paper reinforces the view that it is important to be able to trace elements of the implementation back to the design.

In the early 1990s, there was no single, standard approach to designing object systems; rather, there was considerable discussion of the underlying nature of object-orientation. As might be expected from the maturity of AOSD, the current AO situation is similar. Notwithstanding the lack of consensus about most things, there is nonetheless one opinion shared by all researchers on aspect-oriented design—all approaches are based, at least to some extent, on the current standard for object-oriented design, the Unified Modeling Language (UML). UML, as applied to object-oriented software engineering, is well known and well understood. Extending UML to aspect-oriented design requires three additional high-level capabilities of UML. First, we want to modularize crosscutting concerns into separate design models. Aspect-oriented software development is all about modularizing concerns; a design language must support that. Second, we want a means to describe how separate design models should be integrated (composed). Separated concerns need to be integrated into a working system, and designers need to be able to say how that should happen. For example, a designer may want to express the idea that a specific crosscutting behavior should be executed when a certain condition occurs. Finally, we want a design approach that includes the semantics for actually composing (or "weaving," in AOP terms) the designs based on what the designer has previously specified. Composing design models provides a means for the designer to verify the decomposition into separate models and to validate the specification of how the design models should be composed.

Standard UML was not designed with aspects in mind, and so broadly speaking, current aspect-oriented design approaches fall into two categories: extend UML constructs and semantics to deal with aspects, or use standard UML in new ways.

The next two chapters explore these two ideas. Chapter 19, "Generic Aspect-Oriented Design with Theme/UML," by Siobhán Clarke and Robert Walker, is rooted in the notion of multi-dimensional separation of concerns, (as described in Chapter 3, "*N* Degrees of Separation: Multi-Dimensional Separation of Concerns"). Different kinds of concerns, including aspects, are modeled separately and composed at a later stage. For the most part, standard UML is used to model each individual concern. Theme/UML extends UML templates to allow designers of an aspect to reason about join points without referring to them by name. The main extension to the UML is a new kind of relationship, the *composition relationship,* which allows a designer to specify both how the design models relate to each other and how they should be composed.

Theme/UML extends standard UML. This has the advantage of providing linguistic structures close to the user's conceptual notions of aspects, but the disadvantage of requiring extending standard UML tools. Chapter 20, "Expressing Aspects Using UML Behavioral and Structural Diagrams," by Tzilla Elrad, Omar Aldawud, and Atef Bader, describes an approach that stays within standard UML, relying on advanced features of UML statecharts to express aspects. Concurrent statecharts describe different behaviors, some of which may crosscut. This chapter shows how to use standard (though advanced) features of statecharts, including event broadcasting, to achieve implicit weaving. This has the benefit of allowing the use of standard UML tools but adds the additional complexity of using UML constructs in novel ways.

Other aspect design approaches avoid adding constructs to the UML by using stereotypes of existing UML constructs that map the AspectJ model. Many of these approaches are strongly tied to varying versions of AspectJ and depend on it for their semantics. These also have the advantage of allowing designers to use existing case tools, and they are familiar to existing AspectJ programmers. References to design approaches that take this perspective can be found at [2]. Ultimately, we need to gain experience with the different approaches to aspect-oriented design. It is important that this experience is assessed in conjunction with studies on different aspect-oriented programming models (and indeed, aspect models across the whole development lifecycle) to gain insight into traceability and other ilities. Standardization would be useful, but considerable work is needed to agree upon the basic aspect model before standardization is appropriate.

Chapter 21, "Concern Modeling for Aspect-Oriented Software Development," by Stanley Sutton, Jr. and Isabelle Rouvellou, discusses the necessity of having a model of the concerns of a system that is independent of development artifacts and the software lifecycle. Such a model needs links into all development artifacts, allowing the analysis of these artifacts for properties such as traceability, impact of change, and applicability for reuse. From a software engineering perspective, such a model is an important addition to a developer's toolset; this kind of analysis is critical for understanding the system as a whole and for managing its evolution. This sounds great in theory, but does such a model exist? The model described in the chapter, Cosmos, represents a good basis from which to evaluate and evolve concern schema. Cosmos speaks to the core of a fundamental difficulty we have in our field: What is a concern? How do we characterize it? How do we recognize it when we come across it? Focusing on schemas like Cosmos helps the AOSD community gain a common understanding of exactly what a "concern" is—an important goal towards converging on standards for supporting technologies.

The theme of concern modeling is echoed at the programming level in Chapter 22, "Design Recommendations for Concern Elaboration Tools," by Gail Murphy,

William G. Griswold, Martin P. Robillard, Jan Hannemann, and Wesley Leong. Here, the focus is on elaborating concrete concerns in code—once a programmer has identified a concern of interest, a tool should help find all code that relates to that concern. The benefits of such a tool are clear—when all the code for a concern can be clearly identified, modifying it becomes less problematic and the impact of modifications more readily identifiable. This chapter describes a study of three existing concern elaboration tools and presents a set of challenges and recommendations for the kinds of issues a concern elaboration tool should handle.

This part includes some experimental studies relating to the efficacy of aspect-oriented programming. Chapter 23, "An Initial Assessment of Aspect-Oriented Programming," by Robert J. Walker, Elisa L. A. Baniassad, and Gail C. Murphy, reports on two experiments that assessed how easy aspect programs are to debug and modify. Though the work was based on an early version of AspectJ, it nonetheless highlights some interesting points that remain relevant. The scope and extent to which aspects impact the base code is fundamental to understanding the program as a whole. Programmers need a language that provides a narrow, well-defined interface between the aspects and the base, with constructs that provide appropriate levels of encapsulation for crosscutting code. From a software engineering perspective, this oft-cited work has been highly influential in many ways. Languages like AspectJ have evolved that provide considerable improvement in these areas. In addition, this work serves as an example as to the kinds of studies that can be performed, with many researchers building from or analyzing the methods and the results.

Chapter 24, "Aspect-Oriented Dependency Management," by Martin Nordberg III, analyzes aspect-oriented programs to assess the level of dependencies between modules that are introduced by aspects. Given some of the hand-waving claims relating to the modularization capabilities of aspect-oriented programming, it is always refreshing (indeed, essential for software engineering) to view these claims from different perspectives. In general, when examined from the perspective of levels of coupling, aspect-oriented programming appears to perform well in reducing coupling between modules, but, interestingly, this is not true in every case. Based on studies of different patterns of software, the chapter provides guidelines for when to use standard object-orientation, aspect-orientation, or a combination of both. In the rush of (justified) enthusiasm for the aspect-oriented paradigm, we recognize a danger of treating it as the ideal hammer for every nail (and screw). More studies such as those described in this chapter will help us refine the technology to achieve the greatest benefit.

Chapter 25, "Developing Software Components with Aspects: Some Issues and Experiences," by John Grundy and John Hosking, presents further experience of combining the use of aspects with existing established approaches—in this case, with the current "sharpest tool in the programmer's toolbox" [Chapter 24], component-based programming. An acknowledged difficulty with component-based software engineering relates to specifying how components that have been designed without specific knowledge of each other should nevertheless work together, especially when knowledge of the internal details of components is required. This chapter combines components with aspects, using aspects to encapsulate crosscutting behaviors, thereby removing from a component any intimate knowledge of other components. Results appear encouraging, though potential disadvantages are readily acknowledged. Nonetheless, this trend towards experimenting with combinations of existing paradigms is to be encouraged, as much can be learned from the advantages and disadvantages of any approach, and much can be gained by combining the best of all.

Chapter 26, "Smartweaver: A Knowledge-Driven Approach for Aspect Composition," by J. Andrés Díaz Pace, Marcelo Campo, and Frederico Trilnik, takes a small step towards combining the aspect paradigm with knowledge-based engineering. Here, a tool provides guidance to a programmer relating to the tasks that need to be completed and templates to be filled in to achieve some of those tasks. The authors have ambitious goals for their tool; we look forward to monitoring their progress. Further exploration of how agents can support the aspect-oriented software engineering process is to be welcomed.

Having introduced the full set of papers in this part of the book, it is time to consider the coverage of current AOSD research against software engineering in the large. At the start of this introduction, we characterized the range of the software engineering field. Clearly, aspects do not currently permeate it all. (This is not to say that it is necessary or even appropriate that they do so.) Nevertheless, it is worthwhile to determine which areas are not addressed by aspects and to assess whether any perceived gap is one that should be filled. Take, for example, ensuring that a new system integrates with existing business process—a task we included as a necessary one to achieve a successful deployment of software within an organization, and therefore within the remit of software engineering. Intuitively, we might suggest that this is partly a management task and partly a business process-engineering task, and therefore aspects would not help. On the other hand, it might be considered partially an analysis task that might impact the design of a system, and therefore aspects are appropriate. Another example of a software engineering area not addressed in this part is testing. Encouragingly, work is emerging in examining different approaches to unit-testing aspect programs [1]. In general, we envision that further aspect activity will emerge across the broad scope of software engineering (including both development activities and quality "ilities").

Notwithstanding current limitations and potential gaps, we are excited by the range and momentum of current aspect-oriented software engineering research, especially when we consider the age of the field. Clearly, more needs to be done. The object-oriented paradigm seems a good role model for many reasons, not least because of its success. We suspect one reason for the pervasiveness of objects in current software development practice is a common, standard understanding of the relevant constructs. Such a common understanding currently eludes the aspect community, but is likely to develop over time. As aspect-oriented software development becomes mainstream, the range of supporting tools available to software engineers will grow, complementing and supporting each other across the lifecycle. Core principles will be absolute, making a move from one aspect-oriented language to another (regardless of the stage of the development lifecycle each language supports) as straightforward as moving, for example, from C++ to Java, or from UML to C++—particulars of the language need to be learned, but not the fundamental, core principles. We look forward to watching the aspect-oriented paradigm improve software engineering.

REFERENCES

1. AFANTI PROJECT. http://www.fit.ac.jp/~zhao/afanti.html.

2. ASPECT-ORIENTED MODELING 2002. *Workshop on Aspect-Oriented Modeling with UML (AOSD)*. Enschede, The Netherlands. http://lglwww.epfl.ch/workshops/aosd-uml/index.html.

Chapter 17

Engineering Aspect-Oriented Systems

GORDON S. BLAIR, LYNNE BLAIR, AWAIS RASHID, ANA MOREIRA, JOÃO ARAÚJO, AND RUZANNA CHITCHYAN

Aspect-oriented software development (AOSD) techniques aim at providing means for the systematic identification, modularization, and composition of crosscutting concerns throughout the software lifecycle. A number of aspect-oriented programming approaches are available, such as AspectJ [5], composition filters [8], adaptive programming [58], and Hyper/J [61]. The concepts are also being applied at the earlier stages of software development. At the requirements engineering stage, [7, 34, 70, 76] provide means for handling aspectual requirements. Similarly, a number of aspect-oriented specification [2, 28, 29, 74, 82] and design [7, 21, 36, 77, 79] approaches have been proposed. With a range of techniques available to a software engineer at each stage, the task of engineering an aspect-oriented system poses significant challenges. At each development stage, the software engineer needs to employ the most suitable aspect-oriented technique for the application being developed. The choice of technique can be dictated by a number of factors including system requirements, organizational practices, constraints imposed by the tools or development environments, and the nature of the crosscutting concern. The last implies that multiple techniques may be employed at each stage in conjunction with each other. This hybrid view of separation of concerns has previously been advocated by multi-paradigm approaches [14, 23] and more recently for aspect-oriented programming techniques [66].

As AOSD techniques mature, there is a need for guidelines supporting the development of well-engineered aspect-oriented systems. It is the aim of this chapter to provide such guidelines for key phases of the software lifecycle. The guidelines are aimed at describing the distinguishing characteristics of AOSD approaches at each stage and their suitability for the application or concern being modularized.

By making these guidelines available, we aim to support the software engineer in choosing the optimal technique or set of techniques at each stage. Note that aspectization should not be a *forced* phenomenon. Conventional separation of concerns techniques (e.g., object-oriented approaches) should be used if crosscutting concerns can be cleanly modeled without having to encapsulate them in a separate unit. For instance, a crosscutting concern could be embodied in the choice of specific system architecture rather than an individual unit [70]. However, when this clean separation of a crosscutting concern is not possible, aspect-oriented techniques should be used.

The structure of the chapter mirrors the typical software lifecycle, considering AOSD at each stage. In particular, Section 17.1 considers aspects and requirements engineering, with Section 17.2 addressing aspect-oriented specification. Design and implementation issues are then addressed in Sections 17.3 and 17.4, respectively. Section 17.5 addresses the important issue of software evolution and aspects, highlighting the issue of dynamic aspects. Section 17.6 then examines the potential problem of aspect interactions, and Section 17.7 presents some concluding remarks.

17.1 REQUIREMENTS ENGINEERING

Broadly scoped requirements and constraints form good candidates for aspectization at the requirements level. However, currently only a small set of requirements engineering techniques specifically aim to provide new abstractions and composition mechanisms to modularize and compose such concerns. Other requirements-level approaches achieve separation of concerns through the separation of functional and non-functional requirements. Non-functional requirements are constraints that affect several components of a system and are associated with quality of service (e.g., usability, security). Thus, they can be seen as good candidates for aspects.

Goal-oriented approaches [57], such as KAOS [25] and i* [86], are good examples of methods where non-functional requirements play a major role. A *goal* is an objective that the system under consideration should achieve. It can be formulated at different levels of abstraction, and it covers functional and non-functional concerns. The i* framework identifies and models organizational requirements and adopts the goal and *softgoal* modeling concepts. A softgoal represents a non-functional requirement that we expect to satisfy within acceptable limits.

There are other mechanisms, such as problem frames [43] and viewpoints [32], which manage concerns during requirements. Problem frames focus on the environment in which a system is located instead of the system itself or its interfaces. Problem frames are concerns that can be handled as aspects. Separation of crosscutting properties has been considered in PREView [76], a viewpoint-oriented requirements engineering method. A PREView viewpoint encapsulates partial information about the system. Requirements are organized in terms of several viewpoints, and analysis is conducted against a set of concerns intended to correspond broadly to the overall system goals. In applications of the method, the concerns that are identified are typically high-level non-functional requirements.

Approaches explicitly created to handle aspectual requirements are those presented in [7, 34, 68, 70]. Grundy proposes an aspect-oriented component requirements engineering (AOCRE) method targeted at component-based software development [34]. He has developed a categorization of diverse aspects of a system that each component provides to end users or other components (namely user interface, collaboration, persistence, distribution, and configuration). Baniassad and Clarke [7] propose Theme to provide support for aspect-oriented analysis and design through Theme/Doc and Theme/UML, respectively. In this section, we will focus on the analysis part of the approach and leave the design part to be analyzed in Section 17.3. Analysis is carried out by first identifying a set of actions in the requirements list that are, in turn, used to identify crosscutting behaviors. The authors define actions as sensible verbs for the domain. An action is a potential *theme,* which is a collection of structures and behaviors that represent one feature. The aspect-oriented requirements engineering (AORE) model [68, 70] relates concerns to requirements to see which concerns crosscut the stakeholders' requirements and qualify as candidate aspects. The model supports separation of the specification of aspectual requirements, non-aspectual requirements, and composition rules in modules representing coherent abstractions and following well-defined templates. The composition rules employ informal and often concern-specific actions and operators to specify how an aspectual requirement influences or constrains the behavior of a set of non-aspectual requirements. The modularization makes it possible to establish early trade-offs between aspectual requirements, thereby providing support for negotiation and subsequent decision-making among stakeholders. At the same time, early separation of crosscutting requirements facilitates the determination of their mapping and influence on artifacts at later development stages. Further support for traceability in the AORE model is provided by the PROBE framework [48], which generates proof obligations based on standard linear temporal logic that should hold for an aspect-oriented system from the initial aspectual requirements and their associated trade-offs. The temporal logic assertions can be used as input to formal methods tools such as model-checkers or as the basis for deriving test cases.

Given such a range of alternatives, how do we select what best satisfies an organization and its project needs? The decision process consists of two main steps. The first step is to select a subset of candidate approaches from the whole set of existing ones. The guideline to help us in achieving this is dictated by a set of organizational constraints, ranging from budget limitations to existence of expertise on particular approaches.

The second step is to choose one specific approach or an integration of several from the reduced set. The guideline here needs to take into consideration the development process we would like to use. The criteria that may influence our decision are:

Support for aspectual concepts.   Does the approach support the basic AOSD concepts directly?

Activities of lifecycle.   Which activities of the development process are supported?

Composition rules.   Does the approach provide explicit rules to compose aspects with requirements?

Handling conflicts.   Does the approach provide a method to identify and resolve conflicting aspects?

Maturity.   Has the approach been used in real projects?

Mapping to later artifacts.   Does the approach foresee how the aspectual requirements are mapped onto design and implementation artifacts?

Tool support.   Does a tool support the approach?

Table 17-1 shows the results of applying these criteria to the approaches mentioned here.

Table 17-1   *Comparing the Approaches*

Criteria Approach	Support for Aspectual Concepts	Activities of Lifecycle	Composition Rules	Handling Conflicts	Maturity	Mapping to Later Artifacts	Tool Support
KAOS [25]	No	RE+specification	No	Yes	Yes	Yes	Grail
i* [86]	No	Org. req.+RE	No	Yes	Yes	No	OME
Problem frames [43]	No	RE+architecture	Yes	No	Yes	Yes	No
PREView [76]	No	RE	No	No	Yes	No	JPREView
AOCRE [34]	Yes	RE for CBS	No	No	Partially	Yes	JComposer
AORE [68, 70]	Yes	RE	Yes	Yes	No	Yes	ARCaDe
Theme [7]	Yes	Analysis and design	Yes	No	No	Yes	Theme/Doc

Considering this comparison table, the main issues that may help us in our decision are:

KAOS.   KAOS is an established reference on goal-oriented approaches for requirements engineering. One of its main advantages is using a formal language (first-order temporal logic with real-time constraints) to specify critical parts of the system, besides allowing informal modeling. KAOS uses goals to detect and manage conflicts among requirements. It has been used in several industrial projects [57].

i*.   The i* framework is very effective at identifying and modeling the business domain of an organization. It does not directly support mappings to later activities of the software lifecycle, but recent work is being developed to derive UML models from i* models [17, 71].

Problem frames.   Problem frames categorize software development problems. As the author does not provide a systematic way to use the concepts, the approach may be difficult to learn and apply. Recent work combines problem frames with software architectures [37].

PREView.   PREView has already been used in small- and medium-sized safety-critical systems. As such, it has the advantage of proposing a stable set of concepts and a reliable method. Beyond alerting the requirements engineer to the risk that viewpoint requirements and concerns may cause inconsistencies, the approach does not identify the mapping or influence of crosscutting properties on artifacts at later development stages.

AOCRE.   AOCRE supports modularization of aspectual requirements during component-based software development. The strength of the approach is its focus on handling crosscutting concerns in component-based systems. Its major drawback is the lack of clarity on how to identify aspects for each component. Also, it lacks mechanisms to handle conflicts and omits how aspects and components are integrated together.

Theme/Doc.   Theme/Doc supports the requirements analysis activity by providing an approach to identify base and crosscutting behaviors. Having a tool that supports lexical analysis of the requirements to identify the major actions of a domain and relate them with the original requirements is an interesting feature. Having the major actions related between them through the requirements is a good basis to help identify behaviors that may be crosscutting.

AORE.   In the AORE approach, the separation of composition information from the aspectual and non-aspectual requirements makes them highly independent of each other, thereby providing an improved separation of concerns. This also improves the reusability of the aspects in some instances. Since the composition rules operate at the granularity of individual requirements, it is possible to identify and manage conflicts at a fine granularity. This optimizes the task of the requirements engineer identifying negotiation points for the stakeholders. The identification of the mapping and influence of a requirement-level aspect promotes traceability of broadly scoped requirements and constraints throughout system development, maintenance, and evolution. However, the approach is in its infancy, needing to be validated in real projects.

17.2 SPECIFICATION

There is an emerging body of research in the area of aspect-oriented specification. In this section, we present some of the key research in this area with our emphasis being placed on *formal* approaches. The reason for this is twofold:

◆ Formal approaches enable the early identification of problems in aspect-oriented software development through the use of formal analysis and verification techniques.

◆ The work also indirectly supports the emergence of a more rigorous foundation for AOSD through the emergence of an underlying semantics.

There is also, however, an expanding body of research on less formal approaches, such as approaches centered on UML. The interested reader is referred to the literature for a treatment on this subject, such as [3, 22]. Some key works will also be considered in the following design section.

Some of the most important research in this area has been carried out at the Ecole des Mines de Nantes. In early work, Fradet and Südholt define a generic framework for AOP based on *program transformation* [33] (a similar approach is also advocated by Lämmel [56]). In particular, aspects are considered to be "program transformations acting on the syntax tree of the component program." Aspect weaving is then defined generically as the repeated application of such program transformations until a *fixpoint* is reached (i.e., until the transformation of the program is equivalent to the program itself).

In subsequent work, they offer a formal definition of crosscuts based on the concept of *execution monitors* [29]. Execution monitors are concerned with the observation of events emitted during program execution or, more generally, patterns of events. On discovering a particular pattern, a particular action is executed (an aspect). A formal definition is provided for this *event-based model,* and a domain-specific language is then derived based on this formalism. A Java prototype is also described that, interestingly, is systematically derived from the language definition (by a translation from Haskell to Java). More recent work by this group, presented in [28], has further extended this approach to allow for the analysis of interactions between aspects; we include it in this section for completeness, but this work will be revisited in Section 17.6.

Frequently, work within the specification domain attempts to build on previous research to provide a theory of aspects. For example, Katz and Gil examine the relationship between aspects and *superimposition* [47]. Superimposition is a concept developed in the distributed systems community whereby programs are considered as interleavings of subtasks, such as representing the core algorithm and other nonfunctional properties such as liveness. A language called SuperJ has also been developed based on the theory of superimpositions [74]. This language is implemented as a pre-processor to AspectJ.

Other approaches advocate the use of *process algebraic* techniques [2], *multiset rewriting* [59], the use of the *Temporal Logic of Actions* [45], and also the theory of *monads* [26]. Finally, in links with the UML work mentioned previously, Aldawud, Bader, and Elrad consider aspect weaving and *statecharts* [1]. In this work, they achieve what they call *implicit weaving* through the use of the event broadcasting mechanism in statecharts.

Formal verification inevitably brings with it the problem of state-space explosion, which is often alleviated by the use of techniques based on abstractions or symmetries. Within the context of model checking aspect-oriented programs, tools such as Bandera [24] have been used that employ *program slicing* techniques to generate partial models (based on the property to be verified). Some recent research by Ubayashi and Tamai employs this technique [82]. However, this suffers from the drawback of model-checking the already woven code (rather than model-checking taking place prior to weaving). Ongoing work at Lancaster is developing this further by generating a model that retains the aspect-oriented structure of the program for subsequent model checking [10].

A selection of the various techniques outlined previously is analyzed in more depth in Table 17-2.

The key choice here, with respect to which formalism to use, is exactly what is to be formally specified and, hence, what can be verified. If a formal specification of an entire system is required, including the behavior of the base system and the aspects, then the process algebraic approach of [2] is appropriate. Although the referenced work does not currently include tool support for analyzing the specifications, such support is available for the underlying formal notation (CSP). If, instead, specifications of the crosscuts (and subsequent analysis of them) are required, then the approaches based on execution monitors are appropriate [28, 29] (with the latter also providing support for interaction analysis; see Section 17.6). Finally, the work contained in the last two rows of Table 17-2 [74, 82] is different in that support for verification is provided by model checking. This is a very powerful and mature verification technique but unfortunately is one that can suffer from the state-space explosion problem. In this respect, the work of [82] is interesting in the use of program slicing (via Bandera) to reduce the state-space.

Table 17-2 *Comparing the Approaches*

Criteria Approach	Based on . . .	Supports Specification of . . .	Supports Verification of . . .	Programming Language Dependent?	Tool Support?
Formal defn of crosscuts [29]	Execution traces (monitors)	Crosscuts (as patterns)	Program properties—by equivalence rules	No	Yes—2 prototype implementations of framework (Java & Haskell)
Detection & resolution of interactions [28]	Execution traces (monitors)	Crosscuts, inserts, compositions	Aspect independence—by 'laws for aspects'	No	Yes—for detection of interactions
Process algebraic foundations of AOP [2]	Process algebra (CSP subset)	Aspects (behavior), composition	Process equivalence	No	Not at present
Aspects and super-impositions [74]	Temporal logic specification of properties	Super-impositions, properties	Program properties—by established tools	Developed SuperJ/ AspectJ	Yes—via known model checking/ inductive theorem proving techniques
AOP with model-checking [82]	Temporal logic specification of properties	Properties	Program properties by Bandera	Currently Java-based	Yes—via model checking (Bandera)

To summarize, a wide range of approaches has now been developed for the formal specification of aspects, many building on theories emerging from other areas of computing. Further experience is required before a clear consensus can emerge from this work.

17.3 DESIGN

A number of approaches have been proposed to provide support for crosscutting concerns at the design level. Most of these approaches have been developed to augment object-oriented design techniques and UML with facilities for modularization of crosscutting concerns. Some of the key approaches at the design level include Composition Patterns [21, 22] and their successor Theme/UML [7, 22], aspect-oriented component engineering (AOCE) [34, 35, 36], hyperspaces [42, 62, 79], architectural views of aspects [46], and an approach proposed by Suzuki and Yamamoto [77, 78]. Although several other approaches have been proposed (e.g., [39, 41]), they suggest the introduction of specialized UML stereotypes for each particular crosscutting concern. These approaches have been left out of the discussion in favor of the more general approach by Suzuki and Yamamoto [77].

The Composition Patterns approach is based on a combination of the subject-oriented design model [20] for composing separate overlapping designs and UML templates. It is based on the observation that patterns of crosscutting behavior exist with respect to the base designs they cut across. This behavior holds irrespective of the subjects crosscut by the concern. Thus, reusable subjects and concerns can be designed independently of each other. Composition rules are then used to compose these designs together. Presently, the work on Composition Patterns in its entirety and with no significant changes is incorporated into Theme/UML [22], part of the Theme approach [7].

AOCE, at the design level, refines the previously identified aspect-oriented component requirements (from AORE) into design-level aspects. As mentioned in Section 17.1, AOCE is based on the idea that each component in a component-based system uses/provides services from/to other components. A set of UML metamodel extensions and visual notations is employed to make the provided and required aspect details explicit. The crosscutting concerns thus separated are used to categorize components in accordance with their contribution towards the overall system properties and reason about the inter-component services.

The hyperspaces approach proposes using *hyperslices* to encapsulate sets of modules that address concerns in dimensions other than the one used for the dominant formalism. Hyperslices can overlap; that is, a given unit in a hyperslice can appear, possibly in a different form, in other hyperslices. At the composition stage, issues such as overlapping are resolved via composition rules. The model can be instantiated in any formalism, at which time choices may be made as to the mapping between notational constructs and units/modules and as to how hyperslices are represented. Consequently, there are no standard design notations for this model. However, it has been instantiated for the object-oriented formalism [42].

In Architectural View of Aspects [46], aspects are represented as stereotyped packages containing a variety of UML designs pertaining to a certain concern. The elements within each diagram can have certain relations (e.g., uses, defines), while elements that can be bound to other elements in different aspects are color-marked. The notion of a *concern diagram* is introduced, which allows viewing of overlapping concerns in the system being designed. The composition employs the superimposition principle discussed in [74]. Essentially, this design approach is very close to another UML interpretation of the hyperspaces model, augmented with some visual cues (such as concern diagrams) and composition mechanisms (such as superimposition).

Suzuki and Yamamoto propose UML extensions to model aspects and UXF/a, an XML-based aspect description language to provide interchangeability of aspect-oriented models between various development tools (e.g., CASE tools, aspect weavers, etc.). An aspect is depicted as a class rectangle with attributes, operations, and relationships. The attributes are used by the set of operations, which are the weave definitions for the aspect. The signature of these definitions reflects the elements affected by the given aspect.

Like their conventional counterparts, "good" aspect-oriented design techniques should provide a set of notations for encapsulating holistic crosscutting requirements, facilitate understanding of complex systems, and promote reuse and evolution. The resulting designs should exhibit a high degree of traceability, change propagation, reusability, comprehensibility, flexibility, parallel development, and ease of learning and use [19]. Table 17-3 demonstrates the extent to which designs produced with each of the four design approaches discussed previously satisfy these qualities.

Table 17-3 *Evaluation of Selected AO Design Approaches*

Design Tech. Design Quality	Traceability	Change Propagation	Reusability	Comprehen- sibility	Flexibility	Ease of Learning/Use	Parallel Development
Composition Patterns [21, 22]	Good	Average	Good	Good	Good	Poor	Good
AOCE [34, 35, 36]	Very Good	Poor	Good	Average	Good	Good	Good
Hyperspaces [42, 62, 79]	Good	Average	Good	Good	Good	Poor	Good
Architectural Views [46]	Good	Average	Good	Average	Good	Poor	Good
Suzuki & Yamamoto's Model [77, 78]	Average	Average	Average	Average	Poor	Poor	Average

In AOCE, designs do not need to be merged but stay intact and are, therefore, easily traceable across the whole lifecycle. In both the Composition Patterns approach and hyperspaces, crosscutting requirements are clearly traceable to composition patterns and hyperslices respectively but are tangled as designs are merged. Architectural views facilitate traceability through concern diagrams, which show the coarse-level overlapping areas at a glance. They also support designing each crosscutting requirement as a separate aspect and annotate the composed designs with the source. The composed designs are, however, somewhat overcrowded. Suzuki and Yamamoto's model only provides partial support for traceability. Crosscutting requirements are traceable to aspects, which in turn reference affected object elements.

Composition Patterns and hyperspaces support non-invasive changeability, but composition rules need to be reviewed after a change. In AOCE, change is monitored but not effectively propagated. Architectural views refer to superimposition composition rules, which need to be checked for each composition. Suzuki and Yamamoto's model only provides partial support for changeability. UXF/a, however, supports efficient change propagation.

All approaches, apart from Suzuki and Yamamoto's model, support production of highly reusable designs that can be realized using different implementation techniques (high degree of flexibility). Suzuki and Yamamoto, on the other hand, support interchangeability of aspect descriptions between UXF/a compatible tools.

Individual designs involving Composition Patterns and hyperspaces are highly comprehensible, but integrated designs are less so. In AOCE, aspects assist in understanding the relationships between components, but the designs become cluttered due to the high degree of cross-referencing. Similarly, in architectural views, the composed designs could get cluttered with cross-referencing annotations, and while aspects are separated in Suzuki and Yamamoto's model, they still reference base object elements, which reduces comprehensibility.

Ease of using AOCE is impeded by the extra design effort needed but supported by additional run-time reconfigurability and dynamicity. Learning Composition Patterns and hyperspaces is complicated by the need to learn subject-oriented design and associated composition semantics. Architectural views require understanding of using single and composed views and superimposition. It is a similar case for Suzuki and Yamamoto's model, as its heavy reliance on the AspectJ implementation model requires an understanding of AspectJ.

Parallel development is supported by AOCE, Composition Patterns, architectural views, and hyperspaces. Crosscutting concerns and base designs can be developed simultaneously and independently of one another. Suzuki and Yamamoto's model only provides partial support for the purpose because, while designing crosscutting concerns, the designer needs to refer to the objects they cut across.

The decision on which approach to use should be made in accordance with the priorities of the previously mentioned design qualities for a given project on a case-by-case basis.

17.4 IMPLEMENTATION

The initial focus of AOSD on the implementation level has resulted in a range of programming approaches. AspectJ [5] is an aspect language for Java. It supports formulation of the aspect code separately from Java class code. The aspect code is written with reference to *join points* in the dynamic object call graph. An aspect weaver composes the aspects and the classes, and there is additional development support in the form of IDE (integrated development environment) extensions. AOP extensions to other languages have also been developed. AspectS [40], for example, is an aspect language for Smalltalk, while AspectC [4] is an AspectJ-like AOP extension to C.

The composition filters approach [8] extends an object with input and output filters. These filters can be of various types (e.g., dispatch filters for delegating messages and wait filters for buffering messages) and are used to localize non-functional code. JAC (Java aspect components framework) [64] employs reflection and wrappers to support dynamic aspect composition in Java (see Section 17.5). Several other frameworks support dynamic aspect composition, such as AspectWerkz [12] and JBoss [44] (see Section 17.5).

Adaptive programming [58] is a special case of AOP, where one of the building blocks is expressible in terms of graphs. The other building blocks refer to the graphs using traversal strategies. A traversal strategy can be viewed as a partial specification of a class diagram. This traversal strategy crosscuts the class graphs. Instead of hard-wiring structural knowledge paths within the classes, this knowledge is separated.

Hyper/J [61], the programming tool supporting the hyperspaces approach [79], introduces the notion of *multi-dimensional separation of concerns* at the implementation level by capturing each concern as a partial object model in a hyperslice. The hyperslices are composed into hypermodules by means of declarative composition rules. This permits the clean separation of multiple, potentially overlapping and interacting concerns simultaneously with support for on-demand remodularization to encapsulate new concerns at any time.

Figure 17-1 shows the process of identifying a suitable aspect-oriented programming technique when implementing an application. Most aspect-oriented programming techniques support one or more base programming languages. For example, aspect languages are available for separation of crosscutting concerns in Java (AspectJ), C (AspectC), and Smalltalk (AspectS). The Hyper/J tool supports multi-dimensional separation of concerns in Java using the hyperspaces approach. The composition filters approach, on the other hand, has been implemented for Java, C++, and Smalltalk. Therefore, the first natural step in the choice of a suitable technique is to reduce the available set of techniques to those that support the base programming language to be employed in application development. If no suitable technique is available for the base programming language, then a custom language and weaver need to be implemented, as for the SADES object database evolution system [67].

The second step in the identification of a suitable programming technique is not as simple as the first. It is composed of the dynamics of three different factors (Figure 17-1): the nature of the concern being modularized, the system requirements, and decisions made at the design stage. All these factors need to be considered in conjunction with each other; only then can the set of available techniques be reduced to the ones most suitable for the application.

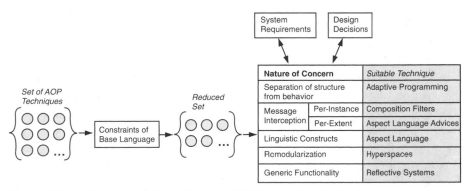

Figure 17-1 *Process of choosing a suitable aspect-oriented programming technique.*

The nature of the concern being modularized can often strongly influence the choice of aspect-oriented programming technique. This is because, although the various techniques tend to be complementary, one can be more suitable for implementing a particular concern. Adaptive programming, for instance, is highly suitable for expressing concerns that involve separation of behavior from object structure. It is very effective in situations where the behavior may be written against a partial specification of a class diagram or a generic specification of the structure of objects (not relating to information specific to individual instances). Examples of such generic specifications include traversal strategies for change propagation and referential integrity semantics in an object-oriented system [66]. These strategies need to know the types of relationships or manipulation operations but do not need to be aware of the information specific to individual relationship instances.

Composition Filters are very effective in implementing concerns involving message interception and execution of actions before and after executing a method. Their key characteristic is the ability to operate at instance granularity and attachment on a per-instance basis. For example, when modularizing relationships in an object-oriented system, a dispatch filter for handling a relationship can be attached to an instance when the relationship is established [66]. If message interception is not required on a per-instance basis, then mechanisms similar to *advices* in aspect languages (e.g., AspectJ), which operate on the extent of a class, are more suitable than composition filters.

Aspect languages are also very suitable in implementing concerns that need to be explicitly represented using linguistic constructs. Expression of such concerns can be simplified if the aspect language is declarative in nature. An example of such a declarative aspect language is the one employed for specifying instance adaptation behavior in SADES (see Chapter 29, "Aspect-Oriented Programming for Database Systems").

Other techniques have their strengths. For example, Hyper/J is very effective in situations involving remodularization of a legacy application. The reflective architecture of JAC, on the other hand, makes it highly suitable for developing generic aspects that can be reused across different applications. However, as mentioned earlier, the choice of a technique is also constrained by the system requirements and the chosen design. Dynamic aspects as in JAC (or frameworks such as AspectWerkz and JBoss) are only suitable for situations where an aspect needs to be adapted and recomposed at runtime. If an aspect does not need any customization at runtime, then for performance optimization, it is better to employ a technique where aspects do not live beyond compile time or are merely reified for some degree of run-time introspection [69], as in AspectJ. The design decisions can also have a similar impact on the choice of a suitable technique. For example, in the SADES implementation, the design decision to separate information about links among entities into relationship objects dictated that these relationship objects be attached to their participating entities on a per-instance basis and, hence, led to the choice of Composition Filters.

17.5 EVOLUTION

Support for evolution is crucially important in the development of computer software. A motivation for this is the well-known fact that somewhere between 60% and 80% of the cost of software stems from the maintenance phase of software development [83].

In addition, economic competitiveness is often dependent on the agility with which new versions of software can be released. Recent trends in software also highlight the importance of *dynamic evolution,* that is, supporting changes to software at runtime without taking the system out of action. This is particularly important in distributed systems, where the complexity and distributed nature of the system make it highly undesirable to stop the system and then build/redeploy the new system. Furthermore, with innovations in fields such as mobile and ubiquitous computing, it is often necessary to support dynamic reconfiguration whereby software configurations can be altered dynamically to match the requirements of the current operating context. An example of this would be to employ caching if a period of disconnection is anticipated. More radically, researchers are currently investigating self-healing systems, where software evolves itself to deal with detected faults in its operation [72].

In theory, AOSD should be well placed to address issues related to evolution (and certainly static evolution). In particular, the separation of concerns inherent in AOSD should facilitate the replacement or upgrading of particular aspects and the introduction of new aspects. Indeed, this is one of the most frequently quoted motivations for the AOSD approach. In practice, however, the state-of-the-art is less positive particularly when dealing with dynamic evolution.

In addressing the state-of-the-art, there are two key issues to consider:

1. How do we support the dynamic evolution of aspects?
2. Can aspects themselves be used to manage this evolutionary process?

In terms of the former, there is now considerable interest in the general area of *dynamic aspects,* that is, being able to weave aspects into a system at runtime (the static approach to weaving exemplified by most current approaches such as AspectJ). In order to understand this area, it is necessary, however, to appreciate the (often misunderstood) relationship between aspects and reflection.

Reflection is a technique to support the dynamic inspection and adaptation of a particular software system [51, 75]. The traditional approach to developing software is based on the principle of abstraction. For example, in the object-oriented paradigm, programmers deal in terms of abstract interfaces without being aware of the underlying implementation details. This is a powerful but ultimately flawed philosophy [50]. In particular, it is often necessary to access underlying details of a system, for example to fine-tune the implementation for a given context such as making space-time trade-offs in the underlying algorithms/data structures. In a reflective system, access is provided to such internal details via a *meta-interface* (or *meta-object protocol*). This interface offers a *causally connected self-representation* of the underlying system— by changing the representation, you are making a change to the actual system implementation.

As a technique, reflection has now gained general acceptance with widespread use in areas such as programming languages [51, 84], operating systems [85], and middleware [9, 55]. From this work, a widespread portfolio of reflective mechanisms has emerged, including *introspection* mechanisms (as found for example in the Java reflection API), *interception/ message reification* (supporting for example the association of pre- and post-behavior with particular object invocations), and *architectural reflection* (supporting the discovery and subsequent adaptation of architectural structures in terms of components and their interconnections). At another level, tools such as Javassist [18] and JMangler [54] support the dynamic adaptation of bytecode.

One problem with reflection is that it can be a rather low-level and hence rather dangerous technique (in terms of maintaining the overall integrity of the system). This is the key to understanding the relationship between aspects and reflection. In particular, the implementation of dynamic aspects inevitably involves the use of particular reflective mechanisms. Aspects, however, provide a higher-level abstraction for the evolutionary process in order to protect the integrity of the application. For example, consider composition filters. The emphasis of this approach is on offering higher-level filtering patterns (e.g., dispatch filters, wait filters, error filters) with strong underlying semantics in order to have a precise understanding of the effects of composition. In order to support dynamic evolution, the approach would typically be implemented using a variation of interception. At this level, however, there is no formal basis to understand the resultant behavior of the system.

In terms of the classic AOP approaches, composition filters are the most advanced in terms of supporting dynamic evolution [8]. In addition, Orleans and Lieberherr report on a language called the DJ Framework, an extension to adaptive programming offering dynamic traversal strategies [60]. Finally, work is currently underway to incorporate dynamic aspects in AspectJ.

There are also a number of experimental languages under development. We feature two interesting examples, JAC and Lasagne:

JAC. JAC (Java Aspect Components) is one example of how reflective mechanisms can be used to construct dynamic aspects [64]. JAC is a component-based framework to support the construction of distributed applications. As with Enterprise JavaBeans, components reside in containers. More specifically, two styles of components are identified: business components containing the standard business logic and aspect components that define crosscutting concerns (the non-functional properties associated with a container). New aspect components can be introduced at runtime. The implementation of this feature exploits dynamic wrappers and also structural meta-data. JAC also features an interesting distributed pointcut mechanism for aspects that may span multiple hosts.

Lasagne. Lasagne is a higher-level component-based approach that supports "the dynamic and context-sensitive combination of aspects on a per collaboration basis" [81]. Like JAC, the approach is based on dynamic wrappers; indeed the current implementation of Lasagne is based on JAC. Each aspect is realized by a set of wrappers potentially hosted on different sites in a network. The key to the approach is the use of composition policies that specify the particular subset of aspects to be employed in different contexts. The approach carries a significant performance overhead and is recommended for use with relatively coarse-grained aspects such as a particular security policy. Lasagne has been applied in a variety of areas including the construction of an adaptive Object Request Broker [80].

A number of pure Java-based frameworks providing dynamic aspect weaving are also being developed. The most prominent amongst these are the JBoss AOP Framework [44], AspectWerkz [12], and PROSE [65]. While these approaches avoid Java language extension, they do require augmented JVMs. JBoss is a reflective and reconfigurable application server that uses the JBoss AOP framework—aspects are implemented as interceptors to provide a set of crosscutting services (e.g., persistence, remote access, etc.), and load-time weaving is used for composition with the help of a custom classloader. The weaver introduces *actual hooks,* that is, only to a set of points of actual interest and not to every possible point of potential interest. AspectWerkz also supports load-time weaving based on introducing actual hooks. It uses a custom-enhanced core Java class loading architecture hooked in directly after the bootstrap classloader. In contrast, weaving in PROSE is based on a JIT compiler, and the weaving scope can be varied between actual hooks and every possible point of potential interest.

Other notable languages offering dynamic aspects include Handi-Wrap [6], AspectS [40], AOP/ST [11], and SMove [49]. Research at INRIA is also investigating efficiency issues in dynamic weaving using the technique of code injection [13].

Interestingly, there has been very little work on employing such (higher-level) techniques in a more language-independent setting, that is, in middleware. Schult and Polze report one technique based on .NET exploiting the underlying CLR to offer language (but not necessarily platform) independence [73]. In general, though, most work in this area simply exposes the underlying reflective mechanisms leaving it to higher layers, such as the application, to preserve consistency.

There is much less research on the second key issue—whether aspects themselves can be used to manage this evolutionary process. However, the authors believe this is potentially a very important approach. This observation stems from previous work by one of the authors on evolutionary mechanisms for databases, as described in Chapter 29.

In selecting from these evolution techniques, an interesting question is which AOP implementation languages support evolution. In terms of the classic AOP approaches, all techniques have the potential to support static evolution. Note however, that this potential will not be realized unless the resultant system has a good architecture/design. Certain language features can also result in undesirable behavior under evolution. One example is with the use of wildcards in AspectJ, where some join points that were previously matched might no longer match, while others might be matched when they should not.

In terms of dynamic evolution, it is clear that of the classic approaches, *at present,* composition filters offer the most comprehensive solution. An increasing number of experimental languages also supports dynamic aspects, typically employing a variation of wrappers and reflection to achieve the necessary level of dynamism. Of this class of language, we consider JAC to be the leading approach, as it is the most mature. Note that the techniques generally have a significant performance overhead because of the level of indirection involved. If this is an important concern, then techniques such as the code injection work mentioned previously should be considered. In general, though, what is required is consolidation of research in this area and for the most promising approaches to be included in the more mature aspect-oriented languages and systems.

17.6 ASPECT INTERACTION

An important area that has not yet been widely targeted by the research community is the (formal) analysis of undesirable interactions between aspects, sometimes referred to as aspect interference. Aspects are, by definition, intended to cut across program code and can be seen as being orthogonal to the underlying base code. However, the aspects themselves need not be orthogonal to one another, and this leads to the potential for aspect interactions (interference), where aspects may cooperate or interact with each other or the base program in unexpected ways.

This problem is not unique to aspect-oriented programming and is well-understood within the domain of telecommunication systems (see [15] and the series of Feature Interaction Workshops [16, 31]). Borrowing the definition of feature interactions from [52], we can say that an aspect interaction occurs if the behavior of one aspect is affected by the behavior of another aspect.

Given the inevitability of aspect interactions, three angles can be considered with respect to providing a solution: avoidance, detection, and resolution, all of which are currently under-researched areas.

One means to address the first of these, avoidance, is the application of the "design by contract" principle, as proposed by Klaeren and colleagues in [53]. This work addresses the issue of whether a particular composition of aspects is valid by using assertions, thus avoiding faulty aspect configurations.

Regarding the second and third categories, interaction detection and resolution, the most significant work has been undertaken in [28], which describes an automatic conflict analysis tool, detecting interactions between aspects. This is based on definitions of two aspect independence properties, where sufficient (but not necessary) conditions are defined to ensure independence. The resolution of detected interactions is achieved manually by using a dedicated composition language that contains linguistic support for conflict resolution.

Work is also underway at Lancaster investigating the detection of aspect interactions by utilizing program slicing techniques [10]. A further intended outcome of this work is identifying a categorization of types of aspect interactions, such as along the lines of those identified for feature interactions in [38]. Also related is work on the resolution of feature interactions, where "feature resolution modules" are implemented as aspects [63].

Issues associated with aspect interactions are also discussed briefly in [27], where a logic meta-programming approach can be used to describe either domain-independent combination rules (based on prioritization) or more specialized domain-specific rules.

The immaturity of this area of work makes it difficult, at this stage, to draw guidelines for the software developer. However, the core observation from this section and from the limited work that has been carried out is the very real problem posed by aspect interactions. While the introduction of aspects helps in the structuring and maintainability of software systems, it does bring with it another challenge, that of dealing with aspects that interact in unexpected ways. As has been stated before, this is not a new problem, having been widely studied within the telecommunications industry. It is also an area about which the AO software developer should be aware. In summary, it is clear that the issue of aspect interaction is an important consideration within the development of aspect-oriented systems; yet, to date, this is an area that is under-researched in the AOSD community.

17.7 CONCLUSION

In its short history, aspect-oriented software development has clearly been driven by the emergence of aspect-oriented languages such as AspectJ. In other words, AOSD has largely been synonymous with AOP. While such languages have helped popularize the subject, this is not a healthy long-term position. In particular, it is vital that a more complete software engineering discipline emerges for AOSD. This chapter is aimed as a stepping stone in this direction.

This chapter has examined the state-of-the-art in engineering support for aspect-oriented systems, looking at areas such as requirements, specification, design, and implementation. Crucial issues such as the evolution of software and dealing with aspect interactions have also been considered. The evidence presented suggests that rapid progress is being made in these areas. Indeed, it could be argued that wider software engineering issues now dominate the literature in this area, such as the strong interest in early aspects [7, 30, 68, 70]. It would be wrong, though, to claim maturity in the topics addressed by this chapter; indeed, the various sections all generally conclude that although many techniques have emerged, further experience is required to appreciate their relative strengths and indeed to consolidate proposals into a small number of key approaches.

Where possible, the chapter has included qualitative metrics to evaluate the various techniques and to offer guidelines to enable software developers to make informed selections. Our argument is that there is no perfect solution; rather, techniques all have their own strengths and weaknesses, and these must be interpreted in a domain-specific manner in conjunction with organizational needs and development constraints such as available tool support. Furthermore, hybrid solutions are often the most appropriate, exploiting the best features of various approaches for different parts of the system development. Consideration of such hybrid solutions and associated composition issues is a key element of ongoing research at Lancaster [19, 66]. We are of the view that these considerations should underpin the aspect-oriented software development process and that effective support for traceability from early aspects to later stages of design, implementation, and evolution should be integrated in such a hybrid environment. Only then can aspect-oriented techniques be exploited to their full potential to develop well-engineered aspect-oriented systems.

REFERENCES

1. ALDAWUD, O., BADER, A., AND ELRAD, T. 2002. Weaving with statecharts. In *Workshop on Aspect-Oriented Modeling with UML (AOSD)*, (Enschede, The Netherlands). http://lglwww.epfl.ch/workshops/aosd-uml/Allsubs/aldawud.pdf.

2. ANDREWS, J. H. 2001. Process-algebraic foundations of aspect-oriented programming. In *Metalevel Architectures and Separation of Crosscutting Concerns 3rd Int'l Conf. (Reflection 2001)*, (Kyoto), A. Yonezawa and S. Matsuoka, Eds. LNCS, vol. 2192. Springer-Verlag, Berlin, 187–209.

3. ASPECT-ORIENTED MODELING 2002. *Workshop on Aspect-Oriented Modeling with UML, (AOSD)*, (Enschede, The Netherlands). http://lglwww.epfl.ch/workshops/aosd-uml/index.html.

4. ASPECTC WEB PAGE. http://www.cs.ubc.ca/labs/spl/projects/aspectc.html.

5. ASPECTJ PROJECT. http://www.eclipse.org/aspectj/.

6. BAKER, J. AND HSIEH, W. 2002. Runtime aspect weaving through metaprogramming. In *1st Int'l Conf. Aspect-Oriented Software Development (AOSD)*, (Enschede, The Netherlands), G. Kiczales, Ed. ACM, 86–98.

7. BANIASSAD, E. AND CLARKE, S. 2004. Theme: An approach for aspect-oriented analysis and design. In *26th Int'l Conf. Software Engineering (ICSE)*, (Edinburgh, Scotland). IEEE, 158–167.

8. BERGMANS, L. AND AKŞIT, M. 2001. Composing crosscutting concerns using composition filters. *Comm. ACM 44*, 10 (Oct.), 51–57.

9. BLAIR, G. S., COULSON, G., ANDERSEN, A., BLAIR, L., CLARKE, M., COSTA, F., DURAN-LIMON, H., FITZPATRICK, T., JOHNSTON, L., MOREIRA, R., PARLAVANTZAS, N., AND SAIKOSKI, K. 2001. The design and implementation of OpenORB v2. *IEEE DS Online 2*, 6.

10. BLAIR, L. AND MONGA, M. 2003. Reasoning on AspectJ programmes. In *3rd German Informatics Society Workshop on Aspect-Oriented Software Development (AOSD-GI)*, (Essen, Germany). http://www.cs.uni-essen.de/dawis/conferences/GI_AOSD_2003/papers/Blair_Monga.pdf.

11. BÖLLERT, K. 1999. On weaving aspects. In *Int'l Workshop on Aspect-Oriented Programming (ECOOP)*, (Lisbon). http://trese.cs.utwente.nl/aop-ecoop99/papers/boellert.pdf.

12. BONÉR, J. 2004. What are the key issues for commercial AOP use–how does AspectWerkz address them? In *3rd Int'l Conf. Aspect-Oriented Software Development (AOSD)*, (Lancaster, UK), K. Lieberherr, Ed. ACM, 5–6.

13. BOYER, F., BOUCHENAK, S., PALMA, N. D., AND HAGIMONT, D. 2001. Aspects can be efficient: Experiences with replication and protection. Tech. Rep. 4651, INRIA.

14. BUDD, T. A. 1994. *Multiparadigm Programming in Leda*. Addison-Wesley, Reading, Massachusetts.

15. CALDER, M., KOLBERG, M., MAGILL, E. H., AND REIFF-MARGANIEC, S. 2003. Feature interaction: A critical review and considered forecast. *Computer Networks: The Int'l Journal of Computer and Telecommunications Networking 41*, 1, 115–141.

16. CALDER, M. AND MAGILL, E. H., Eds. 2000. *Feature Interactions in Telecommunications and Software Systems VI*. IOS Press, Amsterdam.

17. CASTRO, J. F., MYLOPOULOS, J., ALENCAR, F. M. R., AND CYSNEIROS FILHO, G. A. 2001. Integrating organizational requirements and object-oriented modeling. In *5th Int'l Symp. Requirements Engineering (RE)*, (Toronto). IEEE, 146–153.

18. CHIBA, S. 2000. Load-time structural reflection in Java. In *ECOOP 2000—Object-Oriented Programming: 14th European Conference*, (Cannes, France), E. Bertino, Ed. LNCS, vol. 1850. Springer-Verlag, Berlin, 313–336.

19. CHITCHYAN, R., SOMMERVILLE, I., AND RASHID, A. 2002. An analysis of design approaches for crosscutting concerns. In *Workshop on Identifying, Separating and Verifying Concerns in the Design (AOSD)*, (Enschede, The Netherlands). http://www.iit.edu/~akkawif/workshops/AOSD2002/03-chitchyan.pdf.

20. CLARKE, S., HARRISON, W., OSSHER, H., AND TARR, P. 1999. Subject-oriented design: Towards improved alignment of requirements, design and code. In *14th Conf. Object-Oriented Programming, Systems, Languages, and Applications (OOPSLA)*, (Denver). ACM, 325–339.

21. CLARKE, S. AND WALKER, R. J. 2001. Composition patterns: An approach to designing reusable aspects. In *23rd Int'l Conf. Software Engineering (ICSE)*, (Toronto). IEEE, 5–14.

22. CLARKE, S. AND WALKER, R. J. 2002. Towards a standard design language for AOSD. In *1st Int'l Conf. Aspect-Oriented Software Development (AOSD)*, (Enschede, The Netherlands), G. Kiczales, Ed. ACM, 113–119.

23. COPLIEN, J. O. 1999. *Multi-paradigm design for C++*. Addison-Wesley, Reading, Massachusetts.

24. CORBETT, J. C., DWYER, M. B., HATCLIFF, J., LAUBACH, S., PASAREANU, C. S., ROBBY, AND ZHENG, H. 2000. Bandera: Extracting finite-state models from Java source code. In *22nd Int'l Conf. Software Engineering (ICSE)*, (Limerick, Ireland). ACM, 439–448.

25. DARDENNE, A., VAN LAMSWEERDE, A., AND FICKAS, S. 1993. Goal-directed requirements acquisition. In *Selected Papers of the 6th Int'l Workshop on Software Specification and Design*. Science of Computer Programming 20(1-2), 3–50.

26. DE MEUTER, W. 1997. Monads as a theoretical foundation for AOP. In *Workshop on Aspect-Oriented Programming (ECOOP)*, (Jyväskylä, Finland). http://trese.cs.utwente.nl/aop-ecoop97/aop_papers/meuter.ps.

27. DE VOLDER, K., BRICHAU, J., MENS, K., AND D'HONDT, T. Logic meta-programming, a framework for domain-specific aspect languages. http://www.cs.ubc.ca/~kdvolder/binaries/cacm-aop-paper.pdf.

28. Douence, R., Fradet, P., and Südholt, M. 2002. A framework for the detection and resolution of aspect interactions. In *1st ACM Conf. Generative Programming and Component Engineering (GPCE)*, (Pittsburgh), D. S. Batory, C. Consel, and W. Taha, Eds. LNCS, vol. 2487. Springer-Verlag, Berlin, 173–188.

29. Douence, R., Motelet, O., and Südholt, M. 2001. A formal definition of crosscuts. In *Metalevel Architectures and Separation of Crosscutting Concerns 3rd Int'l Conf. (Reflection 2001)*, (Kyoto), A. Yonezawa and S. Matsuoka, Eds. LNCS, vol. 2192. Springer-Verlag, Berlin, 170–186.

30. Early Aspects 2002. *Workshop on Early Aspects: Aspect-Oriented Requirements Engineering and Architecture Design (AOSD)* 2002. (Enschede, The Netherlands). http://trese.cs.utwente.nl/AOSD-EarlyAspectsWS/Papers/AllEarlyAspects Papers.pdf.

31. Feature Interactions 2003. *Feature Interactions in Telecommunication and Software Systems, 7th Int'l Workshop,* (Ottawa), http://www.site.uottawa.ca/ fiw03/.

32. Finkelstein, A. and Sommerville, I. 1996. The viewpoints FAQ. *BCS/IEE Software Engineering Journal 11*, 1, 2–4.

33. Fradet, P. and Südholt, M. 1998. AOP: Towards a generic framework using program transformation and analysis. In *Workshop on Aspect-Oriented Programming (ECOOP)*, (Brussels). ftp://ftp.emn.fr/pub/objet/publications/ ecoop98/aop.ps.gz.

34. Grundy, J. 1999. Aspect-oriented requirements engineering for component-based software systems. In *4th Int'l Symp. Requirements Engineering* (Limerick, Ireland). IEEE, 84–91.

35. Grundy, J. 1999. Supporting aspect-oriented component-based systems engineering. In *11th Int'l Conf. Software Engineering and Knowledge Engineering (SEKE)*, (Kaiserslautern, Germany). Knowledge Systems Institute, Skokie, Illinois, 388–395.

36. Grundy, J. 2000. Multi-perspective specification, design and implementation of software components using aspects. *Int'l Journal of Software Engineering and Knowledge Engineering 20*, 6, 713–734.

37. Hall, J., Jackson, M., Laney, R., Nuseibeh, B., and Rapanotti, L. 2002. Relating software requirements and architectures using problem frames. In *Joint Int'l Conf. Requirements Engineering (RE)*, (Essen, Germany). IEEE, 137–144.

38. HALL, R. 2000. Feature interactions in electronic mail. In *Feature Interactions in Telecommunications and Software Systems VI*, M. Calder and E. Magill, Eds. IOS Press, Amsterdam, 67–82.

39. HERRERO, J. L., SÁNCHEZ, F., LUCIO, F., AND TORO, M. 2000. Introducing separation of aspects at design time. In *Workshop on Aspects and Dimensions of Concerns (ECOOP)*, (Cannes, France). http://trese.cs.utwente.nl/Workshops/adc2000/papers/Herrero.pdf.

40. HIRSCHFELD, R. AspectS home page. http://www.prakinf.tu-ilmenau.de/~hirsch/Projects/Squeak/AspectS/.

41. HO, W. M., PENNANEACH, F., JÉZÉQUEL, J.-M., AND PLOUZEAU, N. 2000. Aspect-oriented design with the UML. In *Workshop on Multi-Dimensional Separation of Concerns in Software Engineering (ICSE)*, (Limerick, Ireland). http://www.research.ibm.com/hyperspace/workshops/icse2000/Papers/ho.pdf.

42. IBM RESEARCH. Hyperspaces. http://www.research.ibm.com/hyperspace/.

43. JACKSON, M. 2000. *Problem Frames: Analyzing and Structuring Software Development Problems*. Addison-Wesley, Reading, Massachusetts.

44. JBOSS. Aspect-Oriented Programming. http://www.jboss.org/developers/projects/jboss/aop.

45. KATARA, M. AND MIKKONEN, T. 2001. Aspect-oriented specification architectures for distributed real-time systems. In *7th Int'l Conf. Engineering of Complex Computer Systems (ICECCS)*, (Skövde, Sweden). IEEE, 180–190.

46. KATARA, M. AND KATZ, S. 2003. Architectural views of aspects. In *2nd Int'l Conf. Aspect-Oriented Software Development (AOSD)*, (Boston), M. AKŞIT, Ed. ACM, 1–10.

47. KATZ, S. AND GIL, Y. 1999. Aspects and superimpositions. In *Int'l Workshop on Aspect-Oriented Programming (ECOOP)*, (Lisbon). http://trese.cs.utwente.nl/aop-ecoop99/papers/katz.pdf.

48. KATZ, S. AND RASHID, A. 2004. From aspectual requirements to proof obligations for aspect-oriented systems. In *12th IEEE Int'l Conf. Requirements Engineering (RE)*, (Kyoto). IEEE (To Appear).

49. KENENS, P., MICHIELS, S., MATTHIJS, F., ROBBEN, B., TRUYEN, E., VANHAUTE, B., JOOSEN, W., AND VERBAETEN, P. 1998. An AOP case with static and dynamic aspects. In *Workshop on Aspect-Oriented Programming (ECOOP)*, (Brussels). http://trese.cs.utwente.nl/aop-ecoop98/papers/Michiels.pdf.

50. KICZALES, G. 1992. Towards a new model of abstraction in software engineering. In *Int'l Workshop on New Models in Software Architecture, Reflection and Meta-Level Architecture*, (Tokyo). http://www.parc.xerox.com/spl/groups/eca/pubs/papers/Kiczales-IMSA92/for-web.pdf.

51. KICZALES, G., DES RIVIERES, J., AND BOBROW, D. G. 1991. *The Art of the Metaobject Protocol*. The MIT Press, Cambridge, Massachusetts.

52. KIMBLER, K. AND VELTHUIJSEN, H. 1995. Feature interaction benchmark (discussion paper for the panel on benchmarking). In *3rd Int'l Workshop on Feature Interactions in Telecommunications Software Systems*, (Kyoto). http://www.docs.uu.se/docs/fi/benchmark.ps.gz.

53. KLAEREN, H., PULVERMUELLER, E., RASHID, A., AND SPECK, A. 2000. Aspect composition applying the design by contract principle. In *2nd Int'l Symp. Generative and Component-Based Software Engineering (GCSE)*. LNCS, vol. 2177. Springer-Verlag, Berlin, 57–69.

54. KNIESEL, G., COSTANZA, P., AND AUSTERMANN, M. 2001. JMangler—A framework for load-time transformation of Java class files. In *1st Int'l Workshop on Source Code Analysis and Manipulation (SCAM)*, (Florence, Italy). IEEE, 98–108.

55. KON, F., COSTA, F., BLAIR, G. S., AND CAMPBELL, R. 2002. The case for reflective middleware: Building middleware that is flexible, reconfigurable, and yet simple to use. *Comm. ACM 45*, 6, 33–38.

56. LÄMMEL, R. 1999. Declarative aspect-oriented programming. In *Workshop on Partial Evaluation and Semantics-Based Program Manipulation (PEPM)*. ACM, 131–146.

57. LAMSWEERDE, A. 2001. Goal-oriented requirements engineering: A guided tour. In *5th Int'l Symp. Requirements Engineering (RE)*, (Toronto). IEEE, 249–261.

58. LIEBERHERR, K., ORLEANS, D., AND OVLINGER, J. 2001. Aspect-oriented programming with adaptive methods. *Comm. ACM 44*, 10 (Oct.), 39–41.

59. MOUSAVI, M., RUSSELLO, G., CHAUDRON, M., RENIERS, M. A., BASTEN, T., CORSARO, A., SHUKLA, S., GUPTA, R., AND SCHMID, D. 2002. Aspects + GAMMA = AspectGAMMA: A formal framework for aspect-oriented specification. In *Workshop on Early Aspects: Aspect-Oriented Requirements Engineering and Architecture Design (AOSD)*, (Enschede, The Netherlands). http://trese.cs.utwente.nl/AOSD-EarlyAspectsWS/Papers/AllEarlyAspectsPapers.pdf.

60. ORLEANS, D. AND LIEBERHERR, K. 2001. DJ: Dynamic adaptive programming in Java. In *Metalevel Architectures and Separation of Crosscutting Concerns 3rd Int'l*

Conf. (Reflection 2001), (Kyoto), A. Yonezawa and S. Matsuoka, Eds. LNCS, vol. 2192. Springer-Verlag, Berlin, 73–80.

61. OSSHER, H. AND TARR, P. 2001. Hyper/J: Multi-dimensional separation of concerns for Java. In *23rd Int'l Conf. Software Engineering (ICSE)*, (Toronto). IEEE, 729–730.

62. OSSHER, H. AND TARR, P. 2001. Multi-dimensional separation of concerns and the hyperspace approach. In *Software Architectures and Component Technology*, M. AKŞIT, Ed. Kluwer Academic Publishers, Boston, 293–323.

63. PANG, J. AND BLAIR, L. 2002. An adaptive run time manager for the dynamic integration and interaction resolution of features. In *2nd Int'l Workshop on Aspect Oriented Programming for Distributed Computing Systems (ICDCS), Vol. 2* (Vienna), M. AKŞIT and Z. Choukair, Eds. IEEE, 445–450.

64. PAWLAK, R., SEINTURIER, L., DUCHIEN, L., AND FLORIN, G. 2001. JAC: A flexible solution for aspect-oriented programming in Java. In *Metalevel Architectures and Separation of Crosscutting Concerns 3rd Int'l Conf. (Reflection 2001)*, (Kyoto), A. Yonezawa and S. Matsuoka, Eds. LNCS, vol. 2192. Springer-Verlag, Berlin, 1–24.

65. POPOVICI, A., GROSS, T., AND ALONSO, G. 2002. Dynamic weaving for aspect-oriented programming. In *1st Int'l Conf. Aspect-Oriented Software Development (AOSD)*, (Enschede, The Netherlands), G. Kiczales, Ed. ACM, 141–147.

66. RASHID, A. 2001. A hybrid approach to separation of concerns: The story of SADES. In *Metalevel Architectures and Separation of Crosscutting Concerns 3rd Int'l Conf. (Reflection 2001)*, (Kyoto), A. Yonezawa and S. Matsuoka, Eds. LNCS, vol. 2192. Springer-Verlag, Berlin, 231–249.

67. RASHID, A. 2002. Weaving aspects in a persistent environment. *ACM SIGPLAN Notices 37*, 2 (Feb.), 36–44.

68. RASHID, A., MOREIRA, A., AND ARAÚJO, J. 2003. Modularisation and composition of aspectual requirements. In *2nd Int'l Conf. Aspect-Oriented Software Development (AOSD)*, (Boston), M. AKŞIT, Ed. ACM, 11–20.

69. RASHID, A. AND SAWYER, P. 2001. Aspect-orientation and database systems: An effective customisation approach. *IEE Proceedings–Software 148*, 5 (Oct.), 156–164.

70. RASHID, A., SAWYER, P., MOREIRA, A., AND ARAUJO, J. 2002. Early aspects: A model for aspect-oriented requirements engineering. In *Joint Int'l Conf. Requirements Engineering (RE)*, (Essen, Germany). IEEE, 199–202.

71. SANTANDER, V. AND CASTRO, J. 2002. Deriving use cases from organizational modeling. In *Joint Int'l Conf. Requirements Engineering (RE)*, (Essen, Germany). IEEE, 32–39.

72. SCHMERL, B. AND GARLAN, D. 2002. Exploiting architectural design knowledge to support self-repairing systems. In *14th Int'l Conf. Software Engineering and Knowledge Engineering (SEKE)*, (Ischia, Italy). ACM, 241–248.

73. SCHULT, W. AND POLZE, A. 2002. Aspect-oriented programming with C# and .NET. In *Int'l Symp. Object-Oriented Real-time Distributed Computing (ISORC)*, (Washington, D.C.). IEEE, 241–248.

74. SIHMAN, M. AND KATZ, S. 2003. Superimpositions and aspect-oriented programming. *Computer Journal 46*, 5 (Sept.), 529–541.

75. SMITH, B. C. 1982. Procedural reflection in programming languages. Ph.D. thesis, MIT, Cambridge, MA.

76. SOMMERVILLE, I. AND SAWYER, P. 1997. *Requirements Engineering—A Good Practice Guide*. Wiley, New York.

77. SUZUKI, J. AND YAMAMOTO, Y. 1999. Extending UML with aspects: Aspect support in the design phase. In *Int'l Workshop on Aspect-Oriented Programming (ECOOP)*, (Lisbon). http://trese.cs.utwente.nl/aop-ecoop99/papers/suzuki.pdf.

78. SUZUKI, J. AND YAMAMOTO, Y. 1999. Toward the interoperable software design models: Quartet of UML, XML, DOM and CORBA. In *4th Int'l Software Engineering Standards Symposium*, (Curitiba, Brazil). IEEE, 163–172.

79. TARR, P., OSSHER, H., HARRISON, W., AND SUTTON JR., S. M. 1999. *N* degrees of separation: Multi-dimensional separation of concerns. In *21st Int'l Conf. Software Engineering (ICSE)*, (Los Angeles). IEEE, 107–119.

80. TRUYEN, E., JØRGENSEN, B. N., AND JOOSEN, W. 2000. Customization of object request brokers through dynamic reconfiguration. In *Tools Europe 2000*, (Mont-St-Michel, France). IEEE, 181–194.

81. TRUYEN, E., VANHAUTE, B., JOOSEN, W., VERBAETEN, P., AND JØRGENSEN, B. N. 2001. Dynamic and selective combination of extensions in component-based applications. In *23rd Int'l Conf. Software Engineering (ICSE)*, (Toronto). IEEE, 233–242.

82. UBAYASHI, N. AND TAMAI, T. 2002. Aspect-oriented programming with model checking. In *1st Int'l Conf. Aspect-Oriented Software Development (AOSD)*. (Enschede, The Netherlands), G. Kiczales, Ed. ACM, 148–154.

83. VAN DOREN, E. 1997. Maintenance of operational systems—an overview. Tech. rep., Software Technology Review, Carnegie Mellon Software Engineering Institute.

84. WATANABE, T. AND YONEZAWA, A. 1988. Reflection in an object-oriented concurrent language. In *3rd ACM Conf. Object-Oriented Programming, Systems, Languages, and Applications (OOPSLA)*, (San Diego, California). ACM, 306–315.

85. YOKOTE, Y. 1992. The Apertos reflective operating system: The concept and its implementation. In *7th Conf. Object-Oriented Programming, Systems, Languages, and Applications (OOPSLA)*, (Vancouver). ACM, 414–434.

86. YU, E. 1995. Modeling strategic relationships for process reengineering. Ph.D. thesis, University of Toronto.

Chapter 18

Aspect-Orientation in the Software Lifecycle: Fact and Fiction

PEDRO J. CLEMENTE, JUAN HERNÁNDEZ, JOSÉ LUIS HERRERO, JUAN MANUEL MURILLO, AND FERNANDO SÁNCHEZ

One of the advantages of aspect-oriented approaches is that they allow software developers to react easily to unanticipated changes in existing software systems, while promoting reusability of already tested and designed software components. Nevertheless, people are reluctant to apply AOP in serious and large projects, not because of a lack of good aspect-oriented programming languages and tools, but because they do not have aspect-oriented modeling and design techniques at their disposal. In this chapter, we share our experience from the national Spanish project "Reusable Software Components for Open Systems." One of the main lessons learned is that aspect-orientation should be taken into account in all the stages of the software lifecycle, in particular, the design level. We show the facts and fictions of AOP when using it with and without an aspect-oriented design. The reader is introduced to aspect-oriented design techniques using two different approaches: an extension to UML and an extension to architectural description languages. While the first approach is relatively mature, the second can be considered an ongoing project that has already produced some significant results. In both cases, software developers have a better understanding of the aspect-oriented system to be developed. This has reduced the developers' fears about applying AOSD techniques.

18.1 INTRODUCTION

As software technology becomes a core part of business enterprises, customers demand a wider range of software systems. This demand coincides with the increasing use of personal computers and today's easy access to local and global communication networks, which together constitute an excellent framework for building complex open distributed systems.

However, quickly producing such systems challenges software developers, whose traditional methods and tools are proving inadequate to the task of coping with new requirements. Enterprise software developers recognize that they cannot address all of a product's requirements in its first release. They will have to deal with numerous revisions during the product's lifetime. This situation, which mainly involves functional extensions, is even harder to manage when the multiplicity of concerns magnifies the application complexity. In order to maintain aggressive profit margins, software companies must reduce their costs when developing new systems. In this new setting, features such as software reusability, adaptability, flexibility, and evolution are becoming mandatory, representing today's major challenges of the software development process.

During the last few years, aspect-oriented programming has emerged as an appropriate technology for developing systems that have to deal with such complexity. One of the main advantages of AOSD approaches is that they allow software developers to react easily to unanticipated changes in existing software systems, while promoting reusability of already tested and designed software components. In this chapter, the results obtained within the national Spanish project "Reusable Software Components for Open Systems" are presented. In the context of this project, aspect-oriented programming models and techniques [11, 13] have been developed to deal with common crosscutting concerns in open distributed systems including issues relating to middleware platforms, coordination, synchronization, exception handling, and thread management. Our experience shows that traditional programmers beginning to use aspect-oriented programming models have difficulties until they acquire the necessary expertise. This is mainly due to the fact that although one can have the best programming models and tools aimed for AOP such as Hypert/J [12], AspectJ [9], or Composition Filters [4], they will never be easily applicable if the software system being developed was designed without considering aspect-oriented concepts. In such cases, the programmer will have to redesign some parts of the system to introduce separation of crosscutting concerns. In many organizations, changing the design is explicitly not a programmer's responsibility.

Although the results obtained from the project were relevant enough from the programming level point of view, we would like to emphasize the main lesson learned: aspect-orientation should be taken into account in earlier stages of the software lifecycle.

In the same way that there is a structured software lifecycle or an object-oriented software lifecycle, we argue that an aspect-oriented software lifecycle is needed. For example, UML was created to provide object-oriented and component-based modeling.

But, where is the methodology that allows aspect-oriented modeling? We have good tools for aspect-orientation at the programming level, but how should aspect-oriented systems be designed and modeled? Once the system has been designed and implemented, is there a correspondence between design and implementation? How do future changes affect both parts? In this chapter, we present our results on these problems. We introduce the reader to aspect-oriented concepts at the design level using two different approaches: an extension of UML with an aspect profile and the introduction of new primitives in architectural description languages (ADLs) to support aspect definition and composition.

The rest of the chapter is structured as follows: In Section 18.2, a case study is presented to highlight the main disadvantages of using AOP without an aspect-oriented design. Section 18.3 outlines the two different approaches we have followed to consider aspects at the design level. Finally, the main ideas presented in the chapter are summarized in Section 18.4.

18.2   ASPECTS AT IMPLEMENTATION LEVEL

The aim of this section is twofold: to describe both the benefits provided by AOP at the implementation level and the drawbacks of using AOP at the implementation level without an aspect-oriented design. For this purpose, we use a simple case study based on the behavior of a broker and its interaction with stock markets and clients. At the end of the section, the reader should conclude that, although aspect-oriented programming help programmers to avoid code tangling at the programming level, aspect-orientation should also be taken into account at the design level.

18.2.1   *Motivating Example*

The case study we have chosen is a simplified version of an online broker interacting with stock markets and clients. The client orders the broker to carry out operations, and the broker interacts with the stock market to buy or sell shares, depending on the client request. In this scenario, three different entities are considered: `Client`, `Broker`, and `StockMarket`. Figure 18-1 illustrates a simplified version of the UML class diagram for this example. Only `Broker` and `StockMarket` classes are shown.

The `Client` is only interested in buying and selling shares. For this purpose, the `Broker` provides the operation `registerOrder` with parameters (not shown in the diagram) to specify the type of the operation (buy or sell), the identification of the company, the number of shares, and an activation condition. The last parameter represents a condition under which the shares have to be bought or sold. The user chooses this condition, normally based on the situation of the market at a given time. A typical example could be "buy X shares of company Y when its value is less than Z." This is the reason why the `StockMarket` class provides an operation to set an alarm and the `Broker` class provides an operation to be informed when this alarm has been triggered so it can perform the required order. Whenever the user invokes `registerOrder`, the broker replicates its state for fault tolerance reasons. When the operation is completed, the state is replicated again. An `ack()` method is provided at the `Broker` side so that it can be kept informed about the details of the operation performed by the `StockMarket`. Distribution-related issues and others are left out for simplicity.

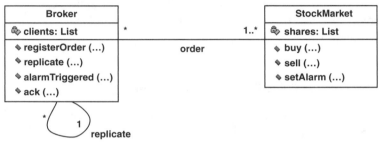

Figure 18-1   *UML class diagram for the Broker example.*

Figure 18-2 shows a sequence diagram for the case in which the client wants to give an order constrained by a condition.

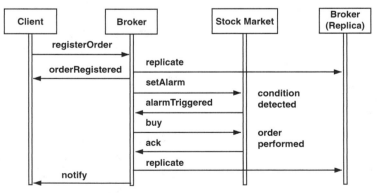

Figure 18-2   *Sequence diagram for buying shares.*

From Figure 18-1 and Figure 18-2, it is easy to see the crosscutting among classes. For example, the methods `setAlarm()` and `alarmTriggered()` are only for coordination purposes. In addition, the `replicate()` method is only for replication issues.

The coordination property cuts across the `Broker` and `StockMarket` classes, while the replication property cuts across different instances of the `Broker` class. Dealing with these properties using conventional languages like Java results in spreading code through many components. In this situation, the source code becomes a tangled mess of instructions for different purposes. A direct implementation in Java or other languages would lead to a set of entities (objects, components, or others) that have the same interface shown in Figure 18-1. This solution would not only hinder reasoning about individual concerns but would also affect features such as reusability, adaptability, and the other -ilities mentioned in Section 18.1.

An AOP approach suggests separating coordination and replication issues to different entities. At the programming level, software developers may choose among different aspect-oriented programming languages and models, such as Hyper/J, AspectJ, or Composition Filters, just to cite a few.

No matter which model is chosen, the appearance of the final application is outlined in Figure 18-3. Although the figure would be the same for many AOP models, AspectJ is used here as a reference for its explanation. The figure shows an overview of the AspectJ code for the case study, merging different elements such as the interfaces of the classes, the placement of join points, and AspectJ pseudocode for those join points.

This code is quite different from that obtained when using traditional development techniques. First of all, the interface of the two classes involved has changed. At the top of the figure, you can see how only those methods related to the functional behavior now belong to the interface. Those methods related to coordination and replication have disappeared. That code is now encapsulated in two different entities called aspects (*Replica* and *Alarm*) (rectangles in the figure). Pseudocode of these aspects using AspectJ can be seen at the bottom of the figure. Different pointcuts are defined in each aspect. Each pointcut defines a set of places in which aspect code has to be injected. The point of execution in which the aspect code should be executed is specified by advice (before and after in this case). Circles in the figure represent the join points between the functional code and the aspect code. For example, the `Apply_Replica` pointcut specifies that after the execution of methods `registerOrder()` and `ack()`, the `replicate()` method must be executed.

Summarizing, code related to crosscutting concerns is separated from functional code. Using the mechanisms provided by AO languages, we can implement the behavior of such concerns in a single modular unit. In the case of AspectJ, the aspect programming construction is the modular unit in charge of encapsulating crosscutting concerns, and it consists of a combination of join points (grouped by the pointcut construction) and advices, besides conventional Java primitives.

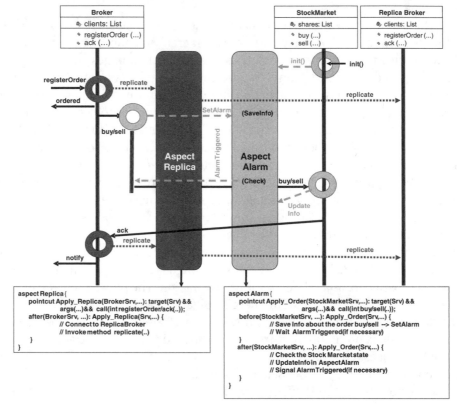

Figure 18-3 *An overview of an AspectJ solution for the case study.*

This AOP implementation simplifies reasoning about the different concerns involved in the behavior of the system. It also improves reusability and adaptability of the different aspects. In summary, the evolution of the implementation is made easier. In the example, changes to the coordination or replication aspects are well localized. Moreover, and depending on the chosen AOP model, it may also be possible to make the changes without stopping the application and re-running it. In this way, things are 'easier' for the programmer.

18.2.2   AOP: Fact and Fiction

The previous example shows the benefits provided by AOP in the software development process: The different aspects intervening in the application have been separated, and therefore productivity is increased while development time and cost are decreased. As such, AOP is coping with the initial requirements of short time-to-market and software evolvability. These are the AOP facts.

Unfortunately, our experience tells us that there is another part of the story: AOP fictions. The *wonderful world* described previously is only an illusion. In fact, the reality is quite different. One begins to realize this when observing what has happened in the example from the point of view of software design: the designer gave a specification to the programmer, and then the programmer was forced to change the design of the application to introduce separation of crosscutting concerns. This has the following negative consequences:

1. As the programmer has changed (part of) the design, coherence with the original overall design cannot be guaranteed. The programmer only has a partial view of the whole system. He doesn't know whether the changes he is introducing are compatible with other parts of the system or not. The problem could be even worse if other programmers are introducing changes as well. For example, the methods `setAlarm()` and `alarmTriggered()` have disappeared from the class interfaces established in Figure 18-1. Other programmers cannot rely on that design to develop their tasks simply because those methods are not available anymore.

2. Owing to the changes introduced by the programmer, the implementation of the system does not correspond with the original design. There is a lack of coherence between implementation and design. Maintenance and evolution of the system becomes difficult. How are the aspect-related changes introduced by the programmer at the implementation level reflected in the design? Thus, the benefit of easier software evolution, one of the main claims of AOP, is reduced.

3. Using AOP, the task of the programmer has been harder than using conventional techniques. In fact, in addition to his normal task, he has been forced to implicitly redesign the system. Thus, the benefit of improved programmer's productivity, one of the claims features of AOP, is reduced.[1]

4. Using AOP, the programmer assumes responsibilities that clearly belong to the designer. This could lead to problems when things go wrong. Who is then

---

1. In our experience, when programmers begin to use aspect-oriented tools, their productivity decreases significantly. This is due not only to the learning curve associated with using a new tool, but also to the cost of having to implicitly redesign the system in the adequate way. At the programming level, a programmer has to discover what different concerns he has to deal with and what concerns cut across groups of functional components in order for them to be encapsulated in the aspect entity.

responsible for this? The programmer or the designer? We experienced this problem when implementing a real AOP version of the case study.

All these problems are a consequence of not having appropriate design techniques. Since the designer has no design tools to specify whether crosscutting concerns must be separated, which crosscutting concerns must be separated, or how crosscutting concerns must be separated, all these responsibilities fall upon the programmer. The lesson learned must not be that AOP should be avoided. AOP complements current programming techniques such as OOP by offering a new concept/entity, the aspect, which captures crosscutting concerns in a modular way. If we want to use AOP in real software projects where several programmers are involved, aspect-oriented design techniques must be provided.

The next section outlines the two different but complementary approaches we have followed for aspect-oriented design.

18.3   ASPECTS AT DESIGN LEVEL

The aim of this section is to demonstrate how the problems stated previously can be overcome by obtaining a correspondence between implementation and design. To achieve this, two different approaches have been followed in our group. The first is extending UML with an aspect profile. In this profile, each aspect is represented with a new stereotype. With this, a notation to describe the behavior of a system based on aspects is provided. However, with UML, there is no way to make formal specifications. This is a requirement for different parts of several systems. In these cases, we introduce aspects at the architectural level.

In Section 18.3.1, using the broker example, we present a rough description of the UML extension. In Section 18.3.2, we outline the work on software architectures and aspects.

18.3.1   Aspects in UML

Although UML does not directly provide elements to define aspects, its semantics can be extended by introducing new *stereotypes, constraints,* and *tagged values.* In the last several years, different approaches to introducing the notion of aspects in UML have been followed. The most recent can be seen in [2]. In [14], a new stereotype is provided to specify aspects, but in a generic way. This stereotype does not provide elements to specify the meaning of individual and real aspects. In [8], three new stereotypes are considered to describe specific aspects: synchronization, distribution, and replication. In [6], aspects are represented as packages that contain standard design models to represent the structure and behavior of the aspect. Extensions to the UML's notion of templates are used to represent those points in a base design where the aspect should be weaved. A new kind of relationship, the *composition relationship,* is used to specify how the aspect should be composed with a base design model. However, in all these cases (and others such as those proposed in [5, 10]), there is a direct extension of the UML metamodel. There appears to have been no explicit effort in any of these approaches to ensure that the extensions (e.g., new stereotypes or metamodel elements) are localized or grouped within the metamodel. This makes understanding the new language constructs at the metamodel level more difficult. An alternative to this view is describing aspects with stereotypes but grouping them in a profile. In [1], the specification of a UML aspect profile is proposed. This work defines the aspect concept in a general way, without specifying the meaning of the new metamodel entities when designing different kinds of aspects. This is the approach we follow in our project, but we include new elements in order to specify different kinds of aspects.

A profile is a predefined set of stereotypes, constraints, and tagged values that specializes UML in a specific domain. A profile does not include additional basic elements. Conversely, it offers mechanisms that help in the application of UML to different domains. In our case, a new UML profile has been created for the application of UML to the generic domain of aspects. To be more precise, four aspects are considered: *synchronization, distribution, replication,* and *coordination.* This new profile has been called Aspect Profile (see Figure 18-4). The first element defined in this profile is a stereotype called <<Aspect>>. It contains a reference to the class or classes with which it is associated. This stereotype is based on the *classifier element* from the *core package.* Deriving from it, there are stereotypes for the aspects of synchronization, replication, distribution, and coordination. Each aspect has its own attributes. Every aspect is associated with one or more classifiers. A class can be related to zero or more aspects. The type of association between a class and an aspect specifies the composition between both elements. The composition stereotypes are based on the *relationship element* from the core package. Because coordination is a more complicated aspect, there are different composition stereotypes for this aspect. These stereotypes are based on the event notifications needed for coordination [11].

When representing a particular aspect, different issues have to be taken into account—on one hand, the static structure and dynamic behavior of the aspect, and on the other hand, the association between classes and their aspects. Next we show how UML has been extended to consider these three issues. Figure 18-5 supports the explanation and illustrates an aspect-oriented solution to the broker example using the proposed UML extension.

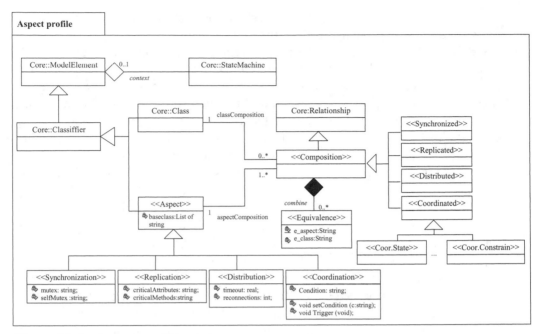

Figure 18-4 *Aspect profile.*

Static structure of aspects. The static structure defines the internal elements of an aspect: attributes and methods. For example, in Figure 18-5, the `<<Replication>>` stereotype contains the set of replicas and the `replicate()` method.

Dynamic behavior of aspects. It is not possible to represent aspect behavior in a normal class diagram. We attach a state chart diagram to an aspect stereotype to represent its behavior. The meaning of the state chart element varies depending on the aspect. In Figure 18-5, the state chart diagram specifies that the broker replicates its state whenever five requests have arrived at the broker. (This somewhat unrealistic situation serves for our purpose.)

Composition mechanism. The association between a class and its aspects is represented by a stereotype. In Figure 18-5, you can see three of them: `<<Replicated>>`, `<<Coord.Constrain>>`, and `<<Coord.State>>`.[2] Other stereotypes exist for distribution issues and other types of notification events. The composition mechanism allows the binding between signatures of methods when necessary.

---

2. They are based on *abstraction dependency* from core package.

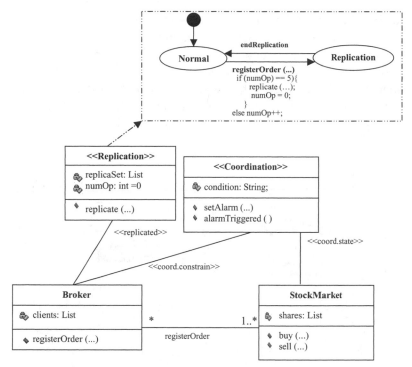

Figure 18-5 *The example with the UML extension.*

18.3.2 Aspects from the Software Architecture Perspective

Another alternative to dealing with aspect-oriented design is concerned with description issues at the level of the software architecture. Although this work is still at an early stage, the first results are being obtained.

Currently, software architects do not have tools to adequately deal with the separation of crosscutting concerns when specifying the architecture of software systems. Current architectural description languages (ADLs) do not provide primitives to specify aspects. Using ADLs, software architects are able to specify the functionality of the system by means of components and the interaction between components by means of connectors. For example, to specify the structure of the broker example from Section 18.2.1, the software architect would introduce two components (`Broker` and `StockMarket`) with their ports and would specify the interaction among them using connectors. However, some concerns (like `Replica` and `Alarm`) cut across the structure of the system. Such concerns must be understood as property specifications crosscutting the description of components and connectors.[3] In order to separately specify such concerns, new elements are required in the ADL. Figure 18-6 shows the specification of the broker example using AO-ADL.[4] The top of the figure (white area) shows how the software architect has specified the `Broker` and the `StockMarket` components and the interaction between them through ports. White ports represent "in" ports, while black ports represent "out" ports. Each connector (`Buy_Order`, `Sell_Order`, and `Buy/Sell_Done`) specifies a complex interaction.

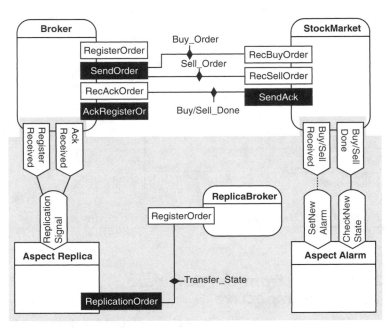

Figure 18-6 *The example using AO-ADL.*

The bottom of Figure 18-6 (grey area) shows some of the elements that our approach introduces to manage the separated specification of crosscutting concerns at the software architecture level. In particular, the figure shows the alternative

---

3. In fact, this is what we mean by crosscutting concern at the software architecture level.

4. AO-ADL is the name given to the aspect-oriented ADL produced by our research project.

followed to separate the `Replica` and `Alarm` aspects (from Figure 18-3) using AO-ADL. The capabilities supported by AO-ADL can be summarized as follows:

1. *Specification of components with interfaces and connections between interfaces.* This functionality is already provided by current ADLs. However, AO-ADL adds a new capability for specifying join points. To support this, we introduce new primitives, allowing the specification of any join point without restriction to a predefined model.[5] Such join points specify the points in which the description of the separated concerns must be "injected." In Figure 18-6, two join points are specified for `Broker`. `RegisterReceived` and `AckReceived` determine the moment in which any input is detected at the `RegisterOrder` and `RecAckOrder` ports, respectively. The aspect `Replica` will affect the `Broker` component at these two points. For `StockMarket`, two join points have been specified as well. `Buy/SellReceived` determines the moment in which any input is detected at the `RecBuyOrder` or `RecSellOrder` ports, while `Buy/SellDone` determines the exact moment in which any output is detected at the `SendAck` port. In this case, these points will be affected by the aspect `Alarm`.

2. *Specification of aspects.* Aspects are the new elements introduced by AO-ADL to modularize the description of the separated crosscutting concerns. Although aspects encapsulate the description of some functionality of the system, they have both a different meaning and a different structure that components. In order to modularize crosscutting concerns, aspects are described with new primitives. Each aspect specifies a set of roles corresponding to the different join points they can affect. The final purpose is to specify *what, when,* and *how* aspect behavior should happen at each join point. This is managed in AO-ADL through a refinement process in which the aspect is totally specified. Figure 18-6 shows the aspects stated by the software architect at the beginning of the process. At this point, the software architect has specified that two aspects are required: `Replica` and `Alarm`. He has also specified the join points affected by such aspects. The connections between join points and roles determine *how* the functionality stated by the aspects operates. A continuous line denotes an asynchronous operation: when the component arrives at the join point, both the component and aspect descriptions will operate asynchronously. A discontinuous line denotes a synchronous operation; that is, when the component arrives at the join point, the flow control interpreting the description of the system will be transferred to the

---

5. We consider that any moment in the life of a system component is capable of being a join point.

aspect, and then it returns to the component. The design of the replication and alarm crosscutting concerns illustrated in Figure 18-6 is the same as that in Figure 18-3. First, the decision to replicate the state of `Broker` is based on the interception of input at the `RegisterOrder` and `RecAckOrder` ports. Next, input at the `RecBuyOrder` or `RecSellOrder` ports is intercepted and blocked until the `StockMarket` is in the correct state. Finally, output at the `SendAck` port is intercepted awaiting a check of the new state of the `StockMarket`. It is important to note that although this is a high-level design, the software architect is implicitly choosing to model crosscutting concerns separately. However, nothing is stated about the internal modularization of the aspects or the AOP language that should be used to implement the software system. In later steps, the aspects will be designed in detail. At this stage, the software architect is able to reason about and include a high-level specification of aspects, making his task easier. Figure 18-7 shows the aspects for the `StockMarket` system in a later stage of design. At this point, the functionality to be injected at the join points (*what* must happen) has been specified through connectors (describing *when* it must happen). The functionality has also been modularized into components. The next step is the specification of the connectors' behaviors.

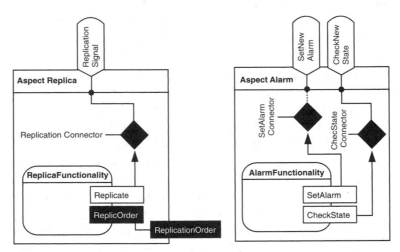

Figure 18-7 *Description of aspects.*

3. *Specification of connectors between join points and aspects.* The purpose of such connectors is to relate the specifications of the whole system. The objective is to maintain coherence with the original system (in which aspects were crosscutting its structure), preserving its semantic. So, such connectors specify *when* and *how*

each aspect occurs. Coordination models and languages already solve a similar problem [7]. In particular, exogenous coordination models such as [3, 11] specify two kinds of components: *functional components* that specify the functionality of the systems and *coordination components* that specify how functional components must coordinate. Coordination components determine when and how the actions implemented by functional components must be performed. The same scheme is being used here. In this model, the functional components are either components that specify the functionality of the system or components (inside each aspect, like `ReplicaFunctionality` or `AlarmFunctionality`) that specify the functionality to be applied at each join point. The coordination components are the connectors between join points and such functionality. These connectors determine two things—first, how (synchronously or asynchronously) the descriptions of functionality and the separated crosscutting concerns must be interleaved in order to obtain the original desired behavior, and second, when (under what condition) they must be interleaved.

For example, in Figure 18-7, the specification of the `Replication` connector states that each time that the `ReplicationSignal` role is applicable (in fact, every time the `Broker` arrives to the `RegisterReceived` or the `AckReceived` join points), the `Replicate` functionality executes. The `SetAlarm` connector states that when the `SetNewAlarm` role is applicable, the `SetAlarm` functionality executes. Additionally, this connector checks the current state of the market and blocks the execution of the service that made the role applicable (`Sell` or `Buy`) until the market satisfies the conditions to buy or sell. As the reader can see, connectors can be complex entities.

Continuing this process, the software architect deals with the detailed design of the system. When it is done, he will be able to give precise guidelines to the programmer about how to manage the separation of crosscutting concerns in the system. In this way, the problems stated in Section 18.2.2 are avoided.

18.4 CONCLUSION

This chapter has illustrated the main lessons learned from the application of AOSD techniques to a real project. Although AOP has important advantages for implementation, to get the real benefit of aspect-oriented technology requires incorporating aspects early in the software lifecycle. Aspects are particularly critical in design. We have examined two different design techniques for aspects: an informal one that extends UML with an aspect profile and a formal one that incorporates aspects in software architectures. The first approach is relatively mature; the second is an ongoing research project that has nevertheless yielded some significant results.

ACKNOWLEDGMENTS

This work has been developed with the support of Spanish Ministry of Science and Technology under contracts TIC99-1083-C02-02 and TIC2002-04309-C02-01.

REFERENCES

1. ALDAWUD, O., ELRAD, T., AND BADER, A. 2003. UML profile for aspect oriented software development. In *3rd Int'l Workshop on Aspect-Oriented Modeling (AOSD)*, (Boston). http://lglwww.epfl.ch/workshops/aosd2003/papers/Aldawud AOSD_UML_Profile.pdf.

2. ALDAWUD, O., KANDÉ, M., BOOCH, G., HARRISON, B., STEIN, D., GRAY, J., CLARKE, S., ZAKANIA, A., TARR, P., AND AKKAWI, F. Eds. 2003. *The 4th Int'l Workshop on Aspect-Oriented Modeling with UML*, (UML), (San Francisco). http://www.cs.iit.edu/~oaldawud/AOM.

3. ARBAB, F. AND MAVADDAT, F. 2002. Coordination through channel composition. In *5th Int'l Conf. Coordination Models and Languages*, (York, U.K.), F. Arbab and C. Talcott, Eds. LNCS, vol. 2315. Springer-Verlag, Berlin, 22–39.

4. BERGMANS, L. AND AKŞIT, M. 2001. Composing crosscutting concerns using composition filters. *Comm. ACM 44*, 10 (Oct.), 51–57.

5. CHÁVEZ, C. AND LUCENA, C. 2002. A metamodel for aspect-oriented modeling. In *Workshop on Aspect-Oriented Modeling with UML (AOSD)*, (Enschede, The Netherlands). http://lglwww.epfl.ch/workshops/aosd-uml/Allsubs/aspUML.pdf.

6. CLARKE, S. 2002. Extending standard UML with model composition semantics. *Science of Computer Programming 44*, 1, 71–100.

7. DE NICOLA, R., FERRARI, G., AND MEREDITH, G. Eds. 2004. The *6th Int'l Conf. Coordination Models and Languages*, (Pisa, Italy). LNCS, vol. 2949. Springer-Verlag, Berlin.

8. HERRERO, J. L., SÁNCHEZ, F., LUCIO, F., AND TORO, M. 2000. Introducing separation of aspects at design time. In *Workshop on Aspects and Dimensions of Concerns (ECOOP)*, (Cannes, France). http://trese.cs.utwente.nl/Workshops/adc2000/papers/Herrero.pdf.

9. KICZALES, G., HILSDALE, E., HUGUNIN, J., KERSTEN, M., PALM, J., AND GRISWOLD, W. G. 2001. An overview of AspectJ. In *ECOOP 2001—Object-Oriented Programming, 15th European Conference*, (Budapest), J. L. Knudsen, Ed. LNCS, vol. 2072. Springer-Verlag, Berlin, 327–353.

10. LIONS, J. M., SIMONEAU, D., PITETTE, G., AND MOUSSA, I. 2002. Extending OpenTool/UML using metamodeling: An aspect-oriented programming case study. In *2nd Int'l Workshop on Aspect-Oriented Modeling with UML (AOSD)*, (Boston). http://lglwww.epfl.ch/workshops/uml2002/papers/lions.pdf.

11. MURILLO, J. M., HERNÁNDEZ, J., SÁNCHEZ, F., AND ÁLVAREZ, L. A. 1999. Coordinated roles: Promoting reusability of coordinated active objects using events notification protocols. In *3rd Int'l Conf. COORDINATION '99*, (Amsterdam), P. Ciancarini and A. L. Wolf, Eds. LNCS, vol. 1594. Springer-Verlag, Berlin.

12. OSSHER, H. AND TARR, P. 2001. The shape of things to come: Using multi-dimensional separation of concerns with Hyper/J to (re)shape evolving software. *Comm. ACM 44*, 10 (Oct.), 43–50.

13. SÁNCHEZ, F., HERNÁNDEZ, J., MURILLO, J. M., RODRÍGUEZ, R. AND HERRERO, J. L. 2000. Adaptability of object distribution protocols using the disguises model approach. In *Int'l Symp. Distributed Objects and Applications (DOA)*, (Antwerp, Belgium). IEEE, 315–324.

14. SUZUKI, J. AND YAMAMOTO, Y. 1999. Extending UML with aspects: Aspect support in the design phase. In *Int'l Workshop on Aspect-Oriented Programming (ECOOP)*, (Lisbon). http://trese.cs.utwente.nl/aop-ecoop99/papers/suzuki.pdf.

Chapter 19

Generic Aspect-Oriented Design with Theme/UML

SIOBHÁN CLARKE AND ROBERT J. WALKER

Requirements such as distribution or tracing have an impact on multiple classes in a system. Their support is, by necessity, scattered across those multiple classes. A look at an individual class may also show support for such crosscutting requirements (or *aspects*) tangled up with the core responsibilities of that class. Scattering and tangling make object-oriented software difficult to understand, extend, and reuse.

Though design is an important activity within the software lifecycle with well-documented benefits, those benefits are reduced when crosscutting requirements are present. This chapter presents a means to mitigate these problems with Theme/UML. Theme/UML is an extension to standard UML to support the modularization of designs into "themes." A theme is any feature, concern, or requirement of interest that must be handled in the system. This chapter focuses on themes that provide a design for behavior that crosscuts other behavior in the design. This chapter also demonstrates how crosscutting themes map to AspectJ and Hyper/J, two implementation approaches that provide a solution for separation of crosscutting requirements in source code. This mapping serves to illustrate that separation of aspects may be maintained throughout the software lifecycle.

19.1 INTRODUCTION

Software design is an important activity within the software lifecycle, and its benefits are well documented [6, 7]. These include early assessment of the technical feasibility, correctness, and completeness of requirements, management of complexity and enhanced comprehension, greater opportunities for reuse, and improved evolvability.

However, in practice, object-oriented design models have been less useful throughout the lifetime of software systems than these benefits suggest. As described in [4], a structural mismatch between requirements specifications and object-oriented software specifications causes a reduction in the expected benefits of design. A single requirement, such as distribution or synchronization, may impact a number of classes in a system, and therefore its support is *scattered* across those multiple classes. Such requirements are described as *crosscutting* requirements, or *aspects* [15]. On the other hand, a single class in a system may show support for multiple requirements *tangled* with the core responsibilities of that class. Scattering and tangling have a negative impact across the development lifecycle with respect to comprehensibility, traceability, evolvability, and reusability.

The *theme design model* [2, 4] removes this structural mismatch with decomposition capabilities that support the separation of the design for each requirement into different design models (called *themes*). Decomposition in this manner removes requirement scattering and tangling properties from software design, thereby also removing their negative impact. Corresponding composition capabilities are supported within the theme design model.

The primary contribution of this chapter is the specification of a means to capture *reusable crosscutting behavior* at the design level with *crosscutting themes*. A crosscutting theme is a design model that specifies the design of a crosscutting requirement independently from any design it may potentially crosscut and how that design may be reused wherever it may be required. Theme/UML provides a means to compose separate, potentially overlapping designs. Crosscutting themes differ from other kinds of themes in that they utilize *templates* (which are parameterized design elements, similar to those found in C++) from Unified Modeling Language (UML) [17]. Support for design themes require non-trivial changes to UML, resulting in an extended language called Theme/UML. Theme/UML includes changes to the UML meta-model, described elsewhere [3]. Section 19.2 motivates the need for modularizing crosscutting concerns at design time and gives some background on the theme design model. The model for designing themes that crosscut the rest of the design is described in Section 19.3, with Section 19.4 providing examples of well-known crosscutting behaviors, designed to be truly reusable.

A secondary contribution is an introduction to how two implementation approaches that support crosscutting behavior (AspectJ [14] and Hyper/J [23]) are supported at the design level by crosscutting themes. This support serves to illustrate that separation of aspects may be maintained throughout the software lifecycle. Suggested mappings to constructs in Hyper/J are illustrated in Section 19.5; those to constructs in AspectJ are illustrated in Section 19.6. Sections 19.7 and 19.8 present related work and conclusions, respectively.

19.2 MOTIVATION

To motivate the need for modularizing the design of behavior that crosscuts other behaviors, we use the simple example of requiring that operations be traced at runtime. Tracing is a particularly pervasive requirement that potentially impacts every operation in every class of a system. Without a means to separate its design, the potential for scattering and tangling across a system is enormous. A simplified design for tracing an operation in class X is contained in Figure 19-1 (using UML [17]).

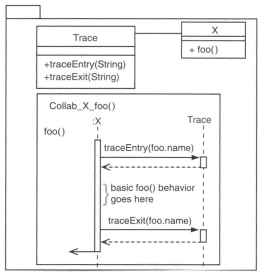

Figure 19-1 *Pervasive trace design.*

From a structural design perspective, the design elements supporting tracing may be separated into a class, `Trace`, upon which any class requiring trace behavior may depend. However, to design the trace behavior of operations, this separation is not possible to maintain. In the interaction diagram, we see that when the `foo()` operation of class X is invoked, it immediately calls the `traceEntry()` operation of class `Trace` with a parameter denoting the name of the entered method, i.e., `foo`. Likewise, when the `foo()` operation has finished and is about to return, it finally calls the `traceExit()` operation of class `Trace`. Any other operations requiring trace behavior would need to be designed analogously.

This design has a number of difficulties. First, any new operation requiring trace behavior must specify an interaction model indicating this—a tedious and error-prone process. Secondly, changing or eliminating the trace behavior design requires changes to all operation interaction models. Finally, reuse of this design in a different system is not straightforward. Structurally, the `Trace` class may simply be copied, but the trace behavior must be redefined in the interaction specification of each operation to be traced.

These problems are mitigated by modularizing the design for crosscutting behavior into a theme. In particular, when modularized, crosscutting behavior specifications can be easily reused in different circumstances.

19.3   CROSSCUTTING THEMES: THE MODEL

Themes that specify designs for crosscutting requirements were introduced, without in-depth discussion, as part of Theme/UML in [4]. Theme/UML supports separate design models as independent views called *design themes* (denoted with a «theme» stereotype on a UML package). Within the model, design themes may specify crosscutting behavior to be composed with other design themes. Crosscut elements are not referred to directly by name, but are reasoned about within the design through the use of parameterized elements. A composition specification mechanism is provided to bind those parameters to "real" elements that will be crosscut. Composition specification is achieved with Theme/UML's composition relationship that allows the designer to identify those parts of the theme designs that are related to each other and that therefore should be composed.

19.3.1   Specifying Templates

The UML defines a template as a parameterized model element that cannot be used directly in a design model [17]. Instead, it may be used as the basis to generate other model elements using a "Binding" dependency relationship. A Binding relationship defines arguments to replace each of the template parameters of the template model element. The UML orders template parameters in a dotted box on the template class. Since a crosscutting theme may potentially have multiple *pattern classes* (classes that are themselves placeholders to be replaced by real class elements), the representation of all the template parameters for all pattern classes is combined in a single box and placed on the theme box. Within this box, template parameters are grouped by class (each class grouped within <> brackets), and ordering is important to support composition specification.

Figure 19-2 illustrates a crosscutting theme with one pattern class, `TracedClass`, denoting that any class may be supplemented with trace behavior. A template parameter is defined for the pattern class, called `_tracedOp()`, which represents any operation requiring tracing behavior. One standard class, called

`Trace`, is also included in the design. The design of tracing behavior is now contained in the `Trace` theme model, with references made to the pattern class and template operation as required.

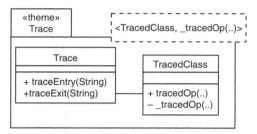

Figure 19-2 *Specifying templates in a `Trace` composition pattern.*

19.3.2 Specifying Crosscutting Behavior

Crosscutting behavior essentially supplements (or merges with) behavior it cuts across. Theme/UML supports merging of operations by allowing a designer to identify operations in different design themes that correspond and should be merged. This means that execution of any one of the corresponding operations results in the execution of all the corresponding operations. This is achieved within the model with the generation of an interaction model realizing the composed (output) operation as delegating to each of the corresponding (renamed) input operations.

This semantics can be explicitly utilized for the specification of patterns of crosscutting behavior. The designer may explicitly refer to the input (i.e., pre-composition) and output (i.e., post-composition) operations separately. The designer defines an input operation as a template parameter and refers to an actual, replacing operation by prepending an underscore to the template name. The generated output operation is referenced with the same name but without the prepended underscore.

As specified by the theme in Figure 19-3 for pattern class `TracedClass`, execution of any operation that replaces the `_tracedOp(..)` template will, in the output theme, result in the execution of `traceEntry()` before the execution of the replacing operation and in the execution of `traceExit()` after the execution of the replacing operation. Note that `_tracedOp(..)` was also given private visibility in Figure 19-2 as defined by merge integration [2, 3]. The ". ." parameter specification of `_tracedOp(..)` indicates that an operation of any signature may replace the template. Possibilities in this specification relate to the scope within which the replacing operation is executed. For example, in Figure 19-3, the active period of the execution of `tracedOp(..)` defines the scope for this operation, and any parameters defined may be used within this scope. The parameter possibilities are defined in Table 19-1. This `Trace` composition pattern theme effectively specifies the merging of trace behavior with any operation replacing `_tracedOp(..)`.

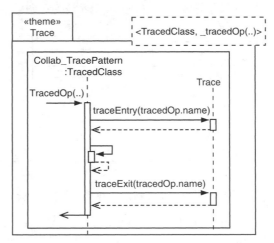

Figure 19-3 *Specifying patterns of crosscutting behavior.*

Table 19-1 *Parameter Scope*

Parameter	Usage
`op()`	In this case, the replacing operation must have no parameters.
`op(..)`	Here, the replacing operation may have any signature.
`op(.., Type, ..)`	Here, the replacing operation may have any signature, but the pattern needs a Type object for execution.

19.3.3 Composition Binding Specification

Theme/UML defines a composition relationship to support the specification of how different themes may be integrated to a composed output, and UML defines a Binding relationship between template specifications and the elements that are to replace those templates. UML restricts binding to template parameters for instantiation as one-to-one. Theme/UML extends UML's notion of binding and includes a `bind[]` attachment with the composition relationship. This attachment defines the (potentially multiple) elements that replace the templates within the crosscutting theme.

Ordering of parameters in the `bind[]` attachment matches the ordering of the templates in the pattern's template box. Any individual parameter surrounded by brackets `{}` indicates that a set of elements with a potential size > 1 replaces the corresponding template parameter.

In Figure 19-4, all classes within `S1` are replacements for pattern class `TracedClass`, with every operation (denoted by `{*}`) in each class (in this example, just `S1.X`) supplemented with the pattern behavior specified for `tracedOp(..)`. Where specific elements from classes replace templates, they may be explicitly named.

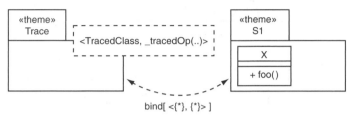

Figure 19-4 *Specifying binding for composition.*

19.3.4 *Composition Output*

As illustrated in Figure 19-4, a composition relationship's `bind[]` attachment may specify multiple replacements for pattern classes and template operations within those classes. Where multiple replacements are specified for a pattern class, the pattern class's properties are added to each of the replacement classes in the output theme. For example, in Figure 19-5, class `X` has class `TracedClass`'s properties. Where multiple replacements are specified for operations, each operation is supplemented with the behavior defined within the pattern theme. Non-template-parameter elements (such as non-pattern classes) are added to each result scope once. Class `Trace` is a non-pattern class defined in the `Trace` theme (see Figure 19-2), and it therefore appears in the output theme.

Wherever a pair of operations has been defined (e.g., `op()` and `_op()`) and referenced within the same scope in a theme (that is, inside the same pattern class), and one is a template parameter for that class, composition applies merge operation semantics. For each operation substituting the template operation, each reference to `_op()` is replaced by the suitably renamed substituting operation, and a new `op()` operation is also defined. Each operation's delegation semantics is realized by a new collaboration as specified within the theme.

Other implications of composition relating to the theme design model not demonstrated in this example are discussed elsewhere [2]. For example, merging generalizations may result in multiple inheritance in the composed theme, where there was only single inheritance in each of the input themes. Multiple inheritance is supported in UML, and therefore the output design is considered to be well-formed from a UML perspective. Multiple inheritance can be eliminated, if so desired, through the process of flattening [26]; this process may be automated during composition.

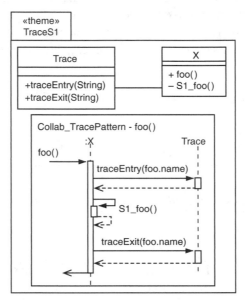

Figure 19-5   *Output from composition with* `Trace` *theme.*

Composition of the design themes can occur during the design phase (via a design composition tool, for example), which would be useful for the purposes of checking the semantics of the composed theme and the correctness of the composition relationships. Implementation may be based on such a composed design, but ideally, composition should be delayed until after the implementation phase, with each design theme being implemented separately and being composed afterwards. We discuss a means of delaying the composition process until after the implementation phase in Sections 19.5 and 19.6, where we map the design to Hyper/J and AspectJ, respectively.

19.4   ASPECTS AS THEMES: EXAMPLES

We now look at some more examples of well-known aspects designed using crosscutting themes. These examples illustrate how crosscutting requirements may be designed independently from any base design, making aspect design truly reusable. The aspects illustrated are synchronization and the Observer pattern.

19.4.1   Library Base Design

The base design on which the aspect examples are applied is a small library design (Figure 19-6). This library has books of which all copies are located in the same room and shelf. A book manager handles the maintenance of the association between books and their locations. The book manager also maintains an up-to-date view of the lending status of book copies.

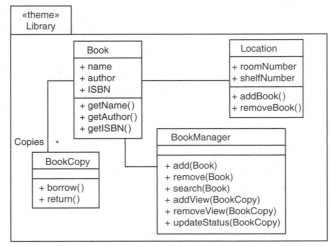

Figure 19-6   *Base library design.*

19.4.2   Example 1: Synchronization Aspect

The first crosscutting requirement is that the book manager should handle several requests to manage books and their locations concurrently. This aspect example, first described in [16], supports the book manager handling several "read" requests concurrently while temporarily blocking "write" requests. Individual "write" requests should block all other services.

19.4.2.1   Pattern Specification

Synchronization of concurrent processes is a common requirement, and therefore, it is useful to design this behavior without any reference to our library example. Figure 19-7 illustrates how this can be achieved. The Synchronize theme has one pattern class, SynchronizedClass, representing any class requiring synchronization behavior.

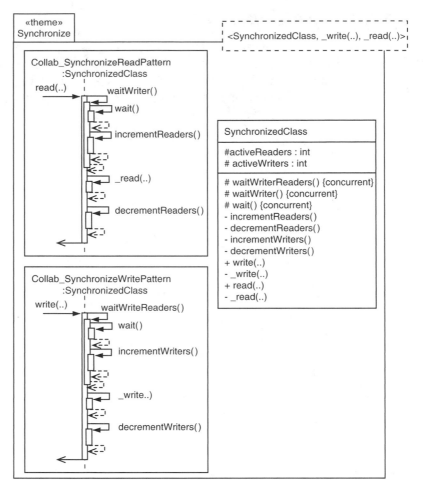

Figure 19-7 *Synchronization aspect design.*

Within this pattern class, two template parameters are defined, called `_read(..)` and `_write(..)`, to represent reading and writing operations. This example also illustrates how non-template elements may be specified within a pattern class to define the inherent crosscutting behavior. These elements are merged unchanged into the composed class. Synchronization behavior introduces a number of such elements, both structural and behavioral, to synchronized classes. Structural properties `activeReaders` and `activeWriters` maintain counts of the number of read and write requests currently in process (for write requests, this number will never be greater than 1). Two interaction patterns define the required behavior for reading and writing. The read pattern ensures that any currently writing process is completed prior to processing a read request. The write pattern ensures that all currently reading and writing processes are completed prior to processing a write request. The designer represents the actual replacing of read and write operations with an "_" prepended to the template parameter name—that is, using _read(..) and _write(..), and the generated operations realized by the interactions as read(..) and write(..). In this way, when a replacing operation is executed in the context of synchronization, the required behavior is clearly defined within the interactions.

19.4.2.2 Pattern Binding

Specifying how to compose the Library base design theme with the Synchronize theme is a simple matter of defining a composition relationship between the two, denoting which class(es) are to be supplemented with synchronization behavior, and which read and write operations are to be synchronized.

In this case, the library's BookManager class replaces the pattern class in the output, add() and remove() operations are defined as write operations, and the search() operation is defined as a read operation (see Figure 19-8).

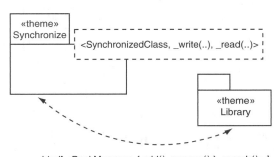

bind[<BookManager, { add(), remove() }, search()>]

Figure 19-8 *Composing* Synchronize *with* Library.

19.4.2.3 Composition Output

Pattern specification and binding, as previously illustrated, are all the designer has to do to define reusable aspect patterns and specify how they are to be composed with base designs. The composition process, utilizing UML template semantics, produces the design illustrated in Figure 19-9, where BookManager now has synchronizing behavior. Note also that the object names in the interactions have been renamed as appropriate.

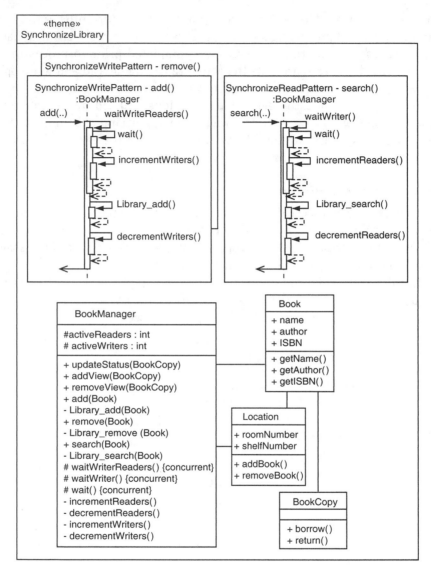

Figure 19-9 `Library` design with `Synchronize`.

19.4.3 Example 2: Observer Aspect

The second example is the Observer pattern [8], which, unlike the synchronization example, describes the pattern of collaborative behavior between more than one object—a subject and observers. This example also illustrates how non-pattern classes may be used within a theme.

19.4.3.1   Pattern Specification

In the `Observer` theme, two pattern classes are defined. `Subject` is defined as a pattern class representing the class of objects whose changes in state are of interest to other objects, and `Observer` is defined as a pattern class representing the class of objects interested in a `Subject`'s change in state (see Figure 19-10).

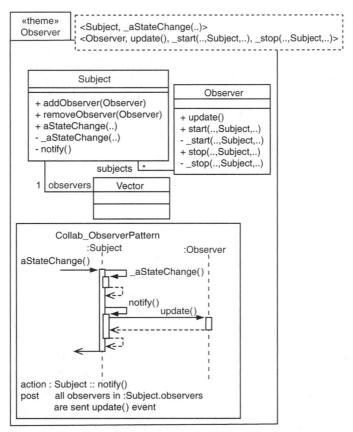

Figure 19-10   *Observer aspect design.*

The interaction in Figure 19-10 illustrates another example of specifying behavior that crosscuts templates, with `Subject`'s template parameter `_aStateChange(..)` supplemented with behavior relating to notifying observers of changes in state. This is achieved by referring to the actual replacing operation with a prepended "_", i.e., `_aStateChange(..)`. Here also is an example of an operation template parameter that does not require any delegating semantics. The `update()` operation in observers is called within the pattern and is not, itself, supplemented otherwise. It is defined as a template so that replacing observer classes may specify the operation that performs this task.

This pattern also supports the addition and removal of observers to a subject's list using `_start(.., Subject, ..)` and `_stop(.., Subject, ..)` template parameters, where each is replaced by operations denoting the start and end, respectively, of an observer's interest in a subject. For space purposes, the interactions are not illustrated here, as they do not illustrate any additional interesting properties of Theme/UML.

19.4.3.2   Pattern Binding

As with the `Synchronize` pattern, the composition of `Library` with the `Observer` pattern is achieved by specifying a composition relationship between the two, defining the class(es) acting as subject, and the class(es) acting as observer. In this example, there is only one of each (see Figure 19-11), `BookCopy` and `BookManager`, respectively.

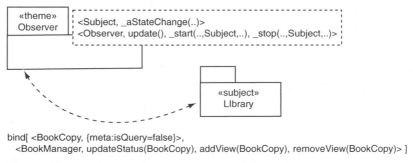

Figure 19-11   *Composing* `Observer` *with* `Library`.

One additional point of interest with this binding is how the meta-properties of a design theme's elements may be queried to assess an element's eligibility to join a set of replacing elements. UML's Operation meta-class defines more properties for operations than most coding languages—for example, in addition to its signature, a designer may specify that an operation is a query operation. Theme/UML supports the discrimination of replacing operations on the basis of any of a design element's properties.

In this example, the `_aStateChange()` template parameter is replaced with all operations within `BookCopy` that have been defined as being non-query—i.e., those operations that affect a change in state that may be of interest to an observer. The keyword `meta` within the set parameter specification denotes that a UML meta-property is queried, and only those operations with `isQuery=false` will replace `_aStateChange()` for the purposes of `Observer`.

19.4.3.3   Composition Output

The output of composing `Observer` with `Library`, illustrated in Figure 19-12, shows `BookCopy` demonstrating subject behavior, with the operations `borrow()`

and `return()` initiating the notification of observers, as they are the only state-changing operations. `BookManager`, as an observer, has defined `updateStatus()` as the operation to be called for notification purposes. Though not shown, `addView(..)` and `removeView(..)` initiate a `BookCopy` adding and removing a `BookManager` from its list of observers.

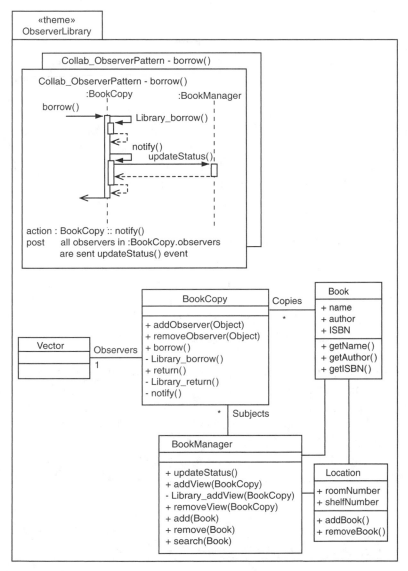

Figure 19-12 *`Library` design with `Observer`.*

19.5 MAP TO HYPER/J

The previous section illustrated the output resulting from the integration of crosscutting themes with base design models. Of course, each output demonstrates the tangling properties aspects are designed to avoid. While composition at the design level is useful to validate the design of a crosscutting theme and its impact on a base design, it is also possible to maintain the separation to the code phase, using an appropriate implementation model.

Conceptually, Theme/UML evolved from the work on subject-oriented programming [10, 18]. Subject-oriented programming evolved into the concept of *multidimensional separation of concerns* (MDSOC) [24], a modelling and implementation paradigm that supports the separation of overlapping concerns along multiple dimensions of composition and decomposition.

Hyper/J[1] [23] is a prototype programming environment to realize the MDSOC paradigm. It facilitates the adaptation, composition, integration, improved modularization, and non-invasive remodularization of Java software components [28]. This section gives a brief introduction to the concepts of and inputs to Hyper/J and demonstrates how Theme/UML constructs map to Hyper/J constructs.

19.5.1 Hyper/J Programming Elements

Hyper/J works with Java `.class` files, supporting sophisticated reasoning about their modularization (and remodularization) and composition. In other words, you may describe the internals of Java `.class` files and describe how you would like this code to be integrated differently. Hyper/J produces new Java `.class` files, where structure and behavior of (parts of) input `.class` files are integrated as defined by the programmer.

The developer provides three main inputs when using Hyper/J: *hyperspace* files, *concern mapping* files, and *hypermodule* files. Each hypermodule specifies a set of *composition relationships* between concerns. Table 19-2 describes these elements and maps them to corresponding design elements in Theme/UML.

In our attempt to map themes to Hyper/J, we have chosen to consider Hyper/J in terms of the full specification of its potential as defined in [23], and not its more limited implementation in the currently available version of the Hyper/J tool.

---

[1] Hyper/J is currently being replaced by CME, the Concern Manipulation Environment.

Table 19-2   *Mapping Hyper/J Program Elements to Theme/UML*

Element	Hyper/J	Theme/UML
Hyperspaces	A hyperspace describes the Java classes to be composed (and by implication, classes not to be composed). Keywords: `hyperspace, composable`.	Each design theme describes the classes available for composition. In the specific case of crosscutting themes, pattern classes are explicitly defined as requiring binding. To map to Hyper/J, all of the classes to be composed would need to be specified within a single hyperspace.
Concern mappings	A concern mapping file describes the pieces of Java within the hyperspaces that map to different concerns (or features) of interest. Keyword: `Feature`.	Each separate design theme, including crosscutting themes, would correspond to a separate concern.
Hypermodules	A hypermodule file describes how integration between concerns of interest should be done. Keywords: `hypermodule, hyperslice`.	A hypermodule is essentially a container for a set of composition relationships. All the composition relationships and `bind[]` specifications for a given composition would be specified within a single hypermodule.
Composition relationships	Within a hypermodule, different kinds of composition strategies may be specified (e.g., merge or override), with the possibility of defining a match relationship for method invocations so that invocation of one results in the invocation of all matched methods. Keywords: `relationships, nonCorrespondingMerge, equate, override, bracket`.	Theme/UML provides for the specification of composition relationships between design elements at all levels of the design hierarchy, from entire design themes to individual methods within design themes. Some Hyper/J composition relationships are expressed as collaboration diagrams. For example, the `bracket` relationship supports the specification of which methods should be executed before and/or after a method to be crosscut with additional behavior; this is applicable to the Observer example of Section 19.4.3.

19.5.2 Observer in Hyper/J

The internals of the `Observer` theme and the `Library` base design may be described using hyperspace and concern mapping files, while the `bind[]` specification of the composition relationship may be mapped to the hypermodule file. However, at a more detailed level, mapping becomes more difficult, as we shall see.

First, we look at the Java source code implementing the classes defined in the `Observer` composition pattern. `Subject` and `Observer` classes are defined in an `Observer` package as follows. (This is a code skeleton that could be generated strictly from the information provided in the crosscutting theme of Figure 19-10. Additional information would be required for a full implementation.)

```
class Subject {
  Vector observers;

  void addObserver(Observer observer) {}

  void removeObserver(Observer observer) {}

  void aStateChange() {
    notify();
  }

  void notify() {
    // All observers in observers are
    // sent update() event
  }
}

class Observer {
  void update() {}

  void start(Subject subject) {
    subject.addObserver(this);
  }

  void stop(Subject subject) {
    subject.removeObserver(this);
  }
}
```

Code supporting the `Library` design model is not illustrated here, although we assume it to be defined within a `Library` package. Each of these packages is considered to be in the space within which we are working; thus, we can define an appropriate hyperspace file as:

```
hyperspace ObservedLibrary
composable class Observer.*;
composable class Library.*;
```

Concern mappings may be defined as:

```
package Observer : Feature Observer
package Library : Feature Library
```

However, this mapping of the reusable `Observer` composition pattern to code is not as straightforward as it may appear. Hyper/J imposes a restriction that operations to be merged must have the same signature. Theme/UML supports a mechanism for specifying considerable flexibility in the signatures of operations that are allowed to replace template operations. For our `Observer` example, the template operations `start(.., Subject, ..)` and `stop(.., Subject, ..)` specify that one of the parameters must be an object of type `Subject` but that there may be any other, arbitrary parameters. This flexibility does not map to Hyper/J. The `Observer` class illustrated here has defined a single `Subject` parameter for both the `start()` and `stop()` methods. This mapping could only occur after examining the signatures of the replacing operations, as defined in the `bind[]` attachment to the composition relationship. The signatures of the template operations in the `Observer` class were then defined appropriately. Therefore, the `Observer` package is not reusable as currently defined. Prior to being merged with any other package, the signatures of all methods with which `start()` and `stop()` are to be merged must be examined, with overloaded methods defined for any methods with differing signatures.[2]

We now consider the hypermodule file, which specifies how the packages should be integrated.[3] The concern mapping identified two features, `Library` and `Observer`, to be composed. A `nonCorrespondingMerge` relationship is defined between the two features, indicating that any elements with the same name in the different features do not correspond and are not to be merged. This is chosen because the correspondences between the `Observer` pattern and elements within any potential hyperslice with which it is to be merged are explicitly defined, and any name matching otherwise is coincidental.

---

2. It is not clear that Hyper/J's bracket declaration would correctly handle overloaded methods; if not, method renaming would be required to differentiate between them.

3. The `nonCorrespondingMerge` and `override` relationships are not currently enabled in the Hyper/J tool, and so this code has not been compiled.

The replacement of the `Observer` and `Subject` pattern classes with `BookManager` and `BookCopy`, respectively, can be mapped directly to `equate` relationships. An `override` relationship may be used to map the replacement of `update()` with the `updateStatus()` method. Each of the methods that are replacements for operations supplemented by crosscutting behavior has a `bracket` relationship defined to specify the invocation of the appropriate methods before or after its own execution. This interactive behavior is gleaned from the interactions within the composition pattern itself, not the composition relationship. One point of note: the `bind[]` attachment to the composition relationship supports reasoning about the meta-properties of operations—in this example, any operations whose `isQuery` property is `false` replaces the `aStateChange()` template operation (refer to Figure 19-11). Since there is no equivalent specification in Hyper/J, the mapping process must examine each of the operations in `BookCopy` and add a `bracket` relationship for any operation that passes the `isQuery` test—`borrow()` and `return()` in this case. Here is the resulting hypermodule specification:

```
hypermodule ObserverLibrary

   hyperslices:
     Feature.Library,
     Feature.Observer;

   relationships:
     nonCorrespondingMerge;

   equate class
     Feature.Library.BookManager
     Feature.Observer.Observer;
   equate class
     Feature.Library.BookCopy,
     Feature.Observer.Subject;
   override action
     Feature.Observer.Observer.update
     with Feature.Library.BookManager.updateStatus;
   bracket "addView" with
     (after Feature.Observer.Observer.start,
      "BookManager");
   bracket "removeView" with
     (before Feature.Observer.Observer.stop,
      "BookManager");
```

```
bracket "borrow" with
  (after Feature.Observer.Subject.aStateChange,
   "BookCopy");
bracket "return" with
  (after Feature.Observer.Subject.aStateChange,
   "BookCopy");
```

```
end hypermodule
```

As we can see, the hypermodule specifying how to integrate the `Library` and `Observer` features has the potential to provide a clean mapping from Theme/UML with simple interactions specified. However, though not illustrated with the `Observer` example, limitations with the `bracket` relationship, as currently defined, may present difficulties for more complicated interactions in the design.

19.6 MAP TO ASPECTJ

As a demonstration of the independence of Theme/UML as a *design* model from any particular *implementation* model, this section looks at the mapping of crosscutting theme concepts to AspectJ.

At the conceptual level, crosscutting theme design and aspect-oriented programming in AspectJ have the same goals. Theme/UML provides a means for separating and *designing* reusable crosscutting behavior, and AspectJ provides a means for separating and *implementing* reusable crosscutting behavior. This section describes a simple approach for mapping crosscutting theme constructs to AspectJ constructs. Other approaches are possible and have been described elsewhere [5]; we discuss these briefly in Section 19.7.

19.6.1 AspectJ Programming Elements

AspectJ is an aspect-oriented extension to Java that supports the implementation of crosscutting code (i.e., aspects) as separate aspect modules. As described in [14], AspectJ adds four kinds of program elements to Java. These are *aspects*, *pointcuts*, *advice,* and *introductions*. Table 19-3 describes these elements and maps them to the corresponding design elements in Theme/UML.

19.6.2 Algorithm for Mapping to AspectJ

The question of how to map crosscutting themes to AspectJ depends on how faithfully one wishes to represent the design-level entities. There are two chief approaches: (1) represent both a crosscutting theme and its composition specification as a single aspect, or (2) maintain the separation of a reusable crosscutting theme from its composition specification.

Table 19-3 *Mapping AspectJ Program Elements to Theme/UML*

Element	AspectJ	Theme/UML
Aspect	An aspect is a crosscutting type, with a well-defined interface, which may be instantiated and reasoned about at compile time. Keyword: `aspect`.	A crosscutting theme is a design equivalent to an aspect.
Pointcut	During the execution of a program, and as part of that execution's scope, there are points where crosscutting behavior is required. These points are *join points*. A pointcut is a *crosscutting set of join points*. Keyword: `pointcut`.	Operation template parameters may be defined and referenced within interaction specifications, denoting that they are join points for crosscutting behavior. These templates may be replaced by actual operations multiple times and are therefore equivalent to pointcuts.
Advice	A piece of advice is code that executes at a pointcut, using some of the execution scope. Keywords: `before`, `after`, `around`.	Within an interaction diagram, crosscutting behavior may be specified on template operation calls. This behavior is equivalent to advice code.
Introduction	An introduction is a programming element, such as an attribute, constructor, or method, which is added to a type that may add to or extend that type's structure. No keywords.	Design elements that are not template elements may be defined within crosscutting themes. These may be classes, attributes, operations, or relationships and are equivalent to an introduction.

The first approach results in aspects that lack reusability and evolvability. It requires that the crosscutting theme be reimplemented for every composition specification that is used; each of these would need to be modified separately should the crosscutting theme need to evolve. The second approach promises a better solution and forms the basis for our analysis in this section.

Difficulties with evolving mapped crosscutting themes would be reduced if we could produce an implementation-level construct that represented a crosscutting theme alone without its composition specification. Then any changes to this crosscutting theme would affect only this one construct. This construct would be more reusable since it would not be specific to a single composition specification.

Abstract aspects potentially provide such a means of separating the code for crosscutting behavior in a reusable way. We therefore provide a direct mapping from uncomposed crosscutting themes to abstract aspects in Section 19.6.2.1. The binding of a crosscutting theme with a base theme is then mapped to concrete aspects that extend these abstract aspects; this is described in Section 19.6.2.2.

19.6.2.1 Uncomposed Crosscutting Themes Map to Abstract Aspects

The following illustrates an algorithm to be applied when mapping a reusable crosscutting theme to AspectJ. We describe the reasoning behind the major features of this mapping next.

Input: A crosscutting theme *CT*.

Output: An abstract aspect *A* corresponding to *CT*.

1. Declare abstract aspect *A*.

2. For each pattern class *PClass* in *CT*:

    2.1. Declare interface *I* in *A*.

    2.2. For each template operation with no supplementary behavior *<op>* on *PClass*:

        2.2.1. Declare corresponding (abstract) method *m* on *I*.

    2.3. For each template operation with supplementary behavior *<_op>* on *PClass*:

        2.3.1. Declare corresponding abstract pointcut *pc*.

        2.3.2. Let *pc* have formal parameters consisting of one to capture the target object (of type *I*) on which *<_op>* is called, plus one corresponding to each of the specified formal parameters on *<_op>*.

        2.3.3. Declare advice on *pc* according to the supplementary behavior.

    2.4. For each non-template operation *op*:

        2.4.1. Introduce method *m* (which implements any behavioral specifications for *op*) on *I*.

    2.5. For each non-template association from *PClass* to some non-pattern class:

        2.5.1. Introduce field *f* on *I*.

3. For each non-pattern class *NPClass* in *CT*:

    3.1. Implement *NPClass* directly if it is not already present.

Figure 19-13 *Algorithm for mapping uncomposed crosscutting themes to AspectJ.*

Pattern classes become interfaces within the abstract aspect. A pattern class (e.g., `Subject`) is a "placeholder" for a concrete class. In AspectJ, the only constructs provided that can act as such a placeholder are an interface or a class.

If we use a class, an inheritance relationship will need to be defined for the concrete replacing class. This is because a pattern class may name operations without providing any constraints upon their behavior, and therefore they need to map to an abstract type in AspectJ. However, a concrete class (e.g., `BookCopy`) that will eventually have to become a subtype of this abstract type may already possess a superclass. It would be necessary to replace any previously defined superclass of the concrete class if we chose to map the pattern class to an abstract class.

On the other hand, mapping a pattern class to an interface allows a concrete class to have added to it a declaration that it implements this interface (e.g., `BookCopy implements SubjectI`).

Non-template operations become introduced methods on those interfaces. An interface maps from a pattern class, so that interface must somehow represent the operations required of that pattern class. Since AspectJ permits method introduction on an interface to propagate to all classes implementing that interface, this is a convenient means to add a method to a concrete class whose name is not known prior to binding. For example, `Subject::notify()` becomes `SubjectI.notify()`, which causes any concrete classes implementing `SubjectI` to implicitly have the `notify()` method introduced on them.

Template operations without supplementary behavior become methods on those interfaces. Once again, an interface mapping from a pattern class must somehow represent the operations required of that pattern class. With a template operation without supplementary behavior, either explicitly placing the corresponding method within the interface declaration or introducing an abstract method onto the interface would suffice. We have taken the former route for the sake of clarity.

Template operations with supplementary behavior become abstract pointcuts plus advice. Advice is an obvious construct to use for designating supplementary behavior to occur on execution of the concrete method bound to a template operation. Advice permits behavior to be specified even on abstract pointcuts. Since the composition pattern is only supplementing the behavior of this template operation, it need only have an abstract pointcut to advise. Thus, `Subject::aStateChange(..)` becomes `aStateChange(SubjectI)` with `after` advice.

19.6.2.2   **Composition Specifications Map to Concrete Aspects**

Now that we have a construct representing uncomposed crosscutting themes, we need to extend it to represent a particular composition specification. The algorithm for performing this deals with many small details that are conceptually straightforward; thus, we do not give a detailed algorithm but instead touch on the highlights of the process.

The elements associated with a `bind[]` specification on a composition relationship are mapped to the appropriate AspectJ constructs. The concrete aspect that results from the composition specification between the `Observer` composition pattern and the base `Library` design is shown in Figure 19-6. We describe the reasoning behind the major features of this mapping next.

Concrete classes bound to pattern classes require `parents` declarations in the concrete aspect.   A pattern class is represented through an interface declared on the abstract aspect. The act of binding a concrete class in the design model to that pattern class causes that concrete class to effectively become a subtype of the pattern class within the context of the composition pattern. Therefore, a concrete class in the implementation must be effectively a subtype of the interface corresponding to the pattern class in order to be "bound" in an analogous manner. To this end, we use AspectJ's ability to add supertypes to a class. For example, `Subject` is represented as the interface `SubjectI`; since `Subject` is bound to `BookCopy`, `BookCopy` must implement `SubjectI`.

Concrete operations bound to template operations without supplementary behavior require introduction of delegating methods on concrete classes.   Each interface (e.g., `ObserverI`) within the abstract aspect, which corresponds to a pattern class, had declared within it a method to represent each template operation without supplementary behavior (e.g., `update()`). Since some concrete class has been declared to implement this interface (i.e., `BookManager`), it must implement each of these methods. The binding of a concrete operation to a template operation is straightforward, save for one point: their signatures can differ. So, even though the concrete class already possesses a method corresponding to that being bound to the template operation (i.e., `updateStatus()`), our concrete aspect must introduce an additional method (i.e., `update()`). This method must possess the signature expected by the aspect and must delegate to the method already possessed by the concrete class.

Concrete operations bound to template operations with supplementary behavior require concrete pointcuts.   Finally, the abstract aspect declared abstract pointcuts that must be made concrete. Each abstract pointcut (e.g., `aStateChange(SubjectI)`) corresponds to a template operation (i.e.,

`Subject::aStateChange(..))` in the design model. For the concrete operations bound to this template operation, the concrete pointcut must capture the execution join points of the concrete operations while exposing the target object and arguments at each join point.

19.6.3 Observer in AspectJ

The `Observer` crosscutting theme (refer to Figure 19-10) with its composition specification to the `Library` theme (refer to Figure 19-11) provides the information required for the structure of an aspect program.

We begin by creating an abstract aspect `Observer` to correspond to the unbound `Observer` crosscutting theme. The `Observer` crosscutting theme has two pattern classes defined; we therefore provide an interface corresponding to each within the abstract aspect. The `Observer` pattern class declares a template operation without supplementary behavior, `update()`; a corresponding abstract method is declared within the `ObserverI` interface on the abstract aspect.

The `Subject` pattern class declares a non-template association to the `Vector` class and a non-template operation called `notify()`. Each of these is introduced to the `SubjectI` interface, which causes them to be introduced to any classes that implement `SubjectI`. (This will be useful when the composition pattern is bound to the base Library theme.)

A template operation with supplementary behavior, namely `_aStateChange(..)`, is declared on the `Subject` pattern class. An abstract pointcut that exposes the instance of `SubjectI` undergoing the state change is therefore declared within the abstract aspect. This pointcut is advised so that the `notify()` operation is called on the instance of `SubjectI` undergoing the state change. Similarly, two template operations with supplementary behavior are defined on the `Observer` pattern class, so two abstract pointcuts plus advice are declared for these.

```
public abstract aspect Observer {
  // ---- type declarations
  interface SubjectI {}
  interface ObserverI {
    public void update();
  }

  // ---- introductions ----
  Vector SubjectI.observers;
  Vector ObserverI.subjects;
```

```
private void SubjectI.notify() {
  // Post: all observers in SubjectI.observers
  // are sent update() event
}


// ---- Pointcuts ----
abstract pointcut aStateChange(SubjectI s);
abstract pointcut start(ObserverI o, SubjectI s);
abstract pointcut stop(ObserverI o, SubjectI s);


// ---- Advice ----
after(SubjectI s): aStateChange(s) {
  s.notify();
}
before(ObserverI o, SubjectI s): start(o, s) {
  s.observers.add(o);
}
after(ObserverI o, SubjectI s): stop(o, s) {
  s.observers.remove(o);
}
}
```

To implement the concrete binding of the Observer composition pattern to the base Library theme, we create a concrete aspect that extends the abstract aspect. Next, the composition relationship's binding specification indicates that BookCopy replaces the Subject pattern class while BookManager replaces the Observer pattern class. Therefore, within the concrete aspect, BookCopy is declared to implement SubjectI, while BookManager is declared to implement ObserverI.

The composition relationship between Observer and Library indicates that all BookCopy operations failing to meet the isQuery meta-property (namely, borrow() and return()) replace aStateChange(), while the updateStatus(BookCopy), addView(BookCopy), and removeView (BookCopy) operations from BookManager replace update(), start(.., Subject, ..), and stop(.., Subject, ..), respectively. To bind both the borrow() and return() methods of BookCopy to the _aStateChange() template operation, the abstract pointcut aStateChange(SubjectI) is implemented to capture all execution join points of the borrow() and returnIt() methods. To bind the updateStatus(BookCopy) method of BookManager to the update()

template operation of the crosscutting theme, we must introduce an `update()` method to `BookManager` that delegates to `updateStatus(BookCopy)`. And finally, to bind `addView(BookCopy)` and `removeView(BookCopy)` to `_start(.., Subject, ..)` and `_stop(.., Subject, ..)`, respectively, we must implement concrete pointcuts to capture all the execution join points for those two methods.

```
aspect LibraryObserver extends Observer {
  // ---- Declarations ----
  declare parents: BookCopy implements SubjectI;
  declare parents: BookManager implements ObserverI;

  // ---- Introductions ----
  public void BookManager.update() {
    // for each BookCopy bc in subjects
    // updateStatus(bc);
  }

  // ---- Pointcuts ----
  pointcut aStateChange(SubjectI copy):
    target(copy) && args(..) &&
    (execution(* BookCopy.borrow(..)) ||
     execution(* BookCopy.returnIt(..)));
  pointcut start(ObserverI obs, SubjectI subj):
    target(obs) && args(subj) &&
    execution(* BookManager.addView(BookCopy));
  pointcut stop(ObserverI obs, SubjectI subj):
    target(obs) && args(subj) &&
    execution(* BookManager.removeView(BookCopy));
}
```

Note that the operation template parameter without supplementary behavior, `update()`, cannot be treated as a pointcut because pointcuts can only be advised; they cannot be made to occur. The interaction diagram indicates that `update()` must be called within the crosscutting behavior. Therefore, references to `update()` are explicitly replaced with references to the operation bound to it.

19.7 MAPPING TO PROGRAMMING MODELS

The examples in the previous two sections illustrate the possibilities for mapping crosscutting theme constructs to Hyper/J and AspectJ programming elements. The advantages of mapping the design to a programming model are twofold. First, from a design perspective, mapping the composition pattern constructs to constructs from a programming environment ensures that the clear separation of crosscutting behavior is maintained in the programming phase, making design changes easier to incorporate into code. Second, from the programming perspective, the existence of a design approach that supports separation of crosscutting behavior makes the design phase more relevant to this kind of programming, lending the standard benefits of software design to the approach.

However, work remains to provide a fully functional set of matching design and programming tools for the aspect-oriented developer. Theme/UML has considerable support for genericity with its use of templates to parameterize crosscutting elements. There are no restrictions (other than on type) as to the elements that may be bound to the templates, except as imposed by the designer—e.g., operations of any signature could replace template operations. However, neither programming model examined currently provides such flexibility. On the other hand, capabilities in programming models such as AspectJ for associating aspects with fine-grained, dynamic scopes such as portions of the control-flow are missing in Theme/UML. We envisage that the maturation of the aspect-oriented software development field will encourage both design and programming approaches to evolve to better enable traceability between the phases.

19.8   RELATED WORK

Conceptually, the Theme/UML model has evolved from the work on subject-oriented programming [10, 18], as is also the case with the work on multi-dimensional separation of concerns [24]. Different themes may be designed (or programmed) to support separate requirements, be they functional (and conceptually overlapping) or crosscutting requirements. Subsequent composition of separated themes is specified with composition relationships (or defined by composition rules in subject-oriented programming). Theme/UML is part of an approach to aspect-oriented analysis and design called Theme. Theme has two parts: Theme/Doc is a set of heuristics and tools for visualisation and analysis of software requirements documentation for the purposes of finding the themes to be designed. Theme/UML is the second part, which is a way to design aspects based on the UML [1]. From the perspective of crosscutting requirements, this chapter has illustrated how the Theme/UML model for crosscutting themes also closely relates to the aspect-oriented programming model [15] as embodied in the AspectJ programming language [14].

In this section, we examine approaches to extending UML, specifically with the AspectJ approach to aspect-oriented programming in mind. We also discuss some other approaches to flexible separation of concerns at the design stage. While there are many approaches to flexible separation of concerns at the programming level, we do not consider these here.

First, there are some interesting approaches that start with the AspectJ mindset and attempt to directly apply its concepts as extensions to UML. Two general approaches to this are evolving. On the one hand, there have been approaches to extending UML with stereotypes specific to particular aspects (e.g., synchronization [11] or command pattern [13]). In such approaches, the constructs required by each particular aspect are stereotyped so that a weaver (like a composer) can determine which elements match the appropriate aspect construct. In both these examples, many of the behavioral details of synchronization and of the command pattern are not explicitly designed in UML—the onus appears to be on the weaver to provide the aspect behavior. The authors of [13] have since further refined their model by building a tool to support building the required application-specific weavers [12]. Other approaches attempt to provide a more generalized way to support aspect-oriented programming in UML. For example, in [22] a new meta-construct called `Aspect` is created, and stereotypes are defined for advice behavior. Operations requiring advice behavior are constrained by the advice stereotypes. Stereotypes for different aspect-oriented constructs similar to those in AspectJ are also the basis for the approach taken in [21]. The Theme/UML model distinguishes itself from these general approaches with its generic approach to designing reusable crosscutting behavior in a manner that is independent of a particular programming environment.

Two approaches that emphasize a more flexible separation of concerns than exists in standard object-oriented design are OORam [19] and Catalysis [7]. In role modelling in OORam, large systems are described with multiple different role models that may be synthesized to create derived models. This is similar to merge integration in theme design. Catalysis also supports the decomposition of software designs along "vertical" and "horizontal" lines, providing the ability to separate both functional and technical kinds of concerns. While both approaches provide advances in the separation capabilities in object-oriented design, neither addresses the specification and composition of patterns of crosscutting behavior.

A focus of work in the field of collaboration-based design is on separation of each of the roles classes may play in different collaborations into different modules. For example, modularization of roles within collaborations is supported by mixins in the work described in [25], utilizing a C++ template class for each role in each collaboration; complete classes are "composed" by placing these mixins in a hierarchy. This work is extended in [20] to overcome problems of scalability by grouping sets of roles within each collaboration. Relative to the Theme/UML model, there are two main drawbacks to these approaches. First, while classes can be mixed together simply by adding mixins to a class hierarchy, individual methods cannot; this is part of the reason tool support is needed in subject-oriented and aspect-oriented programming. Second, whenever the mixins are interdependent, one needs to tangle the dependencies between them by embedding details of the dependencies within each mixin, typically via explicit calls to super-methods and other constraint information. In any situation where prior knowledge of future changes is unknown, such dependencies would require error-prone modifications to pre-existing mixins. As a result, each mixin cannot be designed cleanly and independently as Theme/UML allows.

The need for aspect-orientation across the development lifecycle is described in [9], motivated by agent-based product-line development for e-commerce. A development process is proposed that draws together high-level analysis and design separation techniques and corresponding, supporting implementation techniques. Theme/UML provides a solution to designing crosscutting features in a reusable way that could be considered for inclusion in this development process.

19.9 CONCLUSION

Software design is an important activity in the development lifecycle, but its benefits are often not realized. Scattering and tangling of crosscutting behavior with other elements causes problems with comprehensibility, traceability, evolvability, and reusability. Attempts have been made to address this problem in the programming domain, but the problem has not been addressed effectively at earlier stages in the lifecycle. This chapter presents an approach to addressing this problem at the design stage with Theme/UML. Theme/UML is an extension to the standard UML to support the modularization of a design into "themes." A theme is any feature, concern, or requirement of interest that must be handled in the design. Examples are presented that illustrate the flexible and reusable nature of Theme/UML as a design approach for crosscutting behavior. The chapter illustrates how both separation of aspects and composition with other design models may be specified and demonstrates the impact of possible composition at the design stage. The chapter also shows how the separation may be maintained to the programming phase by mapping the Theme/UML model constructs for crosscutting themes to Hyper/J and AspectJ constructs.

While many of the ideas evolved from subject-oriented programming, the ease with which its concepts are mapped to the aspect-oriented programming constructs in AspectJ for crosscutting behavior illustrates that it is not closely tied to a particular programming paradigm. Therefore, it is insulated from changes to programming environment constructs. In addition, extensions to the UML are minimal—use is made, where possible, of standard UML constructs (e.g., templates). This should make usage of Theme/UML intuitive to UML designers. However, tool support is essential for successful usage, and therefore one of our next primary foci is the inclusion of support for Theme/UML in a design tool. Automation of the mapping to programming environments would also be useful.

REFERENCES

1. BANIASSAD, E. AND CLARKE, S. 2004. Theme: An Approach for Aspect-Oriented Analysis and Design. In *26th Int'l Conf. Software Engineering (ICSE)*, (Edinburgh). IEEE, 158–167.

2. CLARKE, S. 2001. Composition of object-oriented software design models. Ph.D. thesis, Dublin City University.

3. CLARKE, S. 2002. Extending standard UML with model composition semantics. *Science of Computer Programming 44*, 1, 71–100.

4. CLARKE, S., HARRISON, W., OSSHER, H., AND TARR, P. 1999. Subject-oriented design: Towards improved alignment of requirements, design and code. In *14th Conf. Object-Oriented Programming, Systems, Languages, and Applications (OOPSLA)*, (Denver). ACM, 325–339.

5. CLARKE, S. AND WALKER, R. 2002. Towards a standard design language for AOSD. In *1st Int'l Conf. Aspect-Oriented Software Development (AOSD)*, (Enschede, The Netherlands), G. Kiczales, Ed. ACM, 113–119.

6. COOK, S. AND DANIELS, J. 1995. *Designing Object Systems: Object-Oriented Modelling with Syntropy*. Prentice-Hall, Englewood Cliffs, New Jersey.

7. D'SOUZA, D. F. AND WILLS, A. C. 1999. *Objects, Components, and Frameworks with UML: The Catalysis Approach*. Addison-Wesley, Reading, Massachusetts.

8. GAMMA, E., HELM, R., JOHNSON, R., AND VLISSIDES, J. 1995. *Design Patterns: Elements of Reusable Object-Oriented Software*. Addison-Wesley, Reading, Massachusetts.

9. GRISS, M. L. 2000. Implementing product-line features by composing aspects. In *1st Conf. Software Product Lines: Experience and Research Directions*, (Denver). Kluwer Academic Publishers, Boston, 271–288.

10. HARRISON, W. AND OSSHER, H. 1993. Subject-oriented programming—a critique of pure objects. In *8th Conf. Object-Oriented Programming, Systems, Languages, and Applications (OOPSLA)*, (Washington, D. C.). ACM, 411–428.

11. HERRERO, J. L., SÁNCHEZ, F., LUCIO, F., AND TORO, M. 2000. Introducing separation of aspects at design time. In *Workshop on Aspects and Dimensions of Concerns (ECOOP)*, (Cannes, France). http://trese.cs.utwente.nl/Workshops/adc2000/papers/Herrero.pdf.

12. HO, W. M., JÉZÉQUEL, J. M., PENNANEAC'H, F., AND PLOUZEAU, N. 2002. A toolkit for weaving aspect-oriented UML designs. In *1st Int'l Conf. Aspect-Oriented Software Development (AOSD)*, (Enschede, The Netherlands), G. Kiczales, Ed. ACM, 99–105.

13. HO, W. M., PENNANEAC'H, F., JÉZÉQUEL, J. M., AND PLOUZEAU, N. 2000. Aspect-oriented design with the UML. In *Workshop on Multi-Dimensional Separation of Concerns in Software Engineering (ICSE)*, (Limerick, Ireland). http://www.research.ibm.com/hyperspace/workshops/icse2000/Papers/ho.pdf.

14. KICZALES, G., HILSDALE, E., HUGUNIN, J., KERSTEN, M., PALM, J., AND GRISWOLD, W. G. 2001. An overview of AspectJ. In *ECOOP 2001—Object-Oriented Programming, 15th European Conference*, (Budapest), J. L. Knudsen, Ed. LNCS, vol. 2072. Springer-Verlag, Berlin, 327–353.

15. KICZALES, G., LAMPING, J., MENDHEKAR, A., MAEDA, C., LOPES, C., LOINGTIER, J. M., AND IRWIN, J. 1997. Aspect-oriented programming. In *ECOOP'97 Object-Oriented Programming, 11th European Conference*, M. Akşit and S. Matsuoka, Eds. LNCS, vol. 1241. Springer-Verlag, Berlin, 220–242.

16. LOPES, C. V. AND KICZALES, G. 1997. D: A language framework for distributed programming. Tech. Rep. SPL-97-010, Palo Alto Research Center.

17. OBJECT MANAGEMENT GROUP. 1999. The unified modeling language specification. version 1.3.

18. OSSHER, H., KAPLAN, M., KATZ, A., HARRISON, W., AND KRUSKAL, V. 1996. Specifying subject-oriented composition. *Theory and Practice of Object Systems 2*, 3, 179–202.

19. REENSKAUG, T., WOLD, P., AND LEHNE, O. A. 1995. *Working with Objects. The OOram Software Engineering Method*. Manning, Greenwich, Connecticut.

20. SMARAGDAKIS, Y. AND BATORY, D. 2002. Mixin layers: An object-oriented implementation technique for refinements and collaboration-based designs. *ACM Transactions on Software Engineering and Methodology 11*, 2, 215–255.

21. STEIN, D., HANENBERG, S., AND UNLAND, R. 2002. An UML-based aspect-oriented design notation. In *1st Int'l Conf. Aspect-Oriented Software Development (AOSD)*, (Enschede, The Netherlands), G. Kiczales, Ed. ACM, 106–112.

22. SUZUKI, J. AND YAMAMOTO, Y. 1999. Extending UML with aspects: Aspect support in the design phase. In *Int'l Workshop on Aspect-Oriented Programming (ECOOP)*, (Lisbon). http://trese.cs.utwente.nl/aop-ecoop99/papers/suzuki.pdf.

23. TARR, P. AND OSSHER, H. 2000. Hyper/J user and installation manual. Tech. rep., IBM T. J. Watson Research Center. http://www.research.ibm.com/hyperspace.

24. TARR, P., OSSHER, H., HARRISON, W., AND SUTTON JR., S. M. 1999. *N* degrees of separation: Multi-dimensional separation of concerns. In *21st Int'l Conf. Software Engineering (ICSE)*, (Los Angeles). IEEE, 107–119.

25. VANHILST, M. AND NOTKIN, D. 1996. Using role components to implement collaboration-based designs. In *11th Conf. Object-Oriented Programming, Systems, Languages, and Applications (OOPSLA)*, (San Jose). ACM, 359–369.

26. WALKER, R. J. 2000. Eliminating cycles from composed class hierarchies. Tech. Rep. TR-00-09, Department of Computer Science, University of British Columbia.

Chapter 20

Expressing Aspects Using UML Behavioral and Structural Diagrams

TZILLA ELRAD, OMAR ALDAWUD, AND ATEF BADER

Aspect-oriented programming (AOP) is a programming technology, but software engineering is a much greater task than just coding, encompassing elements such as requirements analysis, design, testing, and evolution. The Unified Modeling Language (UML) has emerged as the common CASE methodology for designing object-oriented software systems. Unfortunately, UML lacks explicit mechanisms for modeling interweaving crosscutting concerns. In this chapter, we present a formal design methodology for modeling aspect-oriented elements. Using the event-notification mechanism of statecharts and class diagrams, we show how to model and weave the submodels that represent different concerns. In presenting this methodology, we argue that aspect-oriented modeling improves the quality of software systems for goals such as maintainability, reusability, and traceability.

20.1   INTRODUCTION

Aspect-oriented technology (AOT) is a maturing technology [7, 8, 13] that complements object-oriented technology. AOT is rooted in the idea of separately modularizing concerns, represented by work such as subject-oriented programming (SOP) [15]. In SOP, the different concerns of a software system can be designed and reasoned about in isolation from each other. Finding modular representations for these concerns and developing mechanisms for concern weaving are the main themes of aspect-oriented programming. Recent work in aspect-oriented design [1, 3, 8, 17] has demonstrated the value of deploying aspect technology early in the software life cycle. Crosscutting concerns cause many difficulties for software development. Since these difficulties are present throughout the design process, they must be addressed across its entirety [3]. Initial decomposition of a problem identifies software components and the corresponding concerns that crosscut these components. We want to be able to formally express and model this initial decomposition and carry this model through the software development lifecycle.

Object-oriented modeling is a standard practice in the early stages of software development. Object-oriented modeling has many advantages, frequently outlined in the literature. Similarly, UML [14] enjoys many benefits, including providing structure for problem solving, allowing exploration of a solution space, furnishing abstractions to manage complexity, reducing time-to-market, and managing the risk of mistakes. But what the object-oriented paradigm does not address is the modeling of different design concerns as separate submodels that are easy to maintain and comprehend. Traditional object-oriented modeling techniques usually produce one giant model at the end of the design phase, where multiple concerns have been intermixed. Identifying and modifying a single design concern in a giant model is difficult, impeding the evolution of the software system. Monolithic object-oriented models have motivated researchers in the aspect-oriented community to investigate alternatives. In [2], we demonstrated that when aspects are identified at an early stage of the development lifecycle, their design components become more reusable, and automatic code generation becomes possible. Suzuki and Yamamoto [17] assert that capturing aspects at the design phase streamlines the process of AO development, as it aids learning and documents aspects earlier in the design phase. Clarke and Walker [3] suggest that capturing aspects at the design phase makes round trip development of AO systems possible, helping maintain consistency of requirements, design, and implementation.

Aspect-oriented modeling (AO) ought to have the same relationship to aspect oriented programming as object-oriented (OO) modeling has to object oriented programming. Since UML is the "standard" modeling language for OO, it is natural to try to use it for AO. Most research on AO modeling has taken this approach. Composition Patterns [3] addresses crosscutting requirements in the design phase of the development lifecycle. That approach extends UML to model aspectual behavior, separating crosscutting requirements in design. This supports traceability for crosscutting behavior that is separated at the code level, aiding traceability throughout development lifecycle. Composition Patterns is based on combining ideas from subject-oriented modeling for composing separate designs with UML templates. In the Crichton approach [4], the authors provide a modeling technique to achieve separation of concerns using statecharts. That work differentiates between active objects and passive objects at the operation level. It associates a statechart for classes, and each operation within the class has a statechart describing its behavior. However, both the Composition Patterns and the Crichton approaches require extending UML and the associated CASE tools. In Composition Patterns, UML must be extended to support binding composition relationships and the UML template specifications. In Crichton, UML is extended to support associating operations to statecharts.

Our approach uses standard UML mechanisms. This enables off-the shelf CASE tools to be used with our methodology. The key idea of our work is to use advanced features of statecharts to describe crosscutting behavior and to achieve weaving. Combining behavioral-description UML class diagrams to describe structure and association relationships between objects leads to a complete description of the system model. This enables automatic code generation using existing UML CASE tools.

This chapter presents a design methodology and modeling technique for modeling aspect-oriented software systems using the standard object-oriented modeling language UML. The chapter is organized around the main design methodology components: concepts, notation, and the modeling language component, which are presented in Section 20.2. The process described by the design methodology is addressed in Section 20.3. Section 20.4 addresses the benefits of our methodology. We summarize in Section 20.5.

20.2 CONCEPTS, NOTATION, AND THE MODELING LANGUAGE

20.2.1 Aspect-Oriented Programming

AOP provides mechanisms for decomposing a problem into functional and aspectual components (*aspects*). Aspects are concerns that cut across the functional components. Examples of aspects include synchronization, scheduling, logging, security, and fault tolerance. AOP attempts to modularize aspects and uses a weaving mechanism to combine aspects with the main functional components. In Figure 20-1, we show the difference between OO technology and AO technology.

While aspects can be thought about and analyzed separately from the core functionality, at some point before or at runtime, they must be woven together. In this chapter, we use statecharts as the communication mechanism for the weaving process.

20.2.2 The Unified Modeling Language (UML)

UML [14] is a graphical language for specifying, visualizing, constructing, and documenting the artifacts of software systems. UML is the standard modeling language for object-oriented systems endorsed by Object Management Group (OMG). UML provides several different views of the static and dynamic behavior of a software system. Table 20-1 classifies UML diagrams into inter-object behavior diagrams (use case diagram, class diagram, collaboration diagrams and sequence diagrams) or intra-object behavioral diagrams (statecharts).

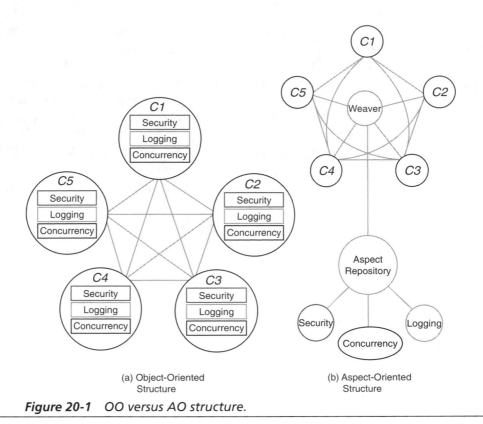

(a) Object-Oriented Structure

(b) Aspect-Oriented Structure

Figure 20-1 OO versus AO structure.

Table 20-1 UML Diagrams

Inter-Object Behavior

Diagram	UML Decomposition Dimension
Use-case diagram	Functional
Class diagram	Static
Collaboration diagram	Dynamic
Sequence diagram	Dynamic

Intra-Object Behavior

Diagram	UML Decomposition Dimension
Statecharts	Dynamic

20.2.2.1 Class Diagrams

UML class diagrams are used to describe the structural (static) view of classes. In our methodology, both core concerns and aspects are represented as classes. Each core class/aspect class in the class diagram is associated with a statechart that describes its dynamic behavior. When describing the structural view of the system, one must define classes. Interfaces depict the role a class (core/aspect) might play. Association relationships between core classes and aspects classes enable them to communicate. These relationships specify how the different components of the system are statically weaved. When combined with statechart communication mechanisms, they lead to an implicit weaving of the aspectual behavior with other components of the system.

20.2.2.2 Statecharts

UML adopted David Harel's statecharts [9] for intra-object behavior modeling. Statecharts are a behavioral language for the specification of real-time, event-driven, and reactive systems. *States* in a statechart are "conditions of existence" that "persist" for a significant period of time [6]. *Events* trigger transitions from one state to another. They maybe guarded by *conditions,* which must be true before transitioning to the next state. *Actions* can occur as the result of a state transition. Transitions are the means by which objects change states in response to events. They follow the following format:

```
Event [Condition] / Action.
```

Orthogonal regions, shown as dashed lines in statecharts, combine multiple simultaneous descriptions of the same object. Interactions between regions typically occur through shared variables, awareness of state changes in other regions, and message passing mechanisms such as broadcasting, propagating, and the IN operator (discussed later) [5]. We choose statecharts to model the behavior of objects and aspects because

1. They provide a rich set of semantics that is suitable for crosscutting concerns.
2. They assume a finite set of states [16], which reduces system complexity.
3. Modeling with statecharts results in full behavioral specifications. This allows semantics-preserving transformations between the design and implementation and thus enables automatic code generation from the design [10].

The unified approach supports the verification and validation of crosscutting concerns at the same level of verifying and validating core concerns.

To support aspect-oriented modeling within the scope of statecharts, we employ advanced statechart artifacts supported by UML. This allows the explicit representation of aspects within the system model and achieves inter-aspect/object communication within the constructed model. In the following sections, we show how to utilize the statecharts to describe the behavior of aspects and objects.

20.2.2.3 Modeling Orthogonal Concerns Using Orthogonal Regions

Statecharts support decomposition of states in an AND/OR fashion, combined with the communication mechanisms to allow communications between states. Broadcast, propagate, and the IN() operator are the main communication mechanisms [5]. Broadcast events are events communicated to more than one orthogonal component. Propagate events are events that are signaled as a result of a transition occurring in one component. The IN() operator returns true if another component is currently in a specific state. In statecharts, states can be broken down hierarchically into three kinds:

- A *Basic state* (leaf) is a state with no sub-states.
- An *Or-State* is a state that can be broken into exclusive sub-states.
- An *And-State* represents an object that is in several sub-states concurrently.

Each of the concurrent sub-states is called an orthogonal component. Statechart models govern orthogonal states whereby an object must be in exactly one state from each of the orthogonal regions. For example, in Figure 20-2 (adopted from [5]), the object behavior is divided into two orthogonal regions (S and T). Component S must be in state A or state B. Component T must be in one of states C, D, or E.

When an object receives an event, it is sent to all orthogonal regions (S, T), and each region responds to that event if the event impacts it (i.e., when a region has a transition labeled with the event name). For example, in Figure 20-2, when the object receives event T3, then in region S, the object transitions to state B (given that the object is in state A), and in region T, the object transitions to state D (given that the object is in state C). The object final state will be {A, D}. If the event does not impact a region, the object simply maintains its current state. In Figure 20-2, if the T2 event is triggered, then region S transits to state A (given that it is in state B), and Region T maintains its current state (as there is no transition that is triggered by T2 in the region).

We achieve implicit weaving and maintain separation of core concerns and aspect concerns though the use of the AND mechanism of the statecharts. This allows us to align orthogonal behavior with orthogonal aspects. By doing so, we guarantee separation of concerns in the design as well as in the implementation.

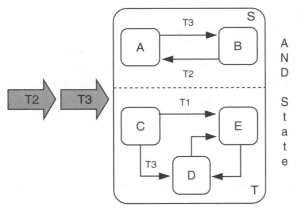

Figure 20-2   *Modeling concurrency in UML.*

20.3   THE PROCESS PRESCRIBED BY OUR METHODOLOGY

An important element of a sound behavioral modeling approach is a rigorous methodology that ensures that the semantics of the constructed model conforms to its implementation and requirements. In this section, we introduce the process prescribed by the design methodology. Section 20.3.1 describes the activities that have to be carried out to apply the methodology. We introduce the methodology by example in Sections 20.3.2 through 20.3.5. Section 20.3.6 outlines the benefits realized by this methodology.

20.3.1   AO Modeling Steps

A methodology's process describes the sequence activities that must be carried out to apply the methodology [11]. It also describes the output of each step. Table 20-2 shows the modeling steps of our methodology. In the following sections, we outline how and when to apply each step and each step's output.

20.3.2   The Concurrent Bounded Buffer Problem

Within the concurrent objects, state transitions may occur if a method is invoked or a timer has expired. Associating aspects to be evaluated when an object method is invoked is troublesome for the system modeler and developer, as the specification and constraints of these aspects are state-dependent. To illustrate the practicality of our design methodology, we apply it to the design and development of a concurrent bounded buffer. In Table 20-3, we outline the requirements that we placed on the bounded buffer system. The buffer has a limited capacity and can handle multiple read requests concurrently, while queuing all write requests. Write requests should block all other services; a blocked service is queued until the buffer is finshed writing. Synchronization and scheduling requirements crosscut the core functionality of the bounded buffer.

Table 20-2   *Modeling Steps*

Step #	Description	Output
1	Identify key core objects in the system.	Core objects
2	Identify crosscutting concerns.	Aspects
3	Identify how objects and aspects relate to each other by defining association relationships between them.	Associations (messages, each message implies an association between participating objects)
4	Model each object and aspect as an autonomous class.	Classes
5	Draw the class diagram based on previous four steps.	Class diagram
6	Identify the set of states for each object in the object structure and the dependencies between them.	A set of states names and state dependencies
7	Use the output of step 6 to describe the behavior of each class in the class diagram using statecharts.	Statecharts (behavioral description)
8	Use broadcasting mechanisms to send messages (events) between object's statechart using associations from step 3.	Implicit weaving
9	Introduce aspects as they arise orthogonally to the system and determine association relationships to existing objects and aspects.	Extensible model that is easy to maintain and comprehend

20.3.3 Analysis and Design

Requirements R6 and R7 in Table 20-3 state that we allow only the put method to proceed when the buffer is in an EMPTY state. Either put or get can be issued when the buffer is in PARTIAL state. And we shall allow only get when the buffer is in FULL state. Requirements R7 and R8 are the synchronization requirements that control access to the bounded buffer. Requirements R3 through R6 are the main scheduling requirements. They impose certain access requirements on the system, for example, that only one writer can access the system at a time, or that more than one reader can access the system at a time. Synchronization constraints and scheduling specifications are the main crosscutting requirements (aspects) that influence the execution of the invoked methods based on the object state. Figure 20-3 shows the state machine for the system with the synchronization requirements and the scheduling policies intermixed with the main functionality of the buffer. Our approach extracts these scattered aspect codes and models as autonomous pieces of behavior. In the bounded buffer statechart shown in Figure 20-3, it is troublesome to associate a condition to a transition. For example, when the buffer is in PARTIAL state and it receives a get event, the buffer has to evaluate the synchronization constraint (if the number of items in the buffer is equal to zero) and the scheduling constraint (if there are any writers accessing the buffer, queue request) before proceeding with the transition. Depending on the outcome of both constraints, the buffer might transit to the EMPTY state or remain in the PARTIAL state. We are able to eliminate the hardwiring of conditions to transitions. This hard wiring is the main cause for tangled design and its consequent tangled code.

Table 20-3   *Bounded Buffer Requirements*

Requirement #	Requirement Description
R1	The buffer will have a limited capacity.
R2	Items in the buffer will be accessed via get and put methods.
R3	The system will allow more than one reader to access the buffer at the same time.
R4	The system will allow only one writer to access the buffer at a certain time.
R5	The buffer will block all requests when a writer is present.
R6	The buffer will block get requests when it's empty.
R7	The buffer will block put requests when it's full.

Steps 1 and 2.   So far, we know that our system is composed of one main object that handles reading from and writing to the buffer. We also know that the buffer requires synchronization and scheduling, which will be modeled as aspects. The outputs from Steps 1 and 2 are shown in Table 20-4.

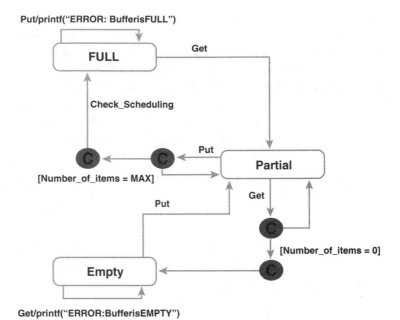

Figure 20-3 *Concurrent bounded buffer statechart with crosscutting concerns intermixed with main functionality.*

Table 20-4 *Output from Step 1 and Step 2*

Step 1	Identify key objects in the system.	`BoundedBuffer` object
Step 2	Identify crosscutting concerns.	Synchronization Aspect, Scheduling Aspect

Step 3. For objects to communicate, they must associate with each other. We have cleanly mapped the states of the bounded buffer to the states of the scheduling aspect by a one-to-one relationship, as shown in Table 20-5.

We have also related the synchronization aspect states to the buffer's states (FULL, PARTIAL, and EMPTY) depending on the number of items in the buffer. This mapping allows the synchronization aspect to block `get` requests when there are no items in the buffer (R7) and to block `put` methods when the buffer has reached its maximum capacity (R8). To prevent deadlocks, synchronization concerns have to be resolved before scheduling concerns. This implies a temporal ordering of the synchronization and scheduling aspects. The output from Step 3 is shown in Table 20-6. These associations are required to enable objects to communicate with each other.

Table 20-5   *Mapping Bounded Buffer States to Scheduling Aspect States*

Bounded Buffer State	Scheduling Aspect State	Description
IDLE	IDLE	There are no requests.
Writing	HaveWriters	A writer is currently writing to the buffer
Reading	Has-a-Readers	Readers currently reading from the buffer.

Table 20-6   *Output from Step 3*

Step 3	Identify how objects and aspects relate to each other by defining association relationships between them.	Association: Scheduling Aspect—BoundedBuffer object. Synchronization Aspect—Scheduling Aspect.

So far, we have identified objects, aspects, and association relationships between them. The next action is described in Section 20.3.4, constructing the class diagram.

20.3.4   *Structural Description Using Class Diagrams*

Class diagrams can be used to describe the static structure of the system (classes, aspects) and define the static relationships between these objects. For objects to communicate, they must associate with each other; therefore, we have to use the associations from Step 3 to connect them. We study the structure of the model using the bounded buffer problem. The bounded buffer system consists of the main functionality object, the synchronization aspect, and the scheduling aspect (from Step 3). Figure 20-4 shows the class diagram for the bounded buffer, which is the output of Steps 4 and 5. Each class in the class diagram defines its own static structure including attributes, methods, and interfaces. The lines between classes denote association relationships. The scheduling aspect is associated with readers' and writers' queues to queue read and write requests when they have to be blocked (i.e., when a `put` request is currently running).

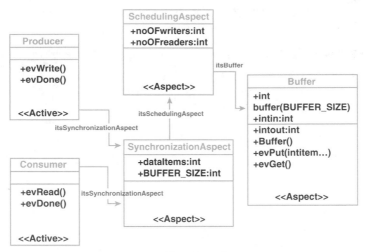

Figure 20-4   *Bounded buffer class diagram.*

20.3.5   Modeling Crosscutting Concerns (Steps 6–8)

The model shown in Figure 20-3 does not align with the main principles of separation of concerns. It is clear that both synchronization and scheduling constraints crosscut the main functionality of the bounded buffer. The conditions are hard-wired to the transition. We need to extract these conditions from the main functionality of the buffer and model them as autonomous pieces of behavior (aspects). By doing so, we guarantee that the bounded buffer's main functionality (design and the associated code) will not be tangled with the synchronization and scheduling aspects. Transitions in the bounded buffer are now controlled by aspects, which can be described by an independent statechart, as shown in Figure 20-5. Notice that extracting these crosscutting concerns (synchronization and scheduling) from the main bounded buffer makes the main functionality easier to understand and reuse, as the buffer deals only with reading and writing items.

We have achieved a unified approach. The states of the buffer, synchronization, and scheduling aspect are now controlled by the same events (`put` and `get`). Producers that trigger the `put` event and consumers that trigger the `get` event can access the system concurrently. The synchronization aspect intercepts events by default as reflected by the arrow going into the aspect state machine region. State transitions are dependent on the aspect's state (and implicitly on the buffer's state). For example, when there are no items in the buffer, the synchronization aspects are in the `EMPTY` state. When a producer issues a `put` event, the following occurs.

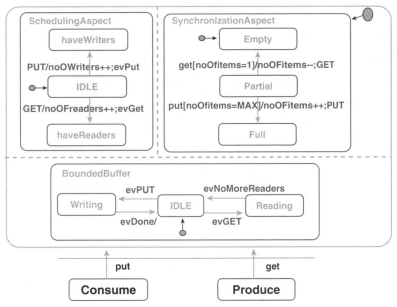

Figure 20-5 *Concurrent bounded buffer statechart with aspects.*

The synchronization aspect intercepts the event, as its region is the only region that has a transition triggered by the put event shown in Figure 20-6 (A). It

- Changes its state to PARTIAL.
- Increases the number of items by one.
- Broadcasts a PUT[1] event.
- The scheduling aspect region is the only region that has a transition triggered by the PUT event.

On a PUT event (see Figure 20-6 (B)), it

- Changes its state to haveWriters (assuming it's in IDLE state).
- Increases the number of writers by one.
- Broadcasts an evPUT event to the buffer.

---

1. Event PUT is not the same as event Put or put.

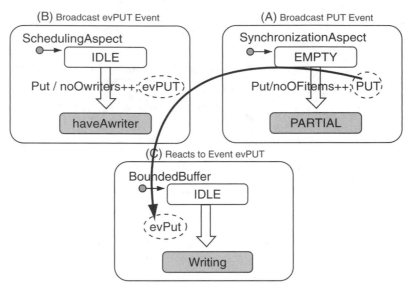

Figure 20-6   *Event broadcasting.*

The buffer is the only region that has a transition triggered by the evPUT event. When the buffer receives the evPUT event (see Figure 20-6 (C)), it

◆ Changes its state to Writing. (That is, it starts writing the item into the buffer.)

◆ When the put operation successfully completes writing the buffer, the buffer broadcasts an evDONE event back to the scheduling aspect.

Figure 20-7 shows the events as they progress from one object to another in response to a producer issuing event evPUT. The sequence of events is as follows:

◆ A consumer object issues the put event.

◆ The synchronization aspect intercepts the event (since its region is the only region that has a transition triggered by the put event), and it changes its state to PARTIAL, increases the number of items by one, and broadcasts the PUT event, as shown in Figure 20-7 (A).

◆ Since the scheduling aspect region is the only region that has a transition triggered by the PUT event, it changes its state to haveWriters (assume that it is in the IDLE state), increases the number of writers by one, and broadcasts the evPUT event, as shown in Figure 20-7 (B).

◆ Once the buffer receives the evPUT event, it changes its state to writing and starts writing the item into the buffer. When writing completes, it transitions back to IDLE state and broadcasts the event DONE, as shown in Figure 20-7 (C).

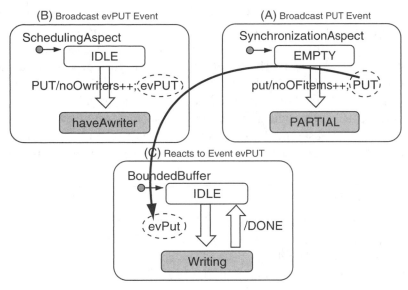

Figure 20-7 *Event broadcasting.*

The scheduling aspect intercepts the event DONE, decreases the number of writers by one, and returns to the IDLE state.

20.4 REALIZING THE BENEFITS OF OUR METHODOLOGY

In this section, we outline the benefits that are realized using this design methodology: implicit weaving, loose coupling, adaptability, traceability, and CASE tool support.

20.4.1 Implicit Weaving

We have demonstrated that we can decompose the overall system behavior into autonomous smaller pieces of behavior (aspect objects and core objects). Weaving is the process of combining different pieces of code (aspects code with core functionality code) into one executable module. We achieve implicit weaving by means of the event broadcasting techniques that send events from one state to another. Implicit weaving has the benefit of reducing coupling, as it maintains separation of concerns at the design as well as the code phase.

20.4.2 Loose Coupling

Propagating events from one object to another increases coupling between them. On the other hand, broadcasting events eliminates coupling but increases overhead. We use unique event names when an object needs to signal an event to another object and do not want another object to respond to that event (synchronous). For example, in the bounded buffer, the synchronization aspect broadcasts the GET event. The scheduling aspect implicitly (no coupling) intercepts this event since it is the only object that is affected by it. The scheduling aspect in turn processes the request and broadcasts the event evGET. The bounded buffer again intercepts the event implicitly, does the actual reading of the item, and, once done, broadcasts the evDONE event to be intercepted by the scheduling aspect. Introducing new events for each interface to an object increases the number of events as the number of objects/aspects increases. Tradeoffs among these different possibilities are application-dependent.

20.4.3 Extensibility

We can add more orthogonal aspects to the system without impacting the existing orthogonal regions (existing aspects or main functionality). To demonstrate this, we introduce the Error Handler aspect to the concurrent bounded buffer. The Error Handler aspect statechart is shown in Figure 20-8 A.

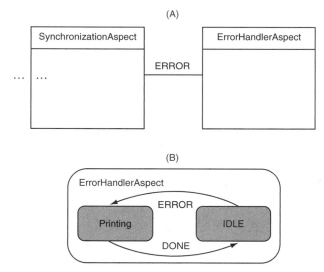

Figure 20-8 *Error Handler aspect.*

We define an association relationship(s) between the Error Handler aspect and the other aspects/objects in the system. Assume that a new requirement has been added to enable the synchronization aspect to generate an error when a request for get is broadcast while the system is in EMPTY state. From this requirement, we can determine that there is an association relationship between the synchronization aspect and error aspects. This association is shown in Figure 20-8 (A); Figure 20-8 (B) shows the statechart for the Error Handler aspect. After the Error Handler aspect has been introduced to the system's class diagram via an association relationship with the synchronization aspect, the synchronization aspect can broadcast events to it. The synchronization aspect now broadcasts the ERROR event when there is a request for GET, when the buffer is in the EMPTY state, or when there is a request for put when the buffer is in FULL state. Nothing else has changed. There is no impact on the scheduling aspect or the buffer itself. If the system evolves so that the scheduler needs the new error service, we first must define an association to then. The schedule can then generate errors simply by broadcasting ERROR events.

20.4.4   *Traceability*

Earlier, we argued that one of the benefits of introducing aspects at an early phase of the development lifecycle is *traceability*: the ability to trace the derivation from requirements through design to code. Table 20-7 shows where the requirements of the bounded buffer have been implemented.

Table 20-7   *Requirements Traceability*

Requirement #	Requirement Description	Implementation
R1, R6, R7	Capacity requirements	Synchronization aspect
R2	Access requirements	Buffer class
R3, R4, R5	Scheduling requirements	Scheduling aspect

20.4.5   *CASE Tools Support for Our Methodology*

Having captured aspects at a high level, including their role, behavior, structure, and crosscutting of classes, we would like to feed the model into existing UML CASE tools. Our research has progressed to the point where we have automatically generated the code for the bounded buffer with Rhapsody [12]. An important property of this code is that it preserves the separation between core modules and aspect modules. This in turn preserves the advantages of aspect orientation at the code level.

20.4.6   *Automatic Code Generation and Round-Trip Development*

As shown in Figure 20-9, the system model consists of static and dynamic behavior [10]. Both have been described so that we can have full automatic code generation (including weaving). We have used UML's class diagrams to describe the static view of the model and UML's statecharts to describe the dynamic view of the model. We fed our model to Rhapsody and automatically generated code from the design.

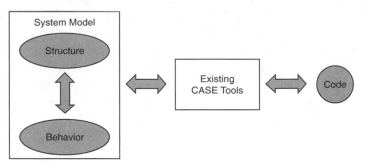

Figure 20-9 *Automatic code generation via existing CASE tools.*

In Figure 20-9, the double arrows between code and system model means round-trip development. Changes to either (code or design) are automatically reflected in the other. This round trip feature is supported by most existing object-oriented CASE tools.

20.5 CONCLUSION

We have argued that aspect-oriented modeling should have the same relationship to aspect-oriented programming as object-oriented modeling has to object-oriented programming. Maturity of AOP leads to aspect-oriented modeling and AO support for all phases of the software development life cycle. Aspect-oriented modeling with UML has been the subject of several recent workshops [18, 19, 20].

ACKNOWLEDGMENTS

This work is supported in part by NSF grant No-0137743. We would like to thank the concurrent programming research group at IIT for its contributions.

REFERENCES

1. ALDAWUD, O., ELRAD, T., AND BADER, A. 2003. UML Profile for Aspect-Oriented Software Development. In *Workshop on Aspect-Oriented Modeling with UML (AOSD)*, (Boston). http://lglwww.epfl.ch/workshops/aosd2003/papers/AldawudAOSD_UML_Profile.pdf.

2. ALDAWUD, O., ELRAD, T., AND BADER, A. 2001. Aspect-oriented modeling to automate the implementation and validation of concurrent software systems. In *Workshop on Specification, Implementation and Validation of Object-Oriented Embedded Systems (SIVOES, ECOOP)*, (Budapest). http://wooddes.intranet.gr/ecoop2001/sivoes2001.htm.

3. CLARKE, S. AND WALKER, R. J. 2001. Composition patterns: An approach to designing reusable aspects. In *23rd Int'l Conf. Software Engineering (ICSE)*, (Toronto). IEEE, 5–14.

4. CRICHTON, C., CAVARRA, A., AND DAVIES, J. 2002. A pattern for concurrency in UML. Tech. Rep. RR-01-22, Oxford University Computing Laboratory. http://web.comlab.ox.ac.uk/oucl/research/areas/softeng/FASE2002.pdf.

5. DOUGLASS, B. P. 1997. *Real-Time UML: Developing Efficient Objects for Embedded Systems*. Addison-Wesley, Reading, Massachusetts.

6. DOUGLASS, B. P. 1999. UML statecharts: A white paper. *Embedded Systems Programming 12*, 1 (Jan.). http://www.embedded.com/1999/9901/9901feat1.htm.

7. ELRAD, T., FILMAN, R. E., AND BADER, A. 2001. Aspect-oriented programming. *Comm. ACM 44*, 10 (Oct.), 29–32.

8. GRAY, J., BAPTY, T., NEEMA, S., AND TUCK, J. 2001. Handling crosscutting constraints in domain-specific modeling. *Comm. ACM 44*, 10 (Oct.), 87–93.

9. HAREL, D. 1987. Statecharts: A visual formalism for complex systems. *Science of Computer Programming 8*, 231–274.

10. HAREL, D. 2001. From play-in scenarios to code: An achievable dream. *IEEE Computer 34*, 1, 53–60.

11. HAREL, D. AND POLITI, M. 1994. *Modeling Reactive Systems with StateCharts*. McGraw-Hill, New York.

12. I-LOGIX. Rhapsody user's guide. http://www.ilogix.com/products/rhapsody/index.cfm.

13. KICZALES, G., HILSDALE, E., HUGUNIN, J., KERSTEN, M., PALM, J., AND GRISWOLD, W. G. 2001. An overview of AspectJ. In *ECOOP 2001—Object-Oriented Programming, 15th European Conference*, (Budapest), J. L. Knudsen, Ed. LNCS, vol. 2072. Springer-Verlag, Berlin, 327–353.

14. OBJECT MANAGEMENT GROUP. 2002. CORBA security service specification, version 1.8. http://www.omg.org.

15. Ossher, H., Kaplan, M., Harrison, W., Katz, A., and Kruskal, V. 1995. Subject-oriented composition rules. In *10th Conf. Object-Oriented Programming, Systems, Languages, and Applications (OOPSLA)*, (Austin). ACM 235–250.

16. Pazzi, L. 1999. Explicit aspect composition by part-whole state charts. In *Int'l Workshop on Aspect-Oriented Programming (ECOOP)*, (Lisbon). http://trese.cs.utwente.nl/aop-ecoop99/papers/pazzi.pdf.

17. Suzuki, J. and Yamamoto, Y. 1999. Extending UML with aspects: Aspect support in the design phase. In *Int'l Workshop on Aspect-Oriented Programming (ECOOP)*, (Lisbon). http://trese.cs.utwente.nl/aop-ecoop99/papers/suzuki.pdf.

18. Workshop on AOM: Aspect-Oriented Modeling with UML. 2002. *1st Int'l Conf. Aspect-Oriented Software Development (AOSD)*, (Enschede, The Netherlands). http://trese.cs.utwente.nl/aosd2002.

19. Workshop on AOM: Aspect-Oriented Modeling with UML. 2002. *5th Int'l Conf. on the Unified Modeling Language—the Language and its Applications. (UML 2002)*, (Dresden, Germany). http://lglwww.epfl.ch/workshops/uml2002/.

20. Workshop on AOM: Aspect-Oriented Modeling with UML. 2003. *2nd Int'l Conf. Aspect-Oriented Software Development (AOSD)*, (Boston). http://aosd.net/archive/2003/program/workshops.

Chapter 21

Concern Modeling for Aspect-Oriented Software Development

STANLEY M. SUTTON JR. AND ISABELLE ROUVELLOU

Separation of concerns is a fundamental principle of software engineering. Of course, concerns are modeled in a variety of guises in contemporary software development, but the modeling approaches used typically depend on the development method, development stage, artifact formalism, and other project-specific factors. Concerns in various representations are also the focus of aspect-oriented software development (AOSD) techniques. However, concerns as such are still not modeled independently, and concern modeling is still not a distinguished activity in software development.

In this chapter, we argue that concerns must be first-class entities and concern modeling must be a first-class activity in AOSD. That is, concern modeling should be an explicit and integral part of AOSD methods, and concerns should be modeled in their own appropriate formalisms, separately from their representations in requirements, design, code, and other software artifacts. We discuss the meaning of *concern* and consider the characteristics of concerns in the life cycle. We show that, while existing modeling approaches address concerns in specific contexts for specific purposes, a general-purpose concern-modeling capability is still needed. We describe requirements for a concern-modeling language and discuss the role of concern modeling in the software process. Finally, we give an overview of a general-purpose concern-space modeling schema, Cosmos, which we illustrate with an example based on the transformation of an individual component into a product family.

21.1 INTRODUCTION

Separation of concerns (SOC) is a long-established principle in software engineering [30]. It has received widespread attention in modern programming languages, with constructs such as modules, packages, classes, and interfaces supporting properties such as abstraction, encapsulation, and information hiding. SOC has also received attention in software architecture and design, with techniques such as Composition Filters [1] and design patterns [12]. While advances in all of these areas have had significant benefits, problems due to inadequate separation of concerns remain [14]. This has led to recent work on "advanced separation of concerns" (ASOC), including subject-oriented programming and design [8, 13], aspect-oriented programming [11, 21], and multi-dimensional separation of concerns [37]. These bring several innovative ideas to programming in particular and to software development in general, which are now beginning to mature and coalesce under the heading of aspect-oriented software development (AOSD).

Surprisingly, concerns themselves have so far remained something of second-class citizens in ASOD. Current ASOD tools provide only limited support for explicit concern modeling. Representations of concerns tend to be tied to particular tools or artifacts, and concern modeling usually occurs only in the context of a particular type of development activity, such as coding or design [8, 22, 37]. A global perspective on concerns, one that spans the lifecycle and is independent of particular development tools or artifacts, has been lacking.

Concerns do not play a second-class role in software development. They arise at every stage of the lifecycle, spanning activities, artifacts, methods, and tools. If AOSD is to be fully realized, concerns must be treated as first-class entities throughout the lifecycle. Concern modeling must be a recognized and essential part of AOSD methods, and concerns must have independent representations on the same level as requirements, architecture, design, and so on.

Sections 21.2 and 21.3 define concerns and give a characterization of concerns in the software lifecycle. In Section 21.4, we argue that general-purpose, independent concern modeling is needed. Section 21.5 presents some requirements for a concern-modeling formalism and discusses some process issues related to concern modeling. Section 21.6 then gives an overview of the Cosmos concern-modeling schema, followed by an example of concern modeling in Section 21.7. Section 21.8 describes related work in the form of four early-lifecycle approaches to software modeling that address concerns in particular contexts. Section 21.9 provides some additional discussion of issues, and Section 21.10 presents a conclusion.

21.2   WHAT IS A CONCERN?

Although most software developers have a good intuitive sense of what a concern is, good definitions of *concern* are hard to come by. *Aspects* are one category of concern: An aspect is a (program) property that cannot be cleanly encapsulated in a "generalized procedure" (such as an object, method, procedure, or API) [21]. A later but comparable definition is that an aspect is a program property that forces cross-cutting in the implementation [11]. These definitions identify a critical property of some concerns that makes separation of concerns problematic in conventional programming languages. However, it is too focused on program structure (and code) to qualify as a general definition of concern. Tarr and others [37] define a concern as a predicate over software units. This definition is not limited to code and appropriately spans the lifecycle, but it is still based on software units.

To promote concerns to first-class status in software development, they must be defined independently of any specific type of software artifact and even of software artifacts in general. One dictionary definition of *concern* is "a matter for consideration" [27]. More specifically to software, an IEEE standard defines the concerns for a system as ". . . those interests which pertain to the system's development, its operation or any other aspects that are critical or otherwise important to one or more stakeholders" [17, p. 4]. We take *concern* generally to be any matter of interest in a software system. This may not seem like a particularly technical definition, but it is open, simple, and intuitive, encompasses other definitions, and is suitable for many purposes. We give some examples in Section 21.7.

Based on this definition, it follows that concerns are fundamentally *conceptual*. They are *not,* in general, artifacts, although artifacts may represent concerns, and artifacts may be of concern (say, as work products in a development task). Concerns are *not,* in general, requirements, although requirements represent concerns and are of concern at many points in a development process. Similarly, a concern model is *not,* in general, a domain model, although a domain model may contribute concerns (or define a domain over which concerns are expressed).

21.3 A VIEW OF CONCERNS

Given the previous definition of concerns as matters of interest in a system, what can we say about them as a prospective domain for modeling? What do we know about them *a priori* based on our overall knowledge of software development and early experience with AOSD?

First, concerns arise at all stages of the software lifecycle. This is implicit in the different purposes, activities, formalisms, and artifacts associated with the different stages of development. A variety of concerns, in various forms, are documented for requirements specification [40, 42], architecture and design [8], coding [13, 22, 37], testing [32], and maintenance and evolution [14].

Individual concerns also span multiple phases of the lifecycle, relate to multiple instances and types of artifacts, and crosscut phases and artifacts in different ways

[4, 32, 37]. For example, a concern for performance may be associated with a set of use cases in requirements, a choice of architectural styles and design patterns that may facilitate performance, algorithms for efficiently implementing specific logical components, and so on.

Finally, concerns are dynamic and relative. The concerns relevant to a particular software product or individual unit change over time, and they also depend on the perspective or purpose of the developer, user, or other stakeholder who considers the software [17, 23, 28, 32].

Based on previous studies, we believe that concern spaces are multi-dimensional; that is, many concerns of multiple types may apply to a particular software unit at any one time [28, 32, 37]. For example, functionality, behavior, performance, reliability, and understandability may all apply to a particular class or method. Additionally, we believe that a concern space is highly structured; that is, that concerns can be organized by multiple relationships of multiple types, that these relationships may be independent or dependent, and that they commonly have a hierarchical or lattice-like organization [32, 33].

21.4 WHY DO WE NEED CONCERN MODELING?

Most, if not all, of software development can be viewed as modeling related to concerns. We don't call the various activities involved "concern-modeling," though, because their primary focus is on other things: requirements, architecture, design, implementation, and so on. The modeling approaches currently used in software development enable the modeling of many kinds of concerns in many forms. However, none of them models concerns in general or in the abstract. For example, none of them allows us to say simply that performance is a concern, although they enable us to say that achieving high performance is a goal or to select an architectural style based on performance properties. In this section, we justify modeling concerns explicitly as first-class entities.

21.4.1 Specification and Analysis of Concerns Across the Development Lifecycle and Artifacts

Concerns, collectively and individually, occur across the development lifecycle and development artifacts. Therefore, we need to be able to specify and analyze concerns across the development lifecycle and artifacts. Concerns exist *ab initio* with respect to the lifetime of a system. Although concerns arise throughout system evolution, the system itself arises from some concerns that preceded it, and these concerns exist before and apart from any representation they may have in the system or associated work products. Concerns also span multiple representations in particular artifacts and formalisms, and the relevance of particular concerns crosses development methods, processes, and stages. We can see examples of this with specific concerns such as performance.

21.4.2 Enhancement of Traditional Development Tasks

Concern models have many potential applications that complement or supplement traditional development tasks. One area of application is based on the analysis and understanding of concerns themselves. Individual concerns may be defined, have associated attributes (e.g., related to ownership, priority, or process stage), be related to other concerns (e.g., to show refinement, motivation, dependence), and be individually or collectively constrained (e.g., to be used exclusively or in combination). Formal representations of concerns would enable analysis for their completeness, correctness, and consistency. In turn, the analysis of concerns can help in assessing the completeness, correctness, and consistency of software artifacts in which concerns are represented.

Another area of application for concern modeling arises from the relationship of concerns to particular work products. Concerns in a first-class model can be associated to particular requirements statements, design elements, code units, and so on. These may be artifacts from which the concerns are derived, in which they are implemented, through which they are affected, and so on. An independent concern model, with meaningful links into an artifact set, can be viewed as a kind of semantic hyperindex to the artifacts (comparable to a topic map [18]). Such a model has many possible uses, including

- Organizing and associating product elements according to the concerns to which they are related (the refinements of [4] would be an extended case).
- Tracing concerns across artifacts and indirectly across associated formalisms, development stages, processes, and organizational units.
- Supporting impact analysis by enabling the determination of concerns affected when artifacts are changed and of artifacts affected when concerns are changed.
- Facilitating the propagation of changes to artifacts linked by shared concerns.
- Supporting rationale capture and analysis by linking artifacts to the concerns that they implement or influence and by semantically linking those concerns to other concerns that may provide motivation for them or receive contributions from them.

- Contributing to reuse by providing a semantic context in which artifacts (or elements of them) can be considered or presented for reuse.

- Enabling additional analyses for completeness, consistency, and correctness of an artifact base with respect to a given concern space.

These applications do not depend on the use of other AOSD technologies or methods. Concern modeling can be used, for example, to facilitate traceability between development stages [26], to analyze a system in preparation for evolution, or to evaluate a candidate component for reuse, all within the context of traditional development methods.

21.4.3 Support of AOSD

Finally, if we are to develop a discipline of aspect-oriented software development based on advanced separation of concerns, it seems appropriate to consider concerns, in general and in the abstract, as first-class entities in their own right. Additionally, concern modeling lends support to specific AOSD approaches. For example, in aspect weaving such as with AspectJ [22], code units that represent a particular aspect such as logging are integrated or "woven" into a base program. However, the base program certainly represents a combination of concerns, and the aspect code, although it typically emphasizes a particular concern, will inevitably involve multiple concerns. For example, logging affects performance and recoverability, and it may serve purposes such as auditing and analysis. Effective aspect weaving thus depends on the compatibility of concerns in the base model and the aspect.

For code composition with Hyper/J [16], Java classes are organized into a multidimensional concern space. Units are related to specific concerns in specific dimensions, and composition is specified in terms of the dimensions and concerns to be integrated. Modeling of concerns is thus a part of the Hyper/J method. An example of the use of Cosmos with Hyper/J, which motivates the integration of concern modeling with other aspect-oriented tools, is given in Section 21.7.

In general, if the goal of AOSD is to enable us to specify the composition and decomposition of systems in terms of concerns, then the specification, analysis, and interrelation of concerns should be a fundamental part of any fully developed AOSD lifecycle. The modeling of concerns, including capturing how they relate to each other and how they are either individually or collectively constrained, is key to allowing a more systematic and therefore manageable use of AOSD techniques. It is a fundamental element to enable AOSD approaches to scale to address composition (and decomposition) of "enterprise" systems (e.g., systems where the relevant level of abstraction is not code units but systems that are very complex because of richness of aspects).

21.5   CONCERN MODELING AS A FIRST-CLASS UNDERTAKING

To make concern modeling a first-class undertaking in software development (AOSD, OOSD, or otherwise), a schema for the modeling of concerns must be adopted, and the activity of concern modeling must be integrated into development processes. In this section, we consider requirements on a concern-modeling schema and discuss issues in integrating concern modeling into the software lifecycle.[1]

21.5.1   Requirements for a Concern-Modeling Schema

Since a concern model is an information model, any language for modeling information or representing knowledge may have some applicability to concern modeling. The initial models we constructed when we began our investigations [33] were informal. Though informal models may be useful for ad hoc or experimental purposes, formal models are more powerful and offer a firmer foundation for an aspect-oriented software engineering discipline. However, different formal languages offer different advantages for different purposes. Thus, while some benefits may indeed be gained by applying existing formalisms to concern modeling, we believe that consideration should be given specifically to the requirements of modeling concerns.

We have identified desirable properties that are useful for a concern-modeling schema, including generality, independence, appropriateness, completeness, and ease of use.

- Generality is important for serving many purposes and allowing users to capture a variety of concerns.
- Independence is important for minimizing the effect of other choices of development methods, tools, and approaches on concern modeling.
- Appropriateness is important for facilitating expressing the kinds of concerns that users have and the kinds of information that they want to express about them.
- Completeness is important for allowing users to express all of the important aspects of a concern model.
- Ease of use is important for facilitating adoption and use.

---

1. Tooling and methods may also be necessary, but these depend in part on which AOSD technologies are adopted, and they are beyond the scope of this chapter.

These desired general characteristics can be addressed through a number of recommendations more specific to concern modeling.

For completeness, it is important to be able to model not only concerns but also relationships between concerns and consistency conditions on concerns. For generality, the schema should allow users to define arbitrary concerns, relationships, and conditions. For completeness and generality, it should be possible to view these relationships and constraints as concerns themselves. Since not all kinds of concerns and relationships can be anticipated, the formalism should include elements for allowing users to define their own kinds of concern. This also supports appropriateness since it would allow specific schemas to be tailored to specific projects. To facilitate ease of use, some specific but commonly useful types of concern and relationship should be included.

To support completeness, generality, and appropriateness, it should be possible to organize concerns in various ways, such as by classifications (including multiple classifications), aggregations, and other groupings.

For independence, a general-purpose concern-modeling schema should be independent from other modeling or implementation languages, artifact types, lifecycle stages, and development methods. For independence and generality, it should also be possible to capture concerns (or related data) that are not necessarily captured in other development formalisms.

In asserting that a concern-modeling schema should be independent, we do not mean to suggest that it cannot be based on or used closely with other languages. Rather, it should be possible for the concern-modeling schema to be meaningful and usable on its own. (For example, a concern-modeling schema may be relational, but it should not depend on the use of relational modeling in other parts of the development process.) Also, while we are advocating a general-purpose concern-modeling schema, it is possible to define more specialized approaches to be integrated with (and dependent on) particular development languages, artifact types, or methods. Within a specialized context, this may increase the appropriateness and ease of use of the formalism.

Finally, many of the potential applications of concern modeling depend on the ability to relate concerns to associated artifacts, that is, artifacts that may represent, define, implement, affect, or otherwise be of significance for the concerns. To some extent, this depends on the nature of the artifacts, such as the ability to reference and access the artifacts and their constituent parts. Where feasible, concerns should be related directly to artifacts, although it may be problematic to establish the reverse relationships, i.e., from artifacts to concerns (as the artifact representations may not accommodate these references). As an alternative, a model of the artifact space may be constructed, analogous to the domain models used in domain specific software architectures (DSSA) [39] (with the artifacts, in effect, as the domain). In this case, concerns are related to the artifact model, and relationships from the artifact model to the concern model can be easily represented. A similar approach is used in UML (v. 1.4 [29]), in which the physical elements of systems are represented by "nodes" and "artifacts," and design elements, such as "classes" and "components," are associated to them.

21.5.2   *Process Considerations*

In general, there are many ways to use concern modeling within a software development process, just as there are many ways to specify requirements or to model architecture. The role of concern modeling depends on the development method and the process objective. The following scenarios suggest the range of possibilities:

◆ In a process centered on using commercial, off-the-shelf software (COTS), a concern model of the system under development (SUD) may be constructed for evaluating the compatibility and potential contribution of candidate COTS products. These products can be characterized in terms of the concerns they address and evaluated against the concern framework of the SUD. The suitability of particular products can be determined based on the consistency or inconsistency of concerns, the range of concerns addressed, the need for tailoring to assure compatibility, and the concerns remaining to be addressed.

◆ In new development, a limited concern model can be elaborated at the start of development to represent the initial concerns that motivate or constrain the project. As development progresses through requirements, architectural design, detailed design, and so on, the concern model can be elaborated. Concerns can be related to the various work products in which they are defined, implemented, or otherwise addressed, and relationships between concerns can be drawn to capture semantic, operational, and other dependencies. The concern model can be analyzed to assess the consistency and coherence of the concerns associated to the project. As the life cycle iterates, changes made at various stages can be validated against the concern model, and the concern model can be used to help propagate updates through both the concern space and the artifact space.

◆ In the retroactive extension of a product line based on an existing product, concern modeling can be used to characterize the potential feature space and to characterize the product variants within that space. An initial concern model can be developed of the existing product. The product can be decomposed into units corresponding to specific concerns. Concerns representing additional features can be identified and related to the existing model, and additional work products can be developed to support implementation of the additional concerns. Variants within the product family can then be specified by selecting concerns of interest from within the product-family concern space. Compositional technologies may then be used to compose a product variant using implementations associated to the selected concerns. This sort of scenario is discussed in more detail in Section 21.7.

As these scenarios suggest, concern modeling may be done before initial development, during development, or as specific needs arise afterwards. It may be done independently of, or in close association with, other development activities. It may be done in one step or incrementally. It may be for particular work products or sets of concerns or comprehensively for a product or complete concern space. Finally, it may be done for general purposes or to address specific problems.

21.6 COSMOS: A CONCERN-SPACE MODELING SCHEMA

Cosmos is a general-purpose concern-space modeling schema that addresses the requirements outlined in Section 21.5.1. Cosmos models software concern spaces in terms of *concerns*, *relationships*, and *predicates*. We give a concise overview and example of Cosmos in this section (see Table 21-1). A more detailed discussion can be found in [36].

Cosmos divides concerns into two main categories, logical and physical. Logical concerns represent conceptual concerns, as "matters of interest"—issues, problems, "-ilities," and so on. Physical concerns deal with the actual things that constitute our systems, such as specific work products, software units, hardware units, and services. Physical concerns are a way to bring the "real world" (to which our logical concerns apply) into the concern-modeling space. They play a role analogous to that of nodes and artifacts in UML [29].

For completeness, and consistent with a multi-dimensional perspective on concerns, predicates and relationships are also classified as concerns. In other words, a predicate over concerns or a relationship between concerns may itself represent a matter of interest. In many situations, though, it is natural to think of predicates and concerns as top-level elements of the concern space, which is how we discuss them here. There is also a fifth kind of concern, concern groups. These represent the idea that groups of concerns may also be of concern. Concern groups are parameterized by the type of concern they can contain. The element type can be any type in the hierarchy of model elements, so specific concern groups can be made inclusive or exclusive as necessary.

Table 21-1   *Cosmos Concern Model Elements: Outline*

Concerns
- ○ Logical
  - ■ Classifications
  - ■ Classes
  - ■ Instances
  - ■ Properties
  - ■ Types
- ○ Physical
  - ■ Collections
  - ■ Instances
  - ■ Attributes
- ○ Predicates
- ○ Relationships
- ○ Groups

Predicates
- ■ // subtypes not elaborated

Relationships
- ○ Categorical
  - ■ Classification
  - ■ Generalization
  - ■ Instantiation
  - ■ Characterization
  - ■ Topicality
  - ■ Attribution
  - ■ Membership
- ○ Interpretive
  - ■ *Contribution*
  - ■ *Motivation*
  - ■ *Admission*
  - ■ *Logical implementation*
  - ■ *Logical composition*
  - ■ *Logical requisition*
- ○ Physical
  - ■ Physical association
  - ■ *Physical requisition*
- ○ Mapping
  - ■ Mapping association
  - ■ *Physical implementation*

Note: Items in normal font are part of the core schema; items in italic font are representative schema extensions used in particular concern models

Logical concerns are further categorized as classifications, classes, instances, properties, and topics. Classifications are for modeling systems of classes and allow for multiple classification of concerns [35]. Classes are for categorization of concerns, for example, by functionality, behavior, or state.[2] Instances represent particular concerns, usually of some class, such as particular functions, behaviors, or states. Properties are characteristics, such as performance, configurability, robustness, that may apply to classes and instances. Topics are groups of concerns of generally different types, typically related to a theme of user interest, such as the classes, instances, and properties that are related to the theme of "logging."

---

2. Classes of concern in Cosmos should not be confused with classes in design notations or programming languages. Cosmos classes serve the purpose of classification of concerns in a taxonomic or ontological sense, which we believe is essential to concern modeling.

Physical concerns comprise instances, collections, and attributes. Physical instances represent particular system elements (such as source files, design documents, workstations). Collections represent groups of these. Attributes are the specific properties of instances or collections, such as the size of a design document or number of files in a directory.

Relationships are divided into four categories: categorical, interpretive, physical, and mapping. *Categorical relationships* reflect fundamental semantics of the concern categories, such as generalization, which relates (sub)classes to (super)classes, instantiation, which relates instances (both logical and physical) classes, and characterization, which relates properties to kinds and instances.

Interpretive relationships relate logical concerns according to user-assigned semantics. One example is contribution, which indicates that one concern (e.g., logging behavior) contributes in some way to another (e.g., robustness). Another interpretive relationship is motivation, which indicates that one concern (e.g., robustness) motivates another (e.g., logging). Such relationships are especially important in understanding the system-specific semantics of concerns.

Physical relationships associate physical concerns, such as composition relationships that associate Java classes in Hyper/J [16] or connectivity relationships among nodes in a network.

Mapping relationships represent (non-categorical) associations between logical and physical concerns, such as the implementation of a logical function by a Java class. These are important (along with interpretive relationships) for purposes such as dependency analysis, impact assessment, and change propagation. They are also important for assessing component reuse and composition potential.

Predicates represent integrity conditions over various relationships and can be classified accordingly. For example, categorical predicates apply to categorical relationships, and interpretive predicates apply to interpretive relationships. Examples of the former are that no concern can be both a class and an instance and that no class can include both logical and physical instances. An example of the latter is that, if one concern motivates another, then the second should contribute to the first (whereas the converse is not required).

21.7 A CONCERN-MODEL EXAMPLE

This section provides an example of concern modeling based on the GPS cache, a general-purpose (software) cache that is intended to be reusable in a variety of applications [19]. The GPS cache is richly functioned and featured. It supports the usual functionality associated with a cache, and it has some less common features such object dependencies, logging, and statistics collection. It is also highly configurable, both statically and dynamically. The GPS cache has been used in web publishing [24] (including IBM web sites for major sports events) and in support of business rule evaluation [9].

We have been interested in the GPS cache as the potential prototype for a "component family," a collection of specialized caches with various, more or less overlapping combinations of features, functions, behaviors, and properties. Our approach to developing this family of caches was based on aspect-oriented ideas and tools. In particular, we wanted to allow a cache to be specified in terms of a particular set of desired concerns and then to enable a cache that addressed those concerns to be composed from reusable, concern-specific fragments of Java code. To achieve this, we used Cosmos for concern modeling and Hyper/J [16] for composition of Java units. This work is described at more length in [34].

Here, we consider our initial modeling of concerns for the GPS cache, primarily as it was programmed, but also including some obvious generalizations. This modeling served two purposes. First, it established a baseline for the concerns that a cache may address and provided a core around which we could organize conceptions and models of what a cache is and how it may be subject to variation [34]. Second, this modeling allowed us to see which concerns were addressed in which parts of the cache code. This provided a basis for decomposing the code into more specialized units that were suitable for recomposition into alternative variants.

Examples of high-level concerns in the implementation of the GPS cache are outlined in Table 21-2, "Selected Concerns from the GPS Cache." (For discussion of relationships and predicates, see [36].)

According to the Cosmos model, concerns are organized as logical or physical, with logical concerns here including concern classes, instances, properties, and topics, and physical concerns including instances, collections, and properties. The top-level concern classes we distinguished included implementation object classes, functionality, behavior, state, properties, and Java units.

Implementation-object classes are concerns in and of themselves and are also used to organize subclasses under other concern classes (such as functionality, behavior, and state). Under functionality, nine different functional areas are associated with the `Cache` class, grouping from one to eight methods (omitted for brevity). Methods in the "printing" group are also included under other groups as they print information relative to those groups.

For the `CachedObject` class, existing methods fall into three groups, and additional groups (not initially used) can be identified by generalization from the `Cache` class; these can be populated later.

Behaviors are grouped into those specific to operations, those aspectual to operations, and those not associated with operations. Behaviors in these groups may be related; for example, the behavior of specific operations to turn statistics logging on or off has an effect on the logging of collected statistics, a behavior that is not associated with any particular operation.

A number of themes occur repeatedly under various kinds of concerns, such as "core," "logging," and others. Such crosscutting concerns represent other dimensions by which the concern space can be organized. For instance, object classes could occur under "core" and under "logging" instead of vice-versa. Topics are one way to represent such crosscutting concerns.

Table 21-2 *Selected Concerns from the GPS Cache*

Logical Concerns: Classes

Object classes
- ○ Cache
- ○ CachedObject
- ○ *Other object classes* . . .

Functionality
- ○ Cache
  - ■ Core
  - ■ Object expiration
  - ■ Operation-enabling
  - ■ Dependencies
  - ■ Object invalidation
  - ■ Operation logging
  - ■ Statistics logging
  - ■ Printing
- ○ CachedObject
  - ■ Core
  - ■ Expiration
  - ■ Dependencies
  - ■ *Other functionalities* . . .
- ○ *Other classes* . . .

Behavior
- ○ Cache
  - ■ Operational
    - ■ Core
    - ■ Object expiration
    - ■ Operation enabling
    - ■ Dependencies
    - ■ Object invalidation
    - ■ Operation logging
    - ■ Statistics logging
    - ■ Printing

- ■ Aspectual
  - ■ Input checking
  - ■ Operation enabling
  - ■ Operation logging
  - ■ Object expiration
- ■ Non-operational
  - ■ Statistics logging
- ○ CachedObject
  - ■ Operational behaviors
    - ■ Core
    - ■ Expiration
    - ■ *Other operational behaviors*
  - ■ *Other behaviors* ...

State
- ○ Cache
  - ■ Objects
  - ■ Dependencies
  - ■ Configurable controls
    - ■ Operation enabling
    - ■ Operation logging
    - ■ Statistics logging
  - ■ Operation log
- ○ Statistics counters

Properties
- ○ Static properties
- ○ Dynamic properties

Java code
- ○ Programmed classes
  - ■ Classes
  - ■ Members
- ○ Decomposed classes
  - ■ *Anticipated*

Logical Concerns: Other Categories

Instances	**Properties**
○ *Omitted for brevity*	○ Generality
Topics	○ Performance
○ Dependencies and transitivity	○ Information hiding
○ Configurable behaviors	○ Concurrency
○ *Other topics . . .*	○ Configurability
	○ Correctness
	○ *Other properties . . .*

Physical Concerns

Instances	**Collections**
○ com.ibm.ws.abr.gps.-Cache.java	○ whimbrel.watson.ibm.com
○ com.ibm.ws.abr.gps.-Cache.class	C:\$Sutton\Caching\Code\Java\Programmed
○ com.ibm.ws.abr.gps.-CachedObject.java	○ *Other collections . . .*
○ com.ibm.ws.abr.gps.-CachedObject.class	**Attributes**
○ *Other instances . . .*	○ com.ibm.ws.abr.gps.-Cache.java.Size
	○ *Other attributes . . .*

In principle, there are many ways that a model of concerns in the cache might be organized and presented. Cosmos supports the modeling of multi-dimensional concern spaces, and concerns in the cache can indeed be described multi-dimensionally. That is, many elements in the cache can be assigned to concerns in multiple classifications, and any of several classifications might be distinguished as the basis of a view of the concern space.

We continued our work on the cache product family by decomposing the cache implementation into small units focused on specific concerns. We then elaborated the concern model to include concerns of interest that were not addressed in the original cache, programming implementations for these. Using Hyper/J [16], and transforming the Cosmos concern-space model into the Hyper/J representations for a hyperspace specification and concern mapping, we composed about alternative versions of the cache. In these we added, deleted, and replaced methods; added, deleted, and replaced fields; changed the behaviors of methods; changed the methods to which particular behaviors were associated; changed aspects associated to methods; introduced and removed features; affected properties such as performance, size, and robustness; and substituted implementation structures. Using the same units, many additional cache variants could be composed to address additional combinations of concerns.

21.8 RELATED WORK

In this section, we consider approaches to modeling at the early stages of the software lifecycle. Early stage activities, such as requirements specification and architectural design, are of particular interest because these are activities whose primary purpose is to introduce concerns into a development project. We consider two sets of modeling approaches: "traditional," non-aspect oriented modeling approaches, and new aspect-oriented modeling approaches.

21.8.1 Traditional (Non-Aspect Oriented) Modeling

Here, we describe some representative modeling approaches in which concerns are identified in the form of requirements or design elements but in which concerns, as such, are not first-class entities. The lack of consideration for concerns as first-class entities is one of the principal motivations for Cosmos.

21.8.1.1 Requirements Engineering: i* and Tropos

i* is a framework for modeling organizations in terms of actors, goals, and dependencies. Tropos is a methodology that applies this to early requirements and provides a basis for extending early requirements to late requirements, architectural design, and detailed design [7, 42].

Tropos emphasizes the need to identify organizational concerns, separate them from implementation concerns, and give them first-class treatment. Toward this end, Tropos posits five main classes of concern: actors, resources, goals, soft goals, and tasks. A particular requirements model contains multiple instances of each of these classes. Properties are not represented directly in the Tropos schema but may be captured in hard or soft goals (e.g., "increase friendliness of customer service"). Tropos and i* incorporate several types of concern relationships, including decomposition, means-ends, and dependency relationships.

21.8.1.2 Requirements Engineering: KAOS

KAOS [5], like i*, offers a goal-dependency model of requirements and takes a view of concerns that is appropriate to requirements and separated from implementation. KAOS also provides some downstream continuity, from requirements to architectural refinement.

In contrast to Tropos, KAOS adopts a more explicitly multi-dimensional perspective on requirements. Conceptually, requirements in the abstract and elements in a model can be associated with different "aspects" (in their terms) such as "why," "who," "when," and "what." Requirements also have a dual linguistic dimension, including both an "outer" semantic net for general types and semantic relationships and an "inner" assertion language for detailed temporal and logical semantics. Goals can be further classified according to their domain, such as robustness, safety, efficiency, and privacy. Goals are also subject to disjunctive and conjunctive refinement. The KAOS system also supports multiple views of the requirements, including refinement, operationalization, entity-relationship, and agent.

As in Tropos, properties *per se* are not a first class construct in KAOS but are represented indirectly by other constructs such as goals and constraints. In addition to refinement, KAOS relationships also include operationalization and responsibility.

21.8.1.3 Architectural Design: ABAS

ABAS are "attribute-based architectural styles" [23]. These styles address specific quality attributes and can be analyzed in terms of these attributes.

ABAS modeling is explicitly multi-dimensional. It incorporates a number of classifications, including classification of architectural attribute information (in terms of external stimuli, architectural decisions, and responses), classification of architectural elements (in terms of components, connectors, and properties), classification of ABAS specification elements (such as problem description and stimulus/response attribute measures), and classification by property. Additionally, parameters in each of the categories of information are subject to multiple simultaneous classifications. For example, stimuli are classified with respect to mode, source, and regularity, and responses are classified with respect to latency, throughput, and precedence.

ABAS, in contrast to the requirements methods described previously, treat properties explicitly and prominently. All architectural styles are classified with respect to the properties of performance, modifiability, and availability. These crosscut the information categories so that the kinds of information used to describe stimuli, architectural decisions, and responses for performance are different from those used for modifiability. For example, performance responses can be described in terms of latency and throughput, and modifiability responses can be described in terms of extent of impact and effort of change.

The sorts of relationships that are emphasized in the requirements modeling approaches (dependency, responsibility) are not highlighted in ABAS. Of course, ABAS describe kinds of physical relationships (connections) among components that observe various architectural styles. Additionally, ABAS include potentially detailed and quantitative analytical models that describe how specific property measures relate to architectural elements and changes to those elements.

21.8.1.4 Architectural Design: DSSAs

Domain-specific software architectures (DSSAs) make (repeated) use of a domain model, reference requirements, and reference architectures common to a family of applications [39]. The domain model usually includes a lexicon, ontology, and taxonomy of terms and entities belonging to the domain. The domain may be characterized in terms of objects, relationships, products, behaviors, and so on. The architecture, depending on the style and representation, typically comprises elements such as components, connectors, constraints, dependencies, responsibilities, and capabilities. The reference requirements are typically expressed in terms of the domain model and linked to elements in the reference architecture.

All the elements of a DSSA—domain model, requirements, and architecture—express concerns of some sort. The domain model defines a domain of concern (or a domain of concerns) but in a way that is abstract from the motivations and objectives of any particular project (i.e., from the things that make a "matter of interest" interesting). Requirements express concerns in the form of specific needs and goals relating to applications in the domain. Architecture begins to introduce concerns about how those needs and goals are to be addressed.

21.8.1.5   Observations on Non-Aspect Oriented Modeling Approaches

The approaches described previously are advanced techniques for modeling software requirements or architecture. They all represent concerns or enable users to represent concerns in a particular form for a particular purpose. For example, ABAS identify concerns in the form of architectural features and properties that are associated with particular architectural styles but independent of a domain. DSSAs, in contrast, present domain-specific concerns in the form of a domain model, requirements, and architecture. Tropos/i* and KAOS support users in specifying concerns in the form of requirements. Thus, the outcome of these approaches is elements specific to requirements and design, even though the concerns they represent typically cut across activities and artifacts from the whole lifecycle. Cosmos is intended to support a concern-modeling approach that can transcend particular activities and artifacts and span the entire lifecycle.

Each of the modeling approaches discussed previously also reflects some explicit or implicit assertion about how concerns of various types should be represented. However, these approaches typically draw on many of the same modeling techniques, such as enumeration, single and multiple classification, views, templates, relationships and associations, abstraction, properties and attributes, and conditions and constraints. These modeling techniques are thus generic with respect to modeling approaches and domains, and Cosmos likewise makes use of many of them.

21.8.2   Aspect-Oriented Modeling

There has been a flurry of recent work in the areas of aspect-oriented requirements engineering and architectural analysis, as well as in the area of more general concern modeling. In contrast to the modeling approaches reviewed previously, a major goal of these recent approaches, as for Cosmos, is to identify concerns or aspects as such. We discuss some examples here.

21.8.2.1 Aspect-Oriented Requirements Engineering and Architectural Analysis

Aspect-oriented requirements engineering (AORE), like all requirements engineering, aims to capture requirements. However, it explicitly recognizes that at least some requirements represent aspects or concerns that will crosscut both requirements and downstream lifecycle artifacts. Thus, AORE approaches include techniques for explicitly modeling aspects or concerns, at least in the context of requirements specification. For example, Brito and Moriera [6] define a process for separation of concerns in requirements that includes steps for identifying concerns, specifying concerns, identifying crosscutting concerns, and composing concerns. Baniassad and Clarke [2] propose the Theme/Doc approach to identify crosscutting behaviors that represent aspects in requirements documentation. Tekinerdogan [38] argues that explicit mechanisms are needed to identify, specify, and evaluate aspects in architectural design. He proposes ASAAM, an Aspectual Software Architecture Analysis Method that provides a set of heuristic rules to allow architectural aspects to be identified based on usage scenarios. Bass, Klein, and Northrop [3] are developing a method to derive a software architecture from required quality attributes and propose that these attributes often represent architectural aspects that can be carried through detailed design and implementation.

21.8.2.2 Concern Modeling

Concern modeling in a still more general sense is now addressed by several approaches. Wagelaar [41] proposes a concept-based approach called CoCompose for the modeling of early aspects. In CoCompose, the concepts involved in a software system are first modeled independently of any implementation; the conceptual models can then be processed to automatically generate an implementation. Lohmann and Ebert [25] propose a generalization of the hyperspaces [16, 37] approach to concern modeling that replaces orthogonal dimensions of concerns with nonorthogonal clusters of concerns and allows a unit to be assigned to more than one concern in a dimension. Lohmann and Ebert distinguish primary and secondary dimensions of concern in which the primary dimensions are based on artifacts and the secondary dimensions represent user interests that are not derived from corresponding artifacts, although these concerns may still be related to artifacts.

Finally, IBM, in part as a successor to Hyper/J [16], initiated development of the Concern Manipulation Environment (CME), a platform for the development and application of cross-lifecycle aspect-oriented technologies [15, 31]. The CME includes a concern-management component, ConMan, which supports general-purpose, multi-dimensional concern modeling, including concerns, relationships, predicates, and various ways to group and associate these. Concerns may be related to artifacts or independent of them, and concerns may be used to organize artifact composition and extraction, to support querying and analysis, and for other purposes with or without artifacts. The CME is now an Eclipse Open-Source project [10].

21.8.2.3   Observations on Aspect-Oriented Modeling Approaches

The aspect-oriented approaches to requirements and architecture analysis take a step toward generality of concern modeling: they enable particular requirements or architectural elements to be specified, and they recognize that these elements represent more general aspects or concerns that crosscut multiple development stages and artifacts. However, concern modeling in these approaches is still focused mainly on particular activities and on artifact representations appropriate to those activities. Approaches such as those in [25] and [41] take concern modeling a further step toward generality. They provide very general notions for the modeling of concerns, although ties to artifacts are still prominent in these models. ConMan in the CME provides the most general and artifact-neutral approach to concern modeling. ConMan, like Cosmos, is a generalization of the hyperspaces approach, although the basic concepts in Cosmos are at a somewhat higher semantic level than those in ConMan. For instance, ConMan includes a wide variety of constructs for grouping concerns, whereas Cosmos has just a few simple constructs for grouping concerns but also includes constructs for semantically categorizing concerns. In the future, we hope to implement Cosmos concepts on top of ConMan.

21.9   ADDITIONAL DISCUSSION

In this section, we address two fundamental questions: Can we achieve a useful degree of formalization for such a general notion as "concern," and what is the nature of the contribution that concern modeling may make to AOSD?

21.9.1   Formalization of the Notion of "Concern"

We have purposely adopted a notion of concern that is general and intuitive. It is therefore reasonable to wonder in what ways and to what extent this notion can be formalized.

We note first that our interest has been primarily with representing concern *spaces* rather than individual concerns. That is, we have focused on categories of concern and on organizational and semantic relationships among concerns rather than on how best to represent the details of particular concerns. The latter does deserve attention, but we expect that different domains of concerns will have different, specialized languages for description. For example, distinct formalisms may be used to describe concerns relating to functionality (perhaps algebraic specifications), performance (perhaps numerical models), and consistency (perhaps Object Constraint Language (OCL) assertions [29]). Moreover, it should be kept in mind that the description of a concern in a concern-modeling schema such as Cosmos is not intended to replace the representation of that concern in other software artifacts. In Cosmos, a concern represents a subject of interest, the details of which should be found mainly in the associated artifacts, such as requirements, architecture, designs, and code, through which system-specific details are defined and implemented.

With regard to the representation of concern spaces, it is possible to introduce a level of formality that is comparable to that found in other sorts of information modeling used in software development, including domain modeling [20, 39], semantic dependency modeling [7, 42], or design modeling [29]. These kinds of modeling typically entail some representation of entities, kinds of entities, properties of entities, and various sorts of semantic or structural relationships among entities. With Cosmos, we have demonstrated that this sort of modeling is possible with concerns.

The level of formality (or formalizability) in the Cosmos schema is sufficient to have allowed us to construct object-oriented models of the schema in UML [29]. In this model, for example, `LogicalInstance` is defined as an extension of `LogicalConcern`, which is defined as an extension of `Concern`, which is defined as an extension of `ConcernModelElement`; operations on instances of the schema (that is, on specific concern models) can take place at any of these levels of abstraction. Given a Cosmos model, it is possible to algorithmically define many sorts of analyses. Questions about a Cosmos model that can be answered by analysis include

- Are there cycles in the concern-class structure?
- Are there classes without instances or instances without classes?
- Does every concern have a motivation or make a contribution?

Additionally, it is possible to define consistency conditions for a concern model. For example, no logical class should contain both logical instances and physical instances, and for any two concerns X and Y, if X motivates Y, then Y should contribute to X. For a UML model of the Cosmo schema, we have defined such constraints using OCL [29].

Thus, it appears possible to formalize modeling concern spaces. As with other sorts of information modeling in software development (and elsewhere), the purpose of such formalization is to take notions that are intuitive and informal and render them precisely. Formalization allows using information not just in one specific tool but in a variety of ways.

21.9.2 Nature of the Contribution to AOSD

AOSD provides new tools and methods for developing software based on concerns. It uses advanced techniques for separation of concerns, with an emphasis on separating and composing crosscutting concerns. In general, AOSD allows for the separate modular representation of information associated with specific concerns. Examples of such information include requirements, designs, and code. In particular, AOSD seeks the modular representation of concerns that might be scattered across conventional representations, such as object-oriented models or code, in which a particular decomposition predominates. AOSD also automates the weaving or composition of concern-specific units according to explicit specifications. In this way, it controls and systematizes the distribution of concern-specific elements across differently organized application architectures. AOSD thus depends on an understanding of concerns and their interrelationships.

Concern modeling allows us to directly represent and reason about concerns and their interrelationships, thereby creating an externalized abstraction for organizing, analyzing, managing, and composing artifacts according to concerns. This affords several advantages with respect to aspect-orientation. It reveals crosscutting relationships among concerns (as when one concern is defined with respect to another). It provides a reference model of concerns that may be organized and distributed in different ways in different artifacts (for example, as when requirements are organized by functional decomposition but designs are organized by object decomposition). Finally, for software rich in aspectual properties, it helps with managing complexity, such as when multiple concerns are tangled within a single artifact, or when individual concerns are scattered across multiple artifacts. All these contributions are important for helping AOSD to scale from individual components and applications to product families and enterprise-level systems.

21.10 CONCLUSION

The notion of concerns has long received attention in software development. However, until now, concerns have remained something of second-class citizens. Although existing software development activities address concerns in specific ways for specific purposes, there has been no effort to model concerns as such, in general and in the abstract.

The advent of aspect-oriented software development and new techniques for advanced separation of concerns have made plain the need to treat concerns as first-class entities and concern modeling as a first-class activity. There are many reasons to do this. They include the need to address concerns that occur across life-cycle stages and artifacts, the ability to enhance traditional development tasks with concern-based analyses and technologies, and the need to support aspect-oriented software development.

If concern modeling is to become a first-class undertaking in software development, then a formalism for the modeling of concerns must be adopted, and the activity of concern modeling must be integrated into development processes. At a high level, the requirements for a concern-modeling formalism are generality, independence, appropriateness, completeness, and utility. The integration of concern modeling into development processes may be done in many ways, but, in general, concern modeling may be done before, during, or after initial development, and it may be adopted comprehensively or incrementally.

Cosmos is a schema designed specifically for general-purpose concern-space modeling. Cosmos models concern spaces in terms of concerns in several categories, relationships of several types, and predicates. A notable example of the use of Cosmos (along with Hyper/J for Java composition) is in the reengineering of a monolithic, general-purpose software component. Decomposing the component according to concerns, we created a varied product line of specialized components tailored according to selected concerns of interest.

Concerns can be considered the essence of software. All software must address and embody concerns, and software development is fundamentally about identifying, realizing, and reconciling concerns. Aspect-oriented software development with concern modeling provides new tools and methods for developing software based on concerns. It allows for the separate, modular representation of information (such as requirements, designs, or code) that is associated with particular concerns, including concerns that might be scattered and tangled in conventional representations (such as object-oriented models or code). It also automates the weaving or composition of concern-specific units according to concern-based specifications, thereby controlling and systematizing the distribution of these units across differently organized application architectures. AOSD thus depends on understanding and leveraging concerns and their interrelationships and constraints. Concern modeling externalizes the abstractions of concerns and their interrelationships and constraints, and it allows them to be specified, analyzed, and understood as independent, first-class entities. Concern modeling is thus fundamental to aspect-oriented software development, and it holds the potential to enhance other approaches to software development as well.

ACKNOWLEDGMENTS

For discussion on MDSOC and Hyper/J, we thank Peri Tarr and Harold Ossher. For sharing his experience with Cosmos, we thank Juri Memmert. For help with the GPS cache, we thank Arun Iyengar and Lou Degenaro. For further discussions on MDSOC, we thank Stefan Tai and Thomas Mikalsen.

REFERENCES

1. AKŞIT, M., WAKITA, K., BOSCH, J., BERGMANS, L., AND YONEZAWA, A. 1993. Abstracting object-interactions using composition-filters. In *Object-Based Distributed Processing*, R. Guerraoui, O. Nierstrasz, and M. Riveill, Eds. LNCS, vol. 791. Springer-Verlag, Berlin, 152–184.

2. BANIASSAD, E. AND CLARKE, S. 2004. Finding aspects in requirements with Theme/Doc. In *Early Aspects 2004: Aspect-Oriented Requirements Engineering and Architecture Design Workshop (AOSD)*, (Lancaster, UK). http://trese.cs. utwente.nl/workshops/early-aspects-2004/Papers/Baniassad-Clarke.pdf.

3. BASS, L., KLEIN, M., AND NORTHROP, L. 2004. Identifying aspects using architectural reasoning. In *Early Aspects 2004: Aspect-Oriented Requirements Engineering and Architecture Design Workshop (AOSD)*, (Lancaster, UK). http://trese.cs. utwente.nl/workshops/early-aspects-2004/Papers/BassEtAl.pdf.

4. BATORY, D. 2000. Refinements and separation of concerns. In *Workshop on Multi-Dimensional Separation of Concerns in Software Engineering (ICSE)*, (Limerick, Ireland). http://www.research.ibm.com/hyperspace/workshops/icse2000/Papers/ batory.pdf.

5. BERTRAND, P., DARIMONT, R., DELOR, E., MASSONET, P., AND VAN LAMSWEERDE, A. 1998. GRAIL/KAOS: An environment for goal driven requirements engineering. *Research Demonstration and Handout, 20th Int'l Conf. Software Engineering (ICSE)*, (Kyoto).

6. BRITO, I, AND MOREIRA, A. 2004. Integrating the NFR framework in a RE model. In *Early Aspects 2004: Aspect-Oriented Requirements Engineering and Architecture Design Workshop (AOSD)*, (Lancaster, UK). http://trese.cs.utwente. nl/workshops/early-aspects-2004/Papers/BritoMoreira.pdf.

7. CASTRO, J., KOLP, M., AND MYLOPOULOS, J. 2002. Towards requirements-driven information systems engineering: The Tropos project. *Information Systems 27*, 6, 365–389.

8. CLARKE, S., HARRISON, W., OSSHER, H., AND TARR, P. 1999. Subject-oriented design: Towards improved alignment of requirements, design and code. In *14th Conf. Object-Oriented Programming, Systems, Languages, and Applications (OOPSLA)*, (Denver). ACM, 325–339.

9. DEGENARO, L., IYENGAR, A., LIPKIND, I., AND ROUVELLOU, I. 2000. A middleware system which intelligently caches query results. In Middleware 2000: *IFIP/ACM Int'l Conf. Distributed Systems Platforms*, (New York). LNCS, vol. 1795. Springer-Verlag, Berlin, 24–44.

10. ECLIPSE.ORG. 2004. Concern Manipulation Environment Project, http://www. eclipse.org/cme.

11. ELRAD, T., FILMAN, R. E., AND BADER, A. 2001. Aspect-oriented programming. *Comm. ACM 44*, 10 (Oct.), 29–32.

12. GAMMA, E., HELM, R., JOHNSON, R., AND VLISSIDES, J. 1995. *Design Patterns: Elements of Reusable Object-Oriented Software*. Addison-Wesley, Reading, Massachusetts.

13. HARRISON, W. AND OSSHER, H. 1993. Subject-oriented programming—a critique of pure objects. In *8th Conf. Object-Oriented Programming, Systems, Languages, and Applications (OOPSLA)*, (Washington, D. C.). ACM, 411–428.

14. HARRISON, W., OSSHER, H., AND TARR, P. 2000. Software engineering tools and environments: A roadmap. In *Conf. Future of Software Engineering*, (Limerick). ACM, 261–277.

15. IBM CORPORATION. Concern manipulation environment (CME): a flexible, extensible, interoperable environment for AOSD. http://www.research.ibm.com/cme/.

16. IBM CORPORATION. Hyperspaces. http://www.research.ibm.com/hyperspace/.

17. IEEE. 2000. IEEE recommended practice for architectural description of software-intensive systems. IEEE Std. 1471–2000.

18. ISO/IEC. 1999. ISO/IEC 13250 topic maps.

19. IYENGAR, A. 1999. Design and performance of a general purpose software cache. In *18th Int'l Performance, Computing, and Communications Conf. (IPCCC)*, (Phoenix). IEEE, 329–336.

20. JACOBSON, I., BOOCH, G., AND RUMBAUGH, J. 1999. *The Unified Software Development Process*. Addison-Wesley, Reading, Massachusetts.

21. KICZALES, G., HILSDALE, E., HUGUNIN, J., KERSTEN, M., PALM, J., AND GRISWOLD, W. G. 2001. Getting started with AspectJ. *Comm. ACM 44*, 10 (Oct.), 59–65.

22. KICZALES, G., LAMPING, J., MENDHEKAR, A., MAEDA, C., LOPES, C., LOINGTIER, J. M., AND IRWIN, J. 1997. Aspect-oriented programming. In *ECOOP'97 Object-Oriented Programming, 11th European Conference*, M. AKŞIT and S. Matsuoka, Eds. LNCS, vol. 1241. Springer-Verlag, Berlin, 220–242.

23. KLEIN, M. AND KAZMAN, R. 1999. Attribute-based architectural styles. Tech. Rep. CMU/SEI-99-TR-022, Software Engineering Institute, Carnegie Mellon University. Oct.

24. LEVY, E., IYENGAR, A., SONG, J., AND DIAS, D. 1999. Design and performance of a web server accelerator. In *INFOCOM '99*, (New York). IEEE, 135–143.

25. LOHMANN, D., AND J. EBERT., J. 2003. A generalization of the hyperspace approach using meta-models. In *Early Aspects 2003: Aspect-Oriented Requirements Engineering and Architecture Design Workshop (AOSD)*, (Boston). http://www. cs.bilkent.edu.tr/AOSD-EarlyAspects/Papers/LohEbe.pdf.

26. MEMMERT, J. 2001. Personal communication.

27. MERRIAM-WEBSTER. Merriam-Webster collegiate dictionary online. http://www. merriam-webster.com/.

28. NUSEIBEH, B., KRAMER, J., AND FINKELSTEIN, A. 1993. Expressing the relationships between multiple views in requirements specification. In *15th Int'l Conf. Software Engineering (ICSE)*, (Baltimore, Maryland). IEEE, 187–196.

29. OBJECT MANAGEMENT GROUP. 2001. OMG Unified Modeling Language specification, version 1.4.

30. PARNAS, D. L. 1972. On the criteria to be used in decomposing systems into modules. *Comm. ACM 15*, 12 (Dec.), 1053–1058.

31. SABBAH, D. 2004. Aspects—from promise to reality. In *3rd International Conference on Aspect-Oriented Software Development (AOSD)*, (Lancaster, UK). ACM, 1–2.

32. SUTTON JR., S. M. 1999. Multiple dimensions of concern in software testing. In *Workshop on Multi-Dimensional Separation of Concerns (OOPSLA)*, (Denver). http://www.cs.ubc.ca/~murphy/multid-workshop-oopsla99/position-papers/ ws13-sutton.pdf.

33. SUTTON JR., S. M. AND ROUVELLOU, I. 2000. Concerns in the design of a software cache. In *Workshop on Advanced Separation of Concerns (OOPSLA)*, (Minneapolis). http://trese.cs.utwente.nl/Workshops/OOPSLA2000/papers/sutton.pdf.

34. SUTTON JR., S. M. AND ROUVELLOU, I. 2001. Advanced separation of concerns for component evolution. In *Workshop on Engineering Complex Object-Oriented Systems for Evolution (ECOOSE) (OOPSLA)*, (Tampa, Florida). http://www. dsg.cs.tcd.ie/ecoose/oopsla2001/papers.shtml.

35. SUTTON JR., S. M. AND ROUVELLOU, I. 2001. Applicability of categorization theory to multidimensional separation of concerns. In *Workshop on Advanced Separation of Concerns in Object-Oriented Systems (OOPSLA)*, (Tampa, Florida). http://www.cs.ubc.ca/~kdvolder/Workshops/OOPSLA2001/submissions/ 05-sutton.pdf.

36. SUTTON JR., S. AND ROUVELLOU, I. 2002. Modeling of software concerns in Cosmos. In *1st Int'l Conf. Aspect-Oriented Software Development (AOSD)*, (Enschede, The Netherlands), G. Kiczales, Ed. ACM, 127–133.

37. TARR, P., OSSHER, H., HARRISON, W., AND SUTTON JR., S. M. 1999. *N* degrees of separation: Multi-dimensional separation of concerns. In *21st Int'l Conf. Software Engineering (ICSE)*, (Los Angeles). IEEE, 107–119.

38. TEKINERDOGAN, B. 2003. ASAAM: aspectual software architecture analysis method. In *Early Aspects 2003: Aspect-Oriented Requirements Engineering and Architecture Design Workshop (AOSD)*, (Boston). http://www.cs.bilkent.edu. tr/AOSD-EarlyAspects/Papers/Tekinerdogan.pdf.

39. TRACZ, W. 1994. DSSA frequently asked questions. *Software Engineering Notes 19*, 2, 52–56.

40. VAN LAMSWEERDE, A. 2000. Requirements engineering in the year 00: A research perspective. In *22nd Int'l Conf. Software Engineering (ICSE)*, (Limerick, Ireland). IEEE, 5–19.

41. WAGELAAR, D. 2003. A concept-based approach for early aspect modeling. In *Early Aspects 2003: Aspect-Oriented Requirements Engineering and Architecture Design Workshop (AOSD)*, (Boston). http://www.cs.bilkent.edu.tr/AOSD EarlyAspects/Papers/Wagelaar.pdf.

42. YU, E. S. AND MYLOPOULOS, J. 1994. Understanding "why" in software process modeling, analysis, and design. In *16th Int'l Conf. Software Engineering (ICSE)*, (Sorrento, Italy). IEEE, 159–168.

Chapter 22

Design Recommendations for Concern Elaboration Tools

GAIL C. MURPHY, WILLIAM G. GRISWOLD, MARTIN P. ROBILLARD, JAN HANNEMANN, AND WESLEY LEONG

A software developer evolving a software system experiences first-hand the consequences of modularity decisions made during earlier development. All too often, the developer must expend a significant effort tracking code pertaining to the software change of interest that was not modularized. We refer to the code related to the change as a concern.

To help with the activity of elaborating a concern, a practicing software developer may use any of a number of existing tools, including standalone search tools, browsers integrated into a software development environment, or compilers.

We believe it is possible to offer more effective support for concern elaboration activity. The authors of this chapter have thus introduced three tools: AspectBrowser [10], AMT [11, 12], and FEAT [22, 23]. A developer using these tools formulates and runs a query over a model of the program and evaluates the query results. The results of the query often cause a developer to refine the query and repeat the process. These actions identify the code of interest. The tools differ in two fundamental ways. First, each tool uses a different model of the program over which queries are run. Hence, the kinds of queries supported by each tool differ. For example, AspectBrowser uses a program model composed of the lexical tokens in the code base, AMT augments the program model used by AspectBrowser with type information, and FEAT uses a program model composed of a graph of structural relationships derived from the code base. In essence, AspectBrowser supports a lexical approach to concern elaboration, AMT provides a combination lexical and structural approach, and FEAT supports a structural approach. Second, the tools differ in their presentation of the query results; these different views impact a developer's investigation. AspectBrowser and AMT provide a Seesoft view [8] of query results that shows a developer the results in the context of the entire code base. In comparison, FEAT shows results in the context of a representation of the concern.

To better understand the task of concern elaboration and how well our tools support that task, we undertook a study in which each tool author applied his tool to elaborate a concern for a change task in three different systems. For each concern elaboration task, we compared the concern code identified and the queries and navigation patterns used by each tool user. From this study, we gained three insights:

- Regardless of the kind of tool support, the participants used the same basic strategy to identify the starting point, called the seed, for concern elaboration and then elaborated the code of interest. For the latter, they largely followed control flow (e.g., calls) in and out of code pieces.

- All of the tools focus on identifying *code* in the program source that pertains to a concern. However, we found that the participants sometimes needed to specify a *condition* in the system, such as "the data has been read in," rather than code: this condition was true at multiple points in the source, and no single point was obviously more appropriate for indicating the concern than another. We refer to the points at which these conditions hold as *execution points*.

- In each case, there was considerable variability about where the edges of the concern lay in the code. It was difficult to clearly delineate what code pertained to a concern because the change task at hand and the tools available led to a different choice about the extent of a concern.

These insights suggest three corresponding recommendations for designers of concern elaboration tools.

1. A concern elaboration tool should support a user in following control flow within the source.
2. A concern elaboration tool should help a user identify points in the source that correspond to conditions in the running system.
3. A concern elaboration tool should allow a user to determine when the concern has been adequately elaborated: the tool should not prescribe where the concern begins and ends.

These recommendations help define the design space for tools intended to aid concern elaboration tasks. Designers of future versions of searching and browsing tools may also benefit from a better understanding of this design space.

Reflecting upon why different descriptions of concerns arose during the study has also caused us to hypothesize that a concern consists of three parts: a core part, an interface, and execution points where the concern can be extended. Understanding more about the form of concerns could help researchers trying to solve problems in software maintenance and aspect-oriented software development [14].

We begin by introducing the tools used in the study. Next, we describe the study format, present the data, and synthesize results from the study. We then relate our work to previous efforts in the area and conclude with a brief summary.

22.1 THE TOOLS STUDIED

22.1.1 AspectBrowser

AspectBrowser assists in the discovery, exploration, and management of crosscutting concerns (aspects). A user identifies a concern by specifying a lexical regular expression that is then matched across the program text. Multiple concern specifications can be built up and visualized simultaneously in a global view [10, 15, 16]. As Figure 22-1 shows, AspectBrowser displays all of the files searched and the concerns found in a Seesoft-like view [8]. The files are displayed in a row of windows, where one row of pixels is equal to one line of source code. Each concern pattern is associated with a color, which is used to highlight each match in the view, visually distinguishing it from other displayed pattern matches. AspectBrowser integrates with the Emacs editor, allowing a developer to navigate to code in an editor: The same color is used to highlight code related to a concern in both AspectBrowser and Emacs. The use of lexical pattern matching permits analysis and visualization independent of programming language.

To help orient the programmer and to manage scale, AspectBrowser uses a map metaphor. Like symbols on a map, the large-scaled view of multiple files in AspectBrowser shows the dispersal of the highlighted concerns across the program text. The proximity of two different highlighted concerns may indicate a plausible relationship between the two aspects. Similar to an interactive map, AspectBrowser views can be customized; for example, the highlighting of a concern can be selectively disabled, or files with no matches can be folded to reduce clutter. AspectBrowser also provides mechanisms to help a programmer remain oriented while immersed in a complex task, including a "you are here" cursor and traversal through all the matches of a concern.

To use AspectBrowser, a programmer launches the tool and specifies a project to be loaded. The project file may have been saved from a previous session, in which case it would include previously defined concern patterns. Based on the task at hand and any prior knowledge of the system, the programmer identifies a concern in the code by postulating a lexical pattern for it (typed into the window above the concern list). The programmer might then click on one or more of the new highlights to bring up the editor to see the code around the matches and how it relates to any previous concern patterns. If necessary, the concern pattern might be refined, or additional concern patterns might be added. To visit all of the code matched by one or more concern patterns, the programmer chooses concerns to navigate from the drop-down box above the main view and then traverses the matches with the arrow buttons to bring up the editor at each match. Such a traversal might be used to make a change at every match (e.g., a variable rename) or to verify that some property holds for the code at every match (e.g., non-interference with another concern).

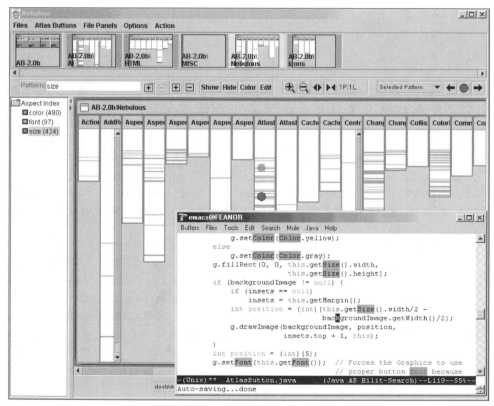

Figure 22-1   *The main view of AspectBrowser. At the left is a hierarchical list of concern patterns. To the right is the concern visualization of one or more directories in the program. Above are operation shortcuts and thumbnail "Atlas tabs" for convenient, visually informed navigation around the system. An Emacs editor is open, showing the highlighting (by color) of the aspects in the text.*

22.1.2 *AMT*

The Aspect Mining Tool (AMT) supports a hybrid approach to concern mining in existing Java or AspectJ [2, 13] software, combining interactive lexical and structural searches over the source code [11, 12]. The lexical searching facility supports pattern and substring matching; the structural searches match type usages in the target code. These two types of searching can be used in combination, such as looking for all creations of a particular object by combining a lexical search for "new" with a type search for the object's type.

Similar to the AspectBrowser, AMT employs a Seesoft-like view, providing the developer with a graphical representation of the code base and the search matches (see Figure 22-2). Each search item can have a different color associated with it. Classes not matching any of the items in a search can be either grayed out or hidden. Since the Seesoft view is a "flat" representation of the system, showing the results only in terms of source files, the tool also offers a tree representation of the class and package hierarchies.

AMT allows the developer to specify the workspace, the collection of files to consider when searching and displaying results. The workspace enables a developer to concentrate on particular parts of a system. The workspace can be formed in two ways: classes or parts of hierarchies can be added using the hierarchical view, or all classes matching a search can be set as the workspace (e.g., all classes matching the lexical token "@author M. Murphy" or all classes containing some usage of the type `EventLogger`). In addition, classes can be removed from the workspace via the Seesoft-like view.

When using AMT, a developer typically first tries to find a good approximation of the workspace and then successively refines the workspace to better fit his or her needs. Then the developer finds a starting point for the concern elaboration task at hand with a lexical search, a structural search, or a combination of both. From there, the developer can perform successive searches to identify the concern extent. The developer can investigate the results of a search with a file viewer built into AMT or an external editor.

22.1.3 *FEAT*

FEAT supports the identification and description of a concern in Java code based on structural queries [22, 23]. Using FEAT, a developer starts with a minimal representation of a concern, or *seed*, and then explores the dependencies to that seed to determine related concern code. When related concern code is found, the developer can add a representation of the concern code to the concern description.

FEAT displays a tree representation of the code that has been identified as contributing to a concern (see Figure 22-3). At the top level, a concern is a collection of classes. Each class can be considered as either being entirely (e.g., class `ChangeAttributeCommand`) or partly involved in the concern (e.g., class `AttributeFigure`). If the latter, FEAT lists which elements of the class—fields and methods (either part or whole)—are included. For parts of method bodies, FEAT represents each code element of a concern with an <action, target> tuple. The action is one of five items: reads (a field), writes (a field), calls (a method), creates (an object), and checks (the type of an object). The target is the field, method, or class upon which the action is performed. For example, in Figure 22-3, the concern described includes calls to method `execute` of class `ChangeAttributeCommand` in method `actionPerformed` of class `CommandMenu`.

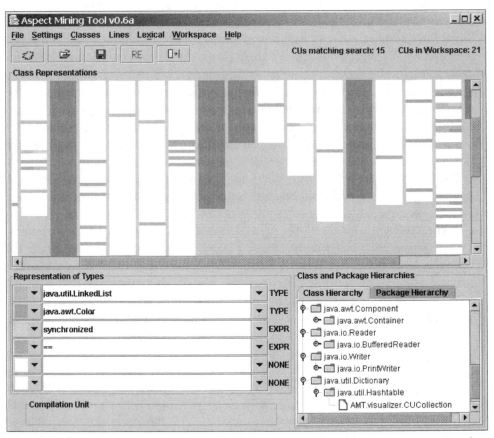

Figure 22-2 *The Aspect Mining Tool. The main window (class representations) shows classes in the workspace, highlighting lines that match the searches (defined in the lower left) with the appropriate colors. Browsable class and pattern hierarchies are shown in the lower right.*

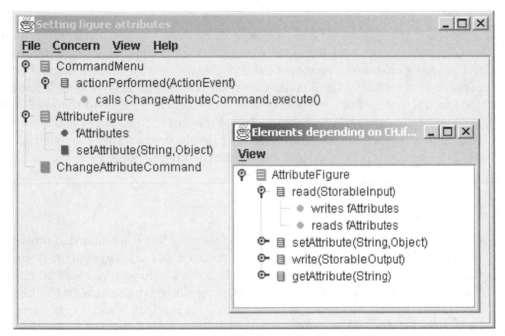

Figure 22-3   *The FEAT tool. The larger window contains the program elements contributing to the Setting figure attributes concern determined to this point. The smaller window shows the result of a query performed on one of the concern program elements. Any of these query results can be added to the concern, a view of the element in the source can be accessed, or further queries can be run.*

From this view, a developer can run structural queries to see whether related elements can also be part of the concern under investigation:

- **Get superclass** returns the superclass of the selected class.
- **Expand class** returns all of the members declared by the selected class.
- **Grab** returns the target element in a code abstraction element. For example, in <reads, *C.f*>, this command would return the field *f* of class *C*.
- **Fan-in** returns all of the elements in a program that depend upon the class, field, or method node that is selected. This query takes into account potential dynamic bindings for method calls and returns conservative estimates.
- **Fan-out** returns all of the different code abstractions for the selected method.
- **Transitive fan-out** returns all of the code elements that the selected method transitively depends upon, including fields, methods, and classes.

The result of one of these queries is a set of program elements presented in a tree structure (see the small window in Figure 22-3). From any window in FEAT, a user can view the source code corresponding to an element, choose to move an element to the concern description, compare the elements to the current concern description, or perform another query based on an element. For example, after viewing the source code for method `getAttribute` of class `AttributeFigure` (in the result window), a user might decide that this method is relevant to the concern and may move this method to the main concern window. A developer continues the investigation until the developer is satisfied with the concern description formed.

22.2 STUDY FORMAT

Our study consisted of three cases, each consisting of a non-modularized (crosscutting) concern to be found to aid a specified change task on a Java system. To ensure the results would be analyzable, a targeted concern was to involve about 10 classes. Each participant contributed one case and was considered to be an expert for the concern on the system. In each case, each participant applied his tool to elaborate the concern of interest and reported five items: the code considered part of the concern, the queries performed in his tool, the strategy he employed with justification, the time taken, and the code viewed as part of the elaboration process. The reports included information about the order in which queries were performed and in which the code was viewed.

For each case, we describe the system and the change task posed. We present the cases in the order in which they were performed.

22.2.1 The Jex Case

Jex is a static analysis tool that produces a view of the exception flow in a Java program based on an analysis of source files [21]. It consists of 57,152 uncommented, non-blank lines of code organized in 542 classes and 18 packages.

To determine the targets of virtual method calls, Jex uses a simplified class hierarchy analysis algorithm [7] based on a user-defined set of classes. Using this algorithm, when a virtual call to method m is detected in the code, all the classes specified by the user are searched, and methods overriding the method signature m are considered a potential target.

The posed change was to perform class hierarchy analysis using a rapid type analysis algorithm [3]. This algorithm does not require a list of classes from the user. Instead, it looks at all the code reachable from a program's entry point(s) and builds the list of potential targets using an analysis of the classes that are instantiated in the program.

The task in this case was to find all of the code in Jex related to class hierarchy analysis, including code involved in discovering which implementations might be selected on a virtual method call.

22.2.2   The AMT Case

The code base for this case was Aspect Mining Tool (AMT) 0.5a, comprising 68,790 lines of code across 727 Java files. The change was to add to AMT the ability to display, via different colors, the code age of each line of code. Earlier work on the Seesoft visualization had hypothesized that such a display might be helpful to developers; for instance, to help a developer identify the age of specific parts of the code, or to help identify code that changed after a specific revision. Code age information is typically available from a version management system.

The task was to identify all code in AMT that might have to change when adding this display mode. Since this scenario was an addition rather than a refactoring task, the participants were also asked to identify portions of code that might change and places where extra code was needed. The task was divided into the following three subtasks:

1. A command-line option was to be added to specify if, where, and how the code age was to be found. For instance, a user might provide the location of the version repository for the system.
2. The code analyzer part of AMT was to be modified to output the age in addition to the type information for each line.
3. The AMT visualizer was to be modified to include a code age view that would be activated by clicking on a toggle button. This view was to ignore all search settings and display the lines of code in different shades of grey depending on their age.

A developer could assume the existence of a module that could provide the code age given a line of source code, a file name, and the version management system location. The age statistics were to be collected, along with the existing type information, during the code analysis phase.

22.2.3   The AspectBrowser Case

The code base for this case came from AspectBrowser 2.0-prealpha and consisted of 19,711 lines of code and 103 Java files. The task chosen for this case excluded the Emacs Lisp portion of AspectBrowser to permit AMT and FEAT to analyze all pertinent code.

This case had the hypothetical task of refactoring the traversal feature in AspectBrowser. The traversal feature moves a red cursor from one match to the next and displays the actual code at that location in Emacs. This feature supports several different modes of traversing through the aspects. The task was to focus on the modularization of the traversal feature through the creation of a class for each kind of traversal. Each of these classes was to inherit a common abstract class.

22.3 DATA

We analyzed the data from each case both quantitatively and qualitatively. Here, we present a summary of the data collected. We synthesize results from the study as a whole in the next section.

In our reporting of the data and results, we distinguish the participants based on the tool they applied. For example, the participant applying the AMT tool is indicated by P_{AMT}. As described earlier, each participant was an expert, meaning they had prior knowledge of the code base for one case. P_{FEAT} was the expert for the Jex case, P_{AMT} was the expert for the AMT case, and P_{AB} was the expert for the AspectBrowser case.

22.3.1 Strategies Used

For the purpose of this study, each participant recorded information about how they used their tool and reported high-level information about the strategies they used. Table 22-1 summarizes the overall strategies used for each case. In the table, we use the term *dependence* to describe the following of a dependence, such as a call from a caller to a callee. We use the term *reference* to describe the reverse, such as determining all callers of a callee.

Despite the differences in the tools used, the participants generally followed a strategy of finding a plausible *seed* for the concern and traversing from that seed the reference/dependence graph to look for related code. Most commonly, the dependences traversed were call dependences.

In general, seeds were chosen based on prior knowledge of the system or through an intelligent guess. When a participant lacked both knowledge of the system and a basis on which to make an intelligent guess, they often resorted to the brute force method of finding the main class—identified by documentation or the presence of a `main` method—and then traversing the control flow from there. At the other extreme, to find a seed for the AspectBrowser case, P_{FEAT} launched the subject tool and used some text out of the traversal feature's tool tip in a text search to find the code that created the tool tip.

Table 22-1 *Strategies Used by Programmers in Identifying Concern Seeds and in Elaborating from Seed*

		Jex	AMT	AspectBrowser
P_{FEAT}	Seed	Knowledge of the application.	Program entry points, plausible name of file.	Word from task description, string shown in GUI.
	Search	Mostly followed dependences. Less frequently, followed references.	Almost exclusively followed dependences. Focused on one part of change at a time.	Followed references to fields. For methods returned, followed both references and dependences. Focused on a class at a time.
P_{AMT}	Seed	Feature programmer's name, word from task description.	Knowledge of application.	Word from task description.
	Search	Followed call dependences and references to data structures encountered.	Read code around search matches or where he knew changes had to occur.	Breadth-first investigation of reference/dependency graph. Recorded calls for later investigation.
P_{AB}	Seed	Plausible name of file, entry point, coding reading.	Program entry point.	Knowledge of application.
	Search	Read code and followed pertinent dependence (call) chains.	Code reading and following of dependencies.	Followed dependences (calls).

Table 22-2 summarizes the number and type of queries performed by the developers in each case. Not surprisingly, prior knowledge was beneficial in concern elaboration. Experts uniformly performed the fewest queries on their own system, even overcoming differences in system size.

The searches performed by the AMT and AspectBrowser participants tended to be of three kinds: (a) explicit naming a specific entity or type, (b) a substring intended to indirectly identify a variety of objects, and (c) finding a comment left behind by the participant. Explicit naming was done when the participant knew what he wanted, as in traversing the control flow.[1] This kind of search tended to be performed later in a task. For example, at the end of the AspectBrowser task, P_{AMT} used explicit naming, searching for `moveCursor`, to ensure his changes were complete. In contrast, at the beginning of the AspectBrowser task, P_{AMT} performed a substring search for `traversal` because the task had described an evolution of the traversal feature of AspectBrowser. The third kind of search, for a comment left behind by a participant, was used by P_{AB} to do some of the bookkeeping required for the study (e.g., `// code mod`). Programmers sometimes do similar marking to keep track of buggy or questionable code (e.g., `// BUG`).

Table 22-2   *Number and Types of Queries Performed by Programmers*

	Jex	**AMT**	**AspectBrowser**
P_{FEAT}	53 queries: 19 fan-out, 15 fan-in, and 19 class.	81 queries: 38 fan-out, 29 fan-in, 14 class.	183 queries: 85 fan-out, 69 fan-in, and 29 class.
P_{AMT}	15 queries: 10 lexical, 3 lexical and type, 1 type only.	3 queries; 3 lexical.	15 queries: 4 lexical, 8 lexical and type, 3 type only.
P_{AB}	19 queries.	19 queries.	12 queries.

Overall, the vast majority of queries in AMT and AspectBrowser were strings meant to locate identifiers, whether by lexical or type matching. In particular, there was little attempt to match on the actual syntax of the program above the identifier level. Although we have seen more aggressive syntax matching in other studies, such as the inclusion of parentheses in string patterns to find method calls [10], we note that the common case pattern was rather simple in our three cases.

Given a seed, FEAT directly supports traversals of references and dependences. The strategy of the participant can thus be seen more through the direction of the query than the content of the query. P_{FEAT} tended to follow dependences more than references. A FEAT query follows only one link of the dependence/reference graph as compared to AMT and AspectBrowser queries, which may result in a number of hits across the code base. Consequently, a larger number of FEAT queries were executed in each case compared to the other tools.

---

1. P_{AB} could have chosen to use the "etags" feature of Emacs for many of these traversals but did not.

22.3.2 Concern Code Identified

For each case, each participant listed the lines of code that he considered to belong to the concern of interest. We compared the concern code identified by each. When the code differed, we questioned the participants as to why they had or had not included the code. The answers to these questions were used to determine which code had been falsely identified as being part of the concern (false positives) and which code should have been identified but had not been (false negatives).

Table 22-3 provides a quantitative overview, at the class-level, of the false positive and false negative code in each case. This table provides a sense of the quantitative differences among the participants' results, showing the significant divergences that occurred.

However, Table 22-3 does not show the false positives and negatives that occur at a finer grain, such as the method or statement level. For example, in the Jex case, P_{AB}'s concern code included a number of false positives related to unnecessary program start-up code and including control flow that was not relevant. A qualitative analysis of the false positives and negatives at the line level, discussed next, provides a better understanding of the differences in the concern code that were identified by each of the participants.

Table 22-3 *Class-Level Breakdown of Identified Concern Code*

	Jex (542 Classes)			AMT (727 Classes)			AspectBrowser (103 Classes)		
	Total	False +	False −	Total	False +	False −	Total	False +	False −
P_{FEAT}	9	0	1	6	1	1	11	2	1
P_{AMT}	5	0	5	6	0	1	15	5	0
P_{AB}	5	0	5	6	0	1	5	0	5

22.3.2.1 False Positives

The false positives—code included in a concern that the expert deemed inappropriate—can be grouped into three categories:

(a) Including functionality unrelated to the change.

(b) Including test code.

(c) Including functionality that is related, but that is unlikely to change, which we call the edges of the concern.

To make categories (a) and (c) more concrete, consider the following examples. A category (a) false positive occurred when P_{AB} in the Jex case included code to determine static calls. However, static calls do not need to be considered for the task of finding code related to determining the targets of virtual calls. A category (c) false positive occurred in the AspectBrowser case, when P_{AMT} chose to include GUI code that triggered the traversal but that did not affect the refactoring task.

When the false positives across all of the cases were discussed, the justifications for cases (a) and (c) were based on a conservative resolution of uncertainties. This reasoning is corroborated by the fact that no expert had false positives—they had no uncertainty about the effect of the code that they had identified and had decided to include as part of the concern.

The inclusion of test driver code, case (b), actually arose as both false positives and false negatives due to the conflicting opinions of experts. The Jex expert was sure that test code did not belong in his concern; the AMT expert was sure that it did.

22.3.2.2 False Negatives

The false negatives—code excluded from a concern that the expert deemed should be in it—can be grouped into five categories:

(d) Missing functionality needed to make the change

(e) Missing utility code that is only used by the concern and that would become dead if the concern was removed

(f) Missing abstract code

(g) Missing related concern code

(h) An alternative but equivalent implementation

False negatives in categories (d) and (g) involve code that is complex, either intrinsically or because of the way that it relates to other concern code. The function of this code was thus misunderstood. As an example of a category (d) false negative, P_{AB} did not include code coordinating the traversal in the concern in the Aspect browser case. An example of a category (g) false negative arose in the Jex case. In this case, replacement of the typing mechanism motivates changing the logging feature so that the logs make sense with respect to the new mechanism. Although the typing mechanism does not depend on the logger for its correct functionality, the typing concern in its broad interpretation cuts into the logger. Due to this subtlety, the logger update was omitted by P_{FEAT}.

On some occasions, P_{AMT} and P_{AB} omitted an interface or field declaration (case (f)), in part because this code was not executable and hence was not judged part of the concern. In another case, FEAT did not show a dependence due to a similar judgment by FEAT's designer, P_{FEAT}. These omissions may occur because of the programmers' primary focus on executable code and their complementary process of searching through the program's control flow.

False negatives in category (h) occurred in the AMT case due to the variety of places that code could be inserted into the program to achieve the same outcome. For example, the code-age feature that was to be added as part of the task could be enabled by a button. The creation of this button can occur virtually anywhere before the AMT display is brought up, as long as it happens before the button itself is inserted into the widget hierarchy. Likewise, the field that stores this button can be declared virtually anywhere in the class, as long as it is scope-visible in all the places it needs to be accessed.

The participants sometimes justified their false negatives by noting that the compiler would have caught their omission. In fact, P_{AB} found his false negatives in the AspectBrowser case when carrying out the subsequent refactoring because the program would not compile after refactoring his identified concern.

22.4 RESULTS

Our study led us to two kinds of insights: recommendations for designers of concern elaboration tools and hypotheses about the nature of concerns. We conclude this section with a discussion of the validity of our study.

22.4.1 Tool Design Recommendations

Our first two recommendations for designers of future concern elaboration tools follow directly from our results.

> *Concern elaboration tools should support a user in following the control flow of a program.*

As we reported, despite the differences in searching supported by the concern elaboration tools studied, all participants tended to use a strategy of following the control flow in the program. Although all of the tools had affordances to help follow control flow, in some cases the lack of explicit support made following the control flow tedious and contributed to mistakes in concern elaboration.

> *Concern elaboration tools should help the user identify points in the source that correspond to conditions in the executing system.*

For some change tasks, it was natural to describe the lines of code related to the concern. For other tasks, in particular those that add code, it was more natural to describe a *condition* in the executing system (e.g., a precondition). These conditions hold at one or more points in the execution, or simply *execution points*. A condition describing a set of execution points might be naturally defined, for example, in terms of the state of an object, the call stack, or a sequence of method calls. To assist code changes and other tasks, tools should map the execution points for a condition to corresponding points in the code.

Our third recommendation is based on our analysis of the differences between concerns identified in the context of the reasons given by the programmers' for those differences.

> *Concern elaboration tools should allow a user to determine the extent of the concern.*

A tool does not exist in isolation. Concern elaboration tools should be expected to work within the context of other development tools. When a participant using a concern elaboration tool knew that a part of the concern could be easily found with another tool, they sometimes chose to limit their exploration with the concern elaboration tool. For example, participants did not include parts of the concern which they knew would be caught by the compiler. The task in which the concern elaboration was posed also affected the extent of a concern that was captured. In a refactoring task, for instance, a developer is typically working with a system that is compilable and for which the compiler can be used to expand the edges of the concern. Our recommendation is that designers of concern elaboration tools should be aware of how other tools might be used to compensate and complement the description of a concern such that a programmer can elaborate a concern cost-effectively within the tool suite. A concern elaboration tool should not prescribe to the user how much of the concern needs to be identified for the task at hand.

22.4.2 Concern Characterization

When we began this study, we assumed that concerns were definite entities that any motivated programmer could reliably identify. In particular, we spoke of a concern as though it were an unformed module that possessed an unambiguous, but possibly messy, interface. This implicit assumption was consistently contradicted by our three cases.

In fact, what we found was that the exact concern was heavily dependent on the particulars of the task—it was not reasonable to define it precisely prior to making an actual change, leading to our third design recommendation. Reflecting on our results, we found that each case taught us something different about the murkiness of concerns.

Concern boundaries are fuzzy. The Jex case involved the *replacement* of a concern's implementation. P_{AMT} wrote:

> *Some details [of the concern's code extent] depend on the actual implementation of the RTA algorithm. From the provided information it is not clear whether the new implementation can make use of (parts of) the helper procedures* `computeRelationships (Method)`. *Since that is implementation dependent, I have marked it.*

This quote shows how the extent of the concern was dependent upon the context in which the concern was identified. Although the task posed to the developers was to find the code related to existing functionality in the system, it was not always possible to clearly delineate the boundaries of that functionality, perhaps because that functionality had not been considered as a unit during any previous development tasks.

Concerns include execution points. The AMT case involved the *insertion* of new code into the concern. P_{FEAT} wrote:

> *It seemed that most of the "concern" code was actually stuff that had to be added, not so much existing code that needed to be changed. That's why I found the "concern code" by navigating parallel structures, and was often confused about what to add and what to leave out.*

That is, the points where the code additions were legitimate depended on the code to be inserted. More importantly, these additions depended on a set of behavioral preconditions that had to be met for the inserted code to behave correctly.

The interface between concerns is a concern. The AspectBrowser case involved the *refactoring* of a concern. Prior to performing the traversal feature refactoring task, P_{AMT} wrote:

> *Are we to identify the complete [concern] or just the part that is relevant for the proposed refactoring task/change?*

> *Later in the conversation, the AspectBrowser expert noted:*

> *[D]ifferent design decisions will ultimately change what would be a concern.*

A couple of insights emerged from this interview with the participants. First, most of the code in the traversal concern would not physically change; the real concern in some sense is the *interface* between the traversal concern and the code that invokes it. On the other hand, the scope of the code in the traversal concern is likely to change from the invokers' classes to a number of new classes. Also, arriving at a sensible design requires a possibly deep perusal of both the traversal concern and the invoking code, as well as an understanding of how the traversal feature might be enhanced in the future. It is not entirely clear whether just the edges of the traversal concern are the concern or if the core of the traversal concern should be included as well.[2] If one can equate Parnas's notion of a *design decision* with a concern, discussions on modularity have weighed in on the side of an interface being distinct from its contents [4, 18, 19, 27].

Based on our experience through the three cases, we would now describe a concern as having the following elements:

◆ A core that determines the behavior of a concern

◆ An interface that may be a concern in its own right and is possibly ambiguous

◆ A set of execution points—states in the execution—that describe hooks at which behavior may be added to the concern

The complete and correct articulation of a concern is fraught with problems and is seemingly unnecessary, at least in support of software evolution tasks. For example, completely characterizing the execution points of a concern depends on a description of all possible changes to a concern. It is also unnecessary because the current change requires only the determination of sufficient execution points to add the code. According to the expert in the AMT case, two different developers need not even derive the same points in the concern.

22.4.3 Study Validity

Our study was exploratory. By using three participants and three tools on three different systems and tasks, we were able to uncover and consider a range of behaviors and issues in concern elaboration. Despite these differences, some commonalities emerged, such as the strategies used to investigate the code bases, and some differences emerged, such as what the participants determined was the edge of a concern and how they did so. The results of our study provide guidance on the functionality designers should consider when building future tools of this type and hypotheses upon which to base further, more in-depth studies.

We have avoided statements about the efficacy of the tools since programmer productivity is known to vary independently of tool use and because we did not

---

2. This distinction was not manifested in the AspectBrowser case results because the ambiguity was arbitrarily resolved before the case was carried out (find the whole traversal concern).

compare our tools with existing, non-concern elaboration specific tools, such as grep. Furthermore, we recognize that we only examined a small part of the programming activity that contributes to productivity. To reflect on efficacy, a much larger study would be required.

22.5   RELATED WORK

We compare our findings to earlier studies on the interaction of programmers with code during a program change task, and we describe the differences between our tools and previous tools intended specifically to help software developers identify features in source code and to assess the impact of a change. Comparisons of the features of each of the tools studied to a wider range of existing tools and previous work can be found in publications specific to each tool [10, 12, 23].

22.5.1   Studies About Program Change Tasks

Several researchers have studied the cognitive processes that programmers use when trying to understand a software system (e.g., [25, 28]). These studies can potentially provide input to developers building tools to support software maintenance tasks, including software change tasks. The work described in this paper does not attempt to study cognition; rather, it assumes searching tools are useful when performing software change tasks and provides specific design recommendations for such tools based on the results of an exploratory study.

Our belief that searching is an important activity is not unfounded. Singer and colleagues studied the work practices of software developers who were evolving a multi-million line real-time operating system [25]. They found that developers frequently performed searches across the source code comprising the system.

Sims and colleagues later studied through a web survey of programmers how and why programmers searched source code [24]. Some of the reasons reported by the 69 respondents included searching to aid the analysis of the impact of a change, maintenance, and feature additions. Of the searches described in these categories, only the impact analysis searches revealed a trend: Programmers often looked for all uses of a variable or a function. Each of the three concern elaboration tools we studied here provides some means of conducting this kind of search, lending credence to the design of the tools studied.

Empirical evidence also exists to suggest that programmers working with no or already-existing tools have difficulty dealing with non-localized pieces of code during software change tasks.

Letovsky and Soloway performed a study in which six programmers of varying experience were asked to make a change to an approximately 300 line of Fortran code system [17]. The programmers were videotaped and asked to think aloud. The researchers found that programmers had difficulty following delocalized plans, essentially changes that included code lines scattered across the code base.

Baniassad and colleagues investigated how developers manage crosscutting concerns—issues that were not well-modularized in a program's structure—that emerge during software change tasks [5]. This study followed eight programmers from industry and academia as they worked on program change tasks on medium-sized systems. They found that crosscutting concerns tended to emerge as obstacles that a developer had to consider when trying to focus on the change. They also found that developers had difficulty determining how much of the code related to a concern they needed to understand, corroborating our observation that concerns are often difficult to delineate.

Some empirical work about the efficacy of the tools described in this paper has been undertaken. Griswold, Yuan, and Kato investigated the efficacy of the map metaphor as embodied in AspectBrowser, in helping a programmer manage crosscutting information when evolving a large system [10]. Robillard and Murphy studied the usefulness of Concern Graphs to guide a change task and the ability of developers to create Concern Graphs using FEAT [23]. This work shows that these tools have promise. The comparison of the use of the tools on common tasks discussed in this paper led to new possibilities for improving these tools.

22.5.2 *Feature Location Approaches*

Some approaches have been proposed to help a developer identify the parts of a code base related to a particular feature. In this literature, the term *feature* is typically used to refer to a unit of functionality in a system.

Researchers have proposed the use of an approach based on comparing execution information collected for test cases exercising a feature with execution information collected for test cases that do not exercise the feature [9, 29, 30]. The completeness of the code identified using this approach depends on the completeness of the test. The tools studied in this paper take a human-centric, static approach to elaborating a concern: a concern may or may not correspond to an easily identifiable executable piece of the system.

Chen and Rajlich advocate the determination of code related to a feature through a systematic exploration of an abstract program dependence graph representation of a system [6]. In their approach, a developer locates a starting component and a tool helps the developer manage the exploration of the dependence graph. This approach advocates a more systematic traversal over more detailed information than the concern elaboration tools in our study. It is unclear if a tool is available to support this approach.

22.5.3 *Impact Analysis Approaches*

Impact analysis approaches are intended to help a developer understand the scope of a software enhancement [1]. Given a seed point in the system's source code that is related to the enhancement, an impact analysis determines points in the system that are transitively dependent upon the seed. The points identified, which are sometimes called the *impact domain*, are intended to help a developer estimate the effort required to make the change and to determine the code that may need to be examined to make the change correctly, amongst other tasks. Early impact analysis approaches focused on call dependencies between modules.

Subsequent work has also considered dependencies in terms of data interactions in the code, as well as other artifacts, such as documents and test cases [20].

Our use of the term *concern* in this paper is similar to the term *impact domain* in that each refers to the scope of effect of a program change task. We use *concern* in a broader sense than *impact domain* in that we include all code related to a change and possible hook points within the code where functionality can be added. Impact analysis approaches typically limit the impact domain to points in the existing code related to the seed point. In contrast, our concern elaboration tools focus on source and do not consider other development artifacts.

22.6 CONCLUSION

We conducted an exploratory comparative study of three concern elaboration tools on three different tasks and systems. Based on the results and our experiences during the system, we synthesized three design recommendations for developers of future concern elaboration tools. These recommendations may also apply to tools, such as browsers within integrated development environments, which are not specifically intended for the task of concern elaboration. We stated our findings as recommendations since, undoubtedly, there is a cost to tool designers—and possibly tool users—in supporting the recommendations. For instance, support for following control flow can be achieved using parsing and control flow graph techniques; these techniques entail a cost in the tool implementation and in the runtime of the tool. For a tool designer targeting, and a user working within, an integrated development environment, the costs of such an approach depend on the resources provided by the environment and may be acceptable. As another example, a tool that allows the user to control the extent of a concern places the onus on the user to determine and evaluate completeness of a concern for the task at hand. A user working on a safety-critical system may prefer a tool with a higher runtime cost that provides a more complete impact analysis. The design recommendations we have stated help to expand our understanding of the design space for concern elaboration tools. Ultimately, tools designers must determine appropriate points in the design space that are effective for software developers.

The results of our study also caused us to hypothesize that a concern can consist of three parts: a core part, an interface part, and a series of execution points. A characterization of the form of a concern can help researchers tackling problems in software maintenance and aspect-oriented software development.

As with any exploratory study, our results need to be subjected to further investigation. The results of this study provide a basis for a more thorough study of the effectiveness of concern elaboration tools and hypotheses for further empirical investigations of concerns.

ACKNOWLEDGMENTS

This research was funded from a number of sources, including NSERC, IBM, and NSF grant CCR-9970985.

REFERENCES

1. ARNOLD, R. AND BOHNER, S. 1996. *Software Change Impact Analysis*. IEEE Computer Society Press, Los Alamitos, California.

2. ASPECTJ PROJECT. http://www.eclipse.org/aspectj/.

3. BACON, D. F. 1997. Fast and effective optimization of statically typed object-oriented languages. Ph.D. thesis, University of California, Berkeley.

4. BALDWIN, C. Y. AND CLARK, K. B. 2000. *Design Rules: The Power of Modularity Volume 1*. MIT Press, Cambridge, Massachusetts.

5. BANIASSAD, E., MURPHY, G., SCHWANNINGER, C., AND KIRCHER, M. 2002. Managing crosscutting concerns during software evolution tasks: An inquisitive study. In *1st Int'l Conf. Aspect-Oriented Software Development (AOSD)*, (Enschede, The Netherlands), G. Kiczales, Ed. ACM, 120–126.

6. CHEN, K. AND RAJLICH, V. 2000. Case study of feature location using dependence graph. In *8th Int'l Workshop on Program Comprehension*. IEEE, 241–247.

7. DEAN, J., GROVE, D., AND CHAMBERS, C. 1995. Optimization of object-oriented programs using static class hierarchy analysis. In *ECOOP'95 Object-Oriented Programming, 9th European Conference*, W. Olthoff, Ed. LNCS, vol. 952. Springer-Verlag, Berlin, 77–101.

8. EICK, S. G., STEFFEN, J. L., AND SUMNER, JR., E. E. 1992. Seesoft—a tool for visualizing line-oriented software statistics. *IEEE Transactions on Software Engineering 18*, 11, 957–968.

9. EISENBARTH, T., KOSCHKE, R., AND SIMON, D. 2003. Locating features in source code. *IEEE Transactions on Software Engineering 29*, 3, 210–224.

10. GRISWOLD, W. G., YUAN, J. J., AND KATO, Y. 2001. Exploiting the map metaphor in a tool for software evolution. In *23rd Int'l Conf. Software Engineering (ICSE)*, (Toronto). IEEE, 265–274.

11. HANNEMANN, J. The aspect mining tool web site. http://www.cs.ubc.ca/labs/spl/projects/amt.html.

12. HANNEMANN, J. AND KICZALES, G. 2001. Overcoming the prevalent decomposition in legacy code. In *Workshop on Advanced Separation of Concerns in Software Engineering (ICSE)*, (Toronto). http://www.research.ibm.com/hyperspace/workshops/icse2001/Papers/hannemann.pdf.

13. KICZALES, G., HILSDALE, E., HUGUNIN, J., KERSTEN, M., PALM, J., AND GRISWOLD, W. G. 2001. An overview of AspectJ. In *ECOOP 2001—Object-Oriented Programming, 15th European Conference*, (Budapest), J. L. Knudsen, Ed. LNCS, vol. 2072. Springer-Verlag, Berlin, 327–353.

14. KICZALES, G., LAMPING, J., MENDHEKAR, A., MAEDA, C., LOPES, C., LOINGTIER, J. M., AND IRWIN, J. 1997. Aspect-oriented programming. In *ECOOP'97 Object-Oriented Programming, 11th European Conference*, M. Akşit and S. Matsuoka, Eds. LNCS, vol. 1241. Springer-Verlag, Berlin, 220–242.

15. LEONG, W. The Aspect Browser web site. http://www.cs.ucsd.edu/users/wgg/Software/AB.

16. LEONG, W. Y. 2002. Using the atlas metaphor to assist cross-cutting software changes. M.S. thesis, University of California, San Diego.

17. LETOVSKY, S. AND SOLLOWAY, E. 1986. Delocalized plans and program comprehension. *IEEE Software 3*, 3, 41–49.

18. PARNAS, D. L. 1972. On the criteria to be used in decomposing systems into modules. *Comm. ACM 15*, 12 (Dec.), 1053–1058.

19. PARNAS, D. L. 1976. On the design and development of program families. *IEEE Transactions on Software Engineering SE-2*, 1 (Mar.), 1–9.

20. PFLEEGER, S. AND BOHNER, S. 1990. A framework for software maintenance metrics. In *Int'l Conf. Software Maintenance (ICSM)*, (San Diego). IESEE, 320–327.

21. ROBILLARD, M. P. The Jex home page. http://www.cs.ubc.ca/~mrobilla/jex/.

22. ROBILLARD, M.P. The FEAT home page. http://www.cs.ubc.ca/labs/spl/projects/feat/.

23. ROBILLARD, M. P. AND MURPHY, G. C. 2002. Concern Graphs: Finding and describing concerns using structural program dependencies. In *Int'l Conf. Software Engineering (ICSE)*, (Orlando, Florida). IEEE, 406–416.

24. SIM, S., CLARKE, C., AND HOLT, R. 1998. Archetypal source code searching: A survey of software developers and maintainers. In *Int'l Workshop on Program Comprehension*, (Ischia, Italy). 180–187. http://www.cs.toronto.edu/~simsuz/papers/iwpc98.pdf.

25. SINGER, J., LETHBRIDGE, T., VINSON, N., AND ANQUETIL, N. 1997. An examination of software engineering work practices. In *CASCON*, (Toronto, Canada). 209–223. http://wwwsel.iit.nrc.ca/seldocs/eassedocs/Cascon97Singer.pdf.

26. SOLOWAY, E. AND ERLICH, K. 1984. Empirical studies of programmers knowledge. *IEEE Transactions on Software Engineering SE-10*, 5, 595–609.

27. SULLIVAN, K., CAI, Y., HALLEN, B., AND GRISWOLD, W. 2001. The structure and value of modularity in design. In *European Software Engineering Conference/ACM Symp. Foundations of Software Engineering*, (Vienna, Austria). 99–108. http://www.cs.virginia.edu/~sullivan/publications/UVa-CS-2001-13.pdf.

28. VON MAYRHAUSER, A. AND VANS, A. M. 1995. Program comprehension during software maintenance and evolution. *IEEE Computer 28*, 8, 44–55.

29. WILDE, N., GOMEZ, J., GUST, T., AND STRASBURG, D. 1992. Locating user functionality in old code. In *Int'l Conf. Software Maintenance (ICSM)*, (Orlando, Florida). IEEE, 200–205.

30. WONG, W., GOKHALE, S., HORGAN, J., AND TRIVEDI, K. 1999. Locating program features using execution slices. In *Symp. Application-Specific Systems and Software Engineering and Technology*, (Richardson, Texas) 192–203. http://srel.ee.duke.edu/PAPERS/locating.pdf.

Chapter 23

An Initial Assessment of Aspect-Oriented Programming

ROBERT J. WALKER, ELISA L. A. BANIASSAD, AND GAIL C. MURPHY

The principle of separation of concerns [6] has long been used by software engineers to manage the complexity of software system development. Many programming languages provide explicit support for separation of concerns by providing different sub-languages for expressing the structure of data versus the functionality to be performed on the data. Pascal [10] is one example of a language with this design. Software specifiers and designers also use the principle when using notations, such as UML [18], which place structure and function information into separate diagrams.

Aspect-oriented programming is a new programming technique that takes another step towards increasing the kinds of design concerns that can be captured cleanly within source code [11]. Aspect-oriented programming provides explicit language support for modularizing design decisions that *crosscut* a functionally-decomposed program. Instead of spreading the code related to a design decision throughout a program's source, a developer is able to express the decision within a separate, coherent piece of code. For example, ensuring that a set of operations do not execute concurrently typically requires spreading code throughout the operations; an aspect-oriented approach allows the synchronization constraint to be specified in one separate piece of code. The aspect code is combined with the primary program code by an aspect weaver. Several different aspect-oriented programming systems have been built, including AML [9], an environment for sparse matrix computation, and RG [16], an environment for creating image processing systems.

The aspect-oriented approach claims to make it easier to reason about, develop, and maintain certain kinds of application code [11]. To begin assessing these claims, we undertook a series of exploratory qualitative studies, including both case studies and experiments[1] [17]. The case study format allowed us to investigate broad usefulness and usability questions surrounding the approach. The experiment format allowed us to focus on more specific questions related to the claims of the technique.

This paper reports on two of the exploratory experiments we conducted to investigate aspect-oriented programming. A particular aspect-oriented programming language created by researchers at Xerox PARC, called AspectJ™ (version 0.1) [1], was used in these studies. This version of AspectJ uses a slightly modified form of Java™ [7] for expressing the core functionality of a program, and supports two aspect languages: `Cool` for expressing synchronization concerns, and `Ridl` for expressing distribution concerns.[2]

Each of the two experiments considered a different programming activity. In the first experiment, we considered whether the separation of concerns provided by AspectJ enhanced a developer's ability to find and fix faults present in a multi-threaded program. The second experiment focused on the ease of changing an existing distributed system. In each case, we compared the performance and experience of programmers working in AspectJ with those of programmers working in a control language: Java in the case of the debugging experiment, and Emerald [3] in the case of the change experiment.

The results of these experiments highlight the importance of the *aspect–core interface* in achieving development benefits with aspect-oriented programming. The aspect–core interface refers to the boundary between code expressed as an aspect and the functionally-decomposed code. This interface is *narrow* when the scope of the effect of an aspect across the boundary is well-defined, and when the aspect can be reasoned about without extensive analysis of the core code. In the experiments, the narrow interface provided by the synchronization aspect language helped the participants to complete assigned tasks. In contrast, the wider interface provided by the distribution concern language seemed to hinder participants.

Our experiments also indicate that aspect-oriented programming may alter the programming strategies used by developers. Specifically, programmers may be more

---

1. We use the term *experiment* similar to Basili: "a study undertaken in which the researcher has control over some of the conditions in which the study takes place and control over (some aspects of) the independent variables being studied" [1, p. 444].

2. Version 0.2 of AspectJ provides more general purpose support for programming cross-cutting concerns [21].

likely to first try to solve a problem related to a concern captured as an aspect by initially focusing on the aspect code. This new strategy tends to help when the programmer's hunch that the problem is pertinent to the concern is correct, and when the aspect cleanly captures the concern. When these conditions do not hold, this strategy may lead to a drop in programmer performance.

Although gathered at an early stage in the evolution of aspect-oriented programming, these empirical results can help evolve the approach in several ways. First, the results can help builders of cross-cutting modularity techniques, such as aspect-oriented programming and the closely related subject-oriented programming [8], improve the usefulness and usability of the techniques. The results can also help bridge to another useful form of empirical study—longer running industrial-based case studies—by helping potential early adopters of the technology determine whether the technique is suitable to address some of their development problems. Finally, software engineering researchers may build on our methods and results to continue experimental studies of both aspect-oriented programming and other separation of concern techniques.

We begin by describing the essential features of AspectJ. We then describe our experimental method and present the results of running each experiment. Next, we describe the insights into aspect-oriented programming that arise from the studies, critique the study format used, and discuss related work on studies investigating the effect of program structure on programming tasks. We conclude with a summary of the work.

23.1 ASPECTJ

AspectJ consists of a slightly modified form of Java, called `JCore`, for expressing the core functionality of a program, plus a set of aspect languages. In version 0.1 of AspectJ, two aspect languages are supported: `Cool` for expressing synchronization concerns, and `Ridl` for expressing remote data transfer and method invocation concerns.

`JCore` is essentially identical to Java, save that the keyword synchronized and the `wait`, `notify`, and `notifyAll` methods have been removed to ensure appropriate separation of synchronization concerns.

`Cool` encapsulates the synchronization aspect of AspectJ programs. A snippet of code called a coordinator is written when coordination is desired for a particular class or set of classes. This coordination can be described on a per-instance or a per-class basis. Each coordinator describes the synchronization on and between methods of the class or classes it coordinates via three constructs: `selfex`, `mutex`, and `guards`. A selfex specification on a method means that only one thread can concurrently execute that method. A mutex specification on two or more methods means that if one thread were executing one of these methods, no other thread could concurrently execute any of the other methods. A mutex specification does not imply a selfex specification. Finally, the guard construct is provided for more complicated, potentially dynamically changing synchronization relationships; they permit the specification and enforcement of essentially arbitrary pre- and post-conditions on the execution of a method. A given method is permitted to simultaneously have a selfex specification and multiple mutex and guard specifications. Version 0.1 limits each class to a single coordinator.

Ridl allows the specification of remote interfaces for classes and the data transfer behavior to be used when these remote interfaces are invoked. Only methods specified in the remote interface can be invoked remotely. The remote interface specifies how the input parameters and return value for each method should be transferred over a network: by passing a copy of the remote object, or by passing a global reference to the remote object. Furthermore, the fields of any of these objects can be individually specified as being passed by copy, passed by reference, or skipped altogether. The rationale behind such specifications is that the implementor of the remote interface has knowledge of the way these objects are being used, and would therefore know whether it were costlier to make multiple communications to a remote host, or to copy an object all at once. Ridl version 0.1 is built on top of Java's Remote Method Invocation (RMI) protocol.

Each JCore class, Cool coordinator, and Ridl remote interface specification must reside in a separate file. At compile time, a tool called an aspect weaver combines these separate specifications into a set of Java classes, which are then compiled to produce executable bytecodes. A tool similar to make performs weaving and compilation only on those classes that are impacted by changes to the source files.

Figure 23-1 shows a portion of a class and its attendant coordinator and remote interface that were used in our studies. Since addBook() alters bookCount while numBooks() returns its value, the two methods should not be called concurrently. The coordinator Query.cool contains a mutex specification to ensure this condition. The remote interface Query.ridl indicates that the book to be added to the query should be passed by copy, while the library from which it came should be passed by reference.

Query.jcore

```
public class Query {
  Hashtable books;
  int bookCount = 0;

  public void addBook( Book b, Library source ) {
    if( !books.containsKey( b ) ) {
      books.put( b, source );
      bookCount++;
    }
  }

  public long numBooks() {
    return bookCount;
  }
}
```

Query.cool

```
coordinator Query {
  mutex{ addBook, numBooks };
}
```

Query.ridl

```
remote Query {
  void addBook( Book b, Library source ) {
    b: copy;
    source: gref;
  }
}
```

Figure 23-1 *Snippets of AspectJ code.*

23.2 EXPERIMENTS

Our main goal in conducting these experiments was to better understand how the separation of concerns provided by aspect-oriented programming affects a programmer's ability to accomplish different kinds of tasks.

23.2.1 General Format

Each experiment was a between-groups study consisting of six trials: In three trials, one pool of participants worked with AspectJ; in the other three, a different pool of participants worked with a control language. We estimated each programmer's relative ability from our previous knowledge of them and a set of informal questions regarding the scope of their previous experience, particularly in regards to object-oriented programming (in Java and Emerald), concurrency, and distribution. The pools were formed to balance abilities; for the debugging experiment, pairs were selected with matching skills (so neither could dominate the trial) and then distributed to balance the pools. Each trial began with training time to allow the participants to familiarize themselves with the environment and the language(s) they were to use. We also gave the participants some refresher material on synchronization and distribution. The participants were then given a ninety minute session in which to tackle the assigned tasks. Two computers were available for use in each trial. The participants were graduate students and professors of computer science, and an undergraduate in computer engineering.

We videotaped the sessions during which participants worked on tasks; the participants were asked to think-aloud during this time. An experimenter was present during the session and was available to answer questions about the programming environment. At 30-minute intervals, or after each task was completed, the experimenter stopped the participants and asked a series of questions:

- What have you done up to now?
- What are you working on?
- What significant problems have you encountered?
- What is your plan of attack from here?

The same basic system—a digital library—was used in each experiment. The library had two main actors: readers and libraries. Readers would make requests to libraries for a particular book. Libraries would search within their internal repositories for the book, and also ask remote libraries to do the same. Each reader could query one library, and each library could directly query at least one other.

The library system was initially written in two languages, AspectJ (with `JCore` and `Cool`) and Java, the control language for the first experiment. These initial implementations were used in the program debugging experiment. A distributed version of the system was then implemented in AspectJ (using `JCore`, `Cool`. and `Ridl`, and in Emerald [3]. Emerald was chosen as the control language for the second experiment because it is an example of an object-oriented language that integrates explicit, but not separate, support for distributed, synchronized programming.[3] To more fairly compare Java and Emerald with AspectJ, synchronization lock classes in each language similar to the synchronization mechanisms of AspectJ were provided to the participants.

Our experimental design was a refinement of a design used to conduct a small pilot study that compared the ease of creating AspectJ programs with Java programs.

23.2.2 Experiment 1: Ease of Debugging

The intent of this experiment was to investigate whether programmers working with aspect-oriented programming were able to more quickly and easily find and fix faults in a multi-threaded program. Our hypothesis was that programmers working with the aspect-oriented programming language, AspectJ (`JCore` and `Cool` components), would be able to more quickly and easily identify the cause of errors and correct them than programmers working in Java, the control language.

Three synchronization errors were introduced into the digital library code. Pairs of programmers, knowledgeable in multi-threaded programming techniques and object-oriented programming, then attempted to correct the faults.

23.2.3 Format

In each pair, one participant had control of the computer with the programming problem, and the other had access to a report describing the symptoms of the faults, and on-line documentation. The teams were asked to fix each fault sequentially. All participants were told that the errors were due to incorrect synchronization within the program.

The faults were cascading, meaning that the symptoms of the first hid the symptoms of the second, and the second hid those of the third. In the first fault, only one reader would make requests while the others remained idle. The participants had to remove per-class self-exclusive coordination on the `run()` method of the `Reader` class so that more than one reader (each in a separate thread) could run. In the second fault, multiple readers would make requests but the system would eventually deadlock. The participants were required to determine that the deadlock occurred

---

3. This support includes simple constructs for object mobility, and transparent object references across machine boundaries.

when two libraries each tried to do a remote search on the other at the same time. Removing per-object self-exclusive coordination on the `remoteSearch()` method of the `Library` class removed the deadlock condition. The third fault allowed more than one reader to check out the same book from the same library. To correct this, the participants had to add per-object self-exclusive coordination on the `checkOut()` method of the `Library` class so that only one reader could check out a book at a particular library at a time.

23.2.4 Results

In both the AspectJ and Java groups, all pairs of participants were able to find and correct all three of the faults. We analyzed videotapes of the ninety minute sessions to extract both qualitative and quantitative data elements such as the participant's views, the time taken, and the number of builds.[4] We first discuss each data element in isolation, and then correlate and summarize the results.

Time.   The times required to correct each of the three faults are shown in Figure 23-2A. In this (and following) figures, a bar, shaded according to the language being used, is shown for each participant and for each assigned task. From Figure 23-2A, we can see that the largest difference in completion times was with respect to the first fault: the AspectJ teams clearly repaired the fault faster than the Java ones. For the second and third faults, there was a smaller difference.

Switching Between Files.   We examined the number of times the pairs switched the file they were examining to determine if the AspectJ users were affected by the coordination specification residing in a different file from the rest of the code. Figure 23-2B shows that the AspectJ pairs typically made fewer file switches than the Java group for fault 1, more for fault 2 and slightly less for fault 3.

Instances of Semantic Analysis.   Figure 23-2C highlights the difference in the number of instances of semantic analysis over the sessions. To determine the number of instances of semantic analysis, we recorded the number of times participants said something to the effect of "let's find out what this does. . . ." The data indicates that the Java pairs more often analyzed the behavior of the code than the AspectJ pairs. In the AspectJ session with the most instances of semantic analysis, the group members openly disagreed as to how much semantic analysis was necessary to solve the second fault:

---

4. The raw data for the quantitative data elements is available at http://www. cs.ubc.ca/labs/se/projects/aop/. The appendix contains tables of the quantitative data referred to in this paper.

A: . . . we *know* it's in the COOL file . . .

B: But we have to know what they do before changing anything.

—AspectJ Pair 2

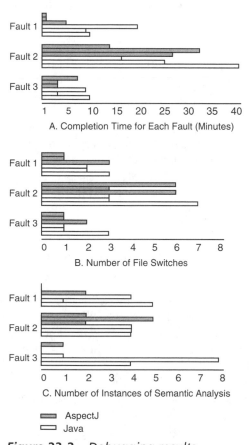

Figure 23-2   *Debugging results.*

Builds.   Overall, the AspectJ and Java pairs spent roughly equal time building and executing their program. The additional time required for weaving AspectJ programs was negligible. The number of builds per fault ranged from one to nine.

Concurrency Granularity.   The Java users specified synchronization constraints by inserting statements about lock objects into methods. Working at the statement level meant that the Java users could attempt to synchronize parts of methods. To alter the concurrency granularity, the AspectJ pairs would have had to have changed the structure of the existing methods. To determine the instances when Java users considered finer granularity locking, we noted when the users attempted to move locks around within a method. Only two of the Java pairs investigated locking granularity. Java pair 1 investigated locking granularity twice in the first fault, twice in the second fault, and once in the third fault. Java pair 3 investigated this once in the third fault. None of the AspectJ participants questioned the granularity imposed by Cool.

Participants' Comments. At the end of the trials, two of the three AspectJ pairs expressed enthusiasm in support of separating the coordination code, and described that the separation directly contributed to their ability to solve the faults.

> It meant that since [the problems] were just synchronization problems we just had to look at the parts that were related to synchronization. We could have spent lots of time looking at the non-synchronization parts, at one point we did look briefly, but it was clear there was nothing about synchronization in that code, and the only way to deal with synchronization was to look in the Cool files.—*AspectJ Pair 2*

The other group, however, expressed that Cool provided a handy way of summarizing coordination of and between methods, but were unhappy with the physical separation of the coordination code.

> The only place I can see there could be an advantage is if you know that you have some modules you are working with that are tested and you are *sure* you can limit the faults to synchronization issues in which case you don't really have to understand the code.—*AspectJ Pair 3*

This pair would have opted instead for the Cool code to have been inserted in pertinent places throughout the code so that the programmer could see in one glance both the coordinator and the method at the same time. Interestingly, although this pair perceived that the separation provided by Cool caused them to look at many files to gain context, this pair switched less between files in total than any of the Java pairs.

Analysis of Results. The three debugging tasks can be categorized two ways: according to the addition or deletion of concurrency functionality, and according to whether there were localized or non-localized reasoning requirements. We say a fault required localized reasoning if the code responsible for the fault was modularized (e.g., part of one class). Non-localized reasoning meant participants would have to look across modularity boundaries for the problem.

The first fault's solution required localized reasoning and the deletion of synchronization code. In this fault, the AspectJ pairs were able to solve the fault faster than the Java pairs. They did so with fewer file switches, and with fewer instances of semantic analysis. This points out that the AspectJ pairs were able to more quickly isolate and remedy the problem causing the fault.

Solving the second fault required non-localized reasoning and involved deleting synchronization code. For this fault, the AspectJ pairs were somewhat faster than the Java pairs, and completed the task with slightly fewer file switching and marginally fewer instances of semantic analysis. Clearly, the AspectJ participants did not benefit as much from the use of `Cool` as they did in the first debugging task when the reasoning required for the problem was more localized.

Fixing the third fault required localized reasoning and involved adding synchronization code. In this fault the AspectJ pairs generally finished faster and performed somewhat fewer file switches. Two of the Java pairs performed significant numbers of instances of semantic analysis, while two of the AspectJ pairs performed none. This may have occurred because the Java participants had to perform analysis to understand how to add locking functionality, whereas using the `Cool` syntax required less analysis.

To summarize, when the solution to a problem required localized reasoning, `Cool` helped programmers focus their efforts. However, when the solution required non-localized reasoning, `Cool` did not provide as clear a benefit. This was regardless of whether functionality was being added or deleted.

23.2.5 Experiment 2: Ease of Change

The intent of this experiment was to investigate whether the separation of concerns provided in aspect-oriented programming enhanced a programmer's ability to change the functionality of a multi-threaded, distributed program. Our hypothesis was that the AspectJ combination of `JCore` for the component programming, `Cool` for synchronization, and `Ridl` for specifying data transfers would make it easier to change such programs compared to a similar program written in Emerald.

23.2.5.1 Format

In this experiment, the participants worked alone. They were asked to address each of three change tasks sequentially. In the first task, participants were asked to add the ability for a reader to check books back into the library after checking them out. The solutions to this problem generally involved adding a method to check books back in, synchronizing that method, and calling it from somewhere within the main program loop. The second task was to assign one library to randomly reject a reader's request to check out a book. Adding this functionality required the determination of a library to make the denial decision, and the addition of a check in the main library code to ask that library if the reader's request for a check-out should be granted. The third task involved enhancing the performance of the code. Here the participants could find and fix any performance lag. However, to try to direct their approach, we seeded an inefficiency into the code: readers read the book byte-by-byte, requiring many messages to be sent if the book were located remotely. Enhancing the performance in this case meant ensuring that the appropriate book object was on the same host machine as the reader reading it. Because the third task was intended to be more open-ended and exploratory than the other two, we treat it separately in the discussion of results below.

The code in the solutions of each of the three tasks did not affect each other.

23.2.5.2 Results

We examined the performance of the participants by examining their approach to solving the problem. In particular, we analyzed the videotape for such data elements as the time spent analyzing the code base versus the time spent writing their solutions. We considered both the absolute time and the proportion of the total time spent on each activity. We also looked at the pattern of activities over time. Finally, we examined the code written by the participants. We describe these data elements individually before synthesizing the results.

Time. Figure 23-3A shows the completion times for the six participants for the first and second tasks. The Emerald participants typically had faster completion times than the AspectJ participants.

Portion of Time. To investigate what could account for the time differences between the Emerald group and the AspectJ group, we examined how the participants spent their time. Figures 23-3B and 23-3C show, as a percentage of total time, how much time was spent coding and analyzing for each activity for each participant. The typical percentage of time spent on coding was slightly greater for the AspectJ trials, while that spent on analysis was greater for the Emerald trials. The remaining percentage of time was spent on a combination of compiling and running the program. The AspectJ participants spent slightly more absolute time observing the program run.

Patterns of Activities. Emerald participants typically began their tasks with extended periods of analysis while AspectJ participants typically began extensive coding attempts with little or no prior analysis.

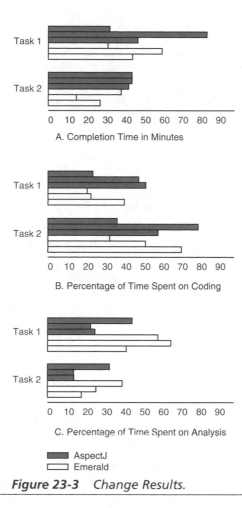

Figure 23-3 *Change Results.*

Code Written. The AspectJ participants wrote between 50 and 150 lines of code, of which two to six lines were `Ridl` code, and two to three lines were `Cool` code. The Emerald participants wrote between 50 and 80 lines of code, of which two to four lines were synchronization code, and one to three lines pertained to the movement of objects.

Task 3: Performance Enhancement. While each Emerald participant successfully made at least one modification to the program that led to a performance enhancement, only two AspectJ participants had sufficient time to attempt this task, and only one of these successfully improved the performance.

AspectJ does not support the identical pass-by-reference semantics of Java[5] because object replication is not automatic. Assuming that `JCore` is effectively Java can lead to surprises when `Ridl` specifications violate the implied semantics of the `JCore` code: when a change is made to an object, the change is not propagated to remote copies of that object. AspectJ participant 2, who unsuccessfully attempted this task, encountered and recognized this difficulty.

Since `Ridl` version 0.1 is implemented on top of Java RMI, copying an object requires that its class implement the `Serializable` interface; to pass a global reference to an object requires that its class provide a remote interface. This causes a serious catch-22 for standard Java library classes that implement neither. The alternative to using such library classes is to encapsulate their instances within "remoteable" versions; however, the `JCore` code would then need to specify explicitly that the "remoteable" version be used. Although we provided such "remoteable" versions for a few classes that we suspected would be needed to complete tasks 1 and 2, the open-ended nature of task 3, combined with the expensive nature of reimplementing most of the standard Java library, prevented us from providing a sufficiently complete set of such versions. Both AspectJ participants encountered problems when the remote interface specifications they attempted involving library classes either failed to compile or caused unexpected run-time exceptions.

Participants' Comments. When the two AspectJ participants who attempted the performance-enhancing task were asked at trial-end what difficulties they had encountered, they both believed that the amount of code analysis required to express a concern in `Ridl` was a factor. One of these participants noted that the separation between `Ridl` and `JCore` was not as clean as desired.

> I get the feeling that `Cool` is pretty close to capturing
> synchronization but that `Ridl` has a way to go . . . it's too meshed
> with Java—*AspectJ Participant 3*

This participant believed that it may be more difficult to separate object mobility issues from the core functional code than separating synchronization issues. The participant characterized object mobility issues as the location of an object at a particular execution point and how an object is passed into a method. These participants

---

5. Although Java is strictly pass-by-copy, since objects can only be accessed via a reference type, objects are effectively passed-by-reference (primitive types are not objects in Java). In other words, if an object is passed to a method, changes made to the object are visible outside that method.

claimed that in order to understand how objects were moving around in the system, it was necessary to thoroughly understand the core semantics that supported the `Ridl` file.

Analysis of Results.   The Emerald participants were able to implement more, faster than the AspectJ participants.

The patterns of activity for the AspectJ participants showed a heavy emphasis on coding quite early in their tasks, as compared to those for the Emerald participants. This may point to the fact that massaging the `Ridl` code seemed like a quick way to solve object-mobility problems when, in fact, it was not. Interestingly, AspectJ participant 1, who successfully attempted task 3, did spend more time on analysis of the core semantics than on coding, while AspectJ participant 2, who unsuccessfully attempted task 3, showed the opposite distribution. This observation lends some credence to the participants' claims that in-depth analysis of the core semantics is required to correctly express a concern in `Ridl`.

The fact that AspectJ participants spent slightly more absolute time observing the program run could also suggest that they perceived that tinkering with the `Ridl` code and watching the program run would keep them from having to deal with the core semantics of the program.

23.3   INSIGHTS FROM COMBINED ANALYSIS

Combined analysis of the results of both the debugging and change experiments provides two key insights into characteristics of aspect-oriented programming that may significantly affect the usefulness and usability of the approach.

23.3.1   Aspect–Core Interface Matters

Separating concepts into different pieces of code does not imply independence of those code snippets. Interaction between the separate pieces is needed to create the behavior of the system. In this discussion, we refer to the boundary between code expressed as an aspect and the functionally-decomposed core code as an aspect–core interface.

Our participants noted the effect of the aspect–core interfaces on the tasks that they performed. For the most part, the AspectJ participants found that the effect of the `Cool` code on the `JCore` code had a well–defined scope: We refer to this as a *narrow* aspect–core interface. The narrow aspect–core interface allowed participants to understand the `Cool` code without inferring or analyzing extensive parts of the core code. Figure 23-4 illustrates the typical analysis necessary; only those methods explicitly mentioned within the coordinator are affected by its synchronization specifications.

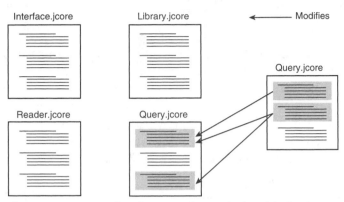

Figure 23-4   *Localized Semantic Analysis with* Cool.

The AspectJ participants in the second experiment had more difficulties with the aspect–core interface between `Ridl` and `JCore`. This interface is wider, meaning it is necessary to look at both the aspect code and large chunks of the core code to understand the aspect code. Figure 23-5 illustrates this point. Because `Ridl` alters the nature of the data being transferred, the potential impact of the remote interface specification extends beyond the method explicitly mentioned therein to include the transitive closure of methods using that method. An extensive analysis is required to ensure that constraints in place within the core code are not violated by the remote interface. As one participant noted,

> `JCore` and `Ridl` interact more than I would like . . . you can't ignore
> `JCore` code in your `Ridl` semantics. . . . I was very often looking at
> the `JCore` implementation so that I could decide what was wise to do
> in `Ridl`.—*AspectJ Participant 3*

The partial separation provided by `Ridl` may have actually hindered the performance of the change tasks by the AspectJ participants. Partial separation should thus not be considered to necessarily bring partial benefit.

By paying careful attention to the design of aspect–core interfaces, builders of aspect-oriented programming environments may be able to help a programmer focus more easily on code relating to a task, aiding the programmer's ability to complete some tasks. Tool support, such as an impact analyzer, might also help a programmer cope with different kinds of aspect–core interfaces. We have provided a high-level definition of the concept of an aspect–core interface; more work is required to refine and characterize this interface.

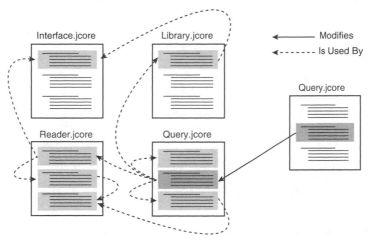

Figure 23-5 *Non-localized Semantic Analysis with* Ridl.

23.3.2 *Aspects May Alter Task Strategies*

All AspectJ participants tended to first consider the aspect files for solutions to perceived coordination or data transfer problems. In the debugging experiments, this strategy was successful, since all of the solutions were solely programmed in the Cool files. However, in the change experiment, it was necessary to understand, and sometimes change, files containing core functionality to complete an assigned task.

As we discussed earlier, the AspectJ participants in the change experiment typically commenced coding much earlier in a task, and spent more time coding overall, compared to the participants in the control group. We observed that the participants initially assumed they could solve the data-transfer problems by looking at and massaging the Ridl files. This presumption may have distracted the participants from analyzing the core functionality code to the extent that was necessary for the task.

The presence of aspect code, then, may alter the strategies programmers use to approach a task. Specifically, programmers may try to tackle problems first in the aspect code, which may be shorter and simpler, rather than gaining a suitable knowledge of both the core functional and aspect code. This behavior alteration could affect the initial usability, and acceptance, of an aspect-oriented programming approach. It also indicates that programmers may have difficulty in performing tasks perceived to be associated with aspect code when the aspect code does not suitably encapsulate a concern. Longer-running studies where programmers are able to gain more experience with aspect-oriented approaches are needed to further investigate this second point.

23.4   EXPERIMENTAL CRITIQUE

Our goal in undertaking an early assessment of aspect-oriented programming was to gather information that could be helpful in directing the evolution of the technology. In support of this goal, we wanted to gather data about both the performance and the experience of programmers using the approach. We chose an exploratory study format in which we compared the results of a small number of programmers using an aspect-oriented approach with others using a control language for several reasons:

- The control groups provided a basis on which to assess the performance of the AspectJ groups,
- The cost of running and analyzing a trial was high so we wanted to balance cost with the maturity of the technology,
- The pool of potential participants and the amount of time available from each participant was limited, and
- We chose to forfeit some precision in measurement in favor of realism [15].

Within these constraints, we took several steps to ensure our results had some validity. To achieve internal validity, we provided the different groups—aspect-oriented versus non-aspect-oriented—with as similar support as possible, limiting variances, as much as possible, to the features of interest. For instance, the lock constructs we provided for use in Java and Emerald provided a mechanism similar to that available in AspectJ.

To address construct validity, we gathered data from multiple sources. One source was the qualitative statements made by the participants during the taped interviews; the other sources were the data analyzed from the tapes. Sometimes the data from the multiple sources was corroborative, other times it was contradictory. Corroborative data strengthened the result under discussion: Contradictory data weakened the result.

The reliability of our experiments was high with respect to the procedures we followed in conducting the experiments and analyzing the data. However, as expected, the skills of the participants varied greatly as finding participants with Java (or Emerald) experience, concurrent programming, and, in some cases, distributed programming was difficult.

The variability in the skills of participants and the modest number of participants limits the generalizability of our results. We chose to make this tradeoff because, in these exploratory studies, we were interested in _how_ the participants worked with the approach; the quantitative data supported the analysis of the qualitative data.

The external validity of the experiments is also affected by the problems we chose as a basis for the experiment and the limited training provided to the participants. The faults seeded into the system for the debugging experiment, for instance, were all synchronization problems that could be solved by altering `Cool` code. We informed the participants that synchronization faults had been seeded into the program; AspectJ participants may thus have been pointed towards the `Cool` code. The performance of all of the participants may also have been affected by being asked to work with either new languages (the AspectJ participants), or with particular constructs (Java and Emerald) introduced to provide a basis of similarity between the languages. Scholtz and Wiedenbeck have shown that programmers experience a drop in performance and their solution process is disrupted when using an unfamiliar programming language [20]. All of our participants likely experienced this effect in differing degrees; our experimental method did not allow us to explicitly quantify or qualify the differences.

The limitations in our studies could be overcome by refining and expanding the experimental method. However, the cost entailed in conducting more controlled experiments must be weighed against the development curve of the technology being studied. Our exploratory study format has provided insights useful for researchers building aspect-oriented programming environments at this early stage of the technology.

23.5 RELATED WORK

Our work in evaluating how the structuring of aspects impacts programming tasks continues a line of inquiry that began with the introduction of structured programming and data abstraction techniques. Curtis and colleagues [5] synthesized two themes from this body of work that considered the effect of control structures and data structures on programming tasks: "structuring the control flow assists programmers in understanding a program" [p. 1095], and "data structuring capability and data structure documentation may be strong determinants of programming performance" [p. 1096].

Aspect-oriented programming builds on this earlier structuring work providing increased support for modularizing the code. Fewer studies have been conducted on the impact of modularity choices on programming tasks.

Rombach reports on controlled experiments that compared the ease of maintaining systems developed in the LADY distributed system language with similar systems implemented in an extended version of Pascal [19]. These experiments showed that the additional structuring information available in the LADY implementations aided the isolation of program faults, and that less rework was required in requirements, design, and coding when adding a new feature. Although the kind of additional structuring provided in AspectJ is different in LADY—LADY provides support for hierarchical structuring of distributed system solutions—the faster times for solving seeded problems in the AspectJ implementation compared to the Java implementation may also be a result of additional structuring information helping fault isolation. We did not see a similar increase in performance for adding new features into an AspectJ program.

Korson and Vaishnavi conducted an experiment to investigate the effect of modularity on program modifiability [12]. They found evidence to suggest that a modular Pascal program was faster to modify than a non-modular version when one or more of three conditions held: modularity was used to localize change required by a modification, existing modules provided some generic operation that could be used in implementing a modification, or a broad understanding of the existing code was required to perform a modification. In our debugging experiment, the localization of concurrency information in an aspect module may have eased the task of adding synchronization information into the system compared to the Java programmers. When the aspect code does not cleanly modularize a concern, as was the case in the change experiment, we did not see a benefit.

Boehm-Davis, Holt, and Schultz investigated four questions relating to the effect of program structure on maintenance activities ranging from the role of structure when modifying a system to whether structure affected the subjective reactions of programmers to a system [4]. The study involved both student and professional programmers making either simple or complex modifications to programs written in either an unstructured style, a functional style, or an object-oriented style. The study showed that the ability of a programmer to abstract information from code was important in the modification process, and that this ability was affected by the structure of the system and the programmer's background. We have discussed how the nature of the separation provided by aspect code can affect a programmer's ability to understand source code during the performance of a task. Our experimental format did not support an investigation of how system structure and programmer's background might impact aspect-oriented programming.

In providing a means of localizing cross-cutting information, aspect-oriented programming shares some features of program slicing [21]. An empirical study by Law of the effect of slicing on debugging tasks found that "the experimental group who [had] obtained the knowledge of program slicing only took fifty-eight percent of the control group's time to debug a one-page C program [13]" [14, p. 43]. Slices differ from aspects in several ways: for instance, slices are typically computed on-demand rather than appearing explicitly as part of the program text, and slices generally describe the inter-dependencies of program statements rather than localizing programming concerns. Further studies are needed to understand how each of these different crosscutting mechanisms impacts the program development cycle.

23.6 SUMMARY

We report on two exploratory experiments we conducted to study the increased program modularization provided by AspectJ, an example of the emerging aspect-oriented programming approach. In these experiments, we compared the performance and experiences of a small number of participants working on two common programming tasks: debugging and change. Some participants worked with AspectJ; other participants used an object-oriented control language. These initial, albeit limited, results suggest that the aspect-oriented programming approach shows promise of being useful and is worthy of further, more detailed study.

We noted the following, typical results. In the first experiment, the AspectJ participants were able to finish the tasks faster than the participants using Java, the control language. The Java participants performed more semantic analysis, and switched the file they were viewing more often, than the AspectJ participants. In the second experiment, the AspectJ participants required more time to complete tasks than the participants using Emerald, the control language. Analysis of the AspectJ participants' activities showed that these participants spent more of their time coding their solutions and less of their time analyzing the existing code base than the Emerald participants.

These results suggest two key insights into aspect-oriented programming. First, programmers may be better able to understand an aspect-oriented program when the effect of the aspect code has a well-defined scope. Second, the presence of aspect code may alter the strategies programmers use to address tasks perceived to be associated with aspect code.

Builders of aspect-oriented approaches may benefit from considering these two key insights. The insights suggest particular characteristics an aspect language may need to exhibit in order to ease the performance of programming tasks. Specifically, aspect languages should enable the writing of aspect code that has a well-defined scope of effect on core functional code, and that suitably encapsulates a concern. These insights may also apply to other cross-cutting modularization techniques, such as subject-oriented programming.

ACKNOWLEDGMENTS

We thank the Xerox PARC Embedded Computation Area group for their comments on and involvement in the studies, the use of the AspectJ weaver, and the fast responses to solving the few problems with the environment that occurred. We also thank Robert Rekrutiak and Paul Nalos for their contributions to experiment setup and design, Gregor Kiczales and Robert Bowdidge for their comments on an earlier draft, and our anonymous experimental participants. This research was funded in part by Xerox Corporation, in part by the Natural Sciences and Engineering Research Council of Canada, and in part by a University of British Columbia Graduate Fellowship.

APPENDIX 23.A

Further raw quantitative data is available at http://www.cs.ubc.ca/labs/se/projects/aop.

Debugging Experiment

Table 23-1   Completion Times (in Minutes)

	AspectJ Trial			Java Trial		
	1	2	3	1	2	3
Fault 1	1	1	5	20	9	10
Fault 2	14	32	26	16	25	41
Fault 3	7	2	2	9	2	10

Table 23-2   Instances of Semantic Analysis

	AspectJ Trial			Java Trial		
	1	2	3	1	2	3
Fault 1	0	0	2	4	1	5
Fault 2	2	5	2	4	4	4
Fault 3	1	0	0	1	8	4

Table 23-3   *Number of File Switches*

	AspectJ Trial			Java Trial		
	1	2	3	1	2	3
Fault 1	1	1	3	2	2	3
Fault 2	6	3	6	3	3	7
Fault 3	1	1	2	1	1	3

Table 23-4   *Number of Builds Performed*

	AspectJ Trial			Java Trial		
	1	2	3	1	2	3
Fault 1	1	1	1	5	1	1
Fault 2	1	6	5	1	5	9
Fault 3	1	1	1	1	1	2

Program Change Experiment

Table 23-5   *Completion Times (in Minutes)*

	AspectJ Trial			Emerald Trial		
	1	2	3	1	2	3
Task 1	32	85	47	46	60	45
Task 2	45	45	43	37	15	27
Task 3	40	—	34	15	20	19

Table 23-6 *Time Spent on Activities (% of Total Time)*

		AspectJ Trial			Emerald Trial		
		1	2	3	1	2	3
Coding	Task 1	24	45	52	21	23	40
	Task 2	36	82	58	33	52	71
	Task 3	19	—	26	21	8	21
Analysis	Task 1	45	23	25	59	66	42
	Task 2	33	14	14	40	26	19
	Task 3	43	—	40	47	54	39
Compilation	Task 1	20	14	11	9	3	4
	Task 2	1	4	20	15	17	6
	Task 3	16	—	14	11	12	11
Execution	Task 1	10	17	13	11	8	15
	Task 2	29	0	8	13	4	3
	Task 3	22	—	20	21	27	29

REFERENCES

1. ASPECTJ PROJECT. http://www.eclipse.org/aspectj/.

2. BASILI, V. R. 1996. The role of experimentation in software engineering: Past, current, and future. In *18th Int'l Conf. Software Engineering (ICSE)*, (Berlin). IEEE, 442–449.

3. BLACK, A., HUTCHINSON, N., JUL, E., AND LEVY, H. 1986. Object structure in the Emerald system. In *1st Conf. Object-Oriented Programming, Systems, Languages, and Applications (OOPSLA)*, (Portland, Oregon). ACM, 78–86.

4. BOEHM-DAVIS, D. A., HOLT, R. W., AND SCHULTZ, A. C. 1992. The role of program structure in software maintenance. *Int'l Journal of Man-Machine Studies 36*, 1, 21–63.

5. CURTIS, B., SOLOWAY, E., BROOKS, R., BLACK, J., EHRLICH, K., AND RAMSEY, H. 1986. Software psychology: The need for an interdisciplinary program. *Proc. IEEE 74*, 8 (August), 1092–1106.

6. DIJKSTRA, E. W. 1976. *A Discipline of Programming*. Prentice-Hall, Englewood Cliffs, New Jersey.

7. GOSLING, J., JOY, B., AND STEELE, G. L. 1996. *The Java Language Specification*. Addison-Wesley, Reading, Massachusetts.

8. HARRISON, W. AND OSSHER, H. 1993. Subject-oriented programming—a critique of pure objects. In *8th Conf. Object-Oriented Programming, Systems, Languages, and Applications (OOPSLA)*, (Washington, D. C.). ACM, 411–428.

9. IRWIN, J., LOINGTIER, J. M., GILBERT, J. R., KICZALES, G., LAMPING, J., MENDHEKAR, A., AND SHPEISMAN, T. 1997. Aspect-oriented programming of sparse matrix code. In *Int'l Scientific Computing in Object-Oriented Parallel Environments (ISCOPE)*. LNCS, vol. 1343. Springer-Verlag, Berlin, 249–256.

10. JENSEN, K. AND WIRTH, N. 1974. *Pascal: User Manual and Report,* LNCS, vol. 18. Springer-Verlag, Berlin.

11. KICZALES, G., LAMPING, J., MENDHEKAR, A., MAEDA, C., LOPES, C., LOINGTIER, J. M., AND IRWIN, J. 1997. Aspect-oriented programming. In *ECOOP'97 Object-Oriented Programming, 11th European Conference*, M. AKŞIT and S. Matsuoka, Eds., vol. 1241. Springer-Verlag, Berlin, 220–242.

12. KORSON, T. AND VAISHNAVI, V. 1986. An empirical study of the effects of modularity on program modifiability. In *1st Workshop on Empirical Studies of Programmers*, (Washington, D. C.). Ablex, Norwood, New Jersey, 168–186.

13. LAW, R. 1993. Evaluating the program slicing technique. *SIAST TODAY 4*, 6 (June), 6.

14. LAW, R. 1997. An overview of debugging tools. *ACM SIGSOFT Software Engineering Notes 22*, 2 (March), 43–47.

15. MCGRATH, J. 1995. Methodology matters: Doing research in the behavioral and social sciences. In *Readings in Human-Computer Interaction: Toward the Year 2000*. Morgan Kaufman, San Mateo, California, 152–169.

16. MENDHEKAR, A., KICZALES, G., AND LAMPING, J. 1997. RG: A case-study for aspect-oriented programming. Tech. Rep. SPL-97-009, Palo Alto Research Center.

17. MURPHY, G. C., WALKER, R. J., AND BANIASSAD, E. L. A. 1999. Evaluating emerging software development technologies: Lessons learned from assessing aspect-oriented programming. *IEEE Transactions on Software Engineering 25*, 4 (July/August), 438–455.

18. RATIONAL CORPORATION. UML summary. http:www.rational.com/uml/resources/documentation/summary/index.jtmpl.

19. ROMBACH, H. 1985. Impact of software structure on maintenance. In *Conf. Software Maintenance (CSM)*, (Washington, D.C.). IEEE, 152–160.

20. SCHOLTZ, J. AND WIEDENBECK, S. 1992. The use of unfamiliar programming languages by experienced programmers. In *People and Computers VII: HCI'92*. 45–56.

21. WEISER, M. 1984. Program slicing. *IEEE Transactions on Software Engineering 10*, 4 (July), 352–357.

Chapter 24

Aspect-Oriented Dependency Management

MARTIN E. NORDBERG III

As the profession of software engineering has matured, better and better means have been devised to manage the ever-increasing complexity of a typical software system, first by separating it into procedures, modules, classes, patterns of cooperating classes, and now introducing crosscutting aspects. However, there is a down side to the division of software into manageable pieces. The sheer number of classes can be daunting, and the dependencies between software modules must be carefully managed. Otherwise, you could end up with a system in which everything depends upon everything else. Such systems are "brittle"—they break in unexpected ways when seemingly unrelated changes are made. Can aspect-oriented technologies not only improve the means for separating software into manageable pieces but also help to manage the dependencies between those pieces? This chapter explores the affirmative answer to that question.

24.1 DEPENDENCY MANAGEMENT PRINCIPLES

Nearly all practicing software developers have felt the painful effects of brittle software—software in which seemingly minor changes in one area break functionality in far distant areas. Like brittle glass that shatters catastrophically on a minor impact, brittle software systems fail in widespread and unpredictable ways on minor changes in one small subsystem. The reason is often poorly engineered dependencies, in which every subsystem depends upon every other, and changes to one have the potential to affect them all. Dependency management is the design discipline of removing or avoiding restrictive, failure-propagating dependencies that shorten the maintainable life of a system and increase its cost over time. Generally, dependency management involves extending the materials metaphor, converting dependencies to a more malleable or flexible form. The goal of software dependency management is to avoid oxymoronic "brittle/soft"-ware.

24.1.1 Dependencies

Fair comparisons between object-oriented programming (OOP) and aspect-oriented programming (AOP) technologies require a clear definition of dependency. Two broad definitions are available:

1. **The compiler's perspective:** Which other modules require recompilation after a developer changes one of them?
2. **The developer's perspective:** Which other modules need to be edited (or might have new bugs) after editing one of them?

In traditional languages, the two perspectives are equivalent. For example, editing a C++ header file generally requires corollary editing and recompiling of some or all files that include that header. The equivalence disappears with the quantification (non-linear mapping from source to binary) that is characteristic of AOSD [5]. From the compiler's perspective, aspect weaving or subject composition languages fare poorly against OO alternatives precisely because of their automated weaving or composition.

This is the era of simpler languages compiled to byte code by GHz workstations, so we focus on the developer's perspective. A dependency, for our purposes, is a pathway for the propagation of software changes. If a subsystem is changed, those that "depend" on it may also need to be changed. Poorly managed dependencies result in excessive maintenance efforts that spread across subsystems like cracks in a windshield. Well-managed dependencies are characteristic of systems that have been prepared to meet their future changes easily and reliably.

24.1.2 Dependency Rigidity

Dependencies have varying levels of "rigidity." For example, Riel [17] identifies several levels of coupling between classes. Primary among them are nil, export (interface), and overt (implementation) coupling. With AOSD, it is possible to refine the list. Considered in relation to a class or another aspect, an aspect may be:

1. Independent (no dependency)
2. Interface-dependent
3. Interface-modifying
4. Implementation-dependent
5. Implementation-modifying

An interface-modifying aspect is one that makes a new or changed interface available to clients but does not make use of existing implementation details. An implementation-dependent aspect makes use of original implementation details in order to augment them (for example, causing a side effect whenever a private method is called). An implementation-modifying aspect changes the behavior of the original class (for example, restricting changes to a member variable to leave it between 0 and 100).

24.1.3 Principles

The first principle for dependency management is trivial: avoid them. The second principle is nearly as simple: Keep the rigidity of each dependency as low as possible. Things become more interesting when we consider the *direction* of a dependency. Several principles for managing dependencies in object-oriented systems have been well articulated by Robert Martin [12]. Three are key, and all deal with dependency direction:

- **Acyclic Dependencies Principle (ADP):** Dependencies must not form cycles.
- **Dependency Inversion Principle (DIP):** Depend upon abstractions; do not depend upon concretions.
- **Stable Dependencies Principle (SDP):** Depend in the direction of stability.

Figure 24-1 summarizes these principles by placing classes on a coordinate system of abstraction versus stability. Well-designed classes or packages in this coordinate system fall on a diagonal from lower left to upper right. Dependencies should be directed upward (DIP) and rightward (SDP).

Some definitions are in order. Abstract and concrete are terms familiar to object-oriented practitioners, but add to their connotation of unimplemented methods the more qualitative concept of encapsulation—how well an abstraction captures one and only one idea. The other dimension, stability, is a counterintuitive one. In most disciplines, stability is a good thing. Even in software development, it's a good thing for library modules, but from the perspective of a development team working on its own code, stability can be a bad thing. Part of the great economic value of software is that it is "soft"—it can be changed rapidly. Stability and rapid change are nearly opposites. In fact, as we see at the bottom of Figure 24-1, the *penalty for change* can be an equivalent and more intuitive way to represent software "stability."

Phrased in terms of change penalty, in concert with the definition of dependency as the change propagation path, the SDP becomes obvious: subsystems that are difficult to change should not depend upon those that are easy to change (and therefore do change frequently). The trick is to distribute a system over the change penalty continuum so that "likely to change" aligns with "easy to change" thus reaping the flexibility benefits that software brings over time. The abstraction-change penalty diagram and the principles behind it are the key tools to explore object-oriented and aspect-oriented techniques for realizing these benefits.

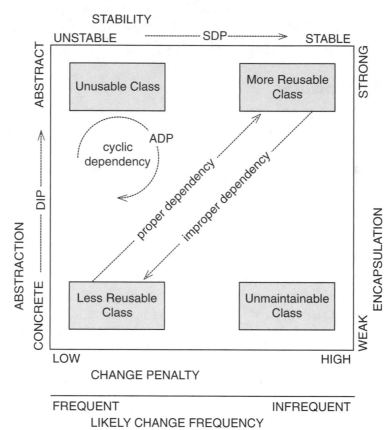

Figure 24-1 *Plotting a design on a coordinate system of abstractness versus instability can reveal how well dependencies have been managed in that design.*

One intuitive difficulty with abstraction-change penalty diagrams is that "good" dependencies are upward in direction, whereas most software design diagrams show downward dependencies. The reason is the even stronger diagramming convention of placing abstract classes above concrete classes, as in an inheritance diagram. This conflict with a designer's intuition is a reminder that inheritance associations are also dependencies. It also illustrates some of the problems of inheritance, such as the "fragile base class problem," where apparently innocuous changes to a base class too readily break derived classes or their clients.

24.2 INDIRECTION AS A GENERALIZED PRINCIPLE: FROM POINTERS TO DESIGN PATTERNS AND BEYOND

It has become a maxim of software design that "any problem can be solved by adding another level of indirection." At it simplest, indirection means the use of a pointer or reference instead of a pointed-to value directly, but over time indirection has come to carry more weight and have deeper meaning. It is instructive to trace the history of indirection, leading to the one problem that cannot be solved by adding indirection— the problem of too much indirection. That problem requires a new *kind* of indirection.

24.2.1 More Than Pointers

Indirection in the form of addressing, pointers, or references is the foundation upon which all significant data structures are built. Since data structures are key to algorithms, indirection is also fundamental to a majority of significant algorithms. More significantly for our purposes, indirection is also fundamental to software engineering principles of modularity based on abstract data types.

However, dependencies are not just references or pointers; they are pathways of change propagation, and today references are so fundamental to software development that our mental model for indirection is wider than simply linking separately stored chunks of data. The semantics of indirection now includes a logical indirection in the *behavior* of the implementation of a separately defined service (polymorphism). The semantics is now widening again to include indirection in the behavior of the clients of a service (weaving or nonlinear composition).

24.2.2 Object-Oriented Indirection

Behavior indirection in object-oriented designs is a powerful dependency management technique. Figure 24-2 illustrates the fundamental idea of an object-oriented "hinge point" [12]—the separation of implementation from interface in such a way that the implementation can be completely changed without affecting clients, as long as the contract of the interface is honored. Object-oriented indirection separates the "what" of a behavior from the "how" of that behavior. In an OO design, a direct dependency can be replaced by dependency upon a more stable and more abstract interface, freeing the implementation of that interface to change without brittle havoc. Interestingly, interface polymorphism has the effect of taking the original indirection of data structures to the extreme: hiding an object's data completely, leaving only a promise of its behavior.

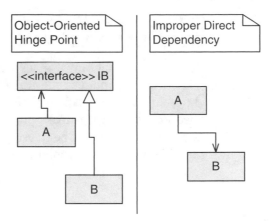

Figure 24-2   *An object-oriented "hinge point" removes an unwanted implementation dependency in favor of a more manageable pure interface dependency.*

24.2.3   Design Patterns and Indirection

Object-oriented indirection is at the heart of many design patterns. Design patterns routinely employ indirection between service provider and service consumer (or service provider and augmented service provider). Each pattern adds extra apparatuses to the OO hinge point in a different way to solve a different problem. Table 24-1 lists many common design patterns, the purpose of the indirection found in them, and the name of the key interface that gives each its characteristic behavior. Most design patterns are, in fact, named after their key interface, an observation that lends weight to the claim that indirection is their central feature.

Czarnecki and Eisenecker [4] describe one key problem with design patterns: "object schizophrenia" or a "lost sense of self." A single domain class is augmented with mechanisms until it becomes a nearly unrecognizable jumble of implementation classes. This is a problem not only for design readability, but also for correct implementation and successful debugging. For example, levels of indirection in patterns like Decorator, Adapter, and Strategy mean that internal calls to the "current domain object" are no longer equivalent to simple calls to "this," "Me," or "self." At debug time, the Observer pattern can be a nightmare because multiple notifications to unknown clients (each hidden behind the same simple interface) can add surprising headaches when tracing through a particular notification or when debugging the interaction or ordering of multiple notifications. Czarnecki and Eisenecker discuss this problem in their chapter on aspect-oriented technologies. Aspect-oriented designs show great promise for overcoming the problem of too much indirection while avoiding improper dependencies.

Table 24-1 *Most Design Patterns Incorporate a Level of Indirection for Some Specific Design Purpose*

Pattern	Indirection	Interface	Ref.
Observer	Decouples event receivers from event senders.	Observer	[7]
Decorator	Allows chained composition of multiple independent fragments of an overall algorithm.	Decorator	[7]
Adapter	Reshapes an existing interface to meet different client needs.		[7]
Extension Object	Dynamically provides multiple interfaces or extensions to a base service.	Extension	[6]
Iterator	Separates the traversal of a data structure from the data structure itself.	Iterator	[7]
Visitor	Allows unanticipated or non-core functionality to be added to a base object hierarchy.	ElementA ElementB ElementX	[7]
Type Object	Allows for dynamically typed object instances.		[9]
Strategy/State	Allows dynamic and potentially multivariate behavior.	Strategy	[7]
Memento	Externalizes the prior state of an object (e.g., for undo) without exposing its details.		[7]
Abstract Factory	Shields the client of an interface hierarchy from construction details and alternative families of implementations.	Abstract Factory	[7]
Property Container	Enables clients to read object attributes by name rather than via compiled interfaces.	Property Container	[2]

24.2.4 Aspect-Oriented Indirection

Recall that object-oriented indirection separates "how" from "what," allowing many answers or an easily changed answer to the "how" for a single "what"—one interface can have many implementations or one easily changed implementation. Aspect-oriented indirection separates "how" from "when" and allows a multi-valued or easily changed "when" for a single "how." In other words, a single implementation can apply at many locations in the execution of code even though it appears only once in the source.

The ability of an aspect-oriented compiler to insert behavior at multiple places in the execution of a program from a single place in the source code leads to the concept of an aspect-oriented hinge point (see Figure 24-3). An aspect-oriented design has the potential to break or avoid unwanted direct dependencies by moving the behavior that requires the dependency into a separate module (an aspect) that depends upon the otherwise directly connected client and service. Where an object-oriented hinge point introduces a new common dependency (the interface), an aspect-oriented hinge point introduces a common dependent (the aspect). With this new dependency management tool, many new design patterns wait to be discovered, and many old and even venerable design patterns may be ready for retirement.

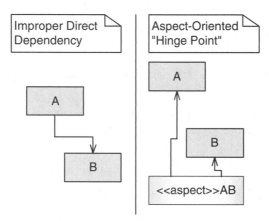

Figure 24-3   An aspect-oriented hinge point, opposite to an object-oriented hinge point, introduces a common dependent rather than a common dependency.

24.3 ASPECT-ORIENTED ALTERNATIVES TO DESIGN PATTERNS

Many established patterns for object-oriented design (even those with dependency management as a key objective) deserve to be revisited in light of aspect-oriented alternatives or improvements.

24.3.1 Visitor

The first design pattern to succumb to aspect-oriented replacement is the Visitor pattern [7] with its infamous cyclic dependency between visitor and element hierarchy, illustrated in Figure 24-4. The improper dependency from `Visitor` to `ConcreteElement` violates all three dependency direction principles—it goes from abstract to concrete, goes from stable to less stable, and forms a cycle. The author has been among those who have proposed object-oriented solutions to this problem [11, 14].

However, the aspect-oriented solution is basic to AOSD and much more effective (see Figure 24-5).

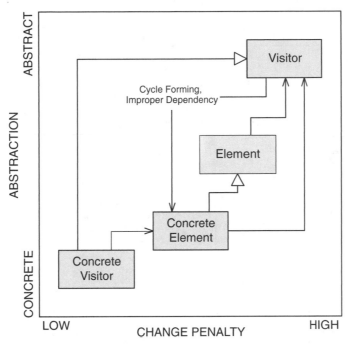

Figure 24-4   *The Visitor pattern shows an obvious flaw when plotted on an abstractness/instability field with all dependencies explicitly shown.*

Interestingly, object-oriented solutions to the cyclic Visitor dependency problem remove the "good" dependencies from Element and ConcreteElement to Visitor. The bad dependency noted in Figure 24-4 from Visitor to ConcreteElement is what makes the pattern what it is. In an aspect-oriented language, where an aspect can augment any class, the good dependency is in a sense left in—every class has a built-in dependency on the language feature of augmentability. The bad dependency, on the other hand, disappears from programmer consciousness (there is no user source code defining what classes may be augmented), though it might be said to remain in the compiler writer's consciousness. (Analogous statements could have been made about polymorphism during the transition from procedural to object-oriented languages.)

Whether the implementation technology is "open classes," "introductions," "composition," or "hyperslices," the ability to *expand* the behavior of an entire class hierarchy after the fact (without changing the original code) is, even by itself, a welcome advance in the design toolbox. When this ability is combined with the ability to *augment* behavior already present in the hierarchy, even more new doors open, and many old techniques may need rethinking.

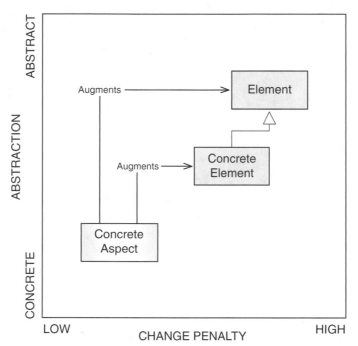

Figure 24-5   *The aspect-oriented solution to extending the behavior of existing classes moves the "weaving" across an element hierarchy that was accomplished by the Visitor pattern from user code to programming language and compiler. This eliminates Visitor's deadly cyclic dependency from the source code.*

24.3.2   Observer

The case against Visitor is easy to make. More surprising is the possibility of replacing the workhorse Observer pattern [7]—surprising because the Observer pattern's whole purpose is to invert or avoid dependencies. For example, Figures 24-6 and 24-7 show the "before" and "after" of applying the Observer pattern to a temperature sensor that notifies a display when the temperature changes. The naïve solution of Figure 24-6 is a design in which the sensor is directly wired to the temperature display in order to trigger display changes. After adding the `Subject` and `Observer` classes of the Observer pattern (see Figure 24-7), this hardwiring is gone, dependencies are all in the right direction, and the code for `TemperatureSensor` is pulled in the direction of greater reusability.

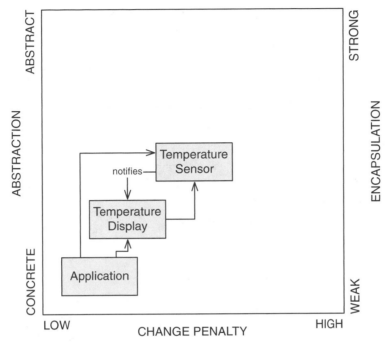

Figure 24-6   *Without the Observer pattern, a temperature sensor keeps a hard-wired reference to a temperature display in order to notify it of temperature changes. This "bad" dependency is in opposition to the ADP, DIP, and SDP.*

The Observer pattern sees use in many applications, particularly in large graphical user interfaces and in message-oriented middleware. A specialized form of Observer is at the heart of Document-View or Model-View-Controller patterns in almost every GUI framework. Why would we want to improve on such a venerable design workhorse? How could an aspect-oriented solution do any better? Table 24-2 lists problems with the Observer pattern and their possible aspect-oriented solutions.

Sadly (for reference-chasing programmers), object-oriented solutions to the problems of Table 24-2 would most likely add another level of indirection. For example, adding a local proxy Observer that receives ordinary events and then publishes them over the network can solve the problem of distributed event sending. Unfortunately, each level of indirection moves the software farther from the real

world or analysis-level view of the problem and deeper into relatively artificial mechanism classes that add overhead to both design comprehension and implementation
debugging.

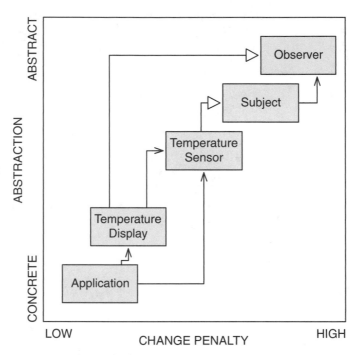

Figure 24-7 *Adding the Observer pattern not only removes the
improper dependency but also pulls some of the code in the direction
of greater reusability (the upper-right corner).*

Figure 24-8 shows a simple aspect-oriented replacement for Observer. The
notification is now orchestrated by a single aspect that weaves itself into
`TemperatureSensor` in order to notify `TemperatureDisplay` of changes. One
immediate benefit is greater reusability for `TemperatureSensor` because all notification code is externalized, freeing clients in different applications to
employ different notification interfaces or none at all. (Recall that reusability is
greatest in the upper-right corner of the abstraction/change penalty graph.)
`TemperatureDisplay` is also more reusable because it no longer needs any knowledge of `TemperatureSensor`. It could easily be wired to different temperature
sensors by different aspects, even if one sensor has a method named `getTemp()` and
another has a method named `getTemperature()`.

Table 24-2 *Problems with the Observer Pattern Are Surprisingly Many But May Have These Aspect-Oriented Solutions*

Problem	Solution
The designer of an event source must decide ahead of time what events will be needed when and with what passed state.	The "obliviousness" inherent in aspect-oriented languages [5] means that an event source designer need not even recognize it as such.
The sender of an event must be designed with the appropriate choice of push or pull and level of detail for changed state information.	Different event receivers can weave different levels of detail into the same event sender code.
Notifications are difficult to accomplish in a single satisfactory thread-safe way.	Clients with different threading models can define aspects with different thread awareness.
Some clients may prefer bundling events for performance or for non-flickering screen updates.	The bundling of events need not be the responsibility of event source or sink but of a connective aspect between them.
Distributed event notification requires much more sophisticated mechanisms for event propagation.	A connective aspect can define the distribution model on top of the event detail, leaving sender and receiver both independent of distribution details.
Registration and corresponding unregistration can be difficult to get right.	Registration and unregistration can appear nearby in a single notification aspect with appropriate related pointcuts or composition rules.
Program comprehension can be difficult when there is a lack of documentation relating to which objects observe which others.	An aspect can declare both the senders and the receivers of an event in a succinct fashion.

There is another way in which the design illustrated in Figure 24-8 is an improvement over Figure 24-7. The techniques and benefits of "aspect-oriented analysis" are mostly yet to be discovered, but notice that the classes and aspects of Figure 24-8 more closely match the physical model that one might conceive for this application: a temperature sensor, a display, and a wire from one to the other. Object-oriented designs tend to become littered with mechanism classes, classes that serve a critical software function but that have no correspondence to real world objects. With aspect-oriented notification, at least, the software module that captures notification itself has a counterpart in the real world (wire, post office, semaphores, kick in the pants, etc.). This seems like a satisfying outcome. As with the aspect-oriented answer to Visitor, the artificial mechanism classes are gone (`Visitor`, `Observer`, `Subject`).

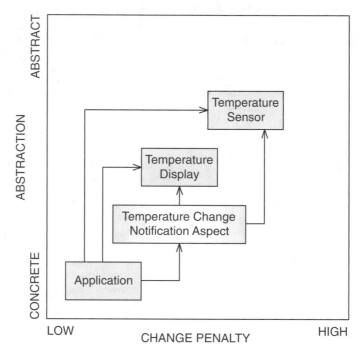

Figure 24-8 *An aspect-oriented alternative to the Observer pattern is a notification aspect that more directly accomplishes the wiring between two objects while decoupling them completely and making each more reusable.*

In some cases, the requirements for the notification might include functionality like asynchronous or idle-time firing of notifications, queuing and elimination of redundant notifications, etc. In fact, it is easy to generate a list of aspects of event propagation:

1. State change propagation

2. Thread safety

3. Bundling of related or redundant events

4. Distribution

5. Delivery guarantees

6. Causality

7. Event tracing

8. Debugging aids

When one or more of these apply, the mechanism classes may be worth keeping but may still be orchestrated by a notification aspect. The AspectJ Tutorial includes an example of applying the Observer pattern in its simplest form to classes that do not in themselves provide notifications [1]. That approach could be readily extended to more sophisticated `Subject` and `Observer` base classes or, better still, to simple `Subject` and `Observer` classes augmented with multiple aspects from the preceding list. Figure 24-9 illustrates the concept of a mixed object-oriented/aspect-oriented Observer design.

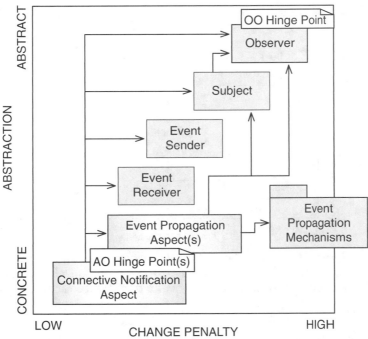

Figure 24-9   *A combined aspect-oriented and object-oriented Observer design has the potential to decouple notification from both sender and receiver and also to decouple multiple aspects of the notification (like thread safety, debugging aids, and notification bundling) from the base Observer implementation and from one another.*

24.3.3 Extension Object

The Extension Object pattern [6] combines the dependency inversion characteristics of the Observer pattern with the extensibility characteristics of the Visitor pattern. Figure 24-10 shows the structure of this pattern in Abstraction/Change Penalty space. A concrete base class, `Subject`, provides mechanisms to dynamically add and query for extensions. A given extension must be downcast to its specific interface (`SpecificExtension`) for use. The pattern as a whole amounts to defining a standard way to *cross cast* from one interface reference to another.

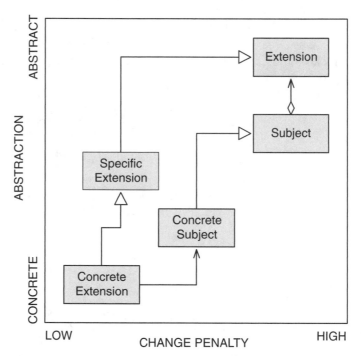

Figure 24-10 *The Extension Object pattern includes mechanism classes (Subject and Extension) to invert the dependency between an original class and its extensions or between partial interfaces to a concrete whole.*

The aspect-oriented alternative to extension objects is extension aspects (see Figure 24-11). This approach eliminates the need for client cross casting from one extension (or base interface) to another by directly injecting the implementation of a specific interface into a class seen by a given set of clients. Besides removing the cross casting from client code, this approach reduces the run-time overhead of the cross cast and the design complexity as measured in number of classes and methods. The core functionality is more reusable since its extension mechanism is not predefined via inheritance from `Subject` and dependence upon `Extension`.

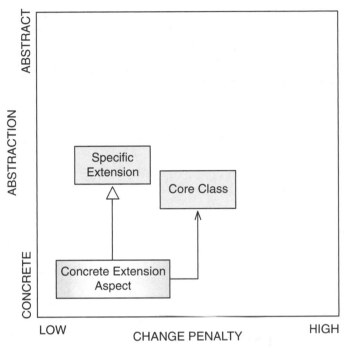

Figure 24-11 *An aspect-oriented extension to an existing class simply augments that class to directly or indirectly realize the desired specific interface, eliminating the run-time cross casting mechanism of the Extension Object pattern.*

An interesting detail is whether the client(s) of the specific extension should be dependent upon the aspect or whether the aspect should be dependent upon the client(s). The second option would lead to a design more like the notification aspect of Figure 24-8 but with a wider connection between client and service. The first option is probably more appropriate if there are several clients or the clients are unknown at compile time. A judgement of the relative stability and abstractness of the client(s) and the extension they make use of would answer the question. Different approaches could even be taken for different extensions of the same core class.

24.3.4   *Virtual Construction*

As a final example, this section describes the use of a factory for polymorphic object construction, which is another design in which object-oriented indirection can be combined with aspect-oriented indirection to improve upon a common design pattern or programming idiom.

The starting point is the simple Factory pattern shown in Figure 24-12. This common idiom for "virtual construction" includes a level of indirection between a client and a set of polymorphic services, one of which is the construction of a product from any given string description of what kind of product is needed. This pattern works nicely for XML deserialization and other situations where objects are to be constructed in memory from their persistent representations. There are two related problems with this pattern:

1. The `Factory` class depends upon every concrete `Product` type and is therefore subject to repeated maintenance.
2. The selection of what kind of product to construct is inappropriately separated from the products themselves.

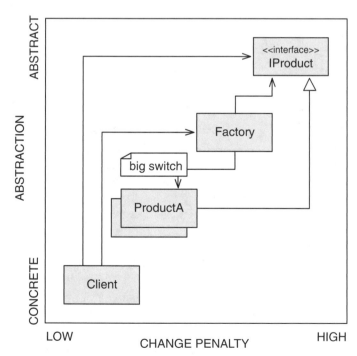

Figure 24-12   *Factories are a common idiom for "virtual construction" of polymorphic objects.*

An aspect-oriented Factory solves these problems and comes closer to the goal of virtual construction: products that polymorphically assemble themselves from given assembly instructions. Figure 24-13 shows the aspect-oriented design, and Listing 24-1 includes the full code of an AspectJ [1, 10] implementation. This solution retains all the elements of the purely object-oriented solution but adds two aspects related to product manufacturing. The object-oriented hinge point, `IProduct`, continues to provide value not only for polymorphic construction but polymorphic behavior after construction. The `Factory` class still appears but no longer knows how to make anything (see `Factory.makeProduct()` in Listing 24-1). Instead, a `VirtualConstruction` aspect located inside each product class performs product selection and weaves itself into `Factory` with the help of a pointcut defined in aspect `ProductManufacturing`.

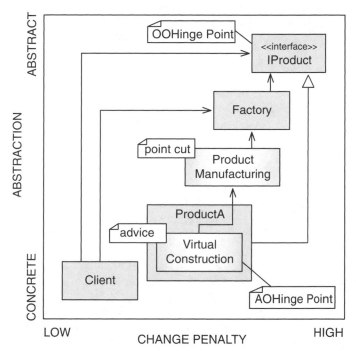

Figure 24-13 *An aspect-oriented factory moves the product selection code into the product modules and therefore comes closer to the goal of "virtual" construction.*

Here are the practical benefits of aspect-oriented virtual construction:

1. When a new product is added, only a single file needs to be added and edited—the code for the product itself.

2. A product may be temporarily or permanently removed without commenting or deleting a block of `Factory` code.

3. The constants that determine product kind need not be exposed outside each concrete product.

4. There is no big `switch` statement in the `Factory`.

These benefits derive from the ability of aspect code to compose itself into a base functionality without any modification of that base functionality. (In this case the base factory has no capability in itself.) This design approaches the ultimate in flexible manufacturing—an empty factory floor that can be reconfigured at will.

Listing 24-1 *An aspect-oriented factory, implemented in AspectJ, moves the product selection code inside the concrete product code, eliminating many of the troubles with maintaining factory code in its object-oriented form*

```
interface IProduct
{
  void beUseful();
  void becomeObsolete();
}

class Factory
{
  public IProduct makeProduct( String whatKind )
  {
    return null;   // aspects required!
  }
}

aspect ProductManufacturing
{
  static pointcut production( String whatKind ):
    target(Factory) &&
    args(whatKind) &&
    call(IProduct makeProduct(String));
}

class ProductA
  implements IProduct
{
  // product "self-assembly" occurs here
```

```
  private static aspect VirtualConstruction
  {
    IProduct around(String whatKind):
      ProductManufacturing.production(whatKind)
    {
      if ( whatKind.equals( "A" ) )
      {
        return new ProductA();
      }
      else
      {
        return proceed(whatKind);
      }
    }
  }

  ProductA()
  {
    System.out.println("new ProductA");
  }

  public void beUseful()
  {
    System.out.println("ProductA.beUseful");
  }
  public void becomeObsolete()
  {
    System.out.println("ProductA.becomeObsolete");
  }
}

// Similar code for ProductB ...

class FactoryTest
{
  public static void main( String args[] )
  {
    Factory factory = new Factory();
    IProduct productA = factory.makeProduct("A");
    productA.beUseful();
    productA.becomeObsolete();
  }
}
```

The fourth benefit in this list, `switch` statement elimination, is often a benefit ascribed to object polymorphism. The `VirtualConstruction` aspect eliminates the `switch` statement left over in the object-oriented solution. In a sense, the aspects of this design cancel out the negative effects of the factory/product indirection by moving construction code back into the various product modules and reversing the dependencies from factory to product.

The aspect idiom of Listing 24-1 incorporates clear aspect-oriented indirection. The pointcut (when the aspect applies) is defined separately from the behavior to be incorporated at that pointcut. In this case, the "when" is defined first in one place, and the "what" is defined separately in multiple places. This is an interesting twist on the usual case of an abstract library aspect that defines the "what" in one place and requires concrete aspects to define the "when," usually in multiple places.

24.4 GUIDELINES FOR ASPECT-ORIENTED DEPENDENCY MANAGEMENT

There are many reasons to choose aspect-oriented designs, but from the perspective of managing unhealthy dependencies, we can derive a number of guidelines from the examples of the preceding sections.

24.4.1 Object-Oriented Indirection

First, the advantages of object-oriented indirection for reducing dependencies are still significant. Choose object-oriented dependency management (often just a simple object-oriented interface to hide an implementation) under these circumstances:

1. **When dependencies cross subsystem boundaries (published interfaces).** At the package or subsystem level, hide private classes behind public interfaces in order to avoid publishing implementation details outside the subsystem.

2. **When an interface has separation-of-concerns value beyond dependency management.** Inside a subsystem, maintain a clear layering of the classes and interfaces to hide external dependencies. For example, classes near the "top" of a subsystem might depend on an XML library, while those near the bottom might depend on a data access library. An object-oriented hinge point in between keeps changes in either external dependency from breaking the whole subsystem.

3. **When behavior is truly polymorphic (has multiple similar services).** If an interface has multiple implementations (e.g., *Product* in the Factory pattern), the need for a polymorphic interface goes almost without saying and is not negated by aspect-oriented techniques.

24.4.2   Aspect-Oriented Indirection

Manage dependencies with aspect-oriented hinge points under these circumstances:

1. **When an object-oriented solution would intrude into un-owned code.**   Often, the lines of modularity in a system have as much to do with organizational divisions as with technical ones. When this is true and a service does not provide needed interfaces, an aspect-oriented design can avoid an ugly direct dependency.

2. **When an object-oriented design would break dependency principles.**   Some object-oriented designs are obsolete (e.g., Visitor) or at least debatable (e.g., Strategy) when aspect-oriented alternatives are available.

3. **When a single object-oriented service design would not meet the needs of all anticipated clients.**   A significant advantage of aspect-oriented designs is that different clients can have different views into a service without cluttering that service with an overly extensible or flexible interface ready for all comers.

4. **When the dependency needs only a simple notification or other "callback" connection between client(s) and service.**   The advantages of aspect-oriented notification come close to making it the default choice in a new design of this kind.

5. **When a service sees use by many similar clients.**   Almost by definition, object-oriented indirection is the better choice for a service with multiple implementations, and aspect-oriented indirection is the better choice for many clients with similar or related behavior.

24.4.3   Combined Object- and Aspect-Oriented Indirection

Finally, there are circumstances when it is best to combine object-oriented and aspect-oriented dependency management techniques:

1. **When an object interface is expected by external code but an aspect-oriented solution makes sense otherwise (e.g., aspect-oriented factory).**   When one concern (e.g., object construction) is best handled by aspects, but other concerns in the same object hierarchy are better modeled by polymorphism (e.g., domain object behavior), the obvious solution is to apply the right technique for each concern.

2. **To provide a reusable target for mechanisms with many optional aspects in addition to a primary client/service connective aspect (e.g., Observer with thread safety, event bundling, and event tracing).**   Sometimes, it may be best to provide a coordinated library of base objects, interfaces, and aspects in order to separate the detailed concerns of a mechanism from a further aspect-oriented application of that mechanism to a particular dependency.

In general, the reasons to combine aspect-oriented and object-oriented indirection amount to minimizing the overall rigidity of a design. There is much yet to learn about the best ways to combine object-oriented and aspect-oriented indirection. Some future book on "Multi-Paradigm Design with Aspect-XX" will be an interesting read.

24.5   MODELING BENEFITS FROM ASPECT-ORIENTED DEPENDENCY MANAGEMENT

The areas of aspect-oriented analysis and design are today in the early stages of exploration [8, 18]. However, there already seems to be an added bonus to aspect-oriented designs for class or component connectivity—the resulting designs more closely match the real world.

Dependency management addresses the theme of connectivity and extensibility between a service and its clients. AOSD naturally moves extensions of base functionality to aspects and makes the core classes more stable, less concrete, and more reusable. In terms of the Open/Closed Principle (which states that modules should be open for extension and closed for modification) [12, 13], classes are the closed part and aspects are the open part in an aspect-oriented design of this type.

Several years ago, software components were hailed as the integrated circuits of the software engineering profession [3]. Component technology has justifiably displaced object technology as the sharpest tool in the programmer's toolbox, but components have not achieved their promise as parts on a shelf waiting for assembly. There are many reasons, but one is that connecting software components is far more complex than connecting electronic or mechanical components. Figure 24-14 suggests that mechanical and electronic parts in relation to their connectors (nuts, bolts, adhesive; wires, pin patterns, bus standards) and assemblies (cars, houses, computers, VCRs) have the correct directionality of dependency. However, software connectors are more concrete and less stable than their mechanical counterparts (see Figure 24-15). The natural dependency from software part to software connector is therefore improper according to the dependency principles. This conundrum is the current justification for many design patterns, Observer being chief among them.

Why are software connectors less stable and more concrete than software parts, in contrast to their electronic or mechanical analogs? Mechanical connectors are defined by their size and shape, strength, adhesive properties, or material—all of which can be standardized without much loss of design flexibility. Electronic connectors add to this list a defined behavior for the signals carried through them. This makes them less stable and abstract than their mechanical cousins. However, the variety of electrical signals (5V 66MHz digital, 12V analog, 120V 60Hz AC, etc.) is still manageably finite and well standardized. Software "signals" through software connectors, however, are as varied as software itself. The variety of information carried between software modules is precisely what makes software so valuable.

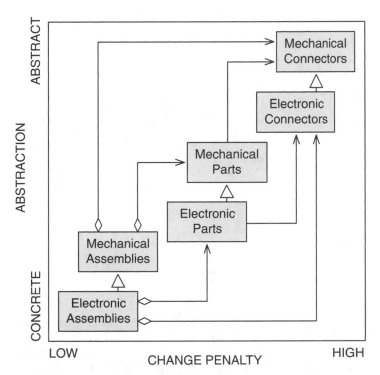

Figure 24-14 *Mechanical and electronic assemblies have dependencies upon parts and connectors that have the proper directionality in stability and abstractness.*

Aspect-oriented software development has the potential to build upon all that we as a profession have learned about object-oriented and component-based development and to solve several remaining issues, like this need for an inverted dependency between part and connector. Aspect-oriented connectors can insert themselves in precise, unanticipated ways into the parts they connect. Like an imaginary engine block with no boltholes, the parts need never have been designed for a particular connection mechanism. Figure 24-16 shows the dependency inversion accomplished by an aspect-oriented solution that pushes connections into aspects and leaves only core functionality in classes, components, or software parts.

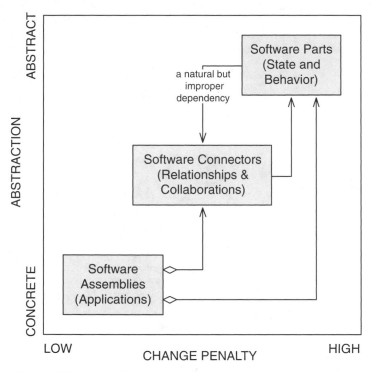

Figure 24-15   *Unlike mechanical or electronic connectors, software connectors (static or dynamic relationships and dynamic collaborations) are more concrete with higher penalties for change. Therefore, the natural dependency of parts upon connectors is improper according to the DIP and SDP.*

Today's aspect-oriented technologies generally provide a declarative definition for "when" functionality applies in the code while keeping an imperative definition for "what" to do there. Tomorrow's technologies will likely make the declarative "when" even more powerful. Our ability to cleanly manage dependencies with aspect-oriented techniques is already a great improvement over long-trusted object-oriented techniques and only promises to improve over time. Software designs that manage dependencies with a skilled mix of object-oriented and aspect-oriented techniques can nicely balance the qualities of practicality, comprehensibility, and flexibility for future change.

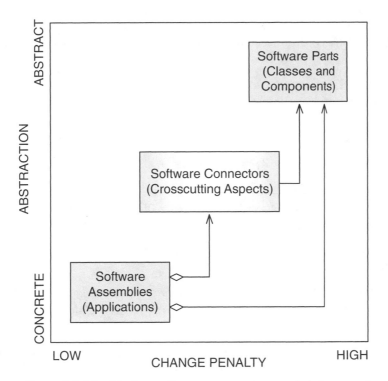

Figure 24-16 *Placing software connectors mainly in aspects successfully inverts the dependency between software parts and software connectors.*

REFERENCES

1. AspectJ Project. The AspectJ primer. http://www.eclipse.org/aspectj.

2. Carey, J., Carlson, B., and Graser, T. 2000. *San Francisco Design Patterns: Blueprints for Business Software*. Addison-Wesley, Reading, Massachusetts.

3. Cox, B. J. 1990. Planning the software industrial revolution. *IEEE Software 7*, 6, 25–33.

4. Czarnecki, K. and Eisenecker, U. W. 2000. *Generative Programming: Methods, Tools, and Applications*. Addison-Wesley, Reading, Massachusetts.

5. Filman, R. E. and Friedman, D. 2000. Aspect-oriented programming is quantification and obliviousness. In *Workshop on Advanced Separation of Concerns (OOPSLA)*, (Minneapolis). http://trese.cs.utwente.nl/Workshops/OOPSLA2000/papers/filman.pdf.

6. GAMMA, E. 1998. Extension object. In *Pattern Languages of Program Design 3*, R. Martin, D. Riehle, and F. Buschmann, Eds. Addison-Wesley, Reading, Massachusetts, 79–88.

7. GAMMA, E., HELM, R., JOHNSON, R., AND VLISSIDES, J. 1995. *Design Patterns: Elements of Reusable Object-Oriented Software*. Addison-Wesley, Reading, Massachusetts.

8. JACOBSON, I. 2003. Use cases and aspects—working seamlessly together. *Journal of Object Technology*, *2*, 4, 7–28.

9. JOHNSON, R. AND WOOLF, B. 1998. Type object. In *Pattern Languages of Program Design 3*, R. Martin, D. Riehle, and F. Buschmann, Eds. Addison-Wesley, Reading, Massachusetts, 47–65.

10. LADDAD, R. 2003. *AspectJ in Action*. Manning Publications, Greenwich, Connecticut.

11. MARTIN, R. C. 1998. Acyclic visitor. In *Pattern Languages of Program Design 3*, R. Martin, D. Riehle, and F. Buschmann, Eds. Addison-Wesley, Reading, Massachusetts, 93–103.

12. MARTIN, R. C. 2002. *Agile Software Development, Principles, Patterns, and Practices*, Prentice-Hall, Englewood Cliffs, New Jersey.

13. MEYER, B. 1997. *Object-Oriented Software Construction, 2nd Ed.* Prentice-Hall, Englewood Cliffs, New Jersey.

14. NORDBERG III, M. E. 1998. Default and extrinsic visitor. In *Pattern Languages of Program Design 3*, R. Martin, D. Riehle, and F. Buschmann, Eds. Addison-Wesley, Reading, Massachusetts, 105–123.

15. NORDBERG III, M. E. 2001. Aspect-oriented indirection. In *Workshop on Beyond Design: Patterns (Mis)Used (OOPSLA)*, (Tampa, Florida). http://www.schwanninger.com/OOPSLA2001/submissions/Nordberg.zip.

16. NORDBERG III, M. E. 2001. Aspect-oriented dependency inversion. In *Workshop on Advanced Separation of Concerns in Object-Oriented Systems (OOPSLA)*, (Tampa, Florida). http://www.cs.ubc.ca/~kdvolder/Workshops/OOPSLA2001/submissions/12-nordberg.pdf.

17. RIEL, A. 1996. *Object-Oriented Design Heuristics*. Addison-Wesley, Reading, Massachusetts.

18. SUTTON, S. M. 2003. Concerns in a requirements model—a small case study. In *Workshop on Early Aspects* (AOSD), (Boston, Massachusetts).

Chapter 25

Developing Software Components with Aspects: Some Issues and Experiences

JOHN GRUNDY AND JOHN HOSKING

Engineering software components is a challenging task. Existing approaches to component-based software development are for the most part focused on functional decomposition. All have the weakness of failing to take into account the impact of crosscutting concerns on components. In this chapter, we outline *aspect-oriented component engineering*. Our approach uses aspects to help engineer better software components. Motivating our work with a simple example of a distributed system, we describe how specifications and designs can use aspects to provide additional information about components and how aspects can be used to help implement more decoupled software components. We show how encoded aspect information can be used at runtime to support component plug-and-play, retrieval, and validation. We also compare and contrast our approach to other component engineering methods and aspect-oriented software development techniques.

25.1 INTRODUCTION

Component-based systems development is the composition of systems from parts called software components. Components encapsulate data and functions. They often provide events and are self-describing, and many can be dynamically "plugged and played" into running applications [1, 7, 36]. In building systems, we often use a mixture of newly built and existing COTS (Commercial Off-The-Shelf) components. For the latter, we usually have no access to source code.

Engineering software components can be quite a challenging task. Components must be identified, and their requirements must be specified. Component interaction is crucial, so both provided and required component behavior needs identification and documentation [18, 32]. Ideally, components are implemented using a technology that supports a high degree of component reuse. Users of components may want to be able to understand and correctly plug-in components at runtime.

We have found problems with most component design methods and implementation technologies. In our experience, they do not produce components with sufficiently flexible interfaces, run-time adaptability, or good enough documentation [11, 12]. A major weakness of current methodology is the inability to describe functional and non-functional characteristics and inter-relationships of the components.

In the past, we used *aspects* (crosscutting concerns) at the requirements level to improve the description of our components [10]. When this proved successful, we applied the concept to component design and implementation [11, 12]. This involves using aspects to better describe the impact of crosscutting concerns on components at the design level. We have made use of these aspect-oriented component designs to help build components with more reusable and adaptable functionality. We have also used encodings of aspects associated with software components at runtime [12]. This process uses aspect information to support dynamic component adaptation, introspection, indexing and retrieval, and validation.

Most aspect-oriented software development uses aspects in similar ways to the way we do. Aspects are used to identify and codify crosscutting concerns on objects. Similarly, some reflective systems use aspect information to support run-time adaptation [25, 30]. Most aspect programming systems weave code into join points of programs [20]. Some design approaches use aspects (or "viewpoints" or "hyperslices") to provide multiple perspectives on the object designs [8, 16, 18, 37].

In this chapter, we provide a summary of our work, applying aspects to the development of software components. We refer readers interested in a more comprehensive discussion of our work to our previously published papers [10, 11, 12, 14].

25.2 MOTIVATION

Consider a collaborative travel planning application that is to be used by customers and travel agents to make travel bookings [12]. Examples of the user interfaces provided by such a system are illustrated in Figure 25-1 (left). Some of the software components composed to form such an application are illustrated in Figure 25-1 (right).

We built this component-based system by composing a set of software components that provide the necessary facilities. These include travel itinerary management, customer and staff data management, system integration with remote booking systems, and various user interfaces. Some components, such as the map visualization, database, and email server, are quite general and highly reusable.

Others components, such as the travel itinerary manager, travel item manager, travel booking interfaces, and integration components, are much more domain-specific.

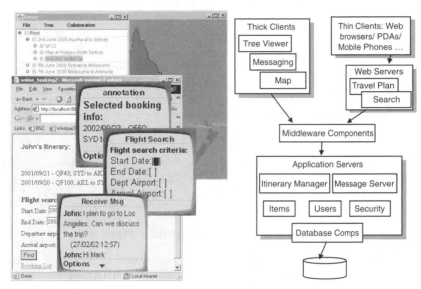

Figure 25-1 *Example component-based application.*

When building such an application, a developer needs to identify and assemble many components. These have usually been built using "functional decomposition"—organizing system data and functions into components based on the vertical piece(s) of system functionality they support. However, many systemic features of an application end up crosscutting many of the different components in the system [10, 20]. For example, user interfaces, data persistency, data distribution, security management, and resource utilization all have pandemic impact. Some components provide such functionalities; others require them [3]. We use the term "aspects" to describe these crosscutting, horizontally impacting concerns.

To illustrate how systemic aspects affect components, Figure 25-2 shows three components from the travel planner system: Tree Viewer, Travel Itinerary, and Database. Aspects User Interface, Persistency, Collaborative Work, and Transactions crosscut these components' methods and state. The Tree Viewer provides user interface and collaborative work support. The Travel Itinerary component requires user interface and persistency support in order to work but provides data to render and store itinerary items. A Database component provides data storage and transaction coordination support but requires transaction coordination. The three components must work together to provide the travel plan viewing, business process, and data management required by the system. Note that several aspects affect each of these components in different ways.

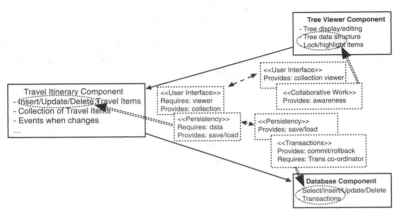

Figure 25-2 *The concept of aspects crosscutting interrelated software components.*

For each aspect that affects a component, we need to provide additional information—a set of *aspect details*. Each aspect detail may also be constrained by one or more *aspect detail properties* that describe detailed functional or non-functional constraints. In our example, we may assert that the Persistency aspect affects the Itinerary manager. We may then specify that the nature of this Persistency impact is that it requires a component providing data storage (a Persistency aspect detail). We may further specify that the data storage provided to it must meet some level of performance constraint. For example, 100 `insert()` and `update()` functions must be supported per second (an aspect detail property constraint for the data storage aspect detail). Other aspect details might specify the kind of awareness supported by the tree viewer (e.g., highlight of changed items), the kind of authentication or encryption used (Security aspect details), the upper bounds of resources used, performance required, or concurrency control techniques they enforce.

In aspect-oriented programming languages [20], aspects support code injection into methods. For example, in AspectJ, pointcuts can specify where to add persistency management, memory utilization, and user interface and distributed communication code [6]. In aspect-oriented design [3, 18, 34, 35], aspects are used to describe crosscutting concerns affecting the components. In dynamic aspect-oriented programming [30, 38, 40], components might be modified at runtime using the aspects to change their parameters or their running code.

25.3 OUR APPROACH

We have developed aspect-oriented component engineering, a new method for developing software components with aspects. The use of aspects provides us with "multiple perspectives" on software component designs. Figure 25-3 illustrates our approach. Component specifications and designs, typically UML diagrams, are augmented with aspect information (1). A key activity is determining whether required aspects are met in proposed component configurations. We also check whether component configurations are consistent with respect to the aspect constraints. When implementing designs, we use the aspect information to help us develop a more decoupled component interaction and dynamic component configuration. This enables us to maximize the amount of component reuse and dynamic component adaptation possible (2). We encode the aspect information about software components in a run-time accessible form (3). At runtime, this information allows components to be introspected—that is, understood by end users and other components. We use this encoded aspect-based information to support dynamic run-time component reconfiguration and adaptation. We have also used it to support component storage and retrieval from a repository and component validation by dynamic test generation and execution (4).

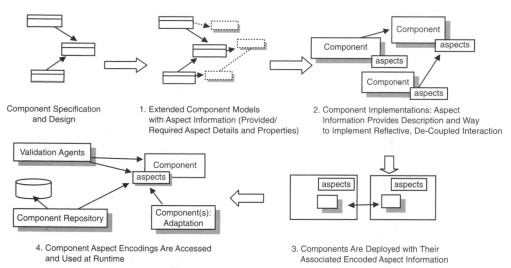

Figure 25-3 *An overview of aspect-oriented component engineering.*

In the following three sections, we briefly illustrate how we use aspects for component design, for decoupled and configurable component implementation, and at runtime.

25.4 COMPONENT SPECIFICATION AND DESIGN WITH ASPECTS

Our approach gives developers a way to capture crosscutting impacts of systemic functionality and associated non-functional constraints as aspects. Note that using aspects is only one approach for doing this. Approaches using some form of multi-perspective or viewpoint representations are also common [1, 8, 13]. Using aspects gives developers a way to categorize the impact of these concerns on different components and different parts of components.

During requirements engineering, we use aspects to document the functional and non-functional properties of a component. These are then grouped using a set of aspect categories. Common categories include user interface, collaborative work, component configuration, security, transaction processing, distribution, persistency, and resource management. Domain-specific aspects can also be used. In the example domain, these include services relating to travel itinerary management, payment, and order processing.

Figure 25-4 illustrates a simple use of aspects when specifying two interrelated software components. In this example, the travel planner's requirements identify several components that must provide extensible user interfaces, where one component provides a user interface that another adapts at runtime. This adaptation is usually the structured addition of a new user interaction "affordance." For example, the travel itinerary construction use case says that new "travel item" construction facilities must be able to be added dynamically to the itinerary planning user interfaces.

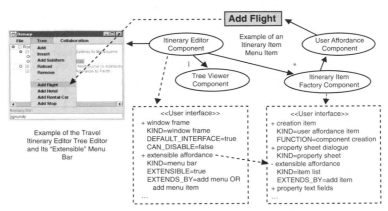

Figure 25-4 *A simple component specification example using aspects.*

Figure 25-4 shows the itinerary editor component, which uses a tree editor and multiple itinerary item creation (factory) components. The aspects of the itinerary editor specify that it provide (among other things) an *extensible affordance* user interface facility. This means other components can extend its user interface in certain controlled ways. Another component, an itinerary item factory, is used to create particular kinds of itinerary items—flights, hotel rooms, rental cars, and so on. This factory requires a component with an extensible affordance so it can add a button, menu item, or drop-down menu item to this user interface for creating different kinds of travel items. In this example, the provided user-interface–extension aspect detail in the itinerary editor aspects satisfies the required one in the factory's aspects. This approach can be used to describe a large range of provided and required component functional and non-functional properties. Developers can then reason about the interrelationships of components.

During design, developers refine component specifications into detailed designs and then design implementation solutions. They also refine the aspect specifications to a much more detailed level. To describe their designs, developers create additional design diagrams. Each diagram focuses on particular aspects affecting a group of related components. An example from the travel planner system is shown in Figure 25-5, an annotated Unified Modeling Language (UML) sequence diagram. This describes component interactions in the travel planning system as a user constructs part of a travel itinerary. In the example, the user interacts with a web-based thin-client interface for the itinerary editor. This in turn interacts with application server-side components. Additional middleware and database components provide the infrastructure for the architecture of this design.

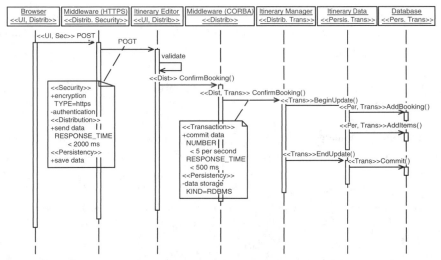

Figure 25-5 *Component interaction design example.*

In this example, we have used UML stereotypes to indicate the aspects affecting each component. Both method invocations and component objects have been annotated in this way. We have used UML note annotations to further characterize particular method invocations between components. These indicate "provided" and "requires" aspect details. Some details are also characterized by adding non-functional constraints. In this example, they include the type of security and data storage required and required performance measures of the distributed system communication.

Such aspect-augmented design diagrams allow developers to capture richer information about their component designs. Developers can augment existing diagrams or create new ones. New diagrams allow them to focus on particular parts of a system or particular component interactions. Our aspects give developers a way to capture and document both functional and non-functional constraints during design.

25.5 COMPONENT IMPLEMENTATION WITH ASPECTS

When implementing software components, some key issues arise:

- ◆ How can reusability of components be maximized? This is desirable to realize the component-based development philosophy of "building systems from reusable parts."

- ◆ How can component interaction be decoupled, thereby minimizing the knowledge required of other components, interfaces, and methods? This allows greater compositional flexibility.

- ◆ How can run-time introspection of components be supported? This allows components at runtime to be understood by other components and by developers (or even end users) who may be reconfiguring a system (for example, plugging in new components).

- ◆ How can run-time adaptation and composition best be supported? This allows dynamically evolving systems.

In our work, we have used aspects to help achieve these goals. We have developed two approaches that make use of aspect information when implementing software components. Figure 25-6 (top) illustrates how information about the aspects affecting a component can be obtained.

The aspect information associated with a component can be queried by other components (1). We have developed two ways of doing this. One has the aspect information encoded using a special class hierarchy of "aspect information objects." The other has aspect information encoded in XML. After obtaining aspect-based information about another component, a client component can then invoke the component's functionality. This can be done by dynamically constructing method invocations (2). Alternatively, it can be done by calling standard adaptor methods implemented by the aspect objects (3).

These translate standard method calls into particular component method calls (4). This approach provides a way of greatly decoupling many common component interactions by the use of a set of standard aspect-oriented interactions.

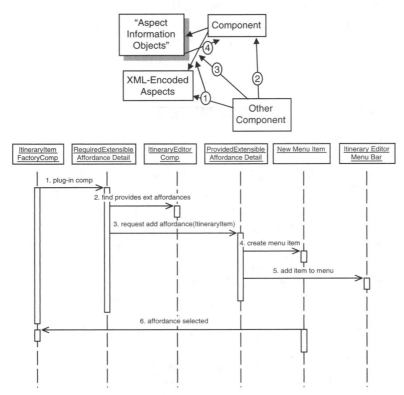

Figure 25-6 *Using aspects to decouple components.*

Figure 25-6 (bottom) shows a simple example of using this decoupled approach. An itinerary item factory component instance wants to add a user interface affordance to the itinerary editor's user interface. The factory component knows nothing about how the editor's user interface is implemented. Neither does it know how its affordance will actually be realized (menu item, button, etc). First, it tells its own aspect information to initialize after plug-in (1). Its required extensible affordance aspect object queries the components related to the itinerary item factory (e.g., the itinerary editor) for its aspect information (2). It then locates a provided extensible affordance aspect object and requests this object to add an affordance to the itinerary editor's user interface (3). This creates a menu item (4) and adds it to the itinerary editor's menu bar at an appropriate place (5). The menu item notifies the factory when it should create a new travel item of a particular kind (6). The provided affordance aspect object knows how to create and add this affordance for its owning itinerary editor component. In this example, it adds a menu item. If the factory were associated with a different component that extended its interface with buttons, a new button would be created and added. This would be done without the factory having any knowledge of how it happened. We have used this approach to implement a wide variety of software components with highly decoupled interactions.

25.6 USING ASPECTS AT RUNTIME

As indicated in the previous section, during component implementation, aspects are codified either using special aspect objects or using XML documents. We make use of these encoded aspects in many ways after component deployment. This is illustrated in Figure 25-7. Client components obtain aspect information from a component and use this to understand the component's provided or required services affected by a particular systemic aspect. They can dynamically compose method calls to invoke component functionality or call aspect object methods to indirectly invoke the component's functionality (1). We have developed a component repository that uses aspect information to index components (2). Aspect-based queries are issued by users (or even other components) to retrieve components whose functions and non-functional constraints meet those of the aspect-based query. We have developed validation agents that use aspect information to formulate tests on a deployed component (3). The agent then compares the test results to the aspect-described component constraints and informs developers whether the deployed component meets its specification in its current deployment context.

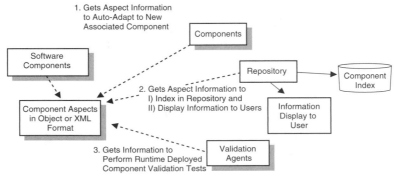

Figure 25-7 *Examples of using aspects at runtime.*

Figure 25-8 (top) shows how several user interface adaptations in the collaborative travel planner have been realized using dynamic discovery and invocation of component functions. The itinerary editor menu has been extended using the mechanism described in the previous section (1). Each itinerary item factory component obtains itinerary editor component's extensible affordance object and requests it to add (in this case) a menu item allowing the factory to be invoked by the user. The dialogue shown at the bottom of the figure is a similar example where a reusable version control component has added check-in and check-out buttons to the button panel of a reusable event history component (2). The version control component also obtains the distribution-providing component and persistency-supporting component of related components in its environment. It uses their facilities to store and retrieve versions and to allow sharing of versions across users. The same mechanism is used to achieve this, but different aspect objects are introspected and invoked. The map viewer has had a collaborative messaging bar added to it dynamically via the same mechanism (3).

The use of aspect information at runtime in this way is an alternative to some of the other dynamic aspect-oriented programming approaches. These use run-time code injection or modification to achieve similar results. However, usually software components are self-contained, and their source code is often not available. Thus, we have tried to provide a way of dynamically changing running components by using aspects to understand component interfaces and behavioral constraints. The implementation of decoupled component interaction by the aspect information allows run-time adaptation.

As a final example of the use of aspects with software components, consider the issue of checking whether deployed components are correctly configured. The operation of most software components is affected by a variety of deployment scenario conditions, particularly the other components they are deployed with. We make use of aspect characterizations of components to enable run-time test construction and validation of component behavior. This approach is useful because many components cannot be adequately validated until they are actually deployed.

Figure 25-8 (bottom) illustrates how we use aspect information to support a concept of *validation agents*. These validation agents obtain aspect information about a component (1) that has been deployed in web or application servers (2). Different validation agents query parts of this aspect information (3) to work out the required constraints on the component's operation. Some agents also make use of deployment-specific test data (4) to formulate tests on the components. Some tests simply check that the component is accessible or that its functions work when invoked. Some check performance of components, transaction support, or resource utilization (memory, CPU, or disk space). Some validation agents run tests (5) by invoking deployed component functionality.

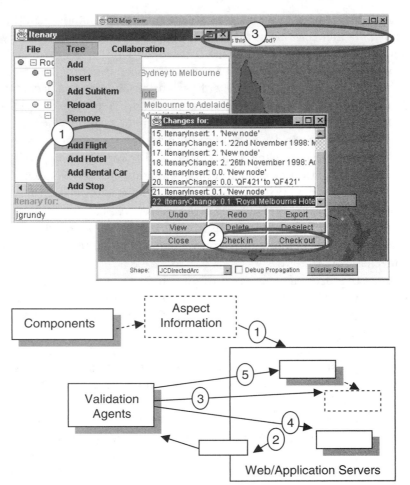

Figure 25-8   *Two examples of run-time usage of aspect information.*

25.7   RELATED WORK

A great deal of work has been done on separation of concerns in software development [16]. Examples of such work include viewpoint-based requirements, designs and tools [8, 13], subject-oriented programming [16], hyperslices, [37] and aspect-oriented programming [18, 20, 30]. Viewpoints, or partial views on parts of software artifacts, have been used for purposes such as requirements engineering, specification and design, and user interface construction and in various software tools. Aspects are in essence a specialization of the general notion of a viewpoint. An aspect captures particular crosscutting concerns on objects or components and thus provides a certain partial perspective on a software system design or implementation. Viewpoints of one form or another have been used in all development methods. These include the many component development methods like Catalysis, SelectPerspective, and COMO [2, 4, 21]. However, in almost all of the current component design methods and implementation technologies, a function-decomposition–centric approach is used. Such an approach results in the tangling of systemic crosscutting concerns in both the component designs and in their implementation code [11, 20, 25]. This is the same kind of problem that aspect-oriented programming tries to address for object-oriented programs. In contrast with these other approaches, we have used characterizations of crosscutting concerns to help design and implement software components in similar way to other UML extensions with aspects [34]. We have used aspect information in a more novel way at runtime to provide a mechanism to dynamically understand and interact with other components.

Hyperslices and subject-oriented programming are similar to aspect-oriented design and programming [16, 29, 37]. They attempt to provide developers with alternative views of crosscutting concerns. Our aspect-oriented component engineering views are specialized kinds of hyperslices. We have deployed this viewpoint mechanism to assist component development in this work. Much recent work has gone into developing techniques to characterize software components. Our work is but one such approach. Some component development methods have introduced specialized views of component characteristics. These notably include security and distribution issues [15]. Our aspects adopt a similar approach but provide a uniform modeling approach for components' crosscutting concerns in general. Some approaches use formal specifications of component behavior [28]. Others make use of characterizations of services that components provide [31]. Some approaches focus on both provided and required functional component services [19, 32]. Our aspects provide an implementation-encoded and run-time-accessible design characterization of software components. We have focused on using common crosscutting concerns as the "ontology" to describe components and some of their interactions. However, we feel that this approach is ultimately complementary to other description approaches.

So far, little attention has been paid to applying aspects to component-based systems. Adaptive plug-and-play components and composite adapters [25, 26] make use of components that implement something similar to the concept of our use of aspect-based decoupled interfaces. These are mixed to help realize the separation of various concerns from component implementations. Component design methods currently provide a very limited ability to identify overlapping concerns between components.

However, the isolation of systemic functions (for example, communications, database access, and security) into reusable components is common in component technologies [27, 32, 39]. This partially addresses the problems of components encapsulating these systemic services. It also enables isolation of these services and access via well-defined component-based interfaces. However, not all aspects can be suitably abstracted into individual components, though some success has been achieved with middle-ware-supporting components [3]. This is due to overlaps and the eventual over-decomposition of systems. JAsCo [35] provides a component-based development method incorporating aspects, which uses the concept of aspect beans and connectors to extend JavaBeans for aspect-oriented composition. This approach is similar to our component aspects but specialized for a JavaBean-based development platform.

One of the main motivations for the use of reflective techniques and the run-time composition and configuration of components is to try to avoid compile-time weaving [30, 38, 40]. This allows running systems and their components to have aspects imposed on them after deployment. This is done typically as before/after method processing. Some technologies also support intra-method code incorporation and component reconfiguration at runtime. Aspects in such systems can be formulated at runtime and added or removed from programs and components dynamically. The crosscutting concerns are encapsulated within the introduced aspect code. Currently, most code incorporation-based techniques have a high amount of expensive performance overhead. A further issue is a current lack of design abstractions. Our aspect-oriented design approach does not preclude implementation with any of these technologies. However, our aim with decoupled interaction and introspection via aspect information was to produce software components that make use of aspect-related services in other components via well-defined component interfaces. This approach allows for controlled and efficient dynamic reconfiguration support via standardized component-supported or delegate aspect object-supported functionality access. In addition, our aspect-oriented component designs provide a consistent set of design abstractions. Our dynamic discovery approach using aspect information has some similarities with the UDDI discovery mechanism developed for web services [24]. A major difference with current UDDI registries is the ability to use categorized functional and non-functional information with our aspect-based approach.

Our use of aspect information at runtime for component repositories and deployed component validation contrasts with most other approaches. Most software repositories use type-based, keyword-based, or execution-based indexing [17]. In these approaches, the component interface, comments, or behavior are used to index and retrieve components. Run-time adaptation can also be well supported by aspects, which is illustrated in our own work and that of others more recently [5, 38]. Using aspects in addition to one or more of these techniques gives further perspectives on components that can be indexed and queried. Current component testing and validation techniques mainly focus on exhaustive functional interface testing [22, 23]. Using aspect-encoded information associated with components allows validation agents to query for expected functional behavior and non-functional constraints. Tests can then be automatically assembled and run and feedback given to developers on whether or not a component meets its aspect-codified constraints in its current deployment situation.

25.8 EVALUATION

We have used aspect-oriented component engineering on a range of problems. These have included the construction of adaptive user interfaces, multi-view software tools, plug-and-play collaborative work-supporting components, and several prototype enterprise systems. We have built some of these systems using our custom JViews component architecture and some with Java 2 Enterprise Edition software components. Using aspects to assist in engineering these components has helped us to design and build more reusable and adaptable components. We have carried out a basic empirical evaluation of aspect-oriented component engineering by having a group of developers design and prototype a set of components. These included experienced industry designers and post-graduate OO technology students. Feedback from the evaluation indicated that the designers found the aspect-based perspectives on their UML designs useful, both when designing components and when trying to understand others people's components and their compositions. Using aspects to assist in developing decoupled components is effective, though it needs good tool support. Run-time validation of software components with aspects is potentially an important long-term contribution of this work.

We have identified several key advantages of component development with aspect-oriented techniques.

- ◆ Crosscutting properties of a system can be explicitly represented in design diagrams. This provides a way for developers to see the impact of these crosscutting concerns on their components and the components' interfaces, operations, and relationships.
- ◆ Adding aspect information allows crosscutting behavior (aspect details) and related non-functional constraints (aspect detail properties) to be expressed together. This allows these to be more easily understood and reasoned about when building component compositions.

◆ Using aspect-oriented designs when implementing software components can result in greater decoupling of components.

◆ Using encodings of aspect information at runtime can provide a useful approach to providing run-time adaptability and run-time accessible knowledge about component behavior and constraints.

However, there are also several potential disadvantages to our approach.

◆ There is possibly considerable added complexity to the specifications and designs. Some of our component designers found that the additional diagrams and aspect annotations come with a high overhead. Others were unclear what aspect details and properties they should use and were unsure whether adding new aspect details and properties to their model was a good or bad thing.

◆ Currently, we have limited tool support for AOCE. Our tools are tuned to producing our custom *JViews* architecture's components, rather than more general J2EE or .NET components. This means that while developers can use aspect annotations in conventional CASE tools, these lack formal foundations and checking. The aspect designs are not yet supported by good code generation or reverse engineering tools.

◆ A considerable amount of effort must be put in by implementers to encode aspect information for association with software components. This can be overcome to a degree by extended tool support and by the use of a component architecture that directly supports aspect encoding and decoupled interaction.

◆ The use of different aspect ontologies by different developers or teams is an issue. Some developers might want to make use of differently named aspect details and properties that express the same information. Of course, developers could agree on the same set of aspects. However, third-party sourced components using different characterizations would need a mapping of one ontology to another. This is a difficult problem to solve in general.

25.9 FUTURE RESEARCH DIRECTIONS

We are developing further extensions to our method and prototype supporting tools to overcome some of these problems. Aspects can be prefixed with an ontology "name-space" (much as XML namespaces can be), and transformations may be defined between different aspect ontologies. This supports translation between different component descriptions. We are investigating the use of an adaptable commercial CASE tool with notations that are more customizable and meta-models to enable integrated support for aspects and the UML. This would also include some formal correctness checking support. In addition, we have been exploring code generation from XML-encoded component characterizations using XSLT transformation scripts. This would generate component skeleton code. We are investigating the use of new .NET reflective technologies to enable efficient run-time weaving of aspect-implementing code with .NET components. This would enable supporting third-party component run-time extensions.

25.10 CONCLUSION

We have been working on using the concept of an "aspect"—a piece of crosscutting systemic functionality—to clearly identify the impact of these concerns on parts of software components and on providing tools to enable developers to represent aspects using augmented component specification and design diagrams. These extended component descriptions allow developers to more easily reason about inter-component provided and required functionality and constraints. We have found that these aspect characterizations provide a useful way of decoupling implemented component interaction. They also provide a practical component description approach. Using encodings of aspect information and making these available at runtime enables more sophisticated component introspection and dynamic component adaptation. It also enables doing better component dynamic validation, storage, and plug-and-play. Developers must balance the potential advantages of this approach with the overhead of describing aspects for components.

REFERENCES

1. ALLEN, P. 2000. *Realizing E-Business with Components*. Addison-Wesley, Reading, Massachusetts.

2. ALLEN, P. AND FROST, S. 1998. *Component-Based Development for Enterprise Systems: Applying the SELECT Perspective*. Cambridge University Press, Cambridge, UK.

3. COLYER, A. AND CLEMENT, A. Large-scale AOSD for Middleware. In *3rd Int'l Conf. Aspect-Oriented Software Development*, (Lancaster, UK). ACM, 56–65.

4. D'SOUZA, D. F. AND WILLS, A. C. 1999. *Objects, Components, and Frameworks with UML: The Catalysis Approach*. Addison-Wesley, Reading, Massachusetts.

5. DUZAN, G., LOYALL, J., AND SCHANTZ, R. 2004. Building adaptive distributed applications with middleware and aspects, In *3rd Int'l Conf. Aspect-Oriented Software Development*, (Lancaster, UK). ACM, 66–73.

6. ERNST, E. AND LORENZ, D. H. 2003. Aspects and Polymorphism in AspectJ. In *2nd Int'l Conf. Aspect-Oriented Software Development*, (Boston, MA). ACM, 150–157.

7. FINGAR, P. 2000. Component-based frameworks for e-commerce. *Comm. ACM 43*, 10, 61–67.

8. FINKELSTEIN, A. C. W., GABBAY, D., HUNTER, A., KRAMER, J., AND NUSEIBEH, B. 1994. Inconsistency handling in multiperspective specifications. *IEEE Transactions on Software Engineering 20,* 8, 569–578.

9. GREEN, T. AND PETRE, M. 1996. Usability analysis of visual programming environments: A 'cognitive dimensions' framework. *Journal of Visual Languages and Computing 7*, 131–174.

10. GRUNDY, J. 1999. Aspect-oriented requirements engineering for component-based software systems. In *4th IEEE Int'l Symp. Requirements Engineering*, (Limerick, Ireland). IEEE, 84–91.

11. GRUNDY, J. 2000. Multi-perspective specification, design and implementation of software components using aspects. *Int'l Journal of Software Engineering and Knowledge Engineering 20*, 6, 713–734.

12. GRUNDY, J. AND HOSKING, J. 2002. Engineering plug-in software components to support collaborative work. *Software Practice and Experience 32*, 10, 983–1013.

13. GRUNDY, J., MUGRIDGE, W., AND HOSKING, J. 2000. Constructing component-based software engineering environments: Issues and experiences. *Journal of Information and Software Technology 42*, 2 (Jan.), 117–128.

14. GRUNDY, J. AND PATEL, R. 2001. Developing software components with the UML, Enterprise Java Beans and aspects. In *13th Australian Conf. Software Engineering*, (Canberra, Australia). IEEE, 127–136.

15. KHAN, K. M. AND HAN, J. 2003. A Security Characterisation Framework for Trustworthy Component Based Software Systems. In *Proc. COMPSAC 2003* (Dallas, Texas). IEEE, 164–169.

16. HARRISON, W. AND OSSHER, H. 1993. Subject-oriented programming—a critique of pure objects. In *8th Conf. Object-Oriented Programming, Systems, Languages, and Applications (OOPSLA)*, (Washington, D. C.). ACM, 411–428.

17. HENNINGER, S. 1996. Supporting the construction and evolution of component repositories. In *18th Int'l Conf. Software Engineering (ICSE)*, (Berlin). IEEE, 279–288.

18. HO, W. M., JEZÉQUEL, J. M., PENNANEAC'H, F., AND PLOUZEAU, N. 2002. A toolkit for weaving aspect-oriented UML designs. In *1st Int'l Conf. Aspect-Oriented Software Development* (Enschede, The Netherlands), ACM, 99–105.

19. KATARA, M. AND KATZ, S. 2003. Architectural Views of Aspects. In *2nd Int'l Conf. Aspect-Oriented Software Development (AOSD)*, (Boston). ACM, 1–10.

20. KICZALES, G., LAMPING, J., MENDHEKAR, A., MAEDA, C., LOPES, C., LOINGTIER, J. M., AND IRWIN, J. 1997. Aspect-oriented programming. In *ECOOP'97 Object-Oriented Programming, 11th European Conf.*, M. Akşit and S. Matsuoka, Eds. LNCS, vol. 1241. Springer-Verlag, Berlin, 220–242.

21. LEE, S., YANG, Y., CHO, F., KIM, S., AND RHEW, S. 1999. COMO: A UML-based component development methodology. In *6th Asia-Pacific Software Engineering Conf. (APSEC)*, (Takamatsu, Japan). IEEE, 54–61.

22. MA, Y. S., OH, S. U., BAE, D. H., AND KWON, K. R. 2001. Framework for third-party testing of component software. In *8th Asia-Pacific Software Engineering Conf. (APSEC)*, (Macau, China). IEEE, 431–434.

23. MCGREGOR, J. D. 1997. Parallel architecture for component testing. *Journal of Object-Oriented Programming 10*, 2 (May), 10–14.

24. MCKINLAY, M. AND TARI, Z. 2002. DynWES—a dynamic and interoperable protocol for web services. In *3rd Int'l Symp. Electronic Commerce (ISEC)*, (Research Triangle Park, North Carolina). http://ecommerce.ncsu.edu/ISEC/papers/09_tari_dynamic.pdf.

25. MEZINI, M. AND LIEBERHERR, K. 1998. Adaptive plug-and-play components for evolutionary software development. In *13th Conf. Object-Oriented Programming, Systems, Languages, and Applications (OOPSLA)*, (Vancouver). ACM, 97–116.

26. MEZINI, M., SEITER, L., AND LIEBERHERR, K. 2001. Component integration with pluggable composite adapters. In *Software Architectures and Component Technology*, M. Akşit, Ed. Kluwer Academic Publishers, Boston, 325–356.

27. MONSON-HAEFEL, R. 2001. *Enterprise JavaBeans*. 3rd Edition, O'Reilly, Sebastapol, California.

28. MOTTA, E., FENSEL, D., GASPARI, M., AND BENJAMINS, R. 1999. Specifications of knowledge components for reuse. In *11th Int'l Conf. Software Engineering and Knowledge Engineering (SEKE)*, (Kaiserslautern, Germany). Knowledge Systems Institute, Skokie, Illinois, 36–43.

29. OSSHER, H. AND TARR, P. 2001. Multi-dimensional separation of concerns and the hyperspace approach. In *Software Architectures and Component Technology*, M. Akşit, Ed. Kluwer Academic Publishers, Boston, 293–323.

30. PRYOR, J. L. AND BASTAN, N. A. 2000. Java meta-level architecture for the dynamic handling of aspects. In *5th Int'l Conf. Parallel and Distributed Processing Techniques and Applications* (Las Vegas). CSREA Press, Bogart, Georgia, 257–262.

31. QIONG, W., JICHUAN, C., HONG, M., AND FUQING, Y. 1997. JBCDL: An object-oriented component description language. In *24th Conf. Technology of Object-Oriented Languages (TOOLS)*, (Beijing). IEEE, 198–205.

32. RAKOTONIRAINY, A. INDULSKA, J., WAI LOKE, S., AND ZASLAVSKY, A. 2001. Middleware for Reactive Components: An Integrated Use of Context, Roles, and Event Based Coordination, In *Proceedings of Middleware 2001*, (Heidelberg, Germany). LNCS, vol. 2218. Springer-Verlag, Berlin, 77–98.

33. STEARNS, M. AND PICCINELLI, G. 2002. Managing interaction concerns in web-service systems. In *22nd Int'l Conf. Distributed Computing Systems Workshops*, (Vienna, Austria). IEEE, 424–429.

34. STEIN, D., HANENBERG, S., AND UNLAND, R. 2002. An UML-based aspect-oriented design notation. In *1st Int'l Conf. Aspect-Oriented Software Development (AOSD)*, (Enschede, The Netherlands), G. Kiczales, Ed. ACM, 106–112.

35. SUVIE, D. AND VANDERPERREN, W. 2003. JAsCo: An Aspect-Oriented Approach Tailored for Component Based Software Development, In *2nd Int'l Conf. Aspect-Oriented Software Development (AOSD)*, (Boston), ACM, 21–29.

36. SZYPERSKI, C. A. 1997. *Component Software: Beyond OO Programming*. Addison-Wesley, Reading, Massachusetts.

37. TARR, P., OSSHER, H., HARRISON, W., AND SUTTON JR., S. M. 1999. *N* degrees of separation: Multi-dimensional separation of concerns. In *21st Int'l Conf. Software Engineering (ICSE)*, (Los Angeles). IEEE, 107–119.

38. TRUYEN, E., VANHAUTE, B., JOOSEN, W., VERBAETEN, P., AND JØRGENSEN, B. N. 2001. Dynamic and selective combination of extensions in component-based applications. In *23rd Int'l Conf. Software Engineering (ICSE)*, (Toronto). IEEE, 233–242.

39. VOGAL, A. 1998. CORBA and Enterprise Java Beans-based electronic commerce. In *Int'l Workshop on Component-Based Electronic Commerce*, (Berkeley).

40. WELCH, I. AND STROUD, R. 1999. Load-time application of aspects to Java COTS software. In *Int'l Workshop on Aspect-Oriented Programming (ECOOP)*, (Lisbon). http://trese.cs.utwente.nl/aop-ecoop99/papers/welch.pdf.

Chapter 26

Smartweaver: A Knowledge-Driven Approach for Aspect Composition

J. ANDRÉS DÍAZ PACE, MARCELO R. CAMPO, AND FEDERICO U. TRILNIK

Many researchers recognize the need to raise the level of abstraction in AOSD. This will enable moving more seamlessly from aspect-oriented specifications to particular aspect technologies, allowing developers to specify their applications using generic aspect models (for example, through a CASE tool), reuse parts of these models in other applications, and employ multiple strategies in mapping these models to specific aspect implementations.

The specification of crosscutting elements in modular units and the designation of elements being crosscut have received much attention and have produced some good solutions. However, the procedures to effectively merge all this information during weaving still require understanding many implementation-specific details. Moreover, this complexity is often compounded by aspect interactions. For example, determining how to weave interacting aspects is still a central issue. Newly added aspects must be prevented from subverting the behavior of existing aspects [17]. In the general case, there are different variants for the weaving, depending on the implementation approaches supporting the aspect infrastructure (e.g., aspect languages or aspect frameworks). Developers have to provide the aspect tool with instructions that direct weaving.

We believe that the specification of aspect-oriented applications is a critical technology. The challenge is not developing a specific tool for a specific AOP language but rather the general issue of guiding developers through weaving. Tools and CASE environments that help developers bridge the gap between aspect-based models and aspect technologies are becoming increasingly necessary.

In this work, we describe *Smartweaver*, an approach for assisting weaving activities in aspect-oriented development [8]. *Smartweaver* is a Java tool that provides semiautomated support to the process of aspect composition. It relies on the *Smartbooks* documentation method [16], which extends framework documentation techniques with *instantiation schemes* specifying how a piece of software should be specialized or used to implement a given functionality. *Smartbooks* can be used for documenting aspect-based models. *Smartweaver* allows developers to express their requirements in terms of classes, aspects, and crosscutting relationships among them. All this information is collected by a special planning engine. This engine is also provided with adequate *Smartbooks* knowledge to implement generic aspect-based specifications using a given aspect implementation. Using this knowledge, the engine produces a list of programming activities to be carried out to get a final application.

This chapter is organized into six sections. Section 26.1 introduces the notion of smart-weaving and the foundations of the *Smartbooks* method. Sections 26.2, 26.3, and 26.4 present the *Smartweaver* approach, centered on an example application involving concurrency, authorization, and logging aspects. The example shows the role that both the developer (final user) and the designer (documenter) play in the process. In Section 26.5, we discuss related work. Finally, in Section 26.6, we draw conclusions and speculate on directions for future research.

26.1   KNOWLEDGE-DRIVEN WEAVING

An ideal tool for aspect-oriented development would allow designers to describe the required functionality for a specific application along with its associated aspects and would then automatically generate the desired application.

Unfortunately, existing technologies are far from providing that kind of assistance. At the current stage of research, an intermediate approach is to have a tool with some core knowledge prescribe to the user which activities should be done to implement a given application. This leads us to the *smart-weaving* concept [8]. Essentially, developers specify their designs through generic aspect models, and then a special engine translates these models to programs in a specific aspect environment. In particular, frameworks [10] are a natural fit for this mechanism. Similarly, *software agents* [3, 21], and specifically, intelligent personal assistants [14], appear to be an interesting alternative for helping developers with framework instantiation. Basically, these assistants can observe human users or interact with them, using the information they glean to make suggestions or even directly alter the result of computations. These agents can employ techniques such as planning [20] to achieve their goals. An agent with adequate knowledge about the different functions that can be implemented using a target framework could guide developers with the programming steps required to implement such functionality. Our idea thus is to provide agent-based guidance for the instantiation of aspect-oriented frameworks. An outline of the proposed architecture is shown in Figure 26-1.

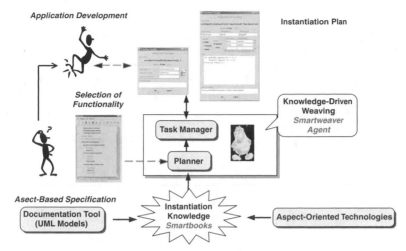

Figure 26-1   *Assisting instantiation of aspect frameworks using the*
Smartbooks *approach.*

The process of framework instantiation can be seen as a composition of relatively simple *programming activities*. However, these activities must be carried out in a meaningful order. The difficulty resides in determining which activities have to be executed for creating a given application and how these activities can be combined to obtain the desired functionality. Pursuing this idea, we have developed an experimental tool, *Hint,* for framework instantiation [15]. Hint shows the user what functionality can be implemented using the framework, allowing the choice of functionality required for the application being implemented. Depending on the selected functionality, Hint elaborates a plan of activities to implement a concrete application. It then guides the user through the instantiation process by effectively executing these activities.

Documentation knowledge is described through predefined instantiation schemes that form part of the *Smartbooks* documentation method. In the next subsections, we briefly explain the *Smartbooks* method and the corresponding engine.

26.1.1   *The* Smartbooks *Documentation Method*

The *Smartbooks* method treats the overall instantiation of a framework as a sequence of basic instantiation tasks such as class specialization and method overriding. The framework designer describes the functionality provided by the framework and how this functionality is implemented by different framework components and provides rules that constrain the ways the framework can be specialized. This knowledge is represented in *instantiation schemes*. The purpose of these schemes is twofold. On one hand, the framework user employs these rules to express the intended functionality of his new application. The user is thus oriented towards defining what his application is supposed to do. On the other hand, the *Smartbooks* engine uses these requirements and the schemes documenting a target framework to guide the user through the process of application development.

Instantiation schemes can be graphically specified using a UML extension called *TOON* (Tasks and Object-Oriented Notation) to express framework structures and instantiation activities associated with them.

26.1.2 *Programming Tasks in* Smartbooks

The schemes of the *Smartbooks* method are directly associated with the concept of *tasks,* programming activities to be carried out by the developer in order to use or specialize a given set of components in the process of implementing a specific function. The execution of these tasks yields either code implementing the desired functionality or a code template to be completed by the programmer.

Smartbooks tasks are classified as *pending* or *waiting tasks* according to their role in the planning process. For example, if the planner finds that the implementation of a given functionality requires the specialization of a component plus overwriting certain methods, the corresponding activities are *pending tasks* (see Table 26-1). The user executes these tasks after an instantiation plan is generated by the tool.

Table 26-1   *List of Pending Tasks Supported by* Smartbooks

Task	Description
DefineClass	Adds a new class definition (from an existing base class).
DefineMethod	Adds a new method to a given a class.
DefineAttribute	Adds a new attribute to a given class.
UpdateClass ·	Modifies the definition of a class.
UpdateMethod	Modifies the definition of an attribute.
ImplementInterface	Makes a class implement a given interface.
Warning	Displays a message explaining a framework constraint.

The second type of task, *waiting tasks* (see Table 26-2), represents decisions required to continue planning. When the planning algorithm finds a waiting task as a precondition of a desired effect, it creates the task and then suspends itself. Once the user completes the task, the algorithm resumes. For example, the user would need to select between a composition or inheritance mechanism when creating a new proxy component.

Table 26-2   *List of Waiting Tasks Supported by* Smartbooks

Task	Description
AskSelection	Presents several alternatives and asks the user for a choice.
GetUserInput	Asks the user to enter a string.
SelectClass	Asks the user to specify a class.
SelectMethod	Asks the user to specify a method for a class.
SelectMethods	Asks the user to specify a set of methods for a class.

26.1.3   *The* Smartbooks *Engine*

As mentioned previously, a specific tool is in charge of collecting all the *Smartbooks* documentation and assisting the user through the process of framework instantiation. The architecture of this tool comprises several components with different responsibilities [15, 16]. The main components are:

Documentation tool.   The documentation tool is used by framework developers to write framework documentation. This documentation corresponds with instantiation schemes, which are internally represented as Prolog rules.

Functionality collector.   The functionality collector is a wizard for helping the user describe the functionality required for the application being developed. This functionality is again expressed as Prolog rules.

Planning Engine.   The Planning Engine uses *least-commitment planning techniques* [20] to build instantiation plans.

Task Manager.   The Task Manager keeps track of the tasks involved in instantiation plans. It is responsible for coordinating the execution, interruption, and cancellation of tasks.

The planning agent takes a list of functional requirements (written as instantiation schemes) and elaborates a list of required instantiation tasks based on the core knowledge provided by the framework designer. During the planning phase, the tool uses a UCPOP-like [18] algorithm called *PHint*. It follows the least-commitment principle. That is, it produces a partially ordered sequence of tasks, delaying decisions as much as possible. This flexibility allows the framework user to delay choosing task execution alternatives until they are needed.

The *PHint* planning algorithm is an enhanced version of the original planning algorithm presented in [15]. *PHint* is able to take advantage of *TOON* diagrams. It incorporates this information to prune the number of action choices. The instantiation tasks defined in these diagrams are seen as partially instantiated action sequences that should be met by the final plan according to the framework prescriptions, thus avoiding unnecessary work during planning.

26.2 A WORKFLOW APPLICATION EXAMPLE

Let us take as a case study a workflow application involving synchronization, scheduling, authorization, and logging aspects. Workflow management arises from automating well-structured, repetitive processes [2]. A flexible and scalable implementation of workflow systems typically requires the modeling of components such as processes, roles, activities, assignments, and resources in terms of independent distributed objects. Here, aspects can naturally provide workflow adaptation mechanisms, representing different strategies to control process execution and resource management.

The functionality required for our example can be informally described as follows. The application defines a workflow model for structured documents, with different users having access to these documents. Users can play different roles (e.g., supervisor, editor, or auditor), and each role has set its own permissions for operations on the documents. During its lifecycle, a document typically goes through a number of predefined states, such as edition, approval, and publishing. State transitions are ruled by events. Therefore, specific tasks may be activated in response to particular event conditions. Initially, a document is empty, waiting for editing. As the editor adds information to the document following certain standards, the document is sent to the auditor for approval. If the auditor considers the document contents relevant to the system, it is marked as ready for distribution. If so, every user potentially interested in this type of document is notified about the event. If not, the document is sent back to the editing phase for revision. However, the auditor may reject the document if defective. In addition, a supervisor can review documents at any time and decide about their status. After certain period of time, some documents may become useless or require modifications. In such cases, a new version of the document is generated. As a result, the old version of the document is no longer available. Old documents are temporarily stored as items pending deletion and are eventually removed from the system. For simplicity, we suppose a supervisor can read, write, or check documents; an editor is only allowed to read or write some documents, and an auditor can read or check other documents.

The aspects identified in the workflow application are

Concurrency. Concurrency deals with synchronization and scheduling issues, controlling document reading and writing from different user sessions. The concurrency aspect also chooses the next reader or writer when a blocking operation completes.

Authorization.   Authorization refers to the security policies regarding document handling. Only authorized users can perform particular operations on specific documents. This aspect is closely related to concurrency because a failure in the authorization process should abort any further user activity, making unnecessary synchronization and scheduling mechanisms.

Logging.   Logging records security exceptions. Every unsuccessful authorization attempt activates the logging aspect to record the user's subsequent actions.

In the following sections, we describe each of the phases developers/designers go through in implementing the workflow application using *Smartweaver*. Our example uses the Aspect-Moderator framework (AMF) [6, 7] as its underlying AOP mechanism, briefly described in the next section.

26.2.1   The Aspect-Moderator Framework

The AMF is a design approach extending the object model, which provides support for a cluster of cooperating objects and their aspect behaviors. A specially designated component called moderator takes the place of the weaver, coordinating the interaction between functional components and aspects. The moderator controls both the activation order and the actual activation of aspects. The approach introduces the concept of aspect bank, where the moderator of a cluster may initially collect all the required aspects and then decide about the integration policies [6] (see Figure 26-2).

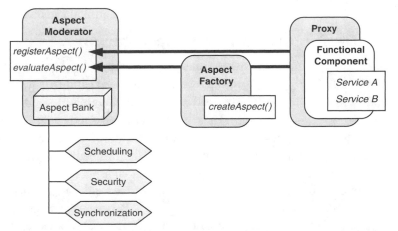

Figure 26-2   *The Aspect-Moderator framework, extracted from [6].*

A proxy object controls the access to the class functionality. This proxy object uses the factory pattern to create aspect objects for each method of the functional component to be associated with some aspects. Aspects are first-class abstractions, and on creation, they are registered with the aspect moderator. Within the proxy, each participating method is guarded by a pre-activation and post-activation phase. These phases are implemented in the aspect moderator. During the former phase, the proxy intercepts requests for access to the functional components and calls the moderator to evaluate all required aspects.

If the pre-activation phase returns successfully, then the proxy calls the actual participating method. Once this execution is complete, the proxy initiates the post-activation phase and again calls the moderator to evaluate the associated aspects. The aspect moderator class is extensible in order to make the overall system adaptable to the addition of new aspects. The framework deals with the weaving of aspects and components at runtime, allowing dynamic composition of aspects with functional components, and thereby avoiding code transformation.

26.3 APPLYING SMARTWEAVER: THE DEVELOPER'S VIEWPOINT

Getting smart guidance for a given application requires two primary activities. First, the developer (or final user) has to specify the design of the target application in terms of UML diagrams extended with some aspect characteristics. After that, the developers interact with the functionality wizard providing additional requirement details. The tool can then suggest a series of programming tasks produce the desired aspect-incorporating functionality.

26.3.1 Design of the Target Application

Developers should use the documentation tool to define the design of the core work-flow components, as well as the crosscutting properties affecting components' functionality. In the line of [5, 19], we have extended conventional UML models to support AOSD features by including additional stereotypes and relationships. Aspects can be seen as special classes defining attributes and operations and incorporating advice operations. Figure 26-3 shows a class diagram with some of the classes involved in the workflow application and its associated aspects.

For example, Figure 26-3 defines concurrency advice for the WFDocument class and also exposes the conditional activation of the WFLogging aspect as a result of evaluating the WFAuthorization aspect. These descriptions may be complemented with more detailed views documenting aspect behavior. Note that in order to specify which aspects crosscut the workflow application, the developers have to previously sketch out the main workflow classes. In the general case, developers can incrementally specify portions of aspect diagrams and define particular properties regarding before/after crosscutting, aspect priorities, or conditional activation, among others. These specifications are based on a new kind of task, more abstract than a programming task, called a *design task*.

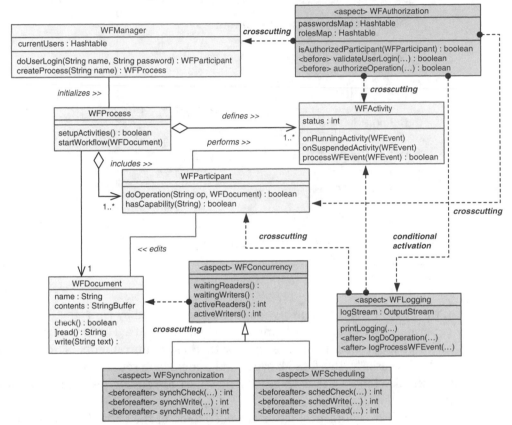

Figure 26-3   *Aspect diagram for the workflow application.*

26.3.2   *Interaction with the Task Manager*

Once aspect models have been defined using the Documentation Tool, it is possible to translate them to schemes expressing a portion of the functionality required by the final application. For example, when running the *Hint's* Functionality Collector, the Functionality Collector begins by presenting the user with the initially available functionality, based on the instantiation knowledge previously provided by the designer (in this case, knowledge of the AMF framework). At first, only high-level functionality is presented to the user. As some items are selected, other options including further information may be displayed so the designer can refine previous selections. Figure 26-4 shows a sample of general functionality items relevant to any aspect-oriented development.

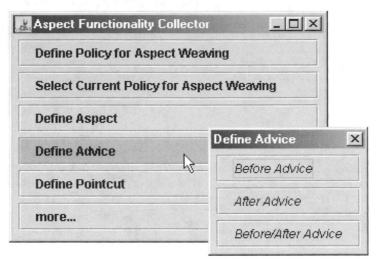

Figure 26-4 *Functionality items suggested by the Hint's Functionality Collector.*

On the basis of the functionality requirements collected by *Hint*, the tool internally generates a set of goals to express these requirements. The engine responds with an implementation plan in accord with these requirements. This plan is presented to the user by the Task Manager, and it includes a set of waiting tasks (representing the developer's design decisions) and a set of pending tasks (representing instantiation actions).

To exemplify this guidance, let us consider some of the activities derived from the definition of a new aspect. In the AMF framework, this functionality requires the definition of an `AspectFactory` class. The planner asks the user for a name for this class. If the class already exists, the planner may initially check for a subclassing relationship. It then presents a task for selecting which methods are to be overwritten. In addition, a task for creating the target subclass may be generated during the checking process. Figures 26-5 and 26-6 depict a possible list of tasks (shown from the Task Manager) for the instantiation of our workflow application.

Finally, the application is shaped through several interactions with the user, either with the diagram editor or the Task Manager. The execution of the tasks suggested by the *Smartweaver* engine can optionally generate code skeletons, which the user can later fill in with more specific implementation details.

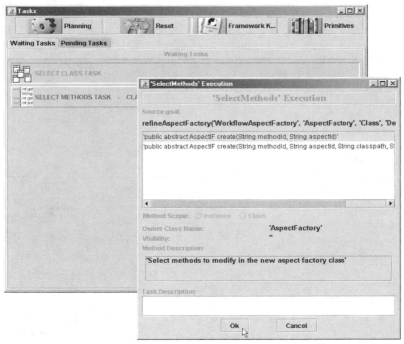

Figure 26-5 *A class-refinement task proposed by the Task Manager.*

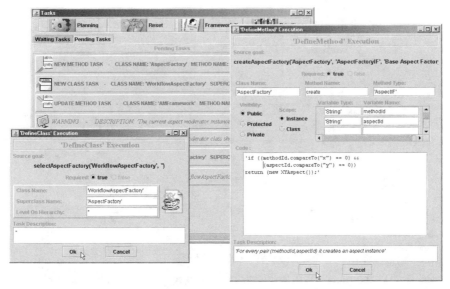

Figure 26-6 *A class-creation task and a method-creation task proposed by the Task Manager.*

To validate the feasibility of this approach, we compared our (assisted) design for the workflow application against the one presented in [7]. Although results are still preliminary, we found a reasonable match between them. The final instantiation of the AMF framework for our workflow application is shown in Figure 26-7.

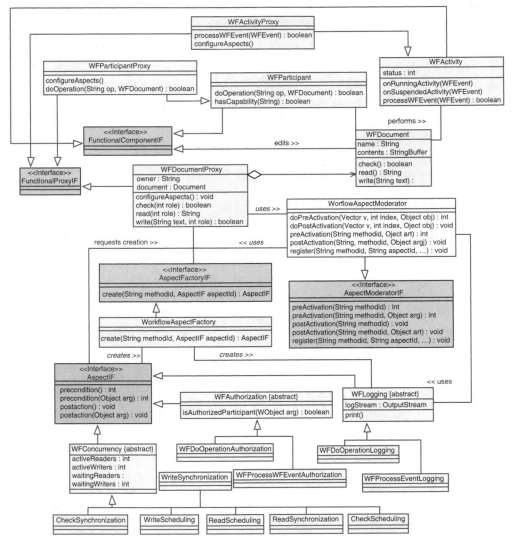

Figure 26-7 *Sketch of the workflow application (gray boxes correspond to AMF classes).*

26.4 DEFINING THE WEAVING KNOWLEDGE: THE DESIGNER'S VIEWPOINT

The designer (or framework documenter) has to provide both a *Smartbooks* representation of a particular aspect technology and mapping rules from generic aspect functionality (refer to Figure 26-4) to enable generating a weaving plan.

26.4.1 Documentation Books of Support Technology

Let us consider how to express AMF-related knowledge in terms of instantiation schemes. Figure 26-8 shows an instantiation scheme described using the *TOON* notation and the associated textual representation. This scheme corresponds to a proxy definition for aspect behavior in the AMF framework. The head of this scheme states that in order to have a functional proxy for a component, the proxy class should implement the `FunctionalProxyIF` interface and wrap the component.

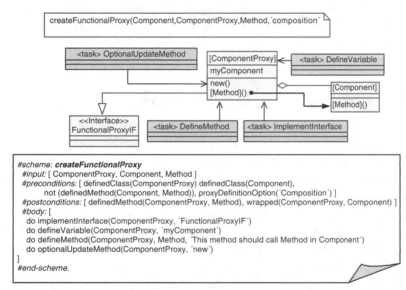

Figure 26-8 *Example of an instantiation scheme for the AMF.*

More precisely, the diagram prescribes that four tasks should be carried out by the user:

1. An *ImplementInterface* task that has to produce a subclass of `FunctionalProxyIF`.

2. A *DefineVariable* task, which must add a `myComponent` attribute for the proxy class.

3. A *DefineMethod* task in charge of overriding a functional method of the component (to incorporate aspect behavior).

4. An *OptionalDefineMethod* task if any update to the constructor is required.

The schema description can also provide explanations about the expected behavior of methods and can specify constraints that must be followed by a code skeleton. For example, the method `[Method]` of `ComponentProxy` in Figure 26-8 should call a similar method in the wrapped class. The kind of tasks presented by the example can be seen as basic tasks or programming tasks because they refer to programming activities associated with framework code. As we have seen before, these tasks are classified as pending or waiting tasks, according to their role in the planning process.

The purpose of the *Smartbooks* approach is to automate, to some extent, the activities dictated by framework documentation. However, the designer arbitrarily fixes the terms used to document the framework functionality. Framework documentation, either automated or not, is usually hard to extract from designers. The method gives little assistance for this process. Good documentation is ultimately a human activity.

26.4.2 Adding Weaving Information

This phase focuses on specifying the ways crosscutting relationships and aspect design tasks should be translated into aspect programming constructs. This depends, of course, on the aspect support available in the environment. As we mentioned before, aspect interaction diagrams include special tasks, with corresponding activities that developers must carry out in order to tune specific details of the aspect-based application. These tasks, so-called *design tasks,* indicate how abstract weaving specifications are mapped to a particular aspect implementation (an aspect framework in our example), which has been previously documented in terms of programming tasks during the previous phase.

The code template of Figure 26-9 illustrates (partially) how the AMF implements before/after advice and conditional activation of aspects according to the design tasks given in Figure 26-3. Boldface code distinguishes those parts defined by means of programming tasks. Note that not everything can be expressed in terms of programming tasks. Some framework constraints are just documented by means of warning messages.

According to the framework design, our aspect-based implementation should basically agree with the following prescriptions:

1. Every method with aspectual advice should be implemented as a separate class, a child of the `AspectIF` interface. After/before behaviors for a given method can

be added by means of the `precondition()` and `postcondition()` methods, defined also by the `AspectIF` interface.

```
DefinePointcut(WFParticipant, WFParticipantProxy, WFAuthorization) :-
  CreateFunctionalProxy(WFParticipant, WFParticipantProxy, 'doOperation(...)','inheritance')
  UpdateMethod(WFParticipantProxy, 'configureAspects(...)'),
  Warning('Method configureAspects() should create aspects using the create(...) method
  AspectFactory and then aspects should be registered with the moderator using the
  method in AspectModerator'),
  UpdateMethod(WFParticipantProxy,
  Warning('Method doOperation(...) should call preActivation(...) in Aspect Moderator and
  postActivation(...) in the same class, to evaluate its associated
```

```
class WFParticipantProxy extends WFParticipant implements FunctionalProxyIF {
  // Constructor
  WFParticipantProxy(String name) { ... }
  protected void configureAspects() {
    //Aspect creation via AMF factory
    WFAuthorization opauth;
    opauth = AspectFactory().create("doOperation","authorization");
    WFLogging oplogging = AspectFactory().create("doOperation","logging");
    ...
    // Registration with the Aspect Moderator
    AspectModerator().register("doOperation","authorization",0,Before,opauth);
    ...
  }
  public boolean doOperation(String op, WFDocument doc) {

    int pre = AspectModerator().preActivation("doOperation","read",...);
    if (pre == RESUME) {
      boolean result = this.doOperation(op,doc);
      AspectModerator().postActivation("doOperation","read",...);
      return (result);
    }
    if (pre == ERROR) {
      this.plugAspect("doOperation","logging",2,AFTER, ...);
      AspectModerator().postActivation("doOperation","read",...);
      return (false);
    }
    return (false);
  }
  ...
} // End class WFParticipantProxy

class WFLogging implements AspectIF
{ ... }

class DoOperationLogging extends WFLogging {
  protected void print (...) { ... }
  public int postaction(Object args) {
    this.print(...);
  }
  ...
} // End class DoOperationLogging
```

```
DefineConditionalActivation(WFAuthorization,
WFLogging, WFParticipantProxy) :-
  UpdateMethod(WFParticipantProxy,
  'doOperation(...)'),
  Warning('Method doOperation(...) should call
  first its corresponding parent method, and
  evaluate preActivation(...) and postActivation(...)
  in Aspect Moderator. Upon return, the method
  should also request the activation of the
  conditional aspect to the Moderator.')
```

```
DefineAfterAdvice(WFLogging) :-
  DefineClass(WFLogging),
  ImplementInterface(WFLogging, 'AspectIF'),
  DefineClass('DoOperationLogging',WFLogging),
  UpdateMethod('DoOperationLogging', 'print(...)'),
  DefineMethod('DoOperationLogging', 'postaction(...)'),
  Warning('Method postaction(...) in class
  doOperationLogging should invoke method print(...)
  somewhere').
```

Figure 26-9 *Mapping aspect design tasks to programming tasks of the AMF.*

2. Regarding aspect composition, a proxy object controls the access to the functionality of its wrapped document. This proxy object uses the factory pattern to create aspect objects using the `create()` method defined by the `AspectFactory` class. Aspects are created for each method of the functional component that has to be associated with aspect behavior. On creation, these aspects should be registered within the aspect moderator by calling the `register()` method in `AspectModerator`.

3. Within the proxy, each participating method is guarded by pre-activation and post-activation phases (methods `preActivation()` and `postActivation()` in class `AspectModerator`). These phases are also implemented in the aspect moderator. During the former phase, the proxy intercepts requests for access to the functional components and calls the moderator to evaluate the required aspects. If the pre-activation phase returns successfully, then the proxy calls the actual participating method. Once this execution is complete, the proxy initiates the post-activation phase and again calls the moderator to evaluate the associated aspects.

Similarly, the code template in Figure 26-10 (partially) illustrates how AspectJ [13] would implement before/after advice and conditional activation of aspects according to the design tasks given in Figure 26-3. Note that the aspect definitions are slightly different from their counterparts in the AMF.

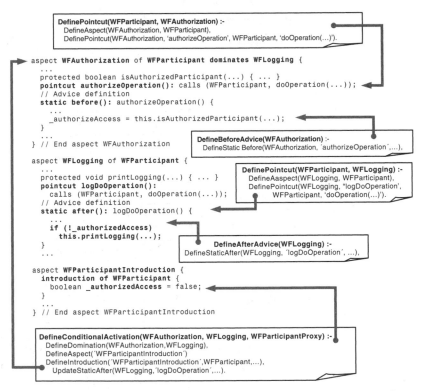

Figure 26-10 *Mapping aspect design tasks to programming tasks of AspectJ.*

Developers can now define several types of advice associated with different methods in the same aspect (class), without needing to split this behavior in separate classes. Advice definitions are expressed in *AspectJ* by means of special designators for crosscutting and pointcuts. Aspects can be instantiated like regular classes, but developers neither explicitly create aspects at runtime nor specify how they are evaluated. If some aspects need finer control over their advice parts when they run, a special modifier called `dominates` can be used to specify that their advice parts should be more specific than another aspect's. Additionally, conditional aspect activation can take advantage of the introduction of parts in order to permit changes in the program by adding or extending classes with new members.

These templates facilitate the work of application developers because they don't require an extensive knowledge about particular implementation mechanisms of AspectJ or the AMF. The specific details are actually hidden by high-level operations documented in the form of design tasks. From the programming perspective, this raises the abstraction level of aspects by explicitly considering aspect programming at the design phase [4].

26.4.3 *Internal Representation of Aspect Requirements*

As we mentioned before, the developer defines several functional requirements (planning goals) to be met by his or her application. The rules of Figure 26-11 give an idea of the kind of information provided to the *Smartweaver* engine as internal representation of these goals.

```
 1.  createAspectModerator('WorkflowAspectModerator', 'AspectModeratorIF', '…').
 2.  selectAspectModerator('WorkflowAspectModerator', '…').

 3.  createAspectFactory('DefaultAspectFactory', 'AspectFactoryIF', '…').
 4.  refineAspectFactory('WorkflowAspectFactory', 'DefaultAspectFactory', 'Class', '…').
 5.  selectAspectFactory('WorkflowAspectFactory', '…').

 6.  createFunctionalProxy('DocumentProxy', 'FunctionalProxyIF', 'Document', 'Composition', '…').

 7.  refineAspect('Concurrency', 'AspectIF', 'Interface', '…').
 8.  createAspect('Synchronization', 'Concurrency', '…').
 9.  createAspect('Scheduling', 'Concurrency', '…').

10.  composeAspect('Synchronization', 'Document', 'read', 'synchRead', 'beforeafter', […]. '…').
11.  composeAspect('Authorization', 'Document', 'read', 'authorizeRead', 'before', […], '…').

12.  conditionalActivation('Authorization', 'Logging', '…').
…
```

Figure 26-11   *Internal representation of planning goals for the AMF.*

Rules 1 and 2 refer to the aspect-moderator definition as a singleton. Rules 3 to 5 describe a similar pattern for the aspect-factory. Rule 6 specifies a proxy that wraps a document in order to incorporate aspectual behavior. Rules 7 to 9 correspond partially to some aspect diagram. Rules 10 to 12, in turn, may come from some aspect interaction diagram. Note that in the case of rules 10 to 12, they say nothing about how aspects should be mapped to framework classes. This enables framework designers to decide which is the best strategy to implement aspects on top of the framework. In particular, the current implementation of the AMF framework prescribes that developers should create a different aspect class for each aspectual advice. For example, the `WFSynchronization` aspect, which conceptually affects several document operations, should be implemented within the framework as an abstract class `WFSynchronization` and three subclasses, `ReadWFSynchronization`, `CheckWFSynchronization`, and `WriteWFSynchronization`, one subclass for each document's operation. In general, the strategies and constraints to map aspectual specifications into framework implementations may vary according to the facilities of the target framework and the developers' experience.

The AMF framework is primarily composed of abstract classes and interfaces, so it can be thought of more as a programming model than a component-based framework. This feature makes the *Smartbooks* method particularly useful because we can express many model constraints not completely captured by code structures as instantiation rules.

26.5 RELATED WORK

There are several promising lines of research on the topic of aspects, frameworks, and UML. For example, we can find approaches that extend UML with stereotypes matching particular aspects, such as synchronization [12], so that the weaver can automatically compose them with functional components. In these cases, many details about specific aspect behavior are somehow not explicitly designed in UML. Other examples propose more general approaches [1, 5], such as so-called composition patterns, trying to support abstract aspect designs.

Theme/UML [5] introduces a UML-based approach to designing reusable aspects based on early research on subject-oriented programming. A design is broken up into "themes," each of which encapsulates a collection of classes, defining a particular viewpoint of a domain and/or providing a coherent set of functionality. The classes in themes may not be complete, containing only the details relevant for the theme's viewpoint and not for the whole system. Then there is a process of theme composition that integrates the classes in separate themes, reconciling differences in views and combining functionality. There are many ways to specify theme composition. The authors just present a basic set of rules, but other mechanisms can be specified according to particular needs. Composition Patterns refer to common patterns of such composition relationships that emerge when the same or similar themes are used in different contexts. This provides an important level of abstraction when specifying composition relationships, thereby improving comprehensibility and reusability. Moreover, changes are localized, which avoids tangling, and traceability is preserved. An experimental environment supporting the approach is under development. An important aspect of these design models, quite similarly to *Smartweaver,* is that they set developers free to decide which technology is more suitable to map designs into implementations.

Recently, Elrad, Aldawud, and Bader have presented a UML profile for generating aspect-oriented code that preserves the modularity of crosscutting concerns [9]. This is a natural generalization of the AMF approach. They specify some requirements to accomplish this goal [1]. First, the profile will enable specifying, visualizing, and documenting the artifacts of software systems based on aspect orientation. Second, the profile will be supported by UML, allowing seamless integration of existing CASE tools. Third, the profile will take into account the modular representation of crosscutting concerns. Finally, the profile will not impose any behavioral implementation for AOSD but will provide a complete set of model elements that enable representing the semantics of the system based on aspect orientation. The methodology is based on using statecharts for specifying the mechanics of weaving.

Fontoura, et. al., describe *UML-F profile*, a tool that explicitly models framework variation points in UML diagrams by expressing the allowed structure and behavior of variation points [11]. UML-F consists of several extensions to standard UML. Here, framework variation points are modeled in terms of tagged values, applicable to both methods and classes. For instance, developers can express that the implementation of a given method may vary depending on the framework instantiation, or they can indicate that a class interface may be extended during the framework instantiation by adding new functionality. UML-F deals basically with three kinds of variation points: variable methods, extensible classes, and extensible interfaces. In addition, OCL specifications are used to describe pattern behavior that should be followed by the variation point instances. The authors suggest a prototypical environment based on Prolog, which supports assistance for both framework development and instantiation. As UML-F focused on the representation of frameworks at design level, several different techniques can be used to effectively implement these designs (e.g., design patterns, meta-programming, and aspect-oriented programming). This approach could be an interesting complement for *Smartweaver*.

Overall, the main difference between the analyzed approaches and *Smartweaver* concerns the way generic aspect models and particular aspect programming techniques are finally combined. The former approaches preserve the independence of particular implementation models because they mostly address the problem of providing appropriate rules (syntax and semantics) to express composition of generic designs. On the other hand, *Smartweaver* is more focused on agent-based assistance for the weaving process. We believe that this kind of assistance represents an interesting advantage in terms of automation levels over more passive design environments.

26.6   CONCLUSION

This chapter reports our experiences with the *Smartweaver* approach, an approach based on the *Smartbooks* method for enhancing aspect-oriented development, with special focus on weaving activities. The smart-weaving notion proposes an earlier incorporation of aspects in the development cycle so that developers can first specify their designs by means of aspect models and then provide different strategies to map generic aspect structures to specific AOSD implementations (programming approaches). With this purpose, we have built an environment to support this process.

A novel aspect of this work is the use of agents and planning techniques to generate sequences of programming tasks to guide developers in the implementation of applications on top of frameworks. Moreover, the agents' assistance can be extended to deal with more abstract design activities. In this line, we have shown an example in which the *Smartbooks* method can be applied to aspect-oriented frameworks based on extending the notion of programming task to higher-level aspect-describing design tasks. As the results obtained with the Aspect-Moderator framework have been encouraging, we are planning to consider other implementation alternatives such as AspectJ and Hyper/J in the future.

We have also described a visual formalism to specify aspect models as an extension of conventional UML diagrams. This formalism is independent of particular aspect implementation technologies. This favors communication among aspect developers and promotes a common documentation model for aspect-based applications. At this moment, a basic CASE environment integrated with the *Smartweaver* engine has been developed. We hope to improve these capabilities in the future, such as by adding more UML models or considering OCL to express *Smartbooks* rules. The final goal is the development of an aspect tool open enough to incorporate specific AOSD approaches. From this perspective, it would be possible to have a general-purpose tool and add such aspect technologies as plug-in packages. This could be complemented with wizards to collect desired functionality.

Finally, the most important contribution of this research is the provision of agent-based assistance during the weaving of aspect-oriented applications. Although a more rigorous and complete specification of aspects models and the *Smartweaver* approach is still a subject of research, we believe the use of agent techniques integrated with CASE tools can open new challenges in the field and can also promote more systematic aspect-oriented practices.

REFERENCES

1. ALDAWUD, O., ELRAD, T., AND BADER, A. 2001. A UML profile for aspect oriented modeling. In *Workshop on Advanced Separation of Concerns in Object-Oriented Systems (OOPSLA)*, (Tampa, Florida). http://www.cs.ubc.ca/\~kdvolder/ Workshops/OOPSLA2001/submissions/26-aldawud.pdf.

2. BACHMENDO, B. AND UNLAND, R. 2001. Aspect-based workflow evolution. In *Workshop on Aspect-Oriented Programming and Separation of Concerns*, (Lancaster, England). http://www.comp.lancs.ac.uk/computing/users/marash/ aopws2001/papers/bachmendo.pdf.

3. BRADSHAW, J. 1997. *Software Agents*. AAAI Press, Menlo Park, California.

4. CLARKE, S. 2000. Designing reusable patterns of cross-cutting behaviour with composition patterns. In *Workshop on Advanced Separation of Concerns (OOPSLA)*, (Minneapolis). http://trese.cs.utwente.nl/Workshops/OOPSLA2000/ papers/ clarke.pdf.

5. CLARKE, S. AND WALKER, R. J. 2002. Towards a standard design language for AOSD. In *1st Int'l Conf. Aspect-Oriented Software Development (AOSD)*, (Enschede, The Netherlands). ACM, 113–119.

6. CONSTANTINIDES, C. A., BADER, A., ELRAD, T. H., NETINANT, P., AND FAYAD, M. E. 2000. Designing an aspect-oriented framework in an object-oriented environment. *ACM Computing Surveys 32*, 1es, 41.

7. CONSTANTINIDES, C. A., SKOTINIOTIS, T., AND ELRAD, T. 2001. Providing dynamic adaptability in an aspect-oriented framework. In *Workshop on Advanced Separation of Concerns (ECOOP)*, (Budapest). http://trese.cs.utwente.nl/ Workshops/adc2000/papers/Constantinides.pdf.

8. DÍAZ PACE, A., CAMPO, M., AND TRILNIK, F. 2002. Smartweaver: Aspect-oriented development using the Smartbooks approach. In *Argentine Symp. Software Engineering (ASSE)*, (Santa Fe, Argentina). 1–21.

9. ELRAD, T., ALDAWUD, O., AND BADER, A. 2002. Aspect-oriented modeling: Bridging the gap between implementation and design. In *1st Conf. Generative Programming and Component Engineering (GPCE)*, (Pittsburgh), D. S. Batory, C. Consel, and W. Taha, Eds. LNCS, vol. 2487. Springer-Verlag, Berlin, 189–201.

10. FAYAD, M. E., SCHMIDT, D. C., AND JOHNSON, R. E. 1999. *Building Application Frameworks: Object-Oriented Foundations of Framework Design*. Wiley, New York.

11. FONTOURA, M., PREE, W., AND RUMPE, B. 2000. UML-F: A modeling language for object-oriented frameworks. In *ECOOP 2000—Object-Oriented Programming: 14th European Conference*, (Cannes, France). E. Bertino, Ed. LNCS, vol. 1850. Springer-Verlag, Berlin, 63–82.

12. HERRERO, J. L., SÁNCHEZ, F., LUCIO, F., AND TORO, M. 2000. Introducing separation of aspects at design time. In *Workshop on Aspects and Dimensions of Concerns (ECOOP)*, (Cannes, France). http://trese.cs.utwente.nl/Workshops/adc2000/papers/Herrero.pdf.

13. KICZALES, G., HILSDALE, E., HUGUNIN, J., KERSTEN, M., PALM, J., AND GRISWOLD, W. G. 2001. Getting started with AspectJ. *Comm. ACM 44*, 10 (Oct.), 59–65.

14. MAES, P. 1994. Agents that reduce work and information overload. *Communications of the ACM 37*, 7 (July), 31–40.

15. ORTIGOSA, A. AND CAMPO, M. 2000. Using incremental planning to foster application framework reuse. *Int'l Journal of Software Engineering and Knowledge Engineering 10*, 4 (Sept.), 433–448.

16. ORTIGOSA, A., CAMPO, M., AND MORIYON, R. 2000. Towards agent-oriented assistance for frame-work instantiation. In *15th Conf. Object-Oriented Programming, Systems, Languages, and Applications (OOPSLA)*, (Minneapolis, Minnesota). ACM, 253–263.

17. PAWLAK, R., SEINTURIER, L., DUCHIEN, L., AND FLORIN, G. 2001. JAC: a flexible solution for aspect-oriented programming in Java. In *Metalevel Architectures and Separation of Crosscutting Concerns, 3rd International Conference REFLECTION 2001*, (Kyoto). LNCS, vol. 2192. Springer-Verlag, Berlin, 1–24.

18. PENBERTHY, J. AND WELD, D. 1992. UCPOP: A sound, complete, partial order planner for ADL. In *3rd Int'l Conf. Knowledge Representation and Reasoning (KR)*, (Boston). Morgan Kaufmann, San Mateo, California. 108–114.

19. STEIN, D., HANENBERG, S., AND UNLAND, R. 2002. An UML-based aspect-oriented design notation. In *1st Int'l Conf. Aspect-Oriented Software Development (AOSD)*, (Enschede, The Netherlands), G. Kiczales, Ed. ACM, 106–112.

20. WILKINS, D., AND DESJARDINS, M. 2001. A call for knowledge-based planning. *AI Magazine 22*, 1 (Winter), 99–115.

21. WOOLDRIDGE, M. 2001. Reasoning about rational agents. *Intelligent Robotics and Autonomous Agents Series*, MIT Press, Cambridge, Massachusetts.

PART 3

Applications

The January/February 2001 issue of the *MIT Technology Review* identified aspect-oriented programming as one of ten "emerging areas of technology that will soon have a profound impact on the economy and on how we live and work." It is pleasant to contemplate the prospect of this prediction; evidence for it can be found in applications built on aspect technology. However, currently most aspect-utilizing applications are research prototypes—a critical stage in technology maturation, but not a marker of a mature technology. In this section, we present several such applications. These chapters serve two purposes: both to inspire readers who view themselves as system builders in the way that AO technology can be applied to system construction, and to anchor those readers that view themselves as developers of aspect technology in the reality of its application.

HARNESSING THE C³

Explicit support for modularizing *crosscutting concerns* (C^3) is the key strength of aspect-orientation. The desired syntax and semantics of both modularizing and composing crosscutting concerns is the central theme of any aspect-oriented proposition. We refer to this critical issue as "harnessing the C^3." Crosscutting concerns are inherent complexities of problem domains; they cannot be completely avoided. This means that for many software systems, there is no way to structure the system to avoid crosscutting complexity. The best we can do is to apply appropriate technology to mitigate the problem. Applications with a variety of crosscutting concerns are always going to be difficult. The prediction is that harnessing the C^3 is significant enough to make a profound impact on the engineering of those applications. The choice an application developer must make is between a system with scattered crosscutting concerns and a system with modular crosscutting concerns.

What improves applications? This field has progressed from calling itself "aspect-oriented programming" to "aspect-oriented software development." This reflects the recognition that aspect orientation must be supported not only at the programming level but also throughout the application lifecycle. Applications benefit from the ability to trace from requirements to a modular implementation of those requirements. The software engineering mechanisms discussed in Part 2 aim to ease aspect-based application construction, serving as steps toward fulfilling the Technology Review prediction. However, the real test of this idea is to be found in applications. As of the writing of this chapter, there are no "killer" aspect-oriented applications. Rather, there are research prototypes that hint at the potential of the technology.

Harnessing the C^3 is achieved by providing new modularization and composition techniques that take advantage of the quantification and obliviousness of AOSD technology. Part 1 surveyed a variety of current languages that differ on their realization of these two properties. While each language may seem to be simply a choice in the design space, in many cases application requirements, such as a need for dynamic adaptability of aspects, distribution, or persistence, drives the implementation technology. Applications that require, say, dynamic adaptability of aspects add this requirement to the technology chosen for the implementation of these applications. This in turn forces the technology or the specific language to reevaluate its bindings between advice and pointcuts. Current innovation may point to the fine-tuning of these two properties to exhibit the "right" degree of power of expression simultaneously with the "right" degree of safety. Harnessing the C^3 in practice is not as simple as it looks in pure theory. Real life applications require compromises. There is a mutual impact of AOSD applications and AOSD's attempt to shape itself toward maturity.

HARNESSING QUANTIFICATION

Quantification allows systematizing properties across an application, but it has the danger of complicating the semantics of components—if we are unsure where an aspect can be applied, we are less certain about the specific behavior of any construct. Real applications need to balance such expressive power with the pragmatics of systems development, either through the use of AOP technology that contains mechanisms for limiting quantification (for example, restricting aspect application to certain regions) or through coding conventions that (less reliably though perhaps more comprehensibly) prescribe when and how to use quantification.

HARNESSING OBLIVIOUSNESS

Ideally, loose coupling between the core and aspects and among aspects themselves is desirable. Obliviousness allows unanticipated changes to a software system to take place without invasive changes to the implementation. Some classes of applications, such as safety-critical systems and medical devices, raise concerns about applicability of obliviousness. A designer of a piece of safety-critical software might feel reluctant to have it "aspectorized" later on. This is true to a lesser degree for all systems. Real applications require compromises. The principle here is that the responsibility for the correctness of a composition between a core and aspects is at the point of making this composition. Unfortunately, this correctness depends on the properties of the core, the aspect, and the desired outcome. This implies that the core cannot be completely oblivious to potential adaptation but at least might need to express some form of abstract requirements, guarantees, or contracts with any potential extensional aspect. The same applies to aspects and interactions between them.

THE CHAPTERS

At the time of this writing, no major AOP application has "a profound impact on the economy and on how we live and work." Our best indication of the potential impact comes from a look at the current set of proto-applications. This section contains chapters that report on different domains for AOSD applications, evaluate the use of the particular AOSD technologies, and suggest future improvements on current technology to support particular application domains. These reports are valuable both for their guidance of the application of AOSD technology and for the feedback they provide to the development of that technology.

The first chapter in this part, Chapter 27, is "Developing Secure Applications Through Aspect-Oriented Programming," by Bart De Win, Wouter Joosen, and Frank Piessens. The paper reports on using AspectJ to develop security components for distributed applications. The paper focuses on the engineering of application-level security requirements such as authentication, auditing, authorization, confidentiality, integrity, and non-repudiation. Modularization of these is difficult to achieve without relying on AOSD technology. At the same time, good modularization is essential for non-invasive adaptation of these requirements. Unanticipated threats to security continue to emerge during the lifetime of system software because initial analyses are often incomplete, because new threats emerge, and because the environment in which the software operates changes. The paper discusses limitations of AspectJ, such as the mechanism to select join points, as well as some essential restrictions in the generalization phase towards the framework. We classify the first as a quantification semantics issue and the second as an obliviousness and semantics issue.

Chapter 28, "Structuring Operating System Aspects," by Yvonne Coady, Gregor Kiczales, Mike Feeley, Norm Hutchinson, and Joon Suan Ong, explores the use of aspects in operating systems. The authors use aspects to implement different variations of prefetching in the FreeBSD v3.3 operating system. The authors note that the original implementation of prefetching displays code tangling and that the implementation of the prefetching concern is not modularized. This results in a system where it is difficult to see the coordination of prefetching activities. The primary functionality of the page fault handling and file-system read-path becomes complicated. To modularize these crosscutting concerns, the authors extended the C language used by the operating system to include aspect-oriented capabilities. The extended language, AspectC, was used to reimplement the prefetching code. The two implementations are compared; the new system exhibits a clear coordination of the virtual machine and file system. The authors speculate that the use of aspect orientation has potential for improving modularity of operating systems structure in general.

In Chapter 29, "Aspect-Oriented Programming for Database Systems," Awais Rashid applies aspect-oriented programming to existing database systems. Domains such as databases for telecommunication and banking systems exhibit both a high degree of crosscutting concerns and a great demand for organization-specific customizations. Such customizations are difficult and expensive when done invasively. Using aspects enables modularizing those concerns, making the overall customization tasks achievable. Aspect orientation also supports manageable evolution of those systems. The chapter outlines how existing database systems may be incrementally evolved to incorporate aspect-oriented technology. Two levels of database crosscutting concerns are explored. The first is the database management system (DBMS) level, and the second is the database itself. For each of these levels, the author implements the modularization of a crosscutting concern typical to that level. Comparisons with non-AOP implementations of these examples demonstrate the advantages of the approach. The chapter concludes that aspect-oriented concepts hold a great promise for database systems and will be embraced by future systems.

Chapter 30 is "Two-Level Aspect Weaving to Support Evolution in Model-Driven Synthesis" by Jeff Gray, Janos Sztipanovits, Douglas C. Schmit, Ted Bapty, Sandeep Neema, and Aniruddha S. Gokhale. This application discusses the effect of applying AOSD techniques to domain-specific modeling and program synthesis. The authors are concerned with computer-aided tools for developing physical systems and devices. Their aspect-oriented domain modeling employs two levels of weaving. The top level is the constraint specification weaver. It is applied to a high-level abstraction of the system. The lower level of weaving is done during model interpretation. Crosscutting concerns can be modularized at the modeling level rather than only at the programming level. Their approach involves three concepts:

Model constraints. These modularize the mutual restrictions of the elements of the model. This contrasts with the traditional implementation of constraint descriptions, where the constraints are scattered throughout the model.

Model pointcuts. Model pointcuts capture quantification capabilities.

Strategies. Strategies define a collection of interchangeable heuristics.

The approach is illustrated by a model weaving of Eager-Lazy Evaluation Constraints. The chapter concludes by evaluating the benefits of using aspect-oriented domain modeling for exploring different design alternatives in domain specific models.

Our final chapter, Chapter 31, "Dynamic Aspect-Oriented Infrastructure," by Andrei Popovici, Gustavo Alonso, and Thomas Gross, presents the use of aspect orientation to implement "application awareness" for distributed applications. Application awareness is characterized by two main requirements: that the computing environment know of all running applications and their properties, and that it provide those applications with the necessary adaptations to local conditions. The variety of adaptations the system may have to deal with creates a fertile environment for aspect technology. Existing platforms lack the support for dynamically applying crosscutting concerns. With a conventional application design, the ability to react to changes is encoded in each appliance before it is deployed. This scattered implementation limits the application to coordinate and orchestrate the desired environment awareness. The authors have developed an AOP tool called PROSE, and they illustrate its use with an application involving the control of distributed robots. Of particular relevance to the development of AOSD is the discussion of the tradeoffs between stub weavers and advice weavers. The chapter demonstrates that with dynamic aspect orientation, one can implement adaptation by weaving aspects through mobile devices when they enter and leave a network. The newly established relationship between application awareness and dynamic aspect orientation has the potential for a productive coupling.

Chapter 27

Developing Secure Applications Through Aspect-Oriented Programming

BART DE WIN, WOUTER JOOSEN, AND FRANK PIESSENS

In this chapter, we report upon our experiences using AspectJ to secure application software in a manageable way. Our case studies illustrate the effectiveness of AOP technology and show encouraging results. However, we also highlight some challenges to be addressed in the further development of aspect-oriented software development technology.

27.1 INTRODUCTION

Invariably, developing a real-life application demands that we consider both functional (i.e., related to the application business logic) and non-functional requirements. Separating the development of different requirements has important advantages in system evolution: As such requirements originate from different concerns (and very often from different stake-holders), they may cause different reiterations over various parts of the software life cycle. Successful separation of concerns thus leads to ease of development, maintenance, and potential reuse. State-of-the-art software techniques already support separating concerns, for instance, by using method structuring, clean object-oriented programming, and design patterns. However, these techniques are insufficient for more complex modularization problems. A major cause for this limitation is the inherently forced focus of these techniques on one view of the problem; they lack the ability to approach the problem from different viewpoints simultaneously. The net result is that conventional modularization techniques are unable to fully separate *crosscutting concerns*.

Aspect-oriented programming (AOP) is an approach that provides more advanced modularization techniques. The main characteristic of this technology is the ability to specify both the behavior of one individual concern and the way this behavior is related to other concerns (the *binding*). In fact, AOP has become a general term to denote several approaches to providing such development functionality. One prominent tool in this space is AspectJ [19]. AspectJ extends Java with mechanisms for expressing advanced modularization capabilities. In AspectJ, a unit of modularization is called an *aspect,* and a unit of binding is a *pointcut.*

This chapter reports the experience of developing security solutions for application software using AspectJ. We highlight both the advantages of aspect technology and remaining open challenges. The chapter is structured as follows: Section 27.2 briefly introduces the domain of application security. Section 27.3 covers two of the several case studies that we have developed. Section 27.4 evaluates AOP technology on the basis of our experience. We compare our work with alternative approaches to engineering application-specific security in Section 27.5, and we conclude in Section 27.6.

27.2 THE DOMAIN OF APPLICATION-LEVEL SECURITY

A classical and increasingly popular example of a non-functional concern is security. Security is a broad domain; we focus our research on the engineering of application-level[1] security requirements including authentication, auditing, authorization, confidentiality, integrity and non-repudiation. Security is a challenging application domain, particularly since many security experts are uneasy about trying to isolate security-related concerns. The primary reason for this discomfort is that security is a pervasive concern in software systems. Indeed, separating security-related concerns such as access control is difficult to achieve with state-of-the-art software engineering techniques.

A major cause of this pervasiveness is the *structural difference* between application logic and security logic. For example, the code to write relevant events to an audit log or the code that realizes an access control model is often spread among many classes. Attempts to modularize security concerns have been ongoing for many years. While the community has succeeded in modularizing the implementation of security mechanisms, *where* and *when* to call a given security mechanism in an application has not been adequately addressed. Furthermore, the crosscutting nature of security relates not only to the diversity of specific places where security mechanisms are to be called but also to the context of calls: Some security mechanisms require information that is not localized in the application. For instance, consider communication encryption within an application: the keys to be used for this purpose are typically linked to a user or principal that is somehow represented

---

1. As opposed to physical security and network layer security.

in the application. Key selection often depends on the specific communication channel and hence requires connection or host information. Initialization vectors and
other security state information is often contained in the security mechanism itself.
Finally, the actual data to protect may be scattered over several locations in the
application.

Application-level security is an appealing but also a difficult candidate for validating AOP techniques because of its inherent complexity. In this validation, it is
important to assess the flexibility for reuse and maintenance that a proposed mechanism provides. Given the prevailing heterogeneity of application domains and
environments, there is a clear need to reuse security solutions. The extra importance
of maintenance may require some further explanation. The Common Criteria [6] and
their predecessors argue for considering security from the start of the system development process. However, history shows that for systems of moderate to high
complexity, the idea of building a secure system from scratch is utopian.
Unanticipated threats always arise during the lifetime of the system, both because the
initial threat analysis was incomplete and because the environment in which the software operates changes. Some form of patching or updating the system is always
necessary. Moreover, building a very secure system from the start makes an application complex and expensive, often beyond the economic resources of the developing
organization.

27.3 AN EXPERIENCE REPORT

The goal of this section is to describe how AOP can be used to implement application
security. We describe two case studies of security aspects. The first is a didactical
example that illustrates the approach; the second applies that approach to a real-life
application, a server for file transfer. We conclude with a discussion that generalizes
these ideas in a reusable security aspect framework.

27.3.1 A Personal Information Management System

Our first example describes a Personal Information Management (PIM) system. A PIM
system backs up the human memory by keeping track of personal information,
including a person's agenda, contact information of friends and business contacts, the
tasks he has to fulfill, and so forth. A Palm Pilot is a PIM. In this case study, we focus
on the important requirement of access control.

Figure 27-1 shows the class diagram of a simplified PIM system. `PIMSystem` is
the heart of the model. Through this class, the system can represent and manage

three different types of information (or PIMUnits): appointments, contacts, and tasks. Besides a common operation represented in the abstract PIMUnit class, each information type requires different fields and operations. Finally, different Persons may perform operations on the system. Implementing access control in this system requires defining both the access control model and the mechanism for enforcing it. In our example, the *owner-based access control model* has the following rules:

◆ The owner (i.e., creator) of a PIMUnit can invoke all operations on that unit.

◆ Contacts are only accessible to their owner.

◆ All other accesses to PIMUnits are restricted to just viewing.

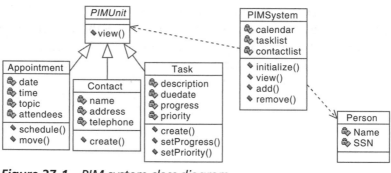

Figure 27-1   PIM system class diagram.

These rules are not complex. However, an object-oriented implementation of this access control model into the PIM context is not straightforward. First, every PIMUnit must be associated with its owner. This can be achieved by inserting an owner attribute into the PIMUnit class, initialized when the unit is created. Then, since access control requires that the real identity of the person responsible for initiating an operation is known, an authentication mechanism must be added to the model. We chose to do this in the general PIMSystem class. Finally, for the actual authorization checks, most operations in the four unit classes must be modified: The signature of the operations must be altered to pass identity information from PIMSystem to the authorization checks. As a result, the initial model has to be changed into a model, as shown in Figure 27-2, where the items in bold represent the places that require changes (both structural and behavioral). Crosscutting is epidemic.

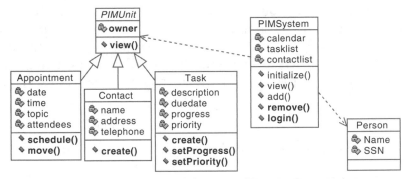

Figure 27-2 PIM system modifications for access control.

Listing 27-1 shows the implementation of the same access control functionality using AspectJ. The first aspect, `Ownermanagement`, is responsible for storage and initialization of the PIM unit owners. To this end, an instance of the aspect is associated (created) with every `PIMUnit` object. Every unit will be decorated with an owner attribute that is initialized by the *after* advice when the unit is created. The `Authentication` aspect is used to authenticate persons and replaces the `login()` method that was introduced in the object-oriented implementation of access control. An attribute is included in this aspect that represents the current user, and an operation initializes this attribute.[2] Finally, the `Authorization` aspect implements the actual access control. Here, an `around` advice verifies the equality of the owner of the unit that is currently being accessed and the current user as identified through authentication and acts accordingly. In this aspect, the `restrictedAccess` point-cut specifies the places for enforcing this verification.

The aspect approach as proposed previously could be considered equivalent to a regular object-oriented implementation, but at first sight it might seem more complex and thus less attractive. However, the integral modularization as described here has a number of essential advantages. First, coping with changes, especially unanticipated ones, is easier because all relevant code is gathered into one place. Second, the proper modularization simplifies scaling when the size of the application increases. This example is not extensive enough to demonstrate this, but for real-life systems,

---

2. For this aspect, several implementation scenarios are possible. In this example, we chose to support only non-simultaneous system interaction by making the currentUser static and thus system-wide. Other strategies, such as simultaneous access of persons, are discussed in [11]. The chosen strategy could also be implemented by associating the aspect with a `perthis()` statement to the `PIMSystem` class.

the difference will be considerable. Third, because of the proper modularization, developers can concentrate on the real core of the problem without having to worry about side issues such as code consistency. Finally, the complete separation of concerns improves the understanding of which security measures are implemented and where and when they are activated. These advantages will be clarified in the following paragraphs.

Listing 27-1   *Access control aspect implementation*

```
aspect OwnerManagement perthis(this(PIMUnit)){
  String owner ; //one per PIMUnit object
  after(): execution(Appointment.schedule(..)) ||
           execution(Contact.create(..)) ||
           execution(Task.create(..)){
    owner = Authentication.getUser() ;
  }
}

aspect Authentication(){
  static String currentUser ; //one per system
  static String getUser(){
    if(currentUser == null) currentUser = <login> ;
    return currentUser ;
  }
}

aspect Authorization(){
  pointcut restrictedAccess():
    execution(* Appointment.move(..)) ||
    execution(* Contact.view(..)) ||
    execution(* Task.setProgress(..)) ||
    execution(* Task.setPriority(..)) ;

  void around() : restrictedAccess(){
    Object currentUnit = thisJoinPoint.getThis() ;
    String unitOwner = OwnerManagement.aspectOf(currentUnit).owner;
    String user = Authentication.getUser() ;
    if(! unitOwner.equals(user))
      System.out.println("Access Denied !") ;
     else proceed() ;
  }
}
```

Consider a possible evolution of the PIM system. Suppose it is used by a company where different participating roles are defined, such as secretaries, managers, and so forth. The original design needs to be changed to reflect the different roles (which can be done by subclassing `Person` with several classes). In such an environment, the access control subsystem might also require an update. For example, secretaries may require full access to all information of their managers. This new requirement affects all access control checks. In the object-oriented security solution, these operations are dispersed among several classes (`PIMUnit`, `Appointment`, `Task`, and `Contact`). This extension requires considerable effort by the software maintainer, along with the possibility of introducing maintenance mistakes. For our aspect implementation, however, the only required change is the modification of the condition of the "if-statement" within the `Authorization` advice so that it includes this new access rule. The changes required to support this extension are more localized.

This example of changing the access control model clearly demonstrates the flexibility gained by the advanced modularization capabilities of aspect-oriented programming. Similarly, other models can be supported equally elegantly. For instance, an ACL (Access Control List) based model would allow the owner to define fine-grained rules for the access rights of each person. In addition, different information confidentiality levels (such as public, confidential, and top-secret) could extend the access control model in order to further restrict information access in the system based on the user's clearance level. The AOP approach can even support a capability-based model, where one can delegate access privileges to others. All these models can be supported without requiring invasive changes in the core application software or unwarranted changes in the aspect implementation.

27.3.2   *An FTP Server*

Our second case study deals with the security requirements of jFTPd [17], a server that (partially) implements the well-known File Transfer Protocol (FTP). The implementation includes several security measures, most of which are imposed by the specification of the protocol. This case study only discusses access control, which is user-based. Users authenticate with a (user name and) password, once per connection, and then the current connection is linked with this user. FTP commands are executed only after proper authorization.

In the implementation of the FTP, `FTPHandler` is the central class in the model that takes care of incoming connection setup requests. For every request, `FTPHandler` instantiates an `FTPConnection` object and assigns the incoming connection to it. From this point onwards, the latter acts as the primary contact point for the connection, which means that it is responsible for reading and answering all incoming FTP requests on the connection. It has a central input operation that delegates each command input to an appropriate suboperation depending on the specific request. At the end of an FTP session, the connection is closed, and the connection object is destroyed.

A user-based access control model can be successfully implemented using AOP technology. We briefly sketch the aspect structure and strategy used.[3] FTP security is session-oriented—the credentials presented at login are used throughout the entire session. Therefore, similar to the `OwnerManagement` aspect of the previous example, an `FTPSession` aspect is associated with the `FTPConnection` class and holds the information from the authentication phase. Furthermore, a second aspect, `FTPConnectionSecurity`, performs two important tasks: In the authentication phase, it checks username/password combinations (and fills in the outcome in the `FTPSession` aspect), and in the various FTP commands of the `FTPConnection` class, it performs the actual access control. Finally, the aspect implementation includes two other aspects for dealing with the representation and initialization of some other security parameters that are not relevant to this discussion. Through the aspect implementation, a complete separation of security-related code is achieved from the initial implementation of the FTP server. In other words, we are able to deploy the FTP server with or without weaving in (i.e., bind and activate) the security aspects.

27.3.3 *Toward a Framework of Aspects*

The deployment of the aspects described in the previous examples depends heavily on the type and implementation of the actual application. For instance, the `Authorization` aspect of Section 27.1 can only be used for `PIMUnit` classes, not for `FTPConnections`. Also, the explicit choice to have system-wide personal authentication in the first case study limits the applicability of that specific aspect. In general, it seems hard to define a single set of aspects that is applicable in a broad range of applications. However, just as Java classes can be made abstract to represent generic behavior, one would like the ability to implement generic aspects that can be reused in several cases. A closer look at the previous aspects reveals two obstacles that hinder their reuse.

- First, the design of (and the mechanisms used within) the specific aspects differs among different cases. An illustration of this is the fact that the number of aspects differs in the two case studies presented in this chapter, although they both cover access control.

- The second obstacle is related to the explicit deployment statements in the definition of an aspect. As an example, aspects that crosscut with `PIMUnits` cannot be applied to `FTPConnections`.

---

3. A more elaborate discussion on this case study is presented in [8].

The key to resolving the first problem is identifying the generic domain concepts and their mutual dependencies while ignoring the particular implementation details of the underlying application. In the two case studies, three common concepts can be identified: (1) an authentication concept that stores information about the subject initiating an access attempt and that guarantees the correct identity of the subject, (2) a resource concept that models resource-specific information required for access control, and (3) an authorization concept that implements the access controls for every attempt to access the resource, possibly based on subject and resource information. In the first case study, the three aspects map nicely onto the previous concepts (notice that OwnerManagement implements the resource concept). In the second case study, both discussed aspects (FTPSession and FTPConnectionSecurity) actually represent distinct parts of the authentication concept and hence should be merged. The authorization concept maps directly; the resource concept has not been used. In short, it is fair to state that the technology does not stop us from generating reusable results.

To address the second problem, AspectJ supports abstract definitions of pointcuts. Specific pointcuts can be instantiated afterwards in an extended aspect. Using this mechanism, it is possible to build a general aspect and redefine the abstract pointcuts based on a specific application.

Combining the two solutions discussed here results in aspect code as shown in Listing 27-2. While the intellectual effort of this generalization phase is nontrivial, it allows the reuse of the core structure of the security aspects. A qualified person properly designs security solutions once. Later, aspect inheritance enables reuse. Furthermore, by continuing this exercise for other security requirements (such as confidentiality, non-repudiation, etc.), a combination of security aspects can be built that form the basis of an aspect framework for security. This framework consists of core structures modeling security requirements, concrete mechanism implementations for these requirements, and abstract pointcuts that must be extended for specific applications. In Listing 27-2, the concrete mechanisms still require an implementation at the places represented by "<. . .>". A more elaborate discussion on this security framework can be found in [31].

Listing 27-2   *Generalized aspects for access control*

```
abstract aspect Authentication perthis(entities){
  abstract pointcut entities() ;
  abstract pointcut authenticationPlace() ;
  private String id ;
  after(): authenticationPlace(){
    id = <authenticate user> ;
  }
}
```

```
abstract aspect ResourceInformation perthis(resources) {
  abstract pointcut resources ;
  ...
}

abstract aspect Authorization{
  abstract pointcut serviceRequest() ;
  void around(): serviceRequest(){
    <check access>
  }
}
```

27.4   DISCUSSION

27.4.1   A Positive Experience

Optimizing the separation between application and security logic is an important objective. Our experience with aspect-oriented programming confirms that this technology enables us to achieve this goal. Several smaller case studies made us confident about the potential of this technology, but the actual implementation of the FTP server lifted our confidence. This is not a toy application. Nevertheless, we were able to fully extract security-related code, producing an isolated basic application. This was done despite the fact that the FTP server was not our own code.

AOP has two important advantages for security. Compared to the well-known technique of modularizing the security mechanism, AOP allows us to raise the level of separation by explicitly focusing on the binding between application and security infrastructure. As a result, the average application developer is no longer involved with security (i.e., he no longer has to invoke security mechanisms himself). This job can be left completely to a focused security expert. A second key advantage relates to the security policy rather than to the infrastructure. Using AOP, the overview of the actual security deployment policy (i.e., defining which mechanisms are used and where they are used) is gathered into a few configuration files. Consequently, compared to object-oriented security engineering, a security expert can more easily verify whether a required security policy is valid within a concrete application.

Some practical limitations of the current tools limit the success of our approach. During different case studies, we experienced some technological restrictions with (version 1.1 of) AspectJ, including limitations of the mechanism to select join points, as well as some essential restrictions in the generalization phase toward the framework. To briefly sketch the first problem, a pointcut is conceptually equivalent to a query on an abstract syntax tree representation of the program. The AspectJ tool provides a set of keywords to describe pointcuts. Unfortunately, some queries (e.g., all the classes that override one or more methods of their parent classes) cannot be expressed using this keyword set, which leads to the construction of less elegant workarounds. Regarding the second problem, aspects, and in particular pointcuts, can be made abstract, but they can only be reused in child aspects of the abstract aspect in which they were defined. In our opinion, the primary cause of this restriction is the forced combination of the specification of behavior and composition logic. Since AspectJ aspects are not fully polymorphic, aspect reuse is hard to achieve. We refer to [10, 12, 31] for a more in-depth discussion of these problems. Some of the restrictions we encountered (e.g., the first one) are due to the current implementation of the tool, while others (the second one) are more fundamental issues that are inherent to the basic concepts behind the tool. As AOP is an active research area, this is what one should expect. Case studies, as included in this chapter, should drive the environments to the next stage. Instead of focusing on specifics related to AspectJ, we will focus in the next paragraphs on the requirements for the AOP domain as a whole.

27.4.2 *Requirements for AOP Environments*

Define the optimal design process.   AOP is a new programming paradigm building on established paradigms such as object-oriented programming. Unfortunately, this hinders the average programmer trying to become productive. Conceptually clean and understandable design processes can help alleviate this problem. Obviously, the rapidly changing character of the AOP technology as it is today does not simplify the development of such clean processes. Even with the existence of such processes, the implementation of security aspects still requires detailed knowledge of the security infrastructure. Apart from enabling improved modularization, AOP technology does not help here.

Watch performance.   With AOP, the modules of a program are composed into an executable artifact. Many tools currently transform an aspect-based program into a classical (class-based) object-oriented program. This results in extra methods and extra method invocations relative to the equivalent handcrafted program. Moreover, execution of a transformed program often requires extra run-time libraries. Development and language support often involve a trade-off between efficiency and ease of use. Historically, the transition from procedural to object-oriented programming involved the same trade-off. The important issue here is that these languages or tools disable some of the optimization capabilities of the programmer and replace them with a more expressive programming model. While we did not experience unacceptable penalties when testing and deploying the aspect-based FTP server, we stress the relevance of this subject matter in the long run, as technology and tools mature.

For AspectJ in particular, the definition of advice on security-sensitive methods results in the insertion by the AspectJ compiler of one or more extra calls. For instance, a before advice is implemented using a method proxy, which requires extra indirection. Therefore, the generated code is less efficient and introduces more overhead than a direct implementation. Unfortunately, this is the price of generality. Building a less general aspect and a more complex combination tool could improve this situation.

Support testing and debugging. Debugging involves code assessment and correction. In a typical design process, all sorts of tests (black box, white box, stress, and so forth) are used to validate modules. Likewise, when using AOP, the programmer should have the ability to test aspects. This testing must include both the behavior of the aspect, which is part of the security infrastructure, and the binding within different environments (the security policy). Testing aspect behavior is comparable to but different from traditional object testing. Testing the binding is difficult. It must include both information about the deployment environment (type information and possibly context information) and specific application binding information (specific state transferred between different aspects). Today, research on aspect testing is in a very early state, and practical tools are non-existent. Locating erroneous code is complicated by the fact that the running code does not correspond to the written code. Fortunately, current AOP research also focuses on tools that provide a clear visualization of the run-time interaction between aspects and the core application.

Toward trusted code. From a security viewpoint, the explicit separation and consequent composition of security aspects and application objects raise the extra risk of introducing new security holes. In particular, the specific combination mechanisms used in the tool and the tool itself must be part of the trusted computing base, and therefore, they are a primary target for attacks. Let us consider the case of authorization: It should not be possible for a client to directly invoke the end-functionality of a server, circumventing the authorization policy. In this respect, security demands absolute guarantees that the combination process (a.k.a. weaving) cannot be bypassed. At the moment, it is not clear how such guarantees can or will be enforced. This is an important topic for further research.

Specifically, in the context of AspectJ, the output of the actual tool cannot be trusted because the original functionality, without the new aspect code, is simply moved into a new method with a special name. Clever attackers knowing the modus operandi of the tool can exploit the code very easily. As explicitly stated by the tool manual, this problem only arises if not all source code is under the control of the

AspectJ compiler. Unfortunately, for practical real-world situations, such as large development processes or dynamic modification of an application, this requirement is often impossible to fulfill.

27.5 RELATED WORK

We first consider alternative ways to add security to an application. Broadly speaking, one can distinguish between the use of component libraries for security and other work that focuses on the security binding.

Over the past few years, several security libraries have been developed to enable the implementation of application-specific security requirements. For example, Sun has released JCA/JCE with basic security primitives, JAAS [20] for authentication and authorization, and JSSE for secured network communication. Other examples include Pluggable Authentication Modules (PAM) [26] and GSS API [21]. We consider them as component libraries: They successfully capture the domain logic into separate modules, enabling flexible component selection and interchange. Unfortunately, the use of component libraries does not improve the control over the inherent crosscutting nature of security.

Ongoing research (e.g., Naccio [13], Ariel [24], and PolicyMaker [3]) addresses a declarative description of security properties for application software. Such security-specific language would be especially valuable to define the binding between application and security mechanisms. In this work, the core challenge is to create the right security abstractions once and for all. We have chosen to focus on a general-purpose aspect-oriented language, and we believe that security abstractions will remain an evolving challenge for the foreseeable future.

Next, we consider related work from a different angle by discussing alternative software engineering techniques to deal with crosscutting concerns. From the viewpoint of software architectures, several approaches have addressed increased independence between application logic and security logic.

By using a number of object-oriented design patterns [16], many security architectures try to be independent of an application structure. This can be achieved to some extent. Also, various security-specific patterns have been proposed [27]. The drawback of this approach is that the structure of the solution becomes more complex and harder to understand. This additional complexity is hard to accept in light of security validation requirements.

Meta-level architectures [4, 25, 29] enable the separate implementation of application and security functionality [1, 33]. They offer a complete reification of the execution of the application: The events of sending a message, starting the execution, or creating objects all get reified into first class entities. As the meta-program has control over these reified entities, it can affect the execution of the core application. In comparison to aspect-oriented programming, this mechanism is in many ways more powerful, but it is also a much heavier burden for the software engineer. Moreover, the development of meta-programs for security is more complex because the programmer is forced to think in terms of meta-entities only indirectly related to the application. Like security patterns, meta-level architectures complicate the security validation process.

Other approaches, such as the CORBA Security Service [2, 23], Microsoft .NET [22], JBoss [30], and others [9, 14, 15], use the basic idea of introducing an interceptor between clients and services, in order to perform access control, for example. They are similar to meta-level architectures in that they intervene in the communication between client and service, but the intervention is less generic (and as such more simplified): the interceptors are mere decorators to the services. In straightforward situations, they can be specified fairly easily, possibly through declarative description. However, when more and more application state needs to be taken into account, writing decorators becomes extremely hard.

Transformations in AspectJ happen on the level of source code, and similar results were achieved in AOSF [28, 32]. Other tools are available that work on the level of bytecode [5, 18]. This has the advantage that aspects can be added even when no source code is available for the application. The disadvantage is that on the level of bytecode, a lot of the application logic is already lost. Reconstructing this logic is hard, and producing correct descriptions of how a series of bytecodes has to be changed to implement authentication is even harder. Needless to say, validating and debugging the result will be challenging. We believe that with the current state-of-the-art, an approach that manipulates source code is important to enable the rapid evolution of various stages in the technology. This will be important in order to experiment with AOP environments of growing maturity, while capturing new requirements as experience grows.

27.6   CONCLUSION

In this chapter, we have discussed our experiences in using aspect-oriented programming to develop security components for distributed applications. We believe that we have illustrated the effectiveness of AOP technology with two application-level security problems, which resulted in examples that are beyond toy-level demonstrations of the technology at hand. In the long run, however, it is clear that support at the level of development processes and environments will be essential for aspect-based technology to become widespread.

We believe that security greatly benefits from enhanced modularization with aspects. The key advantages in this context are the full separation of business and security logic, which allows security experts to concentrate on their core business, and the centralization of the security policy that raises policy verification to a higher level. A recent doctoral thesis [7] discusses the feasibility, merits, and drawbacks of using aspect-oriented software development for application-level security in more detail.

Finally, it is also fair to state that by *only* focusing on security, we have not covered the challenge of combining aspects that result from complementary, relatively unrelated concerns. The use of the technology in such a context, where advanced aspect compositions is clearly required, is the focus of ongoing and future work.

ACKNOWLEDGMENTS

The authors would like to thank Eddy Truyen, Bart De Decker, and the other members of the DistriNet research group for the interesting and inspiring discussions in the context of this work. Furthermore, the Department of Computer Science at the K. U. Leuven deserves our gratitude for giving us the opportunity to conduct this research. Finally, we would like to thank the editors for their useful comments and suggestions for improvements.

REFERENCES

1. ANCONA, M., CAZZOLA, W., AND FERNANDEZ, E. B. 1999. Reflective authorization systems: Possibilities, benefits, and drawbacks. In *Secure Internet programming: Security Issues for Mobile and Distributed Objects*, J. Vitek and C. Jensen, Eds. LNCS, vol. 1603. Springer-Verlag, Berlin, 35–49.

2. BEZNOSOV, K. 2000. Engineering access control for distributed enterprise applications. Ph.D. thesis, Florida International University, Miami, Florida.

3. BLAZE, M., FEIGENBAUM, J., AND LACY, J. 1996. Decentralized trust management. In *1996 Symp. Security and Privacy,* (Oakland, California). IEEE, 164–173.

4. CHIBA, S. 1995. A metaobject protocol for C++. In *10th Conf. Object-Oriented Programming, Systems, Languages, and Applications (OOPSLA)*, (Austin). ACM, 285–299.

5. COHEN, G., CHASE, J., AND KAMINSKY, D. 1998. Automatic program transformation with JOIE. In *1998 Annual Technical Symposium* (New Orleans). USENIX, 167–178.

6. COMMON CRITERIA. 1999. Common criteria for information technology security evaluation, version 2.1. Tech. rep., Common Criteria. http://www.commoncriteria.org.

7. DE WIN, B. 2004. Engineering Application-level Security through Aspect-Oriented Software Development. Ph.D. thesis, Katholieke Universiteit Leuven, The Netherlands.

8. DE WIN, B., JOOSEN, W., AND PIESSENS, F. 2003. AOSD & security: A practical assessment. In *Software Engineering Properties of Languages for Aspect Technologies (SPLAT)*, (Boston). http://www.daimi.au.dk/~eernst/splat03/papers/Bart_De_Win.pdf.

9. DE WIN, B., VAN DEN BERGH, J., MATTHIJS, F., DE DECKER, B., AND JOOSEN, W. 2000. A security architecture for electronic commerce applications. In *Information Security for Global Information Infrastructures*, S. Qing and J. Eloff, Eds. Kluwer Academic Publishers, Boston, 491–500.

10. DE WIN, B., VANHAUTE, B., AND DE DECKER, B. 2001. Towards an open weaving process. In *Workshop on Advanced Separation of Concerns in Object-Oriented Systems (OOPSLA)*, (Tampa, Florida). http://www.cs.ubc.ca/~kdvolder/Workshops/OOPSLA2001/submissions/07-dewin.pdf.

11. DE WIN, B., VANHAUTE, B., AND DE DECKER, B. 2002. How aspect-oriented programming can help to build secure software. *Informatica 26*, 2, 141–149.

12. ERNST, E. AND LORENZ, D. H. 2003. Aspects and polymorphism in AspectJ. In *2nd Int'l Conf. Aspect-Oriented Software Development (AOSD)*, (Boston), M. Akşit, Ed. ACM, 150–157.

13. EVANS, D. AND TWYMAN, A. 1999. Flexible policy-directed code safety. In *Symp. Security and Privacy*, (Oakland, California). IEEE, 32–45.

14. FILMAN, R. E., BARRETT, S., LEE, D. D., AND LINDEN, T. 2002. Inserting ilities by controlling communications. *Comm. ACM 45*, 1 (Jan.), 116–122.

15. FRASER, T., BADGER, L., and FELDMAN, M. 1999. Hardening COTS software with generic software wrappers. In *Symp. Security and Privacy*, (Oakland, California). IEEE, 2–16.

16. GAMMA, E., HELM, R., JOHNSON, R., AND VLISSIDES, J. 1995. *Design Patterns: Elements of Reusable Object-Oriented Software*. Addison-Wesley, Reading, Massachusetts.

17. JFTPD. jftpd, ftp server with remote administration. http://homepages.wmich.edu/~p1bijjam/cs555 Project/.

18. KELLER, R. AND HÖLZLE, U. 1998. Binary code adaptation. In *ECOOP'98 Object-Oriented Programming, 12th European Conference*, E. Jul, Ed. LNCS, vol. 1445. Springer-Verlag, Berlin, 307–329.

19. KICZALES, G., LAMPING, J., MENDHEKAR, A., MAEDA, C., LOPES, C., LOINGTIER, J.-M., AND IRWIN, J. 1997. Aspect-oriented programming. In *ECOOP'97 Object-Oriented Programming, 11th European Conference*, M. Akşit and S. Matsuoka, Eds. LNCS, vol. 1241. Springer-Verlag, Berlin, 220–242.

20. LAI, C., GONG, L., NADALIN, A., AND SCHEMERS, R. 1999. User authentication and authorization in the Java platform. In *15th Annual Computer Security Applications Conference*, (Phoenix, Arizona). IEEE, 285–290.

21. LINN, J. 1997. RFC2078: Generic security service application program interface, version 2. Tech. rep., IETF. http://www.ietf.org/rfc/rfc2078.txt.

22. LOWY, J. 2003. Decoupling Components by Injecting Custom Services into your Object's Interceptor Chain. In *MSDN Magazine 03/03*.

23. OBJECT MANAGEMENT GROUP. 2002. CORBA security service specification, version 1.8. http://www.omg.org.

24. PANDEY, R. AND HASHII, B. 1999. Providing Fine-Grained Access Control for Java Programs. In *ECOOP'99 Object-Oriented Programming, 13th European Conference*, R. Guerraaoui, Ed. LNCS, vol. 1628. Springer-Verlag, Berlin, 449–473.

25. ROBBEN, B., VANHAUTE, B., JOOSEN, W., AND VERBAETEN., P. 1999. Non-functional policies. In *Meta-Level Architectures and Reflection*, P. Cointe, Ed. LNCS, vol. 1616. Springer-Verlag, Berlin, 74–92.

26. SAMAR, V. AND LAI, C. 2003. Making login services independent of authentication technologies. Tech. rep., Sun Microsystems, Inc. http://java.sun.com/security/jaas/doc/pam.html.

27. SECURITY PATTERNS HOME PAGE. http://www.securitypatterns.org/.

28. SHAH, V. AND HILL, F. 2004. An Aspect-Oriented Security Framework: Lessons Learned. In *AOSD Technology for Application-level Security (AOSDSEC)*, (Lancaster). http://www.cs.kuleuven.ac.be/~distrinet/events/aosdsec/AOSDSEC04_Viren_Shah.pdf.

29. STROUD, R. AND WUE, Z. 1996. Using metaobject protocols to satisfy non-functional requirements. In *Advances in Object-Oriented Metalevel Architectures and Reflection*, C. Zimmermann, Ed. CRC Press, Boca Raton, Florida, 31–52.

30. TAYLOR, L. 2002. Customized EJB Security in JBoss. http://www.javaworld.com/javaworld/jw-02-2002/jw-0215-ejbsecurity.html.

31. VANHAUTE, B., DE WIN, B., AND DE DECKER, B. 2001. Building frameworks in AspectJ. In *Workshop on Advanced Separation of Concerns (ECOOP)*, (Budapest). http://trese.cs.utwente.nl/Workshops/ecoop01asoc/papers/ VanHaute.pdf.

32. VIEGA, J., BLOCH, J. T. AND CHANDRA, P. 2001. Applying Aspect-Oriented Programming to Security. In *Cutter IT Journal 14, 2*, 31–39.

33. WELCH, I. AND STROUD, R. 2003. Re-engineering Security as a Crosscutting Concern. In *The Computer Journal 46, 5*, 578–589.

Chapter 28

Structuring Operating System Aspects

YVONNE COADY, GREGOR KICZALES, MIKE FEELEY, NORM HUTCHINSON, AND JOON SUAN ONG

Key elements of operating systems crosscut—their implementation is inherently coupled with several layers of the system. *Prefetching,* for example, is a critical architectural performance optimization that amortizes the cost of going to disk by predicting and retrieving additional data with each explicit disk request. The implementation of prefetching, however, is tightly coupled with both high-level context of the request source and low-level costs of additional retrieval. In a traditional OS implementation, small clusters of customized prefetching code appear at both high and low levels along most execution paths that involve going to disk. This makes prefetching difficult to reason about and change, and interferes with the clarity of the primary functionality within which prefetching is embedded. Here, we explore the use of AOP [4] to improve OS structure [5] by highlighting an AOP-based implementation of a subset of prefetching in the FreeBSD v3.3 operating system. Specifically, we examine an example involving page fault handling and prefetching.

A process generates a page fault by accessing an address in virtual memory (VM) that is not resident in physical memory. Page fault handling begins in the VM layer as a request for a page associated with a VM object. This request is then translated into a different representation—a block associated with a file—and processed by the file system (FFS). Finally, the request is passed to the disk system, where it is specified in terms of cylinders, heads and sectors associated with the physical disk. The division of responsibilities among these layers is centered around the management of their respective representations of data.

Applications associate an access behavior, typically *normal* or *sequential*, with each VM object. Prefetching uses this declared behavior to plan which pages to prefetch, and allocates physical memory pages according to this plan. Allocating pages involves VM-based synchronization, since the VM object's page map must be locked during this operation.

The execution path taken subsequent to the VM layer depends upon the declared behavior of the VM object and requires the file system pay attention to the previously allocated pages. Normal behavior involves checking the plan and de-allocating pages if it is no longer cost-effective to prefetch. Sequential behavior involves requesting a larger amount of data through the regular file system read path, while still ensuring the allocated physical pages are filled.

In the original FreeBSD v3.3 code, the implementation of prefetching is both scattered and tangled. The code is spread out over approximately 260 lines in 10 clusters in 5 core functions from two subsystems. There are clusters of code operating on VM abstractions sitting in FFS functions. This implementation makes it very difficult to see the coordination of prefetching activity, and obfuscates the primary functionality of the page fault handling and file system read paths.

28.1 ASPECTC

The structured implementation of prefetching presented here uses *AspectC* [1]—a simple AOP extension to C. Overall, only a small portion of the code relies on these linguistic extensions. These extensions modularize crosscutting concerns by allowing fragments of code that would otherwise be spread across several functions to be co-located and to share context.

AspectC is a subset of AspectJ [2] (see the article by Kiczales et al. in this issue), without any support for OOP or explicit modules. Instead, we use the C convention of using a file to conceptually delimit a module. Aspect code, known as *advice,* interacts with primary functionality at function call boundaries and can run *before, after* or *around* existing function calls. The central elements of the language are a means for designating particular function calls, for accessing parameters of those calls, and for attaching advice to those calls.

Key to structuring the crosscutting implementation of prefetching is the ability to capture dynamic execution context with the control flow, or cflow, mechanism. Cflow supports the coordination of high-level and low-level prefetching activity along an execution path by exposing specific high-level context, such as function calls and parameters, to lower-level advice.

Figure 28-1 shows three color-coded paths to disk, two of which have been previously introduced: normal and sequential page fault handling. The third is the file system read path. Functions in the (simplified) primary functionality call graph are represented by ellipses labeled with function names.

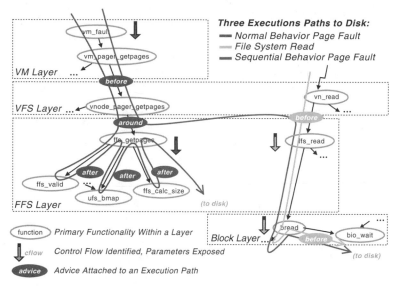

Figure 28-1 *Execution paths to disk.*

28.1.1 Normal Behavior Prefetching in AspectC

Listing 28-1 shows an AO implementation of prefetching along the normal behavior page fault path. To develop this implementation, we first stripped prefetching out of the primary page fault handling. We then made several minor refactorings of the primary code structure to expose principled points for the definition of prefetching advice. In this example, refactoring spawned two new functions, `ffs_valid` and `ffs_calc_size`, from `ffs_getpages`.

This small aspect, `normal_prefetching`, contains two pointcut declarations, which identify and expose important control flow information, and four advice declarations, structured according to these pointcuts.

28.1.2 Pointcut Declarations

A pointcut identifies a collection of function calls and specific arguments to those calls. The first declaration in the aspect is a pointcut named `vm_fault_cflow`, with one parameter, `map`. The details are in the second line of the declaration: this pointcut refers to all function calls within the control flow of calls to `vm_fault`, and exposes `vm_fault`'s first argument, the page map. This pointcut is used by advice to access the page map for planning and allocating prefetched pages. The '. .' in this parameter list means that although `vm_fault` has more parameters, they are not exposed by this pointcut.

Listing 28-1   *Aspect for normal behavior prefetching during page fault handling.*

```
aspect normal_prefetching {

  pointcut vm_fault_cflow( vm_map_t map ):
      cflow( calls( int vm_fault( map, .. )));

  pointcut ffs_getpages_cflow( vm_object_t obj,
                               vm_page_t* plist, int
                               len, int fpage ):
      cflow( calls( int ffs_getpages( obj, plist, len,
                                             fpage )));

  before( vm_map_t map, vm_object_t obj, vm_page_t*
       plist, int len, int fpage ):
           calls( int vnode_pager_getpages( obj, plist,
                                        len, fpage ))
      && vm_fault_cflow( map )
  {
    if ( obj->declared_behaviour == NORMAL ) {
      vm_map_lock( map );
      plan_and_alloc_normal( obj, plist, len, fpage );
      vm_map_unlock( map );
    }

  }
  after( vm_object_t obj, vm_page_t* plist, int
       len, int fpage, int valid ):
      calls( valid ffs_valid(..) )
      && ffs_getpages_cflow( obj, plist, len, fpage )
  {
    if ( valid )
      dealloc_all_prefetch_pages( obj, plist,
                                   len, fpage );
  }

  after( vm_object_t obj, vm_page_t* plist, int len, int
       fpage, int error, int reqblkno ):
      calls( error ufs_bmap( struct vnode*, reqblkno, ..) )
      && ffs_getpages_cflow( obj, plist, len, fpage )
  {
    if ( error || (reqblkno == -1) )
      dealloc_all_prefetch_pages( obj, plist, len, fpage );
  }

  after( vm_object_t obj, vm_page_t* plist, int len, int
       fpage, struct t_args* trans_args ):
      calls( int ffs_calc_size( trans_args ))
      && ffs_getpages_cflow( obj, plist, len, fpage )
  {
    dealloc_noncontig_prefetch_pages( obj, plist, len,
                                       fpage, trans_args );
  }
}
```

Similarly, the second declaration is another pointcut, named `ffs_getpages_cflow`, which allows advice to access the entire parameter list of `ffs_getpages`. This pointcut is used by advice for de-allocating planned pages.

28.1.3 Advice Declarations

Advice in this aspect are shown as four color-coded ellipses associated with normal behavior page fault handling in Figure 28-1. Each is labeled as executing `before` or `after` the function directly below it in the call graph. Places where control flow information is exposed are indicated by small arrows adjacent to specific functions.

The first advice in the aspect is responsible for the high-level planning and allocating of prefetched pages according to the object's behavior. The header says to execute the body of this advice before calls to `vnode_pager_getpages`, and to give the body access to the `map` parameter of the surrounding call to `vm_fault`.

In more detail, the first line of the header says this advice will run *before* function calls designated following the ':', and lists five parameters available in the body of the advice. The second line specifies calls to the function `vnode_ pager_getpages`, and exposes the four arguments to that function. The third line uses the previously declared pointcut `vm_fault_cflow`, to provide the value for `map` associated with the particular fault currently being serviced (that is, from a few frames back on the stack). The body of the advice is ordinary C code.

The next three declarations implement the low-level details associated with retrieval. There are three conditions under which the FFS layer can choose not to prefetch. In each case, the implementation of the decision not to prefetch results in deallocation of pages previously allocated for prefetching. Each of these instances of *after* advice uses `ffs_getpages_cflow` to provide access to the necessary parameters and to ensure the advice runs only within the control flow of an execution path that includes `ffs_getpages`. This is important because `ufs_bmap` is part of many other execution paths in the system.

28.1.4 Implementation Comparison

The key difference between the original code and the AOP code is that when implemented using aspects, the coordination of VM and FFS prefetching activity becomes clear. We can see, in a single screenful, the interaction of planning and canceling prefetching, and allocating and deallocating pages along a given execution path. Structuring the code this way—as path-specific customizations—has helped us refactor several other prefetching aspects, including one for sequential behavior page fault handling and another for file system reads [3].

28.2 CONCLUSION

In its original implementation, prefetching in FreeBSD v3.3 is tangled—spread throughout the code in an unclear way. Implemented with AOP, the crosscutting structure of prefetching is clear and tractable to work with. This structuring hinges on the ability to identify and capture dynamic execution context. This result suggests that proper use of AOP may enable improving OS modularity beyond what is possible with procedural and OO programming.

REFERENCES

1. AspectC web page. http://www.cs.ubc.ca/labs/spl/projects/aspectc.html.

2. AspectJ project. http://www.eclipse.org/aspectj/.

3. COADY, Y., KICZALES, G., FEELEY, M., AND SMOLYN, G. 2001. Using AspectC to improve the modularity of path-specific customization in operating system code. In *8th European Software Engineering Conference* (Vienna). ACM, 88–98.

4. KICZALES, G., LAMPING, J., MENDHEKAR, A., MAEDA, C., LOPES, C., LOINGTIER, J. M., AND IRWIN, J. 1997. Aspect-oriented programming. In *ECOOP'97 Object-Oriented Programming, 11th European Conference*, M. Akşit and S. Matsuoka, Eds. LNCS, vol. 1241. Springer-Verlag, Berlin, 220–242.

5. NETINANT, P., CONSTANTINIDES, C., ELRAD, T., AND FAYAD, M. 2000. Supporting aspectual decomposition in the design of operating systems. In *Workshop on Object-Orientation and Operating Systems (ECOOP)*, (Cannes, France). http://www.tu-chemnitz.de/informatik/osg/ecoopooosws/ecoop-ooosws 2000/papers/p5.ps.

Chapter 29

Aspect-Oriented Programming for Database Systems

AWAIS RASHID

29.1 INTRODUCTION

Today, database systems are central to the operation of most businesses. The volatile nature of business, especially in domains such as banking and telecommunication, implies that database systems need customization and evolution in line with changes in organizational and application requirements. Often, the concerns that need to be customized are crosscutting in nature. For instance, the transaction model governs the transformation of the database from one consistent state to another. The transaction policy is intertwined with locking, recovery, cache management, and synchronization policies [16, 28]. Similarly, the schema evolution model governing the modification of the conceptual structure of the database crosscuts the transaction model, the data storage and access mechanisms, and the version management policy [28, 29]. Organizations and applications have highly specialized, "local" requirements for such concerns. For example, one application might need a conventional isolation-based transaction model [8], while for another, a cooperative transaction model [36] might be the right choice. Similarly, for one organization or application, it might be desirable to only simulate data conversion on schema evolution [33], while for another, physical data conversion might be better [19].

In the presently dominant "one solution fits all" database design, such customizations can be expensive: systems lack the modularity necessary to localize the impact of changes. Trade-offs between modularity and efficiency, and granularity of services and number of inter-service relationships result in these concerns being spread across many parts of the database management system (DBMS) [31].

657

This results in systems with a largely fixed set of features, which compromises customizability. Organizations find themselves choosing either the costly and risky strategy of developing a new database system or revising their organizational and business practices to be compatible with their current database [23].

Layered architectures for database systems [12, 22] provide only a partial solution to the customization problem [31]. The intra-layer and inter-layer interactions in such systems simply shift the code-tangling problem to a different dimension [20]. For example, in the layered architecture proposed by Haerder and Reuter [12], concurrency control is spread across two different layers, with lock management and recovery mechanisms in the lower layer and transaction management in the higher layer. Consequently, customizing the locking or recovery mechanism in the lower layer has an impact on the transaction management component in the higher layer [31].

Aspect-oriented programming (AOP), with its inherent support for modularization and composition of crosscutting concerns, is an obvious solution to these customizability and evolution issues. This chapter discusses the application of AOP concepts to database systems and highlights how this can transform the way we develop and employ such systems. We focus on the potential of AOP techniques to improve customizability, extensibility, and maintainability of database systems. Like all other systems, database systems will benefit from an improved separation of crosscutting concerns throughout the software lifecycle. However, this chapter only provides an in-depth view of the role of aspect-oriented *programming* techniques in this context.

Section 29.2 introduces a general database model for an object-oriented database. We use the model as a basis for examples of crosscutting concerns at two levels: the DBMS level and the database level. We demonstrate how the crosscutting nature of these problems can adversely affect the customizability, extensibility, and maintainability of the database system. Section 29.3 offers a description of how aspect-oriented programming techniques can be employed to modularize and compose such concerns. The discussion draws mainly on concrete examples from the SADES object database evolution system [24, 30, 31]. SADES was built using a combination of three aspect-oriented programming techniques: an aspect language, composition filters, and adaptive programming [25]. Several examples are also derived from AspOEv: a customizable aspect-oriented evolution framework for object-oriented databases [11, 29]. Section 29.4 offers a discussion of the pros and cons of the proposed uses of AOP in database systems. Section 29.5 discusses other approaches to modularization of crosscutting concerns in database systems. We conclude in Section 29.6 by outlining how existing database systems may be incrementally evolved to incorporate the aspect-oriented approach.

29.2 CROSSCUTTING CONCERNS IN OBJECT-ORIENTED DATABASE SYSTEMS

The various concerns in an object-oriented database system are illustrated in Figure 29-1. Usually, an object database programmer or maintainer writes code in an object-oriented programming language for persistent objects and their class/type definitions in the same fashion as transient objects and classes/types. The exception to this style is that operations on persistent objects are encapsulated within transaction boundaries. The DBMS-level concerns are responsible for keeping the persistent and transient space consistent, both during database operation and its maintenance and evolution, in a fashion that is transparent to the application.

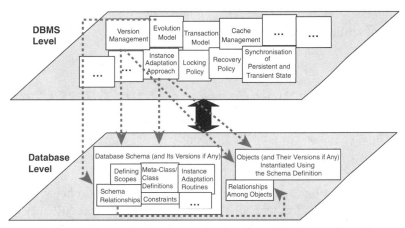

Figure 29-1 *Concerns at the DBMS level and database level in an object-oriented database system.*

The concerns in Figure 29-1 are divided into two levels, driven by the desire to separate data management concerns from the data itself. Some concerns such as distribution and security have been omitted for simplification:

- **DBMS-level concerns:** Pertaining to software components for managing data and meta-data (e.g., the schema) stored in the database. These concerns differ from concerns in other domains as they operate on both transient and persistent elements.

- **Database-level concerns:** The data and meta-data (e.g., the schema) residing in the database. These concerns differ from crosscutting concerns in other domains because they are spread across persistent entities (objects, classes, metaclasses, etc.) and, hence, are persistent in nature. This persistent nature is their distinguishing characteristic and needs to be taken into account by techniques used to modularize them. They also require an appropriate representation at the meta-level within the database to enforce necessary typing constraints.

Figure 29-1 also illustrates the intertwined nature of concerns at the two levels. The crosscutting relationship between the concerns tends to be multi-dimensional in nature. For instance, the evolution model cuts across the instance adaptation approach, the transaction model, and the version management policy. At the same time, the instance adaptation approach crosscuts the evolution model, the version management policy, and the locking scheme. Furthermore, at times, there is a dependency between the two levels (shown by the dashed lines in Figure 29-1) with a crosscutting concern at one level influencing its counterparts at the other level.

29.2.1 Crosscutting Concerns at the DBMS Level

Evolution of object databases imposes its own set of crosscutting concerns. The evolution problems are amplified by the close integration of object databases with object-oriented programming languages and the existence of complex user-defined data types. Changes to a class definition can invalidate not only its own objects but also definitions of its subclasses, their instances, and application behavior bound to the older class definition. Let us consider two examples of crosscutting evolution concerns at the DBMS level in detail: *instance adaptation* during object database evolution and the *evolution model* itself.

29.2.1.1 Instance Adaptation Approach

Instance adaptation is the process of simulated or physical object conversion across compatible class definitions on schema evolution. Instance adaptation is a crosscutting concern at both the DBMS level and the database level. It is essential to distinguish the *instance adaptation approach* from an *instance adaptation routine*. The former exists at the DBMS level. It is the code that bears a close relationship with the schema evolution model and defines the instance adaptation strategy for the system. The latter exists at the database level. It is the code specific to a particular class or its historical representation (depending on whether the evolution model supports change histories) and defines adaptation semantics for instances of the particular class definition. It can be an error handler [33], an update or backdate method [19], or a transformation function [20]. In other words, the instance adaptation approach identifies the type of routines to be used for instance adaptation and, on detection of interface mismatch between the accessed object and the class definition, invokes the appropriate routine with the correct set of parameters.

Figure 29-2 shows the various elements in an object-oriented database system over which the instance adaptation approach needs to quantify (i.e., interface mismatch messages from the objects) and those with which it is tightly integrated (i.e., the evolution model, the version management approach, and the instance adaptation routines). This illustrates the crosscutting nature of the instance adaptation approach and how parts of it, for example, the detection of interface mismatches, are scattered across other concerns.

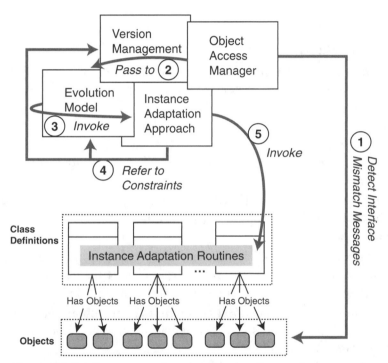

Figure 29-2 *Sequence of operations leading to instance adaptation in an object-oriented database.*

An instance adaptation approach simulating object conversion might be suitable for one system, while one that physically converts objects might be more appropriate for another [32]. At times, a hybrid approach might be desirable. However, the closely knit relationship with the evolution model and the instance adaptation routines (refer to Figure 29-2) results in a "fixed" instance adaptation approach whose customization or replacement by a new approach to suit local needs is expensive because

- Such a change can have a large ripple effect on the evolution model, as it is tangled with the instance adaptation approach.
- At the database level, corresponding instance adaptation routines exist within each class definition or each historical representation of a class (see Section 29.2.2.1). Consequently, customization of the instance adaptation approach at the DBMS level can trigger the need for changes to all or a large number of classes or their historical representations.

29.2.1.2   Evolution Model

The second example of a crosscutting concern at the DBMS level is the *evolution model*. An object-oriented database system can employ one of several different evolution models:

- *Schema modification* [3, 10], where the database has one logical schema to which all changes are applied. No historical representations of class definitions are kept.
- *Schema versioning* [14, 21], which allows several versions of one logical schema to be created and manipulated independently. Change histories are maintained at a coarse granularity.
- *Class versioning* [19, 33], which keeps different versions of each type and binds instances to a specific version of the type. Change histories are maintained at a fine granularity.
- Other models such as *context versioning* [2], which are based on versioning partial, subjective views of the schema, or on superimposing one model on another (e.g., [24]).

Similarly to the requirements for instance adaptation, organizations can have highly specialized needs for evolution models. For one organization, it might be inefficient to keep track of change histories, hence making *schema modification* ideal. For another, maintenance of change histories and their granularity might be critical. The requirements can be specialized to the extent that custom variations of existing approaches might be needed. As shown in Figures 29-1 and 29-2, the schema evolution model is intertwined with other concerns, for instance, the instance adaptation approach and the version management mechanism. This makes such customizations virtually impossible. Even if the evolution model were decoupled from the instance adaptation approach and other overlapping concerns, most database system regard the schema evolution model and the schema implementation model as being mutually integral. Consequently, there is no clear distinction between the two. Customization of the evolution model can invalidate the whole schema and, in fact, the whole database.

29.2.2 *Crosscutting Concerns at the Database Level*

Analysis of two crosscutting concerns at the database level, *instance adaptation routines* and *links among persistent entities,* illustrates how lack of modularization can adversely affect the customizability, maintainability, and extensibility of a database system.

29.2.2.1 Instance Adaptation Routines

Consider the instance adaptation routines in an object database evolution system that employs a class versioning model for evolution and a simulation-based instance adaptation approach. This is the approach taken by the ENCORE system [33]. As illustrated in Figure 29-3, all the versions of a class are members of a *version set*. When the addition of an attribute or method generates a new class version, error handlers are introduced into all the previous class versions in the version set. These error handlers are triggered when an interface mismatch is detected between an object instantiated using an older class version (e.g., `Person_V1`) but accessed using a newer definition (e.g., `Person_V3`). The handlers simulate a conversion by returning a default value. Now consider the scenario where the behavior of the `address` handler in Figure 29-3 (c) needs to be modified. Since the handlers are introduced into the class versions directly, such a change impacts both `Person_V1` and `Person_V2`.

The example in Figure 29-3 presents a very simple scenario that does not take inheritance of handlers from versions of superclasses into account. The situation is complicated by the fact that a large number of hierarchically related class versions can come into existence over the lifetime of the database. Let us assume that the instance adaptation approach at the DBMS level can be customized, for example, to use update/backdate methods [19] that physically convert the objects to bring them in line with schema changes. Such transitions produce a large ripple effect on the version sets of all classes as the handlers are removed and update/backdate methods introduced.

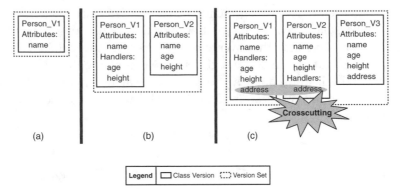

Figure 29-3 *Crosscutting instance adaptation routines at the database level: (a) Initial class version; (b, c) Derivation of new class versions due to additive changes.*

29.2.2.2 Links Among Persistent Entities

Another example of crosscutting concerns at the database level is that of links among persistent entities. Examples of such links are association and aggregation relationships among objects, version derivation links among object or class versions, inheritance relationships among classes (or their versions), and scoping relationships between classes and their members. Traditionally, information about links is embedded within the entities themselves. For example, following the database evolution theme, consider the meta-class that defines the structure and behavior of class objects in an object-oriented database. As shown in Figure 29-4 (a), the inheritance links are implemented as collections of references to superclass and subclass objects. Figure 29-4 (b) shows a simplified schema evolution scenario from a case study of a database central to the functioning of an adult education organization [23]. Prior to evolution, the class `Person` has two subclasses: `Tutor` and `Principal`. The subclasses collection in the `Person` class object contains references to the two subclass objects, while the superclasses collections in the subclass objects include references to the `Person` class object. When a new non-leaf class `Staff` is introduced, we must

♦ Remove all the references to subclass objects from the `Person` class object.

♦ Update all subclass objects to remove the reference to the `Person` class in their respective collections of superclass references.

♦ Add a reference to the `Person` class object to the superclasses collection in the `Staff` class object.

♦ Add references to older subclasses of `Person` to the subclasses collection in the `Staff` class object.

◆ Add a reference to `Staff` to the subclasses collection (not shown in Figure 29-4 (b)) in `Person` and to the superclasses collection in each of its former subclasses.

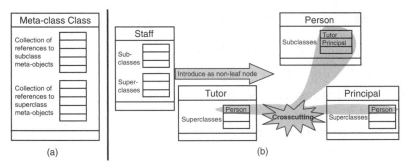

Figure 29-4   *(a) Traditional structure of a meta-class in an object database. (b) Modification of inheritance links in a schema evolution scenario.*

The number of entities affected on modification of a connection is $m + n$, where m and n represent the number of participating entities at each edge of the relationship (in this case, superclasses edge and subclasses edge). Consequently, introduction of new links or removal of existing links among entities (in the schema or otherwise) is expensive. Similarly, extensions to the set of metaclasses to include new types of entities in the system can also have a huge impact on existing data and meta-data, as metaclasses are often also linked using the same mechanism.

29.3   AOP IN OBJECT-ORIENTED DATABASE SYSTEMS

The discussion in Section 29.2 highlighted how crosscutting concerns, if not effectively modularized, inhibit the customizability, maintainability, and extensibility of a database system. AOP techniques, with their inherent support for modularization and composition of crosscutting concerns, are an obvious solution to the problem. Several aspect-oriented programming techniques have been proposed. These range from aspect language mechanisms [3] to filter-based techniques [6] to traversal-oriented [18] and multi-dimensional approaches [34]. The choice of a particular AOP technique is dictated not only by the system requirements or the nature of the concern being modularized but also by the constraints imposed by the domain and the development environment [25]. Sections 29.3.1 and 29.3.2 discuss the use of some of these AOP techniques for the four crosscutting concerns discussed in Sections 29.2.1 and 29.2.2.

29.3.1   DBMS-Level Aspects

This section discusses modularization of the instance adaptation approach and the evolution model using AOP techniques.

29.3.1.1 Modularizing Instance Adaptation

General approach.   As a first example of the use of AOP at the DBMS level, let us consider the modularization of the instance adaptation approach. From Figure 29.2, we can observe that the features that need aspectization are:

- Interception of interface mismatch messages
- Invocation of the instance adaptation routines
- References to constraints of the evolution model and the version management approach
- Call-backs from the evolution model

Composition filters [6] are based on message interception and are an appropriate mechanism for intercepting interface mismatch messages. Figure 29-5 illustrates an output dispatch filter attached to an object that traps interface mismatch messages for delegation to the weaver performing composition of the instance adaptation routines. (We discuss this in greater detail in Section 29.3.2.1.) The instance adaptation routine to be invoked can be determined from the property name that caused the interface mismatch and returns the results to the application.

We use *introductions* (as in aspect languages such as AspectJ [3]) to modularize the references to constraints and behavior in the evolution model and the version management mechanism. The code specifying the instance adaptation behavior (simulated conversion, physical conversion, etc.) is introduced into the evolution model and reflectively invoked at the appropriate point in the evolution model control flow.

Concrete implementation in SADES.   We have employed the previous approach to modularize the instance adaptation approach in the SADES object database evolution system [24, 30, 31]. Composition filters (used for capturing interface mismatch messages) have been implemented as first class objects, and the method invocation mechanism has been adapted to keep track of entities with attached filters. This ensures that all messages to and from an object are routed through the attached input and output filters. SADES offers a simple, declarative aspect language modeled on AspectJ [3] to specify the behavior of the instance adaptation approach. SADES uses an evolution model based on superimposing schema modification on class versioning. As a self-descriptive system, class definitions in the evolution model follow the same versioning semantics as the rest of the system. The aspect language specifies the aspects with reference to these versioning semantics and supports

- Specification of join points where composition is to be carried out in the class versions.

◆ Definition of new methods for the class versions.

◆ Redefinition of existing methods in the class versions (this is somewhat similar to an around advice in AspectJ, though not identical).

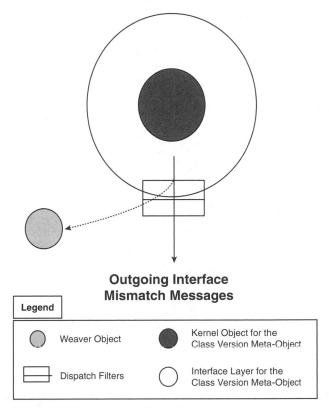

**Outgoing Interface
Mismatch Messages**

Legend			
⬤ (gray) Weaver Object		⬤ (dark) Kernel Object for the Class Version Meta-Object	
⬚ Dispatch Filters		◯ Interface Layer for the Class Version Meta-Object	

Figure 29-5 *Interception of interface mismatch messages for weaver invocation.*

SADES employs its own aspect language instead of using an existing language such as AspectJ for three main reasons:

◆ As an object database evolution system, SADES requires access to the low-level functionality of its underlying database system, Jasmine [13]. Consequently, it uses the interpreted Jasmine database language ODQL extensively. At the same time, to avoid performance deterioration due to ODQL interpretation, some of the SADES functionality is written in C and C++ [26]. Operating within these development constraints requires a custom aspect language and weaver.

◆ The instance adaptation approach needs to be customized by the database application developer or maintainer. A declarative aspect language eases this task.

◆ The language is also used to define aspects containing instance adaptation routines at the database level (see Section 29.3.2.1.). These aspects require a weaver aware of their persistence. Such weavers are not otherwise available.

The key element of the instance adaptation aspect in SADES is the *redefinition* of the `invokeAdaptationRoutine` method in the `Root` version for the class `SADESRoot`, the superclass of all classes whose instances are stored in the database:

```
crosscut SADESRoot:Root(
redefine   SADESSurrogObjVer invokeAdaptatioRoutine
           (String propertyName,
           SADESSurrogObjVer theValue,
           Integer readWrite)
{<code for the instance adaptation approach to be used>})
```

The `invokeAdaptationRoutine` method is called by the evolution model to execute the adaptation approach. Since SADES is built on top of Jasmine, the instance adaptation routine requires a reference to the Jasmine replica (instance of `SADESSurrogObjVer`) of the SADES object. This is provided through the `theValue` argument obtained from the interface mismatch message. The invocation of an adaptation routine returns a Jasmine replica, which is then wrapped as a SADES object before it is sent to the application.

29.3.1.2 Modularizing the Evolution Model

General approach. The approach discussed in Section 29.3.1.1 provides a good degree of decoupling between the instance adaptation approach and the evolution model. A similar approach can be employed to modularize elements that overlap with other concerns. However, customization of the evolution model cannot be achieved without decoupling it from the implementation model. One approach is to specify the schema implementation (and its evolutions) in the form of class versions. Other types of evolution approaches can then be implemented as aspects projecting suitable schema views on this fine-grained historical representation. As shown in Figure 29-6, the aspect encapsulating the instance adaptation approach is woven into an abstract evolution model. The abstract model offers customization points (in a fashion similar to hot spots in object-oriented frameworks [9]) to be realized by an evolution model defining the view required by an application.

The *schema modification* aspect resolves all application references to persistent classes to the latest class version (as shown by the dashed dark gray arrows in

Figure 29-6). The class versions are invisible to the application. All instances can also be resolved to belong to the latest class version. This can be done in an immediate or deferred fashion. In the latter case, the database system would need to refer to previous versions of the classes until all instances have been adapted to the latest class definitions.

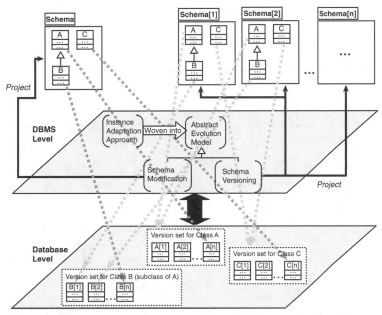

Figure 29-6 *Using aspects to project different schema views to applications.*

The *schema versioning* aspect can project multiple views incorporating different versions of each class from the underlying schema implementation. Applications can be bound to different schema versions and do not necessarily need to be updated to use the latest class definitions. However, references to the actual class versions are resolved at runtime (depicted by the indirect dashed light gray arrows in Figure 29-6), as a reference to class A could refer to A[1] in one application and A[2] in another. An object is bound to a particular class version and must be dynamically adapted when it is accessed by an application using a schema version with a different version of the class.

Concrete implementation in AspOEv. The previous approach has been used to support customization of the evolution model in the AspOEv framework. Figure 29-7 illustrates the architecture of the AspOEv framework [11, 29]. The programming language Vejal has been defined to decouple the evolution model from the schema implementation model. Vejal is based on a versioned type system and provides inherent support for multiple co-extant versions of a class. This class versioning mechanism is used as the schema implementation model. The AspOEv framework is an integral part of the interpreter for Vejal. Applications and database-level instance adaptation aspects are written in Vejal, whereas the framework and its concrete instantiations are implemented in AspectJ. We use AspectJ because the framework is being developed in Java, and AspectJ is currently the most stable aspect language for Java.

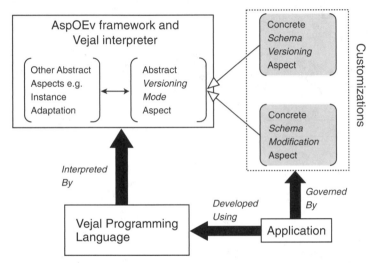

Figure 29-7 *Customization of the schema evolution model in the AspOEv framework.*

The abstract `Versioning Mode` aspect provides a set of protected abstract methods. These are realized in a sub-aspect defining the evolution model to be employed by an application. At present, two such realizations have been carried out to support schema versioning and schema modification. In the `Schema Versioning mode`, instead of duplicating every single class on disk each time a schema version is updated, only the classes that have changed are allocated new version numbers. This means that references to classes have to be indirect (versionless) on disk because `Person` could refer to `Person[1]` or `Person[2]`, depending on the schema version in use by an application. In the `Schema Modification` mode, only one schema version exists in the database. This provides optimizations when change histories are undesirable. All on-disk references to classes now refer directly to resolved classes, rather than the indirect references of the schema versioning model.

The various evolution model aspects in AspOEv also define some pointcuts and a corresponding set of advice. These mainly pertain to resolution of object references on retrieval from the database. One such advice is the `postLookup` advice in the `Schema Versioning` aspect, which ensures that `Persistent Root` objects (all classes whose instances are to be stored in the database inherit from the `Persistent Root` class) read from the database are adapted as necessary to the current schema version. Note that other objects are handled by a lazy object cloning mechanism. The `postLookup` advice is a good example of an advice that only advises one method but still usefully separates a peripheral and configuration-specific concern from the core functionality, in this case a lookup method. Since the advice forms part of an aspect addressing a crosscutting concern, its use is not out of step with good aspect-oriented programming practices.

29.3.2 *Database-Level Aspects*

AOP techniques can also be used to modularize crosscutting concerns at the database level and to reduce the customization impact of a corresponding aspect at the DBMS level. In this section, we look at modularization of the two database-level concerns discussed in Section 29.2.2: instance adaptation routines and links among persistent entities. In each case, we first discuss the general approach describing the use of AOP techniques in the context of the particular concern is discussed, and then its concrete realization in object database evolution systems.

29.3.2.1 Modularizing Instance Adaptation Routines

General approach. Instead of defining the instance adaptation routines directly within the class versions on evolution (refer to Figure 29-3), they can be encapsulated in an aspect and introduced into the appropriate class versions when instance adaptation is required. Figure 29-8 (a) shows one such aspect (in pseudo code) encapsulating the `address` handler from Figure 29-3. Figure 29-8 (b) shows, in bold, the modifications required to the aspect if the behavior of the `address` handler needs to be modified. The impact of the change is localized: Unlike the scenario in Figure 29-3, only one aspect needs to be modified. The changes are propagated to the class versions during weaving. Furthermore, if the instance adaptation approach at the DBMS level is customized, the impact of the change is limited to the aspects. For instance, if a conversion-based approach using update/backdate methods [19] is employed, the version sets of all classes do not require modification. Instead, only the aspects containing the handlers need to be replaced. It is also possible to generate the aspects containing update/backdate methods from the handlers and vice versa.

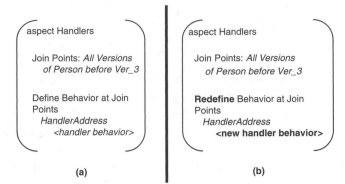

Figure 29-8 *(a) An aspect defining the address handler. (b) Changes to the aspect on modifications to the handler.*

As discussed in Section 29.3.1.1, the weaver for the aspect language is invoked using composition filters (refer to Figure 29-5). The intercepted interface-mismatch messages are delegated to the weaver, which, in turn, dynamically weaves the instance adaptation routines into the particular class version. The routines are then invoked by the instance adaptation approach to return the results to the application.

Concrete implementation in SADES. We used the previous approach to modularize the instance adaptation routines in SADES. The declarative aspect language used to specify the instance adaptation approach (refer to Section 29.3.1.1) was also used to specify the instance adaptation routines. The SADES aspect weaver accounts for the fact that the aspects encapsulating instance adaptation routines do not expire at compile-time or when the application stops execution but can be modified after they have been woven. The weaver therefore provides support for unweaving already composed aspects or their modified parts and reweaving them. Optimizations for the weaving process (e.g., on-demand weaving and selective weaving) are also supported in order to reduce weaving overhead [27].

29.3.2.2 Modularizing Links Among Persistent Entities

General approach. Besides instance adaptation routines, Section 29.2.2 highlighted the crosscutting nature of links among persistent entities. The composition filters approach can also be employed to separate information about links into relationship objects instead of embedding this information within the entities. Composition filters have been chosen because of their effectiveness in message interception (in this case, relationship manipulation messages) and attachment on a per-instance basis. Mechanisms such as AspectJ advice [3], which operate on the *extent* (the set of all instances) of a class, are not suitable for relationship manipulation [25].

As shown in Figure 29-9, an input dispatch filter intercepts any relationship manipulation messages and directs them to the relationship objects. Since the relationship information is no longer embedded within the participating entities, it can be modified in an independent fashion. It is also possible to introduce new relationships or remove existing ones with localized changes.

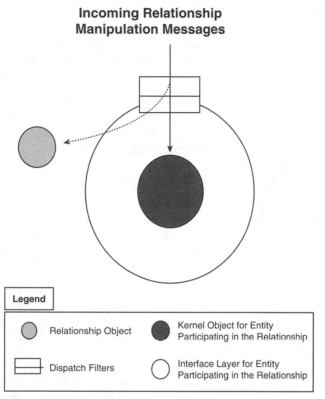

Figure 29-9 *Separation of relationships from related entities using composition filters.*

Concrete implementation in SADES. The composition filters implementation in SADES was discussed in Section 29.3.1.1. It has been employed to modularize relationships in the system.

29.4 *EVALUATION OF THE ASPECT-ORIENTED APPROACH*

The advantages and disadvantages of the aspect-oriented approach can be discussed by comparing the aspect-oriented solution discussed in Section 29.3 with the non-aspect-oriented approach described in Section 29.2.

The use of AOP to modularize the instance adaptation approach makes it possible to customize it to specific needs as changes are localized to the aspect. It also makes it possible to switch to an entirely new instance adaptation approach by replacing the existing aspect. Such changes are expensive, if at all possible, in the non-AO approach, as the instance adaptation approach is tangled with several other DBMS-level concerns. In case of the SADES implementation, all the instance adaptation customizations can be carried out at runtime, as the aspect weaver for the language supports dynamic weaving. This removes the need to bring the system offline to incorporate changes; in SADES, all evolution operations can also be carried out dynamically. A simulation-based approach using error handlers and a conversion-based approach employing update/backdate methods has been successfully implemented in SADES [32]. Encapsulation of the instance adaptation approach also opens up the possibility of multiple instance adaptation strategies coexisting in the system to support context-sensitive adaptation. These concepts are being explored in the AspOEv framework [11, 29] whose instance adaptation mechanism extends the one implemented in SADES.

In the case of the AspOEv framework, effective separation between the schema implementation model and the schema evolution model coupled with the use of aspects makes it possible to customize the evolution model employed by the system. This is a significant advantage, as schema evolution models in object-oriented database systems have traditionally been "fixed," resulting in organizations having to fit their evolution needs around the model and not vice-versa.

In a fashion similar to the instance adaptation approach, the use of AOP localizes changes to the instance adaptation routines. Furthermore, the impact of any changes to the instance adaptation approach is limited to the aspects encapsulating the instance adaptation routines. This makes customization cost-effective. This is in direct contrast with the non-AO approach, where changes to the instance adaptation approach can trigger the need for changes to many or all class versions in the system.

The use of AOP also results in cost-effective changes when manipulating relationships among schema entities, for example, inheritance or version derivation relationships between class versions. In SADES, this has resulted in significant reduction in change impact—at times as high as a fourfold reduction [31]. The use of composition filters to modularize relationships also improves the extensibility of the system, as introduction of new metaclasses requires only introduction of new relationship objects. This extensibility has been exploited in SADES to seamlessly introduce a new metaclass `Aspect` that defines the structure of aspects specified in the SADES aspect language. This makes it possible to store the persistent aspects encapsulating the instance adaptation routines in the database.

The reliance on dynamic weaving and delegation-based approaches in the AO solution results in performance overhead at runtime. In particular, dynamic weaving of instance adaptation routines in SADES each time an incompatibility is encountered might be perceived to increase the maintenance overhead instead of reducing it.

However, this is not the case. The overhead associated with dynamic weaving pays off in terms of localized changes and automatic propagation of changes through the weaver. Moreover, as discussed in [27], the SADES weaver uses on-demand and selective weaving to reduce the weaving overhead. An aspect is rewoven only if it has not been modified since the last time it was woven. This need to reweave is identified by a simple timestamp check.

In summary, the use of AOP to modularize crosscutting concerns in an object-oriented database system offers significant benefits in terms of improving the customizability, evolvability, and extensibility of the system and opens up possibilities for dynamic context-sensitive adaptation of the system behavior. However, the composition overhead, especially in the case of dynamic weaving and delegation, can be significant. Nevertheless, this can be reduced by applying code optimizations, for instance, using linguistic reflection [15], and improving weaver efficiency through on-demand, selective weaving [27].

29.5   OTHER APPROACHES TO MODULARIZING CROSSCUTTING CONCERNS IN DATABASE SYSTEMS

Modularization of crosscutting concerns has also been considered in other database systems. Most notably, the Generic Object-Oriented Database System (GOODS) [16] employs a meta-object protocol to separate policies for inter-task synchronization of object access, locking, transaction management, and cache management from the object access manager. Custom approaches can be implemented by refining existing meta-objects through inheritance. However, some overlapping concerns such as the transaction model and the locking scheme are not completely untangled and cannot be customized with a localized impact. This is in contrast with the use of aspect-oriented approaches discussed in this chapter, as these have been effective in localizing changes to overlapping concerns.

The Open OODB framework [35] offers a meta-architecture comprising some kernel modules and interface definitions to be respected by *extender modules*. The latter implements custom application-specific policies for features such as persistence, transaction management, distribution, querying, and change management. The functionality of extender modules is plugged in using advice-like interceptors defined for existing methods in the system. The Open OODB architecture, therefore, pursues the same philosophy—development of customizable and extensible object-oriented database systems—as the aspect-oriented approach presented in this chapter. While the former relies on traditional object-oriented modularity for the purpose, the latter makes use of the additional modularization support offered by aspect-oriented techniques, thereby reducing the complexity encountered in modularizing crosscutting policies.

Genesis [5] offers a DBMS compiler to synthesize systems from a library of pre-existing modules. The synthesis is based on parameterized types and rule-based algebra. Unlike Genesis, which focuses on an architecture to build component database systems, the aspect-oriented approach presented in this chapter can be used to provide customizability in existing database systems without re-architecting them.

The Transparent Schema Evolution System (TSE) [21] employs object-oriented views to simulate versions of schema. All objects are associated with one underlying global schema, and the schema versions are implemented as views defined on the global schema. Objects are thus directly shared across the various schema versions. Changes to the global schema are implemented using inheritance and virtual classes. Virtual classes represent the incremental change and are generalizations or specializations of modified classes. Introduction of a new class whenever a new feature is needed is termed as "abusing inheritance" by Meyer [17], who advocates that "a class should always define a significant abstraction, and if we are just adding a property that we initially forgot, we should simply update the class definition." Introduction of virtual classes in TSE can also compromise substitutability semantics of object-oriented systems. An object-slicing approach complemented by multiple classification and dynamic reclassification is employed for instance adaptation. The proposed dynamic reclassification approach can violate the type-system rules of the object-oriented programming language being used. This is in contrast with AspOEv, where the schema implementation is based on a language with a versioned type system. Therefore, typing semantics are preserved, and incremental changes are introduced through versioning.

In the *hologram approach,* an object is implemented by multiple instances representing its many-faceted nature [1]. These instances are linked together through aggregation links in a specialization hierarchy. This makes objects dynamic since they can migrate between the classes of a hierarchy. This is similar to the dynamic instance adaptation approach discussed in this chapter.

Event-condition-action rules have been employed in active database systems [7] to modularize broadly scoped constraints. In the approach discussed in this chapter, aspects have been used to separate instance adaptation constraints from the evolution model and project schema views to be used by applications.

29.6   CONCLUSION

This chapter has presented some examples of crosscutting concerns in database systems. Two object database evolution systems, SADES and AspOEv, have been used as a basis for discussing how such concerns can be effectively modularized with AOP techniques. Such modularization results in improved customizability, extensibility, and maintainability. A range of crosscutting concerns exists in database systems, and the discussion in this chapter has barely scratched the surface. Interested readers are referred to [28] for a more detailed discussion on the synergy between AOP and database systems and how the two technologies can offer mutual benefits.

Like all new technologies, the introduction of aspect-oriented concepts in database systems must be approached with caution and in an incremental fashion. One possible approach is to initially employ aspects for internal system optimizations. After such optimizations have been successfully implemented, the concepts can be exposed to the application programmer. This approach was effective during the development of SADES, where AOP techniques were initially employed internally for reducing the impact of schema changes before exposing the aspect language to the application programmers for customizing the instance adaptation mechanism. Another factor to be taken into account when introducing aspect-oriented techniques in database systems is the dependencies among the various crosscutting concerns being modularized. One must identify the concerns that build on the functionality offered by other concerns. The latter can then be implemented in lower system layers, exposing their functionality to the former that reside in higher system layers [25].

Commercial acceptance of the concepts presented in this chapter largely depends on the efficiency and correctness of weaving mechanisms. Therefore, the development of techniques for efficient weaving and its verification requires extensive research. Nevertheless, aspect-oriented concepts hold great promise for database systems and are bound to be increasingly adopted in this domain.

REFERENCES

1. AL-JADIR, L. AND LEONARD, M. 1999. If we refuse the inheritance . . . In *Int'l Conf. Database and Expert Systems Applications (DEXA)*. LNCS, vol. 1677. Springer-Verlag, Berlin, 560–572.

2. ANDANY, J., LÉONARD, M., AND PALISSER, C. 1991. Management of schema evolution in databases. In *17th Int'l Conf. Very Large Data Bases (VLDB)*. Morgan Kaufmann, San Mateo, California, 161–170.

3. ASPECTJ PROJECT. http://www.eclipse.org/aspectj/.

4. BANERJEE, J., CHOU, H. T., GARZA, J. F., KIM, W., WOELK, D., BALLOU, N., AND KIM, H. J. 1987. Data model issues for object-oriented applications. *ACM Transactions on Information Systems (TOIS) 5*, 1, 3–26.

5. BATORY, D. S. 1988. Concepts for a database system compiler. In *7th ACM Sigact-Sigmod-Sigart Symposium on Principles of Database Systems* ACM, 184–192.

6. BERGMANS, L. AND AKŞIT, M. 2001. Composing crosscutting concerns using composition filters. *Comm. ACM 44*, 10 (Oct.), 51–57.

7. DITTRICH, K. R., GATZIU, S., AND GEPPERT, A. 1995. The active database management system manifesto: A rulebase of ADBMS features. In *2nd Int'l Workshop on Rules in Database Systems (RIDS)*. LNCS, vol. 985. Springer-Verlag, Berlin, 3–20.

8. ELMASRI, R. AND NAVATHE, S. B. 2000. *Fundamentals of Database Systems (3rd Ed.)*. Addison-Wesley, Reading, Massachusetts.

9. FAYAD, M. AND SCHMIDT, D. C. 1997. Object-oriented application frameworks. *Comm. ACM 40*, 10, 32–38.

10. FERRANDINA, F., MEYER, T., ZICARI, R., FERRAN, G., AND MADEC, J. 1995. Schema and database evolution in the O2 object database system. In *21st Int'l Conf. Very Large Data Bases (VLDB)*. Morgan Kaufmann, San Mateo, California, 170–181.

11. GREEN, R. AND RASHID, A. 2002. An aspect-oriented framework for schema evolution in object-oriented databases. In *1st AOSD Workshop on Aspects, Components, and Patterns for Infrastructure Software (AOSD)*, (Enschede, The Netherlands). http://www.st.informatik.tu-darmstadt.de/staff/Ostermann/aosd2002/ACP4IS.pdf.

12. HAERDER, T. AND REUTER, A. 1983. Concepts for implementing a centralized database management system. In *Int'l Computing Symp. Application Systems Development* (Nuernberg, Germany).

13. JASMINE. 1996. The Jasmine documentation. 1996-1998. Computer Associates International, Inc. and Fujitsu Limited.

14. KIM, W. AND CHOU, H. T. 1988. Versions of schema for object-oriented databases. In *14th Int'l Conf. Very Large Databases (VLDB)*. Morgan Kaufmann, San Mateo, California, 148–159.

15. KIRBY, G. N. C. 1992. Persistent programming with strongly typed linguistic reflection. In *25th Hawaii Int'l Conf. System Sciences*, (Kauai, Hawaii). IEEE, vol 2., 820–831.

16. KNIZHNIK, K. A. 2003. Generic object-oriented database system. Tech. rep., Institute for Systems Programming, Russian Academy of Sciences. http://www.ispras.ru/~knizhnik/goods/readme.htm.

17. MEYER, B. 1998. Tell less, say more: The power of implicitness. *IEEE Computer 31*, 7 (July), 97–98.

18. MEZINI, M. AND LIEBERHERR, K. 1998. Adaptive plug-and-play components for evolutionary software development. In *13th Conf. Object-Oriented Programming, Systems, Languages, and Applications (OOPSLA)*, (Vancouver). ACM, 97–116.

19. MONK, S. AND SOMMERVILLE, I. 1993. Schema evolution in OODBs using class versioning. *ACM SIGMOD Record 22*, 3, 16–22.

20. PULVERMUELLER, E., SPECK, A., AND RASHID, A. 2000. Implementing collaboration-based designs using aspect-oriented programming. In *Technology of Object-Oriented Languages and Systems (TOOLS USA)*, (Santa Barbara, California). IEEE, 95–104.

21. RA, Y. G. AND RUNDENSTEINER, E. A. 1997. A transparent schema-evolution system based on object-oriented view technology. *IEEE Transactions on Knowledge and Data Engineering 9*, 4, 600–624.

22. RAMAKARISHNAN, R. 1997. *Database Management Systems*. McGraw Hill, New York.

23. RASHID, A. 2000. A database evolution approach for object-oriented databases. Ph.D. thesis, Lancaster University.

24. RASHID, A. 2001. A database evolution approach for object-oriented databases. In *Int'l Conf. Software Maintenance (ICSM)*, (Florence). IEEE, 561–564.

25. RASHID, A. 2001. A hybrid approach to separation of concerns: The story of Sades. In *3rd Int'l Conf. Meta-Level Architectures and Separation of Concerns (Reflection 2001)*. LNCS, vol. 2192. Springer-Verlag, Berlin, 231–249.

26. RASHID, A. 2001. Multi-paradigm implementation of an object database evolution system. In *Workshop on Multi-Paradigm Programming with OO Languages (MPOOL, ECOOP)*, (Budapest). John von Neuman Institute for Computing, 3-00-007968-8, 1–9.

27. RASHID, A. 2002. Weaving aspects in a persistent environment. *ACM SIGPLAN Notices 37*, 2 (Feb.), 36–44.

28. RASHID, A. 2003. *Aspect-Oriented Database Systems*. Springer-Verlag, Berlin.

29. RASHID, A. 2003. A framework for customizable schema evolution in object-oriented databases. In *Int'l Data Engineering and Applications Symposium (IDEAS)*, (Hong Kong). IEEE, 342–346.

30. RASHID, A. AND SAWYER, P. 2000. Object database evolution using separation of concerns. *ACM SIGMOD Record 29*, 4, 26–33.

31. RASHID, A. AND SAWYER, P. 2001. Aspect-orientation and database systems: An effective customization approach. *IEE Proceedings-Software 148*, 5 (Oct.), 156–164.

32. RASHID, A., SAWYER, P., AND PULVERMUELLER, E. 2000. A flexible approach for instance adaptation during class versioning. In *Symp. Objects and Databases (ECOOP)*. LNCS, vol. 1944. Springer-Verlag, Berlin, 101–113.

33. SKARRA, A. H. AND ZDONIK, S. B. 1986. The management of changing types in an object-oriented database. In *1st Conf. Object-Oriented Programming, Systems, Languages, and Applications (OOPSLA)*, (Portland, Oregon). ACM, 483–495.

34. TARR, P., OSSHER, H., HARRISON, W., AND SUTTON JR., S. M. 1999. *N* degrees of separation: Multi-dimensional separation of concerns. In *21st Int'l Conf. Software Engineering (ICSE)*, (Los Angeles). IEEE, 107–119.

35. WELLS, D. L., BLAKELY, J. A., AND THOMPSON, C. W. 1992. Architecture of an open object-oriented database management system. *IEEE Computer 25*, 10 (October), 74–82.

36. ZHANG, Y., KAMBAYASHI, Y., JIA, X., YANG, Y., AND SUN, C. 1999. On interactions between coexisting traditional and cooperative transactions. *Int'l J. Cooperative Information Systems 8*, 2-3, 87–110.

Chapter 30

Two-Level Aspect Weaving to Support Evolution in Model-Driven Synthesis

JEFF GRAY, JANOS SZTIPANOVITS, DOUGLAS C. SCHMIDT, TED BAPTY, SANDEEP NEEMA, AND ANIRUDDHA GOKHALE

An important step in solving a problem is to choose the notation. It should be done carefully. The time we spend now on choosing the notation may be well repaid by the time we save later avoiding hesitation and confusion. Moreover, choosing the notation carefully, we have to think sharply of the elements of the problem which must be denoted. Thus, choosing a suitable notation may contribute essentially to understanding the problem—George Pólya [37].

Since the inception of the software industry, models have been a beneficial tool for managing complexity. In fact, the first commercial software package that was sold independently of a hardware manufacturer was an application for constructing flow chart models, i.e., ADR's AUTOFLOW [1]. In numerous disciplines, models are constructed to assist in the understanding of the essential characteristics of some instance from a particular domain. Mechanical engineers, architects, computer scientists, and many other professionals create models to provide projected views over an entity that has been abstracted from the real world. As tools for creative exploration, even children erect models of real-world structures using Legos, Tinker Toys, and other similar materials.

As Polya points out in the opening quote of this chapter, the notation chosen to represent our abstractions contributes to the ease (or difficulty) with which we understand the essence of a problem. Selecting the correct modeling abstractions can make the difference between a helpful aid and an irritating hindrance to comprehension. In models for computer-based systems, tool support can also offer assistance in comprehending complex systems.

In addition to improving comprehension, models are also built to explore various design alternatives. In many domains, it is often too costly (in both time and money) to build variations of the real product in order to explore the consequences and properties of numerous configuration scenarios. For example, a model of the Joint Strike Fighter aircraft, along with configurations of various hostile scenarios, permits the simulation of an aircraft before it has even left the production line [46]. Models can be the source for simulations or analyses that provide a more economical means for observing the outcome of modified system configurations. The level of maturity of a chosen modeling tool can greatly influence the benefits of the modeling process, which is especially true when a modeling tool can make changes throughout a model's lifecycle.

As Gerald Sussman observes [42], in traditional system development, "Small changes in requirements entail large changes in the structure and configuration." It is desirable to have changes in the requirements be proportional to the changes needed in the corresponding implementation. Unfortunately, crosscutting requirements (such as high availability, security, and scalability in distributed systems) tend to have a hard-to-manage, global impact on system structure.

Our work involves the construction of models that represent a system in a particular domain. From these domain-specific models of systems and software, various artifacts are generated, such as source code and simulation scripts. We have found that model-based approaches can help to solve problems that often accompany changes to system requirements. For example, Neema et al. offer an approach for synthesizing models represented as finite state machines into a contract description language, which is then translated to C++ [34]. The benefit of this technique is that very small changes to the state machine models often result in large transformations of the corresponding source code. Thus, a single manipulation of a higher-level abstraction may produce multiple transformations at the concrete level, resulting in a conservation of effort when compared to the equivalent effort needed to make the same modification at the implementation level.

Aspect-oriented software development (AOSD) is growing in depth and breadth. The techniques espoused by AOSD researchers generally provide new capabilities for modularizing crosscutting concerns that are hard to separate using traditional mechanisms. This chapter summarizes our work in applying AOSD techniques to domain-specific modeling and program synthesis. The use of weavers, which are translators that perform the integration of separated crosscutting concerns, is described at multiple levels of abstraction. Our research on aspect-oriented domain modeling (AODM) employs the following two-level approach to weaving:

- ◆ At the top level, weavers are built for domain-specific modeling environments. The concept of applying AOSD techniques to higher levels of abstraction is covered in Section 30.1, where we describe our Constraint-Specification Aspect

Weaver (C-SAW).[1] This section also provides an overview of Model-Integrated Computing (MIC). An example of AODM is described in Section 30.2.

- ◆ The second level of weaving occurs during model interpretation. Synthesis of source code from models typically proceeds as a mapping from each modeling element to the generation of a set of semantically equivalent source code statements. When a library of components is available, the model interpreter can leverage a larger granularity of reuse by generating configurations of the available components. It is hard, however, to synthesize certain properties described in a model (e.g., those related to Quality of Service (QoS)) due to the closed nature of the components. An aspect-oriented solution can instrument components with features that are specified in the model. Section 30.3 presents an approach and an example for generating AspectJ [28] source code from domain-specific models.

The chapter concludes with summary remarks and a description of current and future work in this area.

30.1 MODEL-INTEGRATED COMPUTING AND AOSD

To support this focus on the development of interacting subsystems with multiply redundant design requires the development of languages that allow description of the function and relationships between different parts of the overall system. These descriptions "let go" of the specific logic of individual processes to capture the interactions that are necessary for the redundancy and robustness of multiple processes. When stated in this way we see that it is the description of constraints between functional units of the system that are the essential parts of the collective description of the system—Gerald Sussman [42].

The aim of domain-specific modeling (DSM) is similar to the objective of textual domain-specific languages (DSL) [45] in that expressive power is gained from notations and abstractions aligned to a specific problem domain. A DSM approach typically employs graphical representations of the domain abstractions rather than the textual form of a traditional DSL. A program in a DSL is also usually given a fixed interpretation, but a model created from DSM may have multiple interpretations. For

---

1. According to *Webster's Revised Unabridged Dictionary,* a crosscut saw (or c-saw) is "a saw, the teeth of which are so set as to adapt it for sawing wood crosswise of the grain rather than lengthwise."

example, one interpretation may synthesize to C++, whereas a different interpretation may synthesize to a simulation engine or analysis tool.

Like DSLs, domain-specific modeling raises the level of abstraction to highlight the key concerns of the domain in a manner that is intuitive to a subject matter expert or systems engineer. A domain-specific visual language (DSVL) [18] can decouple designers from specific notations, such as UML [5]. In domain-specific modeling using a DSVL, a design engineer describes a system by constructing a visual model using the terminology and concepts from a specific domain.

30.1.1 Model-Integrated Computing

An approach called model-integrated computing (MIC) [25] has been refined at Vanderbilt University over the past decade to assist the creation and synthesis of computer-based systems. A key application area for MIC is those domains (such as embedded systems areas typified by automotive and avionics systems) that tightly integrate the computation structure of a system and its physical configuration. In such systems, MIC has been shown to be a powerful tool for providing adaptability in frequently changing environments. An example of the flexibility provided by MIC is documented by Long et al. [31], where an installed system at the Saturn automobile factory was shown to offer significant improvements in throughput by being able to adapt to changes in business needs and the physical environment. Other example domains where MIC has been successfully applied are the DuPont chemical factory [14], numerous government projects supported by DARPA and NSF, electrical utilities [33], and even courseware authoring support for educators [22].

An instance of the type of domain-specific modeling supported by MIC is implemented using the Generic Modeling Environment (GME) [30]. The GME is a modeling environment that can be configured and adapted from meta-level specifications (called the *modeling paradigm*) that describe the domain [35]. When using the GME, a modeler loads a modeling paradigm into the tool to define an environment containing all the modeling elements and valid relationships that can be constructed in a specific domain [26].

The process for applying MIC is shown in Figure 30-1. The left-hand side of this figure describes the task of creating new modeling environments. From meta-level specifications, new modeling environments are generated using meta-level translators. (Note that this process is self-descriptive—the meta-level specifications are also created with the GME.) These meta-level specifications define the domain *ontology*, the specifications that identify the pertinent entities of the domain, and their related associations.

After a modeling environment has been generated, a domain expert can create models for the particular domain associated with the environment (see the middle of Figure 30-1). Once a model has been created, it can be processed by domain interpreters, which traverse the internal data structures that represent the model and generate new artifacts. These interpreters can synthesize an application that is customized for a specific execution platform and can generate input to analysis tools. The synthesis/interpretation task is represented by the right-hand side of Figure 30-1.

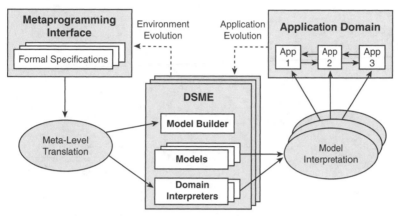

Figure 30-1   *Process for applying model-integrated computing.*

An example of a meta-model is shown in Figure 30-2. In the GME, a meta-model is described with UML class diagrams and constraints that are specified in the object constraint language (OCL) [48]. At the meta-modeling level, OCL constraints are used to specify the semantics of the domain that cannot be captured with the static relationships defined by a class diagram. The meta-model of Figure 30-2 specifies the entities and relationships among collaborators in a middleware publisher/subscriber service, such as a CORBA event channel [24]. For instance, the meta-model contains the representation of several types of connecting ports, as well as various methods (e.g., call-back or notify) that are needed to realize the event channel. Constraints are not explicitly shown in this screenshot, but an informal example of a constraint for Figure 30-2 would state, "Every data object that is attached to a call-back and compute method must also be associated with a corresponding notify method." The meta-model can itself be interpreted to produce a new modeling environment. In fact, this particular meta-model defines the ontology for the subset of the Bold Stroke [39] avionics models that we present in Section 30.2; that is, Figure 30-6 is an instance of the meta-model of Figure 30-2. The environment generated from this meta-model provides semantic checks to ensure that the constructed models conform to the semantics of the meta-model [43]. Other mature meta-modeling environments include MetaEdit+ [36] and DOME [23]. A similar approach that also uses OCL has been adopted recently in the Kent Modeling Framework (KMF) [6].

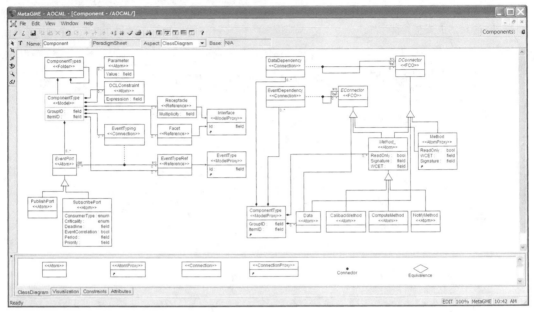

Figure 30-2   *A GME meta-model for Bold Stroke Avionics Mission Computing.*

30.1.2   Crosscutting Concerns in Domain Modeling

A distinguishing feature of AOSD is the notion of crosscutting, which characterizes the phenomenon whereby some representation of a concern is scattered among multiple boundaries of modularity and tangled among many other concerns. Aspect-oriented programming (AOP) languages, such as AspectJ [28], permit the separation of crosscutting concerns into aspects. We have found that the same crosscutting problems that arise in code also exist in domain-specific models [16]. For example, it is often the case that the meta-model forces a specific type of decomposition, such that the same concern is repeatedly applied in many places, usually with slight variations at different nodes in the model (this is a consequence of the "dominant decomposition" [44], which occurs when a primary modularization strategy is selected that subjects other concerns to be described in a non-localized manner).

A concrete example of crosscutting in models is shown in Section 30.2 based on the meta-model in Figure 30-2. An abstract illustration of the effect of crosscutting constraints is presented in Figure 30-3. In this figure, a hierarchical decomposition is evident. This decomposition has forced another concern (represented by the checkered boxes, all pointing toward the existence of a global crosscutting constraint) to be distributed across the hierarchy of the model. This results in much redundancy and replicated structure because the concern is tailored to the context of numerous nodes in the model.

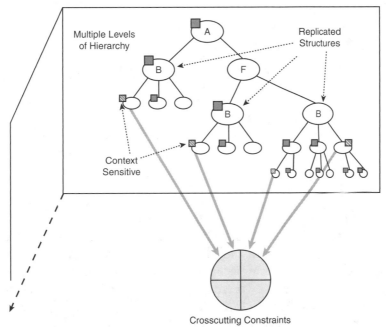

Figure 30-3   *Crosscutting constraints in domain-specific modeling.*

There are several different types of constraints that may be applied throughout a model. Figure 30-4 shows a set of resource constraints that indicate specific hardware resources needed by software. Several of the models created using the GME tool contain thousands of components, with several layers of hierarchy. In the presence of a dominant decomposition, the constraints of a complex model become tangled throughout the model, which makes them hard to understand. The AODM approach can isolate the crosscutting constraints to modularize these global system properties more effectively.

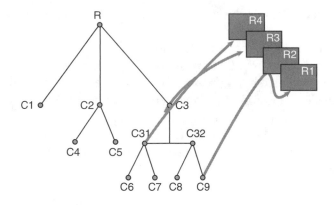

```
Constraint Resource () {
      C31.assignedTo (resources()->R4) implies
      (C3.assignedTo (resources()->R3) and
         ((C9.assignedTo (resources()->R1) or
           (C9.assignedTo (resources()->R1))}
```

Figure 30-4 *Crosscutting resource constraints.*

30.1.3 Model Weavers

Our approach to AODM requires a different type of weaver from those that others have constructed in the past, such as the AspectJ weaver [28], because the type of software artifact processed by our model weaver differs from traditional (programming language) weavers. Programming language weavers support better modularization at a lower level of abstraction by processing source code, but a domain-specific modeling weaver processes the structured description of a visual model. In particular, this new weaver requires the capability of reading a model that has been stored in the Extensible Markup Language (XML). This weaver also requires the features of an enhanced constraint language. The standard OCL is strictly a declarative language for specifying assertions and properties on UML models. Our need to extend the OCL is motivated by the fact that we require an imperative language for describing the actual model transformations. We have created the Constraint Specification Aspect Weaver (C-SAW) to provide support for modularizing crosscutting modeling concerns in the GME (please see the C-SAW web page at http://www.gray-area.org/Research/C-SAW).

Our approach to model weaving involves the following concepts:

Model constraints. This type of constraint appears as attributes of modeling elements. It is these constraints that are traditionally scattered across the model.

These constraints are typically represented by a specialized entity in the meta-model, such as the `OCLConstraint` meta-type in Figure 30-2.

Modeling pointcuts. A *modeling pointcut* is a new modular construct that specifies crosscutting concerns across a model hierarchy. Each modeling pointcut describes the binding and parameterization of strategies to specific nodes in a model. A modeling pointcut is conceptually similar to a pointcut in AspectJ [28]. Like an AspectJ pointcut designator, a modeling pointcut is responsible for identifying the specific locations of a crosscutting concern and offers the capability to make quantifiable statements across the boundaries of a model [11]. Quantification permits statements such as, "For all the places where properties X, Y, and Z hold, then also make sure that property A and B are also true, but not property C." In the context of modeling pointcuts, the general notion of quantification refers to the ability to make projected assertions and transformations across a space of conceptual representation, such as models or even source code.

Strategies. A *strategy* is used to specify elements of computation, constraint propagation, and the application of specific properties to the model nodes. (Note: We refer to "model nodes" as being those modeling elements that have a definition in the meta-model and serve as visualization elements in the domain model.) The name "strategy" is inspired by the Strategy design pattern [13]. We use this term to define a collection of interchangeable heuristics. Strategies are generic in the sense that their descriptions are not bound to particular model nodes. Each weaver that supports a specific meta-level GME paradigm has disparate strategies. A strategy provides a hook that the weaver can call to process node-specific constraint application and propagation. Strategies therefore offer numerous ways for instrumenting nodes in the model with crosscutting concerns. Section 30.2.2 provides an example strategy for assigning eager/lazy evaluation within a CORBA event channel.

These three items differ in purpose and in application, yet each is based on the same underlying language. We call this language the embedded constraint language (ECL). The ECL is an extension of the OCL and provides many of the common features of OCL, such as arithmetic operators, logical operators, and operators on collections (e.g., `size`, `forAll`, `exists`, `select`). However, a unique feature of ECL that is not in OCL is a set of reflective operators for navigating the hierarchical structure of a model. These operators can be applied to first class model objects (e.g., a container model or primitive model element) to obtain information needed in either a strategy or pointcut.

Figure 30-5 shows the use of model weaving with C-SAW. In this figure, the solid arrows represent the output from tools that generate, or transform, a model. The GME can export the contents of a model in the form of an XML document (see step 1 in Figure 30-5; in this case, the exported XML is related to the meta-level paradigm from which the model was constructed, such as the one in Figure 30-2). In our approach, the exported XML representing a model is often devoid of any constraints. The constraints are not present in such cases because they are modularized by the pointcuts and strategies.

The input to the domain-specific weaver consists of the XML representation of the model, as well as a set of modeling pointcuts provided by the modeler (step 2). In Figure 30-5, these entities are positioned to the left of the domain-specific weaver. The output of the weaving process is a new XML description of the model (step 3). This enhanced model, though, contains new concerns that have been integrated throughout the model by the weaver and that can be reloaded into the GME (step 4).

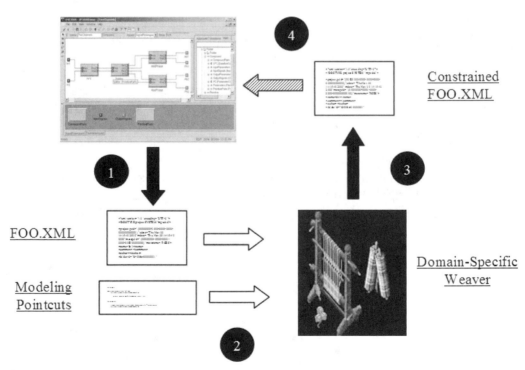

Figure 30-5 *Process of using a C-SAW model weaver with the GME.*

There are several key benefits of the Aspect-Oriented (AO) approach described previously. For example, consider the case of modeling an embedded system where constraints often have conflicting goals (e.g., latency and resource usage). In a non-AO approach, latency and resource requirements would be scattered and tangled throughout the model. As a result, it would be hard to isolate the effects of latency or resource constraints on the design. However, by using aspects to represent these concerns, designers can apply modeling pointcuts separately to see how the system is affected in each case. In this way, areas of the system that have more difficulty meeting a requirement may be given more relaxed constraints, while the constraints on other parts of the system may be tightened.

In general, AODM enables designers to isolate and study the effects of concerns (such as constraints) across an entire model. This approach is desirable with respect to application-constraint tuning because the separation of concerns provided by the modeling pointcuts improves the modular understanding of the effect of each constraint. The plugging/unplugging of various sets of modeling pointcuts into the model can be described as creating "what if" scenarios. These scenarios help explore constraints that may have conflicting goals. The insertion and removal of design alternatives is analogous to AspectJ's ability to plug/unplug certain aspects into a core piece of Java code [28].

Our previous work [16] investigated the idea of a meta-weaver framework that used generative programming techniques [9] to produce new model weavers based upon the strategies specified for a specific domain. The framework could therefore be instantiated to produce a specific weaver for a particular domain (e.g., avionics) and could also be instantiated with different strategies to generate another weaver for an additional domain (e.g., automotive electronics). The details of the meta-weaver framework are described in Gray et al. [16].

30.2   EXAMPLE: MODEL WEAVING OF EAGER-LAZY EVALUATION CONSTRAINTS

*The point of time at which the resources are acquired can be configured using different strategies. The strategies should take into account different factors, such as when the resources will be actually used, the number of resources, their dependencies, and how long it takes to acquire the resources. Regardless of what strategy is used, the goal is to ensure that the resources are acquired and available before they are actually used—**Michael Kircher** [29].*

This section introduces a modeling domain and an example to explain the process of model weaving with C-SAW. Section 30.3 expands on this example by presenting an approach for generating AspectJ code from models.

30.2.1 *Modeling Bold Stroke Components in GME*

Boeing's Bold Stroke project [39] uses COTS hardware and middleware to produce non-proprietary, standards-based component architecture for avionics mission computing capabilities, such as heads-up display, navigation, data link management, and weapons control. A driving objective of Bold Stroke is to support reusable product-line applications [8], leading to a highly configurable application component model and supporting middleware services. There have been efforts within the DARPA MoBIES and PCES programs to model the structure, behavior, and interactions of subsets of applications built from Bold Stroke components. A modeling effort for a subset of Bold Stroke components has been conducted using the GME.

Figure 30-6 represents a simple model that contains five components. All of these components have specified parameters (e.g., frequency, latency, Worst-Case Execution Time (WCET)) that affect end-to-end QoS requirements. The first component is an inertial sensor. This sensor outputs the position and velocity deltas of an aircraft. A second component is a position integrator. It computes the absolute position of the aircraft given the deltas received from the sensor. It must at least match the sensor rate such that there is no data loss. The weapon release component uses the absolute position to determine when to deploy a weapon. A mapping component is responsible for obtaining visual location information based on the absolute position. A map must be constructed such that the current absolute position is at the center of the map. A fifth component is responsible for displaying the map on an output device. The specific values of component properties are likely to differ depending on the type of aircraft represented by the model; for example, the latencies and WCETs for an F-18 are often lower than those of a helicopter. The core modeling components describe a product family with the values for each property indicating the specific characteristics of a member of the family. Gu and Shin provide a more detailed description of WCET within the context of Bold Stroke [20].

The internals of the components in Figure 30-6 permit their realization using the CORBA Component Model (CCM) [40]. The CCM provides capabilities that offer a greater level of reuse and flexibility for developers to deploy standardized components [47]. Each of the components in Figure 30-6 has internal details in support of the CCM that also are modeled. For instance, the contents of the Compute Position component are rendered in Figure 30-7. This figure specifies the interactions of entities within a middleware event channel, such as a call-back function, notification procedure, and local data store (Position). The ports and Receptacle/Facet entities provide the connection points to other components and events.

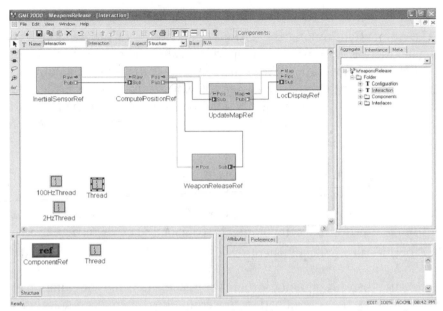

Figure 30-6 A GME model of the Bold Stroke component interactions.

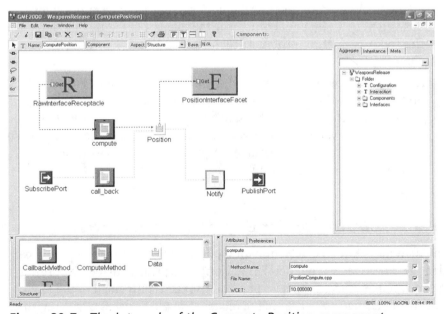

Figure 30-7 The internals of the Compute Position component.

30.2.1.1 Eager/Lazy Evaluation

In the interactions among the various components in the weapons deployment example, there is a protocol for computing a value and notifying other components of a completed computation. These interactions are the result of a publish/subscribe model that uses the CORBA Event Service, which consists of suppliers who publish events to an event channel that then delivers the events to the appropriate consumers in a timely and reliable manner [21]. The typical scenario for these interactions is:

1. One component (*C*) receives an event from another component (*S*), indicating that a new value is available from *S*.
2. *C* invokes the `get_data()` function of *S* to retrieve the most recent data value from *S*. *C* performs a computation based upon the newly retrieved value.
3. *C* notifies all other components that subscribed to the event published by *C*.

Because there are situations where early acquisition and computation of data can waste resources, the determination concerning how often a computation should be made is an optimization decision.

- In an eager evaluation, all the steps to perform the computation for a component are done at once. An eager evaluation would follow the three steps listed previously in a strict sequential order (see the top part of Figure 30-8 for a depiction of the eager evaluation protocol) each time an event is received from a supplier component.
- A lazy evaluation is less aggressive in computing the most recent value. The second step from the previous list is performed late; that is, the value from the supplier and the actual computation are performed after a client component requests a data value. The computation is therefore performed only when needed, not during each reception of an event from a supplier. The concept of a lazy evaluation is shown in the bottom part of Figure 30-8.

30.2.2 Strategies for Eager/Lazy Evaluation

The manner by which a determination of eager/lazy evaluation is made can be modeled as an aspect. The determination is typically made according to some optimization protocol, which is spread across each component of the model. If it were essential to change properties of the model, it would be necessary to revisit each modeling element and modify the eager/lazy assignment of each node. The dependent

nature of the eager/lazy evaluation on properties in the model makes change maintenance a daunting task for non-trivial models.

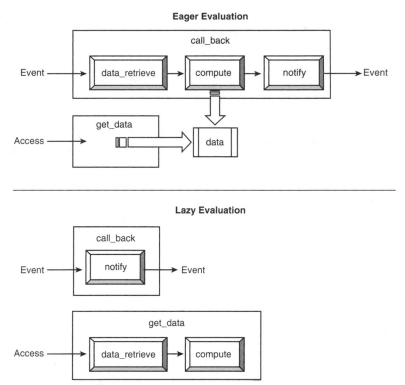

Figure 30-8   *Description of eager/lazy strategy.*

It would be useful to be able to separate the criteria used to assign an evaluation.
Such separation would support changeability and exploration of different protocols. A
specific strategy for determining eager/lazy evaluation is given in Listing 30-1. This
listing shows how the EagerLazy strategy simply determines the location of the
start and end nodes of a range of elements within the model to which the strategy is
applied. It also finds the context of folders and models that will be needed during the
distribution of the concern. The parameterization of the start and end nodes—and
also the latency threshold—enables this strategy to be called by a modeling pointcut
in numerous ways. This AO design permits the weaving of different constraints into
the model in a more efficacious manner by quantifying over the model space and
parameterizing the heuristic that is applied. Without such capabilities, a modeler
would have to visit every node of the model that is affected by the concern and manually apply the modification.

Listing 30-1 *Eager/lazy strategy specified in the ECL*

```
defines EagerLazy, DetermineLaziness;

strategy EagerLazy(EndName        : string;
                   latencyThreshold : integer)
{

  declare components, interactions, startNode,
          endNode : node;

  components   := findFolder("Components");
  interactions := findModel("Interaction");

  startNode    := self;
  endNode      := components.findModel(EndName);

  startNode.DetermineLaziness(components, interactions,
                              endNode, latencyThreshold);

}

strategy DetermineLaziness(components, interactions,
                           endNode : node;
                           latencyThreshold : integer)
{

  declare static accumulateLatency : integer;
  declare        latency           : integer;
  declare        currentID, endID  : string;

  if (accumulateLatency < latencyThreshold) then
    AddConstraint("EagerLazy", "assignment = lazy");
  else
    AddConstraint("EagerLazy", "assignment = eager");
  endif;

  latency          := self.compute.latency;
  accumulateLatency := accumulateLatency + latency;

  getID(currentID);
  endNode.getID(endID);

  if(currentID <> endID) then

      self.BackFlow(components, interactions, endNode,
                    latencyThreshold);

  endif;
}
```

The `DetermineLaziness` strategy is invoked on the start node (because the strategy works backwards, the start node is actually the node that is nearest to the end of the interaction). This strategy performs a simple computation to determine the evaluation assignment for the current node. The intent of the strategy is to assign a component to an eager evaluation until the latency threshold is exceeded. After the threshold is exceeded, all subsequent components are assigned as lazy. If the current node is not the end node of the interaction, then the strategy named `BackFlow` is fired (this strategy is not shown in order to conserve space). The `BackFlow` strategy collects all of the suppliers of the current node (this is done by finding the components that are on the current component's data flow and serve as suppliers) and invokes a continuation on the collection.

A simple modeling pointcut is shown in Listing 30-2. This specification binds the `EagerLazy` strategy to the data flow path starting with the "InertialSensor" component (the "start" node) and ending with the "LocDisplay" component (the "end" node). The specific parameter for the latency threshold could be changed, which would weave in different constraints into the base model. Of course, the start and end nodes of the data flow can be changed, too. A more complex declaration of the starting and ending node could also be denoted, such as a declaration on properties of the nodes like whether or not a node has a publisher or consumer port.

Listing 30-2 *Modeling pointcut for eager/lazy evaluation*

```
aspect EagerLazyWeaponsComponents
{
  models("")->select(m | m.name() = "InertialSensor")->
                    EagerLazy("LocDisplay", 20);
}
```

The effect of applying the `EagerLazy` strategy across the set of modeled components can be seen in Figure 30-9. This figure displays the modifications made to the internals of the Update Map component. The internals of Update Map are similar to those of Compute Position, as shown in Figure 30-7. In this case, a new constraint has been added (called `EagerLazy`), and the specific value of this constraint is "`assignment = Lazy`" (this can be seen in the "Constraint Equation" box in the bottom-right of Figure 30-9).

For application developers who are creating new instantiations of Bold Stroke, a model-based approach provides a facility for describing component configuration, assembly, and deployment information at higher-levels of abstraction with visual models as an alternative to hand-coded XML representations. Additionally, the availability of model weavers like C-SAW permits the rapid exploration of design alternatives, which are captured in constraints that specify crosscutting global properties of the modeled system.

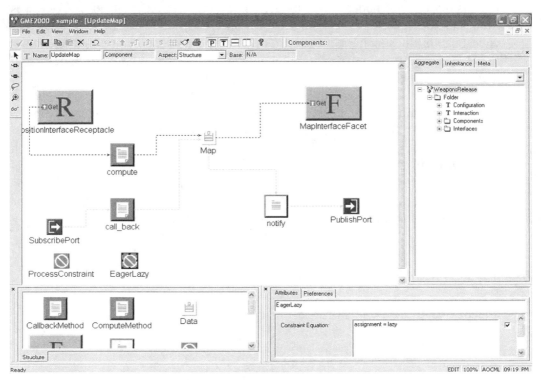

Figure 30-9   *Effects of eager/lazy strategy within Update Map component.*

30.3   GENERATING ASPECT CODE FROM DOMAIN-SPECIFIC MODELS

The traditional approach for generating artifacts from a domain-specific model involves the construction of an interpreter, or generator, which is then used to traverse a tree-like representation of the model. The actions performed at each visited node result in the synthesis of a new representation of the model. The GME provides a rich API for extracting model information.

Often, the generated artifact is represented as source code in a programming language, such as Java, C++, or C. In such cases, the interpreter has built-in knowledge of the semantics of the domain and the programming language to which it is mapped. The interpreter may also be aware of a library, or set of components, from which the synthesized implementation instantiates. When an interpreter produces a source code artifact that relies on pre-existing libraries of components (i.e., the libraries are static and not a part of the generated artifact), it can be hard to map crosscutting properties of the model into the component. This is typically true even if the component library is available in source form (unless there is provision within the interpreter to parse and transform the component library itself during the model synthesis). The reason is that the component, during generation-time, is often treated as being *closed* to modification—the granularity of the component representation is typically at the interface level, not the individual statements within the component implementation.

An aspect-oriented approach can assist in the generation of component customizations that extend the component with properties declared in the model. The focus of this section is to introduce a generation technique that relies on an aspect-oriented language to encode the extended features that are added to a component.

30.3.1   *Synthesizing Aspects*

It is possible to generate the configuration of Bold Stroke components from domain-specific models in such a way that specific parts of each component are weaved together as an aspect. This goal fits well with the OMG's Model Driven Architecture (MDA) [4, 12] and also the concept of "fluid" AOP, which "involves the ability to temporarily shift a program (or other software model) to a different structure to do some piece of work with it, and then shift it back" [27].

A technique for realizing this objective is the generation of AspectJ [28] code from models, as shown in Figure 30-10. In this figure, the model (top-left of figure) and modeling pointcuts (top-right of figure) are sent through a C-SAW weaver that constrains the model. Here, modeling pointcuts represent the description of crosscutting concerns that are to be woven in the model [16]. The constrained model (bottom left of figure) can then be sent to a GME interpreter/generator that generates the aspect code. This figure illustrates that two stages of weaving are performed. A higher level of weaving is done on the model itself, as illustrated by the Bold Stroke example in Section 30.2. This weaving instruments a base model with specific concerns (often represented as model constraints) that typically crosscut the model. The second type of weaving occurs from the aspect code that is synthesized and later processed by the AspectJ compiler. Thus, we achieve weaving at both the modeling level and the implementation level.

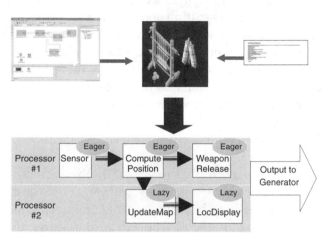

Figure 30-10 *An MDA view of aspect code generation.*

The amount of generated code produced from the aspect generator would actually be quite small. The assumption is that the core of the available components would already exist. Another assumption would be the existence of several different aspects of concern. These assumptions are in line with the work that other researchers are doing toward the goal of making a library of components and aspects available for a subset of the CORBA Event Service, such as the FACET work [24] at Washington University written using AspectJ. As an alternative, the AspectC++ weaver [32] could be used on the original C++ Bold Stroke components. For other languages, adaptations to a program transformation system, such as the Design Maintenance System (DMS) [3], could be integrated within the model interpreter. We have shown on a separate project how such a transformation engine can be used to perform aspect weaving at the code level [19].

An example of a core library of components can be found in the Java code in Listing 30-3. This listing represents an abstract `Component` (a) and a `LocDisplay` component (b). The abstract component defines the required methods for the domain—the same methods that can be found in models like Figure 30-6. The `LocDisplay` subclass, for clarity, simply provides stubs for each method implementation.

Listing 30-3 (a) Component.java *(from component library)*

```java
public abstract class Component
{

  public abstract void call_back();
  public abstract int  get_data();
  public abstract void init();

  public abstract void data_retrieve();
  public abstract void compute();
  public abstract void notify_availability();

  protected int _data;

}
```

Listing 30-3 (b) LocDisplay.java *(from component library)*

```java
public class LocDisplay extends Component
{

  public void call_back() {
    System.out.println("This was LocDisplay.call_back"); };

  public int get_data() { return _data; };

  public void init() { };

  public void data_retrieve() {
    System.out.println("This is LocDisplay.data_retrieve!");
    UpdateMap map = new UpdateMap();
    map.get_data();
  };

  public void compute() {
    System.out.println("This is LocDisplay.compute!"); };

  public void notify_availability() {
   System.out.println
       ("This is LocDisplay.notify_availability!");

};
```

Example aspects are coded in Listing 30-4. The `Lazy` aspect contains abstract pointcuts. Other aspects (e.g., various other forms of Eager/Lazy, etc.) refine the definition of the pointcuts through extension. The `Lazy` aspect exists in a library of reusable aspectual components. This abstract aspect captures the notion of lazy evaluation, as described earlier in Section 30.2.1.1. The callback "after" advice simply forwards all notifications to client components without making any effort to retrieve data and compute the intention of the component.

Listing 30-4 (a)   Lazy *Aspect (from aspect library)*

```
abstract aspect Lazy {
  abstract pointcut call_back(Component c);
  abstract pointcut get_data(Component c);

  after(Component c): call_back(c)
  {
    System.out.println("after:call_back (Lazy)!");
    c.notify_availability();
  }

  before(Component c): get_data(c)
  {
    System.out.println("before:get_data (Lazy)!");
    c.data_retrieve();
    c.compute();
  }
}
```

Listing 30-4 (b)   *Concretization of* Lazy *Aspect with* LocDisplay

```
aspect LocDisplayLazy extends Lazy {

  pointcut call_back(Component c) : this(c) &&
                execution(void LocDisplay.call_back(..));

  pointcut get_data(Component c) : this(c) &&
                execution(int LocDisplay.get_data(..));

}
```

The `LocDisplayLazy` aspect, shown in Listing 30-4, illustrates the type of code that is expected to be generated by the GME model interpreter. This code is straightforward to generate. In fact, to synthesize the `LocDisplayLazy` aspect, all that is needed is the name of the class and the type of eager/lazy evaluation to weave. These properties are readily available to the model interpreter responsible for generating the aspect code. The code generator produces the concrete pointcuts that are needed to accomplish the weaving of the lazy evaluation concern with the `LocDisplay` component.

To summarize the idea, it is assumed that the code shown in Listing 30-4 (a) exists in a library of reusable aspects. The model synthesis step produces code, such as that shown in Listing 30-4 (b), which represents the weaving of a particular concern as a result of model properties.

30.4 CONCLUSION

Our work on C-SAW has demonstrated the benefits of aspect-oriented software development (AOSD) and aspect weaving at different levels of abstraction. Applying aspect-oriented techniques at the level of domain modeling is known as aspect-oriented domain modeling (AODM). AODM yields several benefits that support improvements for exploring different design alternatives in domain-specific models. When these design alternatives are captured as constraints that crosscut the modeling boundaries, separating those constraints as aspects and then weaving them into a base model significantly improves the capabilities for changing properties of the base model. At the implementation level, generative techniques can be used to synthesize models into executable applications. Programming language weavers, such as AspectJ, are essential for customizing prefabricated components from the various concerns that are described in the model.

For the AODM approach to evolve to the next level of maturity, it is necessary to have an extensive library of reusable aspects. We believe that much research is still needed within the AOSD community in general regarding the idea of large-scale aspect reuse and composition.

30.4.1 Future Work

The current specification of modeling aspects is done using a textual language, such as the one shown in Listing 30-1. Future research will be conducted on the modeling representation science required to specify model aspects using graphical formalisms. These visual representation techniques and tools will permit the specification of aspects in a manner that is consistent with the abstraction used in the specification of the base model; that is, both aspects and models will be represented graphically within the same environment, rather than the current situation where aspects are specified textually. We are also investigating the feasibility of using the meta-weaver with other meta-modeling tools [17].

30.4.2 Related Work

There is an increasing interest among researchers toward applying advanced separation of concerns techniques to non-code artifacts [2]. In particular, AOSD techniques have been investigated at all levels of the development lifecycle, including requirements engineering [38]. Several researchers have investigated the application of AOSD concepts within the context of the UML [7, 10]. These efforts have yielded guidelines for describing crosscutting concerns at higher levels of abstraction. In this regard, they have common goals with the work described in this chapter. These efforts differ from our work, however, because we have been concentrating on the idea of building actual weavers for domain models.

Within the context of distributed real-time embedded systems (DRE), the C-SAW techniques described in this chapter are being integrated within the CoSMIC tool suite developed at Vanderbilt University [15]. CoSMIC extends the GME to provide a modeling environment to assist in the configuration and assembly of DRE component middleware—in particular, systems that have QoS requirements and are assembled from components constructed using concepts from Real-Time CCM [47]. Other research efforts related to CoSMIC and aspect weaving are the Virginia Embedded Systems Toolkit (VEST) from the University of Virginia [41] and the AIRES tool from the University of Michigan [20].

VEST is a toolkit that is built as a GME meta-model [30]. It supports modeling and analysis of real-time systems and introduces the notion of prescriptive aspects to specify programming language independent advice to a design. A distinction between VEST and our C-SAW is in the generalizabilty of the weaving process. C-SAW is constructed to work with any GME meta-model (including VEST itself), while the strength of VEST lies within real-time system specification. Additionally, the VEST prescriptive aspect language is not as rich as our ECL. According to Stankovic et al. [41], the structure of prescriptive aspect is limited to the form, "**for** *<some conditional statement on a model property>* **change** *<other property>*," which is comparatively less powerful than the ECL capabilities demonstrated in Listing 30-1. The AIRES tool also has a focus on modeling of Bold Stroke scenarios. The focus of AIRES is on analysis of real-time properties, but does not adopt an aspect-oriented approach to modeling.

ACKNOWLEDGMENTS

We recognize the support of the DARPA PCES program in providing funding for the investigation of ideas presented in this paper.

REFERENCES

1. APPLIED DATA RESEARCH. 2002. Software products division records (CBI 154). Tech. rep., Charles Babbage Institute, University of Minnesota, Minneapolis. http://www.cbi.umn.edu/collections/inv/cbi00154.html.

2. BATORY, D., SARVELA, J. N., AND RAUSCHMAYER, A. 2003. Scaling step-wise refinement. In *25th Int'l Conf. Software Engineering (ICSE),* (Portland, Oregon). IEEE, 187–197.

3. BAXTER, I., PIDGEON, C., AND MEHLICH, M. 2004. DMS: Program transformation for practical scalable software evolution. In *26th Int'l Conf. on Software Engineering (ICSE),* (Edinburgh, Scotland), IEEE 625–634.

4. BÉZIVIN, J., FARCET, N., JEZEQUEL, J., LANGLOIS, B., AND POLLET, D. 2003. Reflective model driven engineering. In *UML 2003 Conference,* (San Francisco), Springer-Verlag, Berlin, 175–189.

5. BOOCH, G., JACOBSON, I., AND RUMBAUGH, J. 1998. *The Unified Modeling Language Reference Guide.* Addison-Wesley, Reading, Massachusetts.

6. CLARK, T., EVANS, A., AND Kent, S. 2003. Aspect-oriented meta-modeling. *The Computer Journal* 46, 3 (Sept.), 566–577.

7. CLARKE, S. AND WALKER, R. J. 2001. Composition patterns: An approach to designing reusable aspects. In *23rd Int'l Conf. Software Engineering (ICSE),* (Toronto). IEEE, 5–14.

8. CLEMENTS, P. AND NORTHROP, L. 2001. *Software Product Lines: Practices and Patterns.* Addison-Wesley, Reading, Massachusetts.

9. CZARNECKI, K. AND EISENECKER, U. W. 2000. *Generative Programming: Methods, Tools, and Applications.* Addison-Wesley, Reading, Massachusetts.

10. ELRAD, T., ALDAWUD, O., AND BADER, A. 2002. Aspect-oriented modeling: Bridging the gap between implementation and design. In *1st ACM Conf. Generative Programming and Component Engineering (GPCE),* (Pittsburgh). LNCS, vol. 2487. Springer-Verlag, Berlin, 189–201.

11. FILMAN, R. E. AND FRIEDMAN, D. P. 2000. Aspect-oriented programming is quantification and obliviousness. In *Workshop on Advanced Separation of Concerns (OOPSLA)*, (Minneapolis, Minnesota). http://trese.cs.utwente.nl/Workshops/OOPSLA2000/papers/filman.pdf.

12. FRANKEL, D. 2003. *Model Driven Architecture: Applying MDA to Enterprise Computing*, Wiley, New York.

13. GAMMA, E., HELM, R., JOHNSON, R., AND VLISSIDES, J. 1995. *Design Patterns: Elements of Reusable Object-Oriented Software*. Addison-Wesley, Reading, Massachusetts.

14. GARRETT, J., LÉDECZI, A., AND DECARIA, F. 2000. Toward a paradigm for activity modeling. In *Int'l Conf. Systems, Man, and Cybernetics*, (Nashville, Tennessee). IEEE, vol. 4, 2425–2430.

15. GOKHALE, A., SCHMIDT, D. C., NATARAJAN, B., GRAY, J., AND WANG, N. 2004. Model-driven middleware, In *Middleware for Communications*. Q. Mahmoud, Ed. Wiley, New York, 163–187.

16. GRAY, J., BAPTY, T., NEEMA, S., AND TUCK, J. 2001. Handling crosscutting constraints in domain-specific modeling. *Comm. ACM 44*, 10 (Oct.), 87–93.

17. GRAY, J., LIN, Y., AND ZHANG, J. 2003. Levels of independence in aspect-oriented modeling. In *Workshop on Model-Driven Approaches to Middleware Applications Development (Middleware)*, (Rio de Janeiro). http://www.gray-area.org/Papers/MAMAD-2003.pdf.

18. GRAY, J., TOLVANEN, J. P., AND ROSSI, M., Eds. 2003. *DSM03, Workshop on Domain-Specific Modeling (OOPSLA)*, (Anaheim, California). http://www.cis.uab.edu/info/OOPSLA-DSM03/.

19. GRAY, J., AND ROYCHOUDHURY, S. 2004. A technique for constructing aspect weavers using a program transformation system. In *Int'l Conf. on Aspect-Oriented Software Development (AOSD)*, (Lancaster, UK). ACM, 36–45.

20. GU, Z., KODASE, S., WANG, S., AND SHIN, K. 2003. A model-based approach to system-level dependency and real-time analysis of embedded software. In *Real-Time Applications Symposium*, (Washington, DC). IEEE, 78–87.

21. HARRISON, T., LEVINE, D., AND SCHMIDT, D. C. 1997. The design and performance of a hard real-time object event service. In *12th Conf. Object-Oriented Programming, Systems, Languages, and Applications (OOPSLA)*, (Atlanta). ACM, 184–200.

22. HOWARD, L. 2002. CAPE: A visual language for courseware authoring. In *2nd Workshop on Domain-Specific Visual Languages (OOPSLA)*, (Seattle). http://www.cis.uab.edu/info/OOPSLA-DSVL2/Papers/Howard.pdf.

23. HONEYWELL, INC. Domain modeling environment. http://www.htc.honeywell.com/dome/.

24. HUNLETH, F., CYTRON, R., AND GILL, C. 2001. Building customizable middleware using aspect oriented programming. In *Workshop on Advanced Separation of Concerns in Object-Oriented Systems (OOPSLA)*, (Tampa, Florida). http://www.cs.ubc.ca/~kdvolder/Workshops/OOPSLA2001/submissions/01-hunleth.pdf.

25. KARSAI, G. 1995. A configurable visual programming environment: A tool for domain-specific programming. *IEEE Computer 28*, 3, 36–44.

26. KARSAI, G., MAROTI, M., LEDECZI, A., GRAY, J., AND SZTIPANOVITS, J. 2004. Composition and cloning in modeling and meta-modeling languages. *IEEE Transactions on Control System Technology* 12, 2 (March), 263–278.

27. KICZALES, G. 2001. Aspect-oriented programming—the fun has just begun. In *Workshop on New Visions for Software Design and Productivity: Research and Applications*, (Nashville, Tennessee). http://www.hpcc.gov/iwg/sdp/vanderbilt/position_papers/gregor_kiczales_aspect_oriented_programming.pdf.

28. KICZALES, G., HILSDALE, E., HUGUNIN, J., KERSTEN, M., PALM, J., AND GRISWOLD, W. G. 2001. Getting started with AspectJ. *Comm. ACM 44*, 10 (Oct.), 59–65.

29. KIRCHER, M. 2002. Eager evaluation. In *European Conf. Pattern Languages of Programs* (Kloster Irsee, Germany). http://hillside.net/europlop/EuroPLoP2002/papers/Kircher.zip.

30. LÉDECZI, A., BAKAY, A., MAROTI, M., VOLGYESI, P., NORDSTROM, G., SPRINKLE, J., AND KARSAI, G. 2001. Composing domain-specific design environments. *IEEE Computer 34*, 11 (Nov.), 44–51.

31. LONG, E., MISRA, A., AND SZTIPANOVITS, J. 1998. Increasing productivity at Saturn. *IEEE Computer 31*, 8 (Aug.), 35–43.

32. MAHRENHOLZ, D., SPINCZYK, O., AND SCHRÖDER-PREIKSCHAT, W. 2002. Program instrumentation for debugging and monitoring with AspectC++. In *5th Int'l Symp. Object-Oriented Real-time Distributed Computing*, (Washington DC). IEEE, 249–256.

33. MOORE, M., MONEMI, S., AND WANG, J. 2000. Integrating information systems in electrical utilities. In *Int'l Conf. Systems, Man and Cybernetics*, (Nashville, Tennessee). IEEE, vol. 1, 8–11.

34. NEEMA, S., BAPTY, T., GRAY, J., AND GOKHALE, A. 2002. Generators for synthesis of QoS adaptation in distributed real-time embedded systems. In *1st ACM Conf. Generative Programming and Component Engineering (GPCE)*, (Pittsburgh). LNCS, vol. 2487. Springer-Verlag, Berlin, 236–251.

35. NORDSTROM, G., SZTIPANOVITS, J., KARSAI, G., AND LÉDECZI, Á. 1999. Metamodeling—rapid design and evolution of domain-specific modeling environments. In *Int'l Conf. Engineering of Computer-Based Systems (ECBS)*, (Nashville, Tennessee). IEEE, 68–74.

36. POHJONEN, R. AND KELLY, S. 2002. Domain-specific modeling. *Dr. Dobb's Journal*, 26–35.

37. PÓLYA, G. 1957. *How to Solve It*. Princeton University Press, Princeton, New Jersey.

38. RASHID, A., MOREIRA, A., AND ARAÚJO, J. 2003. Modularisation and composition of aspectual requirements. In *2nd Int' Conf. Aspect-Oriented Software Development (AOSD)*, (Boston), M. Akşit, Ed. ACM, 11–20.

39. SHARP, D. 2000. Component-based product line development of avionics software, In *1st Software Product Lines Conference (SPLC-1)*, (Denver, Colorado). Kluwer International Series in Engineering and Computer Science (576), 353–369.

40. SIEGEL, J. 2000. *CORBA 3 Fundamentals and Programming*. Wiley, New York.

41. STANKOVIC, J., ZHU, R., POORNALINGAM, R., LU, C., YU, Z., HUMPHREY, M., AND ELLIS, B. 2003. VEST: An aspect-based composition tool for real-time systems. In *Real-Time Applications Symposium* (Washington, DC). 58–69.

42. SUSSMAN, G. J. 1999. Robust design through diversity. In *DARPA Amorphous Computing Workshop*. http://www.swiss.ai.mit.edu/projects/amorphous/workshop-sept-99/robust-diversity.pdf.

43. SZTIPANOVITS, J. AND KARSAI, G. 2002. Generative programming for embedded systems. In *1st ACM Conf. Generative Programming and Component Engineering (GPCE)*, (Pittsburgh). LNCS, vol. 2487. Springer-Verlag, Berlin, 32–49.

44. TARR, P., OSSHER, H., HARRISON, W., AND SUTTON JR., S. M. 1999. *N* degrees of separation: Multi-dimensional separation of concerns. In *21st Int'l Conf. Software Engineering (ICSE)*, (Los Angeles). IEEE, 107–119.

45. Van Deursen, A., Klint, P., and Visser, J. 2000. Domain-specific languages: An annotated bibliography. *ACM SIGPLAN Notices 35*, 6 (June), 26–36.

46. Vocale, M. L. 2000. JSF virtual battlefield. *CodeOne Magazine*. Lockheed Martin Aeronautics Company. http://www.codeonemagazine.com/archives/2000/jul_00.html.

47. Wang, N., Schmidt, D., and O'Ryan, C. 2001. Overview of the CORBA component model. In *Component-Based Software Engineering: Putting the Pieces Together*, G. Heineman and W. Councill, Eds. Addison-Wesley, Reading, Massachusetts, 557–572.

48. Warmer, J. and Kleppe, A. 2003. *The Object Constraint Language: Getting Your Models Ready for MDA*. Addison-Wesley, Reading, Massachusetts.

Chapter 31

Dynamic Aspect-Oriented Infrastructure

ANDREI POPOVICI, GUSTAVO ALONSO, AND THOMAS GROSS

31.1 INTRODUCTION

Researchers have already recognized that adapting a system's software is important for supporting mobile applications [22, 25]. Faced with variations in bandwidth, location, disparity of available services, or the presence of other mobile devices, applications must adapt their behavior to their execution context. According to a taxonomy by Satyanarayanan [26], possible adaptation strategies range between two extremes. At one end, the *laissez faire* approach stipulates that an application running on a mobile node is entirely responsible for modifying its behavior in response to external stimuli. For example, if the light level diminishes, a text editor would recognize this change and might increase the font size. At the other end, the *transparent adaptation* strategy places the entire responsibility for adaptation on the computing environment where the application runs (e.g., the operating system and the network infrastructure).

Within this classification, the notion of application awareness [13, 26] denotes that the computing environment (i) is aware of the applications running within its boundaries and (ii) provides the applications with the necessary adaptations to the local conditions. From an engineering point of view, the question is how to design systems capable of exhibiting application awareness. This chapter attempts to answer this question and describes how to use aspect-orientation [6, 9, 33] to implement application awareness.

An illustrative example of application awareness is a neighborhood that requires encrypted communication within its boundaries. When a mobile computing device enters this space, the environment should be able to adapt the device accordingly. To meet this objective, it should suffice that one node in the system (e.g., a base station associated with the location or one of the peer devices) has the required functionality. This device sends a run-time extension to the new device, which immediately and transparently becomes capable of encrypted communication. Participants should not be required to carry with them all the software needed for encryption. This functionality should be a property of the computing environment and should be delivered on demand.

Using current technology, this level of application awareness is difficult to achieve since typical adaptations are crosscutting concerns. Existing platforms for mobile computing [2, 11] lack the support for dynamically applying crosscutting adaptations. Approaches like configurable middleware platforms [3, 7] open the definition of the infrastructure but have the disadvantage of being tailored to a particular purpose. We present here an approach that provides generic support for adaptation when each mobile device carries with it its own platform for dynamic aspect-oriented programming (AOP) [5, 14, 15, 16, 21].

In this chapter, we demonstrate the feasibility of this approach and its suitability for application awareness. Although the techniques we describe are generic, we assume for the discussion a Java-based environment. We start in Section 31.2 with an application scenario. Based on this scenario, we address in Section 31.3 the problem of providing an AOP platform for a single node. Section 31.4 gives a concrete example of this type of support. Once each node is prepared for application awareness, we can apply adaptations to all nodes of a network. In Section 31.5, we address the problem of ensuring that an entire community of mobile nodes can be adapted correctly. In Section 31.6, we give additional examples of how to use this technology.

31.2 APPLICATION SCENARIO

Consider a manufacturing plant where a large number of mobile devices, robots, and possibly "smart" artifacts (appliances for short) executes tasks to collaboratively manufacture goods, control quality, receive production schedules, and order sub-parts needed in the production process. The tasks the robots execute are broken down into basic (parametrizable) macros. Macros are available in the firmware of each robot and reflect its capabilities and functionality. They ensure a deterministic behavior of the robot (by taking into account input from various sensors). For example, to avoid relying on the precision of the motors, a macro may control the movements of a robot's wheels so that the robot follows a guidance line on the floor.

A simplified setting of this type is illustrated in Figure 31-1. Assume that quality problems have been detected in production hall H_2. To identify the source of a drop of quality in the production process, it is required to continuously monitor all activities within H_2 (messages received or sent by robots, service calls, macro executions, sensor inputs, etc.). With a conventional application design, the ability to react to changes is encoded in the appliance before it is deployed. Hence, the flexibility of the appliance is limited to what designers could foresee and what is reasonable to embed within the application. Thus, conventional design implies taking the appliance of interest offline to add the necessary functionality (logging in this case).

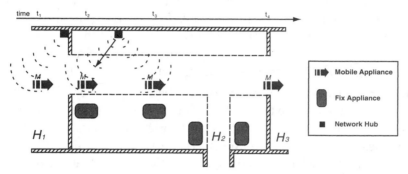

Figure 31-1 *Mobile appliance traversing a production hall.*

The form of application awareness we describe addresses this problem by allowing any mobile device that enters the production hall to be adapted on the fly. Consider a mobile appliance M located in production hall H_1. At this point, it does not have the monitoring functionality needed in H_2, as the type of logging needed for quality assurance could not be foreseen when M was initially deployed. Upon entering production hall H_2, the application-aware production hall detects M's presence and sends a run-time extension e that adds the necessary monitoring functionality in M. Extension e modifies M's execution during its presence in H_2 such that all relevant activities are recorded in a base station associated with H_2 and used by the functionality in e. When M leaves H_2, the monitoring extension is discarded. Fixed devices are treated accordingly: they are detected by H_2 at deployment time, and the monitoring extension remains until the corresponding appliance is redeployed in another production hall or monitoring is no longer required. The list of extensions that can be used in a similar manner includes the following:

Control.   In certain locations, one might want to change the execution of a robot's task. This change may be necessary when macros initially programmed to follow a simple guidance line in H_1 encounter a forking in H_2. Given the potential differences in geometry and external factors, adapting a robot task to a new location results in consistently changing the parameters of the macros under execution, interlacing the execution of existing macros with executions of other macros, or reacting to sensor events in a different way than initially foreseen. Because all these changes must be consistent, aspect-oriented programming is extremely well suited for expressing behavior-changing extensions.

Logging. In difficult or important situations, one may want to record all movements performed as well as all events detected by the robot sensors. That way, if an accident or failure occurs, one can replay a part of the sequence of movements to see if the failure can be reproduced or at least be better understood. This feature is particularly interesting if the failure is due to the interaction between different robots: the system can be instructed to feed the events previously captured by each robot's sensor and replay the sequence of movements of all robots at the right relative time, thereby reproducing the interaction between them.

Remote replication and coordination. When the precision of the robot hardware is high, it is possible to use the extension to monitor all the moves and feed these move operations to an identical robot in a remote location (or to a collection of identical robots in other locations). That way one can either duplicate the work or follow up on what is being done. It is also possible that the replication of the work takes place at a scale different from what is being done by the original robot. The only feature needed is the ability to amplify or reduce the extracted sequence of movements to adjust it to the new scale. Replication of movements may be further enhanced with coordination.

31.3 APPLICATION AWARENESS USING ASPECT ORIENTATION

Application-aware platforms pose interesting challenges to the application designer. For example, intercepting the communication between devices translates into dynamically adding crosscutting functionality for all incoming and outgoing messages for various communication protocols (remote invocations, web services, etc.). The case is similar for expressing coordinated processing, where the body of a large number of application methods must be bracketed at runtime with transactional functionality. Similarly, fine granularity logging may require recording the state of each robot; this task implies capturing the changes to a large number of fields and propagating updates to a nearby database.

Building an application-aware network using traditional software development techniques is hampered by the lack of support for (1) expressing crosscutting concerns and (2) expressing run-time extensions. In previous work [18, 19, 21, 23], we argued that aspect-oriented programming can make this task significantly easier to solve. In particular, we have identified the following requirements to an AOP platform to be suitable for application awareness:

- Extending the functionality of a running application by dynamically injecting the behavior appropriate to the current location (or networking environment)
- Extending multiple applications running on separate nodes of a network (e.g., to ensure they can later interoperate)
- Gracefully dealing with new nodes entering or leaving the network by dynamically applying extensions addressing crosscutting changes
- Making adaptations secure by providing the appropriate protection from malicious services that may use application awareness as a trapdoor for getting access to sensitive local data

With these requirements in mind, we propose dynamic AOP as the most appropriate way to design application awareness. Dynamic AOP is the ability of an AOP platform to weave and unweave aspects to/from applications at runtime without interrupting operations. Dynamic AOP allows one to model the extensions (e.g., as described in the production hall scenario) as aspects.

31.3.1 Design Alternatives for Dynamic AOP

In a Java-based application, the application code passes several stages before being executed. First, the sources are compiled, and corresponding class files are produced. Class files are loaded at runtime into the Java Virtual Machine (JVM). Loading implies that the code is verified for well-formedness and then transformed into a JVM-internal format. In a further, optional, step, the code is compiled using a Just-In-Time (JIT) compiler into the native language of the current host where it is executed.

Depending on when weaving is done, we distinguish between compile-time weaving (see Figure 31-2 (a)), load-time weaving (see Figure 31-2 (b)), or JIT-time weaving (see Figure 31-2 (c)). Compile-time weaving currently offers extended support for application development [4]. However, load-time and JIT-time weavers are more appropriate for expressing run-time changes, as these weavers provide "late" binding of aspects and application classes and allow extending an already running application. In addition, they do not require the source code of the original application. Load-time platforms like JAC [16] and Hyper/J [32] and run-time weavers like PROSE [21] offer preliminary support for this type of adaptation.

Since most of the modern JVMs [29, 30] use a JIT compiler, let us consider in more detail a JIT-time weaver (Figure 31-2c) that instructs the JIT-compiler to insert advice code when transforming the bytecode into native code. Figure 31-3 (a) illustrates how the weaving process works. We consider weaving the advice defined by an aspect *A* through the code of an application class C that declares two methods `foo` and `bar`. For simplicity, we consider the case that *A* specifies the weaving of the code `print("enter")` before all executions of C.foo. When translating C's bytecode into native code, the JIT compiler adds the code for `print("enter")` (in bold characters in the figure) at the beginning of the code corresponding to `foo`.

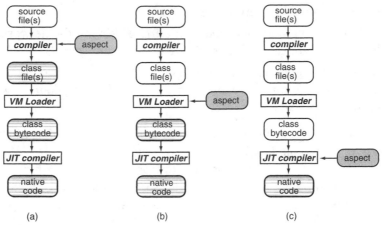

(a)   (b)   (c)

Figure 31-2 *(a) Compile-time weaving, (b) Load-time weaving, and (c) JIT-time weaving.*

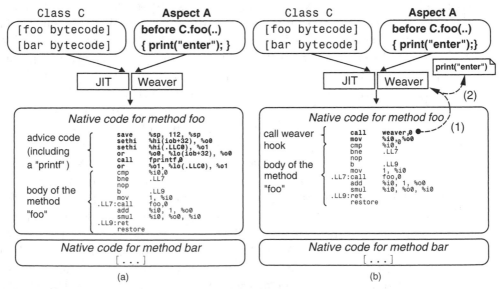

Figure 31-3 *(a) Full-code weaving and (b) Stub weaving.*

So far, we have implicitly assumed that the actual advice code is woven at the matching join points. We denote this approach as full code weaving and the corresponding weavers full-code weavers. What happens if an aspect *A* must be woven after the bytecode-loading and JIT-ing is over? JIT-time weavers would have to recompile all classes and methods that contain affected join points. Similarly, load-time weavers would have to unload and reload all classes containing join points for *A*. To avoid this problem, a dynamic weaver can add minimal hooks (or stubs) instead of the advice code. Stubs must be woven at all potential join points in C's code (such as field changes, method boundaries, exception throws and handlers, etc.). Figure 31-3 (b) illustrates this situation. Unlike in Figure 31-3 (a), only two lines of code have been added to at the beginning of the native code corresponding to foo. Every time foo is called, the weaver component is notified (step 1). When this happens, the weaver checks whether any advice must be executed and eventually executes all advices corresponding to the reached join point (step 2). This approach is taken, for example, by JAC [16] and Handiwrap [5]. We denote this second type of weavers as stub weavers. Stub weavers may lead to a significant increase of the resulting code size (since code is added at locations where no advice is needed). Stub weavers are less efficient than full-code weavers because executing advice goes through at least one layer of indirection. However, they have the advantage of avoiding recompilation or reloading of the application code by providing minimal hooks at all potential points.

The trade-offs between the various types of weavers are presented in Table 31-1. Given the various design alternatives (e.g., full-code weaving vs. stub weaving, load-time weaving vs. JIT-time weaving), we can use this table to choose the most appropriate weaver for a given type of application. Based on this information, we now demonstrate how to build a weaver that can address application awareness.

Table 31-1 *Properties of Various Weaver Types*

Full-Code Weavers	**Stub Weavers**
Reduced code size	Large code size
Mix advice and base code	Advice and base code separate

Load-Time Weavers	**JIT-Time Weavers**
Portable	Less portable
Less efficient	Efficient
May require reload	May require re-compile

31.4 MEETING APPLICATION-AWARENESS REQUIREMENTS WITH PROSE

To show that dynamic AOP can be used for expressing application awareness, we developed PROSE (PROgrammable extenSions of sErvices), a system in which aspects are first-class Java entities and all related constructs are expressed using the base language, Java. The first version of PROSE was based on the debugger interface of the JVM [21]. The second version [19] is a JIT-based stub weaver based on IBM's Jikes Research Virtual Machine [1]. The PROSE experience has shown that dynamic AOP can be efficient and can be provided at a low implementation cost. In addition, by carefully selecting the features of the dynamic AOP platform, one can fully address the requirements of application awareness. The next section gives an overview of this system.

31.4.1 Addressing Application Awareness in PROSE

31.4.1.1 Addressing Security

For application awareness, security is a very important feature. Just like Internet browsers that control the code they download from the network, the AOP support embedded in each node must guarantee that a foreign advice cannot damage the local system. In this respect, stub weavers offer a better choice than advice weavers. The reason is that a full-code weaver mixes advice and base code, and this makes the verification of the code origin at a later point in time a difficult task. By contrast, stub weavers separate advice code from the base code. This way, the advice code (potentially originating from a foreign host) can be kept in a sandbox. This setup allows well-understood security models (such as the Java Security Model [31]) to be enforced. It was for this reason that we have chosen the stub-weaver approach for PROSE.

31.4.1.2 Addressing Performance

Under normal operations (no woven aspects), the dynamic weaving platform should not lead to significant performance degradation (performance is a key requirement when dealing with online and mobile systems). Our decision to implement PROSE using a JIT-time approach was based on measurements using SpecJVM [27] and JavaGrande [8] benchmarks. The results are summarized in Table 31-2. They show that a JIT-time weaver slows down application execution less than 10% when considering all field operations and method calls as join points. The good performance of a JIT-time weaver was to be expected, as native code hooks can be programmed extremely efficiently. According to our measurements [20], JIT-time weavers compare favorably with load-based approaches, which incur larger overheads at each join point. With a JIT-time weaver, we also obtained encouraging results when expressing CPU-intensive adaptations like orthogonal persistence and transactional processing [18].

Table 31-2 *Relative Overhead with AOP Support for Method Boundaries, Field Sets, and Field Gets*

Benchmark	Relative Overhead
Java Grande Benchmark Suite	
LUFact:Kernel	103.15 %
Crypt:Kernel	103.24 %
SOR:Kernel	98.74 %
SparseMatmult:Kernel	100.23 %
Average	**101.44 %**
SPECjvm 98 Benchmark Suite	
check	103.04 %
jess	110.19 %
db	105.17 %
jack	107.84 %
javac	113.51 %
Average	**107.95 %**

31.4.1.3 Addressing Portability and Cost

The advantage of a small performance overhead (mainly due to the efficiency of native code) is balanced by the disadvantage of a reduced portability. By contrast, load-time stub weavers are usually portable from one JVM to another, as they are essentially replacements for a standard JVM classloader component. To address this restriction, we divided the AOP support provided in PROSE into two modules.

31.4.2 PROSE Architecture

System modules. The *AOP engine* is a replaceable module that uses the support for weaving provided by the *execution monitor,* a module that is tightly integrated with the JVM and its JIT compiler.

Figure 31-4 gives an overview of this architecture. In the upper layer, the AOP engine accepts aspects (1) and transforms them into basic entities like join point stop requests (2). It activates the stop requests by invoking methods of the execution monitor (3). The execution monitor is integrated with the JVM. When the execution reaches one of the activated join points, the execution monitor notifies the AOP engine (4), which executes an advice (5).

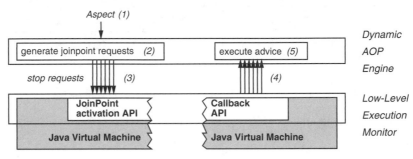

Figure 31-4 *PROSE architecture.*

Following a conventional design approach, we kept in the execution monitor only the most frequently used functionality. Our goal was to show that this functionality can be provided at a low (implementation) cost. Indeed, in our first prototype, the execution monitor consisted of only 1600 lines of code added to the JVM core. If this support were available in every JVM platform, application providers could program their own AOP engines on top of the execution monitor.

The execution monitor.   The execution monitor support is integrated with the JVM. It contains the functionality for activating join points (used when a new aspect is added to the system) and the callback functionality for notifying the AOP engine that a join point has been reached (used at runtime).

When a new aspect is added to the system, the AOP engine activates join points using the join point activation API of the execution monitor. It specifies as parameter a class member (e.g., field or method) that uniquely identifies the join point to be activated. When an activated join point is reached, the execution monitor notifies through the callback API the AOP engine (each AOP engine implements an appropriate interface) by passing a join point object to the AOP engine.

The passed join point object contains methods for the inspection of local variable values, of thread states, of return values, etc. This design implies making the stack layout visible to the join point object passed to the aspect engine. This is needed because the join point interface allows gathering information of the local environment (e.g., local variables).

Stack visibility is just one of the problems that must be solved when providing an execution monitor. For consistency and efficiency reasons, a tight integration of the execution monitor with several components of the JVM is needed.

One example is the division of a method's body into basic blocks. A basic block is a code sequence in which the stack layout remains unchanged. Basic blocks are used by the garbage collector to inspect the stack and to collect object references. When adding join point stubs, a method call may occur at a location where no basic block boundary was detected during bytecode analysis. As a consequence, JIT-level AOP implies the additional cost of adapting the bytecode analyzer of the JVM. In general, all information related to join points must be as close as possible to the internal representation in the JVM.

The AOP engine.   The main functions of the AOP engine are (1) to decompose an aspect into stop requests and to activate corresponding join points, and (2) to execute a corresponding advice when an active join point is reached. By replacing the AOP engine, one can define an alternative AOP platform, which may differ from PROSE in various ways.

We explain the general architecture of the AOP engine by illustrating the actions for weaving an aspect using PROSE. Then we show the actions taken to execute the corresponding advice. Our example aspect definition encrypts all bytes-array parameters passed to sendBytes-methods. We use PROSE to describe this aspect:

```
(1)  // before methods 'void *.sendBytes(byte[] x)'
(2)  // do encrypt(x)
(3)  class ExampleCut extends BeforeCut {
(4)  void sendBytes(ANY thisObject, byte[] x)
(5)          { encrypt(x); }
(6)  }
```

To weave this aspect, the AOP engine performs several sub-tasks, as illustrated in Figure 31-4. First, it inspects all the classes currently loaded by the JVM and gathers all methods $m_1 \ldots m_n$ that match the signature '*.sendBytes(byte[] x)'. For all generated stop requests, it activates method entry join points using the join point activation API of the underlying execution monitor.

Upon entry in $m_1 \ldots m_n$, the execution monitor calls the AOP engine. The AOP engine guarantees that all run-time conditions defining the reached join point are met (e.g., the aspect may be defined using control-flow crosscutting mechanisms [4]). If all the dynamic checks are passed successfully, the advice can be executed.

Finally, the AOP engine executes the encrypt method. If classes are loaded by the JVM at a later point in time, the actions done for aspect weaving are repeated accordingly on each new class in the system.

31.5 WEAVING ASPECTS IN A COMMUNITY OF NODES

31.5.1 Aspect Distribution

In the production hall scenario, we want to weave aspects at runtime through several nodes accessible through the local networks (fixed or mobile).

For this purpose, we distinguish two roles for nodes. *Aspect base* nodes contain a database of aspects. They discover new nodes joining the network and send aspects to the newcomers. *Aspect receivers* carry the component that receives aspects from aspect bases. We assume that each aspect receiver has PROSE activated on its JVM. When it obtains an aspect from an aspect base, it immediately inserts the aspect using the PROSE API. Aspect receivers also discard aspects when they leave a network or lose contact with the aspect base.

By appropriately assigning aspect base and aspect receiver roles, one can achieve adaptations of various service communities. At one extreme, each node can contain an aspect base. When it joins a new community, it distributes its aspects and receives others from the existing nodes. This type of organization is appropriate for creating an application-aware system infrastructure in entirely ad-hoc communities. At the other extreme, each physical location (e.g., a production hall) may have a base station as aspect base. All other nodes (e.g., the mobile nodes) are aspect receivers. This organization is appropriate for adaptations that correspond to infrastructure and organizational requirements. Between the two extremes, many other configurations are possible.

31.5.2 Lifecycle of Aspects

Application awareness must be designed for device mobility. This requirement implies that aspects must transiently adapt a service (for as long as the service is working in a given network). To model this behavior, the aspects must be *leased* to each node (i.e., to the adaptation service of a node). It is the responsibility of each aspect base to keep alive the functionality it has distributed among nodes. When a node leaves a given space, the leases on the aspects acquired in that space fail to be renewed, and corresponding aspects are revoked. Each aspect sender keeps track of its aspect activity (what nodes where adapted at what point in time) and may implement a simple roaming algorithm to deal with nodes migrating between areas.

31.5.3   Software Architecture Issues

Aspects range from service-generic to fully service-customized. For generic aspects, no specific information on services implementation is needed. For instance, one can replace the communication layer of a service with a new one that encrypts data without any particular knowledge of the adapted service. Specific adaptations may require either a black-box view (information on particular interfaces) or glass-box view (knowledge on how a service is implemented) of the service to be adapted. We assume that each aspect base has many aspects ranging from generic to service-specific. This approach, also followed by [17], accommodates incremental evolution of the software at every node (because generic aspects still work even if the node application has changed).

31.6   USAGE EXAMPLES OF AOP IN APPLICATION AWARENESS

31.6.1   Location-Specific Functionality for Robotics

We describe here the software architecture of the robots we use for experimenting with application-awareness (see Figure 31-5 (a)). A robot is equipped with a differential drive powered by two separate motors. A front bumper is attached to a touch sensor. Two optical sensors directed to the ground can be used to sense the ground markup. The system is physically distributed on two hardware components (see Figure 31-5 (b)). At the bottom, the RCX controller available in Lego's Robotics Invention System [10] is running the LeJOS operating system [11]. At the top, an iPAQ PDA is executing a robot task in Java. The program running on the RCX is very small (less than 11 Kbytes) and can efficiently control the hardware (adjust movements to sensor inputs). For its rapid reaction, it is called "spine." Conversely, the full-fledged Java program running on the iPAQ is called "brain." The brain is in charge of executing robot tasks by decomposing them into basic macros and sending the macros for execution to the spine.

Spine functionality.   The spine is provided with macros dependent on the robot's physical design (by robot design we mean the physical attachment of motors and sensors and their functions). A typical macro example is a forward move. Internally, this macro would start both wheel motors at the same time and with the same power. However, precise commands may produce imprecise results (the command to move forward for 30 seconds does not precisely delimit where the robot stops). For this reason, macros may take into account sensor inputs. This feature can be used to stop the macro execution when a marker is detected on the floor.

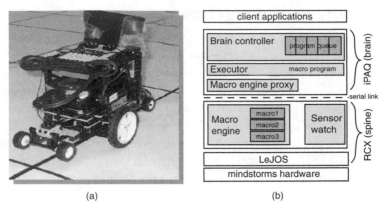

(a) (b)

Figure 31-5 *(a) A transporter robot and (b) software architecture of the robot.*

The *macro engine* is responsible for executing macros. Before each macro execution, the API of the macro engine can be used to specify what events (sensor inputs) the current macro should be sensitive to. The execution of each macro either terminates normally (e.g., after the motors have been activated for 30 seconds), or when an expected event is detected. In both cases, the macro engine saves the state of the macro and notifies the brain application. The brain application may decide to continue the execution of the macro or start the execution of a new macro.

Brain functionality. Robot tasks are Java programs running on top of the brain application. Internally, they call the API of the macro engine. Because the macro engine resides on the RCX controller, robot tasks use a *macro engine proxy* that exposes the same API as the macro engine itself. A robot task may declare handlers to be executed when an event is encountered. It must also specify what macros should be executed, in which order, and with what parameters values. Depending on how sophisticated the available macros are, a brain program may consist of just one macro (e.g., "find the exit of the maze") or a sequence of basic macros ("move forward until the touch sensor is active, turn, move forward"). For example, the following code is a simple sequence of macros that instructs the robot to turn in place until it can move forward:

```
(1)     beginSensitive(sensor1,handler1);
(2)     while (sensor1Active) {
(3)         turnRight(90);
(4)         forward();
(5)     }
(6)     endSensitive(sensor1);
```

Because the brain is much more powerful in terms of computational resources than the spine, a large number of simple macros increases the programmability of a robot. As part of the brain, the *executor* maintains the progress and state of the currently running task. Internally, it uses a state machine model reflecting transitions between execution modes (executing a macro, executing a handler, executing a sensitive macro, etc.). The overall functionality of the brain (executing tasks, enqueueing new tasks for later execution) is exported as a Jini [2] service to application clients.

Adaptation example. As a first adaptation example, we reconsider the monitoring aspect described earlier. We created an aspect that can be woven through the Java-based brain of moving robots. For each invocation of a macro, the aspect logs the time when the command was issued, its duration, and the identity of the robot. Whenever an event is received by an event handler (e.g., after having activated a sensor with a `beginSensitive` command), the aspects may log the values of the sensor inputs, as well as all invocations of Java methods within the control flow of the handler method. This data is first locally stored and then asynchronously sent to a base station. Thus, one can connect to the base station and query the database that stores all operations performed by robots being monitored by the base station.

The extension can be added or removed as needed. If the robot is moved to a different location, that location's aspect sender can add a new aspect that indicates where the data must be sent for persistent storage. Within the same location, the aspect can be exchanged for a new one that indicates that the data must be sent to a program that shows the movements in a graphic display. A clear advantage of this form of adaptability is that devices only need to carry their basic functionality.

More sophisticated adaptation examples imply changing the behavior of the robot. This is the case when a robot using line-following macros enters a location with different semantics of the guidance lines. Since robot tasks are built out of many macro calls, this type of adaptation requires consistently changing the parameters sent to a subset of macros and handlers. Programs, macros, and sensor handlers are separate entities; the semantics of sensor inputs may differ from one location to another. In addition, behavior adaptation may require simultaneous changes of several distinct robots. For this reason, dynamic AOP is highly useful in consistently expressing behavior changes. Both for monitoring and for behavior changes, dynamic AOP provides obliviousness (the robot program is not aware of the aspect and must not explicitly prepare for it) and has the ability to simultaneously change many parts of several executing tasks in one atomic weaving operation.

31.6.2 *Other Examples of Application Awareness*

While application awareness is used to perform dynamic adaptations in the space domain, it can be also used to perform adaptation in the temporal domain. One interesting application area would be to apply hot fixes to long-running web services, both mobile and fixed. A hot fix is an extension applied to a running application server that affects the behavior of a large number of deployed and running components. Hot fixes can be used for fixing bugs or security breaches or dealing with unexpected changes in network traffic, server availability, or client-specific services [34]. We have encountered such a case in the HEDC [28] project.

HEDC, the HESSI Experimental Data Center, is a multi-terabyte repository built for the recently launched HESSI satellite. HESSI observes the sun and builds catalogs with events of interest such as sun flares. In HEDC, scientific users are confronted with large catalogs that they need to browse and update. At a certain point in time, an older servlet-based web service for browsing database tuples was reintroduced. Since the main system had evolved in the meantime, the web service resulted in performance degradation for all users (including those who were not browsing the catalog via the web). The analysis identified the problem: for each http request, a *session object* was created that incurred a significant workload on the database server.

Fixing the problem (adding pooling for session objects) revealed how useful aspect-oriented application awareness can be. This solution is desirable for the following considerations. First, the problem has a clear crosscutting concern: It requires replacing code (e.g., `new Session()`), which is scattered through multiple servlet classes, with code that reuses sessions from previous invocations. Second, in a service environment, the load on the database can be decreased considerably when the first corrections are applied directly, without taking the service offline. This second issue is addressed by the ability of the application-aware infrastructure to apply crosscutting run-time changes. Third, a large web application is usually distributed on several nodes of a network (e.g., to ensure high availability); hence changes have to be applied simultaneously on several nodes. For this third problem, the aspect support for node communities offers a practical solution.

31.7 CONCLUSION

Dynamic aspect-orientation can play a significant role in the development of application awareness. We have encountered a number of scenarios where adaptations cut across a mobile system that needs to be adapted. With dynamic AOP support, one can implement adaptation by weaving aspects through mobile appliances when they enter (or leave) a network (section). There are various ways to provide dynamic AOP support in a Java-based application. We have studied the situation in which the AOP support is provided at the Just-In-Time compiler level. This solution requires minimal changes to the JVM and offers high performance at a low implementation cost. Our experiments in the area of mobile computing and service infrastructures suggest that this cost is worth paying. The aspect-oriented support allowed a small team to design and implement challenging prototypes. Based on this experience, the results are a first encouraging step towards providing full support for application-aware adaptations in mobile environments or in web services.

ACKNOWLEDGMENTS

Research supported, in part, by the National Competence Center in Research on Mobile Information and Communication Systems (NCCR-MICS), a center supported by the Swiss National Science Foundation under grant number 5005-67322.

REFERENCES

1. ALPERN, B., ATTANASIO, C. R., BARTON, J. J., BURKE, M. G., CHENG, P., CHOI, J. D., COCCHI, A., FINK, S. J., GROVE, D., HIND, M., HUMMEL, S. F., LIEBER, D., LITVINOV, V., MERGEN, M. F., NGO, T., RUSSELL, J. R., SARKAR, V., SERRANO, M. J., SHEPHERD, J. C., SMITH, S. E., SREEDHAR, V. C., SRINIVASAN, H., AND WHALEY, J. 2000. The Jalapeno virtual machine. *IBM Systems Journal 39*, 1, 211–238.

2. ARNOLD, K., SCHEIFLER, R., WALDO, J., O'SULLIVAN, B., WOLLRATH, A., O'SULLIVAN, B., AND WOLLRATH, A. 1999. *JINI Specification*. Addison-Wesley, Reading, Massachusetts.

3. ARREGUI, D., PACULL, F., AND WILLAMOWSKI, J. 2001. Rule-based transactional object migration over a reflective middleware. In *Middleware 2001: IFIP/ACM Int'l Conf. Distributed Systems Platforms*, (Heidelberg). LNCS, vol. 2218. Springer-Verlag, Berlin, 179–196.

4. ASPECTJ. The AspectJ programming guide. http://dev.eclipse.org/viewcvs/indextech.cgi/~checkout~/aspectj-home/doc/p% rogguide/index.html.

5. BAKER, J. AND HSIEH, W. 2002. Runtime aspect weaving through metaprogramming. In *1st Int'l Conf. Aspect-Oriented Software Development (AOSD)*, (Enschede, The Netherlands), G. Kiczales, Ed. ACM, 86–98.

6. BERGMANS, L. AND AKŞIT, M. 2001. Composing crosscutting concerns using composition filters. *Comm. ACM 44*, 10 (Oct.), 51–57.

7. CLARKE, M., BLAIR, G. S., COULSON, G., AND PARLAVANTZAS, N. 2001. An efficient component model for the construction of adaptive middleware. In *IFIP/ACM Int'l Conf. Distributed Systems Platforms*, (Heidelberg). LNCS, vol. 2218. Springer-Verlag, Berlin, 160–178.

8. JAVA GRANDE FORUM BENCHMARK SUITE. http://www.epcc.ed.ac.uk/computing/research_activities/java_grande/index_1.html; http://www.javagrande.org.

9. KICZALES, G., LAMPING, J., MENDHEKAR, A., MAEDA, C., LOPES, C., LOINGTIER, J. M., AND IRWIN, J. 1997. Aspect-oriented programming. In *ECOOP'97 Object-Oriented Programming, 11th European Conference*, M. Akşit and S. Matsuoka, Eds. LNCS, vol. 1241. Springer-Verlag, Berlin, 220–242.

10. LEGO. 2002. Lego mindstorms robotics invention system. http://mindstorms.lego.com.

11. LEHMAN, T. J., COZZI, A., XIONG, Y., GOTTSCHALK, J., VASUDEVAN, V., LANDIS, S., DAVIS, P., KHAVAR, B., AND BOWMAN, P. 2001. Hitting the distributed computing sweet spot with TSpaces. *Computer Networks: The Int'l Journal of Computer and Telecommunications Networking 35*, 4, 457–472.

12. LEJOS. Lejos project homepage. http://lejos.sourceforge.net.

13. NOBLE, B. D., SATYANARAYANAN, M., NARAYANAN, D., TILTON, J. E., FLINN, J., AND WALKER, K. R. 1997. Agile application-aware adaptation for mobility. In *16th Symp. Operating Systems Principles (SOSP)* (Saint Malo, France). ACM, 276–287.

14. ORLEANS, D. AND LIEBERHERR, K. 2001. DJ: Dynamic adaptive programming in Java. In *Metalevel Architectures and Separation of Crosscutting Concerns 3rd Int'l Conf. (Reflection 2001)*, (Kyoto), A. Yonezawa and S. Matsuoka, Eds. LNCS, vol. 2192. Springer-Verlag, Berlin, 73–80.

15. OSTERMANN, K. 2002. Dynamically composable collaborations with delegation layers. In *ECOOP 2002—Object-Oriented Programming: 16th European Conference*, (Málaga, Spain), B. Magnusson, Ed. LNCS, vol. 2374. Springer-Verlag, Berlin, 89–110.

16. PAWLAK, R., SEINTURIER, L., DUCHIEN, L., AND FLORIN, G. 2001. JAC: A flexible solution for aspect-oriented programming in Java. In *Metalevel Architectures and Separation of Crosscutting Concerns 3rd Int'l Conf. (Reflection 2001)*, (Kyoto), A. Yonezawa and S. Matsuoka, Eds. LNCS, vol. 2192. Springer-Verlag, Berlin, 1–24.

17. PONNEKANTI, S., LEE, B., FOX, A., HANRAHAN, P., AND WINOGRAD, T. 2001. Icrafter: A service framework for ubiquitous computing environments. In *3rd Int'l Conf. Ubiquitous Computing (UBICOMP)* (Atlanta). Springer-Verlag, Berlin, 56–75.

18. POPOVICI, A. 2003. PROSE: A study on dynamic AOP. Swiss Federal Institute of Technology, Zurich. Dissertation No. 15176.

19. POPOVICI, A. AND ALONSO, G. 2002. Ad-hoc transactions for mobile services. In *3rd VLDB Int'l Workshop on Transactions and Electronic Services (TES)*, (Hong Kong). LNCS, vol. 2444. Springer-Verlag, Berlin, 118–130.

20. POPOVICI, A., ALONSO, G., AND GROSS, T. 2001. AOP support for mobile systems. In *Workshop on Advanced Separation of Concerns in Object-Oriented Systems (OOPSLA)*, (Tampa, Florida). http://www.cs.ubc.ca/~kdvolder/Workshops/OOPSLA2001/submissions/13-popovici.pdf.

21. POPOVICI, A., ALONSO, G., AND GROSS, T. 2003. Just in time aspects: Efficient dynamic weaving for java. In *2nd Int'l Conf. Aspect-Oriented Software Development (AOSD)*, (Boston), M. Akşit, Ed. ACM, 100–109.

22. POPOVICI, A. AND FREI, A. AND ALONSO, G. 2003. A proactive middleware platform for mobile computing. In 4th ACM/IFIP/USENIX International Middleware Conference, (Rio de Janeiro, Brazil).

23. POPOVICI, A. AND ALONSO, G. AND GROSS, T. 2003. Spontaneous container services. In European Conference for Object-Oriented Programming (ECOOP), (Darmstadt, Germany).

24. POPOVICI, A., GROSS, T., AND ALONSO, G. 2002. Dynamic weaving for aspect-oriented programming. In *1st Int'l Conf. Aspect-Oriented Software Development (AOSD)*, (Enschede, The Netherlands), G. Kiczales, Ed. ACM, 141–147.

25. SATYANARAYANAN, M. 1996. Fundamental challenges in mobile computing. In *15th Symp. Principles of Distributed Computing (PODC)*, (Philadelphia, PA). http://www.cs.cmu.edu/afs/cs/project/coda/Web/coda.html.

26. SATYANARAYANAN, M. 1996. Accessing information on demand at any location. mobile information access. *IEEE Personal Communications 3*, 1 (Feb.), 26–33.

27. STANDARD PERFORMANCE EVALUATION CORPORATION. 2001. Spec JVM98 v1.04. http://www.spec.org/osg/jvm98/.

28. STOLTE, E. AND ALONSO, G. 2002. Efficient exploration of large scientific databases. In *28th Int'l Conf. Very Large DataBases (VLDB)*, (Hong Kong). Morgan Kaufmann, San Mateo, California, 622–633.

29. SUGANUMA, T., OGASAWARA, T., TAKEUCHI, M., YASUE, T., KAWAHITO, M., ISHIZAKI, K., KOMATSU, H., AND NAKATANI, T. 2000. Overview of the IBM Java just-in-time compiler. *IBM Systems Journal 39*, 1, 175–193.

30. SUN MICROSYSTEMS. Java 2 platform, standard edition, v 1.4.2 API specification. http://java.sun.com/j2se/1.4/docs/api/.

31. Sun Microsystems. Java security model. http://java.sun.com/security/.

32. Tarr, P. and Ossher, H. 2000. Hyper/J user and installation manual. Tech. rep., IBM T. J. Watson Research Center. http://www.research.ibm.com/hyperspace.

33. Tarr, P., Ossher, H., Harrison, W., and Sutton Jr., S. M. 1999. *N* degrees of separation: Multi-dimensional separation of concerns. In *21st Int'l Conf. Software Engineering (ICSE)*, (Los Angeles). IEEE, 107–119.

34. Truyen, E., Joosen, W., and Verbaeten, P. 2002. Consistency management in the presence of simultaneous client-specific views. In *Int'l Conf. Software Maintenance*, (Montreal). IEEE, 501–510.

Index

Register
Your Book

at www.awprofessional.com/register

You may be eligible to receive:

- Advance notice of forthcoming editions of the book
- Related book recommendations
- Chapter excerpts and supplements of forthcoming titles
- Information about special contests and promotions throughout the year
- Notices and reminders about author appearances, tradeshows, and online chats with special guests

Contact us

If you are interested in writing a book or reviewing manuscripts prior to publication, please write to us at:

Editorial Department
Addison-Wesley Professional
75 Arlington Street, Suite 300
Boston, MA 02116 USA
Email: AWPro@aw.com

Visit us on the Web: http://www.awprofessional.com

Wouldn't it be great

if the world's leading technical publishers joined forces to deliver their best tech books in a common digital reference platform?

They have. Introducing
InformIT Online Books
powered by Safari.

▪ Specific answers to specific questions.

InformIT Online Books' powerful search engine gives you relevance-ranked results in a matter of seconds.

▪ Immediate results.

With InformIT Online Books, you can select the book you want and view the chapter or section you need immediately.

▪ Cut, paste and annotate.

Paste code to save time and eliminate typographical errors. Make notes on the material you find useful and choose whether or not to share them with your work group.

▪ Customized for your enterprise.

Customize a library for you, your department or your entire organization. You only pay for what you need.

Get your first 14 days FREE!

For a limited time, InformIT Online Books is offering its members a 10 book subscription risk-free for 14 days. Visit **http://www.informit.com/online-books** for details.

informit.com/onlinebooks

InformIT Online Books

informIT

www.informit.com

YOUR GUIDE TO IT REFERENCE

Articles

Keep your edge with thousands of free articles, in-depth features, interviews, and IT reference recommendations – all written by experts you know and trust.

Online Books

Answers in an instant from **InformIT Online Book's** 600+ fully searchable on line books. For a limited time, you can get your first 14 days **free**.

Catalog

Review online sample chapters, author biographies and customer rankings and choose exactly the right book from a selection of over 5,000 titles.